THE SOLDIER KINGS

The House of Hohenzollern

Books by Walter Henry Nelson

SMALL WONDER:
The Amazing Story of the Volkswagen

THE GREAT DISCOUNT DELUSION

THE BERLINERS:
Their Saga and Their City

The Soldier Kings

THE HOUSE OF HOHENZOLLERN

Walter Henry Nelson

LONDON
J. M. DENT & SONS LTD

First published in Great Britain 1971

Printed in Great Britain
by
Lowe & Brydone (Printers) Ltd, London
for
J. M. DENT & SONS LTD
Aldine House · Bedford Street · London

Permission to quote from the following copyrighted material is gratefully acknowledged:

Winston Leonard Spencer Churchill, *Thoughts and Adventures*. New York, Macmillan, 1942; London, Thornton Butterworth, 1932.

Gordon A. Craig, *The Politics of the Prussian Army, 1640–1945*. New York and London, Oxford University Press, 1955; New York, Galaxy Book, Oxford University Press, 1964.

Gerhard Ritter, *Carl Goerdeler und die deutsche Widerstandsbewegung*. Stuttgart, Deutsche Verlags-Anstalt, 1954.

ISBN 0 460 03997 0

For H.L.

Contents

THE SOLDIER KINGS

The House of Hohenzollern

Illustrations appear following page 256.

1

A Glittering Experience

PRUSSIA, said Lord Acton, was not a giant, but an athlete; its champions were the Hohenzollerns. It was this family that developed the muscles of that state and later flexed them; the Hohenzollerns transformed a weakling that was mocked into a giant that was feared and even respected. Theirs came to be the sport of kings: the aggrandizement of their lands and peoples, which meant their wealth and power. Theirs, however, was also a triumph of the spirit, for the obstacles they needed to overcome would have daunted lesser men. The land of Brandenburg, with which they commenced the process of building Prussia, was remote, unfruitful, backward, and landlocked; further, the family possessions remained for centuries awkwardly scattered and virtually indefensible. Despite such disadvantages, despite a lack of wealth or natural resources, the Hohenzollerns brought forth a kingdom which became an empire. German unity, which had not existed since Charlemagne, was re-created in 1871, almost 900 years later, under a Hohenzollern King of Prussia. The Hohenzollerns rose from obscurity to become German emperors, ruling a prosperous German Reich; having attained fame and fortune, they remained at peace for more than forty years.

They surprised everyone; no one in Europe ever expected this obscure family, possessed only of marginal lands, to attain to such great heights. For centuries they remained unexceptional; suddenly they rose to startling heights. The Prussian eagle began "to spread its wings," as the historian G. P. Gooch put it, in the seventeenth century; "four Hohenzollern rulers in the space of a century and a half put Prussia on the map." The greatest of these was Frederick II, who made Prussia a great power by means of unabashed and audacious aggression; this Frederick, whom they called the Great, stands for the Germans beside Bismarck "in the national Walhalla . . . incomparable in resolution and resource. . . ." His great deeds had great consequences. If he had not succeeded in making Prussia a great power, there might never have been a Bismarck, says Gooch, and without Bismarck, Gooch argues, "there could hardly have been a Hitler and a Third Reich." [1]

So astonishing was the rise of Brandenburg-Prussia that European courts regarded Frederick the Great as a brash *arriviste,* just as his father, the real founder of Prussianism, had been the butt of jokes all over the Continent. It consistently amused the courts of Europe to look down on the Hohenzollerns, snickering that they were pretentious and uncultivated *nouveau riches* who were trying to exceed their proper station in life. Since they were regarded as having become too big for their breeches, attempts were made at slapping them down; when even the mightiest of these attempts failed, the Hohenzollerns loomed bigger yet. Older princely families often could not reconcile themselves to the success the Hohenzollerns achieved; when they became German emperors, they continued to outrage many of the courts, especially many German ones which found their lands now forcibly Prussianized. Prince Günther of Schwarzburg-Sondershausen, for example, exploded when it was suggested in the 1870's that he visit the Kaiser in Berlin; that Hohenzollern could come visit him, said this head of an ancient Thuringian family, but he would never venture to the capital. Hohenzollerns, spluttered the old prince, were nothing but "mushrooms" which had shot up "in a night." [2]

Such superior attitudes, however, availed no one. If the family had shot up like fungi, they proved indigestible to all; the compost on which the Hohenzollerns fattened amounted to dead wood, particularly that of the decaying Habsburg tree. Hohenzollern vitality was enormous; the Habsburgs came to be no match for them, even when their armies vastly outnumbered those of Prussia.

The first Hohenzollerns to arrive in the Mark Brandenburg are described by British historian A. J. P. Taylor as "ruthless, unprincipled military adventurers"; they were, Taylor claims, "the most backward and despised of the Electors" * who "had nothing great in their past, and no long-standing connection with the Electorate they had acquired." [3]

Their humble beginnings and initial lack of connection with Brandenburg are beyond dispute, but neither are to their discredit, for the Hohenzollerns were go-getters who became self-made men. They may have been adventurers, but that merely underlines the magnitude of what they ventured and what they ultimately attained. They were empire builders and frontiersmen as well as soldiers, great achievers as well as grand autocrats. They were aggressors in an age when cynical aggression was the rule; they may have been as ruthless in their pursuit of power as all other kings, but they were often more successful. Ultimately, the Prussia they shaped became an intriguing mass of apparent contradictions: It was a preserve of royal absolutism, yet also a *Rechtsstaat,* a state under laws which even the mighty obeyed; it was a shrine to the doctrine of the divine right of kings, even in the twentieth century, but was endowed with the enlightened notion that a king was his state's first servant, not merely its master; it was a vast prison for political liberals, yet also a safe refuge for victims of religious persecution, even for Jews; it was a garrison state which became a hatchery of aggressive wars, yet liberals within it periodically hailed its soldier kings as though liberalism, peace, and concord might be secured by Prussian guns.

Theirs is a success story, nor does the fall of the House of Hohenzollern diminish its achievement. Like many a millionaire when the bubbles burst, the Hohenzollerns were simply caught short in 1918 and were wiped out in the crash that followed. Madame de Pompadour's remark *"Après nous le déluge"* might have been uttered by Kaiser William II, the last reigning Hohenzollern in Germany, for the collapse of his house so convulsed his realm that it did in fact eventually unleash a flood.

* Electors (in German, *Kurfürsten*) were a small, select group of princes and bishops privileged to cast a vote for the Emperor of the "Holy Roman Empire of the German Nation," an elective position which, in practice, came to be held by successive Habsburgs for centuries.

This was called Nazism; its ebb swept away everything the Hohenzollerns had built up so diligently, so ruthlessly, and always with such loving care: the state; the way of life; the attitude of mind called Prussia. When the Hohenzollerns were finally forced to flee in 1918, after 500 years on their throne, there was no one left to laugh superiorly, for all German princes everywhere had toppled with them. The Hohenzollerns not only left behind them the memory of great deeds and impossible achievements, the stuff of that legendary "Prussian glory" which intoxicates many Germans even today, but also left behind a creation they had indirectly helped to shape and which remains with us yet: the German character. *Die Schule der Nation* ("the school of the nation") for a long time meant only one thing to the Germans: the German army—more particularly, the army of the King of Prussia, the army which the Hohenzollerns built and perfected. Their Hohenzollern ruler was more than just head of the state: He was their supreme warlord (*oberste Feldherr*) and, incidentally, the first bishop in the state church. He taught them not only on the drill field, but in school and church as well. Over the centuries and largely through the aegis of the army, the House of Hohenzollern gradually developed into the schoolhouse of the German people, imbuing first the Prussians and, later, all Germans with beliefs and attitudes, with patterns of thought and action, which were useful to the Hohenzollern state. Thus these rulers helped mold the best and noblest, as well as the most wretched, features of that unique and tortured, puzzling and contradiction-ridden race, that strange population of mystics and warriors, poets and policemen, philosophers and robots, sycophants and men of principle, martyrs and bootlickers, creative geniuses and destructive bullies. Being their lords, the Hohenzollerns proved to be exemplars—but also microcosms—of them all.

Throughout the centuries the Hohenzollerns had taught their subjects obedience well. Three times these subjects rebelled against their lords, but only three times: in 1448, in 1848, and in 1918. The last uprising was less against the Hohenzollerns than it was against continuing the war; had William II handled the crisis better, his dynasty might have survived, even if he himself had had to leave the country. The first two rebellions, separated by 400 years almost to the day, were quelled in the one instance and allowed to fizzle out in the other, and only led to the Hohenzollerns' increasing their power. Except for these few times, the subjects of this house accommodated themselves to the rule of a sometimes benevolent but often brutal junta of military aristocrats and court officials. The dynasty, after all, had for most of its years been so successful that those who yearned to trim its powers seemed malcontents. Even before the Thirty Years' War began in 1618, Brandenburg had been greatly enlarged in size; the year the war started, the duchy of Prussia came under the control of the Hohenzollern Elector of Brandenburg. Despite all that the lands suffered during the war, they endured less than other German lands and then staged a remarkable recovery under a brilliant young ruler who came to the throne in 1640. By the start of the eighteenth century the electorate had been elevated to a kingdom, a century before Napoleon Bonaparte raised other German princes to kingly rank. The father of Frederick the Great, who became king shortly thereafter, may have been a monstrous parent, but he was a wonderfully devoted father to his army; he created a marvelous machine which all Europe underrated but which his son did not. No sooner had this son, Frederick II, come to the throne than he set this machine in motion, triumphing so brilliantly that Napoleon later remarked, "Prussia is hatched from a cannonball." Greatly enlarged in size by the end of the eighteenth century, Prussia even survived complete disaster at the hands of Napoleon, as well as dismemberment and occupation by the French; ultimately, Prussian soldiers helped liberate Europe from Napoleonic rule, fighting alongside Wellington at Waterloo. Half a century later, under the guidance of Bismarck, the Hohenzollerns defeated the Austrians, flabbergasting all Europe; in one stroke, they had eliminated all Habsburg influence in Germany and had Prussianized two-thirds of all the Germans. The remaining third was added after 1871, when a German Reich was proclaimed, fulfilling that age-old dream of German patriots and liberals: the dream of German unity. Oddly, neither this dream nor the new imperial dignity pleased the King of Prussia who became emperor, for Prussia was sacred to him while Germany was not. The character of the Hohenzollern fief was being changed, he feared; most Hohenzollerns had a horror of all change.

Never uneventful, the times of the Hohenzollerns constituted a period of monumental attainments, of enormous heroism over vast odds, of survival in the face of great coalitions of enemies, and of a period of feverishly exciting growth. Because most of the Hohenzollern era was a time of expansion, it constituted Prussia's—and Germany's—"frontier heritage"; it has the glamor for Germans today that the Old West has for Americans. Brave men, bold deeds, large prizes—these constitute one side of its coin. Harshness, brutality, and blood—these constitute the other. Even today, the Germans have not entirely recovered from the glittering experience. Even now, the words *Preussens Gloria* ("Prussia's glory") excite many of them with visions of the Great Elector rushing to liberate his lands from the Swedes, of Frederick II's decimated grenadiers triumphing with only courage for their weapon, of Zieten's cavalry thundering to surprise a foe, of the Old Dessauer bargaining with heaven before charging into the cannon mouths at Kesselsdorf, of Blücher's armies revenging themselves on Bonaparte, of Moltke defeating the Habsburgs at Königgrätz and the French before Paris, of the unprecedented *fin-de-siècle* prosperity the German Empire enjoyed after a Hohenzollern became Kaiser in 1871. The enchantment of it all has not vanished; there is something chimerical about the Hohenzollern name even today, at least for the Germans. Only a minority would welcome a monarchy again, but more Germans than one might expect would like to see a Hohenzollern act at least as ceremonial head of state. In November, 1968, exactly fifty years after Kaiser William II fled Germany forever, the newspaper with the largest circulation in West Germany, *Bild-Zeitung,* polled its readers, asking whom they would choose as President of the Federal Republic, if they had the opportunity. The man whom the party delegations subsequently elected, Gustav Heinemann, came in second, with 14.3 percent of the popular vote. Almost *four times* as many readers (55.6 percent) voted for someone not officially in the running: the claimant to the vanished imperial crown of Germany, Prince Louis Ferdinand of Prussia, grandson of the last Kaiser, and head of the House of Hohenzollern today.

2

From Lazy Gretel to a Great Elector

PART of the business of kings is to produce babies. Royal houses need to grow by means of conquests, whether in love or war; both the marriage bed and the battlefield require heirs to fill them. Enough children had to be brought into the world so that at least some of them would survive childhood. The Hohenzollerns took this aspect of their job as seriously as they took most others, being in general uncommonly devoted to their sense of duty. One early Hohenzollern, John George, sired twenty-three children, the last of these being born shortly after the father had died of his exertions at age seventy-three; in the eighteenth century, a relative noted with satisfaction that the work of producing babies in the Berlin Palace "went on night and day." The family tree, therefore, came to be luxuriant.

All these Hohenzollerns originally sprang from the first-recorded member of the family, Burchard I (or Burchardus), about whom nothing is known except that he was killed on August 29, 1061, together with a kinsman, Wezil. This obscure early member of the family lived in South Germany, in what is today called the *Land* (or state) of Baden-Württemberg. He and those who followed him were *Schwaben*—Swabians—and these South Germans have a reputation for industry and business cunning which is legendary. Piling up gold and possessions and amassing lands are said to count most for the *Schwabe.* If ever there was a German who "lived to work, rather than worked to live," then this is the Swabian. "Money comes first" is said to be his motto, and he is said to be little interested in anything but what is his or what he can make his own by dint of work or guile. Several Hohenzollerns seemed to have had large quantities of Swabian blood in their veins.

The Swabian castle of Burchard I was called Zolorin or Zolre and was perched atop a mountain south of Tübingen. One explanation of the origin of the family name traces it to *Zoll,* meaning a customs or toll charge which the counts of Zolorin or Zolre may have levied on traders passing through these lands, as was the custom elsewhere. Others believe the name may have derived from *Söller,* which means a balcony or loft and which could have described its perch atop the mountain; still others trace it to *mons solarius* ("sun mountain"), the Latin name for the hill, for in Roman days it contained a shrine to a Germanic sun-god.

The family whose name evolved to Zollern and eventually to Hohenzollern ("High," or mighty, Zollern) might have stayed in South Germany forever, had not an early descendant of Burchard championed the cause of the Hohenstaufen Emperor Frederick I, who was called Barbarossa, or Redbeard. This emperor was a sort of Germanic King Arthur, regarded as the very embodiment of all knightly virtues, and was the leader of the Third Crusade. After Barbarossa had drowned accidentally during this expedition, his son and successor rewarded Frederick III of Zollern for his services by making him Burgrave of Nuremberg in 1191 (or possibly 1192); as was customary, Frederick III styled himself Frederick I, being the first of his line and name to assume that position.

Thus it was that the family moved away from Swabia, to Franconia.* The title *Burggraf* ("burgrave"), literally meant fortress count (*Burg* = fort; *Graf* = count); it signified a military governor of a city whose task it was to protect the emperor's castle or fortress within that city, as well as to administer justice. Nuremberg, however, became a *Reichsstadt,* meaning that it was granted the rank of a free imperial city, which led the

* The Zollern-Hohenberg line, also directly descended from Burchard I, remained behind but was extinct in all its branches by 1486. The later Swabian Hohenzollerns were descended from the Frederick who established the Franconian line of the family after moving to Nuremberg. (A younger line, Zollern-Schalksburg, died out in 1408.)

citizens to govern themselves and even to assume the job of defending the imperial fortress in the town. The burgrave was compelled to build himself a castle of his own, whereupon the citizens walled themselves in, in order to lock him out. In Nuremberg they even built a wall around the burgrave's castle during one of his absences, which meant he could enter it only with their permission.

By conquest, marriage, and outright purchase, however, the fortunes of the Hohenzollerns flourished in Nuremberg. They added other Franconian lands to their possessions, notably the towns of Ansbach and Bayreuth. Finally, services rendered by another one of their line to yet another emperor secured for them the most important of their possessions, the Mark Brandenburg, far to the north, from which they would eventually fashion the kingdom of Prussia and, later on, the German Empire.

The Mark (march, or frontier region) Brandenburg consisted of about 10,000 square miles of land and was about the size of Sicily or a fifth that of England today; it was first settled by Germans after the conquests of Charlemagne had extended the Frankish Empire to the world of the Slavs. Margraves, or border counts, were established in forts and fortified towns throughout this region, to protect the empire against incursions of Slavs; the *Nordmark* or *Altmark* ("North" or "Old Mark") was the most important of these buffer regions. Men were mobilized for its defense under Albert the Bear, a member of the Ascanian House; every ninth man had to serve, and every robber was given the choice of soldiering or being hanged. Albert the Bear conquered the hill fort called Brandenburg and converted its Wendish (*i.e.,* Slavic) ruler to Christianity; by the time he and his successors had finished colonizing and converting the region, most of the Wends had disappeared. Peasants from western Germany were brought in to populate the region, being offered 60-acre homesteads, twice what they might have hoped to have back home. This generosity was necessary, for the land was twice as difficult to cultivate, much of it consisting of sand, swamp, and marshes, and open to rapacious raids by robber barons who lived throughout the region and who were the highwaymen and extortionists of the times.

Armies as we know them were unknown at the time, but the Ascanian rulers did command so many men who were armed for the defense of the mark that Brandenburg came to be one of the most important portions of the empire. A hundred years before the Ascanian House died out, the margraves of Brandenburg had already received the rank of electors as well. This occurred in 1230. By 1320 the Ascanians were gone, and the mark fell into the hands of the Bavarian Wittelsbachs, who cared nothing about it. Otto the Lazy, a drunkard, sold the lands to Emperor Charles IV and spent the proceeds on wine, drinking himself to death in Wolfstein Castle in Bavaria, rolling as "deep as possible in every sort of debauchery," as one account puts it. The region thereupon fell to the Luxemburgers, who were no better. Ultimately, they pawned the lands as one might pawn a ring; Brandenburg was repawned several times until the pawn tickets ended up in Hohenzollern pockets.

Frederick VI was Burgrave of Nuremberg in the early fifteenth century and had helped Emperor Sigismund attain imperial rank; Sigismund, who had inherited Brandenburg from the Luxemburgers, made Frederick VI governor (*Statthalter*) of the region in return for a loan of 100,000 gold guldens. Frederick had fought alongside Sigismund in the past, and the emperor wanted a man like him to assert imperial law in lands overrun and terrorized by Junker landowners, then little more than robber barons.*

Frederick Hohenzollern arrived in the Mark Brandenburg in 1412 and invited the rebellious, independent-minded Junkers to dine with him, hoping to use persuasion rather than force. They, however, were for the most part intractable; one of them said he would not give in "even if it rained Nurembergers." He was compelled to eat his words, for Frederick was just as stubborn in his determination to put down all rebelliousness and lawlessness. He sent for Franconian knights from Nuremberg, then for a huge cannon nicknamed Lazy Gretel (*Faule Gretel*), borrowed from Thuringia. Gretel impressively knocked

* Junker derives from *Jungherr,* the early meaning of which was young master or young lord (today: young gentleman); it was applied to the sons of the landowning nobility in the eastern territories of the empire. The Prussian army's term for officer cadets, *Fahnenjunker* ("flag Junker") reflects this original meaning. As the term came to mean Prussian landed nobles in general, the nineteenth century came to call landed conservatism *Junkertum,* or Junkerism.

down walls 24 feet thick, as at the Friesack castle of Dietrich von Quitzow, after which the Junkers surrendered. Frederick did not punish them for their rebelliousness, for he was a magnanimous man, as many a Hohenzollern tends to become once he has had his way. He kept his cannon close at hand but began a round of dinners again.

In return for a further loan of 200,000 gold guldens, the emperor invested Frederick on April 17, 1417, with permanent possession of the Mark Brandenburg as well as with the joint titles of margrave and elector. The new ruler, who retitled himself Frederick I, proved more than an able man. A contemporary scholar called him "a model of morality and uprightness, such as is seldom seen in so high a place"; he was filled with virtues and a "zeal for justice." [4]

A man of such quality, however, was needed for imperial affairs elsewhere and could not be wasted stuck in the backwater called Brandenburg. Frederick I remained in the mark only a few years and never returned there again after 1426, leaving behind a son called John the Alchemist.

The Hohenzollerns (as they had begun to call themselves in the thirteenth century) had, within about 200 years, promoted their fortunes well. That Swabian instinct for bettering one's position and that Swabian capacity for hard work had taken an insignificant family off a castle on a remote crag first to the governorship of a large and prosperous city, then to the ownership of neighboring towns, and finally to sovereignty over 10,000 square miles of a poor but strategically important land. From counts of Zollern, they had become burgraves and then margraves and electors, the latter title a tremendous honor and one which conferred power and influence as well as dignity on the house. The Nuremberg, or Franconian, Hohenzollerns thus became the fathers of all the major lines of the house: the Brandenburg line, which came to be the most important; the Ansbach and Bayreuth lines which remained important only until they were ceded to Prussia in 1791; and the Swabian line, the second major branch of the family. This latter, which also stemmed from Burchard I and was founded by Burgrave Frederick II of Nuremberg (who died in the mid-thirteenth century), was equally as long but not as spectacularly successful as the Brandenburgers, though it produced all of Rumania's kings from the nineteenth to the twentieth century: Carol I, Ferdinand, Carol II (best remembered for marrying Magda Lupescu), and Michael, whom the Communists ousted in 1947.*

The animosity existing between the Hohenzollern burgraves and the imperial city of Nuremberg has already been mentioned; it produced in the Hohenzollerns a distinct antiurban tendency. To be sure, they were not the only princes who disliked the cities of the time, being unable to break their independent spirit, for the fifteenth century in Germany was a time of constant friction between the urban patricians and merchant oligarchies on the one hand and the aristocracy on the other. The issue was simple: The aldermen who ruled the cities wished to retain their privileges and their freedoms, while the princes wished to impose their authority on them. Unfortunately for the cities of the Mark Brandenburg, however, the urban oligarchies were threatened not merely by their prince and by the Junker aristocrats, but also by a rebellious commons, represented by members of lower guilds, as well as by other burghers. The opposition in the towns was, therefore, divided, and divided they fell.

The Hohenzollerns had first entered the Mark Brandenburg to assert their authority over the independent Junkers and to subjugate any who continued to be rebellious or refractory; they had to spend the following decades subjugating the towns. Frederick's son, John the Alchemist, began the process, siding with the aldermen against rebellious burghers at Prenzlau, the city of Brandenburg, Stendal, and Salzwedel. Members of the guilds and the commons were compelled to swear allegiance to the patrician aldermen; several rebellious burghers were executed and others banished. John the Alchemist had succeeded in making the ruling urban classes dependent on him and his power if they wished to retain their own. But John was dispirited by the conflicts and turned the affairs of the mark over to his brother in 1440; this brother, Frederick II, a man of steel, quickly earned the sobriquet of *Eisenzahn* ("Iron Tooth").

Frederick II was not satisfied with the fact that the aldermen were dependent on his power. The very fact that they gov-

*** It also produced princes of Hohenzollern, of Hohenzollern-Hechingen, and of Hohenzollern-Sigmaringen.**

erned their own towns vexed him. When he first came to the throne, his antiurban bias was made plain right away, for he confirmed the rights and privileges of the twin cities of Berlin-Cölln not in the customary and solemn manner by invoking heaven itself, but only in "simple words," as the town clerk noted. Berlin-Cölln had assumed considerable power, for the aldermen had united the two city administrations, had established a common court and town hall, had elected their own judges, and had become members of that trading fraternity, the Hanseatic League. The guilds, however, had been denied any share in the government of the twin cities, and they and the commons made the mistake in 1442 of asking Frederick to champion their cause. They wanted the joint administration abolished, asked that separate town councils be reestablished for Berlin and Cölln, and generally pleaded for assistance in their quarrel with those who denied them their civic rights. It was natural for them to turn to a prince who seemed to stand above the quarrel and who had armed men who might intervene with success, for where else could they turn? What they perhaps failed to realize was that Frederick Iron Tooth, if he intervened, would do so for his own reasons and not theirs; it was not in the interests of the House of Hohenzollern to champion the cause of freedom, but rather the elevation of its own power. Having become sovereign over a rebellious land and over independent-minded towns, Frederick needed to assert his sovereignty. The Mark Brandenburg itself needed to be subdued or, it might be said, actually conquered, before the Hohenzollerns could go on to subdue and conquer anyone else.

In February, 1442, Iron Tooth entered the city of Berlin-Cölln with an armed force. At gunpoint, as it were, he compelled the councilors to deliver the key to the cities to him, dissolved the council, and appointed two new ones, one for each town. He issued a decree which called for the annual election of new town councils, the members of which were to be drawn mainly from the guilds and commons; he himself had veto rights over every councilor chosen and could install substitutes if he saw fit. All alliances which Berlin and Cölln had made with other towns were nullified, and six months later the margrave took further steps to ensure his electoral rule over the towns. Their right to choose their own judges was abolished, as was their joint town hall; further, the cities had to cede to the margrave a portion of land in Cölln, on the island embraced by the arms of the Spree, for a fortress of his own. This came to be called the Zwingburg, a fort designed to force the citizenry to obey, a Coercion Castle, translated literally. A first stone was laid in 1443, and construction began in earnest in 1447; the Hohenzollern castle which grew from this was to remain standing for more than 500 years, nor was its character to change for much of that time.

The relationship between the urban citizenry throughout the Mark Brandenburg and their Hohenzollern margraves and electors began on a sour note; in the important towns of Berlin and Cölln, the relationship soon deteriorated further. Not only was the construction of the Hohenzollern Zwingburg within their walls an ugly sign that electoral rule was there to stay, but it seemed to the citizens like an affront, even like a provocation. In 1448 they revolted.

Opening a sluice, they attempted to flood the foundations of the Zwingburg with Spree water; then they stormed the palace itself, forced its doors, ransacked its rooms, and destroyed papers in its archives. They arrested the judge whom the margrave had appointed, held him prisoner, and refused to release him after the margrave had demanded his freedom.

They then sought to obtain support from other towns in Brandenburg which had grievances against the elector and sent word to many of them that their ruler was a tyrant who was trampling not only on their civic rights and prerogatives, but on their personal freedoms as well. But only three or four other towns had the courage to join them in defying electoral rule, and these were not enough.

The margrave, meanwhile, was also seeking support from the towns in Brandenburg. He toured the mark, addressing citizens in one town square after another, making impassioned and apparently eloquent pleas for their help in crushing the rebellion, asking them for men at arms, as well as expressions of loyalty. He also played on their rivalries with Berlin and Cölln; Spandau, Bernau, and several other towns which had been jealous of the prosperity and former independence of their neighbors, offered to join forces with Frederick Iron Tooth. Soon the twin cities were ringed by allies of the elector—and by 600 armed knights who stood by to crush them. Faced with such odds, Berlin and Cölln surrendered; as noted, they surrendered for 400 years. By 1452 opposition had been so well broken that the towns even resigned from the Hanseatic League. But the opposition of other towns to certain measures of the electoral rule continued for a time thereafter, under Frederick's successor. Frederick Iron Tooth had in his later years increased his lands, by purchase, by about 50 percent, buying the New Mark from the Teutonic Order, a quasi-religious order of knights which resulted from the Crusades and which ruled portions of Prussia. They needed funds, and Frederick used this need to purchase from them valuable land to the east of his North or Old Mark, which eventually would help link Brandenburg with East Prussia. Some further purchases increased the Hohenzollern possessions in the region toward the southeast. Directly to the north lay Pomerania, which Frederick could not conquer but against which he warred, becoming an indirect casualty of that struggle. While besieging Uckermünde, Frederick Iron Tooth was dining when a cannonball crashed into the room and through the table directly in front of him. The experience would have been enough to unnerve any man; it destroyed Frederick's hearing, impaired his memory, and made him reflect on the mortality of man. Naturally pious, he withdrew to meditate; within a year he was dead. The electorate of Brandenburg went to his brother from Ansbach. This was Albert, called Achilles because of his prodigious strength and warlike nature. Tall, muscular, Roman-nosed, Albert went far in the Mark Brandenburg. He completed the process of subduing the towns which had begun under him to be unpleasant about taxation, and he even conquered Pomerania. He and his son, John, called John Cicero in later years, consolidated the power of their house with considerable success.* Albert Achilles' rule was even distinguished, in that he took a real interest in government and administration, regulated state employees and paid them fixed wages, and even instituted a system of accounting when few were keeping accurate records of this kind. He

* The belief that John was called Cicero because he delivered brilliant orations in fluent Latin is without foundation. He spoke no Latin at all. Nor was he even called Cicero in his time. Philipp Melanchthon (1497–1560), Luther's great champion, the great educator, created this pleasant fiction.

foreshadowed many a later Hohenzollern, for the house was always as filled with bookkeepers and officials as it was with soldiers, the dynasty being generally distinguished for the interest it took in sensible, efficient, honest, and, above all, frugal administration.

It was the custom in Albert Achilles' time to divide lands equally among the sons upon the ruler's death; Albert was far-sighted enough to see that this deplorable custom weakened a family by forever fragmenting its lands among more and more relations. The *Dispositio* (or *Constitutio*) *Achillea,* published in 1473, with which he freed the House of Hohenzollern from this tradition, became famous and in his day was almost a revolutionary document. It stipulated that the House of Hohenzollern would henceforth divide its possessions in the following manner: The eldest son would always receive the Mark Brandenburg intact, and any second and third sons would receive Ansbach and Bayreuth respectively; if there were more than three sons, suitable bishoprics should be found for them, and if either the Bayreuth or the Ansbach lines died out, then Brandenburg would take possession of the vacant Franconian holding. This testament of Albert Achilles not only ensured that the family possessions would not be fragmented over succeeding generations, but for the first time established formally that the Brandenburg line was foremost.

One of the sparks which ignited the Protestant Reformation in Germany was unwittingly struck by a Hohenzollern. John Cicero died in 1499, when Luther was only sixteen years old; he was followed by his son, Joachim I. In accordance with the provisions of the *Dispositio Achillea,* one of Joachim's brothers became an ecclesiastic. This was Albert, and no sooner was he ordained a priest than he was made an archbishop (in his teens) and, presently, a cardinal, as well as the Elector of Mainz, on the Rhine, in 1514. (Thus, during this time, the House of Hohenzollern cast two votes in the electoral college.) Deeply in debt to bankers in Augsburg named Fugger, the young cardinal set up Johann Tetzel, the preacher, in the business of selling indulgences, which provoked Luther into publishing his ninety-five theses in 1517. The cardinal, however, seemed not very disturbed by the Lutheran movement and was so generous in his attitude that Luther even suggested to him he ought to take up the new faith and become secular ruler in Mainz. It was not until the Peasants' Revolt (1524) that Albert took a decisive stand against Protestantism. Elector Joachim I, on the other hand, was so passionately orthodox a Roman Catholic that his marriage broke up over his beliefs. Elizabeth of Denmark, his wife, had been found out by him to be a secret Protestant; when he threatened to wall her up for the rest of her life, she fled the Berlin Palace at night with only a maid and one groom for companions, finding shelter with John the Steadfast in Saxony.

Three years before she left Berlin, an incident occurred which illustrates the character of this particular Hohenzollern. Joachim was somewhat of an irresolute weakling, but he was interested in learning (he founded the university at Frankfurt an der Oder in 1506) and one branch which particularly fascinated him was astrology, which he pursued from a small observatory he had built onto his palace. The court astrologers one year predicted to him that the entire Mark Brandenburg would be destroyed by a great flood on July 15, 1525, and Joachim, who was a prudent and cautious man, arranged for the rescue at least of his court.

There was no time to build an ark, only crates and boxes; these were hurried onto a wagon train the moment the clouds broke at noon on the promised day. The procession clattered off to the highest point in the region, the Kreuzberg, but Joachim must have known he was clutching at straws for, while Mount Ararat looms 14,000 feet above its plain, the Kreuzberg is only 217 feet high. Joachim, Elizabeth, and their entire court sat drenched atop this hill throughout the afternoon, while troops surrounded it to keep the commoners at bay. Ultimately, of course, the rains ceased, and the sheepish nobles sloshed back to their carriages for the ride home. Crowds of locals reportedly were amused by the spectacle of their bedraggled, soaked betters. No sooner had the cavalcade arrived in the palace courtyard than the rain started to pour down again. Suddenly, a bolt of lightning crashed down into the wagon train; Joachim fainted, as though thunderstruck. When the cold rain on his face finally awakened him, he learned that the lightning bolt had killed his coachman. "Aside from that," commented a laconic chronicler, "the weather did no further damage." [5]

A real calamity occurred in Germany that same year: the Peasants' Revolt and its bloody suppression by the nobles. Germany had already been declining in economic importance for some time because of the discovery of new worlds across the seas; these explorations led a land of boom to sink into a backwater. The body blow came as a blow to the spirit. Luther delivered it by siding with the princes against the peasants, although it had been his ideas which had fired their hunger for human rights. From the moment Martin Luther publicly advocated the *massacre* of the insurgent peasantry, he became a pawn of despots. Germany came to be wrested from the enlightening clutches of the Renaissance, but even more damage was done than that. The merchant class ended up siding with the princes, especially since these were now dignified by heading the church as well. A counterweight to princely power was aborted in Germany, killed before it was even born. The greatness of Lutheranism—its assertion of the inviolability of the human conscience—assumed secondary importance in Germany; of greater importance was Luther's claim that all established authority, even that of tyrants, had to be obeyed absolutely.

Casimir, the Hohenzollern who ruled Bayreuth at the time, obeyed Luther's call to massacre the peasantry; he swept upon them like an avenging angel, hanging them by the score. "Unhappy mortals," he shouted at them, "will you shake the world to pieces, because you have much to complain of?" His brother George, who ruled nearby Ansbach, was more merciful, spared those peasants he captured, and even tried to get Casimir to do the same. By way of reply, Casimir warned George not "to let the dog learn to eat leather"—lest he chew through leash and muzzle.

One Hohenzollern had made an early break with the Roman Catholic Church, again with fateful consequences for the house and for the history of the lands it would rule. In 1510, Albert, one of Albert Achilles' grandsons who was destined for an ecclesiastical life, was elected grand master of the Teutonic Order (*Deutscher Ritterorden*). The knights of this order originally entered far-off Borussia ("bordering on Russia") at the invitation of a Polish duke; they were then a charitable religious order devoted to missionary work. They Christianized Borussia (*i.e.*, Prussia) by the simple expedient of slaughtering almost all its heathen Prusi population, who spoke a language resembling Latvian or Lithuanian, after which they repopulated the region with German Christian farmers and townsfolk. Gradually, great cities were established in this remote fief, and both culture and commerce flourished, until the order's influence reached to Estonia. As time went on, however, the presence of these Germans vexed the Poles, just as the glitter of the cities the Germans had built aroused their cupidity. In the fifteenth century the Poles recaptured some of the Prussian lands from the aristocratic squatters whom they had invited into the region, and the order was forced to cede West Prussia along with Danzig, as well as to acknowledge the hegemony of the Polish king over the rest of their lands. Albert of Hohenzollern became grand master at the nadir of the order's fortunes. He had been elected by the knights in the hope that he might obtain for them money and troops with which to fight Poland. Albert actually started a war against the Poles in 1519, but the help he had expected did not materialize, and he was defeated, forced again to make a humiliating peace. The Teutonic Order remained as before vassals of the King of Poland, with each grand master pledged to go to Warsaw to do homage and to swear that the knights would "love those whom Poland loved and hate those whom Poland hated." [6]

The Reformation secretly interested Grand Master Albert, though his order was of course Roman Catholic. In 1522, Andreas Osiander, the Nuremberg preacher, had converted him;[7] a year later Albert visited Martin Luther himself, at Wittenberg. "Give up your vow as a monk, take a wife, abolish the Order," said Luther. "Then make yourself hereditary Duke of Prussia." [8] Albert thought it over in silence for a time, then roared with laughter at the irony implicit in the advice. He'd been elected grand master to protect the order and was now being asked to break it up. Nothing loath, however, he proceeded to do just that. In 1525 the order was dissolved, and the King of Poland confirmed Albert as Duke of Prussia, conferring on him a banner bearing the Prussian black eagle. The marriage he contracted had one unfortunate result: His son and successor was mad. Upon the death of this insane Duke Albert Frederick, the Elector of Brandenburg assumed the rank of Duke of Prussia as well. That happened in 1618 and marks the date when the state of Brandenburg-Prussia was first formed. But the two were not contiguous, nor was Brandenburg contiguous with lands it had obtained in the West, the Cleves-Jülich lands. The Hohenzollerns ruled over large territories, but they were unable to govern them effectively because they were scattered from Poland to the Rhine. Every time they wished to travel from one to the other of their possessions, they had to pass through someone else's pasture. No wonder they came to develop a wish to gobble those pastures up. Before they were able to do anything about that, however, their own lands were ravaged by other armies, for the horrors of the Thirty Years' War were now being unleashed on Germany. Brandenburg proved virtually indefensible, for it contained not a single city which was much more than a day's march from a frontier. Further, it was already in a state of economic decline when the war broke out, for trade routes had shifted in the decades which had passed, and many of these routes now no longer traversed Brandenburg at all. The war also reduced the fortunes of the state; indeed, it reduced much of its lands to ashes and its population to a condition of barbarity. At Tangermünde, for example, where the very first Hohenzollern in the Mark Brandenburg had dined the rebellious Junkers to persuade them to be loyal to the law, there was now so great a famine that "men ate human flesh," the records say; "nay, human creatures ate their own children." [9]

Two generations of men were being herded into the slaughter of this conflict. Elector George William, who acceded to the throne in Brandenburg in 1619, tried his best to straddle the fence; it turned into a rail, and he was ridden out on it. He was a disaster in a time of calamity, for when Brandenburg needed a Hohenzollern who was a Great Elector, it got only George William, the Great Elector's father. "On the whole," wrote Thomas Carlyle, "George Wilhelm did what is to be called nothing, in the Thirty-Years War; his function was only that of suffering." [10]

He was a Protestant whose brother-in-law was Gustavus Adolphus of Sweden, yet he was completely at the mercy of

Adam von Schwarzenberg, his strong-minded adviser, a man who was loyal to the Catholic Habsburgs and very likely in their pay. As a result, he pursued middle-of-the-road policies, occasionally vacillating from one side to the other, until almost everyone, with a nice impartiality, began ravaging and sacking his lands.

Germany was a cripple before the war began; that cripple was now being bled to death. The conglomerate of states which formed the empire had been declining economically and was virtually on the road to destruction before the war ever started, but the war accelerated the process of disintegration until it finally killed off whatever importance Germany had enjoyed before.

This was not one war, but four separate wars, escalating in ferocity and bloodshed, partly religious in character, but mainly concerned with territorial and dynastic questions. The Bohemian phase of the war, with which the conflicts were all unleashed, began when Protestant Bohemian nobles deposed King Ferdinand, who later emerged as Emperor Ferdinand II, and replaced him with a Protestant king, Frederick V, "The Winter King." Catholic forces under Maximilian, Duke of Bavaria, and under Count Johannes Tilly defeated the Protestants in 1620 to 1623, but the intervention of the Danish king, who was leader of the Protestants, opened the second, or Danish, phase of the struggle. Albrecht von Wallenstein became commander of the imperial (*i.e.,* Catholic) forces and, over a period of four years, defeated the Danes, who withdrew from the war in 1629. A year later, King Gustavus Adolphus of Sweden landed on the coast of Pomerania, north of the Mark Brandenburg, ostensibly to protect the Protestants being oppressed by Catholics in Germany; in this third phase of the war, he obtained the backing of Catholic France, which hoped the conflict would reduce the power of the House of Habsburg. Terrible battles followed, with Tilly being mortally wounded in 1632 and Gustavus Adolphus being killed later the same year. Wallenstein, who commanded a huge private army, and the emperor, whose cause he ostensibly served, became estranged; ultimately, Wallenstein was assassinated, and though the emperor was not behind the murder, he rewarded the assassins handsomely. In 1634 the Catholic forces triumphed over the Swedes at Nördlingen, and a year later, the Peace of Prague was signed, to which Brandenburg acceded, being allowed freedom of worship. This peace, however, did not end the war, for it now seemed to the French as though the Habsburgs had triumphed, and France openly entered the conflict on the side of the Swedes. From 1635 to 1648 the war continued in its final phase, this being the bloodiest, and spread into Scandinavia, the Netherlands, Italy, and the Iberian Peninsula, although most of the conflict raged as before over German lands. Ultimately, the Franco-Swedish forces were triumphant, and the House of Habsburg began its decline as France became the dominant power in Europe. The Treaty of Westphalia (1648) officially ended the war, at least in Germany, though it continued in the case of France and Spain for almost eleven years longer.

As a war, it was worse than most; in fact, it was worse than any. Rival armies crisscrossed towns and farmlands, destroying at random and in a hysteria of hatred born of desperation. While the struggle was ostensibly religious, this proved soon enough to be a cloud of bunkum behind which the rival armies wheeled. Torture and bestiality were the rule, largely owing to the war's religious pose; further, the soldiers lived almost without exception off the land by means of outright robbery and murder and often starved as much as did the peasants from whom they stole. Trees were festooned with hanging bodies; dead men were found with grass in their mouths; jailed prisoners, who might have expected to be safe from war, feared for their lives at the hands of hungry jailers. Village and town stank of death; contagion—even the plague—blew about with soot and ash. Peasants whose homes lay outside fortified towns were butchered, their women raped and mutilated, their animals killed or driven off. To be seen by soldiers meant to be impressed into service or murdered; the citizenry were used by whoever came upon them first. Brutalized over three decades of butchery and privation, soldiers lost all sense of mercy, and the populace lost all hope. While some towns (such as Dresden and Hamburg) miraculously escaped being ravaged, many virtually ceased to exist. According to some estimates, Magdeburg lost 90 percent of its population; Wolfenbüttel lost seven-eighths; Colmar lost half; Berlin and Cölln, which first lost a quarter of its people, was soon also reduced by 50 percent. The state of

Württemberg lost five-sixths of its population, while Bavaria lost 80,000 families. The city of Chemnitz was reduced from 1,000 inhabitants to 200. The Swedes alone destroyed 18,000 villages, 1,500 towns, and 2,000 castles. Where 21,000,000 people had lived in 1618, only 13,500,000 survived.

In Brandenburg, Elector George William's policy was one of appeasement; he ended up being devoured by his Swedish brother-in-law, who had waited in vain for him to support the Protestant cause. Gustavus Adolphus' armies swept over Brandenburg after seizing Pomerania, captured towns such as Frankfurt an der Oder, Küstrin, and even Spandau, which lay directly outside Berlin and Cölln. When Tilly led his imperial forces against nearby Magdeburg, George William was hesitant about letting Gustavus Adolphus relieve that city by passing through his territories (despite the fact that the archbishop there was a Hohenzollern); as a result, Tilly captured Magdeburg handily and then slaughtered virtually every one of its 40,000 men, women, and children. When George William finally acceded to the Treaty of Prague in 1635, this made him an enemy of the Swedes, whose troops remained encamped throughout his territories, nor did the emperor help George William drive them out. By 1638 George William had had enough and left his people in the lurch, which meant in the hands of Schwarzenberg. He himself took up residence in far-off Königsberg, East Prussia, where he remained until his death. Schwarzenberg was inherited by his son and successor, who dealt with him.

While Brandenburg was in the thick of war, the elector's son, Frederick William, was sent to Holland at the age of fifteen, partly for an education, partly for safety. So impoverished was the House of Hohenzollern by this time that his mother, the electress, had to skimp on food in order to pay for the journey. Frederick William was accompanied by a guardian named Leuchtmann, an ardent Calvinist, and, at his own request, by a friend, Werner von der Schulenburg. With them, he traveled to Leiden, where he attended the university for some years, becoming proficient in languages and science, deeply interested in the development of trade and commerce, and even somewhat experienced in war. This came about because the young man visited Frederick Henry of the House of Orange, a relative, at his Schenkenschanz camp, where he fought the Spaniards; there he received some practical instruction in military tactics, which he later put to good effect. Leaving the camp, he went to The Hague, where a group of Dutch aristocrats had invited him to a meeting of a "Midnight Society." Schulenburg warned him that the nobles were known sybarites, but Frederick William was not to be deterred: he wanted to see for himself, and he didn't want to pass judgment on hearsay. Sure enough, he walked right into an orgy and, to everyone's surprise, walked right out again. The participants pleaded and tried to hold him back; he refused to stay, but raced back to the Schenkenschanz camp, where he blurted out what he had seen to his Prince of Orange. Frederick Henry was enormously impressed that so young a man would find the strength to tear himself away from such old temptations. "Anyone who can learn so much self-control so early," he told Frederick William, "will accomplish something great."

He did. More than 100 years later, the greatest of the Hohenzollerns, Frederick II, whom they called Frederick the Great, opened his coffin to gaze at his features, still well preserved, touched the dead hand and told his attendants, *"Messieurs, celui-ci a fait de grandes choses"*—"Gentlemen, this one performed great works!" [11]

What this young man accomplished was nothing short of amazing. When he became Elector of Brandenburg, at the age of twenty, he found a country so ravaged it might as well be called destroyed: it took two years of effort just to make the farmland fruitful again. The Hohenzollern domains were reduced to nothing: split up; still occupied by Swedes; at the mercy of a hostile Habsburg emperor; its towns devastated; its population drastically reduced and utterly exhausted. The elector could not even govern from Berlin, for the palace roof was in danger of collapsing, nor was there food enough in the town to feed him and even a modest court. As for the "German nation"—that patchwork of principalities—it seemed to be utterly finished. Eight years after Frederick William acceded to the throne in Brandenburg, the Treaty of Westphalia left the empire standing, but its power was gone. Westphalia freed the German princes to conduct their own affairs, making each an absolute ruler responsible to none, although nominally under imperial rule. This meant that the nation was not merely divided, it was shattered. In Germany, there were now 51 imperial cities, 45 imperial towns, 77 major principalities, and 1,475 independent states ruled by imperial knights: a total of 1,800 political entities. Westphalia secured absolutism; it created 1,800 absolute rulers, many of them petty despots. It froze 1,800 political entities into a kind of enchanted medieval trance. The people waited for someone to break the spell; a legend grew to the effect that this would be the greatest German emperor of them all, Frederick Barbarossa, said to be seated, slumbering and waiting, inside a mountain, his red beard grown through the table in front of him, down to the floor.

To rebuild the Mark Brandenburg took ferocious energy, faith, and determination, as well as all the natural optimism of youth. These things Frederick William possessed in abundance. Handsome, with a strong nose and mouth, alert blue eyes, and a strong athletic body, he was not only intelligent, but filled with vigor and animated by religious faith. The reconstruction of Brandenburg required that he extricate himself from the war, well before the Treaty of Westphalia was signed. This he accomplished in 1641, the year after he became elector, when he effected an armistice with the Swedes. To do so, however, he had to give up hope of gaining western Pomerania, then under Swedish control; this meant he had to give up hope of gaining Stettin, an important harbor which would have given him an access to the sea at the estuary of the Oder River. He had been anxious to have that ever since he had observed maritime and naval power in Holland; he entertained the impossible hope of making his devastated possessions into another prosperous Netherlands.

Schwarzenberg, however, was conniving at subverting his plans; he actually persuaded the officers of Frederick William's army that they owed their allegiance to the emperor and got them to deny the elector their oath. A loyal officer named Burgsdorf seized the fortress of Küstrin on the elector's behalf, arresting treasonous officers, but the matter was not settled yet, although the infantry officers did give their oath of allegiance to the new elector. Schwarzenberg, however, continued to have the emperor on his side, and Frederick William was still far away in Königsberg while Schwarzenberg was in Berlin; finally, fortunately, the disloyal adviser collapsed at dinner in March, 1641, and died—"from grief of mind and disturbance of his feelings," as the doctors diagnosed afterward.[12] Frederick William's cousin, the Margrave Ernest von Brandenburg Jaegerndorf, was appointed to replace him. Against the emperor's express wishes, he dismissed a great many troops and even demanded that the officers provide an accounting of the goods and moneys they had extorted from the people. At this, the officers mutinied; one of them threatened to blow up Spandau Fortress rather than hand over such a list to civilians. Frederick William acted with dispatch, to the surprise of all those who remembered his father, and arrested some of the rebellious officers, dismissing others. Meanwhile, the Brandenburg peasantry had risen up against the Swedish troops, who had committed great barbarities; it was this rising that caused the Swedes to accede to peace with Frederick William in July, 1641. All these turmoils took their toll; the Margrave Ernest was exhausted by them and resigned, dying a year later. The loyal Burgsdorf took charge for a while; then, in March, 1643, Frederick William entered his *Residenzstadt,* Berlin, and took all affairs of state into his own strong, energetic hands.

He found a city in which the citizens had been reduced to eating cats, dogs, and rats—and some of them human corpses. In the Brandenburg countryside, agriculture had ceased to exist as farms had been laid waste and farmers murdered; as it had been 200 years before, robber barons and freebooters of every kind roamed the land. Demoralization was general, as were fatalism, cynicism, and opportunism. Seeking a breathing spell in which to rebuild the country, the elector sought to ally himself with Sweden by marriage: to become the husband (king consort) of Queen Christina, his cousin. This was opposed, however, by Swedish court circles, not to speak of the King of Poland, with whom Frederick William needed to deal most delicately for the time being; even Queen Christina did not seem enchanted by the idea, referring to her Hohenzollern suitor as "the little Burgomaster."

Frederick William turned to more immediately pressing matters. He required a professional, standing army to achieve freedom of action; to obtain that, he required funds by means of taxation. His Prussian estates were refractory, reluctant to submit to his tax collectors, and, being for the most part Lutheran, hostile on religious grounds to the Calvinist elector. Frederick William did not want to crush the estates; he favored keeping their privileges but saw the clear necessity of uniting his domain. He had no choice and began forcibly collecting taxes, asserting his preeminent position and compelling the estates to submit.

In 1646, Frederick William revisited Holland, his great love; it was there that he fell in love for the first time. The girl was Louise Henriette, daughter of the Prince of Orange. Frederick William had actually met her when she was a girl of twelve, but he had ignored her then and subsequently, for it had been rumored that she was in love with a Frenchman—or possibly with a Pomeranian named Otto von Schwerin. This did not prove to be the case; further, they fell in love. Frederick Henry of Orange gave his blessing to the match. The wedding took place in a hurry, in December, 1646, because Frederick Henry was ill and wanted to be alive to enjoy it.

Louise Henriette was an extraordinary woman: gentle, affectionate, yet very strong-willed and knowledgeable in political affairs. Frederick William, on the other hand, was given to rages, as was almost every Hohenzollern; most of them were "choleric," given to sudden bursts of anger, explosions, apoplectic fits and furies, foot stampings, fist bangings, and slamming of doors. Louise had a comment about everything that went on, good comments too, but they provoked quarrels. "Govern you then, Madame!" Frederick William would splutter, throwing his electoral hat to the ground at her feet. "It seems my covering is to be a *coif,* not this!" [13] Yet it all was half in jest, for he valued her advice and on occasion even left Privy Council meetings to seek Louise out in her apartments, to ask what she thought of the matter under discussion. She was devout, sincerely religious, as was her friend, the one who had been thought to be her suitor: Schwerin. Together they modified and eased the elector's tendency to rule with a heavy fist; together they tried to create harmony in a country torn with internal dissensions and religious strife. Furthermore, it was she who urged the elector to repopulate the decimated lands with hardworking, thrifty Dutchmen. These were brought in by means of enormous concessions: They were free of all taxation, could govern their own communities, could gather free lumber from the royal forests, paid very little rent for the ground they worked, and were allowed in certain cases to pass on their holdings to their children. Of course, the local German peasants and townsfolk objected to such preferential treatment. The continual arbitration of disputes which the elector needed to supervise turned out to be an education in statecraft. At firsthand, Frederick William learned the truth about his people: how they had been preyed upon by hordes of extortionary officials; how they had been discriminated against in terms of the lands they were allowed to work.

Once again, he moved decisively and imaginatively. He reduced the number of his officials, those who had profited from the peasantry, reduced the privileges of those remaining, offered to rent out his fisheries and vineyards, removed rank restrictions as they pertained to the holding of lands, removed oppressive duty payments and even freed the tenants from personal service to himself.

Meanwhile, he was building up a standing army at the expense of the Junkers on the estates, who wanted private armies under their own local control rather than a "national" army under the command of the elector personally. Even loyal Burgsdorf opposed the elector, as did most other Prussian nobles. Burgsdorf was thrown out of office as military adviser, partly because of his opposition, partly because Electress Louise found him coarse and vulgar; three generals in sympathy with Frederick William took his place.

Gradually, the elector united his scattered domains administratively. The refractory spirit of the estates gave way to his determined will; the size of his new standing army, his strong personality, and his growing power brought success in foreign affairs. He was a practical man, so he tore up a treaty with Poland and asserted his rights over ducal Prussia. He was said to be ruthless, cynical, unscrupulous; indeed, Carlyle calls him "one of the shiftiest of men," although he adds, "not unjust by any means." Clearly, he made the most of opportunity; his greatness lay in the fact that he made the most there could be made of the Mark Brandenburg.

Some of his efforts at enlarging the prestige of his state seem today vaguely theatrical or quixotic. With so few funds that he was dependent on other states, he went so far as to try and build a Dutch-style navy, even to begin attempts at colonizing. In 1682, he formed an African company and began settling the Guinean coast. He organized a fleet of twenty-eight vessels with more than 500 guns; he even won a naval victory over the Spaniards and went on to establish an East Indian company, for trade with India. Such expeditions affected Brandenburg very little, but they are more than historical curiosities, for they show the breadth of the man's imagination, his daring, and his interest in commerce and in the prosperity not only of his court but of his people.

Of greater importance was the fact that Frederick William finally rid his lands of Swedes—who had come back into them while Frederick William was fighting at the emperor's side against Louis XIV, far to the south of Germany. Louis had been Frederick William's sometime patron, and indeed, the elector was often to vacillate between allegiance to the French "Sun King" and the Habsburg emperor, but the cruelties of the French invaders of the Palatinate and his sympathies with Holland, then at war with Louis, caused Frederick William to go to Strasbourg in late 1674. There tragedy struck: his eldest son, Charles Emil, died of wounds, this being the son on whom Frederick William had pinned his hopes. The French, wishing to draw off the elector's forces, succeeded in interesting the Swedes in attacking Brandenburg while the elector and his troops were away, despite the fact that they had just signed an agreement with Frederick William, in which each guaranteed the other against attack. A cheap victory over prosperous lands which they coveted was too tempting for the Swedes; they invaded Brandenburg, tore the land apart, inflicting savage cruelties on the local citizens.

Far from rallying to the elector, his Junker lords and nobles in Brandenburg grasped this opportunity to wrest what power they could away from him, specifically again in the matter of raising "private" local armies of their own; to their amazement and consternation, the Brandenburg peasants spontaneously rose up in defense of Frederick William and the electorate, forming military units of their own and marching under hand-painted "electoral" flags, singing: "We are only peasants and little land have we; but we give our blood for our lord right cheerfully!"[14]

On June 5, 1675, Frederick William began the long march from Alsace to Brandenburg. He was fifty-five years old, suffered from gout and was in considerable pain, yet he rode in the saddle with his men for three weeks. He had 6,000 cavalrymen, 1,200 foot soldiers, and three guns; facing him were 16,000 Swedes. These were divided into three units, the central one of which the elector decided to attack, so as to stab the heart. The battle took place on June 16 and 17, the elector having driven the Swedes back on Fehrbellin (which gave the battle its name) during the night. The Swedes counterattacked, threatening the outnumbered Brandenburgers, whereupon Frederick William personally rushed forward at the advancing Swedes, sword raised, shouting as many a king had done throughout all ages past: "Forward! Your prince and captain conquers with you—or dies like a knight!" Immediately, Frederick William was surrounded by Swedish soldiery. An aide was killed at his side, attempting to shield his lord, whereupon dragoons broke in to rescue the elector. The personal intervention carried the day, however, for the Brandenburgers attacked with renewed force, compelling the Swedes to retreat to Fehrbellin. Asked by his aides to raze the occupied town by fire, Frederick William replied, "I have not come to destroy my country, but to save it."

The next day the Swedes retreated from Fehrbellin; then the peasants everywhere rose against their torturers and drove them out of the elector's territories. By 1677 Frederick William had captured Stettin and swept the Swedes from Pomerania. He thought he had his outlet to the sea at last, but he was wrong. At the Peace of Nymwegen (1678) the French insisted he surrender western Pomerania to the Swedes and, since Emperor Leopold I refused to support his claims, Frederick William was forced to sign.

His final encounter with the Swedes came in 1679. Unsatisfied, they had this time invaded not Brandenburg, but Prussia, again scourging the land like a plague, moving on Königsberg and threatening to capture it. Frederick William, racing 60 miles a day, reached Königsberg to find it still untouched; he found out upon his arrival that the Swedes were suffering from trichinosis, having gorged themselves on local pigs. Frederick

William had left Berlin at Christmas, 1678; he had covered more than 400 miles in two weeks, then raced his troops an additional 100 across the snow and ice in 1,200 wooden sleds to strike the Swedes and send them out of Prussia.

These military victories, especially the one at Fehrbellin, are what caused him to be called the Great Elector, although he might have earned this title for his enlightened policies as well. Certainly there was something grand, not merely great, about the man. It evidenced itself in his liberalization of the laws to benefit agriculture, industry, and commerce; it evidenced itself in his ability to form a semblance of a modern state, with centralized authority (down to a postal system) and a regular paid standing army. It evidenced itself also in his religious tolerance. Although he was a devout Protestant, he permitted Catholics and Jews in his territories. He was a practical man always, the type who liked the company of bourgeois merchants, and he had a merchant's sense of what his state required. His spirit showed itself again when France abrogated the Edict of Nantes in 1685, thus withdrawing the rights of its Protestant minority and sending thousands of Huguenots searching for new homes. Frederick William immediately condemned the French action and offered asylum to any Huguenot who wished to come.

With a stroke of the pen, Frederick William had brought new, exceptionally vigorous blood to the Mark Brandenburg. Five thousand French Huguenot artists, artisans, craftsmen, and merchants settled down in Berlin alone, bringing its population to 25,000 (it had been less than 6,000 in population when Frederick William became elector). They were not the only ones to be invited in. Dutch farmers had come already; now more Hollanders arrived: painters, sculptors, and architects. They helped him fortify his city (a massive undertaking which ringed Berlin with a huge wall it took a quarter century to build); they built the Friedrich Wilhelm Canal which linked the Oder River with the Spree, thus giving his lands an outlet to the sea at last: in Hamburg, to which the waterways led.

Louise had died, giving his hand three "farewell" squeezes upon her deathbed; he missed her dreadfully. The servants heard him murmur, looking at her portrait, "Louise, Louise, how much I miss your counsel!" He would miss it even more in later years, after marrying Dorothea of Holstein-Glücksburg, the widow of the Duke of Brunswick. Businesslike and practical, it was she who built Dorotheenstadt, then a suburb of Berlin, as a quarter for nobles; it was she also who gave the city its Unter den Linden avenue. But she was also hard and harsh; she almost turned out to be the apotheosis of the wicked stepmother. Charles Emil still lived when she married his father; strong, obstinate, and willful, he was not one for her to push around. But then Charles Emil died at Strasbourg and she turned with venom on the princeling who still lived.

Often violent, yet usually just, Frederick William was Brandenburg's version of Louis XIV, a "Sun King" for a distant northern land. He never built a Berlinese Versailles, but like Louis, he regarded himself as the embodiment of the state and of his people, the very expression of the popular will. The remark attributed to Louis XIV, "I am the state," could have been uttered by Frederick William of Hohenzollern, the Great Elector; he also believed his state and himself were divinely ordained and inseparable. He set the stamp of absolutism on Brandenburg and the House of Hohenzollern, having subdued his estates and centralized his administration; he set the seal of militarism on the state as well, from which it never recovered. Majestic, portly, with a strong hooked nose, covered with a fine Louis XIV wig, he even looked the glorious embodiment of the best sort of seventeenth-century ruler, much concerned with the well-being of his state, which meant to him his land and peoples, in every conceivable way. He had attained power when the fortunes of the Hohenzollerns and of the Mark Brandenburg were at their lowest ebb; he raised them and set the course for greatness. Under him, enlightened policies threw flecks of light on a canvas otherwise dark. The state was graced with a patron of arts and science, of industry and education; it was now catching up, having been earlier bypassed by the Renaissance. Yet the shadow he cast was there as well, the darker for all the light he brought: He set the course for the modern, militaristic and absolutist Prussian state. He died in 1688, less than forty years after the execution in England of King Charles I, it being said in later years that absolutism might never have left its stamp on

Germany had someone, somewhere, sometime, executed a Hohenzollern king. No one ever did, and so the future Hohenzollerns, often lesser men than the Great Elector, had free reign to do as they liked.

3

The Deformed Dandy

THE course of the House of Hohenzollern—indeed, that of Prussia and Germany—after the Great Elector's death was being decided while he was still alive: not by him, not in accordance with his wishes, but by a clumsy nurse. It was the year 1657, when the Great Elector was in his prime: thirty-seven years old, great deeds to do yet, and thirty-one more years to reign. A third child, Frederick, had been born that year to Electress Louise, on July 11. This infant was the electress' second surviving child, her firstborn having died within a year of his birth, in 1649, and her second, the aforementioned Charles Emil, being two years old and heir apparent upon the birth of the third son.

The infant Frederick was about six months old when his parents bundled him up and put him in charge of a nurse, so that he could accompany them on a winter's trip to Königsberg, in Prussia. This was a journey of several hundred miles, done in a coach. To understand what this might have been like, it is best to keep in mind the fact that the words "travel" and "travail" are related; these were not trips; they were tortures. Even 100 years later the roads were so filled with potholes that one was better off to ride a horse cross-country than venture out on them; they were called corduroy roads and with good reason. All this is central to the point. The carriage bounced about until the careless nurse in question lost control of the infant prince. The infant Frederick fell down—or fell backward in her arms—injuring his back so badly that he afterward grew crooked, misshapen, and looked somewhat like a hunchback.

Being the weakest child, frail, seemingly helpless, he was pampered, at least by Louise Henriette, the gentle, kindhearted electress. She encouraged him to be studious as he grew older, had him carefully taught music and drawing. After all, he hardly seemed fit for anything else, especially not for the martial pursuits of the Hohenzollerns. Even Charles Emil, a rough and somewhat boorish boy, was affectionate and kind to Frederick; his life might have been pleasant and peaceable enough had not both his mother and his brother died. Electress Louise died first, in 1666, when Charles Emil was eleven years old and Frederick was nine. Two years later, when the Great Elector married Dorothea of Holstein-Glücksburg, Charles Emil and Frederick very soon were relegated to second place in her affections, if indeed she was capable of having them. They were her stepsons, and she had other sons by the Great Elector. She favored these: Philip, born a year after she married Frederick William, and Albert, born three years later.

When Charles Emil died in Strasbourg at the age of nineteen, Dorothea turned on the weak Frederick, whom fate had suddenly made heir apparent. She intrigued against him, hoping to gain the electorate for Philip, her eldest son, or at least to gain for her own children valuable lands reserved to the elector. Her attitude was a great burden to Frederick, especially since his father also seemed inconsolable about Charles Emil's death and about the prospect of having this weak, crooked boy as his successor. Frederick William's heavy Hohenzollern hand—that family predilection for anger and sternness—had been restrained by the Electress Louise; the extent of her beneficent influence on him was fully apparent only now that she was gone. In his old age, coupled to the cold, businesslike, managerial Dorothea, he turned harder and colder yet, especially toward his misshapen son, who seemed to detract from his own glory.

In boyhood, Frederick had formed an attachment with his cousin, Elizabeth Henrietta of Hesse-Kassel; he remained faithful to her over the years and wished to marry her. This was contrary to his stepmother's intrigues, as was almost anything he planned; they quarreled bitterly. Gossip about their quarrels developed into ominous rumors. It was said Dorothea would have liked him out of the way, rumored she would just as soon have him dead. Talk that it would not be difficult for her to obtain a poison must have reached Frederick, too, causing his precipitate action after one bitter quarrel with Dorothea, when she shouted, "You shall repent this, sir!" He didn't wait, but fled Berlin at night, accompanied only by a valet and his tutor, Eberhard von Danckelmann, racing off to Hesse-Kassel, to the home of his aunt and the cousin he wanted to marry.

Schwerin, the devout and noble friend of Frederick's mother, finally persuaded the Great Elector to let his son marry Elizabeth Henrietta after all, despite Dorothea's opposition; the wedding took place, but that did not end Dorothea's intrigues. She may on at least one occasion actually have tried to poison him; this occurred shortly after his marriage to Elizabeth, perhaps to forestall any further Hohenzollern heirs along that line. The event in question occurred during a dinner Frederick had with his stepmother, after a cup of coffee. Whatever was in that cup made him feel ill, and he retired to another room, where he underwent violent spasms. He was in an alarming state and, furthermore, badly frightened, for he was convinced he had been poisoned and was dying. A physician was summoned but took a while to arrive; meanwhile, Danckelmann acted on his own and administered an emetic. Frederick recovered, thanks to that drug; Danckelmann had saved his life, as he afterward told everyone. Then Frederick hurried to leave the Berlin court, fled to safety in the country, and asked his father for permission to remain there. From this time, around 1680, until his father's death eight years later, Frederick remained removed from the evil influence at court—or at least from the evil suspicions lurking there.

Elizabeth Henrietta died in 1683 (again there were unconfirmed rumors of poisoning); a year later Frederick decided to marry Sophia Charlotte of Hanover, once more against the wishes of his stepmother, Dorothea, who even slandered the bride, casting doubt on her virginity. Angry at these insults, Frederick again withdrew, took his new wife with him, and ended all contact with his father's court.

This had strong political repercussions, with aftereffects in the time of Frederick the Great. As heir apparent, Frederick was strongly pro-French: Louis XIV was the godfather of his first child, a daughter. Louis, however, was well aware of the hostility between Electress Dorothea and young Frederick, as well as of the influence Dorothea had gained in Berlin. Having his difficulties with the Great Elector, Louis bribed Dorothea with lavish gifts, so that she might influence her husband's policy to be more Francophile than it then was.

Frederick's Hanoverian bride, Sophia Charlotte, was strongly opposed to France and very much championed an alliance between Brandenburg and the Habsburg emperor, Leopold. Frederick had taken a strong dislike to Emperor Leopold ever since the peace of Nymwegen, but that was long past, while his enmity with his stepmother was fresh. Furthermore, the fact that Louis XIV lavished gifts on his stepmother swung Frederick around to the emperor's cause.

At this very time the emperor and the Great Elector were quarreling about some Silesian duchies which the Hohenzollerns claimed and which the Austrians refused to surrender. To settle the matter, Leopold suggested to Frederick William that he accept instead a small parcel of land, Kreis ("district") Schwiebus, which was contiguous to Brandenburg near Frankfurt an der Oder; it was a matter of Frederick William's accepting Schwiebus or getting nothing at all. These deliberations occurred three years before the Great Elector's death; he was sixty-five years of age, tired, in no mood to quarrel, and ready to settle for something at least, so he accepted. But the matter was not settled with that agreement. Even as the Austrian ambassador in Berlin was offering Schwiebus to Frederick William, he was also secretly intriguing to get it back. The heir apparent, out in the country, was short of funds, owing to his alienation from his father's court; the Emperor Leopold had a solution for all of this young man's financial worries. He offered to pay him an allowance if he would agree to return Schwiebus to the Austrians as soon as he became elector. Frederick signed, partly to get the cash, partly to revenge himself against his stepmother with this underhanded alliance to the Habsburgs; this was at about the same time that Frederick William signed, accepting Schwiebus, without ever knowing his son was promising to give it away. Carlyle described the treacherous deal with the heir apparent by saying that Leopold's plan was "actually not unlike that of swindling money-lenders to a young gentleman in difficulties, and of manageable turn, who has got into their hands." [15]

Two years later, Frederick William died; the thirty-one-year-old successor became Elector Frederick III of Brandenburg. For seven years, he refused to return Schwiebus to Emperor Leopold but finally gave in to threats—and to an overriding ambition which loomed larger than Schwiebus ever had. "I must, I will and I shall keep my word!" he announced on surrendering Schwiebus—after seven years of trying to welsh on the promise. Then he charged "posterity to prosecute" the Hohenzollern claims in Silesia, "if God shall one day send the opportunity"—which happened when Frederick the Great seized that opportunity.

The overriding ambition of the new elector was to become a king. He yearned to be regal, as his father had been, but he wished to be royal in fact: to wear a king's crown, which his father had never dared covet. Already, upon his accession to the electoral throne, he had revenged himself on his parents by ripping up his father's testament, which had bequeathed lands to his father's other sons, those whom he had had with Frederick's stepmother. He then commissioned a magnificent equestrian statue of the Great Elector; this was created by Andreas Schlüter in 1698. In the year of his accession, 1688, a second son was born to Sophia Charlotte (the firstborn having died in infancy); this child was named Frederick William, in honor of the Great Elector. Ironically, this boy was to grow up despising his father, perpetuating a heritage of alienation, even of outright hatred, which plagued the House of Hohenzollern throughout the generations.

The reign of the Elector Frederick III was, in one sense, a long career of overcompensation for the hump on his back and the treatment he had received in childhood. Since his body was regarded as less than beautiful, he would hide it in richness and beauty. If his presence in the court seemed less than Olympian, he would teeter about in high-heeled shoes, elaborate wigs, costly garments, and turn the city around him into a majestic court, cost what it might. He was less interested in ruling well than reigning gloriously, in consequence of which he turned over the affairs of state to Eberhard von Danckelmann, the man who saved his life. Danckelmann was his prime minister for the first nine years of his reign (after which he was ousted, thanks to the electress' intrigues): the first order of business, the only one that mattered, was the affair of the royal crown.

Only the Holy Roman Emperor—the Habsburg, Leopold I—could make him king; fortunately for Frederick, Leopold was in need of allies at the time Frederick came to power, for he was forging a coalition to thwart the ambitions of Louis XIV. Joining this Grand Alliance may well have given Frederick some personal satisfactions as well, for it again gave him a chance to strike at least a symbolic blow at his father and stepmother, whom the French had in the one case subsidized and in the other bribed; also it gave him a chance to revenge Brandenburg for Nymwegen. Frederick placed his troops at the service of the emperor, and six months after acceding to the throne, he personally and with reported bravery led Brandenburg troops in action near Bonn, covering the passage of William of Orange to England against a French attack.

Frederick's troops remained in the service of the emperor for years; Brandenburg had 30,000 well-drilled and well-disciplined soldiers, a sizable force in those days and one which Leopold appreciated. Frederick used 8,000 of them to bargain for the kingship, being ever more anxious for it as the end of the seventeenth century approached, for the nearby Saxon elector had achieved that goal in 1697 by becoming King of Poland as well, and the Duke of Hanover had risen in 1698 to become elector. Everyone around him, it seemed, was getting promoted; indeed, the Saxon had surpassed him, while the Hanoverian was crowding in.

Frederick, however, could not become King of Brandenburg, for that land lay within the Holy Roman Empire and, with one exception, the only king within that empire was the emperor himself.* All other rulers were electors, dukes, princes, margraves, and the like. If Frederick, therefore, wanted a royal

* The King of Bohemia was the only king, separate from the emperor, within the empire, but by this time the King of Bohemia was in fact the Habsburg emperor. That one of the electors was a king derived from the fact that the author of the Golden Bull, a charter of 1356 which defined the position of the electors, was the Holy Roman Emperor Charles IV, himself King of Bohemia. Thus the King of Bohemia became one of the four lay and three clerical electors established by the Golden Bull; the others were the archbishops of Mainz, Cologne, and Trier, all on the Rhine, and the Duke of Saxony, the Margrave of Brandenburg, and the Palatine of the Rhine.

crown, he would have to become king outside the empire, just as the Saxon elector had done. This, in fact, meant outside his own lands.

Prussia, of which he was hereditary duke, seemed to be the best—indeed, the only—solution, but how could he be King of Prussia when, in fact, he ruled mainly in the Mark Brandenburg? Further, the western half of the old Teutonic Order lands of Prussia had been reclaimed by Poland. West Prussia was now ruled by the Polish king. How could Frederick, therefore, become King of Prussia when in fact he would have dominion only over half of it?

Such considerations created a dilemma which might have proved insurmountable to anyone less ambitious than the Elector Frederick III. Determined as he was to raise himself to the rank of king, he brought to bear upon the problem the simple brilliance of a single-minded man, substituting the word "in" for the preposition "of." He would become King *in* Prussia, not of it; at the same time, he would remain the Margrave of Brandenburg, within Brandenburg itself. This seemed to bother no one, especially as he would reign principally in Berlin and not in Prussia at all—and, when there, only over half of it. He himself was pleased, for he would now be spoken to as "Majesty" and not merely as "Serene Highness" (*Durchlaucht*), the form in which he had been previously addressed.

Permission for him to assume the royal title was granted in November, 1700; the emperor, Leopold I, apparently regarded the matter as petty and was indifferent to the issue. (Frederick's cause had been successfully pleaded in Vienna by an aristocratic Jesuit priest named Father Wolf, who apparently had hopes his intercession might allow for the future insinuation of Jesuits into Protestant Brandenburg.) On December 17,1700, the margrave and elector, Frederick III, set off for Königsberg for the coronation. His train consisted of 1,800 carriages, divided into three squadrons as it were: Sophia Charlotte, the queen-to-be, riding in the second and Frederick William, the twelve-year-old crown prince-to-be, riding in the third. More horses were assembled for this journey than Frederick's capital had inhabitants: 30,000 horses in all, positioned along the route, which stretched more than 400 miles. The whole land had been summoned to celebrate Frederick's elevation: Every village and town through which he passed, both en route to Prussia and on his way back, was festooned; buildings were draped with cloths; even the roads over which his carriages passed were covered with cloths. Every cannon boomed; every soldier and official saluted and cheered; every fountain poured forth wine; every day was a gala. In the castle at Königsberg, the king placed a royal crown on his own head and then another on his wife's. The ceremony had been held in the castle in accordance with Frederick's express wishes, in order to emphasize his independence of the church; after this ceremony was over, a second took place in a chapel, where king and queen were consecrated by two Protestant bishops whom Frederick had specially created for this occasion. These endless formalities seemed to bore the new queen, for she indifferently sniffed snuff throughout them.

The full significance of the coronation of Elector Frederick III—who now had become King Frederick I—may have been lost on the queen, but one astute observer of these events sniffed the full implications of them. Prince Eugene of Savoy, the Habsburg emperor's great field marshal, remarked, when he heard of the coronation, "The imperial ministers who advised the emperor to recognize the King of Prussia deserve hanging!"

The thought that the obscure Hohenzollerns would someday replace the great House of Habsburg as the dominant German power could not have occurred even to Eugene of Savoy; indeed, this must have been far from Frederick's own wildest dreams. Brandenburg-Prussia was merely being elevated to the position it deserved, as far as he was concerned, thanks to the achievements of the Great Elector; furthermore, the crown was a symbol of unity between Brandenburg and Prussia, for there was now less talk of Brandenburg generally, the army being called the Royal Prussian Army and the administration the Royal Prussian Administration.

The new king's return to his capital was as brilliant as his departure from it. Because he wanted to be sure he got a proper welcome back home, he lingered at his country estates for some weeks, giving the residents of the capital ample time for their preparations. They did him honor on May 6. He rode through half a dozen ornamented gates of honor on horseback, followed by his queen in a coach-and-eight, she in turn followed by more coaches, bearing the crown prince and others of the court.

Thousands of citizens cheered, the bells of all churches rang, and 200 cannon thundered from the city walls and from aboard ships on the Spree.

The cannon being fired from the ships recall the Great Elector's fledgling navy. Frederick had added to this ever since becoming elector in 1688. He possessed four large, seagoing yachts built for him in Britain, as well as five gilded galleys, each with eighteen rows of oars. These were regal but sailed nowhere in particular. Later, King Frederick had an even more magnificent yacht built for him in Amsterdam, at a cost of 100,000 thalers. This was moored first in the Spree, across from his daughter-in-law's Montbijou Palace, and afterward was docked near Potsdam. Like everything else around him, the ship was for show, evidence of his importance.

In the years he had waited to be crowned king, Frederick had kept himself busy on various fronts. His desire to make Berlin a city fit for a king had caused him to spend vast sums on public buildings and palaces; he completely changed the appearance of the city. Andreas Schlüter was one of the great artists Frederick invited to the city; this sculptor and architect built Sophia Charlotte a palace (called Charlottenburg today). From 1699, the year it was completed, until 1705, the year of her death, it served as her principal salon. There she surrounded herself with all that was exquisite; it was rumored that she also surrounded herself with lovers and that her courtiers had turned the palace into a huge boudoir. On the sidelines stood a sullen teen-ager, loathing it all. He despised perfumes, found cultivation loathsome, and regarded luxury as a sign of corruption. He smeared his face with bacon fat so that the sun and wind might color his skin like leather. He sneered contemptuously when he saw Sophia Charlotte veil her complexion against the sun and when he saw Frederick, his father, trying to stand tall in high-heeled shoes or hide his hump under the luxuriant curls of his long wig. He was alienated from them both: from his father for being a spendthrift fop and from his mother for being frivolous and, he suspected, an adulteress. He was, of course, the son and heir, the Crown Prince Frederick William, plotting even then to close the pleasure palaces and run his court like a soldiers' saloon. In the midst of the ruffled-lace elegance in which he lived, surrounded not only by courtly gallants but by brilliant minds, Frederick William grew up to become a sadistic boor.

No city outside France was as French as Berlin under King Frederick I; no court copied French gallantries as much. Most conversation and virtually all correspondence were carried on in French; the city even had several French-language newspapers in these years. More Frenchmen than ever poured into Berlin, adding to those *réfugiés* whom the Great Elector had made welcome: tailors; hatters; wigmakers; dancing masters; fencing instructors; teachers of court gallantries, of etiquette, and of French customs. The king was said to have paid some of these as much as he paid his ministers, for what was most important to him were ceremonials, court etiquette, and the like. He was, said his grandson, Frederick the Great, "little in great things, great in little things."

Yet his affectations benefited the capital and the nation in the long run, not just by raising the House of Hohenzollern to regal status, but by raising the cultural life of Prussia. In imitation of France's Académie Française, Frederick established the Prussian Academy of Sciences—and succeeded in getting the philosopher Gottfried Wilhelm von Leibnitz to be its first president. Leibnitz, a friend of Sophia Charlotte's, was also the greatest German scholar of his day, and his arrival in Berlin did the state honor. Frederick had also founded the University of Halle in 1694 and in general he and his queen had welcomed not only men of fashion, but men of accomplishment in arts, sciences, and learning into their distant lands.

No sooner had Andreas Schlüter built Sophia Charlotte's pleasure palace than Frederick ordered an arsenal built for himself. This was to be a copy of the Louvre, with modifications suggested by a French ambassador, François Blondel. This arsenal, the Zeughaus, was placed at the head of Unter den Linden, near the Hohenzollern palace, on which Schlüter also worked. Schlüter remained in the service of the king until Frederick I died and his son chased him out of town; he had been head of the Prussian Academy of Arts, which was established four years before Leibnitz's Academy of Sciences, and the succeeding king had no use for art or artists. As for Leibnitz, he remained in Prussia only until his friend and patron,

Queen Sophia Charlotte, died; after that, he seldom visited Berlin and ultimately died, quite neglected, in Hanover.

All this activity on a wide variety of cultural fronts cost enormous sums. There seems little question that the little king was determined to make Berlin into a kind of Versailles and to make himself into another Sun King, if not by means of solid achievement, then at least by means of glitter. Frederick's other luxuries cost the state just as much. Extravagant furniture for the palace, a collection of diamonds large enough to keep an army of jewelers in business for years, and even a private zoo, which imported lions, leopards, and polar bears into the capital, made him hunt constantly for sources of fresh cash. After the fall of the gifted Danckelmann in 1697, three favorites who were clever at finding money (by piling up the state debt) became dominant in Frederick's court. Because their surnames (Wartenberg, Wartensleben, Wittgenstein) all started with the same letter, they were called the three W's, which in German sounds like the three Woes (*die drei Wehen*). They doubled the household expenditure in the royal court, enriching themselves meanwhile, and were finally exposed and ousted in 1711, thanks to an investigation conducted by the only one around who was interested in saving money: the crown prince, Frederick William. This prince was horrified at the extravagance he witnessed all around him; a good example of it was shown him when he married and his father arranged a wedding feast which required 640 calves, 100 oxen, 1,102 turkeys, 650 ducks, 1,000 doves, and 7,200 eggs. Worse yet was the fact that the Prussian army depended entirely on subsidies from foreign patrons; this meant the state enjoyed no freedom of action at all. That was demonstrated in 1700, when the Second Northern War broke out and, a year later, when the War of the Spanish Succession began. In the first-named, Charles XII of Sweden had defeated Peter the Great of Russia at Narva and not only had conquered Poland, but had set up camp on the Prussian border, in Saxony. The matter of the Spanish succession began when Charles II died; the French, the Habsburgs, and the Bavarians contested over his inheritance. That war expanded when the Dutch and English joined in, for Louis XIV had recognized the Stuart pretender as King of England when William of Orange died in 1702.

Frederick I felt his real interests lay in the conflict between Sweden and Russia, for this might enable Prussia to emerge with valuable territories in the East, on the Baltic, where he still needed an outlet to the sea; it might even give him western Pomerania, if the Swedes were defeated. But he was unable to commit himself to the Russians because his funds would not allow him freedom of action; he needed the Russians to subsidize his armies, and this they refused to do. On the other hand, the Habsburg emperor *was* willing to pay subsidies if Prussia fought alongside the Austrians, British, and Dutch, against the French. Committing himself to this cause, Frederick thought, would promote his claims to some of the lands belonging to the Orange family and make himself the champion of Protestantism and defender of German interests, as his father had been. Accordingly, Prussian troops fought with considerable distinction throughout the War of the Spanish Succession, battling alongside Marlborough at Blenheim and elsewhere and finally bringing to Prussia small portions of Orange lands from Switzerland to the Netherlands. Ultimately, Prussia was also drawn into the Russo-Swedish War, but that came after the death of this king and shortly after the accession of his son.

The last years of "King Aesop" (as Sophia Charlotte referred to Frederick I)* were not happy ones. He and his crown prince shared few interests and even less affection. Russian and Polish troops had disregarded the neutrality of the empire in the Northern War and had invaded Swedish Pomerania, an act which served to underline the inability of Prussia to act decisively even in her own backyard. Frederick's troops were committed in the West, and his exchequer was so depleted that he could raise no further forces to defend the eastern frontiers of Germany. Frederick's people, whose fortunes had been mortgaged by the king, resented his spendthrift court. Berlin was beginning to look splendid, but the increase in magnificence was not matched by one in general prosperity. True, Brandenburg-Prussia looked more prosperous and orderly than did many

* Sophia Charlotte also had a nickname for herself: She liked to call herself "the first Prussian republican," by which she referred to her preference for untitled intellectuals over court aristocrats, but this title was merely an intellectual pretension.

other German states: Its roads, however wretched, were better and better-marked; its inns were cleaner and safer; its agriculture flourished. But many, if not all, of these benefactions derived from the reign of the Great Elector and from the policies of Danckelmann; in later years there had been nothing but mismanagement under the three Woes. The natural industry, thrift, and probity of his people—and of the Dutch and Huguenot immigrants —had helped the state; Frederick I had only hindered it. His achievements were cultural, artistic, or of a kind requiring little effort. (For example, it was he who, in 1709, by a stroke of the pen, united Berlin, Cölln and its suburbs into one city named Berlin, which then had a population of 57,000.)

He took some joy in being a grandfather, particularly at the birth of the boy who would later become Frederick the Great. Crown Prince Frederick William had been married to Sophia Dorothea of Hanover in 1706, at the age of eighteen, seven years before he acceded to the throne; of this couple it was said that the job of producing babies "went on night and day." Of the several children which were born before the death of Frederick I, only two survived: Wilhelmina, born in 1709, and Frederick, born in 1712. (The couple's other children were born after King Frederick I died in 1713.)

Frederick I at least had the joy of seeing one surviving grandson, born a year before he himself died, and to see this grandson christened with his name. It is clear he doted on the child. Little "Fritz's" umbilical cord was placed in a gilded silver capsule marked with the inscription: *"Friedrich, Prince de Prusse et d'Orange et né le 24 Janvier 1712 à 11&1/2 heurs du Matin."* [16] A letter which the king wrote on August 30, 1712, when Fritz was seven months old, shows the same pride; it was addressed to one of the most celebrated *grandes dames* of history, Electress Sophia of Hanover. "Your Electoral Serenity," the king wrote, "will without doubt share our joy that the little prince, Fritz, now has six teeth and without being incommoded in the slightest. One can discern predestination from this, for all his brothers had died of this; this one, however, gets them without any trouble, like his sister. . . ." [17]

The recipient of this letter was Frederick I's *former* mother-in-law, because after the death of Sophia Charlotte, the king had remarried in 1708, at the age of fifty-one, five years before his death. This third marriage (Sophia Charlotte had been his second wife) was a disaster, contributing to the woes of his declining years.

King Frederick I had undertaken this union for a curious reason. His son, the crown prince, had fathered only one child prior to 1708, and this infant had died within a year. He worried whether there would be an end to the House of Hohenzollern's male, Brandenburg line (this explains his great joy in later years, when Fritz arrived). It was suggested to King Frederick during a holiday at Carlsbad that if the young crown prince was not capable of siring strong offspring, then the fifty-one-year-old king was still man enough to do it—despite the fact that he was sickly, weak, and "taking the waters" at the spa. A twenty-four-year-old princess, Sophia Louisa of Mecklenburg-Schwerin, was found for him. He married her, brought her to Berlin in style, only to find the crown prince and his wife producing babies successfully: the aforementioned Wilhelmina and, later, little Fritz. That, of course, was a source of consolation to him; what was not was the fact that his new wife proved to be a fanatic, puritan Lutheran—as well as going mad. She showed herself mentally unstable very soon, whereupon she retired to her apartments in the palace, the king estranged from her; soon she was over the hill and required watching. For a time, they must have seemed a bizarre pair in the palace: the weary, aging, and deformed king and his unbalanced wife, tottering, teetering about in luxury, lace, and debt. Ultimately, she did him in. One morning, escaping from the attendants who guarded her, she ran amok through the palace corridors until she reached the king's bedroom, into which she crashed, quite unexpected, dressed only in her white undergarments. Frederick woke up with a start, for she had literally crashed right through the glass door to his room; he was confronted with an apparition in white, blood streaming over her clothes, a frightening specter. In fact, he took her to be just that: He thought she was the "White Lady," the ghost of Countess Agnes von Orlamünde, the Hohenzollern family spook, who often appeared to announce death to the family members. He keeled over, never rose again, and died a few days later. His life, which had been a parade of compensations and trivia, thus ended as it had been lived: with a hollow note of the preposterous about it, yet something sad as well. In his palaces of pleasure, as he himself felt in his later years, everything had been essentially joyless. It was to prove even more so after his death.

4

A Mania for Freaks

POSTULATE, if you will, a child born to wealth and privilege, surround him from birth onward with flatterers and fawners, never or rarely compel him to do anything he has not a mind to do, indulge his every whim and caprice, allow him to gratify every malicious impulse and sadistic streak, never or hardly ever let him hear the word "No," change his schoolmasters each time he has exhausted one of them with his obstinacy, then add to that a character which is rude, petty, avaricious, vengeful, and vulgar, and what do you have? You have, to say the least, a spoiled brat whom you would not care to see run around with absolute power over life and limb. Yet that is precisely what this kingdom got when King Frederick William I of Hohenzollern acceded to the throne. He was an impossible child; he grew up to become an improbable king. Everything described in the foregoing was in him, making him a monster at times—most of the time, in fact—yet there is no denying the paradox that this brat turned into a great king. He never won anyone's affections, and no one ever suggested calling him Frederick William the Great, but great he was in fact and in accomplishments, good for his people, too, in the way that a good, strong dose of castor oil may be said to be a blessing.

The House of Hohenzollern had come a long way. It had begun with a small fief in South Germany and moved from there to prosperous Nuremberg, of which the early Hohenzollerns became military governors. From there the Hohenzollerns had moved north—to nothing, which meant to the wilds of the Mark Brandenburg. They had become electors, which was something, but even so their electorate was backward, poor, and despised, and they did not count highly among those who cast their votes from time to time to choose the next Holy Roman Emperor of the German Nation. Then, they had become kings—*in* Prussia, residing in Brandenburg for the most part—something again, but not much, considering how paltry the kingdom was compared with others then existing. The first king "in" Prussia, the puzzling little Frederick I, had been so enchanted with his kingship that he concentrated on adorning it and on enjoying it: nothing more. It was still very little to be king in Berlin, but it would soon count for more. The modern Prussian state of recent memory, the one which triumphed and became the nucleus for the modern German Reich of the Kaisers, was created by the "monster" under discussion; it seemed right that he should have been named after his grandfather, the Great Elector, who had prepared the ground for him.

There was no growth of modern Prussia. This new king, Frederick William I, and his son, Frederick the Great, *made* Prussia; it was, says Britain's A. J. P. Taylor, "as artificial as the making of a canal." [18]

Whatever Prussia was not, it was becoming something under the Hohenzollerns. Something was being forged which was more than a state or a kingdom; it was a secret weapon: a force in European affairs. Its potential was completely overlooked by every contemporary monarch in Europe; what was being built up in so remote an area was an autocratic state machine, powered by a mighty army. The fuel driving it was the obedience of its people, learned in large part from Luther, who sanctified obedience, and from King Frederick William I, who beat it into them.

Nations, like plants, can grow organically, which means slowly and healthily, feeding from a common ground: the popular will. A great maturing process is at work in such cases. Given time, the "tree of liberty" (to use Jefferson's phrase of 1787) is here refreshed with "its natural manure"—that is, "the blood of patriots and tyrants." Both the British and (later) the French have had the heady experience of lopping off a monarch's head; the kings who followed never looked or acted quite the same. As noted, no Hohenzollern ever lost his head, speaking literally at least, nor did the subjects of these Hohenzollerns ever consider committing such an act of *lèse-majesté*.

The state of Brandenburg-Prussia was not maturing; its growth was forced. Marvelous creations can be formed when nature is pressed artificially: large and gorgeous, unnatural and freakish. The Hohenzollerns forced the growth of their lands, using the fertilizer they knew best how to apply: brute force and blood. The means were usually ruthless, often terrible; the result was awesome, the end predictable. A brilliant but freakish experiment in statecraft was being hurried along. The Hohenzollerns were like botanists hungering for fame and success; their subjects came to be the mutants they created. Oddly enough, the "Luther Burbank" who helped create the freakish growth was Martin Luther himself. He gave the Germans a national language by means of the German-language Bible, but, says Taylor, "he also gave to Germany the Divine Right of Kings, or rather the Divine Right of any established authority." [19] The rulers had become the heads of the church, as well as of the state and of the army; it was not a condition which encouraged liberal growth. What this meant in Brandenburg-Prussia is that the citizens came to be taught one lesson in school, home, church, and barracks square: obedience to constituted authority. Obedience toward *die Obrigkeit* ("those above," or those in authority) had received the sanction of religion, as well as the compelling force of the state.

Had the Hohenzollerns been different sorts, they might have set the nation's course differently. Instead, they were for the most part contemptuous of their people, suspicious of their landed gentry, severe to their officers, brutal to their soldiers, and spiteful to their officialdom. Religion was to them the padlock on the chain they bound about their people; it chained them, too, making most of them unable to entertain a single liberalizing thought. What a haunted family they were may be seen from the heritage of family hatreds which dogged them: son alienated from parents or despising, even loathing, them; the parents reciprocating in kind. It developed into a cancer of the soul, but perhaps a cancer which was unavoidable. The relationship between king and crown prince anywhere is that between one who wishes to live on so that he might continue to reign and one who wishes he could reign instead, which at least suggests he might wish his father dead. Among the Hohenzollerns, this relationship often became uglier still, for the family had more than its fair share of rancorous, vain, egomaniacal men, always easily angered, men who were harsh, often brutal, seldom opposed. Vindictive to their children, resentful toward their parents, they were often oblivious—certainly contemptuous—of the interests of their subjects. Had parliamentary restraints been allowed to develop, the Hohenzollerns might have been checked; instead they had carte blanche from the beginning to the end, thanks in large part to the obedience drummed into their people, in even larger part owing to the military dictatorship with which they oppressed their lands. They bred a proud and energetic people until it developed a disproportionate number of bullies and lickspittles.

Such was the thing created. The king who did the most to start the process going was born on August 14, 1688, a few months after the death of his grandfather, the Great Elector, after whom he was named. He was pampered in his first years but, being robust, did not grow to become namby-pamby; he grew to be impossible instead. His grandmother, Electress Sophia of Hanover, invited him to her home when he was five years old but had to send him back again, for he was forever fighting with his cousin Prince George, the Hanoverian who later became George II of England. From time to time, young Frederick William returned to Hanover on visits; each time he did, he disgraced everybody, tussling on the floor with George, whom he detested and whose nose he bloodied, though George was twice his age. Back in Berlin, others were not having it much easier with the child. His first governess, Dame de Montbail, and the assistant governess were frightened out of their wits by his strange behavior while he was still a small child. On one occasion, obstinately refusing to spit out a shoe buckle in his mouth, he swallowed it, either accidentally or for spite; a physician got it out of him after the entire palace was reduced to a hysterical state. (The buckle, made of silver, was later deposited in a Berlin museum, carefully tagged to show when His

Majesty had downed it: December 31, 1692, when he was four years old.) On another occasion, when Dame de Montbail had ordered him to do something he found offensive, the young prince ran away from her and toward the window, threatening to let himself fall three stories unless she let him have his way. (It is not clear whether he leaped onto the windowsill and threatened to jump or whether, as another account has it, he actually flung himself out, hanging onto the ledge only with his hands, threatening to let himself drop.)

Very early in life, he developed a loathing for finery; this is the time when he greased his face with bacon fat to tan it like a soldier's. Ordered to put on a gold brocade dressing gown one morning, little Frederick William showed what he thought of it by throwing it into the fire. He was just as obstinate, or even more so, when it came to his studies. A distinguished, somewhat solemn general was appointed to be his governor when he was seven years old; this was Count Alexander von Dohna, commissioned to teach the boy Latin. He found the task impossible. Those trying to teach him piano and the flute were even worse off, for he hated music and refused even to try. Teachers of art fared little better, though he did enjoy coloring in drawings which others had sketched, a practice he continued throughout life.

His first teacher, Friedrich Cramer, actually had a profound influence on the boy, though not necessarily a salutary one. Cramer was very learned and proud of it, but also possessed of a temper he found difficult to control. An example of how it might flare up was given when a French abbé named Bouhours had written a tract entitled "Is It Possible for a German to Possess Sense and Wit?" Cramer, who had no doubts about the matter, exploded and fired off a reply. The same volatility of temperament, the same tendency to go off half-cocked at the slightest provocation were to be noted in Frederick William in his later years, as was the same tendency to champion things German against things French. His dislike of the French must have been sharpened by his next teacher, a Frenchman named Rebeur, a pedantic and dreary taskmaster, who required the prince to copy out endless extracts from classical works or the Old Testament, leading him forever afterward to loathe all learning.

In the face of his refractory and rebellious nature, Queen Sophia Charlotte, flighty and frivolous as usual, could do nothing but indulge. She even wrote instructions to Frederick William's governor, Count von Dohna, not to oppose his charge; Frederick William, in later years, admitted that his mother had spoiled him outrageously, even accused her of it, but by then it was too late. The one thing she most thoroughly disapproved of in him was his avaricious nature, the fact that he hated to spend money; she also disliked the fact that his awkwardness in the face of the opposite sex caused him to be rude to the ladies of the court.

"Good heavens!" she wrote to a confidante, Mademoiselle Pöllnitz. "Avaricious at such a tender age; other vices may be surmounted, but this one increases with the years! What perverseness of heart to behave badly to the sex which ought, at the very least, to be the object of politeness in men!"

Frederick William's two youthful loves were drilling soldiers and economies. He saved his pocket money to form a company of young cadets, all nobles, whom he drilled himself, not gently either, for he was once seen dragging one of his soldiers, a young duke, by the hair. When he was eight, he kept a ledger entitled "Account of my Ducats"; it was the only book he cherished. Another youthful love which played a part in keeping alive a lifelong loathing was Caroline of Ansbach, five years his senior. She treated him not as a suitor, but as a boy, inspiring an aversion to women in later life; furthermore, she married his detested cousin the future George II, fueling hatreds which lasted for life, for neither cousin could ever bear the other.

When Frederick William was sixteen, his father let him travel to Holland and England. His mother was especially anxious for him to make the trip; it might broaden him, educate him, do something for him. Indeed, it might have, and it might have conceivably changed the course of the state he was to rule. A ship had already been obtained by the Duke of Marlborough which would carry Frederick William to England when news reached the crown prince that his mother had died on February 1, 1705; he returned to Berlin, and the trip was never made, neither then nor later. On his return, his father delighted him by giving him an infantry regiment to command: real soldiers of his own, at last, that which he craved most. One member of the regiment, whom Frederick William noticed straightaway, was the tallest man there, the regiment's judge advocate, a bailiff's son with the imposing name of Ehrenreich Bogislaus Creutz. Frederick William made him his private secretary, three years later argued his father into raising him to the nobility, and, upon becoming king, made him a minister. Frederick William had made an early encounter with what would become an obsession, the greatest indulgence he permitted himself: tall soldiers. "He who sends me tall soldiers," he admitted in later years, "can do with me whatever he likes."

The next year, 1706, the crown prince joined the Duke of Marlborough and Prince Eugene of Savoy in the aforementioned War of the Spanish Succession, that conflict which dragged on from 1701 until 1713–14. That year also, Frederick William married Princess Sophia Dorothea of Hanover, the sister of his detested cousin George. Once again, in 1709, Frederick William went to the field of battle, in his twenty-first year, rejoining Marlborough and Prince Eugene and witnessing the Battle of Malplaquet, the worst slaughter of the war, in which between 36,000 and 39,000 men were killed; it so impressed him that ever afterward he celebrated its anniversary in Berlin.

The glass door had been shattered, and the White Lady, actually the mad queen, had dispatched King Frederick I. Frederick William, now called King Frederick William I, gave his father a fine funeral. Nothing was spared, no parsimony displayed; it was just as the old king would have liked it. At the funeral, however, they could find nothing nobler to call the deceased than the Magnanimous. He had certainly been just that, as every courtier knew. Now came the reckoning.

No sooner was the burial over than the new king hastened to the palace to strip off the peruke he had been compelled to wear and which he had worn on this occasion as a last sign of respect to the old man: no more perukes; no more fancy coats even; no more luxuries. He announced he would forgo a coronation; he remembered all too well how much the last one had cost. Stripped down to his shirt sleeves, he helped the servants tear down all the palace draperies, curtains, and wall hangings, to throw out all upholstered furniture, even all carpets—"dust catchers all," he called them. His father's diamonds, wines, coaches, and wild beasts were sold, the beasts and gems going to Augustus the Strong of Saxony, who also inherited his father's master of ceremonies, a protocol and etiquette expert no longer needed in Berlin. The king moved himself and his family into a bare, almost bourgeois five-room suite and turned the rest of the building into offices, so that he could watch his officials personally and pounce on them if they were lax. The first letter he is known to have written as king shows the role he intended to play (and reiterates his childhood loves, soldiers and economies). "Tell the Prince of Anhalt," he wrote, "that I am minister of finance and commander in chief to the King of Prussia." * He was everything else as well. He ran the entire economy, all church affairs, educational matters, justice, and the police—anything which might benefit from his touch. He was certain everything would.

General Friedrich von Grumbkow, then just thirty-five years old (twelve years older than his king), was placed in charge of all affairs of state, while Prince Leopold of Anhalt-Dessau was put in charge of the army. The latter was a soldier of the blood-'n'-guts variety, a veteran of famous battles (Blenheim, Malplaquet, among others); the former was a courtier in military dress, a onetime groom of the bedchamber who had doubled as an infantry lieutenant. By 1703, ten years before Frederick William I elevated him to run affairs, Grumbkow had risen to first cupbearer at the court—and to general—at the age of twenty-five. Like Prince Leopold, who was a war-horse, Grumbkow had *been* at Malplaquet, but not much more: He had spent the action hiding in a ditch. He was never a fighter: At Stralsund, he pleaded a sprained leg when the fighting started; where others joined in, he was a voyeur.[20] The great Prince Eugene is said to have told him more than ten times, "You will die either in a dungeon or a palace," to which Grumbkow, ever the hypocritical courtier, is said to have replied, "I predict the latter; I shall try my very best to merit it." [21]

In fact, Grumbkow died in the disfavor of his king, just before the king's own death, after having survived brilliantly

* Note the King *of* Prussia. Technically, there was no King of Prussia until the partitioning of Poland during the reign of Frederick the Great brought in West Prussia as well, but the term "of" was nevertheless used much earlier, being arrogated as it were.

throughout the entire reign of Frederick William I, taking outrageous bribes from both Austria and France (these, of course, being rivals) and championing few interests but his own. His was the only establishment in Berlin during Frederick William's reign which could be called lavish: Grumbkow was permitted it since he was charged with entertaining foreign dignitaries; he was the Perle Mesta of his day. He was also a glutton and a prodigious drinker; his nickname was Biberius. It is hard to ascribe any nobility to Grumbkow; his great merit was that he could keep his choleric king amused. Every ruler needs a crony and a kitchen cabinet, it seems; Grumbkow was sufficiently coarse to hold his own with this king. Few rulers, however, elevate such cronies beyond the kitchen: Grumbkow made it into the center of power. For a time, he was in charge of virtually everything, under the king, and proved a rival to Prince Leopold even in military affairs; Grumbkow was one of Frederick William's perplexing weaknesses, like the one he had for tall soldiers. Finally, he wore even Frederick William's patience to a frazzle. When he died, the king remarked, "Now people will at last stop saying that everything is done by Grumbkow! If he had lived a fortnight longer, I would certainly have had him impeached." [22]

The rivalry between Grumbkow and Prince Leopold developed into a fierce feud, one which the king apparently encouraged, although he took Grumbkow's side on three occasions when it flared into duels. Grumbkow, of course, would not fight, being a coward; the king at last prevailed upon Prince Leopold to forget the matter and even to lie publicly that Grumbkow was "an honest man." Leopold came to be so disgusted that he retired to his private lands and to service under Prince Eugene for the last ten years of Frederick William's reign.

The importance of Prince Leopold of Anhalt-Dessau to the House of Hohenzollern and to the power of Prussia can hardly be overstated. From 1693, when he was seventeen years old, until he fought his last battle at the age of seventy, he was in service both as a battlefield commander and as a military innovator and trainer. The superb Prussian army, which Frederick William established and which Frederick the Great subsequently used, was primarily the creation of Anhalt-Dessau. He was a cousin to King Frederick William, his mother being a sister of the Great Elector's first Dutch wife and a princess of the House of Orange. He had the personal courage to marry a common chemist's daughter over the enormous objections of his family; he triumphed there as elsewhere, for she turned out to be such a success that she ran the affairs of the state of Anhalt-Dessau as regent while Prince Leopold was away. Like Frederick William, he was bluff, unpretentious, unrefined, and at times coarse; these characteristics inspired the friendship of the king and the loyalty of his officers and men. He had come to know Frederick William at the Battle of Malplaquet, when Prince Leopold was assigned to Marlborough's camp and Frederick William was just crown prince; there they formed a friendship which proved important to Prussia, for Frederick William soon charged Prince Leopold with training and drilling the Prussian army. His philosophy of war was simple: "Fire well, reload quickly; intrepidity and spirited attack are the surest road to victory." [23] He introduced the iron ramrod, a great advance in musketry; he also reintroduced marching in cadence, which allowed columns to be wheeled and maneuvered about, permitting the creation of a military machine. (Marching in step had somehow been forgotten for centuries, ever since the Romans practiced it; France's Marshal Maurice de Saxe rediscovered the technique, and it was quickly taken up by France, Britain, and Prussia.)

Frederick William and Prince Leopold rapidly discovered they had other interests in common: Both were devout Protestants, and both were inspired by the same view of religion. They were righteous and devout; this made them harsh and brutal. They were God-fearing; this made them stern, often merciless. Theirs was a harsh God; they served him by tolerating neither weakness, idleness, nor error in others. Both men proved brilliant in their fields; both men proved themselves brutes, however. A story which Frederick the Great once heard about them from a garrulous old veteran sheds light on the characters of both. "I have a very good joke I must tell your Majesty," the old soldier told Frederick William's son. "When the King, your father, was still Crown Prince, I used to serve him as orderly. One day we were travelling with the Prince of Dessau to Potsdam. At Zählendorf * they found a cow-herd sleeping with his

* Zählendorf, then a village, is today Zehlendorf, part of Berlin proper; Potsdam lies outside Berlin and was a favorite residence of the Hohenzollern rulers.

cattle, and as they had nothing better to do for the moment, they thought it capital fun to cut the tails off the poor animals, which they did, every one of them." [24]

It was not much different with their soldiers. Neither the king nor his military trainer had time for niceties. They used beatings to turn their recruits into terrified, but superbly drilled automatons, just as the king used beatings to punish anyone else who displeased him by not working hard enough.

No sooner had Frederick William acceded to the throne than he asked for a roll of the royal household to be brought to him. There were 141 courtiers on the list. Before the eyes of the horrified lord marshal of the court, King Frederick William I picked up a pen and crossed out the entire list. (Eventually he reduced the court to a dozen.) "Gentlemen," one general blurted out afterward to the frightened courtiers, "our good and kind master is dead, and the new king sends every one of you to the devil!" Anyone who remained in service had to strip off his peruke and French court dress and replace them with the pigtail, blue coat, and white leggings of the Prussian army uniform. So military was the atmosphere in the Hohenzollern palace that the handful of pages serving at table were assisted in this duty not only by the king's twelve royal huntsmen, who also had to do such extra work, but even by grenadiers. So small was the court that the king's valets, who had daily access to him, assumed an exaggerated importance; as a result, one valet, Eversmann, received regular bribes from Vienna and London, so that he might intrigue in favor of those courts.

The reduction in the court was not merely niggardly, but primarily prompted by Frederick William's intelligent assessment of the state economy. His father had left Brandenburg-Prussia deeply in debt; the son determined to make it prosperous and to pay all his father's obligations. It was toward this latter purpose that he sold his father's diamonds and most of his stud (the stables were reduced from over 1,000 horses to 30, and most of the rich harness was sold as well). He sold the expensive palace furniture, although he prudently kept and even increased its stock of silver (platters, vessels, and a gold and silver table service), calculating that he could turn this into cash in a time of need.

Utility was the keynote of this king's reign. Whatever did not serve a useful purpose was ruthlessly cast out of Prussia: Sculptors like Schlüter were chased out; architects still working on the palace were given three years to finish up and then expelled from town; the only painters who were allowed to remain were hacks who agreed to produce a stipulated number of canvases a year for a set sum. This partly inspired Oswald Spengler after World War I to declare that Prussianism and Socialism had much in common; they did indeed, from this point of view. Frederick William I would have wholeheartedly endorsed the statement in Karl Marx's *Das Kapital*: "Nothing can have value without being an object of utility. If it be useless, the labor contained in it is useless, cannot be reckoned as labor, and cannot therefore create value." Frederick William insisted that every activity, private or public, had to produce "a plus" as he put it: something extra. Marketwomen were ordered to keep their fingers busy knitting socks; pastors who preached for more than one hour were fined. The kitchen expenses of the palace, like all others, had to be presented to him daily, down to the last lemon and measure of milk. That Swabian instinct for piling up treasures was given constant expression by this particular Hohenzollern king. He liked to note the slightest squandering of money, as when on one occasion he wrote "One thaler too many!" on an accounting of dinner expenses which ran to 31 thalers and 16 groschens. "The true and only philosopher's stone," the king wrote, giving another expression to that same Swabian temperament, "is that the money remains in the country!" On another occasion, he put it more succinctly: "Money's the thing!"

He may have been "minister of finance to the king," as he had said, but he was a soldier first and foremost. He wore a uniform and sword every day, abjuring the fineries of the eighteenth century. He also carried a rattan stick which, even more than a scepter, came to be the symbol of his particular reign. With it, he belabored everyone, often regardless of rank. He did this because he felt himself surrounded by rascals and scoundrels, because he regarded himself to be literally the father of his people and charged with thrashing them if necessary, and because he considered idleness, sloth, luxury, and the like to be the worst possible sins, sure evidence of depravity and of the devil's work. He took walks through his capital—through almost-deserted streets, for most people fled to their homes and barred their windows at news of his approach. If he saw someone idling, he seized the man and thrashed him personally; if he heard quarreling inside a burgher's house, he burst open the door, charged in, and beat the quarrelers. Yet he apparently did all this without conscious malice and would never have believed anyone so foolish as to report that his people feared and hated him; such sentiments would have been perverse.

Once on a Berlin street he caught hold of a man who had fled from his approach and whom he had called to a halt. Grasping him, the king asked the frightened wretch why he had run away.

"I was afraid," the miserable creature stammered.

"Afraid? Afraid!" Frederick William shouted, red-faced and apoplectic. "You are supposed to love me! Love me, scum!" Whereupon he beat the fellow about his head and shoulders with his cane.

But he was impartial; he did much the same to everyone, commoner or aristocrat. He demanded that everyone be "good Christians, industrious citizens, and brave soldiers," little more and certainly nothing less; he himself would determine whether they measured up. An embezzling aristocrat, Councilor Baron von Schlubhut, was ordered hanged by the king after a court had sentenced him only to imprisonment; Schlubhut protested to Frederick William "that this was not the fashion of the country thus to deal with a Prussian nobleman" and promised to make good the money, whereupon the king, livid with rage, screamed, "I will have nothing to do with your tainted money!" and had him hanged outside the council chamber, before the eyes of all the other councilors.

Everyone was frightened to death—and with good reason. Frederick William kept two pistols by his side in his chambers, loaded with salt, it is said, and fired them off at his valets if they did not move quickly enough. One valet lost an eye as a result; another had his foot severely injured. So feared was he that one official who was summoned to his presence fell dead of fright before the king had said anything at all to him. Another was savagely beaten and called a "rascal and a scoundrel" because, having been asked what his new title was, he had elegantly replied, "I am Your Royal Majesty's Privy Councilor Blank" when he ought simply to have said, "I am called Privy Councilor Blank." Even the officers in his army were belabored with his cane, in full view of their men. When he beat one major on such an occasion, the humiliated officer drew his two pistols, fired one at the ground in front of the king's horse and then killed himself by firing the other through his own temple.

Of course, he was more than eccentric, though it would be incorrect to write him off as mad. He took a bankrupt nation and, by personally watching over everything, rattan cane poised, made it prosperous and its army the best in Europe. He had his wild eccentricities, but he was logical as well and, without a doubt, brilliant. His single-mindedness and ferocity of will and temperament produced an enormous achievement. Wishing to root out all human error at all costs, he began the work of making the Prussian civil service virtually incorruptible, a job his son extended; he was impartial in the administration of justice and favored no one, being harsh to all.

Early in his reign, he established a General Directory form of government, this *Generaldirektorium* amalgamating all military, financial, and administrative activities. It became the most powerful and important arm of the king's government, Foreign Affairs and Justice being two other departments which never received quite as much attention from the king. The General Directory was, in turn, subdivided; above all was the president of the General Directory: the king, of course.

No one dared contradict him or even advise him honestly, with one notable exception. The closest Frederick William got to establishing a real cabinet, in which questions of state actually could be discussed, was his *tabagie* or *Tabakscollegium*. The members of this body met every night with the king for his favorite recreation, smoking pipes, which gave this collegium its name. It would convene at about five or six and remain in session until late at night, or even into the early morning hours. Most of its members were generals, but it also included ministers and foreign ambassadors, as well as certain personal favorites of the king, such as a Dutch general named Ginckel. Servants were excluded from the room, so that the conversation and behavior could be unrestrained. A sideboard of cold meats and cheeses was available, although the king excused himself briefly at about eight to dine with the queen, after which he returned to his cronies. Long Dutch pipes were smoked, and each man had before him a jug of ale from Brunswick, along with a tankard. Everyone needed to drink hearty to please the king and even to suck an empty pipe if he could not smoke a full one. (Frederick William often smoked as many as thirty pipes in an evening.) The meetings were educational as well. A lecturer read aloud from newspapers and journals, not only German but also French and Viennese, and then had to explain to the assembled company whatever they might not understand in them. This lecturer was for a long time Jakob Paul von Gundling, who was the king's walking encyclopedia, having to accompany him everywhere, and who became the butt of all the king's lifelong hatred of pedants, teachers, savants, *Schwarzscheisser* as he called them: men who "shit black"—that is, black ink.

Poor Gundling was his court jester and fool, the victim of vicious tricks in which the other members of the *tabagie* joined, though at the same time Gundling was constantly being elevated in rank, if not in importance. With each elevation, he would be humiliated all the more. He was promoted to president of the Academy of Sciences, as the great Leibnitz's successor; it was a meaningless post, this being a reign in which the academy ceased to function and in which the royal library did not add more than a handful of books in a quarter of a century. He was raised to be master of ceremonies at court and ordered to dress in the uniform of that former etiquette expert who had moved to Saxony on the accession of Frederick William I: an enormously elaborate uniform with white goats' hair, ostrich feathers, and high heels. Gundling was publicly invested in that office while attired in this fashion; during the ceremonies the king and his *tabagie* cronies presented him with an ape dressed exactly the same way. They even announced to all those present that this was Gundling's bastard child and then forced Gundling to embrace and "acknowledge" it. At sessions of the *tabagie,* Gundling was ordered to read aloud insulting articles about himself, which the king had caused newspaper editors to print; he was also made dead drunk almost every evening, prompting further mischief on the king's part. On one occasion, while Gundling was drunk in his uniform of chamberlain, the *tabagie* members cut off the ceremonial key which was his badge of office and which hung about his neck; when he was awakened, the king threatened to punish him as a soldier is punished upon losing his gun. Mercifully, he spared the man's life, but Gundling was compelled to walk about for a week with a gilt wooden key three feet long hung around his neck, after which the original was returned to him. At Königswusterhausen Palace near Berlin, where the *tabagie* often assembled, Gundling awakened in his bed on one occasion to find with horror that several small bears were nearly crushing him to death; these had been placed in his room (nails clipped) by the king's drinking companions. Gundling spat up blood for days. On yet another occasion the king ordered four grenadiers to seize Gundling and to lower him to the moat at this same palace, jerking him up and down onto the ice until he had broken through it, while the king and his fellows roared with laughter from a window overlooking the scene. Gundling never had any rest; often, when he returned home, he found the door to his room literally bricked up and had to sleep wherever he could. Finally, Gundling tried to escape, but he was hauled back, tried for desertion and threatened with death; the wretched Gundling, trembling for his life, found out it was all a big joke after he had been sentenced—only to be promoted in rank and income. Announcing that Gundling long merited the title of count, the king promoted him—but only to baron. Finally, the king maliciously gave Gundling the freedom of the royal wine cellars; he could drink all he wanted. It was the only freedom Gundling had ever enjoyed in the Hohenzollern court, and it promptly killed him.[25] He died at the age of fifty-eight in 1731, apparently from excessive drinking—or so the physicians explained the ulcerous condition of his stomach, after a postmortem examination had taken place. The king's final prank took place at the funeral. Gundling, on the king's orders, was buried in great style—inside a wine barrel.

In one way or another, most members of the Hohenzollern court underwent comparable treatment during the reign of Frederick William I. An example of how the king treated his court when he was in a *good* frame of mind occurred on Sundays, after the afternoon church services. As soon as the service was over, the entire court had to file past the king, who was seated on horseback while they rode past him in carriages. Frederick William addressed them in a friendly manner, but the surest sign of the king's approval came if he greeted one of those passing by, not with kind words, but by silently raising two fingers to his forehead, making the sign of the cuckold, that of horns. Many a wife is said to have fainted in the carriage when the husband beside her was saluted in this remarkable fashion.

Most remarkable of all, however, was the king's passion for tall soldiers. Once he was king, he quickly formed what came to be called the Potsdam Giants' Guard.*

He called them his *lange Kerle,* his "long fellows," and they were recruited from among his own subjects, bought in other states, received as gifts from foreign courts or from anyone who wished to be in his good graces, or they were dragooned and kidnapped, not just in Prussia but almost anywhere in Europe. As many as 1,000 kidnappers worked for the king to abduct any man over six feet tall; as much as 12,000,000 thalers are said to have been spent between 1713 and 1735 on purchasing those whom the press-gangs could not waylay. No man at all who traveled in Prussia during this reign was really safe, for any man might be forcibly impressed into the Prussian army, but those who were *tall* men had no chance at all. Even distinguished foreign diplomats who happened to be tall were kidnapped and impressed into the Giants' Guard; if protests were made, then the king would regretfully release these with apologies, but the practice never stopped. His recruiting officers, in search both of regular soldiers and giants, roamed as far as Italy; both a tall priest from the Italian Tyrol and a monk from a monastery in Rome were kidnapped and put in the

* Vehse's *Memoirs* includes the following, interesting as conjecture but questionable, seeming more justification than explanation:

"The well-known Chevalier Zimmermann . . . quotes, on the authority of the privy councillor Von Schlieben, who was present at the opening of Frederic William's will, the following passage from it: 'During the whole of my life, I was obliged, in order to escape from the jealousy of the Austrian court, to make a display of two passions which I did *not* possess: one, a preposterous love of money, and the other, an unmeasured love of tall soldiers. Only for the sake of these two glaring foibles, they allowed me to hoard a large treasure, and to raise a strong army. Now, as they are both called into existence, my successor needs no longer to wear a mask.' "[26]

guard, the priest while he was reading mass to villagers. One of the tallest was an Irishman named Kirkland, spotted by the Prussian ambassador in London, who paid 9,000 thalers for him from his previous employer and who engaged him for three years as his valet. This, of course, was a mere pretext, nor did Kirkland know the ambassador's identity; in ignorance, he sailed with him to Germany and was duly enlisted in the guard. (The ambassador was unable to return to London because of this incident.)

"The most beautiful girl or woman in the world," the king is quoted as having remarked on one occasion, "would be a matter of indifference to me, but soldiers: they are my weakness!" [27] He had meant that he was not a libertine; indeed, he was puritanical when it came to sex, but there is no escaping the conjecture that he was more than that. In any event, soldiers were not his only weakness, if his main obsession. Tobacco was another addiction, as was the hunt; he drank and ate lustily, principally loving oysters, of which he sometimes downed 100 at a sitting; he was also addicted to washing his hands, which he did countless times throughout the day, and changing his shirt, which he did often, displaying a mania for cleanliness, uncommon in his time, and hinting at a sort of Pontius Pilate complex.

A Dominican priest named Bruns, who became chaplain to the Roman Catholics in the Giants' Guard regiments, told in his diary of the indescribable despair felt by those who had been dragooned into it. Of the 4,000 men in this Giants' Guard, half were Catholics, and almost every one of these was there against his will. There were, says Bruns, Frenchmen, Italians, Spaniards, Portuguese, Hungarians, Slavs, Croats, Poles, Bohemians, Englishmen, Irishmen, Russians, Turks, Swedes, Danes, Ethiopians, "and other foreigners from Asia, Africa and America." Priests, princes, counts, doctors of law, and physicians were among those who had been impressed into service. Conditions were so wretched that mutinies were constant. The soldiers, says Bruns, were always trying to burn the town of Potsdam down and kill the king, in the hope of obtaining their freedom. Others mutilated themselves or committed suicide or killed others in order to be killed in turn. Horrible punishments were meted out by way of reprisal, he says, and invariably the offenders were foreigners and Catholics, which caused the king to demand that Bruns explain why those soldiers of his faith were "so evil." Father Bruns stoutly pointed out that this should occasion no surprise, since they were mostly foreigners who had been taken by force and often brutally. He quotes the king as replying, "I myself never forced anyone. If any were forced to become soldiers, then that was the fault of the recruiting officers, to whom I never gave such an order. Furthermore, I pay them well and none of them suffer from deprivation." Father Bruns admitted this was so; despite the high pay the guards received, their despair was even greater. They had, after all, been recruited not for a few years, but were compelled to serve, on pain of death, for the rest of their natural lives, until on the king's pleasure they were retired.[28]

Peter the Great, whom Frederick William admired and who was one of the godfathers of Crown Prince Fritz, sent King Frederick William I "eighty Muscovites notable for their tallness" in the first year of his reign; later, he sent him 150 more and then, in accordance with an agreement arrived at during a visit Peter made to Berlin, shipped an annual consignment of Russians of exceptional height to the Potsdam Blues. On Peter's death, the czarina continued the bequest, ordering her provincial governors to send to Potsdam "all the tall men that could be found in their respective districts, of six foot four inches high or upwards." [29]

The Russian court was not the only one which bound Frederick William by means of his mania; it was common knowledge in every court in Europe that where diplomacy or threats failed, tall soldiers succeeded. The Austrian emissary in Berlin, Count Friedrich Heinrich von Seckendorff, wrote Prince Eugene in Vienna to send him two dozen "of the finest, tallest, and youngest men," for with these, "I should be able to do more . . . than with the most powerful arguments." [30] The men arrived, and the king signed a pact with the Austrians. The same was tried by the British on one occasion. They sent fifteen tall Irishmen, "very agreeably received," it was noted. In 1715 the Saxon minister sent King Frederick William a birthday gift of two expensive Turkish pipes, a large package of tobacco—and had the lot delivered by a seven-foot-tall messenger, asking that the king graciously accept both the gifts and "the Cupid who brought them." This sort of bribery was so flagrant and so successful that foreign diplomats rounded up reserves of tall fellows and, rather than use up the whole lot to solicit just one favor, offered the king only a few at a time, keeping the remainder as reserve stock.

Augustus the Strong, King of Poland and Elector of Saxony, had put together a minor version of the same Giants' Guard, and it was in 1730, on a visit to the Saxon capital of Dresden, that Frederick William first caught sight of it. What most captivated him, however, was an eight-foot-tall but dim-witted Swede; Frederick William pestered Augustus for days until he finally gave him the Swede and twenty-four other "long fellows." The Swede was brought to Potsdam, where he was to be a star attraction, but no matter how hard he tried, the king could not get him to drill like a Prussian grenadier; even beatings did not help. Furious with the enormous ox, the king chased him out of the guard and out of Potsdam, surely one of the few occasions, perhaps the only one, when a man was so soon discharged from these regiments. The Swede stumbled on, until he came to Berlin, but he was not bright enough to make a living and, ultimately, starved to death in the capital.

It was in his own domains, where Frederick William could do as he liked, that the most flagrant manhunting took place. When the University of Halle protested bitterly about an abduction of a law student, the king merely snorted, by way of reply, "No fuss—he is my subject!" He cited the Bible to justify abductions; in I Samuel 8:11–16, "the manner of the king that shall reign over you" is described: "And he will take your . . . goodliest young men, and your asses, and put them to his work."

Violent death was frequent, for those who fled from their abductors were often killed in flight. "A life for a life" was, however, the king's code, and overzealous recruiters came to be punished under it as well. One man who was nearly executed was a lieutenant colonel, a Baron Hompesch, who had tricked a Jülich carpenter into a box (to measure its length) and had then tied it shut, carting the box with the man inside to Potsdam. Since he had neglected to drill air holes, the box became a coffin, and Hompesch was sentenced to death for causing the death of his "recruit." In Hompesch's case, however, the king was merciful, perhaps because he was moved by the man's zeal; he commuted the sentence to life imprisonment.

The Giants' Guard initially consisted of 1,200 men and contained 3,030 when it was disbanded by Frederick William's successor; as Chaplain Bruns noted, it contained 4,000 at certain times. The first contingent was formed from the 30,000 soldiers Frederick William had inherited; each original member had to be at least six feet tall in his stocking feet. Later, as press-gangs brought in real giants, front ranks were created for the tallest, some of whom were nearly nine feet tall. When they marched with their pointed helmets, which resembled bishops' miters, they sometimes reached more than ten feet in height. The king's special favorites were painted life size, the paintings being hung about the palace; when Jonas, a onetime Norwegian blacksmith, died, the grief-stricken king had him sculpted in marble.

Baron Bielfeld's *Lettres familières* describes an evening spent among the tall officers of this Giants' Guard. "All these corpulent machines are great wine-bibbers," he writes, describing how the evening at the colonel's home moved from heavy drinking through dinner to a dance. "I looked this way and that," says Bielfeld, "expecting to see some ladies enter; and I was stupefied when one of these descendants of Anak, a giant of ruby and weather-beaten countenance, proffered me his hand to open the ball. I could not be but greatly embarrassed when the proposition was made to me to dance with a man! But they gave me little time for reflection, for dance I must. The commanders of the regiment danced, all the officers danced; and towards the end this masculine ball became very animated, thanks to the repeated bumpers of champagne. . . . About eight in the evening most of these terrible warriors declined the combat, their huge limbs no longer able to encounter Bacchus and Terpsichore, and they went staggering off." [31]

The great weakness of the guard was morale. About 250 deserted each year; those who were caught mutinying had their noses and ears sliced off and spent the remainder of their lives in Spandau Prison. Bounties were put on deserters, and any village in which one was found (without having been turned in) was heavily fined. Nevertheless, it was said that Amsterdam in those years "was filled with" uniformed Prussian soldiers, deserters all. Nor did the recruiting sergeants have an easier time of it than those they chased, for they were murdered on the highways and in taverns, and peasants attacked them with axes and dogs.

The Blues, with their enormous waxed mustachios, were ceremonial units, used for the purpose of guarding the palace and public buildings; the king loved them too much to send them out to fight. They were his toy soldiers, and he drilled them personally. So sharp was his eye, so able was he to spot the slightest imperfection in a line, so keen was he about the smallest detail and irregularity that the Blues were said to move not in precision, but in perfection. "At the word of command, only one click was heard in the line, one measured step in marching, and one report in platoon firing." [32] The techniques worked out on this Giants' Guard by means of merciless drill, endless terror, and frightful beatings were afterward incorporated throughout all Prussian regiments, until King Frederick William I had forged a military machine which knew no equal at the time. He could say, "No one can resist us," [33] even though he had no proof that this was so. Frederick William played soldier but did not go to war.

Thus it was that the Prussian army then being forged frightened no one in Europe. It was said that Frederick William's recruiting agents were both the plague and the fair game of the entire continent, but their activities annoyed the European courts only when they were too brazenly conducted within foreign kingdoms. The statesmen of the time were intent on watching, with enormous amusement, the king's mania for acromegaloid freaks; they failed to see that the toy he was building was deadly. George II of England dismissed Frederick William as "my brother, the drill sergeant" (brother-in-law, that is, for Frederick William was married to George's sister); the Prussian king, in turn, referred to the King of England as "my brother, the comedian" or "my brother, the red cabbage." As for the Prussian army the "drill sergeant" had built with Anhalt-Dessau, all Europe called it "an army of deserters." They sloughed it off, and this was a bad mistake. This was the army with which Frederick William's son would upset all Europe; this was the army which eventually would enable the House of Hohenzollern to build an empire for itself.

5

"God Knows I Am Too Tranquil!"

FREDERICK WILLIAM I suspected everyone—on treasonous ambitions, selfish motives, partisan interests, or, often enough, simply not loving the king enough. He kept his government responsible only to him and firmly kept the Junkers out of power. He wanted no Prussian Runnymede, nor did he want an aristocratic court, with all the folderol that meant. He felt more comfortable among the bourgeoisie, once even called himself "a true republican," liked to have homely dinners at the King of Portugal Hotel, where Frau Nicolai, the hotelier's wife, prepared his favorite dish: pork and cabbage. Eleven ministers of state were commoners during his reign, officers were often promoted from the ranks, and commoners even became diplomats. Once he received a complaint from a Baron von Strunckede to the effect that Baron von Pabst, whose title was more recent than his own, had sat ahead of him in church; the king replied, "This is all nonsense; in Berlin there are no ranks. . . . If Pabst sits above me in Church, I am still who I am; my extraction remains always the same."[34] Had he learned this from his mother, who also had called herself the "first Prussian republican," and even the "first republican queen"?

The bourgeoisie had grown rich in commerce and industry; the king ennobled them and let them marry into the old landed families. His only command to the aristocracy in this respect was that they not marry daughters or widows "of *poor* citizens or peasants" or "disreputable" people. Money was the thing, even here, particularly since many in the nobility had become somewhat less than noble. The profligate reign of Frederick I and the dandified fashions of Paris had stripped them of dignity and of the respect of the masses, which they in turn treated as a mere canaille, as a rabble.

Still, out on their farmland estates, they could become focuses of power if allowed to administer their regions; consequently, Frederick William stripped them of this right. He allowed them a role in his army, for it was under them that locally recruited regiments were raised, but he selected for his bureaucracy an army of the middle class, rather than of the nobility. This legion of lawyers, this regiment of scribes and officials would, he knew, be loyal to the king, for they were utterly dependent on the king's purse.

Thus the varied elements which were to make up Prussian society in the future began to take up their special roles. The emerging middle classes either found employment within the state bureaucracy or profited by cooperating with the state machine. The tradesmen and merchants among them needed the king's goodwill to ensure the success of their enterprises; since an overproportion of these had to do with supplying the army, this bourgeoisie came to be a class of royal agents and profiteers of the new militarism. As for the workers and the peasants, they existed merely in the sense that livestock then existed in Prussia. They made up a faceless mass, an economic force, but not a political one. They slaved, or they served in the army, ignored by all outside their class. The French Revolution, after all, was still some years away.

No counterforce could develop to the growing absolutism of the Hohenzollerns. The Junkers and the standing army dominated the country and prevented the development of prosperous towns and of a prosperous peasantry until late in the nineteenth century. The economic backwardness of the nation contributed to the power of the Junkers; in most of the state, the population density was one-third, or even one-fourth, that of Saxony, Württemberg, Holland, or France. This tended to confirm the power of the Junkers in their remote estates, isolated as they were from any liberalizing influences and protected as they were from liberalizing pressures. Serfdom was the condition of the majority of the subjects of the King of Prussia and would remain so until Prussia's temporary, complete collapse under Napoleon Bonaparte compelled the state to institute some minimal reforms.

The pattern of Hohenzollern absolutism was not created by Frederick William I, although he perfected it; it was initially set by the ruler for whom he was named: Frederick William, the Great Elector. It was he who had first established the standing army which was to become the dominant force in Prussian society; it was he who had confirmed the power of the Junkers on their estates while reducing their power over the nation as a whole. A coalition between monarch and the estates had been forged by the Great Elector; it effectively prevented all liberal change in the state. The Great Elector had established the foundations on which his successors built up Hohenzollern power; F. L. Carsten makes the point that while he had been overshadowed by Louis XIV during his lifetime, "yet his work outlasted that of the French king by generations." [35]

The relationship between the Junkers and their Hohenzollern monarch came to be symbiotic. The estates dominated the land, thanks to the continuing unimportance of the Prussian towns, and the monarch made common cause with them. For their part, the Junkers' interests were entirely class interests, not regional ones. They never were linked to an urban gentry, as were portions of the English aristocracy. The absence of such a link in Prussia proved to be "the vital chink in the armour of the Estates," [36] which prevented them from forming an alliance against the Hohenzollerns; this enabled the Hohenzollerns to use the Junkers' class interests in order to engage their loyalty to the crown. The Hohenzollerns maintained the Junkers in power; the Junkers maintained the Hohenzollerns. This Prussian nobility had never felt any obligation whatever to the people it either oppressed, enslaved, displaced, or killed; the Junkers of the time were estate managers with the refinements of range bosses and often the humanity of privateers. Since they cared so little about defending their own freedoms from the crown, they cared absolutely nothing about the freedoms of others; in the future, they would oppose their sovereign only on matters of economic importance to their class, when his interests or those of the nation clashed with the interests of their barnyards.

Everything began to hum efficiently in the Prussia of King Frederick William I, for everything was whipped along by a horde of faceless administrators who were, in turn, whipped on by the king. Frederick William redeemed the Prussian lands his father had pawned and which had been decimated by a plague in 1709. Protestant homesteaders were brought in to repopulate them in 1732. Religious refugees from Salzburg arrived by the hundreds in Berlin, to be resettled in East Prussia, where their descendants remained until they were expelled in 1945. Wilhelm Strathmann, the ambassador of Brunswick in Berlin at the time, noted that Frederick William was so moved by the condition and the religious fervor of the Salzburgers that "tears ran down His Majesty's cheeks" when he met them.[37] The Salzburgers repopulated the decimated areas and increased their yield; eventually, revenues from these farmlands were to double, and agriculture was to provide half the national income. Crown Prince Fritz wrote Voltaire a letter about the manner in which his father had made these lands fertile. The king, he said, had traveled East to see with his own eyes "the devastation brought upon the land by disease and want and filthy greed of local administrators," had been shocked by the sight of "twelve or fifteen deserted towns, between four and five hundred uninhabited villages, fields everywhere reverting to wilderness." With admiration, Fritz said his father had turned this region into one where "fertility and abundance reign," and Voltaire was no less generous in his praise. "A vast desert," he wrote, had been reclaimed by means of policies "very different from those followed by other princes of his time."

"Every day His Majesty gives new proofs of his justice," wrote the Saxon ambassador in Berlin, who then went on to describe how the king had treated the official in charge of the Potsdam posthouse after several passengers of a post coach had failed to obtain admittance to the building at six in the morning. The king, without identifying himself, joined the passengers in knocking at the door and, finally, in smashing in some windows. This brought the postmaster to the door, whereupon "His Majesty let himself be known by giving the official some good blows of his cane . . . [driving] him from his house and his job after apologizing to the travelers for his laziness." The ambassador concluded, "Examples of this sort, of which I could relate several others, make everybody alert and exact."[38]

Whipped on by a drill sergeant of a king, the administrators made Prussia prosper. Local tax collectors, with enormous police powers and great influence over agriculture and commerce throughout the kingdom, helped reduce the power of the Junkers in the provinces even more. These were the officials who, under Frederick William I, completed the work of subjecting the entire kingdom to central authority, until all provincial powers were eliminated and the Hohenzollerns reigned and governed absolutely.

The main business of Prussia, however, remained the army. All the Hohenzollern rulers were soldier kings, but the one who liked to be called *the* soldier king was Frederick William I. "Fifty thousand soldiers are worth more than one hundred thousand ministers," Frederick William said,[39] and he proceeded to add to that number, increasing the Prussian army from the 30,000 he had inherited to 80,000 at the time of his death. It became the fourth largest standing army in all Europe, though Prussia ranked thirteenth in terms of population; this alone should have given the other European courts cause for alarm, but it didn't, for the soldier king was mocked as a coward who never fought a war.* By the time Frederick William I died, five-sixths of the income of the kingdom went to support the army.† A separate recruiting fund was created. Captains received lump sum payments with which they were to recruit men for their companies and then maintain them; the king divided the entire nation into cantons, and each of these was to supply soldiers for a particular regiment, which lessened rivalry between recruiting officers. The army was mainly recruited from the peasantry, and soldiers had to serve for twenty years, a prospect which drove some peasants to suicide. "Once a grenadier,

* With one brief exception. Two years after acceding to the throne, Frederick William's troops fought a brief war against the Swedes, at Stralsund, acquitting themselves well. By the Treaty of Stockholm (1720), Prussia obtained at last an important outlet to the sea, at Stettin on the Baltic, as well as acquiring the eastern half of Swedish Pomerania.

† Later, it was much the same. In 1786, three-fourths and, in 1806, five-sevenths of the state income went to support the army.

always a grenadier," the king said, but he was intelligent enough to know what it would do to agriculture to have all the farm boys conscripted into the army. Once soldiers had been sufficiently well drilled, therefore, they were allowed to go home on furlough for nine months of the year, during which time they remained under regimental authority and were free of the authority of local courts or police. Regiments were brought to full strength for only three months of the year, during spring and fall training periods. Barracks and forts were built by the king, but for the most part the soldiers were quartered in private homes, receiving rooms which burghers were compelled to allocate for this purpose. Soldiers were everywhere; every fifth inhabitant of Berlin was in uniform.

Government officials were everywhere as well, and their work was regulated by the king with military precision, down to the last detail. Frederick William had, in a matter of a few days, written a book of regulations for them, which consisted of 297 paragraphs, divided into 35 chapters, and which set down the exact duties of every state employee from minister to watchman. Government officials were recruited from outside the provinces in which they were to work; this was meant to eliminate favoritism and prevent extortion. The king instructed the officials not to tour their lands on farm horses, for these could be used more productively on farms; they were to use dog traps instead. No inspectors were to venture onto farms during harvesting or plowing; they might distract the peasants from their labors. The king even issued detailed instructions on how plowing and threshing were to be done, how wolves were to be hunted, how gardeners and millers were to be trained. He made certain that grain was stored up in good seasons and sold in bad; he reclaimed marshes and wastelands; he imported artisans and skilled workers; he encouraged industry and commerce; he put "Prussian order" into everything. The word "responsible" became enshrined; every official knew precisely for what he was responsible and precisely what punishment awaited him in case he failed. A little gallows, which the king had drawn alongside the word "responsible" in his book of regulations, made the point quite clear.

He was no gentler with his Junkers. "But this I *credo*," he once said. "The Junkers' authority will have to be ruined, for

I mean to establish my authority like *un rocher de bronze* [a rock of bronze]!" On another occasion, he wrote, "They [the Junkers] shall dance to my tune or may the Devil take them; if they don't, I shall treat them as rebels, I shall hang them and roast them like the Tsar!"[40]

"God knows I am too tranquil!" he was given to say. "I think it would be better if I were more choleric." He meant he was too gentle, too forgiving, to those who vexed him; that claim actually held true in foreign affairs. As noted, foreign courts thought him a coward because he never used his army; the British sneered that he "only acted the wolf in his own fold," and Peter the Great remarked that Frederick William was peaceful not because he disliked fishing, but because he was afraid of getting his feet wet. In fact, Frederick William was no coward; he merely lacked confidence. He knew that his kingdom was ridiculed and that his court was the laughingstock of Europe, thanks to his own eccentricities and buffooneries; he felt—indeed, he was—out of his league whenever he dealt with royalty. He saw himself as bluff, aboveboard, honest, and plainspoken; he saw Prussia as being surrounded by older courts filled with elegant scheming councilors, with sly and subtle diplomats, all versed in dissembling and flattery. He wasn't wrong: The King of Prussia was indeed a country bumpkin surrounded by city slickers. Afraid only of losing all he had amassed, he wanted at all costs to avoid entangling himself with other courts, for that might allow the schemers to cheat Prussia out of its growing treasure. He knew his limitations very well indeed. He told his son, "Beware of imitating me in all that touches diplomacy, for I have never understood anything of that."[41]

He was an apoplectic balloon filled with hot air, poisonous gases, and much thundering, but little else. To portray him is to enter the world of fantasy: Frederick William was growing year by year in girth, until at death his waist measured 102 inches, possibly more, and he weighed 273 pounds. But he was *short,* so this ponderous, bloated mass was grotesque in the extreme: It supported a short neck and a large head, the complexion of which was described as exhibiting "red, green, blue, and yellow shades." His appearance was regarded as truly terrifying at home, although it terrified no one abroad. He thought his army of 80,000 and his sizable war chest ought to win him advantages in foreign affairs, but he could not even get concessions out of Emperor Charles VI, whose side he championed loyally throughout his reign.

"I'll not depart from the Emperor unless he kicks me out," he said.[42] The emperor never went that far, but he certainly never showed himself grateful to Prussia for its loyal support. He treated Frederick William cavalierly* when Prussia pressed its claim to the duchies of Jülich and Berg, at the Rhine: At first, Charles offered a compromise, then welshed on his promise, and finally did not bother to give Prussia anything at all. Frederick William was simply never taken seriously, as the French ambassador in Berlin noted when he said, "Thanks to his instability, the King of Prussia is neither useful to his friends nor dangerous to his enemies." Frederick William found all this inexplicable, not to say frustrating. "This world is past my comprehension," he told Prince Leopold of Anhalt-Dessau. "God grant me a speedy and peaceful end so that I shall have done with all this knavery. It can be endured no longer." Insecure as he was, he ended up whining that he was misunderstood. When one of his hussar squadrons, fully armed and equipped, deserted en masse, his comment was, "Now the whole world will think I treat my people badly!" Finally, he said that he no longer wanted any power at all. "I only want to find a pretty, lonely place in a foreign land far from my own," he said, "where I could live in peace, for I'm just no use to anything in this world and everything is a burden to me, wherefore I want to live a philosophic life." [43]

There was no time, however, for philosophizing; there was always too much to do, too much to oversee, and too many orders to issue. Though he loved to be called the "Soldier King," his people called him "the greatest sand caster in the empire," after the amount of sand needed to dry the endless instructions issuing from his pen. Nothing escaped his notice, nor anyone his eye. It was his habit to accost people in the streets and ask them to identify themselves by name and occupation. If they gave the desired straightforward answer, they survived the encounter; if not, they got thrashed. "Who are

* As though Frederick William were "the Prince of Zipfel-Zerbst," the king was given to complain.

you?" he asked, following that with, "Look me straight in the eyes, man!" A timid answer awakened his wrath; a courageous one sometimes aroused his admiration. One tattered young man whom the king accosted one day identified himself as a theology student. "Where from?" the king thundered. "Berlin, Your Majesty," was the reply. "Aha!" the king shouted, "the Berliners are a good-for-nothing lot!" The student never flinched, but shot back, "Yes, it is true; most of them are, but I know two exceptions." Puzzled, the king asked, "And who might those two be?" whereupon the student answered, "Why, Your Majesty and myself, of course!" The king's eyes widened; he laughed; he had scholars give the boy an examination, then saw to it that he got a chaplaincy.[44]

This sort of rough-and-ready answer appealed to the king. It was to his credit that he never welcomed flatterers. As a matter of fact and typically, he had laid down regulations against them in 1723, casting some more ink and sand again: "We do not by any means want flattery, so people are always to tell us nothing but the plain truth." [45] He did not often get it, but that was because he inspired such a holy terror in everyone with his sudden rages, with that Hohenzollern family temper referred to earlier. Those whom he could *not* bully, such as other kings, were a different matter; he could relax and enjoy their company, especially that of Peter the Great and of Augustus the Strong. Those two were made in his mold, at least in some ways; unlike Frederick William, both were libertines, but like him, both were earthy.

Peter came for a visit on September 19, 1717; he had been in Berlin before, but always briefly and without his court. This time, en route home from Paris, he had brought a small army with him. It consisted of about 400 "ladies" of the czarina's suite—"ladies when there is occasion," reminisced Princess Wilhelmina in her *Mémoires*; she was then nine years old, and said the ladies had acted "as chambermaids, cooks, washerwomen" as well. Queen Sophia was reluctant to greet them; these women were a randy, tatterdemalion lot, a surprising number of them with babies in their arms and all of these replying, on being interrogated about their infants, "The czar did me the honor." Two days before the czar's arrival in Berlin, Peter had stopped off in nearby Magdeburg, where he had been greeted by the celebrated Samuel Cocceji, the man who in later years would reform the entire Prussian legal code; he had flabbergasted Cocceji and the other officials by his attitude while listening to their speeches of salutation. Throughout these ceremonies, Peter stood between two of the ladies of his court, his arms thrown about their shoulders, his hands openly fondling their breasts.

That was just a starter. Frederick William himself witnessed the czar's reception of a favorite niece, the Duchess of Mecklenburg. No sooner had the young duchess entered the room than her uncle, the czar, took her up into his arms, swept her into the next room, a bedchamber, and there took his pleasure of her without so much as closing the door to prevent the duke, her husband, from watching.*

The czarina was described by Wilhelmina as having "a little stumpy body, very brown" and without either "air nor grace: you needed only to look at her, to guess her low extraction." She was, in fact, a Lithuanian peasant girl who had been a camp follower of the czar's armies, having been made the czar's wife and afterward the czarina because she saved Peter's life on one occasion. Her dress, Wilhelmina recalls, "was loaded with silver and greasy dirt," as well as with tiny diamonds, "very ill mounted." She walked with "a jingling, as if you heard a mule with bells to its harness," for the front of her dress was a mass of little metal objects: medals, holy relics, portraits of saints, and what-not. She made a remarkable contrast with the czar, for he was very tall and, in Wilhelmina's eyes, handsome in a "savage" way and dressed in a nautical outfit, simply cut. At the czar's request, he and his court were housed at Montbijou Palace, which Peter thought more relaxing than the Berlin Palace. Before Peter's arrival, Queen Sophia had carefully stripped Montbijou of all its breakable *objets d'arts* and crystal; she knew from previous visits what a Russian invasion meant. Despite these precautions, four days of housing these visitors took their toll. The Montbijou guest apartments had to be completely redecorated after the Russians left.

* The duke, however, had a thick skin; he and the duchess invited Czar Peter to visit them in Mecklenburg after Peter left Berlin. Russian troops had just evacuated the duke's lands after helping him subdue a rebellion, and he was thus heavily indebted to the czar. Two years after being swept up in her uncle's arms, the duchess left her husband and went to live in Moscow.[46]

Presents were exchanged. Czar Peter received that elaborate yacht which Frederick William's father had purchased from Holland; he also coveted what Carlyle coyly refers to as an "Antique Indecency," this being a Russian fertility charm, probably a phallus, which he discovered in a chamber of curiosities in Berlin. Frederick William was delighted to get rid of the horrid thing, then was taken aback when Peter, with great good humor, forced the czarina to kiss the object before all those assembled. "Off with her head!" (*"Kopf ab!"*) Peter shouted in German, suggesting this would be her fate if she hesitated. Finally, another exchange was made: Russian "long fellows" for German armorers and drill sergeants, the latter neatly summing up the nature of Prussian exports in these years.

Frederick William was delighted with his guest—and delighted to see him go as well. He liked Peter; the robust nature of the man, his earthiness, savagery, and military air appealed to him more than the cultivated manners he witnessed among the French and Austrians. Brandenburg-Prussia, after all, was half-*Eastern,* the lands originally settled by Slavs, the whole sweep of his terrain resembling the windswept lands of Russia. Peter's amorous activities, however, found no response in Frederick William, for the Prussian king always remained a puritan and a prude; he liked the czar's lustiness, but not his lust. When his guests left Berlin to travel to the duchy of Mecklenburg, Frederick William had them escorted to Potsdam and on to the border. Suddenly he was overwhelmed with the expenses incurred during this state visit. He told his officials they could spend 6,000 thalers on Peter's trip to Mecklenburg —"not a penny more, understand that!" Before they left, he also issued instructions that Peter be told differently. "Let it be known that this has cost me thirty or forty thousand," Frederick William said.[47]

If Peter was a trial, he was only a preparation for Frederick William's later visit to Augustus, King of Poland and Elector of Saxony. This took place in 1728, nine years later, when Crown Prince Fritz was sixteen and able to accompany his father.

Meanwhile, Frederick William's uncle—the Hanoverian George I of England—had died; the death affected Frederick William deeply. When he spoke with the British ambassador to

Berlin, he broke into a flood of tears, none of them feigned, although perhaps occasioned not only by the death of the first George, but by the prospect that his hated cousin George II (that "red cabbage") would now become king.

His mood was not improved by a recent embarrassment he suffered at the hands of Augustus. This had come about thanks to the king's mania for tall soldiers. A Prussian officer, a Captain Natzmer, had entered Saxony to recruit "long fellows"—that is, to induce tall Saxon soldiers to desert, this being a common method of Prussian recruiting then. But the Saxon court, like others, no longer was amused when the king's mad hobby extended to their lands. Prussian recruiters had been arrested in several lands, and Augustus had personally denounced their incursions onto Saxon territory. When Captain Natzmer was spotted, he was pursued and chased across the frontier into Brandenburg, whereupon the Saxon posse crossed the border, arrested him, and dragged him back for trial, after which he was hanged. This so infuriated Frederick William that he sent a message to Baron von Suhm, the Saxon representative in Berlin, threatening to hang Suhm by way of reprisal, whereupon Suhm fled to Augustus' court in fear of his life. There he was chided for being a coward, and a message was sent from Augustus to Frederick William, asking in outraged terms what the devil Frederick William meant by such threats to Suhm, such "flat insult to the Majesty of Kings." [48] Ever the classic blusterer, Frederick William collapsed; he protested he had been misquoted by a blundering official and had never meant to hang Baron von Suhm at all.

Thus Frederick William was in an agony of spirit: His relations with Saxony (*i.e.,* also with Poland) were at a new low, and his despised cousin had become King of England. Furthermore, he now worried endlessly about being assassinated and was continually fretting about his ailments, real and imaginary. Bluster alternated with bathos, self-assertiveness with enormous depressions, periods of vigorous activity with times when the king was dispirited, resigned and passive. In fact, the symptoms he showed indicate that he suffered "pronounced manic-depressive cycles," [49] as one historian put it.

This awful climate was now made even worse by one August Hermann Francke, of Lübeck, who had helped found the University of Halle, who had established a famous orphanage there, and who, most important, was a prominent disciple of Philipp Jakob Spener, an exponent of Pietism, a movement aimed at reforming Lutheranism. At the age of sixty-four, close to death, he was in Berlin, expounding on the religious life to Frederick William and his family.

Francke, says Princess Wilhelmina, "entertained the King by raising scruples of conscience about the most innocent matters. He condemned all pleasures; damnable all of them, he said, even hunting and music. You were to speak of nothing but the Word of God only; all other conversation being forbidden." Francke preached constantly at Frederick William, and the effect, says his daughter, was to exaggerate "the evil" of his melancholy humor.

"The King treated us to a sermon every afternoon," she wrote in her *Mémoires,* "his valet-de-chambre gave out a psalm, which we all sang; you had to listen to this sermon with as much devout attention as if it had been an apostle's. My Brother and I had all the mind in the world to laugh; we tried hard to keep from laughing; but often we burst out. Thereupon reprimand, with all the anathemas of the Church hurled out on us; which we had to take with a contrite penitent air, a thing not easy to bring your face to at the moment. In a word, this dog of a Francke led us the life of a set of Monks of La Trappe.

"Such excess of bigotry awakened still more gothic thoughts in the King. He resolved to abdicate the crown in favour of my Brother. He used to talk, He would reserve for himself 10,000 crowns a-year; and retire with the Queen and his Daughters to Wusterhausen. There, added he, I will pray to God; and manage the farming economy, while my wife and girls take care of the household matters. You are clever, he said to me; I will give you the inspection of the linen, which you shall mend and keep in order, taking good charge of laundry matters. Frederika [then thirteen], who is miserly, shall have charge of all the stores of the house. Charlotte [then eleven] shall go to market and buy our provisions; and my Wife shall take charge of the little children and of the kitchen."

No sooner said than—almost—done: The king sat down and prepared a set of instructions, more ink and sand again, for the crown prince. The *tabagie* was horrified: It seemed the king might actually go through with these mad plans. Most especially frightened were the two Austrian agents in Frederick William's inmost circle, these being Grumbkow and Count Seckendorff, for their power in Berlin would dwindle to nothing if Crown Prince Fritz assumed the throne, since his pro-British sympathies were known. Seckendorff and Grumbkow hit upon a plan to divert the king from such ideas and, perhaps, even to cure his melancholia: A visit to the court of Augustus the Strong at Dresden was the medicine they prescribed.

Seckendorff and Grumbkow were experts at deceiving the king, as the whole history of their relationship with him shows. As a matter of fact, Seckendorff established himself in the Berlin Palace by means of such deception. Grumbkow, who felt he needed an ally in the *tabagie,* so as to bring the number of Austrian agents in the king's innermost circle to two, had sent for Seckendorff, who had known the king in the War of the Spanish Succession and during the Stralsund campaign. Yet it would not do for Grumbkow to invite Seckendorff; that might arouse the king's suspicions. It was, therefore, arranged for Seckendorff "accidentally" to stroll by the palace at just the hour when the king was accustomed to lean out of one of its windows to survey the scene. Delighted to spot his old friend, Frederick William asked Seckendorff how long he was planning to stay in Berlin. Just two or three days, en route to Scandinavia, said Seckendorff. Frederick William invited him to live in the palace and remain a bit longer; Seckendorff remained to stay. He was such an obvious schemer and conniver that everyone, even the queen, cut him dead; only the king was oblivious of the man's nature and of the fact that Seckendorff used him toward Austria's ends. He refused to think ill of the count, being enchanted by the way Seckendorff could listen inexhaustibly to the king's tedious, repetitive, and vulgar stories.

Now that the matter of the Dresden visit had arisen, Seckendorff and Grumbkow decided to use the same technique again. This time the man "accidentally" visiting Berlin was a former Prussian field marshal, just in from Augustus' court in Warsaw. He patched up the quarrel about Baron von Suhm and suggested Augustus would be delighted to have Frederick William in Dresden for the carnival season. This was followed by a formal invitation from Augustus. Frederick William accepted.

The Austrian agents were pleased; they felt sure Augustus' gay, licentious court would seduce Frederick William from Pietism, plans for retirement, and even seduce Prussia from Britain. As it turned out, Augustus tried to have Frederick William seduced, quite literally.

6

An "Angel" in Torment

THERE comes a time in every boy's life when he realizes his father is less than perfect: no boy ever had better cause to feel that way than the Crown Prince Fritz. His father believed he was "more perfect than most other kings"; in fact, Frederick William I had the manners of a barroom brawler, the instincts of a ruffian, and the uncontrollable temper of so many Hohenzollerns. To top it all off, he was downright sadistic toward his son. When it came to ill-treatment, this king was a true democrat: Everyone got his fair share and full measure, regardless of rank.

Children were no exceptions. There were plenty of offspring to irritate the choleric king. Though she loathed her husband, Queen Sophia Dorothea submitted constantly to his loutish assaults; she bore him enough progeny to form a football team, with a few left over: fourteen children in all.* Frederick William didn't ever take a mistress, as so many other kings did; one rather suspects Sophia Dorothea would have been grateful had he done so.

* Of the eleven which survived their first few years, those of more than passing interest are: Wilhelmina (1709–58), later Margravine of Bayreuth and author of colorful memoirs; Frederick (1712–86), crown prince, later King Frederick II; Louisa Ulrica (1720–82), later Queen of Sweden and mother of subsequent Swedish kings; Augustus William (1722–58), father of Frederick the Great's successor; Henry (1726–1802), who commanded forces under his brother; Ferdinand (1730–1813), who also served under his brother and who was the father of the colorful Prince Louis Ferdinand of Hohenzollern. Frederica, Philippina, Sophia, and Amalia were daughters of lesser historical importance.

Crown Prince Fritz, as previously noted, was not Sophia Dorothea's first child, but her first surviving male offspring; thus his birth had given rise to great joy in Berlin. He was born a year before his father became king and was baptized Friedrich Karl, "Frederick" after his grandfather and "Charles" after Charles VI, Holy Roman Emperor, one of his godfathers (another being Czar Peter the Great).*

He was a Sunday child—therefore believed to be both lucky and endowed with a sixth sense, then thought to include the faculty of seeing ghosts. He was a beautiful child: with large, blue, sparkling eyes, which would throughout his lifetime spellbind visitors. He certainly seemed predestined for good fortune; as his grandfather noted, he survived his teething months, and furthermore, an old palace tree suddenly shot up 31 feet and produced more than 7,000 blossoms, as though to hail the advent of this prince.

He was given over to women for the first years of his life: to a Frau von Kamecke and a Dame de Roucoulles, the latter being the very same French Huguenot refugee who, as Dame de Montbail, tried twenty-five years earlier to train the impossible young Frederick William. This prince was everything that particular one had not been: Young Crown Prince Frederick, whom they called Fritz or Fritzken,* was quite simply "an angel." Alert, bright, endearing, and very affectionate, he won everyone's heart, even his father's, during these years. Indeed, the king almost crushed the infant in his arms, directly after birth. It was Dame de Roucoulles whom he called "dear Mama" (*cher Maman*). She had a profound influence on him, and with characteristic loyalty, he sent her letters, gifts, and money for years after being taken out of her charge.

Fritz showed little interest in soldiering. This troubled the Soldier King, his father, a great deal. Yet when the Stralsund campaign was under way, Fritz was found caught up in the fever of the preparations going on all about him: troops marching off, military bands playing, the sounds of grenadiers' boots and rifles stamping, banging and clanging all around him. He was seen, at the age of four, beating on a little military drum,

* The emperor afterward referred to the crown prince as "Charles Frederick."
* A diminutive which in Germany today would be Fritz*chen*.

a sight which brought joy to the king's heart, was taken as a good omen, and immediately immortalized in a painting by a French immigrant, Antoine Pesne, "The Little Drummer," in which Fritz makes as if hurrying off to war, gently restrained by his sister, Wilhelmina, then six or seven, while a Moorish page shields both of them with a parasol and a grenadier stands guard in the distance.

Little else is known of Fritz's first few years of life, until the age of seven, when his education began in earnest. Lieutenant General Count Finck von Finckenstein and Lieutenant Colonel von Kalkstein were named tutor and assistant tutor respectively, along with a preceptor, Duhan de Jandun, and other specialist tutors as occasion warranted. Duhan had caught the king's eye at Stralsund, where he had been a soldier, but he soon proved more than a military man and was responsible for broadening the prince's mind and channeling it into philosophical interests. Fritz loved him, thought of him as his mentor, and at the age of fifteen wrote him a letter, in wretchedly misspelled French, which showed his sentiments.

"My dear Duhan," it says, "I promise to you that when I shall have my money in my own hands, I will give you annually 2,400 crowns every year, and that I will love you always even a little more than at present, if that be possible."

He needed an outlet, an object for his affections, for the first signs of paternal displeasure had manifested themselves in an instruction, impatiently worded, that the prince should "not be so dirty." The king knew exactly what was good for his son, down to the smallest detail, just as he knew exactly what was good for his people. Frederick William had no doubt whatever that he himself was always in the right and always knew best; it was an assurance born not so much out of any royal arrogance, but rather out of an all-too-common obtuseness. He had a precise picture of what his son and heir should become; he should become, of course, an exact carbon copy of his father. This time, however, Frederick William could specify the course of instruction and training and therefore eliminate all educational errors which had been made with him and which he, thanks to his wisdom and great strength of will, had overcome in later life. Two sets of detailed instructions were accordingly issued by the king to Fritz's tutors, one dating from 1718, when they were appointed, and the other from 1721, when the prince was nine years old.

"A proper love and fear of God" were to be instilled in the prince. "No false religions or sects" were even to be "named in his hearing," with the exception of Roman Catholicism, about which he would have to know ("impossible to be ignored"), yet for which he must be given "a proper abhorrence . . . and insight into its baselessness and nonsensicality."

Fritz was to be kept in every way from "inflated and overweening pride," be taught "frugality and humility," and, "under pain of my highest displeasure," should never be flattered.

As for academic studies, under no circumstances was Fritz to be taught Latin, considered dead and useless by the king; he was to be taught a good style in both French and German; ancient history was to be treated only briefly, the main emphasis being placed on events during the previous 150 years ("taught most accurately"). Geography, mathematics, arithmetic were to be taught, as also "artillery [and] economy, to the very bottom." Fortification and other branches of military science were to be taught in detail, "so as to make him from a boy acquire the qualities and the knowledge of an officer and a general . . . with a true love for the profession of a soldier."

"Both the governors," wrote the king, "are to be particularly careful . . . to impress him with the conviction that nothing on earth is so calculated to earn glory and honor for a prince as the sword; and that he would appear before the world as a contemptible fellow if he did not love it, and did not seek his only glory in it."

The governors were, furthermore, to make the prince "disgusted . . . in every possible way" with "idleness, from which prodigality and extravagance arise." Toward that end, Fritz "is never for a moment to be left alone, either by day or by night, one of the governors is always to sleep in his chamber." If Fritz fell into "certain vicious excesses," which the king said were common to young people of that age, "the governors are to answer for it with their heads."

These, then, were the general rules for the education of this prince. Much that seems right and sober and proper was in them, but all their virtues were turned sour by the king's heavy hand.

In 1721 the king again penned a set of instructions, these meant to govern his son's every waking minute.

"On Sundays," he prescribed, "he shall rise in the morning at seven; as soon as he has put on his slippers, he is to fall on his knees and say a short prayer aloud, so that all those who are in the room may hear it. This being done, he shall speedily and quickly dress, wash properly, and have his hair tied and powdered; dressing and the short prayer not lasting longer than fifteen minutes, so that all may be over by a quarter past seven. Then he is to breakfast in seven minutes' time."

After that, more prayers, with servants and Duhan in attendance, Duhan to read a chapter from the Bible, and all to sing "some godly hymn," all that to be finished by a quarter to eight. From then until nine, Gospel studies, after which Fritz was to attend the king at church and at luncheon.

"The rest of the day he may spend as he pleases," the king wrote. "In the evening, he is to come and bid me good-night at half past nine, then immediately go to his apartment and undress and wash his hands as fast as he can," whereupon more prayers and hymns, until he is in bed by half past ten.

"On Mondays," the king continued, "he is to be called at six, when he shall get up at once, without even another turn in bed, but briskly and at once get up." Morning prayers were to follow, as on Sundays. "This being done, he shall as rapidly as possible get on his shoes and spatterdashes [*i.e.,* leggings]; also wash his face and hands. . . ." While his hair is combed out and queued ("but not powdered"), "he shall at the same time take breakfast and tea, so that both jobs go on at once, and all this shall be ended before half past six." After more worship, history lessons by Duhan were set by the king from seven to nine, whereupon Christian religion was to be taught until a quarter to eleven. "Then Fritz rapidly washes his face with water, hands with soap and water; clean shirt; powders, and puts on his coat; about eleven comes to the king . . . until two. . . .

"Directly at two, he goes back to his room. Duhan is there, ready, takes him upon the maps and geography from two to three. . . . From three to four, Duhan gives a treatise on morality; from four to five, Duhan shall write German letters with him and see that he gets a good style. About five, Fritz shall wash his hands and go to the king: ride out, divert himself in the air and not in his room, and do what he likes, if it is not against God."

The regimen for Monday was changed slightly for the other days of the week, in terms of subject matter to be taught. On Wednesdays, as on Saturdays, there was the chance of a half-day holiday, although Fritz could forfeit Saturday afternoon in favor of more study and review, if he failed to pass examinations held Saturday morning, to show whether he had "profited" by what was taught throughout the week.

The king ended his instructions to Finckenstein, Kalkstein, and Duhan with "one general rule which cannot be too much impressed upon you":

"In undressing and dressing, you must accustom him to get out of, and into, his clothes as fast as is humanly possible. You will also look that he learn to put on and off his clothes himself, without help from others, and that he be clean and neat and not so dirty."

These rules were meant to be broken; Fritz was certain of that. They aroused opposition in him; in them was the seed of the strife between himself and the king. The prohibition against Latin, for example, awakened a curiosity about and interest in that language. Fritz never learned more than a smattering of it, but even in later life he showed an affection for that which was forbidden him in youth. *"O tempora, O mores!"* he wrote once, adding, "You see I don't forget my Latin!"

A subtutor under Duhan was once teaching the prince that forbidden tongue when the king unexpectedly burst into the room. Latin books, dictionaries, and grammars were scattered before the horrified, outraged eyes of Frederick William, among these being the *Aurea Bulla,* the Golden Bull of Emperor Charles IV.

"What is this?" Frederick William roared, his face livid with anger. "What are you doing here?"

"Your Majesty, I am explaining *Aurea Bulla* to the prince!"

the terrified tutor replied, cowering before the king's wrath.

"I'll *Aurea Bulla* you, you dog!" Frederick William screamed, flailing at the tutor's head and shoulders with his cane until the terrified man fled the room.

It was a sign of more than disobedience: of subversion, perhaps. If Latin were being taught the prince, what might come next? Sure enough, unmistakable signs of rebelliousness and filial disrespect, of refractoriness, were discovered: Far from loving military studies and playing at soldiers, Fritz loved poetry and, worse yet, playing the flute! This despite the fact that, at the age of five, he had been given a company of cadets to drill and also despite the fact that, at the age of nine, he had received a Hohenzollern version of a doll house: a scale model of the Zeughaus, that arsenal on Unter den Linden, complete with miniature cannon and other machinery of war. The king began to feel that all his hopes were evaporating. At the age of seven, Fritz had surprised and delighted his father by mounting guard outside his rooms, dressed in the uniform of a musketeer. What joy there had been in the paternal heart on that occasion! But now all seemed different. Frederick William began to mutter that Fritz was becoming an "effeminate fellow" (*effeminierter Kerl*). The very sight of him troubled the king, for Fritz affected clothes which were far too dandified, "Frenchified," and wore his hair, not in the pigtail of the Prussian grenadiers, but in soft curls about his face and neck.

For that, at least, there was a remedy: a barber, promptly summoned to do his work under the very eyes of the king. Tears ran down Fritz's cheeks when the barber attacked his locks; the tears seemed to be evidence that he was being properly shorn, and so the king buried his face in a newspaper until the job was done. The barber thereupon took mercy on the prince, combed his locks back so that they appeared to be trimmed off regulation-style but could be shaken down whenever Fritz wanted, for which the prince was ever afterward grateful to this man.

The king wanted his son to be straightforwardly honest, but his constant nagging was teaching the prince dissimulation instead. Fritz found that safety lay in making a great hypocritical show for his father; it was an education in slyness which profited him a great deal later on. Fritz and his sister Wilhelmina even devised a code language in which they could communicate warnings and alarms; the codeword for their father was "Stumpy," and a fair enough description it was.

Fritz claimed in later years that his interest in reading had been stimulated by Wilhelmina. "Do you know from whom I learned to accustom myself to work and from whom I developed my love of studying?" he asked one of his intimates in 1758, when he was king. "It was my sister! When she noticed that I had no desire to read or busy myself and that I preferred to run around aimlessly, she said to me one day, 'Aren't you ashamed of yourself, dear brother, constantly to be running about? I never see you with a book in your hands. You neglect your abilities, and what sort of role will you play when you are finally called upon to play one?' These words and some tears which followed touched me so much that I began to read, although I began by reading novels.

"But orders had been given," he continued, "to prevent me from reading; I was therefore compelled to hide my books and to take precautions not to be caught reading them. When my governor, Marshall Finck [*i.e.*, Count Finck von Finckenstein], and my servant slept, I would climb out over the bed of my servant and sneak very, very silently into another room, where a nightlamp burned beside the fireplace. Bundled up beside this lamp, I read Pierre de Provence's book . . . and others, with which my sister and others supplied me. . . .

"My father regarded me at first as a kind of human clay, out of which might be formed whatever one wished. But how disappointed he came to be in this! He did everything he could to make me a hunter, but I never became one. . . . You can imagine what beautiful scenes there were; I was covered with accusations and humiliations; my lack of attention and indifference were ridiculed; and my father called out, full of despair and agony of heart, 'That boy will never amount to a thing!'

"He specifically did not wish me to read, yet I read as much as all the Benedictines put together. He did not wish me to dance, yet I did it and even came to love dancing. . . . My father wished me to become a soldier, but he could never have dreamt that I would become it some day to such an extent as now. . . ."[50]

The prince, in short, liked what the king did not like, adopted those mannerisms of which the king disapproved, and had interests the king thought immoral and ungodly. The father's growing vexation burst into the open when Fritz was twelve. This happened at a dinner given by Grumbkow, which both the king and the crown prince attended, Fritz being seated at his father's side. Frederick William began one of his endless lectures, his moral preachments, much of this lesson being directed at the son whom he regarded as ungodly, unaffectionate, disobedient, willful, and insolent. As he spoke, Frederick William began idly to tap his son's ear, as though for emphasis; each point he made was being lightly drummed home on the boy's head. Soon the king became more animated and the taps more severe; presently he raised his voice and slapped the boy to drive home his moral lessons. A moment later the king was completely out of control. He began boxing Fritz's ears, slapping his cheeks, pulling his hair; then he leaped up and started heaving plates against the wall. Grumbkow, ever the diplomatic courtier, began to do the same with the plates in front of him, as though all this behavior were due to the wine or merely a big joke, but it fooled no one. Crown Prince Fritz stood next to his father, shaking, his face white not so much with fear as with contempt. This lasted. Two years later, Fritz spoke in secret, separately, to the ambassadors of Great Britain and France. What would their attitude be if the king died or— The ambassadors wrote to London and Paris, saying they did not dare to commit to paper all the things the crown prince had said. Did he have in mind a coup to overthrow the king, or did he believe his father was going mad?

Fritz had reached manhood—that is to say, puberty. The king interrogated a cleric about the prince's knowledge of religion; when he was told that his son understood the letter, if not the spirit, of the Gospels, Frederick William announced that that was good enough. He dismissed Duhan and the other tutors when the boy was about fifteen and put the prince into the guards. Four officers, one of whom was told never to leave the prince's side, were appointed as his overseers. The king wanted to know even the slightest irregularity in Fritz's conduct.

* * *

In October, 1723, when Fritz was nearly twelve years old, his maternal grandfather, George I of Great Britain, had arrived in Berlin.

Queen Sophia Dorothea, George II's sister, was an ambitious, scheming woman, fiercely loyal to her children, especially to Fritz and to Wilhelmina; she had in mind a double marriage which would unite the Prussian and English families closely. Her plan was for Wilhelmina to marry the Duke of Gloucester (also Duke of Edinburgh and later Prince of Wales); Fritz was to marry Amelia, one of the daughters of George I's son. What course European history might have taken had the Prussian and British monarchies been united in this marriage is fascinating to conjecture on; however, nothing came of the double marriage.* When it was first broached, Frederick William approved of it, but the double marriage proposal later turned into another area of conflict between the king, on the one hand, and the queen (together with Wilhelmina and Fritz), on the other.

Wilhelmina was fourteen when George I and "Fred" (Frederick Louis, Wilhelmina's "intended") arrived in Berlin. She made a favorable impression on them, speaking English and being told she had "quite the English air and made to be their [*i.e.*, England's] Sovereign one day." Wilhelmina knew this was quite a compliment. "It was saying a great deal on their part," she notes, "for these English think themselves so much above all other people that they imagine they are paying a high compliment when they tell anyone he has got English manners." Such, in any case, was the impression she had of George I's suite; George I himself struck her as having "Spanish manners . . . of extreme gravity." He was obviously in ill health, for at supper he keeled over and remained unconscious on the floor for an hour. He stayed in the palace for four more days after that, watched young Fritz drilling his company of cadets, and

* On the accession of George II, the Duke of Gloucester did indeed become heir apparent (as Prince of Wales), but his death was to precede that of his father, so that Wilhelmina would never have become Queen of England even if the marriage had taken place. The other half of the double marriage, that of Fritz to Amelia, would of course have made an English princess royal the Queen of Prussia in the eighteenth century, 100 years or so before that actually took place (Kaiser William II's mother being Queen Victoria's daughter). As it turned out, when the double marriage failed to materialize, Amelia retired into spinsterhood and never married at all.

on October 12 prepared to sign the double marriage treaty. Then he went hunting with Frederick William, the treaty never signed, while Queen Sophia Dorothea stayed home, not feeling well. As a matter of fact, she had for some months been enlarging in size, feeling ill, faint and puzzled, for no one knew what was the matter with her health. Suddenly, in the night of November 8, she experienced the most fearful pains—gas pains, it was thought—whereupon the king was called to her bedchamber, along with nurses and attendants. To everyone's amazement, her discomfort was not due to gas at all: She was having a baby! The birth was so sudden that the king had to act as midwife. The queen had had a dozen children before and ought to have known the symptoms; the fact that she hadn't made for great gossip and amusement in court circles for some time to come. The baby was Anna Amalia, whose fate was later to be bound up with the tragic figure of Baron Friedrich von der Trenck.

In the year 1724, that of the Grumbkow dinner, the year after George I's visit and the double marriage negotiations, when Fritz was twelve, the Pragmatic Sanction of the Holy Roman Emperor Charles was universally promulgated. This was a document, first published in 1713, in which Charles proclaimed that his female heirs and descendants for the throne of the Holy Roman Emperor were to become eligible as though they were males. This was done for Maria Theresa, then seven years old, who was to become Fritz's adversary in later life. Her father, the emperor, spent his last years hunting out signatories to this document, for it was after all only a scrap of paper unless he could get the consent of other states. Loyal to the emperor as always, Frederick William signed, but a few others did not, one of them being Augustus of Saxony, who was holding out for a price.

On May 3, 1725, just thirteen years of age, Fritz was made a captain in the guards; the next year, promoted to major, he led his regiment of 2,400 "long fellows" out on parade. It was for this military service that his hair had to be shorn, regulation-style; no further nonsense, effeminacy, dandyism, Frenchified behavior were to be permitted him. Whatever might be said of book learning, however desirable a "good style" in French and

German might be, it was as nothing compared to the army in Frederick William's mind; the Prussian grenadiers' drill was considered the noblest and loftiest pursuit, its absolute perfection the worthiest goal for a man's life.

The fact that Fritz was now a soldier did not, however, make him the apple of his father's eye. In 1722, Sophia Dorothea had blessed the king with a second son who was now surviving infancy quite well: Augustus William, still a toddler as Fritz entered the Blues and therefore very much doted upon by his father, even as Fritz had been during those early, amenable years. Fritz was in his teens; those are difficult years for a boy and doubly difficult for a father if he has little tolerance and understanding, whereas little Augustus William was not difficult at all, just fetching. Furthermore, since he was not crown prince or heir apparent, no parties circled around him, as the king suspected was the case with Fritz, there always being people in a royal court who make up "the crown prince's party," ensuring their future, siding with the heir apparent against the king.

Gradually, the Prussian court came to be more filled with intrigue than any other in Europe, or so ambassadors in Berlin reported home. There was, on the one hand, the British camp, made up of the queen, Wilhelmina, and Fritz; opposed to their interests were Grumbkow and Seckendorff, both Austrian agents and both *tabagie* cronies of the king. While the king's ear was the target of both camps, the cards were hopelessly stacked in favor of the emperor's agents. The pro-British party was alienated from Frederick William on personal, family grounds; furthermore, Grumbkow and Seckendorff fed the king's hatred for his heir apparent each evening, during those smoking and drinking sessions of the *Tabakscollegium*.

Queen Sophia Dorothea was an enemy of her husband from the start, after just a few months of being mistreated. Early in their marriage, the king threatened to divorce her; her reply was, "Believe me, I set no store by my own life. You embitter it too much for me to mourn for it." As he did with his children, he also accused her of not loving him enough; this idea, she told him, was only one of "the malignant phantoms of your imagination." [51] The only time he treated her more than civilly was when her mother left her 3,000,000 thalers. "To obtain control of this sum," one ambassador reported, "the king lavishes endearments on the queen and nothing is too much to put up with. The moment the money is transferred to his treasury, no doubt this will become less apparent." A privy councilor was sent to Hanover to fetch the money, but the queen's brother (again that damnable George) refused to hand over a penny. "To hell with all Hanoverians!" the king shouted as a toast in front of his queen afterward and dropped all tenderness.[52]

Matters were made all the worse when the king heard that Fritz had referred to his army uniform as a shroud and that he had complained that discipline in the Prussian army was too brutal; furthermore, on one occasion when he should have been pursuing the manly sport of hunting, he was found under a tree reading a book. Always this boy showed himself rebellious and unaffectionate, or so the king thought, and ever since the incident at the Grumbkow dinner party Frederick William never bothered to hide his feelings about his son. He had at first been worried about the crown prince, then been vexed by him, soon claimed to be broken hearted, and at last hated the boy thoroughly. In his heart, he wished Augustus William might succeed him as King of Prussia, but how could this be done? One avenue lay open, and the king, losing his temper, showed that he at least entertained the monstrous idea. On one occasion, he made as if to strangle Fritz with a curtain cord and almost succeeded in doing so.

It was at this juncture that the trip to Dresden took place. The king had not intended to take Fritz along; he only agreed to do so at the last minute, on the urging of Augustus, his host. It was to be Fritz's first venture outside his immediate environment, into "the world."

What a world this was! The Saxon elector and Polish king was reputed to have had the most pleasure-loving court in all Europe; it was world-famous for its profligacy, elegance, degeneracy, luxury, and playfulness. Augustus was called the Strong for both his large size and his legendary virility; the number of his bastard offspring is known to have come to 354. He not only outperformed Frederick William in bed, but in majesty as well. He was fifty-eight years old at the time (Frederick William was forty), yet much more vigorous both physically and mentally. Even his royal title was older; he had become King of Poland before Frederick William's father became King "in" Prussia.* Indeed, he was everything the Hohenzollern king was not: He was charming, gay, and healthy in both mind and body.

The king arrived in Dresden on January 14, 1728; Fritz arrived a day after. Frederick William declined Augustus' invitation to stay with him and moved into simpler quarters instead, as the guest of the Dresden city commandant, Field Marshal Wackerbarth, who was a friend from Stralsund days. Frederick William had come with only a few attendants, Grumbkow among them, and wanted no fuss. When Fritz arrived in Dresden with his two tutors, Finckenstein and Kalkstein, he was quartered with Field Marshal Count Flemming. Soon Frederick William moved over there as well, for in the middle of the night of the seventeenth, Wackerbarth's house burned down, almost on top of the King of Prussia, forcing him to abandon it in his nightclothes, clutching a box of his treasures.

Dances and lavish dinners took up four weeks and a day, this being the carnival season. There were plays to be seen, operas, fireworks, cannon salvos, animal baitings, hunts; of all these, Frederick William seems to have enjoyed the dinners the most. The Dresden cuisine was infinitely better than that of Berlin, for Augustus' tastes ran to more than pork and cabbage. Frederick William, growing ever fatter, made the most of the enormous banquets served. He especially enjoyed Augustus' loving cup which, when raised to one's lips, fired off a harmless shot; it was this kind of practical joke which the King of Prussia enjoyed the most.

He found another of Augustus' practical jokes less amusing. The kings of Poland and Prussia were one evening walking through the palace on their way to an entertainment, when Augustus the Strong led Frederick William into a side room, suggesting he have a look at the furniture. The room interested Frederick William; it was richly ornamented and "in quite exquisite taste," as Wilhelmina describes it. As he stood there, surveying the room, a curtain at one end of it was swept aside,

* The Hohenzollerns rose to royal rank partly thanks to Augustus the Strong. When this Protestant Elector of Saxony turned Roman Catholic so as to become King of Poland, the religious balance of power in North Germany was disturbed. It therefore became desirable to elevate a Protestant elector to redress this imbalance.

revealing a beautiful, nude woman lying enticingly on a luxurious bed. Nothing was hidden from view, for the seductress' body was brilliantly illuminated by great numbers of candles; only her eyes were masked, making her even more mysteriously appealing. Frederick William froze in his place, not knowing what to do.

Augustus, of course, was less clumsy; for one thing, he had arranged this tableau to see if Frederick William's sexual appetites could be aroused. He was a man of great gallantry and considerable charm and now showered his talents upon the mysterious lady. He approached her and begged her to unmask; he said he hoped she would not refuse, since two kings were asking her for this favor. She succumbed, took off her mask, and revealed a beautiful face. (Wilhelmina called her "more beautiful than they paint Venus and the Graces . . . whiter than snow, and more gracefully shaped than the Venus de' Medici," a "treasure" and a "goddess"; Baron von Pöllnitz, of the Prussian court, said she had "one of the loveliest faces in the world.")

She was too much for Frederick William. When Augustus assessed his reaction, Frederick William politely harrumphed, "It must be admitted, she is very beautiful," but then immediately turned away in embarrassment. In so doing, he caught sight of something which made him freeze in horror: His son Fritz was standing in the room, staring at the beauty on the bed. Frederick William leaped forward and clapped his hat over his son's face and hustled him out of the room and out of temptation's way; later, he summoned Grumbkow and complained bitterly that Augustus had wanted to tempt him. Grumbkow assured his king that it was all a joke, but Frederick William was deadly earnest. If Augustus ever tried anything like that again, he would leave Dresden immediately, he said, ordering Grumbkow to carry this message to his host. Augustus roared with laughter when Grumbkow delivered Frederick William's warning and then immediately and generously apologized to the Prussian king. It was clear there was no arousing Frederick William's sexuality.

It was different, however, with Crown Prince Fritz. The sixteen-year-old boy had caught what was very probably his first sight of a naked woman, and, as Wilhelmina wrote, this experience "did not inspire in him so much horror as in his father." Fritz promptly obtained "the cabinet Venus" from Augustus the Strong in a rather singular manner.

He struck a bargain with Augustus. There was at the Dresden court a certain Countess Orzelska, a favorite (and presumed to be a mistress) of Augustus, with whom young Fritz had fallen hopelessly in love. She had a bizarre history: Her mother was a French milliner in Warsaw; her father was Augustus himself. After she had grown up, she had been taken as mistress by a soldier named Rutowski—and this Rutowski was another one of Augustus' 354 bastards. Rutowski afterward introduced the girl to Augustus, which meant he was surrendering his half sister to his (and her) own father. Fritz, who was much coveted by the ladies at the Dresden court, had singled this Countess Orzelska out not only because of her beauty and gaiety, but also because she was irresistibly Bohemian. She walked about in men's clothes and was, according to Pöllnitz, somehow very "grand" and "extremely open-handed." Augustus, who liked the courtly and handsome Crown Prince Fritz a great deal and who indulged every one of his whims in Dresden, was nevertheless jealous and wanted to be the sole recipient of Countess Orzelska's attentions. And so he gave Fritz the "cabinet Venus" instead, she being named Formera. It appears, however, that Fritz may have had the best of the bargain: After Formera, the Countess Orzelska also gave herself to the young prince.

Either from one of these two ladies or possibly from someone else in Dresden, the Crown Prince Fritz *appears to have* contracted venereal disease. Wilhelmina, whose memoirs are only partly reliable, claims he definitely did; Prussian historians generally deny it vehemently. Yet while Wilhelmina exaggerates to emphasize the lurid, this does not mean her statement in this case is necessarily untrue. In any event, Fritz took ill upon his return to Berlin, becoming "a mere shadow." Circumstantial evidence, based in part on his later life, in which he showed a marked indifference toward women, led to the belief that the Berlin doctors botched the cure, that they operated on his penis in such a way as to make it impossible for him to have sexual relations afterward, without however castrating him or influencing his hormonal balance. Historians have battled about it, but Fritz's sister at least did not doubt that this was so.

During his illness, Fritz for the first time in years received some kind attentions from his father. The king told Prince Leopold that one only appreciates how much one loves one's children when they are sick; the moment Fritz was well again, his hatred of his son flared up all the more.

Fritz was compelled to sit at the end of the table; he was banished from his father's sight except during meals; even at that distance ("at thirty paces"), the king said, he could see that the boy's head was filled with evil thoughts. He began to throw plates at Fritz and at Wilhelmina during dinner; they learned to duck.

Fritz was in a torment. He wished at all costs to reconcile himself with his father, but nothing he tried worked. If he answered his father politely and humbly, his father accused him of lying; if he replied boldly and stood his ground, his father exploded at his rebelliousness. Meanwhile, he tried to make his private hours bearable and even pleasant, mainly by music. An instructor was secretly hired and taught the prince the flute, perfecting him in that instrument—a difficult task, since the instructor had to sit inside a chimney in the prince's room, just in case the king ventured in. In September, 1728, Fritz wrote his father an abject, humble letter, pleading to be put again in his good graces. In it, he said that his conscience was clear but that if unintentionally he had done anything "to anger my dear Papa, I herewith most humbly crave his pardon and hope that my dear Papa may relinquish the cruel hatred which I perceive in all his treatment of me; I could not otherwise resign myself to it, since I always used to think I had a gracious father, and now I have to see the contrary is the case. . . .[53]

His father replied promptly, in a letter (although they lived in the same palace, a few yards from each other). The letter used the third person singular in addressing the prince, this being a form the Hohenzollern kings used in addressing inferiors:

> His obstinate wicked head, which does not love his father, for when one does do everything [required], particularly loving one's father, then one does what [the father] wishes, not only when [he] is there to see it, but also when he is not there. Further, he knows full well that I can't abide an effeminate fellow

who has no inclinations worthy to be called human, who disgraces himself being able neither to sit his horse properly nor hit his target, and who is also offensive in his person, dressing his hair like a fool and not getting it cut, and I have reproved him in all this a thousand times but always in vain and without no improvement in nothing. Furthermore, he is arrogant, conceited and proud, does not speak with the people but for a few exceptions, and makes no effort to be pleasant or affable, and who grimaces his face as though he were an idiot and won't do anything unless forced, doing nothing from filial love, and having no other desire than to follow his own stubborn head, which is no use to him or anyone else. This is my answer.

FREDERICK WILLIAM[54]

Shortly thereafter, at Wusterhausen, Fritz made one more attempt to reconcile himself with the king. It was at dinner, and Fritz, obeying his father's command that he keep up with the others in the manly art of drinking, had been drinking far more than was his custom. He began to tell Suhm, the Saxon ambassador in Berlin, who sat next to him, how intolerable his life was; he asked Suhm to get Augustus to urge King Frederick William to let Fritz travel abroad. His voice began to be heard above the other conversations, although the queen gave him frantic signals to lower his tone. Fritz, very drunk, continued speaking of how wretched he was, punctuating this every now and then with the cry, "And yet I love him!"

"What is he saying?" the king called out, having caught the sound of Fritz's voice.

Suhm was anxious to placate the king and avoid a scene. He told the king that Fritz was just a little drunk and didn't make much sense.

"*Ach,* he's just pretending!" the king replied. "I want to hear what he has to say!"

Suhm said that the prince had declared his love for the king, whereupon the king sneered, "So he pretends!" At this the queen rose to go from the table and signaled to Fritz to leave as well. Fritz got up, begged his father to let him have his hand, and then covered it with kisses, trying to embrace him the next moment. The queen left the room alone, in disgust, but the other guests shouted, "Bravo! Long live the crown prince!" and Fritz, overcome with drink and emotion, fell to his knees before his father, clasped Frederick William's knees in his arms, swore that he only wished to love and obey his father, and spoke hysterically of enemies who were slandering him to the king, for he knew what Grumbkow and Seckendorff were doing. Tears poured down the prince's cheeks; the guests again hailed the filial devotion being shown, and Frederick William finally was touched enough to grunt, "All right, all right, just see that you turn out an honest fellow." The prince was helped to bed, and the king remained in a jolly mood for the rest of the evening. The next day, however, Frederick William was persuaded by others, very likely the two Austrian agents, that Fritz's performance had just been a hypocritical pretense.[55]

Matters went from bad to worse. Accused at one point of being pro-British, Fritz replied to the king, "I respect the English, for the people there love me," whereupon the king grasped him and beat him savagely. "There is a general apprehension of something tragic taking place before long," the British ambassador reported.[56]

Fritz wrote his mother he could no longer stand the treatment he was receiving. "I am in uttermost despair," he wrote her. "The King has entirely forgotten that I am his son. I am driven to extremity. I have too much honor to endure such treatment and am resolved to put an end to it one way or another."[57]

Hearing of this, Frederick William merely mocked the prince. "Had I been treated so by my father, I would have put a bullet through my head, but you do not even have the courage to do that." Then he told him that those who suggested things might get better were in truth his enemies. "For on the contrary, you'll find out I shall get harder every day." And so it proved. One night, as all the family lined up to kiss the king before going to bed, Fritz hesitated. Frederick William grabbed his son by the hair, dragged him to the ground, and forced him to kiss his boots. "I treat you as my child, not as an officer!" he shouted.[58]

The British, meanwhile, kept the issue of the double marriage alive, but insisted it would be a *double* marriage or none at all. This didn't please Frederick William; he had decided not to have an English princess marry Fritz for the simple reason that he didn't want anyone putting on "English airs" in Berlin; the king's obstinacy in this matter made it impossible for Wilhelmina to marry the Prince of Wales. A compromise was almost found by means of which the double marriage was saved, but Frederick William changed his mind about that, three times in two days. Grumbkow was plotting actively to subvert the marriage; some of his letters, which proved Grumbkow's treasonous activities, came into the hands of the British envoy, who showed them to King Frederick William. Finally, Frederick William had proof positive that Grumbkow was a foreign agent and a traitor and that the double marriage was being undermined for reasons not necessarily in Prussia's best interest. Frederick William, however, cast only a glance at the letter, threw it down angrily, shouted to the British envoy, "I've had enough of this affair!" and barged out of the room.[59] He could not admit to himself or to anyone that he had been deceived. It was on this note of self-deception that the double marriage was finally called off. As for Fritz, the king's frustrated anger now burst out on him afresh. Though he had been reduced in rank briefly from lieutenant colonel to ensign, he had been restored to colonel and, at eighteen, went with his father to some Saxon maneuvers. There King Frederick William seized his son in full view of all the troops, dragged him by the hair, kicked him, beat him savagely, and sent him off, disheveled and bleeding, as well as in despair. Only escape from Prussia could now save this prince, and this is just what Fritz began to plan. The aftermath would be more horrible than what he had lived through before.

7

"The Man Is Mad!"

The suggestion, which has so often been made, that Frederick the Great was probably a homosexual derives in part from his relation with Hans Hermann von Katte, a lieutenant in the Potsdam guards. Its proponents cite for confirmation not only the prince's declared "love" of Katte, but also his later inability to love any woman. There is, however, no proof to substantiate this allegation; Fritz may or may not have had a homosexual relationship with Katte, although the lack of proof leads one to dismiss the suggestion. (Voltaire later reinforced it, claiming that Frederick the Great in his later years had homosexual relations with his soldiers.)

Crown Prince Fritz's love for Katte was certainly not sparked by homosexual tendencies; the prince, naturally affectionate and being denied warmth in the palace, needed a friend on whom he could lavish his own capacity to love. Fritz had few champions in Berlin or Potsdam; Katte was a loyal friend of his own generation.

There had been one other such friend, Lieutenant Peter Christoph Karl von Keith, a descendant of Scottish nobles who had settled in Pomerania and whose name was pronounced *kite* in Prussia. Keith was the most prominent of a group of young officers who befriended the crown prince—at considerable risk to themselves, for the prince's friends *ipso facto* became the king's enemies. With Keith and the others, Fritz did what all other young men of his age are given to do: He amused himself—that is to say, he broke windows, caroused, and "roistered about." When Keith was transferred to a regiment at Wesel, on the Rhine, Fritz discovered Katte, whom he had known only casually before. Katte was more than Keith had been, for Fritz could do more than amuse himself with Katte; he could engage himself intellectually with Katte as well. The lieutenant was by all accounts a remarkable person, with interests which ranged from mathematics to philosophy and art; he had studied law at Halle (Berlin did not yet have its own university); he possessed wit, charm, high spirits, and considerable courage. He also had a somewhat fearsome countenance, which Wilhelmina found distinctly ugly; he had a pockmarked face and great, dark eyebrows, these giving rise to a verse sung about him in schooldays, predicting that anyone with such sinister brows would end up either hanged or broken on the wheel.* As it turned out, the jingle proved prophetic.

Fritz was now practically under room arrest, which meant under constant watch. A Colonel von Rochow and Lieutenant Dietrich Keyserlingk had been appointed his guardians—really his guards—for rumors that the prince planned an escape had reached the king's ear. His displeasure with the prince knew no bounds during this time. Frederick William had virtually stopped thinking of him as a human being; indeed, when Queen Caroline of England (the beloved Caroline of Frederick William's youth) asked Frederick William for a portrait of his son, the king replied that any picture of a long-tailed ape would serve the purpose.

Sometimes at night, while Fritz was being watched in the Potsdam garrison, Katte would secretly break into his room and spend an hour or so, this again giving rise in later years to those rumors of homosexual conduct, although apparently they just talked. It must be remembered that Fritz had a highly intelligent mind and a lively curiosity; Katte, eight years older and better-educated, fascinated Fritz and allowed him to sharpen his wits. They spoke of religion and philosophy, both disdaining the first and being fascinated by the second; they spoke, in short,

* *Wer solche Brauen hat*
Wie der Ritter Katt',
Der endet am Galgen
Oder unterm Rad.

as young men always speak, both of weighty matters, such as the nature of the universe, and of lighter ones, such as the gossip of Berlin and Potsdam. Soon they also spoke of the prince's plans.

The crown prince had been actively entertaining thoughts of escape for some months and had even petitioned his uncle George II for asylum in England. This troubled George, for he wanted, on the one hand, to accommodate the prince and, on the other, to do nothing which would so infuriate Frederick William as to draw him closer still to the Habsburg emperor. He advised Fritz to be patient and do nothing rash; Uncle George would, in return, pay his considerable debts. Fritz had been forced to borrow 7,000 thalers because his father gave him a miserly allowance; he told the British his debts amounted to 15,000, and although they spluttered a bit, they paid him the full sum. This gave Fritz a surplus which was to help finance his escape, other funds being derived from some jewels which he sold.

The opportunity for an escape finally came, because the king was taking precautions against it. On July 15, 1730, Frederick William had left Potsdam for a long tour of German states and had taken Fritz along to keep a close watch over him.

His trip was undertaken on the emperor's behalf, to promote the Pragmatic Sanction previously mentioned. Before joining the journey, the crown prince gave Katte, who remained behind, all his worldly goods: jewels, rings, books, and a portable desk filled with papers. Katte planned to apply for leave, ostensibly to go on recruiting business; he was then to join Fritz en route, perhaps at Cannstatt, near Stuttgart. Keith, now stationed on the Rhine, was to join them in a dash across the river and into France. The King of France had already told Fritz he would be safe there; Fritz was certain George II would later on provide refuge across the Channel. A younger brother of Lieutenant Keith, a page who rode beside the king's carriage, joined the conspiracy.

The prince traveled in a carriage behind the king's and was guarded by three officers: Rochow, old General Buddenbrock, and old Colonel Waldau. At Leipzig a lavish dinner was prepared by the town commandant, General Hopfgarten, but this official's welcome to the King of Prussia was so elaborate and his address so simperingly hypocritical that it outraged Frederick William, who charged on, abandoning the uneaten meal.* At the next stop, Count Seckendorff joined Frederick William's party, bringing along picnic lunches, which were the kind of meals the king enjoyed most. When traveling, he liked to stop en route, eat under the trees, rush off again, and, at night, even requisition a barn and sleep on straw. Frederick William kept up an exhausting pace while traveling, hardly ever stopping at any town for more than a day and often covering surprising distances without a rest. The wretched roads and their potholes never slowed him down a bit; his carriages just lurched over them and jolted along, bouncing and joggling down the roads as though the Furies were pursuing the party. The king raced through ten towns to get to Ansbach, where he stayed a week, for this was now the home of his sixteen-year-old daughter Frederica, recently married to the margrave there. There Fritz bought himself two French-style coats for his flight to France, one of them bright red, a color his father detested. He even attempted escape at Ansbach, but since this proved impossible, he made plans to escape later on. Meanwhile, Katte had written him to say that he was unable to get leave and that they would have to flee separately, joining Keith in either France or Holland.

One would have thought that the crown prince would behave with the utmost circumspection, but it appears he was too foolhardy, boastful, or perhaps inexperienced to do so. As the prince's carriage headed toward the Rhine (across which lay France), Fritz pulled his red coat out and put it on right in front of the eyes of his three guardians. Rochow remonstrated; the prince had better make certain the king never saw that coat. Fritz shrugged, remarked he had bought it only because the weather was colder than expected, and pushed it out of sight. The party headed for Mannheim on the Rhine, where the Elector Palatine resided. Rather than drive on all the way to that city in one day, the king had for once ordered an early halt, in a village called Steinfurth, where he commandeered a couple of barns, placing himself and his party in one of them and the

* Hopfgarten (as Frederick William afterward reported) said that if King Augustus of Saxony had but known, he would have wished for wings to fly to meet the Prussians and would have "in the Polish manner" bowed so low as to grasp Frederick William's feet. Such florid talk always nauseated Frederick William.

prince and his wardens in the other. A fresh start was to be made at five in the morning.

Fritz ordered the page Keith to bring him horses at three. Shortly after two, Fritz got up quietly and dressed, putting on his red coat, its pockets bursting with all his possessions. Rochow's valet, Gummersbach, who lay next to the crown prince, awakened and asked what Fritz was doing. "I'm getting up," Fritz replied coolly. "Don't ask silly questions." But the valet persisted. Didn't the prince remember that this red coat was supposed to remain hidden? Fritz shrugged off the remark with, "I just happen to feel like wearing it," then stepped outside. The valet instantly woke up Colonel von Rochow, who got dressed in a hurry and went out to see what was going on. He found Fritz standing about in the red coat, engaged him in a friendly conversation, and waited to see what would happen. At three thirty, Keith showed up, leading two saddled horses. Rochow asked for whom these were meant, and Keith replied they were for himself and another page, being readied for the journey. "His Majesty is not leaving until five today," Rochow reminded Keith. "Take the horses away."

As Keith led them off, Fritz's other guardians appeared; a moment later, Seckendorff himself showed up, his eyes wide at the sight of the red coat. Rochow made light of the matter. "How do you like His Royal Highness in that coat?" he asked, as if it were a joke. Then he added, "Of course, His Majesty must never see it!" Rochow and the two other guardians led the prince back to the barn, took the coat off him, and prepared to depart in the prince's own carriage; because it was somewhat heavier and slower than the king's, it needed a head start.

The prince should have reached Mannheim ahead of the king, but in fact, the king's carriage got there three and a half hours ahead of Fritz's; what delayed Fritz and his guardians is still a mystery. It was eleven thirty in the morning of August 4, 1730, that Fritz and the three officers finally pulled into Mannheim, to accompany the king on a sight-seeing tour.

In the course of that day, the crown prince managed to slip a note to the page Keith, ordering him to obtain two more horses in Mannheim and to have them ready for the next day. But Keith had begun to crack as a result of his early-morning encounter with Rochow; he knew that if he were ever caught again trying to help the prince, it would mean his head. From Steinfurth to Mannheim he had ridden next to the king's carriage, trembling and shaking both from fear and remorse of conscience, for who was he to counter the wishes of kings? The next day was a Sunday, and Keith attended church along with the royal party; this apparently affected him so profoundly that, immediately afterward, he fell upon his knees before the king and confessed everything.

Frederick William controlled his rage; he was not in Prussia, where he could do as he liked, but was a guest who needed to observe proprieties. He told Rochow, Buddenbrock, and Waldau they would pay with their heads if the prince failed to reach Prussian territory, "alive or dead."

Three more stops had been scheduled before they finally reached Prussia's Rhineland territory at Wesel, where Lieutenant von Keith was stationed; at each of these, Frederick William managed to suppress his impatience and rage, so as not to embarrass his hosts. As for Fritz, he was unaware that the page had confessed everything, although the king once turned to him and said, sarcastically, "I am surprised you're still here. I thought you'd be in Paris by now." Fritz, puzzled, made light of it. "I would have been there, had I wanted to be," he said. Then he slipped a note to the page: "Things look bad. Arrange for us to get away."

Two days later, on August 8, more fuel was heaped onto the fires in the king's breast. He was handed a letter Fritz had written from Ansbach to Katte; it had been misdirected to that officer's cousin, a captain, who sent it on to the king.

"In two days I shall be free," it said. "I have money, clothes, horses; my flight will undoubtedly succeed, and, if I should be pursued, I shall seek an asylum in a monastery, where no one shall find out the arch-heretic under the disguise of a cowl and a scapular. You will immediately follow me with the things I have entrusted to your keeping, even if we should only meet beyond the sea: go by Leipzig and Wesel to Holland; there you will hear from me."

Boiling with rage, the king nevertheless controlled his temper until his party traveled by ship down the Rhine to Wesel. Near Mainz, the king finally exploded. He seized Fritz, hit him in the face with his cane until his nose bled, cursed him as a deserter and a traitor, until Buddenbrock intervened to stop the beatings. Fritz and the page Keith were placed on a separate yacht from the king's, under close guard. Still, Fritz somehow managed to smuggle out two letters, one for Lieutenant von Keith and the other for Katte in Berlin. "Save yourself, all is lost!" read the one to Keith. Fritz even pleaded with Seckendorff, his archenemy, to help him "in this labyrinth," and Seckendorff actually obliged, trying to calm the king, perhaps out of pity, but very likely because he knew this prince was still probably going to become king some day. Fritz had loyally not begged help for himself, but for Lieutenants von Keith and Katte; his chief misery, he had told Seckendorff, was that they should come to grief because of him. "Well, if he confesses everything and tries to conceal nothing," the king told Seckendorff, he might have mercy, adding, "But I know he won't."

In fact, the king had become convinced there was more to this business than Fritz's wish to escape harsh treatment. No doubt, he thought, it was the fault of England, of George II, and signified a plot to overthrow Frederick William and to place Fritz on the Prussian throne by foul and bloody means. He was filled with such thoughts when he next confronted the prince at Wesel, on Prussian soil.

"Why were you going to desert?" the king asked his son.

"Because you have been treating me not as a son, but as a slave."

"Then," replied the king, "you are nothing but a mean-spirited deserter who has not a shred of honor in him!"

"I have as much honor as you!" Fritz replied. "I have done nothing but what you have told me a hundred times you would do in my place!"

Infuriated by these words, Frederick William drew his sword and lunged at his son, quite prepared to run him through; he was prevented from this only by the Wesel commandant, General von der Mosel, who threw himself in front of the prince, saying, "Sire, kill me, but spare your son!" Fritz was hurried out of the room, and the king shouted that he never wanted to see him again and told others to interrogate the deserter. Colonel von Derschau, who thoroughly disliked the prince and who was a *tabagie* crony of the king's, was made chief inquisitor, and Frederick William drew up the questions to be asked. Fritz was now formally under arrest and guarded by armed soldiers.

It wasn't long before all the European courts knew of the prince's arrest. Rumors circulated that certain powers might undertake to rescue him. To prevent this, the king ordered the prince to be taken to Küstrin Fortress, east of Berlin. Fritz was clapped into a closed carriage and surrounded by a troop of soldiers, who had orders to kill him if he tried to escape. No stops were to be made en route; if the prince wished to relieve himself, the king ordered, he was to be permitted to do so only in open countryside, where there were no hills, ditches, trees, or bushes to shelter him from the constant observation of the guards.

Berlin was in a turmoil throughout. Katte quickly got Fritz's money and papers to the queen. Knowing that the king would demand to see Fritz's portable desk and its contents when he returned, she and Wilhelmina burned all of the prince's incriminating letters, some of them virtually treasonable under the circumstances, and they then filled the desk with between six and seven hundred innocent letters, which these two women, working night and day, managed to forge before the king returned.

Orders had arrived for the arrest of Katte. Why Katte had not immediately fled remains a mystery; he made preparations to do so, but never left. "You *still* here, Katte?" asked his major the day before Katte was arrested. "I leave this night," Katte replied, but he didn't go. Colonel Pannewitz, who was charged with arresting him the following morning, hoped he would not find him in Berlin, but he was still there, and the order had to be carried out. Keith had better luck, or more resolution. He sped to The Hague, from where the German secretary to Lord Chesterfield spirited him to England. When Frederick William learned of this, he had an effigy of him cut in four, nailed onto a gallows, and he then confiscated what little property Keith had owned.

The day before Katte was arrested was August 15, the king's birthday, and Queen Sophia gave a ball in honor of it. In the middle of this, she received a letter from the king which turned her "pale as death." What it contained is not known, but another letter of the king's to Frau von Kamecke at the palace refers to it: "I have unfortunately the misfortune that my son wanted to desert. . . . I have had him arrested, I have written to my wife; you must break it to her in a roundabout fashion even if it takes a few days, so she won't get ill. Meanwhile, pity an unhappy father. . . ."

Frederick William was concerned about the queen's health because she was pregnant, but his solicitude didn't prove very sincere. When he reentered the Berlin palace on August 27 and saw the queen, he announced to her, "Your worthless son is no more; he is dead!"

"What!" Queen Sophia cried out in despair. "You have had the barbarity to kill him?"

"Just so!" the king lied. "What I want now is that sealed desk of his. . . ."

She went to fetch it, moaning, "My God, my son!" After Frederick William had opened it and studied the letters, he was even more furious, for there was nothing in them which incriminated the British.

An incredible scene followed. The queen and all her children assembled to plead for mercy to be shown to Fritz, for in the interval they had found out he was not dead after all. They kissed the king's hands, weeping and moaning; even four-year-old Prince Henry was on his knees before Papa.

No sooner did the king spot Wilhelmina than he lost all control of himself again.

"Infamous scum!" he shouted at her. "You dare show yourself before me? Go keep your scoundrel of a brother company!"

Wilhelmina says that Frederick William "became black in the face, his eyes sparkling fire, his mouth foaming." He grasped her with one hand, hit her several times in the face with his fist, so that she fell backward, struck on the temple, and unconscious. The king, still "in a frenzy," tried to kick her, while the queen, the other princesses, and all the attendants ran around shrieking and trying to prevent him from doing so. Two ladies revived Wilhelmina with cold water; she only reproached them for it, saying death would be a thousand times better. "The queen kept shrieking," Wilhelmina reports, "her firmness had quite left her: she wrung her hands, and ran in despair up and down the room. The king's face was so disfigured with rage, it was frightful to look upon. The little ones were on their knees, begging for me. . . ."

All this took place in ground-floor palace rooms, before windows. A crowd of Berliners had collected outside, attracted by the noise; the noise had also called out the palace guards, who tried to disperse the onlookers. The king told Wilhelmina she would be walled up for the rest of her life for being an accomplice to "high treason," and he even accused her of having had a love affair with Katte and of having borne him several children. "That is not true!" her governess interjected. "Whoever has told Your Majesty this has told a lie!" At that moment, Katte passed by, being escorted to the palace by four soldiers, for interrogation by the king. "Pale and downcast," writes Wilhelmina, who watched him through a window, "he took off his hat to salute me." Hearing that Katte had arrived, the king prepared to leave his distraught family. "Now I shall have proof about the scoundrel Fritz and the scum Wilhelmina," he shouted, leaving the room, "clear proofs to cut the heads off them!" [60]

At Küstrin Fortress the crown prince was placed in a sparsely furnished cell which had one window, high up; his cell door was locked, bolted, and guarded day and night. He wore prison dress, was given neither a knife nor a fork (his food was served to him already cut up), and no one was allowed to speak to him. Two officers were ordered to search his cell each day and to bring him a chamber pot; they were to remain with him while he made use of it. Only one candle was allowed him, and this had to be snuffed out at seven in the evening. No reading matter except the Bible and a prayer book was to be permitted him. He was denied all information about the fate of his co-conspirators, although he already knew of Katte's arrest. This alone put him in agonies, and he pleaded constantly for Katte, saying he alone had been responsible.

This failed to help, for the king was determined to get the "truth" about how the attempted escape tied in with a British plot to put Fritz on the throne. He was prepared to extract such a confession by torturing both Katte and his own son, and was dissuaded from this course only by Grumbkow and Seckendorff. A commission was then appointed to interrogate the prince; it was given a list of 178 questions which the king had drawn up. The crown prince appeared before the commission after two weeks of solitary confinement and answered their questions frankly and even cheerfully, openly admitting his guilt. Frederick William then told the commission to ask him further questions, all of them designed to trap him. The prince, however, proved to be more than a match for them. Asked if he thought he deserved to be king, he replied, "I cannot be my own judge." Asked if he deserved to live, he answered, "I submit to the king's mercy and pleasure." Asked finally if he would be ready to save his life by renouncing the succession "as he has rendered himself unfit to succeed to the throne by forfeiting his honor," the prince avoided replying directly by saying, "I do not set such store by my life, but His Majesty will not show such great severity toward me." The prince then tried to cast oil on the troubled waters by writing a humble plea in which he said he realized he had been at fault in everything from the very start, but had no criminal intent and was distressed mostly by the grief he had brought the king, to whose "will and mercy" he submitted himself. Frederick William tore the statement up as soon as he received it. Furious at having failed to trap his son, he ordered that Fritz's imprisonment be made more harsh and that Fritz be told that no one in Berlin even remembered him, that the queen no longer wished to hear his name, and that Wilhelmina was being kept "under lock and key."

His rage was being fed by foreign newspaper articles which claimed the crown prince had tried to flee because his father had wanted him to embrace Roman Catholicism, in order that he could marry Maria Theresa of Austria. "God knows I could never be such a rascal," Frederick William protested and then ordered that anyone in his kingdom who repeated that story have their tongues cut out. His rage also extended to a sixteen-year-old girl named Dorothea Ritter, the daughter of a minor official, who had once received some ribbons and music sheets from the prince. Convinced immoral conduct, not mere kindness, was behind this, the king had her examined by doctors, who reported that her virginity remained intact. This disappointing news so infuriated Frederick William that he had the girl publicly whipped in front of the town hall, then in front of her father's home, and then "at all corners of the town." Afterward her father was dismissed from his post, and she was incarcerated "for life" (in fact, she was released three years later).

A court-martial had been assembled to try Lieutenants von Katte and Keith (the latter *in absentia*). Lieutenant General Count von der Schulenburg was president of the fifteen-man court; he was ordered to restrict himself to the written record, the result of the interrogations. The court deliberated for four days; it then sentenced Katte to life imprisonment, although it was well aware of the fact that the king wanted him sentenced to death. The king found this verdict unacceptable and imposed the death sentence. Out of consideration to Katte's family (two of Katte's grandfathers were field marshals), the king wrote that "although by rights Katte for his crime of *lèse majesté* deserves to die by tearing with red-hot pincers and hanging, he shall nevertheless . . . be put to death by the sword. When the Court Martial acquaints Katte with this sentence, they shall tell him that His Majesty is very sorry, but that it is better he shall die than that Justice should perish from the earth." When Katte's father, a lieutenant general from Königsberg, pleaded for clemency, Frederick William listened sympathetically and then replied, "What can we poor fathers do? Your son is a scoundrel; so is mine." [61]

The sentence of death by beheading was not merely imposed for revenge. It was also meant to be a lesson, not only to other officers of the king's own guards (the *garde gens d'armes*), but to the king's nobles as well. During the reign of Louis XIV, there had been a bloody uprising of the nobles against their king (this revolt was called the Fronde); there was not likely to be one in Brandenburg-Prussia, where the nobles had long ago surrendered their freedoms, but Frederick William was not taking any chances, especially since the crown prince's cause was known to have enlisted their sympathies. Katte, therefore, had to die, partly so that justice should not "perish from the earth" and partly to reassert Hohenzollern power in its lands. So that the lesson might also prove salutary to the crown prince, the king ordered that Katte die in Küstrin and that Fritz be forced to watch. "If there is not room enough outside his window, take him [Fritz] to another place where he will have a good view," the king wrote.

The character of the crown prince is revealed by the torment he underwent when he realized that his plot to escape his father's rages was costing another man's life. On September 2 he submitted to the commission interrogating him a declaration which was subsequently passed on to the king. In this, the crown prince stated that he alone was guilty, that Katte was not only innocent of plotting the escape but had been "seduced" into it by Fritz, and that, if the king were determined to impose the death sentence on Katte, then it ought properly be carried out on Fritz instead, for his guilt was all the greater, since he was the king's son.[62]

A plea from Katte's grandfather, Field Marshal Count von Wartensleben, having already been denied, the king was certainly in no mood to listen to one coming from his hated son. Katte himself issued one final appeal for clemency and, when this failed, wrote his father a farewell letter in which he said he hoped he would be able to console himself with his surviving sons. Then Katte prepared for death with the utmost composure.

Frederick William personally supervised every detail of Katte's execution; he even ordered that the body and severed head be left lying outside the prince's window for some hours after "the executioner has wiped his sword." It was to take place at seven in the morning of November 6, 1730. The crown prince was awakened at five and told the news. He had not heard it before; he had not even been told the verdict of the court-martial. He cried out, "Jesus, take my life for his!" and then fell down sobbing. In the two hours left, he begged to be allowed to write the king, offering to renounce the crown if Katte's life were spared, but it was all in vain. At seven, he was led by his jailers to the window. The morning was cold and gray; the soldiers were already in position; then Katte was led out between two prison chaplains. He looked up to Fritz's window. "My dear Katte!" the prince called out. "I beg your forgiveness . . . a thousand times." He threw Katte a kiss. Katte looked at him and replied calmly, "No need for forgiveness. It is easy to die for a prince so easy to love." * Spurning a blindfold, Katte knelt down at the scaffold. His head was severed with one stroke of the headsman's sword. Crown Prince Fritz, whose view of the scaffold was mercifully obscured, collapsed into the arms of his jailers and remained in a fever and delirium for the remainder of the day.[63]

Fritz was certain that he would be next. Indeed, his life was in extreme danger, for his father was seriously considering the execution of his son. Fritz was a Prussian officer who had attempted to "desert"; the only penalty for this was death. The fact that the court-martial declared itself incompetent to try the heir apparent did not matter; the king himself would be expected to impose the death penalty. Frederick William, however, was not inflexible, at least not when extreme pressure was applied on him. This pressure was now coming from all quarters. The British, Russian, Polish, Swedish, German, and even Austrian courts were attempting to move the king to mercy. Old General Buddenbrock even made the dramatic gesture of tearing open his tunic to bare his breast, exclaiming, "If Your Majesty must have blood, take mine, but that other blood you shall not have as long as I have voice to speak!" Even Grumbkow and Seckendorff were coming around to side with the prince, at least to the extent of pleading for mercy.

Of these events the prince knew nothing. His fears remained acute. Chaplain Müller of the *gens d'armes* came to the prince's cell after Katte's execution and found him ill and feverish, whereupon he offered the prince a medicinal powder to be taken with water. The prince refused it, fearing it might be poison; he accepted it only after the pastor had taken half the powder himself. Still, even this did not end the prince's fears, for the pastor might have been sent to prepare him for death.

* Katte's last words were: *"La mort est douce pour un si aimable prince."* The translation offered here is not literal, but it provides the sense of the declaration. *La mort est douce* could also be translated as "death is gentle" and *aimable,* in its older sense (the word dates to the fourteenth century) means "one who deserves to be loved," a kind and "pleasant" person. There appears to be no ground for Thomas Carlyle's translation, which has been repeated by many historians, "Death is sweet for a prince I love so well."

It soon turned out, however, that Chaplain Müller's mission was to determine whether the prince was truly contrite and had abandoned the "pernicious" belief in predestination. Fritz was quick to grasp the fact that the King would not treasure a soul won cheaply, and so he argued with Müller and only allowed himself to be "persuaded" point by point, slowly over the days that followed. King Frederick William watched his son's progress and was as pleased as a revivalist preacher is after having wrestled successfully for the soul of an especially obstinate sinner. On November 17, eleven days after Katte's death, a commission headed by Grumbkow visited Fritz and recorded his statement of complete submission to the king's will. On the following day, Grumbkow had a friendly private talk with the prince, and on the day following, Fritz gave his solemn oath on the statement previously recorded. Grumbkow's friendliness played a large part in dispelling the prince's fears. It seemed to him likely that he was going to be spared after all; for what other reason would his former enemy become so friendly? Certainly Grumbkow would not risk royal displeasure by displaying kindness to someone the king planned to execute as a deserter. It seemed obvious that Grumbkow wanted to bask in the warmth of "the Rising Sun" (as the king sarcastically called Fritz) after Frederick William left the scene. That might be anytime, everyone knew, considering Frederick William's illnesses, his enormous weight, his apoplectic nature, and the frightening way his face turned all sorts of colors, even black.

Shortly after having sworn his submission to his father, Fritz was told the plans his father now had in mind for him. He was to go to work as a junior clerk in the *Kriegs- und Domänenkammer* ("War and Crown Land Board") at Küstrin and learn all about the lands he might someday inherit. He was to sit at the bottom of the council table and was specifically forbidden to dance, listen to music, dine out, entertain, buy light summer clothes, order Hamburg oysters, burn candles after nine in the evening, or speak to strangers in the absence of the men appointed to watch over him. He was also not to read anything but devotional books, and if he spoke of anything but business, he was to be told to be silent. No future plans were to be discussed, nor any politics; even geometry, military engineering, and other such subjects were forbidden him. He was to learn how manure was spread, how lands were plowed and sown, how taxes were collected, and how profits were to be realized from local enterprises.

He entered this work with good humor and was clever enough to feed his father exactly what his father wanted to hear. He wrote the king reports about a local glassworks, telling him the good news that it ought to produce "a plus" of more than 857 thalers that year; he told him that he had killed eight wild boar and two sows in a hunt; he wrote about a fabulous "long fellow" he'd spotted and how wretched he felt at not obtaining him for his dear Papa; he said he'd be the happiest man on earth if Papa would send him the new infantry regulations to read; and he reported that he had shipped the king a large cut of especially juicy pork he'd obtained nearby. Meanwhile, he amused himself by writing somewhat silly poems to a colonel's wife at Küstrin, who replied to these halfheartedly amorous overtures with verses of her own, which she said (to restrain the prince) her husband had helped her compose.

This flirtation, which apparently never went beyond the writing of verses, was perhaps occasioned more by Fritz's love of himself and his ability to write poems than by anything else; Fritz had a great opinion of his talents and his looks and loved to display both to admiring eyes.

After Fritz had served at Küstrin for a year, Frederick William showed himself to his son for the first time since he almost ran him through with a sword at Wesel. Fritz threw himself at his father's feet and surrendered himself to a long lecture. Twice more that day Fritz flung himself publicly at his father's feet, moving onlookers profoundly and touching even his father's heart. It was Frederick William's birthday; Fritz's gift of filial devotion and submission prompted him publicly to forgive the crown prince. He embraced Fritz and said, "Behave well, as I see you mean to do, and I will take care of you." As the king's carriage drove off, Fritz was in tears. "I would never have believed until now," he told one of his companions, "that the King felt the least affection for me. At this moment, I am convinced he does."[64]

Forgiveness apart, Frederick William could not restrain his criticisms of the prince's character. Fritz had asked his father to be allowed to rejoin his regiment. The king replied:

"What's the use? If I really tickled your heart, if I sent you a master of the flute from Paris with a dozen or so instruments and books of music, together with a troupe of actors and a large orchestra, if I ordered you Frenchmen and Frenchwomen, also a couple of dozen dancing masters and a dozen coxcombs, this would be sure to please you more than a company of grenadiers; for in your opinion, grenadiers are just scum, but a fop, a *petit-maître,* a Frenchy, a *bon mot,* a hack comedian, a scratch quartet: there's something much more noble, fit for a king—that's princely dignity!" [65]

Nevertheless, he allowed Fritz to show himself again in Berlin, in gray civilian clothes, on November 20, when Wilhelmina's marriage to a distant cousin, a son of the Margrave of Bayreuth, was celebrated. (Wilhelmina had accepted this choice of her father's, having been told what the alternative would be: Fritz would remain a prisoner at Küstrin; she would be imprisoned in the fortress at Memel; and her governess would be publicly whipped, the officer delivering this warning adding that nothing would please him more than to see blood pouring down pretty Fräulein von Sonsfeld's naked back.)[66]

The wedding was magnificent. Seven hundred couples danced for three days, and Frederick William kept the bridegroom drunk most of the time, "to deepen his character and educate him." The king had not spent so much money since he buried his father. Perhaps he was celebrating not the marriage, but the final *coup de grâce* this had given to the queen's plans for a double marriage with Britain. In fact, the queen was in utter despair. She even begged Wilhelmina to be as "a sister" to her husband, so that the marriage could some day be annulled on the grounds that it had never been consummated, after which she might still marry the Prince of Wales.

Fritz appeared at the ball given after the wedding, icy-cold to his sister and uncivil to her husband; in fact, he was plagued by the thought that his freedom was being purchased by this marriage. Wilhelmina did not get much more affection from her mother. She later wrote that the queen "had in fact no love for her children except insofar as they served her ambitions. . . ." Frederick William, on the other hand, now lavished tendernesses on the daughter he had earlier called "infamous scum." When she left, he said he was so completely "overcome" with "sadness of heart" that he could not even bear to say farewell to her husband; afterward, as she noted, the king "took no further notice" of her and never fulfilled any of the promises of "wonderful benefits" he had assured her she would get.

Shortly thereafter the prince attended a troop review with his father and was greeted by great ovations from the people; then Prince Leopold of Anhalt-Dessau and a group of generals petitioned the king that Fritz be allowed to rejoin the army. On November 30, Fritz again wore a uniform. Frederick William seemed pleased. Still, he told an official that something ought to be done about Fritz's "waddling gait" and his habit "of constantly rocking forward on tiptoes." [67]

Fritz was posted at Ruppin and Nauen, far away enough from his father to make life bearable. The flute was taken up again; this was to be the instrument which afforded him the greatest comfort and relaxation throughout his life. He also interested himself in trade, agriculture, and administration—and, oddly, in building somewhat of a reputation as a rake. Women were suddenly alleged to be his biggest expense, although canny Seckendorff recognized that Fritz wanted a reputation more than action in this field. "It is said," Seckendorff remarked, "that the flesh is weaker in him than the sinful spirit, from which it would follow that the Crown Prince seeks a vain renown rather than satisfaction." * [68]

In 1731, when the crown prince was nineteen, the king busied himself with finding a wife for his son. He picked Elizabeth Christine of Brunswick-Bevern, the only Protestant princess connected with the Habsburgs, being a niece of the empress. The marriage was engineered by Seckendorff and Grumbkow to tie Prussia more closely to the Austrians. The king, however, wrote his son that he had surveyed the Continent for the right choice. Elizabeth, he said, was "well brought up, modest and

* Luise Eleonore von Wreech, the colonel's wife at Küstrin, was rumored to have had a child by the crown prince. Grumbkow told Seckendorff that if this were true, her husband would disown the infant; significantly, when it was born, he did not do so. Grumbkow added the comment that "His Majesty in secret is rather pleased" about the affair. In fact, the king had for a long time feared that the "effeminate" prince might be homosexual. The pregnancy of Frau von Wreech seemed to prove otherwise, as well as provide hope that there would be a continuation of the line once Fritz married.

retiring, [as] women ought to be . . . not ugly; not beautiful either. . . . She is a God-fearing creature and that is everything."[69]

Privately, the prince was outraged. He said he'd prefer the greatest whore in Berlin to this uneducated, stupid princess (whose reputation was known to him); couldn't the king at least find someone with whom he could *talk?* Writing to Grumbkow, who had become his confidant, Fritz threatened suicide, then warned of subsequent infidelity or divorce. He insisted Grumbkow get the king to reverse his decision, but Grumbkow refused to invite "destruction" by doing so and warned the prince that the king had once expressed the fear that Fritz would yet "come into the hands of the executioner."

The crown prince gave in, there being nothing else he could do. His father burst into tears of joy at the news, said this was the happiest moment of his life, and ordered Fritz to Berlin for the betrothal ceremony. When this was over, Fritz left the city to take command of his regiment. Then he wrote Seckendorff that there would never be "petticoat rule" in his house. "So when I marry," he wrote, "I shall let Madame go her ways and as far as I am concerned I shall do as I please. And long live freedom!"

In Berlin the queen told Wilhelmina, "Your brother is in despair at having to marry her, and he has some reason. She is a proper goose. Whatever you ask her, she just says 'yes' or 'no,' with a stupid laugh that makes you feel quite ill." Princess Charlotte, Wilhelmina's younger sister, joined the fun with her own appraisal: "The other day I was present at her toilette. She stinks like the plague. I was nearly asphyxiated. I think she must have ten or eleven fistulas. . . . I also noticed that she is misshapen: her bodice is padded on one side and one hip is higher than the other." Seckendorff wrote to Vienna that she wasn't all that bad: A few dancing lessons and some other instruction would improve her; furthermore, her pimples were bound to go away, her pockmarks would probably fade, and her neck would grow less scrawny, whereupon she might be quite beautiful.[70]

In fact, it is difficult to decide how ugly she was, although portraits (predictably) show her as pretty. The crown prince wrote Grumbkow, "I am sorry for the poor girl. There is going to be one more unhappy princess in the world." In one letter to Wilhelmina, he called her "a decent sort," said he wished her no ill, but added, "I can never love her." In another letter, he said, "I do not hate her as much as I pretend. I affect complete dislike, so that the King may value my obedience all the more. She is pretty, complexion lily-and-rose, features delicate, face altogether that of a beautiful person. True, she has no breeding and dresses very badly. . . ." [71] His appraisal of his bride is more trustworthy than those of the queen or Princess Charlotte, for the queen was so embittered about the failure of all her marriage plans that she was, as G. P. Gooch put it, delighted to "rub salt into the wound." [72] Seckendorff's comments, however, can be taken more seriously, for the bride was, after all, his own choice, and he might be expected, therefore, to be inclined to paint a favorable portrait of her, even to Eugene of Savoy.

The king was delighted with the engagement; he was, however, displeased with the fact that Fritz seldom wrote to his fiancée. "What am I to write to her?" Fritz protested, but obeyed. The king noted the increase in letters and announced that "the lovers are thoroughly in love." The wedding was set for June 12, 1733.

It took place at the home of the bride's grandfather, the Duke of Wolfenbüttel. When it was completed, the crown prince wrote Wilhelmina, "Thank God it is all over!" He spent an hour in bed with his bride, then left her, got dressed, and joined the festivities in the palace garden. As soon as these were over, he rejoined his regiment. Elizabeth stayed in the Berlin Palace, where the queen and the princesses ignored her and where the king went so far against his principles as to have her taught dancing, philosophy, and ancient literature. Some historians claim that the postnuptial hour was the last time Fritz ever entered his wife's bed. Later, in private letters, he commented admiringly about Elizabeth's sexual equipment, but this may have been written for effect. For the rest of his life, Frederick seems to have remained almost ascetically celibate. He enjoyed having certain women around him, but they had to have wit as well as beauty, and his flirtations with them remained intellectual. The true facts about his sexual life may always remain a mystery. What is known is that his body was examined by a Swiss physician after he died and that this physician claimed Frederick had been mutilated by clumsy doctors who tried to cure his venereal disease, making him impotent. Several Prussian doctors promptly denied these allegations, whereupon Frederick's corpse was hurriedly shoved out of sight. There are no other "eyewitnesses." All his life long, Frederick took care that no one, not even his valet, ever saw him naked.

Now that he was married, back in favor, and over twenty-one, he had left behind his life as Prince "Fritz"; the Crown Prince Frederick was now master of his own house. This was a ruined lakeside castle named Rheinsberg some distance north of Berlin, which the king had given him along with funds for its restoration; here Frederick would spend the happiest years of his life. A former army captain, the painter Georg Wenzeslaus von Knobelsdorff, helped him rebuild and decorate the place; significantly, all its frescoes were allegories concerning the glorious "dawn" when Frederick would emerge as the enlightened "philosopher king." When Rheinsberg was finished, Elizabeth joined him there, remaining for five years. She was a pitiful creature, although she awakened little compassion in Frederick. He showed her great courtesy, but never affection; no sooner was he king than she was, in effect, banished from his sight. She never abandoned her love for him and never could understand why he failed to love her. The reason was perhaps beyond her comprehension. Quite simply, it was that she was not bright enough for Frederick. He greatly respected her for the way she always tried to please him and for her gentleness, but the spark of love was missing. This union, says Gooch, was "the mating of the eagle and the dove";[73] in fact, it was the marriage of a kindly but drab *Hausfrau* to one of the most brilliant men of the times. She resigned herself to her fate and was pleased at least with a few signs of courtesy, gallantry, and respect from her husband. He gave her an allowance of 40,000 thalers a year; she gave more than half of it away to the poor. When she died at eighty-one, she left behind her own epitaph: "It has pleased God to watch over me in such a way that I have never knowingly committed an action which has in any way diminished the happiness of another person." It was quite something to be able to say in good conscience; it was something no "eagle" like Frederick could ever have written.

In the summer of 1734, Frederick was allowed to join the Prussian forces on the Rhine, in the War of the Polish Succession. This minor conflict arose because there was now competition for the Polish throne, Augustus the Strong having been succeeded by his son, Augustus III, who claimed it from Stanislaus Laszczynski. The main theater of war was in Italy; the Rhine campaigns, which Frederick joined, were unimportant. (Augustus III was crowned in Cracow in 1734 and recognized as king in Warsaw in June, 1736.)

No sooner did Frederick receive news that he was to join the war than he characteristically dashed off two poems about warfare, later noting that there seemed to be more mud than poetry to the business. At the siege of Philippsburg, where he received his baptism of fire, he and others rode through a small woods being strafed by cannon fire; observers who were there claimed that, although trees were shot down to the right and left of the prince, he calmly continued chatting with his companions without pausing once.

He was learning more than just coolness under fire; he also learned tactics at the feet of Prince Eugene of Savoy, one of the most brilliant commanders of the age. Frederick was twenty-two when he joined Prince Eugene's camp; the old war-horse was seventy. A man of phenomenal bravery who bore the marks of thirteen wounds, he had also been a statesman of distinction, as well as a patron of the Enlightenment. This "noble knight," as he was often called, was a master of military science, an expert at the art of movement, brilliantly inventive and audacious, and a leader who understood soldiers' psychology so well that he inspired his own forces while striking fear into those of his enemies. Almost single-handedly, he restored Habsburg power after the ascendancy of France following the Thirty Years' War. Seventeen major victories under Eugene of Savoy raised Austria, already the dominant German state, into the ranks of the great powers. He was considered to be a genius by his contemporaries, as well as one of the first "Europeans," for he was culturally a Frenchman (a patron of Rousseau and other writers of the French Enlightenment), loyally a German and

Austrian, and full of admiration for English commerce and Italian art. He understood the importance of Prussia, which he hoped to use against the French along the Rhine, and he also understood the importance to Austria of Crown Prince Frederick, especially since this young man was so Francophile that, it was rumored, he planned to make the French ambassador in Berlin, Marquis de la Chétardie, his prime minister when he became king.

"A great deal depends," Eugene wrote to the emperor in Vienna, "on winning the Prince, who one day can make more friends in the world than his father has, and will do as much good." [74] But King Frederick William I had sent his own instructions to Prince Eugene, concerning his son: "He can be treated lightly, but he should not be accorded an imperial bodyguard, because he should not be allowed to get any higher opinion of his own importance than he already has." Then, a few days later, Frederick William personally came riding into the camp, suffering so much from gout that it was thought he was dying. Eugene had long discussions with Crown Prince Frederick; the young man wanted to know all about war and politics, while the old man wanted to win Frederick to the Habsburg cause. He succeeded in obtaining from Frederick an agreement that he would abide by the Pragmatic Sanction after acceding to the throne; Frederick asked in return that the emperor remove his old enemy, Seckendorff, from Berlin and intercede once again to get Frederick William to improve his treatment of the crown prince. The emperor replied that he had already shown his affection by writing to the King of Prussia in his own hand, asking him to spare his son's life, and that he had often helped Frederick with money. He didn't offer to write again, but he agreed to remove Seckendorff.

All this, however, would not in later years marry Frederick to Austria. He may have received a good many lessons directly from Prince Eugene, but the greatest lesson he learned in the Austrian camp during the War of the Polish Succession was the complete disorganization and confusion of the Austrian armies. He had come to the war as an ally and had stayed as a spy. Later in life, he expressed himself tersely about Prince Eugene's last, less-than-brilliant campaign: "What a humbling reflection for our vanity. That a Condé, an Eugen, or a Marlborough should have to witness the decline of their mental powers before their physical powers. The greatest geniuses end up as imbeciles. Poor humanity, boast of your glory if you dare!" [75]

During this campaign, Frederick also noted that Prince Eugene had recently begun to be "a drill demon," like Anhalt-Dessau. He had found out early that everyone seemed willing to learn from Prussian army methods, even if no one liked them.

After the king recalled his son from the front, Frederick returned to Rheinsberg, where he spent the years from 1735 to 1740, making the restored castle a magnet for intellectuals, artists, and wits, strangely left at peace by the choleric king.

The king suffered and seemed to be dying. His joints burned, were as tender as open wounds; dropsy swelled his enormous body even more; his arteries, lungs, kidneys, and heart were diseased. Still, despite these ailments, he embarked on a tour of the East Prussian farm provinces, spurning all comforts, and took Frederick along to complete the prince's education. Again he raced across wretched roads, sleeping in barns and hardly ever resting at any stop. The journey just about killed him, but it brought about a remarkable change in the relationship between father and son. By the time it ended, so had the last vestiges of their feud, and they now spoke to each other in friendly terms. Their relationship had always included love, as well as hatred and contempt; Frederick desperately wanted his father's affection and respect, while the king wanted no more than what he called a properly obedient son. Now that Seckendorff had left Berlin and Grumbkow had died, the relationship could mellow and take its natural course, for there were no longer any Austrian agents around who kept the king's rages well fueled with slander.

Returning to Berlin, Frederick William prepared himself for death with remarkable aplomb. For years he had been frightened of dying, but mainly because of what he thought it would mean to his kingdom and the House of Hohenzollern. Both, he suspected, would go to the dogs, meaning to the dog Fritz. Now that the slanderers were gone, father and son could have the relationship which came naturally to them, one of love, and which ought to have been theirs all along, had not others subverted it. The king was at ease about his kingdom's future; he even remarked to his generals how fortunate he was to be able to entrust his lands to such a son as Frederick.

The king had himself moved to Potsdam, in order to die there, he announced. His chief preacher, a man named Roloff, came to help him prepare. Frederick William knew that his royal prerogatives would not avail him in heaven and that he would stand before the throne of God not as a former king, but as the equal of any beggar; still, he was sanguine, for he suspected that he would be greeted with great rejoicing and would fare handsomely, having kept God's commandments at all times. Roloff diplomatically suggested that all men were sinners and that even Frederick William was no exception; be that as it may, the king replied, for a king, he had been more perfect than most. Since Roloff did not immediately agree, the king demanded to know *one* example of actions less than just or pious. Roloff bravely provided several, among them the oppression of the king's subjects, who were brutally taxed and compelled into construction schemes against their will, as well as the peremptory hanging of Baron von Schlubhut, that self-confessed embezzler, who had offered to make good the money he had taken and who had been executed without ever standing trial. The king protested: Councilor von Schlubhut may not have had a trial, but he had certainly received justice. Roloff, however, insisted the punishment had been too harsh and had smacked of tyranny.

The king argued, but Roloff insisted he must repent without any reservations whatever. How could he expect forgiveness in heaven, Roloff argued, if he would not show it to all his enemies on earth before he died?

Well, that was asking a bit much, the king said, considering what scoundrels they were, but he would do it nevertheless. He would even forgive the queen's "detestable brother" and let her write George II, advising him of this, after Frederick William had died. Roloff shook his head; forgiveness must not be delayed, he insisted. That was too much for the dying man. He told the preacher to stick to his preaching and to let the king handle "affairs of state" as best he knew; then he dismissed him.

Frederick came from Rheinsberg on several occasions to see

his father, careful not to overdo the visits lest the king think his son was impatient for him to die. The king carefully instructed the prince in matters of state and gave precise directions concerning his funeral. There were to be three volleys from the grenadiers, he dictated, and care was to be taken that they were well fired, not ragged (*"nicht plackeren"*); simplicity was to be the keynote of his burial, as it had been of his reign.

Practical to the very end, the king checked out the size of his coffin and had it shoved next to his bed, where it would be handy. His favorite hymns were sung to him by his family and his generals; he joined in the singing. When they reached a line referring to the dead leaving the world as naked as they had entered it, Frederick William stopped the singing and corrected the text. "Not quite naked," he said. "I shall have my uniform on."

In the early morning hours of May 31, 1740, the king roused himself and demanded his wheelchair. In it, he first visited his youngest son, Ferdinand, recovering from measles, bidding him a tender adieu; then he had himself rolled into the queen's room and told her to get up, advising her he would die that day. He summoned his ministers and told them he wished to abdicate in favor of the crown prince. The royal stables could be seen from the room in which the king was seated, and he ordered the horses to be brought out; once they were on display, he told Leopold of Anhalt-Dessau, his oldest friend, and Colonel von Hacke, his adjutant general and another favorite, each to choose a horse for himself, the best of the stables, as farewell gifts. Prince Leopold was too overcome with emotion to do more than point to the first horse he saw, whereupon the king remonstrated that he had picked the worst of the lot and pointed to another which he could guarantee was better. Leopold was dumb with grief and fought back tears; the king comforted him and told him not to weep. "This is a debt we all have to pay," he said.

Too weak to make himself heard to all those assembled, the king dictated his intention to abdicate to an old general, who repeated it aloud. Afterward the king was told it would have to be put on paper, then signed and sealed, but Frederick William fainted a moment later, and the document was never needed.

Back in bed, he lingered on for hours. He watched his last changing of the guard. At eleven in the morning, the Calvinist court preacher, Cochius, was summoned to pray beside the king's bed. "Not so loud!" Frederick William snapped at him. He called for a mirror, to have a last look at himself, and murmured, "Not as worn out as I thought." He called a doctor, the surgeon of his Giants' Guard, and asked him to feel his pulse, to tell him how much longer he had to live. "Alas, not long," the doctor replied. "The pulse is gone." That seemed nonsense to the king. "Impossible," he insisted, raising his arm. "How could I move my fingers like this if my pulse were gone?"

The effort exhausted the king. He fell into a faint, from which he never recovered; just before he closed his eyes, he uttered his last words: "Lord Jesus, to thee I live; Lord Jesus, to thee I die; in life and death, you are my gain."

It was between three and four in the afternoon that this remarkable man died, at the age of fifty-one. That same day, heralds proclaimed his son to be the new king. The news of Frederick William's death shot around Potsdam and the capital as though an enemy had vanished from the Berlin city gates. For the rest of the day and well into the night, people laughed, cheered, and celebrated, embracing one another in the streets. Their agony was over; of that they were convinced.

8

"Save Yourself, All Is Lost!"

No figure looms larger in the gallery of the Hohenzollerns than Frederick II, who earned the name of Frederick the Great both in war and peace and who ultimately was enshrined in German hearts simply as "Old Fritz," *der alte Fritz.* He was for Prussia what Napoleon was for France or Julius Caesar for Rome; had he failed, the Hohenzollern lands would have been partitioned among the European powers: Brandenburg-Prussia might have disappeared, and the history of Germany and Europe would have been profoundly altered. He gambled everything—his lands, his peoples, and certainly himself—on making Prussia into a major European power. He almost lost this gamble several times, and had he not been as lucky as he was brilliant, his kingdom would have been destroyed. Indeed, this soldier king brought it to utter ruin; for a time, as he admitted, his lands resembled those his great-grandfather, the Great Elector, had inherited after the Thirty Years' War. Afterward, he raised them again, as the Great Elector had done, until Prussia achieved its greatest glory and Berlin vied with Vienna and Paris as a seat of major power.

This Frederick II was the one who brought modern Prussia into the world, although its seed had been planted by his father. The only tool he used, the only one he had, was his inheritance: his father's army, that weapon forged so well but hardly ever used. Unscrupulous and ruthless, he was at the same time a just ruler and a brilliant, gifted personality; recklessly ambitious and fiercely autocratic, he was also for a time the repository of liberal hope throughout Europe. Yet it became his ironic destiny that his ambition overwhelmed his enlightened, libertarian instincts. He could have been more than a father of his country: he could have led Prussia through the Enlightenment and set it on the road toward a liberal reform. Instead, both Prussian militarism and Hohenzollern absolutism were strengthened throughout his reign and later came to be enshrined, because both seemed to have worked so brilliantly under this king.

What Frederick II was to become could not even have been guessed when Frederick William I died. No one knew what to expect of the crown prince suddenly become king; there were only suspicions, as well as fears that he would blunder. The old king had told his son before he died that he would sit in his grave in Potsdam and laugh if he bungled his job and made a mess of his inheritance; this vision was to haunt Frederick II for many years. As for his father's ministers and generals, these all questioned his ability, shared his father's doubts, and wondered nervously what the state and they themselves might receive at the hands of this new king.

They had seen little of him for five years. These Frederick had spent at Rheinsberg, rhyming, reading philosophy, playing the flute, corresponding with Voltaire, and surrounding himself with undistinguished cronies, even artists, poets, and the like. Would he prove himself a silly ass and send the country to the dogs? They feared he might be a new version of his own grandfather, his namesake: concerned mainly with elegance and ceremonials, leaving the nation deeply in debt.

To their great surprise, the cheering in Berlin had not consoled Frederick on his father's death. For one thing, his grief was real; for another, he realized the people were not so much cheering his accession to the throne as cheering his father's demise. To the court's amazement, mere mention of his father's death threw Frederick II into tears. He sobbed, moaned, charged about distractedly, nor was anyone allowed to console him. One would have thought he'd lost a friend. Only gradually did he quiet himself, become grave, dignified, gentle. He asked his mother to stop calling him "Your Majesty." "Always call me son, Madame," he said, "a name more precious. . . ." The drama swirling about him touched his poetic, even his theatrical, nature. Grave and wet-eyed, he assembled his generals and ministers, each of these wondering how long he would last. He thanked them for "the splendid army" they had helped build up; they wondered what this flutist, essayist, and poet would do with 80,000 soldiers and a war chest of 8,000,000 thalers. They offered to swear allegiance to the new king, but he waved this aside. "Between men of honor," he said gently, "there is no need for oaths." Then he made them feel even more at ease by saying there would be no personnel changes at all; his father's advisers and officers would become his own. Prince Leopold of Anhalt-Dessau asked if he and his sons would remain in their positions of authority; Frederick replied that they would certainly keep their jobs but added pointedly, "As for authority, I know of none in Prussia save the sovereign's." That was a note of sternness no one had expected. Almost as an afterthought, Frederick remarked that he had heard charges against some of them, "of undue avarice, harshness, and arrogance." He didn't want to go into these in detail, he said quietly, but they were to see that there were "no further grounds for these." Before they left, he commented that if there had ever been a distinction between the interests of the king and of his kingdom, this was now gone. Henceforth, these interests were identical. "Should the two nevertheless conflict at any time," he said, "the interests of the country shall come first."

They had heard what seemed like pretty generalities and veiled threats; none of them knew what the young king might mean by these words. He might yet prove an esthete who had inherited a huge army to no purpose, a dilettante placed on a throne of absolute power toward no end.

Certainly the courts of Europe failed to be impressed by him. Not only was he an unknown quantity, but what little was known of him hardly inspired awe. Furthermore, he was his father's son, and Frederick William I had been a standing joke among the European monarchs. They had several times betrayed Frederick William and broken alliances with Prussia; they had cheated him out of payment for the pacts he entered into; they had treated him more than cavalierly: They had treated him with contempt. That Hohenzollern fief, the former margraviate of Brandenburg, had never played a role of major importance; it had been the plaything of other states or their instrument. So absurd had the Hohenzollern court seemed under Frederick William that Baron Pöllnitz in Berlin had handsomely supplemented his income for years by sending a gossip column to the European courts, revealing the latest gaucheries to be observed in Prussia. These juicy tidbits were served up at dinner parties all over Europe and made the subscribers to Pöllnitz's letters choke with laughter. What could they expect from the son of such a buffoon?

The fact that Frederick II was the darling of the European intellectuals didn't help either. It merely tended to lower his prestige with statesmen and generals, at home and abroad. Led by Voltaire, whose favor Frederick had curried from Rheinsberg, Europe's intellectuals were fascinated by the charming anomaly: a poet presiding in Prussia of all places; an elegant essayist issuing edicts; a flutist to whose tune marched 80,000 troops! These intellectuals loved him in much the same way as other intellectuals later loved John F. Kennedy, and for the same reasons: He had "style" and elegance; he was cultured and literate; most important, he loved them.

What none of them knew—neither the intellectuals nor his advisers and generals—was that "a fever," as he later put it, was beginning to rage within him or that he had the brilliance to transmute this fire into the stuff of which greatness is forged. A dream visited his nights, just as a recurring nightmare had haunted his father, but while the father never revealed the nature of his nocturnal torment, the son frankly revealed his own vision. It was, of course, about his father. In it, Frederick William and a guard of soldiers were coming to arrest him on charges of not having loved his father enough. Just before the arrest took place, the dream shifted to a battlesite, where once again old Frederick William confronted his son. Here the father said he was satisfied with his son's actions. In the dream, Frederick II replied to his father, "I am content; your approval means more to me than that of the whole world."

How could he win the dead king's approval if not by avenging him? How could he best avenge the father if not by throwing back into the teeth of Europe's rulers the very laughter they had expended on Prussia? Frederick came to be determined to make Prussia great and, in so doing, to make himself great as well. Or, perhaps, it was the other way around: Making himself great would make Prussia all the greater. The two were intertwined and inseparable in his mind, bound together with the ribbon of vanity. "I was young, had plenty of money, a big army, and wanted to see my name in the newspapers," he was to quip later in explanation of his first military campaign; while much truth lay in that confession, the lie in it was the flip tone. In fact, he was in deadly earnest—and deadly secretive. His plans were still uncertain, and events would provide the impetus to bring them to fruition; in the meantime, he bided his time.

Nevertheless, he certainly intended to see his name in the newspapers immediately and went about it swiftly. Within three weeks of his father's death, he had taken the court of Prussia out of the gossip columns and onto the front pages. Each new report from Berlin was the sort one might wish for from a "philosopher king," as he was now everywhere being called; each new edict was a perfect gesture to one group or another, as though plotted by public relations counsel. All were enlightened decrees, all reflected his sincere sentiments, all nevertheless were calculated to win public favor.

It was relatively easy to produce enlightened decrees; he had only to reverse some of his father's policies to create a good impression. Two days after his father died, Frederick had the Berlin *Gazette* publish his statement to the ministers; it told his subjects that "it is not our purpose that you [the ministers] should in future enrich us and oppress our poor subjects." This alone was in startling contrast with Frederick William, who hoarded barrels filled with coins in the palace basements. On June 6, four days later, he ordered the recall of the philosopher Christian von Wolff from Marburg. Wolff had been forced to leave the University of Halle by Frederick's father and for reasons very characteristic of that soldier king. The philosopher had feuded with the Pietists at Halle for a decade, but the king had taken no notice of this argument until Wolff appealed to the courts. Wolff's enemies then approached the king and translated the issues for him into practical terms. They told Frederick William that if the courts recognized Wolff's determinism, it would be impossible to punish any soldier for desertion, since he could claim he had acted as it was predetermined he should act. Frederick William suddenly realized what was at stake, fired Wolff from the university, and ordered him to leave Prussia at once on pain of death. In recalling Wolff, Frederick II announced he was "a man who seeks for the truth and loves it [and who] ought to be esteemed by all mankind." Then he went a step further and wrote Pierre Louis Moreau de Maupertuis, the Parisian astronomer and mathematician, offering him the post of president of the Academy of Sciences, which the Frenchman accepted immediately. He also authorized the Berlin publishers Haude and Spener to print a new gazette—without censorship, for "muzzled gazettes make dull reading," Frederick said.*

Most spectacular was an early decree abolishing torture. Frederick was the first European monarch to do so, over the protests of his judges, who immediately predicted that every thief and ruffian in Germany would flee to Prussia and that they would never be able to get the truth from offenders without this weapon. Punishments in Berlin had been ghastly, as indeed they had been elsewhere. A celebrated example, dating to 1718, just twenty-two years earlier, is provided by two employees in the Berlin Palace who had stolen some palace gold. These men, Runck and Stieff, were broken on the wheel, while 30,000 citizens watched; this meant they were tied to a cartwheel, limbs extended along its spokes, while the wheel was slowly spun, blows with metal bars breaking the prisoners' bones, one by one, until they died. Nor were they even given the *coup de grâce,* the term deriving from blows mercifully directed at the victims' chests or stomachs, which killed them faster.

Such was the punishment for serious offenders, yet lighter crimes brought heavy punishments as well. It had earlier been customary to punish coachmen who exceeded the speed limits by caning them twenty-five times and to cut off the hands of those who damaged trees or grapevines. Such practices and the one of pinching with red-hot irons were not Prussian or German, but common throughout much of Europe. For Frederick II to abolish them was revolutionary in the extreme.

He also struck off the books the traditional punishment for infanticide; murderers of infants were henceforth simply to be

* A ministerial decree issued with royal sanction reduced the effect of this, however. No censorship would be observed on local home news, but in the case of foreign news, the king's directive was to be taken with "a grain of salt," lest foreign monarchs be offended.[76]

beheaded, rather than drowned in leather sacks they had been forced to sew themselves. He also abolished the public humiliation of unwed mothers, which had been the single greatest cause of infanticide. Then he added harsh punishments for those who mistreated soldiers, as well as for those found "too zealous" in recruiting; this won him the love both of the army and of those who hated soldiering. Another edict abolished a host of hated aristocratic and even royal hunting privileges, which won him the devotion of the farmers. Afterward he chaired a meeting of Freemasons and declared religious freedom for all, even offering to build mosques if they were required. In his country, he said, "everyone must go to heaven in his own way"; that statement thrilled all Europe.

Next, merchants and tradesmen found themselves both surprised and flattered when their new king asked for their advice; he said he wanted recommendations on how commerce and industry might be spurred. Consumers, in turn, were made happy when Frederick II alleviated the hardships resulting from the previous severe winter by opening grain warehouses to the needy (a move Frederick William had refused to make while those hardships were mounting, being too ill to supervise distribution personally and fearful there might be corruption); he also imported grain in bulk, sold royal game cheaply, and established financial relief for those most severely affected. Furthermore, Frederick offered plans to spur housing and employment and, in general, showed every kind of proof that he was vitally and personally interested in the welfare, prosperity, and happiness of his subjects.

As though additional evidence were needed of his enlightened intentions, there then appeared *Anti-Machiavel,* a broadside which he had written earlier but which only appeared after he became king, being published abroad with the help of Voltaire. It created a sensation, though it contained little that was really new; what was newsworthy about it was the fact that it had been written by a king. It was taken as Frederick II's liberal political platform and even Voltaire, that archcynic, believed in it.

Three weeks of reform preceded his father's state funeral, on which occasion Frederick William's beloved "long fellows" fired a final salute to their recruiter and "drill sergeant." Frederick II reviewed the guard on this occasion; immediately afterward he disbanded his father's toy. Some of the giants chose to remain in Prussian service; since they were freed from their slavery by the new king, most chose to go home. This move, prompted by two considerations, was also well received everywhere. Frederick William had repented of this monstrous toy in his final agonies, telling his son he would have disbanded the guard long before, had not false pride prevented him; he urged him to dismiss the chained monsters. (One of the grenadiers was reportedly brought to the king's deathbed in his last hours, to display a gorgeous new uniform; Frederick William stared at him for a time, then turned his face to the wall, and is said to have groaned, "Vanity of vanities!" [77]) But it was not only his father's wish he was obeying. These regiments cost the state more than a quarter of a million thalers a year in upkeep, not to speak of the sums expended in recruiting the giants. Frederick learned that he could raise sixteen new battalions for his army with that money, and this he immediately proceeded to do.

To the delight of his ministers and generals, Frederick II kept his word and fired none of them. Grumbkow's son-in-law, Baron Podewils, was even named foreign minister. Even the gossipy Pöllnitz stayed on. "Entertaining at table," Frederick II said about him, adding, "Should be locked up between meals."

He settled a few old scores generously. Katte's bereaved father was promoted to field marshal and elevated to count; Keith, who had fled to Britain, returned and received a modest position; the family of Münchow (the Küstrin Fortress governor who had risked royal wrath by befriending his prisoner) were granted jobs. In no case, however, was there real favoritism. His old cronies at Rheinsberg found out that the king paid them in poems of affection; promotions went to those who merited them. They had expected it "to rain ducats" [78] now that their boon companion was king; those who waited for the shower were left high and dry. The Rheinsbergers called the day of Frederick's accession *la journée des dupes*—the day they were duped—and were left in no doubt that cronyism was finished. The Margrave of Schwedt found this out when he ventured an improper joke in front of the king, thinking Frederick would enjoy it now as much as Crown Prince Fritz had enjoyed such jokes at Rheinsberg. Frederick turned an icy stare on the offending Henry of Schwedt and gravely replied, *"Monsieur, à présent je suis roi!"* ("Monsieur, I am now king!")

Knobelsdorff sniffed the wind and got busy. Frederick II said that buildings—not toy soldiers—were his "dolls" and ordered him to build an opera house for Unter den Linden; thus Knobelsdorff earned by accomplishment what would not come by friendship alone. Frederick's two closest friends at Rheinsberg remained his intimates but were also not given major posts. One of these was Baron Dietrich Keyserlingk (whom Frederick called Caesarion); he was the young officer who had been appointed along with Rochow to guard him years earlier and who had become a friend. "My dear Caesarion," Frederick II said to him, "you're a dear fellow, you are well read, have a pleasing wit and a nice singing voice, but your advice is that of an imbecile." A French Huguenot, Charles Étienne Jordan, who had been Frederick's secretary and literary adviser at Rheinsberg, stayed on as secretary; although he had expected to become president of the academy, he became only vice-president under Maupertuis. Closest of all was Michael Gabriel Fredersdorf, the only person to whom King Frederick II ever fully confided everything, the only individual with whom he ever completely relaxed. Fredersdorf also stemmed from the days of horror, a souvenir of Küstrin; he had been a lowly private in a regiment commanded by Major General Kurt Christoph von Schwerin, the officer who had battled most for the crown prince and Katte on the courts-martial convened to try both of them. Schwerin, noting that Fredersdorf was an accomplished flutist, had plucked him from the ranks and sent him to Küstrin to keep the crown prince company; Fredersdorf and the prince were inseparable ever afterward. To Fredersdorf, Frederick never played the lord; Fredersdorf, in turn, had the happy faculty of accepting the crown prince and, later, the king almost as his equal, without ever seeking to profit from the relationship, for which Frederick was grateful. Fredersdorf, as a result, became a confidant of the king and not just what he was: the king's chamberlain and valet.*

Frederick enjoyed being king enormously.

* The fact that a king would feel such affection for his valet again fed gossip of a homosexual relationship, but this seems to derive from the fact that such a friendship was very unusual, not from the slightest supporting evidence.

"Adieu!" he said in a letter written at the time. "I must now write to the King of France, compose a solo for flute, make up a poem for Voltaire, alter some army regulations, and do a thousand other things!"

He sparkled; he glittered; he was a gadfly. Voltaire was enchanted with such a friend. "Already you are beloved in your own dominions and in Europe," he wrote the king. Then he asked Frederick not to overwork himself, "in the name of the human race, to whom you have become a necessity. . . ."

The French ambassador described Frederick as "the prettiest, daintiest Majesty in the world": about five feet seven inches in height, graceful and somewhat negligent in his movements (although he was somewhat plump, with hips "too high" and legs "too thick"). He had curly hair, blue eyes, and a tanned face. His hands, loaded with rings in accordance with the fashion then, were very white. The ambassador said his expression was lively, pleasant, "noble"; his smile indescribably winning; his charm "irresistible" in conversation; his gaze, radiant with attentive intelligence, calculated to loosen the most diffident tongue. This latter became famous as the "Frederician gaze." Such sparkling eyes had not been seen in the Berlin court since Frederick's grandmother, Sophia Charlotte, had charmed Berlin with them.

Frederick unilaterally discarded the title given by the emperor to the Hohenzollern kings in Brandenburg-Prussia. He changed his title from King "in" Prussia (*rex Borussorum*) to King "of" Prussia (*rex Borussiae*), the term popularly used but never before formally proclaimed. Then he turned his youthful, Frederician gaze on a field of action, unsheathing his sword. Europe ignored the act, because the issue seemed so unimportant. In fact, however, it had its larger meaning. King Frederick II was testing himself.

The matter concerned Herstal, an insignificant town near Liège which in 1732 had fallen to Prussia but which, with the support of Liège's prince-bishop, had resisted Prussianization, since none of its citizens wanted to be subject to Frederick William I's recruiters. Frederick William had sent in troops and had forced the town to swear allegiance to him, but the townspeople afterward ignored their oath, and Prussia was obliged to occupy this little place with so many troops that it was willing to sell Prussian rights over it for 125,000 thalers, although there were no buyers at the time.

Frederick II, having acceded to the throne, insisted that unruly Herstal swear allegiance to him personally, but Herstal flatly refused to do so and claimed allegiance to the Prince-Bishop of Liège. Frederick asked his ministers what a philosopher king was to do in the face of such overt rebellion. They counseled caution, lest any precipitate action bring on a war. Frederick promptly showed contempt for their counsel, a contempt which would last. He told them to mind their politics, which they understood, but not to attempt to begin talking about war; that would be "like Iroquois discussing astronomy." The insult so shocked the ministers that one privy councilor collapsed of a stroke and died some weeks later. The others were soon only slightly less affected, for Frederick now stopped consulting them entirely and chose to deal directly through private diplomatic agents. He handed the Prince-Bishop of Liège a two-day ultimatum, and when he received a testy reply that no one sent an ultimatum to a prince of the empire, Frederick responded by sending in three battalions of Prussian grenadiers and one squadron of dragoons, not into Herstal, but into Liège. They occupied the bishop's lands, levied funds to pay occupation costs, and posted the king's orders. The distraught prince-bishop requested help from Austria and France with which to repel the invaders; they sent him only words of support. Six weeks later the prince-bishop surrendered to his fate. Frederick forced him to pay 250,000 thalers for insignificant little Herstal, twice what he had refused to pay eight years earlier.

It had been a great coup—in a teacup, to be sure; still, even Voltaire was delighted and clapped his hands. His *roi philosophe* had outtalked the prince-bishop, using "two thousand good arguments," Voltaire remarked, referring to the number of Prussian troops.

The Prussians had put the prince-bishop under siege on September 11; on that same day, Frederick for the first time entertained Voltaire in a Prussian castle near Cleves. Frederick had malaria, a disease common at the time to those who lived in the marshy and swampy region of Berlin and Potsdam. Voltaire found the king in an almost bare room "sweating and shivering under a wretched blanket [and] muffled up in a dressing-gown of coarse blue duffel."

"I could only admire and keep quiet," Frederick wrote of this meeting with the man he most worshiped, while Voltaire also confessed himself captivated. "I met one of the most charming men in the world," wrote Voltaire. Frederick, he said, "would be everywhere sought after if he were not king; a philosopher without austerity; full of sweetness and obliging ways; not remembering that he is king when he is with his friends; indeed so completely forgetting it that he made me too almost forget . . . that here I saw sitting at the foot of his bed a sovereign who had an army of 100,000 men. . . ."

On October 20 the prince-bishop acquired Herstal at gunpoint and for ransom. That same day, Emperor Charles VI died; eight days later the Czarina of Russia, Anna Ivanovna, also died. Frederick had been so ill that none of his advisers and friends dared break the news of the emperor's death to him. They finally gave the job to the valet, Fredersdorf. Far from prostrating the ill king, it proved such a strong tonic that he leaped out of bed and gave his fever "the sack," as he put it.

"The emperor is dead," he wrote Voltaire the day he heard of it. "His death alters all my pacific ideas, and I think that next June it will be rather a matter of gunpowder, soldiers, and trenches, than of actresses, ballets, and spectacles. The time is arrived when the old political system can undergo a complete change. . . ."

These were not idle boasts or merely youthful visions. Reports of a Prussian military buildup soon reached Vienna, Paris, London, and other cities; while most capitals speculated on their meaning, few in fact worried. The issue which concerned all of them most was the succession in the empire. While some states wished to preserve the empire, others saw the death of Charles VI as a chance for breaking imperial power. Maria Theresa, his daughter, had succeeded her father, but unable to become emperor, she was now trying to get the states of Europe to recognize her husband, Francis, as emperor and to preserve the empire territorially as her father had wished and, indeed, decreed through the Pragmatic Sanction. She watched the Prussians mobilize but never dreamed they would be a threat to her. Frederick II, she thought, would be as loyal to the empire as his father had always been; no doubt she could treat him as contemptuously and cavalierly as Charles VI had always treated Frederick William I. At the most, she thought, Frederick might conceivably threaten her duchies of Jülich and Berg, on the Rhine, which the House of Hohenzollern had been trying to regain for decades; surely, however, France would never allow the Prussians to invade lands lying so close to their frontier.

Frederick, however, was not planning to move against Jülich and Berg. Small game, that; it would surprise no one; such an action was the kind Europe expected of little Prussia. Fame and fortune—the newspapers again—lay elsewhere and called for bolder strokes. Frederick had his eyes fixed on Maria Theresa's richest province, a land of lush farms, vast underground deposits of coal and minerals, and prosperous cities. This was Silesia. Taking it meant stabbing Austria, to which Brandenburg owed allegiance, in the back.

"When sovereigns wish to come to a rupture," Frederick II wrote some years later, "it is not the question of the contents of the declaration which restrains them. They take their sides, they make wars, and they leave to some lawyer the task of justifying them." [79]

In fact, some lawyer had actually handed Frederick justification for the attack, although this was an academic exercise which did not influence Frederick's decision. No sooner had Emperor Charles VI died than Chancellor Ludewig of the University of Halle sent Frederick a learned study on which Ludewig had lavished 40 years, which set forth Prussia's rights in Silesia. These rights were based on a pact made 400 years earlier, which had since lost any meaning, though Frederick II's grandfather had attempted to assert his claim, leaving behind instructions to his successors to carry the work forward.

When it became apparent that the Prussians were massing along the Silesian border, Maria Theresa instructed her envoy in Berlin to find out what was going on. No one, however, could tell him, for Frederick even kept his own ministers in the dark. A week before the Prussian soldiers crossed the frontier, the Austrian ambassador in Berlin murmured to the king, "The Silesian roads are terrible at this season." Frederick II replied archly, "The worst one will risk on them is a few splashes of mud."

No one could believe he would really dare to invade Silesia. Such an action would be an outrageous breach of the international order, an act of flagrant and unprovoked aggression—in fact, the kind of act almost every eighteenth-century monarch would have liked to commit, being restrained only by custom. Further, an invasion of Silesia seemed improbable even on military grounds. It was December; wars were fought in spring and summer, when one needed to contend only with enemies, not also with mud, snow and ice.

Frederick II, however, boldly announced his decision to invade and seize Silesia, doing so on December 10. He coupled this with an impertinent offer. If Maria Theresa would surrender all Silesia to him in a peaceable manner, then Frederick would vote for her husband in the imperial election, would help finance Austrian rearmament, and would also guarantee her other possessions in Germany. He did not really expect her to accept, nor did she. On December 13, Frederick attended a great court masquerade ball at the Berlin Palace, danced with all the ladies, and later that night set out for Silesia at the head of his troops. "The man is mad!" said Louis XV when he heard of the move.

In fact, the invasion made a great deal of sense to Frederick. The death of the czarina, more than that of Charles VI, had made it possible, for now Prussia had nothing to fear from the East, at least for some time. Ruled by an infant successor, the Muscovite court had pulled tight its Byzantine curtains and conspired behind them, never peeking out, which gave Prussia a free hand, thought Frederick. As for France, he guessed it would support rival claimants to the imperial throne, rather than Maria Theresa's Francis. Furthermore, barely two regiments of infantry, totaling 3,000 men, occupied and guarded Silesia, while Frederick was marching into it with 40,000 Prussian troops.

Now the superb war machine which his father and Prince Leopold had trained and which he had inherited was rolling—or, rather, sloshing through the Silesian mud. Resistance never materialized. Three fortified towns tried to make a stand; these were simply bypassed, left isolated, to be picked off later on. By the time Breslau, Silesia's capital, was taken on January 1,

1741, not a single shot had been exchanged, and the only casualty had been a soldier's wife, who had fallen into a river and drowned. Silesia was conquered in six weeks.

That sort of success is likely to turn the head of any young man; it was enough to surprise even Frederick. This act of unprovoked aggression had of course tarnished his public image as a philosopher king; as though to make up for his conquest of Silesia, he treated the conquered especially well, almost as though he had liberated them. Protestants were offered the protection of a Protestant (in fact, an atheist) king, after having suffered discrimination at the hands of the Catholic Habsburgs; Catholics in Silesia were granted full religious freedom. The king's decrees, posted everywhere, assured the civilian population they would not be hurt, molested, annoyed or disturbed "in the peaceful possession of their goods." Frederick swiftly and severely punished any of his soldiers who mistreated a civilian, and he generally maintained tight discipline throughout the campaign. Noting that it was not as bad as they had feared, many Silesians treated the Prussians almost as saviors, especially as Habsburg rule often was less than enlightened. This became apparent when Frederick entered the capital, Breslau.

Breslau was defended by a garrison of its town militia, which had sealed the city gates. The advancing Prussians, under General von Münchow, approached the first barrier; Münchow boxed the ears of a sentry who resisted, and the city surrendered the next day. That slap was the only blow exchanged during this entire action. On January 3, 1741, Frederick II, elegant in blue velvet trimmed with silver, rode in on a gray horse, preceded by four colossal Prussians in scarlet liveries (footmen, formerly of the Giants' Guard), and took up residence with Count Schlegelberg, in a mansion on the Albrechtstrasse, where he gave a grand ball twelve days later for the Silesian nobility. When Frederick rode into the city, he had been wildly cheered by the populace; after he had been there for a time, he had won over the aristocracy as well. "I never saw such enthusiasm," wrote one Prussian observer.

Others were less charmed about the invasion. The British ambassador in Vienna huffed "that the new King of Prussia deserved to be politically excommunicated." [80] The Austrians were so enraged that they hired assassins to kill this upstart king before he caused more mischief.

Upstart he was; he even admitted it. It was during this campaign that he had repeated his remark about yearning for publicity and hoping for fame, confidentially, to be sure, in a letter to Jordan dated March 3: "My youth, the ardour of burning passions, desire for glory; nay, to conceal nothing from you, curiosity, and finally, a secret instinct; and the pleasure of seeing my name recorded in the newspapers, and, perhaps, at last in history: all these have seduced me." [81]

Frederick II had predicted a completely successful end to the campaign on January 17; some brief skirmishes a few days earlier had resulted in only minor casualties. "The whole conquest has cost us only twenty men and two officers," Frederick noted when these were done. He had no inkling then of the slaughter that would follow when Austria sought revenge.

The Austrians were busy mobilizing a force of 15,000 men under General Adam von Neipperg; by mid-February this force was assembled across the mountains from Silesia, in Bohemia. But winter had come on hard now, the mud had turned to ice, and snow was falling; Frederick was certain that the Austrians would never march in weather such as that. He did not yet appreciate that two could play the game of the unexpected.

Neipperg led his army into Silesia during a furious blizzard in the beginning of April, swiftly relieving the city of Brieg, one of those beleaguered outposts which had come under siege by the Prussians after first having been bypassed by Frederick's soldiers. The two armies met on April 10, at nearby Mollwitz. This was to be the young king's first major battle, and he decided to lead the Prussian troops himself, to the horror of his field marshal, Schwerin, for the officers now needed to concern themselves not only with the battle, but also with the protection of their king.

The Prussians advanced on the enemy in accustomed fashion: cannon out front; cavalry on the flanks; and in the center two lines of Prussian infantry, spaced 300 yards apart. They struck before the Austrian cannoneers were ready, causing the Austrian cavalry to stampede. It charged the Prussians at full gallop and quickly disposed of the Prussian cavalry, for this weak force was easily overwhelmed. (Anhalt-Dessau, who thought less of cavalry than infantry, had never built the Prussian horsemen up as he had the grenadiers.) In a moment, the Austrian cavalry had plowed into the Prussian infantry and shoved them out of formation. Soldiers milled about, horses reared, and what had seemed perfect order became utter confusion. Frederick, seeing his disintegrating front, was convinced all was lost. Impetuously, he charged among his men, trying to rally and inspire them, like Henry at Agincourt. "Brothers, children, lads!" he shouted. "Your country's honor! Your king's life!"

It was no use. Infantrymen were so confused in the melee that some of them were even firing into their own lines. In despair, Frederick allowed his officers to get him off the battlefield. He rode away surrounded by an escort; he rode away so fast that he outdistanced his guards, who lost him for ten hours. Frederick, whose intrepidity in later years became legendary, was in despair.

Relieved of their responsibility for the king's safety, Schwerin and his officers reassembled their troops. Now it was the turn for the Austrian cavalry to be floundering about; they were stuck in a marsh, while the Austrian infantry, which ought to have attacked while the Prussians were confused, had frozen in their tracks when they lost sight of their horsemen.

Schwerin reassembled and unleashed his terrifying weapon: the Prussian grenadiers whom Anhalt-Dessau had drilled. No one in Europe had ever encountered formations of them in battle before.

"I never saw anything more beautiful," wrote an Austrian officer afterward, commenting about the way these soldiers marched forward shoulder to shoulder, flags flying, fifes blowing, spotless in white uniforms and blue coats.

"They marched with the utmost composure," he continued, "arrow-straight, their front like a plumb-line, absolutely level, as if they had been on parade, their side-arms glittering with the most superb effect in the declining sun, their volleys sounding without pause like a continuous growl of thunder." [82]

It wasn't only beautiful, however; it was almost eerie to see these grenadiers approach without wavering, each man killed replaced instantly by one who moved up, so that the front rank was never broken. Confronted by this sight, the Austrian infantry first broke ranks, then began to huddle together, presently fell apart, and finally ran away in terror.

The Battle of Mollwitz had taken eight hours. Nine thousand men were dead, missing or wounded, more or less evenly divided between the two sides. Victory had been won—less by Frederick than by Field Marshal Count Schwerin; the king, knowing nothing of the outcome, kept riding furiously throughout the day. By nightfall he had reached Oppeln, not knowing that the Austrians had captured it; he had to turn about and race off when the sentries at the gate began to fire at the solitary horseman in Prussian uniform. They, of course, never imagined this was King Frederick II of Prussia; had they known it and killed or captured him, much would have been different afterward.

After leaving Oppeln behind, Frederick rode back across the Neisse River to a town called Löwen; there he learned that Schwerin had triumphed in Mollwitz. He could hardly believe his ears.

He had gone for forty-eight hours without rest or food, not only exhausted and half-starved but despairing all the while. Although he wrote down in detail everything that had happened during this campaign, he never wrote down a word about his wild, solitary ride in the night or spoke to anyone about it. One can only imagine his state throughout.

In the widow Panzern's little shop on Löwen's marketplace, Frederick ate roast chicken, drank coffee, and restored his spirits. Refreshed, as well as exhilarated by news of Schwerin's victory, he returned to Mollwitz. That battle, he said later, had been his "school"; never again would he deem a battle lost when it was only half over.

Mollwitz was just as much of a lesson for the rest of Europe. In fact, Mollwitz created a sensation. The little state of Prussia had played David to a Habsburg Goliath. Many were now ready to draw the necessary conclusions. One by one, most great powers drew away from Austria. Louis XV, who had called Frederick "mad," now allied France with Prussia, and Frederick found himself feted everywhere. He loved the role so much he even gave the new French envoy, Marshal Charles de Belle-Isle, a chance to watch the Prussians in action as they neatly and swiftly besieged and captured Brieg.

There followed months of diplomatic activity as the European powers regrouped and Austria rearmed. Under new leadership in the field, the Austrians overran Bavaria and threatened the French troops in Bohemia. Frederick worried and, reneging on a secret pact he had temporarily made with Maria Theresa in October, 1741, attacked the Austrian province of Moravia. There, in mid-May, 1742, he fought his second major battle, at a place called Chotusitz in the valley of the Elbe River.

Frederick had spent a year perfecting his cavalry; he was as determined to have them redeem themselves after Mollwitz as the Austrians were determined to have their infantry redeem themselves after the same battle. Old General Buddenbrock, in his seventies, led the charge of the Prussian cuirassiers; he did it so effectively that the Austrian cavalry collapsed under the impact, although they somewhat outnumbered the Prussians in the field.

Instead of snow as at Mollwitz, there now swirled a blanket of dust, kicked up by the horses' hooves. Once again, thousands of Prussian infantrymen floundered blindly about while fresh assaults of Austrian hussars plunged through them. These hussars rode right through the Prussian lines, set fire to the town of Chotusitz in their rear, and then were unexpectedly canceled out of the action. Some of them had begun to plunder the Prussian camp in the rear of the lines, and some were cut off from the battlefield by the very fires they had started.

Again, as at Mollwitz, the Prussian grenadiers regrouped, and their discipline proved its worth. They lined up with parade-ground smartness and marched ahead, into the Austrian guns. Whole ranks of them were cut down and slaughtered, even dying in perfect unison, while others stepped forward to take their places. It terrified the enemy; it seemed the dead were rising up before them, never to be stopped.

Then Frederick ordered in a reserve of twenty-one battalions equipped with fast-firing light artillery. These fresh troops, on Frederick's right wing, threatened to encircle the Austrian forces; to save what they could, the Austrians fled. They left behind 3,000 dead and wounded and another 3,000 missing. Again the victory was Prussia's; again Prussian casualties (which this time included a general and three colonels) amounted to more than 4,000 men or, roughly, 1,000 an hour, for the four-hour battle. "Who would have thought," wrote Frederick to Jordan after the battle, "that the disciple of Jordanesque philosophy, Ciceronic rhetoric, and Baylean dialectic was destined for the role of warrior . . . that Providence would choose a poet to overturn the European system and upset all the calculations of kings?"

While Count Seckendorff was still in the Berlin Palace, he had written to Prince Eugene of Savoy of a conversation he'd had with Frederick, then crown prince.

"He told me that he is a poet and can write a hundred lines in two hours," Seckendorff reported. "He could also be a musician, a philosopher, a physicist, or a mechanician. What he will never be is a general or a warrior."

Frederick had proved otherwise. The specter of his father was not seated in Potsdam, laughing, now. In July, 1742, Britain mediated a pact between Prussia and Austria which gave Frederick II all Silesia, except for the principality of Teschen with Troppau and Jägerndorf on the Moravian border. In return, Frederick paid some debts of Charles VI, promised to tolerate Catholicism in his lands, and agreed to withdraw from the War of the Austrian Succession, which his attack on Silesia helped to unleash.

That, to be sure, left his new French allies holding the bag. Having obtained what he had wanted, Silesia, Frederick now betrayed the French, as he had earlier betrayed the Austrians. His separate peace left Louis still in the war and very much in the lurch. Concerning this, Frederick had few qualms; the French had acted "like fools," he remarked. To Voltaire, he compared his action to that of a man who obtains a divorce from a wife he finds too weak and too unfaithful. Yet who, in fact, had been unfaithful? Frederick had betrayed more than his pact with Louis; he had betrayed the ideals of his youth and the hopes of his friends. When he had acceded to the throne, London's *Gentleman's Magazine* remarked, "The present king of Prussia's accession to the throne hath given his subjects such an happy prospect of a mild, gracious and glorious reign. . . ." The mildness, the graciousness, had seemed to vanish overnight; what was being born was what Prussian historians ever afterward called Prussia's glory. Frederick himself put it this way, again in a letter to his confidant Jordan: "Let the ignorant and envious babble. . . . My object is glory. Of this I am more enamored than ever." On another occasion, he wrote: "We have undergone fatigues from bad roads and worse weather. But what are fatigues, cares, and danger compared to glory? It is so mad a passion that I cannot conceive how it happens that it does not turn every man's brain." To Voltaire, he confessed the obsession in these words: "I would willingly resign my occupations to another were it not for the phantom of glory that visits me so frequently." Then he admitted: "The desire for glory is indeed a great folly, one of which man cannot easily rid himself, once he is possessed by it."

His master stroke, by which he had first won Silesia and then successfully withdrawn from a general war he had helped start, proved to be a watershed for many of his intellectual admirers. He had succeeded, but he was not trusted after that. His separate peace with Austria and his betrayal of France had even disgusted those intellectuals who, like Voltaire, had excused him the Silesian aggression. To these Frenchmen (and the only intellectuals who counted during the Enlightenment were French), Frederick's pact with Austria married him to everything they loathed: the Habsburgs, who symbolized the reactionary old order of absolutism, clericalism, Catholicism. France, even under the Bourbons, they regarded as being at least the seedbed of liberal thought; when Frederick broke faith with France, he broke faith with the future.

Frederick prepared his defense and called it "Judgment of the Public upon Those Who Follow the Unhappy Calling of Politics"; it failed to impress. Even his own subjects were disillusioned. They grumbled that whatever economic gains Silesia might bring, the king seemed to be spending them as fast as they materialized. They noted sourly that some of his early reforms had not been implemented, that 10,000 men had been added to the army as soon as the Giants' Guard had been dissolved, and that now, two years later and after the Silesian War had brought them peace, Frederick was building up his army to a record strength of 140,000 men. Furthermore, even though he was only thirty years of age, the Frederick who returned from the field of battle seemed to have become more autocratic than ever, more crusty and cantankerous than they liked. They did not know that the worst—and, to be sure, the best—was yet to come.

9

"Shall I Never Rest?"

Two of his predecessors filled Frederick II with admiration, and with good reason; they were Frederick William, the Great Elector, and his own father, King Frederick William I. Despite the terrible sufferings he had endured at the hands of the latter, Frederick pays him generous praise in his family history, the *Histoire de la Maison de Brandebourg*. He knew that his own great success was largely due to the machine his father had created and to the wealth he had amassed and left behind. Frederick William I had built the administrative and bureaucratic apparatus which made Prussia function domestically; he had asserted his power over the Junkers like *un rocher de bronze* until all opposition had ceased to exist; he and Anhalt-Dessau had trained the beast which Frederick now unleashed on Europe.

The surprise conquest of Silesia and, more important, the utter defeat of the Austrian armies at Mollwitz and Chotusitz had raised—or, more precisely, catapulted—Prussia to importance. True, even the Brandenburg of the Great Elector had been a state of some importance after the Thirty Years' War; during that elector's forty-eight years in power, he had made his domain into a force to be reckoned with in northern Europe. But to say that is to define its limits: Brandenburg was a force up North, but not in the affairs of Europe as a whole. Under the Great Elector, its armies remained small, and its economy continued to be primitive. Frederick II's father had raised up both; in fact, the Hohenzollern who most enjoyed being called the soldier king went down in history as one of the greatest Prussians in domestic, peacetime policy. Prussia became a beehive of activity during his reign; he saw to it that everything in the kingdom, as well as everyone, worked, and worked well; he restored his lands and gave them a measure of prosperity such as they had not known before. Yet as it turned out, it was his peculiar vanity, his passion for soldiers whom he could never bring himself to use, that had the greatest and most lasting effect. Perhaps, if he had not bequeathed his son an army of 80,000 men, Frederick II would have raised it, but it might have been too late, for in fact, the army was available to him at precisely the most propitious time in history, immediately after he came to the throne. As he himself recognized unerringly, the death of both the Austrian emperor and the Russian czarina enabled him to upset the balance of European power and to venture a stroke so bold as to outrage and finally to amaze all Europe: his attack on the Habsburg Empire.

It is not enough to accept Frederick II's explanation for his seizure of Silesia. The desire for glory was in him and gave him the courage to risk attacking the very empire to which Prussia had long been loyal. But there were sounder reasons for it as well. Despite everything Frederick William I had done to extract the last ounce of produce from his lands, these lands remained for the most part very poor, and very little could be done about them. They were as they had always been: sandy, marshy, swampy, and forested. Furthermore, they remained as scattered as ever, as difficult to defend, as hard to rule. Frederick II described his inheritance as more an electorate than a kingdom; there was nothing cohesive about it; it was neither fish nor fowl; in fact, Frederick called it an hermaphrodite. If Prussia was ever to become a proper kingdom, as well as a prosperous one, it urgently needed more land, which meant more natural resources and more people. It needed to be consolidated; the attack on Silesia was the first move in that process. Such, then, was the economic reason for Frederick's aggression; it caused Bismarck to remark, "Frederick the Great stole Silesia, yet he is one of the greatest men of all time."

Still, it was theft. "When every allowance has been made for ancient claims and for the fact that moral considerations meant little to any eighteenth-century ruler except Maria Theresa," writes G. P. Gooch, "the rape of Silesia ranks with the partition of Poland among the sensational crimes of modern history."[83] It unleashed rapaciousness across all Europe, as, one after another, dynastic wars were triggered off. "The whole world sprang to arms," writes Macaulay. "On the head of Frederick is all the blood which was shed in every quarter of the globe. The evils produced by his wickedness were felt in lands where the name of Prussia was unknown, and in order that he might rob a neighbour whom he had promised to defend, black men fought on the coast of Coromandel and red men scalped each other by the Great Lakes of North America." *

The cynical attack on Silesia also had a profound effect on the personality of Frederick II; what remained of the young idealist of Rheinsberg was being eroded. Frederick II had begun to feel himself as absolute and autocratic ruler, as well as master of his destiny; battles were beginning to chill him.

Frederick's friend Knobelsdorff was among the first of the old Rheinsberg court to note the change with dismay. He and the king were to build a Forum Fridericianum in Berlin, inspired by the classical architecture of Greece; the opera on Unter den Linden was to be its cornerstone. No soon had this been completed than Knobelsdorff noted with dismay that Frederick no longer shared his vision, to say nothing of the old close friendship. Knobelsdorff had become less a friend than one of that army of servants executing the king's wishes. These Frederick II had by now become accustomed to snapping out; less and less did he have time or inclination to consult anyone. He wore a uniform constantly: the "shroud" of his youth was smothering his enlightened ideals. Affecting the homespun simplicity of his father, he spurned the robes of state, called a crown "merely a hat that lets the rain in," began to dress rather theatrically in wrinkled, unadorned uniform coats, and in later years could be spotted in every state function by the fact that he was the one who did *not* glitter. The elegant, Frenchified dandy of earlier years was turning into a cranky, cynical, and

* The reference is to Britain's colonial wars. Prussian activity in Europe enabled Britain to seize French territories abroad. The relationship was mutually advantageous, for Britain drew off French strength from Europe during the Seven Years' War, which came later in Frederick's reign.

increasingly misanthropic Prussian officer. The ideas of the Enlightenment had not won new lands for the House of Hohenzollern, while aggression had. The First Silesian War which followed the invasion had cost 20,000 casualties (dead, wounded, and deserted) and 5,000,000 thalers; with these, Frederick II had secured a province which contained more than 1,000,000 people—and these paying more than 4,000,000 thalers a year in taxes. As for the arts, the king saw no reason why they could not be pursued with the left hand while the right held a sword. He managed it. He composed music and played it, wrote poems and essays, even dramatic sketches, in bewildering profusion, prepared his bulky *History* and ran the government. He also played host to Voltaire, who had arrived not only to read from his works to a worshipful Berlin court, but also on a diplomatic errand: to win Prussia back to France. Voltaire was enchanted with what he saw. "I am in France here," he remarked. "French is the only language: German is used only with soldiers and horses." This visit was brief, but what he encountered (everyone seemed to know his poems by heart, as he noted) inclined him later to come for a protracted stay.

Meanwhile, Frederick had negotiated the marriage of his sister Louisa Ulrica to the Swedish throne, while another sister, Amalia, was shunted away to become abbess of a Protestant home for spinsters. Amalia was suspected of having had a love affair with a young officer on Frederick II's staff, Baron Friedrich von der Trenck, who suffered a terrible fate at the hands of the king. The motivation behind the king's persecution of Trenck is hard to decipher, for Frederick's views about sexual transgressions were almost notoriously liberal. Frederick abolished all Prussian laws against fornication and unwed motherhood and, even within his own circle at court, protected any ladies who had become pregnant outside marriage. Yet Trenck's affair with Amalia seemed to have aroused in the king a violent dislike of the officer, possibly in part caused by the fact that Trenck was known to be in correspondence with his cousin, an Austrian officer and noble.* Whether or not Baron von Trenck's

* Both Trencks were dogged by tragedy. The Austrian Trenck retired in disgrace from the Austrian army in 1731 and several years later joined the Russian army. There he was sentenced to death for disobedience and brutality, this later being commuted to imprisonment. On his release and return to Vienna, he was so hounded that he sought refuge in a convent, after which he

affair with the Princess Amalia was real or imagined by Frederick II, Trenck was arrested in 1743 and placed in Glatz Fortress, from which he escaped after three years. A vengeful manhunt followed, initiated by the king. In 1754, Trenck was kidnapped by Frederick's agents in Danzig, returned to Prussia, and placed in Magdeburg Fortress. He remained there for ten years, chained by the neck, arms, and legs in a solitary cell. He was freed on Maria Theresa's initiative at the end of the Seven Years' War, and in later years, drawn by his hatred of Frederician absolutism, Trenck visited Revolutionary France. There he came to be arrested as an Austrian spy and was guillotined at the age of sixty-eight. "None of the Trencks is worth anything," commented Frederick II.[84]

The Trenck affair was a Frederician anomaly, certainly not an example of Frederician justice. He planned to reform the Prussian legal code and, in the meantime, issued a decree authorizing every single one of his subjects, of whatever rank or station, to seek an audience with him personally. This was by no means window dressing for his autocratic form of government; people actually came before him with their requests and pleas, every single day of his life from that year on, so long as he was not away at war.

The Silesian campaign showed up all the strengths and weaknesses of the Prussian forces. After Mollwitz, Frederick remarked, "Our infantry are heroes to a man; as for our cavalry—the devil won't accept it as a gift." Now that the war was over, at least temporarily, an intensive effort was made at improving the cavalry. War games were begun; as performance improved, Frederick excluded all foreign observers from them. He wanted his forces to surprise all Europe when next they had to be put into action.

Frederick had noted one other shortcoming of the Prussian army: the ignorance of its officers. Under Frederick William I, a system of universal education had begun, but while this eliminated a good deal of downright illiteracy, it didn't affect the

---

was amnestied and put in charge of irregular troops. At the Battle of Soor, in the Second Silesian War, Trenck's men were accused of looting, rather than fighting, and he himself was charged with allowing Frederick II of Prussia to escape. He was sentenced to death by the Austrians but later had the punishment reduced to life imprisonment. He died at the age of thirty-eight, in jail.

low educational standards of the upper classes. Frederick II's officers were drawn from the Junker landowning aristocracy; as previously noted, these were by no means cultivated landed gentry, but ranch managers more at home in muddy fields than in the classics. Taylor refers to them as "barbarians who had learnt to handle a rifle and, still more, bookkeeping by double entry"; when they came to Berlin to join the army, he says, it "was merely to leave the threshing floor for the barrack-room." [85] They needed to be educated, broadened in their vision, and made into strategists and tacticians, not merely battlefield commanders.

Frederick underestimated the determined Maria Theresa; he did not realize she would never let his aggression go unpunished as long as she had troops in the field. As a matter of fact, Maria Theresa was so infuriated with Frederick's thievery that she said she would rather lose an entire province to Bavaria than a village to Prussia. By the autumn of 1743, however, Frederick began to sense that his position in Silesia was not as secure as he wished. Austria, at war with France and with the emperor (now the Bavarian puppet, Charles VII), was strengthened by Prussia's withdrawal from the war and was consolidating its position. Frederick felt there was a real danger that Louis XV of France might pull out of the War of the Austrian Succession (following Frederick's own example), leaving Austria immeasurably strengthened and possibly prompting Austria to seize back the province Frederick had stolen. His position was made even worse by the fact that England had entered the war against France in 1743.

Accordingly, Frederick signed a twelve-year pact with Louis XV, who was happy to have allies, even such an ally as had deserted his cause a short while earlier. In August, 1744, Frederick wrote a memorandum to the courts of Europe, explaining why he was about to take to the field; he postured as the champion of the emperor, of ruling princes everywhere, of law and of constitutions, even of peace. "His Majesty takes up arms," he wrote, "only to restore liberty to the empire, dignity to the emperor, and tranquillity to Europe." This was nonsense, of course; the Second Silesian War was solely aimed at securing for Frederick the prize he had stolen. It began with an invasion of Bohemia and the capture of Prague; at the same time, Frederick urged the French to move more boldly in the West.

But the French let their Austrians escape, nor did they pursue them as they raced eastward to meet Frederick's threat in Bohemia.* By autumn the Austrians' one and only skilled battlefield commander, Field Marshal Count Otto Ferdinand von Traun, and his forces swarmed all over Bohemia, harassing the Prussians. Traun refused the Prussians the kind of pitched battle at which the Prussian grenadiers excelled; instead, he sent in Hungarian hussars to raid, harass, and plunder. Soon the Prussians were short of supplies, weakened, diseased, and demoralized. In three months, from October to December, 17,000 men deserted from the Prussian forces, most of these having been impressed against their will. (Frederick's policy was one of impressing all captured soldiers into his own army.)

"We no longer have an army," one of his administrators confessed. "All we have is a rabble barely held together by habit and the authority of their officers; and the officers themselves are disaffected. . . . At the slightest further reverse, or for that matter a continuation of the war at this season, we may expect wholesale revolt, such as one would have thought impossible under Prussian discipline."

The reverses did, indeed, continue. The Prussians were forced to evacuate all Bohemia and to retreat to Silesia. But Traun harassed them there as well, and the Prussians, who were still unable to fight this war of maneuver, barricaded themselves in forts while Frederick raced back to Berlin. There he worked feverishly to shore up his reserves and to seek a new avenue of success.

This presented itself in the form of an ailing, cantankerous sixty-nine-year-old man whom Frederick had dismissed from his mind as a has-been, a leftover from his father's days: Prince Leopold of Anhalt-Dessau. The old war-horse, who still knew a thing or two, was sent to Silesia at the head of a relief expedi-

* Louis XV had taken to the field only because his mistress, the Duchesse de Châteauroux, wanted him to play the hero; no sooner had he got into action than he contracted a fever which his confessors pretended was fatal. They refused him the final absolution of the church until he got rid of his mistress. He was delighted to do so, the duchess being too ambitious and spirited for his tastes; shriven and cured, Louis abandoned war and returned to his other women.

tion, along with one of his sons, himself a skilled commander.

This expedition must have seemed a strange sight as it headed south, for the "Old Dessauer" was not only aged, but also ailing and compelled to travel over the wretched roads in a cart, bouncing and cursing to himself, for he was bedeviled throughout by waspish and critical messages from Berlin, whence the young king was observing his progress. Worse yet, Prince Leopold's son was ailing, too. Barely able to sit his horse, Prince Maurice, aflame with a fever, jogged alongside his father's cart; the two invalids must have looked less like an avenging force than like the lame and the halt, leading the blindly obedient.

Sick or not, Anhalt-Dessau was the creator of these regiments. He knew what to do with them, and in a record three weeks the two sufferers had cleared all Austrians out of Silesia. They had been helped in this by the obtuseness of Maria Theresa. Instead of sending Marshal von Traun to face the Prussians, she sent in her brother-in-law, Prince Charles of Lorraine, a man whose list of failure was unmatched even in the Austrian forces.

Back in Berlin, however, Frederick found his exchequer empty and the state 4,500,000 thalers in debt. He had no money with which to continue fighting, whereas the Austrians at least faced no financial worries. It was quite an achievement for Frederick II to have brought Prussia to the brink of bankruptcy. His kingdom, during the previous reign, had been spoken about as being unique in Europe simply because it was in the money. Now Frederick William's war chest of 8,000,000 thalers was gone and, with it, much general prosperity. Frederick's subjects were sour, for the taxes needed to pay for the military buildup had become oppressive. It had been earlier thought that Prussia could ill afford Frederick William's 80,000 troops; now, without having grown any richer, it was supporting 60,000 more. Benefits which were supposed to flow in from Silesia had not materialized as yet; Silesia had brought nothing but headaches and two wars. Frederick found it impossible to raise funds from among his people. His own estates finally came up with 1,000,000 thalers, a fourth of the sum needed, but foreign statesmen and banking houses refused him loans or grants. So desperate was Frederick's financial position that Podewils, who had vainly urged caution all along, was sure this was the end of everything for Prussia—possibly even for the Mark Brandenburg itself.

The king was so poor that he was forced to turn his palace's solid-silver furniture into ready cash, using up some more of his father's carefully hoarded reserves. Operating during the dead of night lest the citizenry catch sight of these desperate measures, Fredersdorf shipped all of the palace's trove of silver chairs, chandeliers, mirror frames, chimney gear, and what-not to the Berlin mint to be melted down.

More than financial ruin now threatened, however, for Berlin faced siege and invasion. An enemy force of 110,000 was massing. The threat was so imminent that Frederick issued orders for the civilian evacuation and subsequent defense of the capital. Receiving them, Podewils groaned, "My hair is standing on end!"

Frederick was more sanguine, though he admitted later in his *History* that "No general made more mistakes in this campaign than the king." Occasionally, he lapsed into melancholy and predicted he might have to go into exile. Soon, however, he roused himself and struck a more heroic stance. This came easily, thanks to his considerable egoism.

"Become as good a philosopher as you are a politician," he advised his "wet hen," as he called Podewils. "Learn to confront misfortune with a brow of granite and go through this life renouncing possessions, honors, and vain trinkets, for they cannot follow us beyond the grave. . . .

"I shall win. . . . What ship's captain, having failed in every bid for safety, would not have the courage to blow up his powder magazine? A woman, the Queen of Hungary, refused to despair when the enemy was at the gates of Vienna and her best provinces were gone: should we possess less fortitude?

"As yet, we have never lost a battle. Some fortunate issue may yet raise us up higher than we have ever stood. . . . It is my pride that I have done more than any of my forefathers for the greatness of my house, that I have played a distinguished part among the crowned heads of Europe. To maintain myself therein is, as it were, a personal duty which I shall fulfill, even at the cost of happiness and life. I have no choice now: either I will uphold my power, or . . . have Prussia's name buried with me. . . . If I must perish, let it be with glory, sword in hand!"

Later he told his troops, "I shall win—or none of us shall see Berlin again!" [86] That melancholy pronouncement buoyed up morale. Frederick's plan was to use 65,000 Prussians as bait, so as to lure 80,000 of the enemy into the kind of pitched battle at which his men excelled. He chose the site, a place called Hohenfriedberg, and he devised a strategy of feint and attack. It fooled and then overwhelmed Charles of Lorraine. In three hours, victory was Frederick's. He personally had led a charge of three battalions against the Austrian guns; only 360 Prussians, the king among them, survived this suicidal but successful assault. The sheer ferocity of his army's attack had brought success; one Prussian regiment from Bayreuth alone caused twenty Austrian battalions to flee. At the end of the battle, the enemy had lost 7,650 dead, wounded, or missing; the Prussians, suffering 900 dead and 3,800 wounded, had captured 4 enemy generals, 66 cannon, 76 battle flags, and 6,000 enemy soldiers.

Humiliated by the disastrous outcome, Maria Theresa was determined to wipe out its shame—and then, ever a glutton for punishment, assigned the job once more to the luckless Charles of Lorraine, who had just been beaten.

This time, however, it was the Prussians' turn to be caught by surprise, near a place called Soor. Austrians dominated the crests around a rock-rimmed valley in which the Prussians were encamped. The Austrian generals were jubilant, but Charles of Lorraine, chastened at Hohenfriedberg, was glum even in the face of what seemed to be certain victory. "You don't know the Prussians yet!" he warned.

At four in the morning of September 30, 1745, Frederick received word of large concentrations of enemy cavalry approaching. He leaped onto a horse and rode to an observation post. There was no doubt about it: He was surrounded and trapped. To fight defensively meant to risk annihilation. To attack meant to attempt the impossible: to swarm up and out of the valley onto the crests, each of which was dominated by enemy troops and cannon. Frederick decided to risk it, despite the certain losses.

First to attack were the Prussian horsemen, charging up the steep hills into the Austrian cannons and oncoming cavalry. With each cannonade, more Prussian horses and riders fell, but the rest continued on "with undiminished speed and quite unheeding," as the official Austrian report put it afterward. Buddenbrock's cuirassiers, Frederick's heavy cavalry, now charged up a rocky incline and straight into murderous fire, incurring tremendous losses, but pressing on so ferociously that they gained the crests. Escape from the valley was even ghastlier for the Prussian grenadiers, who had to march uphill and straight into the cannon mouths, disregarding their losses and demonstrating again their apparent total disregard of danger and contempt for death. Everywhere around the valley, bold deeds and great sacrifices bought victory for the trapped Prussians. By noon the horrified Austrians were in full retreat. How could they continue to fight these spectral soldiers, zombies every one of them, it seemed, who would not be halted even in death?

For Frederick, this was a dreadful victory, but a victory nevertheless. Almost 4,000 Prussians lay wounded or dead. The Prussian camp, which had been raided, lay burned, plundered, and ruined, its women and wounded murdered. Frederick lamented the loss of his war chest, his books, snuffboxes, pens and papers, and his whippet bitches, all stolen by Hungarian hussars that day. (His favorite dog, Biche, was returned to him ahead of the other Prussian prisoners of war; Frederick wept with joy when she was let into his room to surprise him a few days later.)

Writing from the ruined camp, Frederick asked Duhan to replace his library of Cicero, Horace, Voltaire, Montesquieu, and others; of Fredersdorf, he requested two new flutes, being unable to exist without them even while on campaign; he also ordered a new jeweled snuffbox exactly like the one a Hungarian hussar had stolen. He was beginning to collect them and, eventually, owned 130. He used to jam several of these snuffboxes into his bulging coat pockets and to finger them like worry beads (although this unconscious act, together with his attachment to the flute, led analysts later to make psychological deductions, associating them with genitals).

More than ever, Frederick relied on comforts other than human. He was lonely, all the more so in that year of 1745, which marked the sudden deaths of his two closest friends, Jordan and Keyserlingk. He came to prefer his whippet bitches to human company; misanthropically, he admitted it. These bitches "were his children," says biographer Edith Simon, "or, as it goes almost without saying scandal would soon hint, his harem." [87] This kennel, which accompanied him everywhere, supplied the kind of doglike devotion craved by an autocrat no longer capable of brooking backtalk. He in turn doted only on Fredersdorf, especially now that Jordan and Keyserlingk were dead. He clucked over his chamberlain like a mother, fussed over and worried about his ailments, and entrusted him with duties which were hardly those of his office. "God protect you," he wrote Fredersdorf immediately after victory at Soor. "See to things in Berlin for me, take your medicine as you should, look after yourself, and get well!" Aside from Fredersdorf, the only man "looking after things in Berlin" for the king was his devoted, secretive secretary, August Friedrich Eichel, described by one envoy as "the true seat of government." Frederick had no *tabagie* cronies nor any real Cabinet. In his reign, Prussia was ruled from the king's private chambers, through Eichel's bureau; government ministers were reduced to mere errand boys. Eichel was so incorruptible that Frederick once remarked that "anybody wishing to find out my intentions would have to bribe me myself." Yet Eichel and, of course, Fredersdorf merely had the power of relaying the king's commands. Frederick was the complete autocrat, and all his officials knew it. They kept their jobs, but little of their pride; they remained in office but never enjoyed power.

"Shall I never be able to rest?" Frederick remarked in November, 1745, as new enemy formations massed against him. "To live like this is not living!" Once again, he dispatched that imposing old man, the Old Dessauer himself, to face the foe, this time an army of Saxons. Prince Leopold and his son, Maurice (thirty-three years old, like the king himself), went off, not quite fast enough for Frederick, who hounded them from his headquarters with more waspish, critical, insulting notes. This nagging from young Frederick II, whom Prince Leopold disliked, infuriated the Old Dessauer, and he stubbornly continued to move forward at his own pace. Finally, on December 9, Frederick sent him a virulent letter, accusing him of disobedience and an excess of caution. "I have no sense of humor in these matters," the king concluded, "and shall be obliged if Your Highness will not take me for some little Prince of Zerbst and Köthen, but just obey orders!"

When he received that, the Old Dessauer exploded. Since he could find no other target for his wrath, he directed it at the enemy. He promptly and ferociously captured the Saxon city of Meissen and then raced about angrily, spoiling for a fight with the main Saxon forces. He found them on December 15, 1745, near a town called Kesselsdorf, but attacking them meant riding into the Kesselsdorf guns, through a valley whose slopes were completely dominated by Saxons. Anhalt-Dessau arranged his forces and then stopped to pray, as was his custom. "O God, let me not be disgraced in my old days!" he is said to have called out to the heavens. "Lord God, help me. Or, if you will not help me, then let us alone to manage it by ourselves and at least do not help those scoundrels the enemy!" Then he charged forward, to win against impossible odds and in the face of terrible casualties. After two hours the Saxons were so terrified that they fled, never stopping in their retreat until they reached the safety of Bohemia. Prince Leopold's momentum was such that his advance never slowed; he promptly captured Dresden and within a week had conquered all Saxony.

Maria Theresa bitterly recognized that defeat was total, and for the second time, she surrendered Silesia to Frederick at a peace signed on Christmas Day, 1745. Frederick was also glad the war was over, for it had exhausted Prussia's exchequer. Still, despite his need for funds and despite the fact that he could have obtained almost any reparations he demanded, he contented himself with 1,000,000 thalers. All he had wanted, after all, was Silesia, for good and all. This he had won, along with the title Frederick the Great, which his people from then on bestowed on their thirty-three-year-old king. In his heart, however, he knew as well as did Maria Theresa that what he had signed was no peace, but only a truce. "Henceforth," he said, "I would not attack a cat except to defend myself. We have drawn upon ourselves the envy of Europe by the acquisition of Silesia, and it has put all our neighbors on the alert; there is not a one who does not distrust us."

The Treaty of Dresden, which ended the war, provided that Frederick recognize Maria Theresa's husband as Emperor Francis I, which meant he was again leaving France in the lurch. When the long War of the Austrian Succession ended in 1748, all signatories recognized Prussia's possession of Silesia; indeed, Prussia alone among all the combatants had emerged with substantial gain. But Frederick knew that he could not count too heavily on declarations. The holding of Silesia had taken two wars; its conquest, only six weeks. Frederick knew he would have to maintain his armies even in the future. As he once put it, "Negotiations without arms produce as little impression as musical scores without instruments." Prussia would have to remain an armed camp and the philosopher king a soldier first of all.

The difference between Austrian and Prussian rule was quickly demonstrated to the Silesians. Under the Austrians, no Habsburg had visited the province for 150 years; Frederick II visited it at least once, and sometimes twice, every single year, staying two weeks each time. It was the same with his other provinces. The king lived in Potsdam, outside Berlin, which pleased him more than the capital did, but it could be said that he lived much of the year in carriages and on horseback, touring the Prussian lands. He went on working visits only, always after having been fully briefed by the reports which poured onto his desk at Potsdam. Clutching in his hands a thick leather notebook crammed with statistics about last year's crop and last year's production, he confronted agricultural and industrial managers with demands about their current yields. He spoke with local officials in towns and villages; he crisscrossed his domains constantly, enduring the rough roads on interminable carriage rides; he walked through muddy fields and spoke with peasants at their work, weighing their vegetables in his bejeweled hands. He was a compendium of economic data, a storehouse of information about the problems besetting different regions, and a constant reminder to his officials that they must redouble their efforts in advance of his next visit. Almost no local appointment could be made without his express approval; he even had to be consulted before the lowest bureaucrat could assume office in some distant town.

Every morning of his life, Frederick II rose at either three or four, after five or six hours of sleep, in order to handle the great mass of work which awaited him each day. His servants were ordered to awaken him at the appointed hour with a wet cloth, to be dropped on his face, for he was inclined to be a late sleeper and usually let the alarm clock run down without rising. But he was determined to discipline himself—once (as an experiment) he kept awake for four days with the help of gallons of coffee (laced with mustard in his later years)—and to attack his mountains of correspondence early in the day. No women, not even chambermaids, were allowed into his rooms; a soldier awakened him, and a footman tied his pigtail while he read the first batch of letters, thumbing them with fingers greasy and wet with perspiration and stained with snuff. He sweated ferociously (his bedclothes and mattress were soaked through each night), and although he wiped himself often with wet cloths, he admitted he looked "a bit of a pig." He dressed each day in the same worn, mended, stained, and sometimes torn uniform jacket and old tricorn hat, the latter kept on throughout his waking hours. After he had studied his letters—petitions from peasants and commoners as well as official memorandums—he heard a report concerning the strangers who had arrived at Potsdam during the night; those who interested him were summoned by a mounted trooper. Then his generals reported to him about military affairs, after which he breakfasted on several glasses of water and as many cups of coffee, munching chocolate in his early years as well. Cherries and fruit of all kinds were always around him; on one occasion, he wrote Fredersdorf that he had the day before eaten 180 thalers' worth of cherries, paying 2 thalers each for the first of the season. Before nine, he played the flute for an hour or two; it was his means of meditation, for his best thoughts, as he once said, flowed to him on a tide of harmony. After this, his Cabinet councilors appeared, one after the other, obtaining the king's decisions on various matters. From ten to eleven, the king received people in audience or strode about the palace gardens. Foreign visitors were forever surprised at seeing shabby commoners peering in through the palace windows, looking for their king, so as to have a word with him; peasants could even be found strolling through the palace gardens, hoping to encounter Frederick during his walks.

At eleven each morning while at Potsdam, Frederick reviewed and, sometimes, personally drilled his guards, mounted on his horse, a practice he continued year after year, even into his aching old age, in pouring rain, swirling blizzards, or blazing heat. Then he retired to lunch at twelve sharp. This being the main meal in Germany, Frederick kept at it for two, three, or sometimes four hours, surrounding himself with guests from all over the world, as well as a few Germans. These dinner parties of his became famous, and during them, something of the young crown prince and the atmosphere at Rheinsberg returned: The conversation was lively and laced with Frederician wit; the food was delicate and elegantly prepared in the French fashion; the visitors were distinguished men of affairs and letters. Frederick liked highly spiced foreign dishes and had twelve highly paid cooks, some of them Italian, French, and Russian, whose performance each day he rated with marks on the dinner menu. He watched over expenditures in the kitchen as sharply as he did over those in the ministries; once, when he received a statement that 25 thalers had been spent on 100 oysters and some other dishes, he scribbled beneath it, "Robbery!", detailed all the costs himself, and concluded, "Everything beyond 12 thalers is barefaced robbery!"

After luncheon, he played the flute for half an hour and then signed letters he had dictated earlier. He insisted that every memorandum and letter be answered the same day; only death sentences were kept for the day following, to be pondered more slowly. Coffee, composition, and reading followed later in the afternoon, or he received more petitioners. Between six and seven in the evening he played the flute in a concert with others, whom he had specially invited. He loved these performances but had stage fright each evening; his hand trembled for fear of producing a false note and shook even more when his instructor coughed gently, for that signified a mistake had been made. Sometimes those playing with him were professional musicians; on other occasions, they were distinguished guests. During a 1770 visit of the Saxon dowager electress, she played the piano and sang, while Frederick and his old flutemaster, Johann Joachim Quantz, played first flute, the Duke of Brunswick first violin, and Frederick's brother and successor, the Prince of Prussia, violoncello.

Supper, which the king attended but disdained to eat, followed from early evening sometimes until past midnight; Voltaire was very impressed with the gaiety and wit displayed during such meals.

Few variations in this daily routine occurred except during wars or trips into the provinces. Military reviews and maneuvers were held in spring and autumn. In mid-June, a ministerial review took place. Each government minister had to present—in brisk, concise, and satisfactory fashion—an accounting of his ministry's work, while the king surveyed him icily from head to foot and occasionally tapped him on the shoulder with the walking stick he carried about. *"Eh bien!"* Frederick would say if satisfied; if not, he would tap the offending minister a bit harder on the shoulder and warn him, "If I catch you tripping again, I shall send you to Spandau [Fortress]!" After the review of the ministers was over, Frederick took a vacation, sipping the healing waters of Bad Pyrmont and Eger, whereupon he had himself bled (four times a year) and, thus strengthened, toured Silesia. The month between Christmas and his birthday he spent in Berlin. This was the social season in Prussia during his reign; he was even sociable enough to visit his queen once in a while during those four weeks and to dine with her. When doing so, he bowed to her as he entered the dining room, bowed when he sat down opposite her, and bowed when he left; that was all, for he never said a word to her, there being nothing to say.

Knobelsdorff's Opera House, which served as a theater as well, cost Frederick 400,000 thalers a year, admission being free, although Berliners of no standing could not even stand in it, since all places were assigned to officials, officers, and soldiers. Johann Sebastian Bach was invited from Leipzig, but few other Germans performed. Frederick once refused to invite a German singer with the remark that he'd "rather hear horses neigh." Foreign singers, especially an Italian called Signora Barberini, on the other hand, were much desired. Barbara Campanini, as she was really named, was beautiful, talented, and fascinating. When she broke her Berlin engagement in order to linger in Venice with one of her lovers, Frederick held the Venetian ambassador to Berlin as hostage until she showed up, whereupon he paid her three times the salary of a Prussian minister. He dined with her often, visited her private rooms, and treated her with such generosity that it was rumored that she was his mistress. This, however, may merely have been idle speculation on the part of the court gossips, for Frederick was as enchanted with her beauty and wit as he was with that of other exceptional women; there is no proof that he ever was intimate with any. She ultimately married the son of his court reformer, Chancellor Cocceji, remaining with him for forty years until Frederick II's death, after which she divorced him.

The most theatrical visitor to Berlin during these peaceful years was, however, Voltaire. Frederick had been trying for years to get Voltaire to move to Prussia for a prolonged stay. The death of Voltaire's mistress and the arrival of 40,000 thalers in traveling expenses persuaded him to come in 1750. "Sire, you are worthy of adoration," Voltaire proclaimed. "You are perhaps the greatest monarch that ever sat upon a throne." Five weeks later, appointed chamberlain, decorated with Prussia's highest medal, the *Pour le mérite,* and given a free household and 5,000 thalers a year, Voltaire wrote a friend, "Either he is the best or I am the most stupid man in the world." A year later he confessed his head had been "completely turned" by "the king's great blue eyes, his charming smile, his seductive voice, his five battles, his pronounced taste for seclusion in which to work at verse and prose, tokens of friendship to make one swoon, a delicious gift for conversation, freedom, complete social equality, a thousand courtesies and attentions which would be captivating even from a private citizen. . . ."

It was not long, however, before the mutual-admiration society dissolved. Voltaire was too avaricious; Frederick too penny-pinching. Voltaire's coffee and sugar supply was cut down; for spite, Voltaire retaliated by burning more candles. Then Voltaire's financial greed led him into an ugly lawsuit with a Berlin financier. Frederick managed to overlook the appetite for money which his cultural lion displayed, but he could not countenance the fact that Voltaire deliberately opposed him in a subsequent quarrel about two members of the Berlin Academy of Arts. Voltaire failed to side with the king's favorite, Maupertuis, and finally outdid himself in recklessness by publishing a lampoon of that academy president. This lampoon was publicly burned on Frederick's orders by the common hangman, and the ashes were sent to Maupertuis, to make amends. Afterward Frederick announced, referring to his friendship with Voltaire, that he had "squeezed the orange dry and thrown the peels away." Voltaire left in March, 1753, and although the two prima donnas continued to correspond until Voltaire's death, they never met again. "You know that you behaved shamefully in Prussia," the king wrote him. "You richly deserve to see the inside of a dungeon. Your talents are no more widely known than your disloyalty and malice." Yet both men continued to share much in common, for they loathed and loved together: hated superstition and ignorance, cherished wit and friendship. When he was eighty-four, Voltaire wrote Frederick, "May Frederick the Great become Frederick the Immortal!" and when he died, the king's funeral oration said Voltaire "would still deserve a place among the small number of mankind's benefactors . . . had he done no more than champion the cause of justice and tolerance. . . ." It was a generous statement to make, considering the fact that Voltaire, after his departure from Potsdam, had published an anonymous and scurrilous book suggesting in coarse language that Frederick's relationships with officers and pages were questionable. (Of Fredersdorf, Voltaire wrote, "Young and handsome, he had served the king in more than one capacity.") Frederick dismissed this as "idle gossip" which he disdained to answer. "I serve the State," wrote the king, "with all the ability and purity which Nature has given me. . . ." [88]

In the summer of 1756, Frederick II had to do more than serve his state: he had to save it, for it faced utter ruin. In whatever direction Frederick faced, he saw enemies who had either already allied themselves against Prussia or were preparing to do so: in the north, Sweden; in the east, Russia; to the west, France; in the south, his old enemies, Austria and Saxony. Prussia by now had a standing army of 150,000 men, but 500,000 soldiers were massed against it. Prussia still had only about 4,000,000 inhabitants and a backward economy little able to sustain a long war; any one of three of his foes (France, Austria, Russia) had far greater resources, both human and economic, and each one of them believed itself ready and able to destroy Prussia single-handedly. Together, they overwhelmed Frederick the Great's kingdom and threatened to wipe it off the face of the map. The Seven Years' War began with a preventive surprise attack by Prussia so as to break this stranglehold; this was motivated by many of the same considerations of national survival which, two centuries later, would motivate Israel's Six-Day War against the Arab states.

Prussia had come to such a desperate condition rather slowly. A year after the Treaty of Dresden, Maria Theresa's traditional policies had been completely revised, thanks to the influence of Prince Wenzel Anton von Kaunitz-Rietberg, her representative at the talks which ended the War of the Austrian Succession. Kaunitz, who has been called the ablest diplomat of the eighteenth century, persuaded her that Austria's enmity toward France and Russia was outdated and that the principal enemy of the House of Habsburg was that upstart, Prussia, and its House of Hohenzollern. These views, at variance with those of most of her other advisers, agreed with Maria Theresa's own, and she urged Kaunitz to implement Austria's new foreign policy.

Accordingly, Kaunitz proceeded to transform France into Austria's ally. This was made easier because Madame de Pompadour and others were now gaining influence at Versailles and the old anti-Austrian party was losing favor; further, the fact that Frederick II had twice deserted the French cause meant that there was no great love cementing the ties between Versailles and Potsdam. If Austria defeated Prussia, then France might be able to fight England successfully; everything could be transformed. Meanwhile, the czarina had developed a hatred of Frederick and had concluded a pact with Austria; everybody was regrouping his alliances. This held true for Prussia as well, for England was anxious to secure George II's German lands, the electorate of Hanover, against French attack; accordingly, England and Prussia signed the Convention of Westminster in 1756, in which Frederick promised to defend Hanover. (This relieved the English, who were fighting the French in India and Canada and wanted to limit the number of their troops on the Continent.) But the Convention of Westminster implicitly violated Frederick's treaty with France, and when this came up for renewal, France refused to consider the matter. Frederick remained sanguine for a while, for he still believed, by then mistakenly, that the French and the Austrians were irreconcilable enemies; he also trusted that his pact with England would deter the Russians from making a move.

He had spies and agents everywhere, and their reports soon enough indicated that his hopes were vain. A huge coalition was being formed against him; Prussia had for its allies only England (busy elsewhere) and Brunswick and Hesse-Kassel. Yet he had never yet lost a battle; this made him more than confident;

it made him cocky. He told Schwerin he had many foes, but no fears; he wrote the Prince of Prussia, his brother, that "Prussian officers who have been through our wars know that neither numbers nor difficulties could rob us of victory. . . ." Then he proceeded to strike the first blow, unleashing the bloodiest war of his century. On August 28, 1756, he invaded Saxony, having first disposed of his 150,000 soldiers around his frontiers. Schwerin, in Silesia, commanded 37,000 men, 26,000 watched the borders of Russia, and 11,000 guarded Pomerania against the Swedes (despite the fact that Sweden had a Hohenzollern queen). Frederick gathered 70,000 men under his own command and marched them into Saxony, where he encountered virtually no resistance. The Saxons retreated to the Bohemian border, and after Dresden was captured and Frederick had inflicted a defeat on the Austrians at Lobositz in northern Bohemia on October 1, the Saxons surrendered and were taken over bodily into the Prussian forces. Administrators were appointed to squeeze Saxony's economy "until the pips flew," and Frederick spent the peaceful winter months in Dresden. "I have not the slightest apprehension," he wrote at the end of October. He felt so confident that he even visited Berlin in January; he did not know it, but that visit would be his last in seven years.

On January 10, 1757, Frederick II drew up an instruction which has gone down in Prussian history as one of the most inspiring and characteristic documents left behind by this great soldier king. "If I am killed," he wrote to Count Finck von Finckenstein, his boyhood friend and now minister for home affairs, "affairs must continue without the slightest alteration and without anyone noticing that they are in other hands. If I have had the bad luck to be captured, I forbid the slightest consideration for my person or the slightest attention to anything I may write in captivity. If such a misfortune occurs, I wish to sacrifice myself for the state, and allegiance must be paid to my brother, who, together with all my ministers and generals, shall answer to me with his head that neither province nor ransom shall be offered for me and that the war shall be prosecuted and advantages exploited exactly as though I had never existed in the world." It was similar to instructions he had issued on March 7, 1741, during the First Silesian War, telling Podewils he would answer for it with his head if he did not obey them: "If by bad luck I am ever captured I command you . . . that in my absence you will disregard my orders, that you will advise my brother, and that the state will stoop to no unworthy act to achieve my liberation. On the contrary, in such an event I order that even greater energy shall be displayed. *I am not king except when I am free. . . .*" *

The possibility of his being captured was by no means remote, for the king was no safer than any of his officers or soldiers. Unlike Louis of France and other monarchs, Frederick II not only led his troops into the field, but led them into the thick of battle, being at their head throughout and valorously exposing himself to enemy fire and enemy sabers. Watching their king risk life and limb alongside them, his soldiers were inspired to feats of astounding bravery; watching him steadfast even in the face of great reverses, his officers and men were moved to match their monarch's intrepidity. More than perhaps any other factor, the king's personal bravery and resolution saved Prussia in the years that followed, for his officers and men not only feared but adored their king and could not bring themselves to let such a monarch down.

That first January of the war brought ominous news of a Russo-Austrian convention. Each signatory promised to provide 80,000 troops for the express and stated purpose of destroying Prussia forever and of restoring Silesia to Austria, "it being impossible for the peace of Europe to be assured," as the document stated, "unless the King of Prussia is deprived of the means of troubling it. . . ." On May 1, France signed a treaty offering large financial subsidies—and 115,000 men—for the recovery of Silesia, prompting Kaunitz to declare: "With God's help, we will bring so many enemies against the insolent King of Prussia that he must succumb." Sweden was lured into the war by the prospect of gaining Pomerania from Prussia, that territory out of which the Great Elector had once chased the Swedes; Russia, with which Frederick had had no grievance, was now thick in the coalition to destroy him. As for Prussia's ally, England, it did not have the ships with which to defend

* Author's italics, this being one of the most famous pronouncements of Frederick II: *"Je ne suis roi que lorsque je suis libre."*

Prussian coasts against the Russians and Swedes, being too deeply committed against France in India and North America.

Schwerin was killed in a battle outside Prague in May; this was a Prussian victory, but it was followed in June by an Austrian one which sent Frederick reeling back to Saxony. This—and a brief occupation of Berlin by Russian and Austrian troops—shook the king's confidence. "Fortune has turned her back to me," he wrote a friend. "I ought to have been prepared for it: she is a woman and I am not a gallant. . . ." He wrote another friend, ". . . you must regard me as a wall broken down by ill fortune for the last two years. I am assaulted from every side. . . . But do not imagine I am weakening. If everything collapses I should calmly bury myself beneath the ruins. In these disastrous times one must fortify oneself with iron resolutions and a heart of brass. It is a time for stoicism. . . ."

Stoicism triumphed, at least that year. Although the Austrian victory in June, at Kolin, had been a disaster, the remainder of that year became glorious for Prussia. The Battle of Rossbach, in which Frederick defeated the French and the imperial army then threatening Magdeburg, was an heroic achievement, the kind which prompted Napoleon Bonaparte to remark that the Seven Years' War was won not by the Prussian army, but by Frederick II himself. It was at Rossbach that General Friedrich Wilhelm von Seydlitz proved himself one of the greatest cavalry commanders of all time. (Seydlitz was such an accomplished horseman that his equestrian feats entered into legend; his most famous one was performed when he rode through the sails of a windmill while it turned at full speed.) He had already distinguished himself by leading a daring charge at Kolin, after which Frederick decorated the thirty-six-year-old officer with the *Pour le mérite* and promoted him to major general; when the Battle of Rossbach dawned, Frederick superseded two senior generals and placed Seydlitz at the head of his entire cavalry, consisting of thirty-eight squadrons. Seydlitz was aided only by the fire of eighteen guns and of seven battalions of infantry (and of the latter, only two fired more than five rounds); facing his horsemen were 64,000 enemy troops. These were routed in just forty minutes by the ferocity of the Prussian attack, Seydlitz remaining at the head of the cavalry despite having suffered grave wounds. The king that night promoted him to lieutenant general and bestowed on him the Order of the Black Eagle, which his grandfather (Frederick I) had created on becoming king in Königsberg. "The affair of November 5," Frederick wrote afterward, "was very favorable. We captured 8 French generals, 260 officers and 6,000 men. We lost 1 colonel, 2 other officers, and 67 soldiers; 223 were wounded. Never could I have hoped for such a result. . . . These terrible times and this war will surely mark an epoch in history."

The defeat—indeed, the utter rout—of 64,000 enemies by a small force of Prussian horsemen made Frederick II the greatest celebrity in Europe and almost a demigod in England. George II hated his nephew, for family reasons, but to the average Englishman who toasted Frederick in The King of Prussia pub, Frederick was the great "Protestant hero" of Europe.

His reputation was reinforced a month later, in a battle which alone, according to Napoleon Bonaparte, was enough to guarantee Frederick II's immortality and rank him among the world's greatest generals. Frederick had raced to Leuthen to attack the Austrians again, for they had captured nearby Breslau. On December 3, 1757, Frederick assembled his officers and spoke to them of his plans, in French; a subaltern recorded his exact words. He thanked them "from the depth of his heart" for their past faithful service and said he was basing his entire battle plan for the next day on their courage and experience alone.

"I am going to break all the rules of war and attack an enemy who is twice our strength and well established on high ground," he said. "I must do it, for if I don't, all will be lost. That enemy must be beaten, or we perish to the last man before his batteries. That is how I see it, and that is how I shall act. But if any of you thinks differently, let him come forward here and now and demand his discharge—and I shall grant it without the smallest reproach." Frederick paused and waited, then broke into a broad smile. "I knew it!" he said jubilantly. "I thought none of you would desert me! From now on I shall have complete confidence in your loyal help and in certain victory. If I am left on the field and not able to reward you for what you are going to do tomorrow, our country will see to that. Now go down the lines and tell your regiments what I have said. And tell them I shall keep a close eye on each of them. Any cavalry regiment failing to charge the enemy at full gallop when it is ordered shall be unhorsed immediately after the battle and made into a garrison regiment. The infantry battalion that even begins to slow up no matter what it encounters shall lose colors and sabers and I shall have the badges cut from their uniforms. And now, fare you well, gentlemen. By this time tomorrow we shall have beaten the enemy, or we do not meet again."

Early the next morning, the king had his 32,000 men marching against the 60,000 Austrians. His enemies were well established between the villages of Leuthen (which gave the battle its name) and Lissa, about 10 miles west of Breslau. In the early afternoon, he captured an Austrian field bakery and 10,000 freshly baked hot loaves by seizing Neumarkt, a village protected by 1,000 Croatian troops, half of whom became his prisoners. Moving on from there, Frederick received the good news that Prince Charles had overruled Field Marshal Daun and removed his Austrian army from its protected position; he was moving to give Frederick battle in open countryside, being confident his superior numbers would bring him victory. Five miles from Breslau, the Prussians encountered the outposts of the Austrian army, a body of Saxon dragoons; Frederick immediately ordered his own cavalry to attack front and flank, sending them fleeing and leaving more than 500 of them captive. The Prussians moved forward for a space; then Frederick and his officers surveyed the countryside from a nearby hill, discovering the main Austrian force about two miles away. Its right wing was impossible to attack, because of the terrain, but the left, near Leuthen, seemed vulnerable. Frederick devised a plan to hide his intentions from the enemy. He would send in his troops with the units staggered behind and slightly to the side of one another, so that most of them would remain hidden from view; finally, they would turn half right and close up for battle, a maneuver only the superbly drilled Prussians could have executed.

The Austrians were watching their flanks, from which they expected the attack to come, since Frederick avoided frontal attacks. When Prince Charles saw what seemed to be ragged, small formations of Prussians moving south toward him, he remarked to Field Marshal Daun that they seemed to be "smuggling themselves out" and had best be left to do it. Then a rider came from the Austrian right wing, saying Prussian cavalry had been spotted and was apparently preparing to attack; help was urgently needed. When a second and more desperate plea for reinforcements arrived, Prince Charles sent Daun off with troops and with the entire Austrian cavalry reserve to save that right wing—miles from where Frederick was really planning to attack.

At one o'clock in the afternoon, Frederick sent in cavalry, as well as infantry, to attack the Austrian left flank. The Austrians repelled the first blow but, when the cavalry, under General Hans Joachim von Zieten, charged again, they began to reel. The Prussian infantrymen were fighting so furiously that Prince Maurice of Anhalt-Dessau even tried to stop them after they had attained their objective. "That's honor enough, lads!" he yelled at them. "Get back into the reserve!" The reply they are said to have given him has become legendary: "Fuck the reserve! Give us more cartridges! More cartridges—quick!"

The Austrian left flank had crumbled, but the center, near Leuthen proper, held and Frederick had no further infantry reserves; moreover, both he and his Austrian opponents recognized that the ferocity of the Prussian attack had exhausted the Prussian soldiers. Seizing the moment, the Austrian cavalry charged the Prussian grenadiers and would have overwhelmed them had it not been for General Driessen, who was waiting with a small body of Prussian cavalry in a hollow, under strict orders from Frederick not to use his men until the Austrians attacked. Driessen allowed the Austrian cavalry to pass him by, then went charging furiously into their rear. The Austrian cavalry commander, General Lucchesi, was killed, and his men were sent fleeing, whereupon Driessen wheeled around and scattered all the remaining Austrian infantry, attacking their rear and their flanks. So intrepid was Driessen's charge that, when Frederick heard the full details, he blurted out, "What? That old fool Driessen?"

By the time the Battle of Leuthen was over, it was dark. Frederick mounted a horse and personally led two battalions of grenadiers along the road to Lissa, to pursue the Austrian survivors. He encountered a mass of them in the village of Lissa proper and directed his soldiers to round them up. Dismounting, the king noted a manor house set back from the main street and, seeing Austrian officers inside, archly walked in, completely unprotected. *"Bon soir, messieurs!"* he said. "Is there room left? I don't suppose you were expecting me?" The enemy officers stood about their dinner table, absolutely thunderstruck. They recognized the King of Prussia immediately; they could easily have seized him and taken him prisoner; his smiling self-confidence paralyzed them. All they could think of doing was introduce themselves. Frederick responded politely, by telling them his own officers would find rooms elsewhere; they could stay where they were. As for himself, he found his own quarters: a bundle of straw in a humble house in the town.

Rossbach and Leuthen were two major victories which would ensure the glory he had always sought, but Frederick knew they did not ensure Prussia's survival. The Russians were gathering their strength, and Frederick knew very well this meant the worst was yet to come. Meanwhile, from that December until well into the next year, Frederick bound up his army's wounds and restored his spirit. Again he wrote poems and epigrams, read philosophy, and consoled himself with the flute. On February 7, 1758, he could write, "I am in for big adventures . . . the kings, the emperors, and the journalists are all on my track, but I hope to defeat the whole lot. I await the event philosophically, knowing that anxiety is useless and that destiny or fortune decide." A few months later, as the Russians began to move west to face his forces, he grew more anxious. "Mine is a dog's job," he wrote on July 28. "If the slightest thing goes wrong, I am lost. . . ." And the atheist even added, "Have masses said for the soul of your friend who is in purgatory. . . ."

The Battle of Zorndorf, where Frederick, again with Seydlitz at his side, confronted the Russians, was one of the bloodiest of the war. Russian resistance was finally broken after hours of close, hand-to-hand combat in which the most horrible butchery killed or wounded 12,500 Prussians and 21,000 Russians, as Seydlitz's cavalry battered itself bloody against three impenetrable Russian infantry squares. Sir Andrew Mitchell, an Englishman who accompanied Frederick II, reported, "We are on the brink of destruction. The Russians fought like devils. The king's firmness of mind saved all. Would to God I was out of this scene of horror and bloodshed." So ghastly had the encounter been that Frederick was compelled to let the Russians escape, his troops being too exhausted to pursue them; the Russians still had plenty of reserves, as Frederick noted, but what they lacked was a battlefield commander who knew how to use them to good effect.

This Prussian victory, which really was more a stalemate than a victory, was followed in Hochkirch by a Prussian defeat at the hands of the Austrians, leaving Frederick dispirited afterward—all the more so because he learned that his beloved sister Wilhelmina had died on the same day. On November 23 he commented, "Our campaign is finished. There is nothing to show on either side beyond the loss of many good fellows, the misfortune of many poor soldiers permanently maimed, the ruin of provinces, the pillaging and burning of flourishing towns. . . ." He began to rail against his enemies, charging them with persecuting him "in such a cruel and atrocious manner," completely ignoring the fact that he himself had set these events in train by invading Silesia. He began to develop a considerable cynicism about the human race. "This war is frightful," he wrote, "it grows more barbarous and inhuman every day. This polished century is still very ferocious, or, to be more correct, man is an untamable animal when he gives rein to his passions. I spend the winter like a Carthusian monk. I dine alone, I pass my life in reading and writing, and I have no supper. . . ." In March, 1759, he confessed that "without some lucky accident there is no way out," for his enemies outnumbered him at least two to one, and he continually had to race from one battlefield to another, often forcing his men to cover 22 miles in a day, in order to shore up yet another sinking front and face still another overwhelming force.

The worst defeat Frederick II endured during this war took place on August 12, 1759, when 50,000 Prussians faced 90,000 Austrians and Russians at Kunersdorf. Although Frederick's troops showed their usual discipline and gallantry, they were completely defeated in a six-hour engagement. Frederick had two horses shot down from under him, and a bullet smashed into a snuffbox in his pocket. When it was over, half his army was left on the ground, and more than 170 guns fell into the hands of the enemy, while the allied Russo-Austrian force lost only 15,700 men. Frederick's surviving force was saved—not by

Seydlitz, whose gallant efforts were in vain that day, but by the sluggishness of the enemy generals, who failed to follow up the defeat by pursuing the Prussians. The next day Frederick was reinforced by 23,000 more Prussians, but his spirits remained so low that he fingered the poison pills in his pockets. "Save the royal family," he wrote home after the Kunersdorf disaster. "I have no more resources left and, to tell the truth, I think all is lost. I shall not survive the ruin of my country. Adieu for ever!"

The failure of the Russians to march on Berlin was "the miracle of the House of Brandenburg," as Frederick called it. A further blessing was the lack of coordination between the Austrians and Russians. As winter approached, Frederick felt he was gaining breathing space. The year had been terrible for Prussia, but it had survived. Stoicism, combined with an incredible capacity for endurance, kept the Prussian forces going. Frederick was exhausted but slogged on, hoping for luck but stating that, if he did not get it, he refused to be any longer "the sport of fortune." He was "tired and disgusted with life," he said, and could merely "groan in silence." To his troops, however, he continued as ever to turn a confident, strong face and to inspire them during battles and afterward with ringing words and fatherly solicitude. He was never remote from them or their torments, but endured everything as they themselves endured, shivering on straw in wintry barns, eating so wretchedly that ever afterward his digestion was ruined.

By 1760 the Russians had retired to the Oder, their troops having consumed all the food and provisions available in the areas they occupied, and Frederick faced only the Austrian forces. Frederick won the Battle of Liegnitz, but the victory changed nothing. "This is not the end of the story," he wrote. ". . . I had my clothes damaged and my horses wounded. Hitherto I am invulnerable. . . ." He added that it had not been much of a victory and that "miracles will be needed to overcome all the difficulties" which he could foresee. His strength, he said, was ebbing, and his physical infirmities were mounting; only he knew the dangers that were still ahead and how hard it was for him to meet them. "I keep all my fears to myself," he wrote a friend. "I tell the public only of my hopes and the little good news there is." He did not know if he would survive the war, he added, and said that if he did, he was resolved to spend the rest of his life "in the bosom of philosophy and friendship." By October he predicted that he would recover Leipzig, Wittenberg, Torgau, and Meissen, but that it would all be of no use, for the enemy would keep Dresden and the Silesian mountains, which would enable them to knock him out during the next year. Once again, he contemplated suicide, saying he knew how to put an end to his misfortunes. "After sacrificing my youth to my father and my mature years to my country," he said, "I think I have a right to dispose of my old age. . . . Brandenburg existed before I was born and will continue to exist when I am dead. At fifty there are so many reasons for despising life. The prospect before me is an old age full of infirmity and sorrow, worries and regrets, ignominy and old age. I have lost all my friends and dearest relatives. I have nothing to hope for. I see my enemies treating me with derision, and in their pride they are preparing to trample me underfoot."

At Torgau, on the Elbe, on November 3, 1760, Frederick fought the last great battle of this war. Only 600 of his 6,000 grenadiers survived the raking cannonades of 400 enemy guns, but Zieten's Prussian cavalry and fresh brigades of foot soldiers finally prevailed, being as undaunted as ever and exhausting the Austrians by the inexorability of their advance. Frederick had three horses shot from under him and was himself knocked down by a bullet. The Prussians lost 13,120 men out of their 44,000 (30 percent), while the Austrians lost only 11,260 (17.3 percent) of their 65,000.* But the Austrians withdrew from Zieten's charge and retired from the field. The terrible battle, which had lasted for only about three hours, so exhausted both armies that no further clashes took place that year. "Next year it will all start again," Frederick noted gloomily after Torgau. Two days later, he wrote, ". . . I am not puffed up by my successes. My enemies crowd upon me . . . [and are not] sufficiently reduced to be compelled to make peace. In fact, the outlook is as black as if I were at the bottom of a tomb. . . ."

The quietest year of the war was 1761, and Frederick could hardly believe that some fresh disaster or some new bloody Prussian—and, therefore, Pyrrhic—victory did not loom ahead. By June 7 he predicted that "this profound calm" would be

* Six thousand of the 11,260 were prisoners.

"the prelude to a violent tempest." He spent his time reading voraciously in his favorite Latin and French books, but his philosophy, he said, was constantly receiving "such shocks that it sometimes gives way." His sufferings made him reflect on the horrors of war. "It is time for peace," he wrote, "else famine and plague will avenge humanity for the plagues and tyrants, and will carry off aggressors and defenders, friends and enemies alike. God preserve us from such things, and have mercy on your soul and mine if we have a soul."

The year passed without a major clash, but Frederick's situation was unchanged. The Great Coalition was still amassed against him and still as determined to crush Prussia for good and all; worse yet, English subsidies, which had helped finance the Prussian armies, were now in doubt. Indeed, January, 1762, dawned as gloomy as any of the previous years, with no cause whatever for hope. Then, on January 5, female fortune finally smiled on the king who said he was not her gallant. Empress Elizabeth of Russia, who hated Frederick passionately, suddenly and unexpectedly died of drink and debauchery. When the news reached Frederick two weeks later, he lashed out with a verse in which he called her Messalina and the "concubine" of Russians and Cossacks; cautiously, he congratulated her successor, Peter III (whose wife came to be called Catherine the Great), on acceding to the throne. He knew Peter was an admirer of his, but he didn't yet realize how great the czar's admiration of Frederick was. Peter promptly withdrew from the war, returned East Prussia (which the Russians had occupied), and even placed 18,000 Russian troops at Frederick's disposal. Frederick was jubilant. He wrote: ". . . we are about to make peace at once and perhaps an alliance, which relieves us of this infamous and devastating horde of [Russian] savages and consequently of the Swedes. . . ." It would not solve all his problems, for the Austrians would "fight until they have spent their last half penny. . . . The war continues and we still have two formidable powers on our hands [Austria and France]. Yet, as two are less than three and four, our situation becomes 50 percent more tolerable." So grateful was he for this turn of events that he wrote Peter III letters such as he would never again write to another human being, filled with simpering praise for the czar's "virtues . . . disinterestedness . . . nobility . . . and many other admirable qualities." These have made Peter "an object of adoration," an almost "divine being"; he told the czar that he could "reckon my heart among your first conquests" and said that all Prussian officers saluted Peter as their "dear Emperor."

Peace with Sweden followed on May 22. "So our tribulations are ceasing," Frederick wrote. ". . . Compare my situation next month with that of last December. Then the state was on its deathbed; we were awaiting extreme unction before drawing the last breath. Now I am freed of two enemies. . . ."

By July 9 Peter had been dethroned and quickly assassinated; Frederick hastened to curry favor with the czar's successor, Catherine. She confirmed the peace with Prussia but withdrew her troops. Russia was out of the war, at least, but the alliance was gone. "I am fortune's spinning top and she mocks me," Frederick noted. Only patience could now prevail, he said.

This proved true soon enough, for France had little stomach for the war anymore, while the English, under a new king and a new prime minister, had withdrawn their support. Frederick faced Austria alone, and the Austrians, as he correctly predicted, would remain "the last champions in the arena."

On October 29, 1762, Frederick's brilliant brother, Prince Henry, fought the last battle of the war at Freiberg, and Prince Ferdinand followed this up by pushing the French across the Rhine. Finally, Maria Theresa had no alternative but to face the facts: If she could not defeat Frederick II and crush Prussia with the help of such a mighty coalition as had been put together, she could never do it alone. Peace negotiations began at Hubertusburg, not far from Leipzig. As these progressed, Frederick wrote home, comparing himself to a man in a stormy sea who finally catches sight of land: "I rejoice so much at this happy prospect [of peace] that sometimes I doubt its reality." The peace, however, was indeed signed, on February 15, and it confirmed the borders of 1756—that is, it confirmed Prussia's possession of Silesia. It also confirmed Prussia's new position among the great powers of Europe.

Frederick was relieved, but he was too exhausted to rejoice. A month later he returned to Berlin for the first time in years, feeling himself a stranger there at the age of fifty-one. He belonged in an old veterans' home, he said; his digestion was ruined, his hair had turned gray, and he was bent over a cane. None of his old friends was around anymore when he returned to his capital. He avoided the public welcome that had been mounted and returned to the palace in the dead of night. "Madame has grown fatter," were his first words to the queen, who greeted him at the gates.

"I am as gray as a jackass," Frederick II noted on his return from the wars. "Every few days, it seems, I lose another tooth and I am half lame with gout." Yet he had achieved the glory he had sought in his youth; he was famous everywhere. In London, an effigy of the king, dressed in Prussian uniform, had been mounted on an ass and been led through the streets; Londoners lay down their capes in front of it, and vast crowds shouted "Hosanna!" as though Frederick were Jesus entering Jerusalem. In Italy, he was venerated as a saint, and candles were lit before his portrait in shopwindows. In Venice, monks of the Monastery of Ss. Giovanni e Paolo split into two factions, the "Prussians" among them battling the "Austrians" with plates, bowls, and tankards; even here, victory went to the "Prussians." In Sicily, Prussian travelers were showered with baskets of fruit and jugs of wine and greeted, wherever they went, by official deputations wishing to express to them the popular regard felt for the Prussian king. Frederick had been popular before, on his accession to the throne, when he had issued so many enlightened decrees; he was now not only popular in many places, but honored and even feared, having prevailed over enormous odds and having battled successfully against the House of Habsburg, which many hated.

Frederick's army alone guaranteed the survival of his state—that had been proved—and so he immediately decided to maintain it on a permanent wartime footing and at a permanent wartime strength of 150,000 men. The Comte de Mirabeau's comment, made later, was beginning to come true: Other states had their armies, but only the Prussian army had a state of its own. Two-thirds of the national income of Prussia and every sixth man in the kingdom were enlisted; by the time Frederick died, his army was almost as big as that of the French, though France was far bigger and richer.

Frederick disbanded some of the "free battalions" he had

been compelled to form alongside his regular troops during the Seven Years' War, and he also cleansed the officer corps of members of the bourgeoisie;* he did not believe they had a sufficient "sense of honor" to serve in such positions. This, above all, is what Frederick demanded of all his officers. Friedrich von der Marwitz described it as a "renunciation of all personal advantage, of all gain, of all comfort—yes! of all desire if only honour remains! On the other hand, every sacrifice for this, for their King, for their fatherland, for the honour of Prussian weapons! In their hearts, duty and loyalty; for their own lives, no concern!"[90] The bourgeoisie, as Gordon Craig points out in his study of the Prussian army, was "driven by material rather than moral considerations and was too rational, in moments of disaster, to regard sacrifice as either necessary or commendable."[91]

What had saved Prussia, if not the sacrifice of all personal interests, the subordination of the individual to the greater cause, and iron, military discipline? As it became clear that Prussia owed its life to such military virtues, it was assumed that these virtues would make the future great as well. Already under Frederick William I, "ministers of state, like generals and colonels, obeyed unquestioningly and carried out orders with military precision and punctuality . . .";[92] this was extended to the rest of the kingdom under Frederick the Great. The top rungs of the administration were staffed by aristocratic officers; the lower ranks were filled with noncommissioned officers or privates disabled in the wars; the population they helped govern fed the army the produce of its fields and the products of its factories or filled its ranks. Because Frederick II personally made all decisions, the state apparatus became merely an instrument he used, not a force which could influence policy and gain self-reliance; because the bourgeoisie was happy simply if it profited, it never strove for any power at all.

The kingdom was becoming in actual fact a military state, for the army was in a sense not subservient to the government or independent of it; the army, in fact, *was* the government, for not only was the king a soldier first of all, but so were most of his administrators and Junker landowners. As long as this

* By 1806 the officer corps contained only 695 nonnobles (in artillery and support units), although it numbered more than 7,000.[89]

was so, Craig says, "the very prestige of the army made . . . reform impossible." Craig continues:

> It was difficult, for instance, to argue that too much discipline was bad for the civil service or, for that matter, for the Prussian people, when the discipline of Prussian troops in the field had won the admiration even of Prussia's antagonists. It was impossible to hope for any real measure of social reform as long as the unity of the officer corps depended upon the protection of the feudal rights of the noble proprietor or as long as hereditary serfdom remained the basis of the canton system. The army moulded the state to its needs; it was now the principal obstacle to political or social change of any kind.[93]

What also stood in the way was the king's reputation in Prussia. It was so enormous that no one in the kingdom questioned the policy of establishing a military state, except a very few disgruntled intellectuals. Most of these fled Prussia, proclaiming it was nothing but a military dictatorship, but the Prussians who remained were content with things as they were. Everyone, even Goethe, who was not a Prussian, revered Frederick II not only as Alexander, but almost as Solomon. For he not only had saved the kingdom from disaster, but had afterward built it up again, driving himself as mercilessly as he had during the war, motivated always by his stated conviction that the "king is the first servant in the state."

A policy of reconstruction and industrialization was begun after the Seven Years' War ended. Royal agents traveled throughout Prussia and totted up the losses the citizens had suffered; partial compensation was made. Army surplus food and fodder were distributed; farmers received cattle, seed grain, lumber, and, often, cash with which to rebuild their homes and their farms. Once again, as in the past, colonists were invited to immigrate, new towns sprang up, marshes were drained, and lands laid waste by war were restored to wood and agriculture. A new Prussian state bank opened in Berlin with capital supplied by the king himself; a program of state subsidies, coupled with strict regulation of manufacture, was begun in order to stimulate production and exports and to lower the need for imported goods. A royally sponsored porcelain industry was established in Berlin; to help it compete, Meissen china from

Saxony was not merely outlawed in Prussia, but was not even permitted to pass through Prussian territory en route elsewhere. Silks, satins, woolens, and cottons were also aided in much the same way and soon became Prussia's largest exports, giving the state by the time Frederick died a trade surplus of 3,000,000 thalers. Canals were constructed, and state monopolies in tobacco, coffee, and salt were established. Silesia's vast underground deposits were exploited. A Silesian mining department made a major start toward coal mining, ironworking, lead mining, and smelting.

A near famine in the 1770's made reconstruction all the more difficult; huge subsidies, established by the king, required huge taxes. When his ministers had earlier complained they could not find any ways of increasing taxation further, Frederick had sought help from abroad. Two Parisian advisers had suggested he adopt a French method: let indirect taxes be collected by independent contractors or collection agents. A hated institution, the *régie,* was set up, using French tax collectors who were paid four times as much as their Prussian counterparts and who were also given a 5 percent bonus on any tax increases they managed to squeeze out. Thus it became inevitable that the growing prosperity was accompanied by resentment against the harsh measures artificially fostering it. This in turn led to an increase in Frederick II's suspicion of his people and to the establishment of Prussia's first secret state police, also modeled after the French example. *Geheime Vertrauensleute* were infiltrated into the underworld, though Frederick refused to extend these agents' mandate to allow them to spy on all levels of society, as the police chief recommended.

Frederick's distrust pervaded many areas of life. As he grew older, he grew ever more autocratic, ever more inclined to keep out of Prussia the liberal thought emerging in France, the very enlightened thought of which he had been the repository and symbol as crown prince. Rousseau said that Frederick's policies deliberately denied the middle and lower classes any chance at political education; indeed, the king's measures began to cast an icy chill over all thought and action. The middle classes, having been allowed to sacrifice their lives in the officer corps, were thrown out of it; the aristocracy, already strengthened by their stranglehold on the army, had been strengthened even more by being allowed into the civil administration. Frederick gave the poorer members of the nobility employment and salaries and strengthened the control they exerted over their feudal farm laborers, restricting that control only for recruitment purposes in that the peasants were protected at least from barbarous exploitation. In his later years, after the partitioning of Poland, his nobles had even greater lands and more serfs, for Frederick had secured a land bridge from the Mark Brandenburg to East Prussia and had finally won West Prussia in the bargain. Frederician triumph had reached its peak.

The capital, adorned with many new palaces and cultural buildings, showed the new importance of the Hohenzollerns' lands, although Frederick himself continued to prefer his small and charming palace in Potsdam, Sans Souci ("Without Care"), built after the Second Silesian War. Bellevue Palace was opened in Berlin in 1785 on a plot owned by Knobelsdorff, who was by then long dead. There the architect had lived after his relationship with Frederick had deteriorated and after the Forum Fridericianum was built, the original plans spoiled by the king's later interference; the lovely French Baroque château which Prince Ferdinand inhabited on Knobelsdorff's former land later became the starting point of most state processions which the Hohenzollern rulers made down Unter den Linden to their Berlin Palace.

Frederick died a year after Bellevue opened. In his last years he had slipped imperceptibly into legend, a wispy, bent old man inhabiting a frail body, animated only by the fiery spirit that still flashed from those hypnotic eyes. Cranky, querulous, peevish, likely to lash out with his silver-headed cane at any clumsy oaf who displeased him, becoming fussy about food (murderously spiced), puttering about his library still in hope that his writings (rather than feats of arms) would assure him immortality, touring the provinces, chastising officials, he was half myth, half wraith, a chimerical leader who had proved himself the greatest Hohenzollern yet and whom the people regarded as both despot and saint. Those veterans who survived his wars worshiped him and called him "Father"; all others called him *der alte Fritz* ("Old Fritz"), and when he entered Berlin, tried to kiss his garments or even lick his boots.

His very accessibility prompted a great deal of love; he was not remote and lofty, as were the Habsburgs or other kings. The austere simplicity of his dress, his stoic disregard for personal comfort, his ascetic appearance—all captured the hearts of his subjects, incorporating as they did homespun Germanic ideals of hard work, simplicity, and directness of speech and manner within the person of an absolute monarch. Literally hundreds of stories and anecdotes circulated about him, throughout Prussia and all Europe, each calculated to increase public adulation, but each at least partly based on fact. His caustic wit shocked and his sense of justice delighted the people, for both were usually very much to the point. Once, commuting a death sentence imposed on a cavalryman found to have committed sodomy with his horse, Frederick II simply ordered, "Transfer to the infantry!" He was quite unable to restrain his waspish tongue; his mocking remarks about other rulers often provoked diplomatic flurries, for they were, of course, passed on as soon as they had been uttered. Yet he was not without warmth and kindness and was genuinely fond of his nephews and nieces. In his last years, when a niece had addressed a particularly pretty speech to him, he told her, "Many thanks, dear child, for the nice things you say to your old uncle. He does not deserve them. He is a decrepit old chatterbox who must be sent by the shortest road to the Beyond, where he can continue his twaddle. . . ." Another nephew, Prince Louis Ferdinand, also remembered and worshiped Old Fritz as a lovable eccentric. When Louis Ferdinand was seven years old and present at the baptism of his younger brother, he heard Frederick the Great, the godfather, say to him, "Young man, when I held you over that same basin seven years ago, the preacher read such a long sermon that I sent you away before he ever finished. You never got properly baptized as a result. That's a shortcoming I intend to rectify today." Whereupon the old king picked up a bowl of baptismal water and dumped it over the boy, drenching him thoroughly.

He was a kind of Connecticut Yankee in his own court: practical, inventive, clever, and, most important, usually just. He once shook up his government, fired officials, and busied himself for months over a case which concerned a village miller who had a grievance against a local lord. He brooked no injustice from anyone, and he even surrendered his own royal prerogatives to this stern interpretation of the law. The case of another miller, who maintained a windmill in Potsdam, has become legendary, especially because it had actually occurred. This man's windmill, clattering about, disturbed the peace at Sans Souci Palace, and Frederick, wishing to silence it forever, attempted to purchase the miller's lands. The man, however, refused to sell; the mill, he told the king, gave him a good livelihood and ensured him a happy old age. Angry at being opposed, Frederick threatened to seize it forcibly and to tear it down, whereupon the miller answered back, "No, you will not! Not so long as there is a court of appeals in Prussia!" Frederick, who all his life had championed the idea that even the king ought to be subject to the law, surrendered. The mill clattered on as before, and the tale, told thousands of times in hundreds of Prussian villages, encouraged all of the king's subjects to believe they had in their autocratic king a champion against royal despotism. (When Napoleon reached Potsdam to visit Frederick's tomb, he was shown the mill and told the tale; he refused to believe it, saying it was incompatible with regal majesty and the prerogatives of kings.)

Leeching officials were sent to jail, no matter what their rank, and honest men were enlisted to serve the state. One time the king found a letter addressed to one of the pages of his chamber, Christian Ernst von Malschitzki, in which the page's mother thanked him for sending her his savings. The king slipped a roll of gold into the page's pocket; on finding it, the page told the king he had discovered gold which did not belong to him. Impressed with his honesty, Frederick promoted him. He eventually died at seventy-six, in 1835, as a colonel, after service as director of the War Office.

Officials and even servants who were quick at repartee and could give back as sarcastic an answer as they had received from the king were rewarded and often promoted. The case of Frederick's coachman, Pfund, is famous in this respect. The king loved to be driven as fast as the carriage horses could manage, always at full gallop; on one occasion, careening about in this manner, Pfund upset the coach and spilled the king into the roadway. Frederick immediately grasped his cane, ready to strike Pfund for his clumsiness; Pfund disarmed him completely by saying, "What? Has Your Majesty never lost a battle?" On another occasion, Pfund had so annoyed the king that Frederick suspended him from his royal duties and assigned him to cart manure from the stables, in a wagon drawn by mules. On being asked by the king how he liked his new work, Pfund replied, "Manure or Majesty, asses or horses: transport remains transport!" He soon got his old job back again. Frederick never could resist a quipster.

Yet he was not just a somewhat lovable and cranky old uncle. He could also be savage in his treatment of those who incurred his displeasure. During one campaign the hereditary Prince of Brunswick bungled in Bohemia, and Frederick came riding up to him at a full gallop, to shout, "Prince, do you know that you are a stupid fool? Whether you are Serene Highness or not, you are to obey orders!" This tirade continued in front of the prince's entire staff, while His Serene Highness turned white as death. Nor could Frederick resist humiliating people or making jokes at their expense at the table. Contemptuous of organized religion and even of religious belief itself, he offended many by his mocking taunts. On Good Friday one year, old Zieten excused himself from the royal table in order to take communion and spend time in seclusion and meditation; at the next meal, the king asked him, "Well, Zieten, how did the sacrament agree with you? Have you well digested the real body and blood of Christ?" Loud laughter followed, but Zieten rose and made such a courageous speech in defense of his faith that Frederick afterward apologized, saying, "Happy Zieten! I wish I could believe like you. Hold fast to your faith. It shall happen no more." That, of course, was only the end of it for Zieten; Frederick never could resist attacks on superstition, as he called all religious worship. Once, when the façade of a Potsdam church displeased him, he had it so altered as to obstruct the light; when the minister and the congregation protested, Frederick dismissed their complaint by acidly remarking, "Blessed are they who have not seen and yet believe."

Inevitably, the king's contempt for churches and for religion led society under him to adopt freethinking ways and, soon, frivolous manners. Frederick, however, remained interested in the philosophical questions which religion posed; he became a Freemason, and he was interested in astrology and even alchemy for a time, although he did not place faith in them after a while.

He once told a friend that he had thoroughly investigated astrology; "the result," he said, "was that I never found anything but old women's tales and absurdity." He joined the Freemasons in 1738, while still crown prince, and eventually founded the Berlin lodge at Charlottenburg, of which he became grand master; later, however, he left the order after a Freemason who was a general had been found guilty of fraud and treason. He eventually turned completely against it because of its religious content; that "religious sect," he said in 1782, "is still more absurd than the others. . . ." His original membership in it was motivated by his idea that society might be justly governed from secret fraternities which concerned themselves with truth and justice; later he dispensed with the fraternities and governed everything himself, using only his own will, judgment, and silver-headed cane.

Gout and piles afflicted him for years, but severe illness had been spared him. In his final years, however, dropsy and a host of other ailments inflicted themselves on him. He became increasingly morose, melancholy, distrustful, and cranky. He coughed constantly, hardly slept a wink at night, yet still continued every day to rise early and review his troops for hours in all kinds of weather, handle a voluminous correspondence, and oversee every affair of state. One of his last acts, in September, 1785, was to conclude a trade pact with the United States of America, negotiated in The Hague, Benjamin Franklin acting for the new republic. That year also, he formed a League of Princes, again to thwart the ambitions of the Habsburgs.

"Tired of ruling over slaves," the king wrote a few months before he died. He called his people canaille or riffraff, and when someone protested that those who had hailed the king in the streets were surely not riffraff, Frederick replied testily, "Put an old monkey on a horse and send it through the streets and they will do the same." He had contempt for his subjects and kept them low; benevolent despot though he often was, despot he remained. It was he who helped seal the future; he made autocracy popular, even if its measures often were loathed. The stern, ascetic, and absolute ruler who posed as servant of the state became the hero figure to be summoned forth in future years; selfless service to the autocratic state came to be the Prussian ideal, thanks in large part to the example he set, for he provided his subjects with an example of stoic endurance and unflinching devotion to duty to the very end, even when coughing blood and grotesquely swollen with dropsy. No wonder they worshiped him. An example of this is provided by the account of one of his subjects who watched the king enter Berlin on a day in May, 1785, a year before Frederick died. The king, he afterward wrote, was "only a man of seventy-three, ill-dressed and covered with dust, [who] was returning from his laborious day's work. But everyone knew that this old man was working for him, had devoted his whole life to the task and had never yet missed a single day. Round about, near and far, could be seen the fruits of his labor, and so the sight of him inspired reverence, admiration, pride, confidence—in short, all the nobler feelings of man." [94]

This statement sums up Frederick's successes. He had identified the public welfare completely with himself in the public mind; his subjects sincerely believed that this old man had worked for every one of them—despite the evidence to the contrary, despite the fact that Junkers still oppressed their serfs, despite the fact that Frederick regarded them as scum. It went even further: They attributed to him and his efforts the fruits of their own labors, the growing prosperity of their lands. These worshipful sentiments remained enshrined in the Prussian people for generations; enshrined along with them were the military virtues of obedience and iron discipline. In 1859 the German novelist Gustav Freytag described the emotions animating the Germans when they volunteered to fight Napoleon Bonaparte in 1815, more than a generation after Frederick II's death, and it is clear from his description that those blazing Frederician eyes still hypnotized and inspired a whole people:

> Frederick became the hero of the nation. The Germans exalted him even more than Gustavus Adolphus. He ruled the minds of men far beyond the boundaries of his limited dominions. In the distant Alpine valleys, among men speaking another tongue, and holding another faith, he was reverenced as a saint both in pictures and writings. He was a powerful ruler, a genial commander, and what was more valued by the Germans, a great man in the highest of earthly positions. It was his personal appearance and manners which made foreigners and even enemies admire him. He inspired the people again with enthusiasm for

German greatness, zeal for the highest earthly interests, and sympathy in a German state. . . . For the Germans became better, richer, and happier, when they were carried beyond the narrow interests of their private life, and beyond their petty literary quarrels, by the appearance of a great character daringly aspiring to the highest objects, struggling, suffering, persevering, and firm. . . . Under him, the grandsons of those citizens who had passed through the great [Seven Years'] war, began for the first time after a century to feel their own powers. . . . He had bequeathed to them the first beginning of a German State. . . . But in the rooms of the German peasants, the picture of the old king, in his three-cornered hat and small pigtail, did not turn his earnest look in vain on the life he had revived; nor in vain had the mothers of the present generation run to the churches to pray for a blessing on his arms. Now it was that the full blessing of his energetic life truly manifested itself. The spirit of the great man lived again in the German people. Fifty years after the return of the king from the seven years' war, three hundred years after Luther strove earnestly to find his God, the German nation roused itself for the greatest struggle it had ever yet successfully carried on. The fathers now sent out their sons and the wives their husbands to the war; the Germans encountered death with a song on their lips, to seek a body for the German soul, a state for the fatherland.

That Frederick II should inspire such feelings is ironic, for he was never a "German"; he was always a Prussian who, often enough, fought other German states and who, in any event, cared nothing for German unity. But the myth is more important than the man, who was important enough.

During Frederick's lifetime, there were only a few men who recognized the essentially despotic nature of his military, autocratic state. Privy Councilor Heinrich von Schön referred to Prussian officials in later years as being more slavish than "West Indian Negroes" because they *willingly* submitted to despotic commands; Frederick II had heard much the same from a British diplomat who once outraged the king by venturing to state that he'd rather be "a monkey in Borneo" than a subject of the Prussian crown. James Harris, later the first Earl of Malmesbury, assessed Frederick in a letter dated March 18, 1776, and addressed to the Earl of Suffolk:

The basis of his Prussian Majesty's conduct from the time he mounted the throne to this day, seems to have been the considering of mankind in general, and particularly those over whom he was destined to reign, as beings created merely to be subservient to his will, and conducive to the carrying into execution whatever might tend to augment his power and extend his domains. Proceeding on these grounds, he has all along been guided by his own judgment alone, without ever consulting any of his Ministers or Superior Officers; not so much from the low opinion he entertains about their abilities, as from a conviction from his own feelings that if he employed them otherwise than as simple instruments they would, in time, assume a will of their own; and instead of remaining accessories endeavour to become principals.

To persevere in this system it was necessary for him to divest himself of compassion and remorse, and of course of religion and morality. In the room of the first he has substituted superstition; in the place of the latter what is called in France *sentiment,* and from hence we may, in some measure, account for that motley composition of barbarity and humanity which so strongly marks his character. . . .

Thus never losing sight of his object he lays aside all feelings the moment that is concerned; and, although as an individual he often appears and really is humane, benevolent, and friendly, yet the instant he acts in his Royal capacity these attributes forsake him and he carries with him desolation, misery, and persecution wherever he goes. . . . If he has failed in small points, resolution and cunning, employed as the occasion required, and always supported by great abilities, have carried him with success through almost every important undertaking he has attempted. . . . He undoubtedly owes this, in great measure, to his superior talents; yet I think we may find another cause in the character and position of his subjects; in general they are poor, vain, ignorant and destitute of principle; had they been rich, his nobility would never have been brought to serve as subaltern officers with zeal and ardour. Their vanity makes them think they see their own greatness in the greatness of their monarch. Their ignorance stifles in them every notion of liberty and opposition, and their want of principle makes them ready instruments to execute any orders they may receive, without considering whether they are founded on equity or not. . . .

Having said this much it is perhaps less wonderful than it generally appears that such a sovereign, governing such a people, should have raised to so great pitch of glory a country which, from its geographical position, its climate and its soil, seems to have been calculated to act a very secondary part amongst the European powers; and it is not difficult to foresee, on its exchanging masters, that its preponderance will greatly sink. . . .[95] *

Frederick II died on August 18, 1786, two hours and twenty minutes past midnight. His last words had been *"Cela sera bon; la montagne est passée."* He had welcomed death—in French, of course, for that was the only language he spoke, except to lowly soldiers and common subjects, whom he addressed in his wretched German. Had he read James Harris' analysis of his people, he would have agreed with much of it, for he had always despised German art, German literature, the German language —indeed, his people.

His valet prepared the corpse; the king's shirts were so rotted with perspiration that the body had to be dressed in one of the valet's shirts for the burial. The rest of his clothes were so shabby that they were sold to a Jewish peddler as rags. When the king's body was moved through the streets, the crowds were strangely hushed. Mirabeau says they were "silent as the grave . . . none mourned. Not a regret, not a sigh, not a word of praise was to be heard. This, then, was what became of so many battles won, so much fame, a reign of almost half a century so full of so many great deeds. All were longing for it to end; all congratulated themselves that it was over."

In later years a great equestrian statue of Frederick the Great was raised on Unter den Linden. Sculpted by Christian Daniel Rauch, the great man's pose is suitably that of a soldier king. Frederick is seated on a horse, his right hand resting, fingers bent back, on his right hip, elbow jutting out so that his cape falls backward regally over the upper arm. His horse stands with its right leg raised as though to paw the ground, as though eager to be off again. The statue freezes action, like a snapshot in metal, showing a moment's pause in a campaign or at some

* The prediction proved accurate enough. As for James Harris' analysis of Frederick II and his subjects, this cannot be dismissed as the work of one who is completely biased against Prussia. Harris (1746–1820) was minister plenipotentiary at the court of Prussia from 1772 to 1776 and so highly regarded in Prussia that, when he was created Baron Malmesbury of Malmesbury in 1788, the King of Prussia (Frederick II's successor) gave him permission to bear the Prussian eagle on his coat of arms. (He was created earl in 1800.)

martial display; Frederick seems to have stopped to assess the terrain or to watch some soldiers march by. At the base of the statue are clustered secondary, smaller figures of the officers who helped him win his wars; one is struck immediately by their robust and manly air, compared with his. The figure on the horse seems like a mummy swaddled in metal cloth, its head like a shriveled prune beneath a huge tricorne hat. The face, with its tightly drawn skin and pointed nose, reminds one less of Caesar, Alexander, or Napoleon than some dusty Egyptian corpse. Its ferrety features contrast grotesquely with the thick legs and dumpy figure of the king, but they bear that characteristic glance which all the Hohenzollerns after Frederick II tried to ape, that "Fritzian look"—waspish, testy and critical, with enough fire in it for it to be called regal. There is in it something malicious, the signature of that sarcastic, spiteful wit he used so often to humiliate subordinates in their presence or kings behind their backs. The face betrays the personality of the man and not the resources within, those hidden depths from which he called forth his courage and his resolution. One sees the shadow side of this great man: how he preened himself, strutting his bitchy wit and cultivated virtuosity before closed circles of admirers; how he flared up viciously at criticism or opposition; how he snapped at and bickered with almost everyone; how he stung and scratched with puns and flip witticisms; how he seemed so often a poseur, in the elaborately rumpled, stained, even patched clothing he wore in later years; how he seemed forever to be hurrying around his bivouacs and music rooms, salons and battlefields, criticizing, nagging, taunting, quipping, twitting, sniggering. That parchmentlike skin drawn over his face contrasts sharply with the faces of the soldiers at the statue's base, men of flesh, blood, and robust appetites, and one gains the impression that the mummy that reigned in Prussia during these years was a bitchy queen. Still, despite everything, events took such a turn after his death that Prussia and the Prussians could sincerely wish that he were still around.

10

Ruin, Rebirth, and Reaction

THE Prussians may have worshiped Frederick the Great, but living with him throughout such a long, stern reign was a little like living atop a Prussian Olympus; after a while, they became exhausted by the rarefied atmosphere. They had had their fill of duty and wanted a little fun. When Frederick II's nephew acceded to the throne at the age of forty-one, they thought they would obtain it.* He immediately made himself popular by abandoning Frederician austerity and by abolishing some of his uncle's most unpopular measures: the *régie* and the state monopoly on coffee and tobacco. He also created a good first impression by abandoning that arrogant Hohenzollern custom of addressing inferiors in the third person singular, as though the "he" being addressed were not a person at all, but an object.

Frederick William II (as he styled himself) was friendly, polite, and interested in furthering the arts; he could play the violoncello well and took an interest in the theater and music. He was tall and portly (he came to be called Frederick William

* The second surviving son of Frederick William I, Prince Augustus William, had been designated Prince of Prussia (the term for heirs presumptive who were not sons of reigning monarchs), but he died at age thirty-six, almost in disgrace, after his elder brother, Frederick the Great, discharged him from the army for blundering in battle in 1757. His fourteen-year-old son then assumed the title. The course of Prussian history might have been very different, had it been possible for Frederick II to name one of his other brothers—specifically the highly talented Henry—as his successor.

the Fat), but it soon became apparent that he had grave shortcomings. Frederick II had noticed them while he was still alive, for the Prince of Prussia's interest in maintaining mistresses was notorious even then. "Let me tell you how matters will be after my death," Frederick the Great said to one of his confidants a year before he died. "There will be a merry life of it at court. My nephew will squander the treasure and allow the army to degenerate. The women will then govern and the state will go to rack and ruin." [96]

The scenario turned out accurate enough. The citizenry, who had longed for an easygoing monarch, very quickly were disgusted. Five months after Frederick William II acceded to the throne, Mirabeau noted: "The contempt for the new king increases daily; people are already past that feeling of amazement which precedes contempt." At first they had been surprised by the king's inactivity, but soon they were shocked by it. "Now," wrote Mirabeau, "they are . . . astonished if it ever happens that some new folly or some old vice has not taken up a whole day. And yet the mania for governing by himself *without doing anything* could never be carried to a higher degree. For the last two months, the king has never transacted business with any of his ministers."

Mirabeau also wrote that "the new king, instead of raising his subjects to him, descends to them. Frederick William hates nothing, and scarcely loves anything; his only aversions are people of mind and intellect. In the royal household, utter confusion reigns supreme. The management is in the hands of the lower servants . . . funds are assigned for nothing. . . . Everywhere, confusion and waste of time. The servants are afraid of the violence of the king, yet they are the first to rail at his incapacity. No paper is in order, no petition is answered; the king never opens a letter himself, as no human power could induce him to read forty lines at a time. . . ." [97]

Frederick William II reigned for eleven years, but he might be said never to have ruled at all, for the state fell into the hands of cronies who were bent only on enriching themselves. Ironically, the Hohenzollern lands increased enormously during this reign, thanks to the second and the third partitioning of Poland, which extended them to Warsaw and beyond, but these were illusory gains which soon vanished. (Ten years later, Prussia's overinflated balloon lost all its wind; even after Napoleon's collapse, Prussia regained only a fraction of these territories.)

Prussia was governed by a strange riffraff, a motley crew of schemers and whores steering the ship of state. Prime among these was the first Prussian Pompadour, the king's mistress, a trumpeter's daughter named Wilhelmina Encke. The others included her "husband" (in name only), a drunk, a glutton, and a vicious schemer named Rietz, who was the Potsdam palace gardener's son and who now became the king's valet and privy steward, as well as an all-powerful intimate of the king; Johann Christoph von Wöllner, an unscrupulous opportunist and profiteer; General Johann Rudolph von Bischoffswerder, who maintained his hold on the king by means of sex drugs and séances; and Wöllner's bizarre secretary, Mayr, who ended up as a religious maniac.

Frederick William had cultivated his taste for debauchery early and had a reputation as a rake by the time he was twenty. That year he was married to Elizabeth of Brunswick-Wolfenbüttel, also twenty, a lovely girl from a distinguished family, who soon found out about his mistresses. "The princess," wrote one contemporary, "thought she had grounds of complaint against her husband. Unfortunately, she was too proud not to feel the slight, and of too warm a temper not to revenge herself. . . ." She disdained to conceal the infidelities she herself now embarked upon and after four years of marriage was divorced by her husband, then still the heir presumptive.* He then married Princess Frederica of Hesse-Darmstadt. By his first wife, he had had one child, a daughter; his second wife bore him seven children, the first being a son and successor.

Neither wife, however, ever enchanted him as did Wilhelmina Encke, whom he had met when she was just fourteen and whom he had educated at his expense. Her older sister was an accomplished courtesan, and she taught Wilhelmina the arts of love so well that when Wilhelmina's education was finished, Frederick William spent 30,000 thalers a year on the girl, though

* A small pension was granted her, and she was ordered to spend the rest of her life in Küstrin; she reportedly tried to escape to Venice on one occasion, but the attempt failed. She died at Stettin in 1840, at the age of ninety-four.

he was still only heir presumptive and did not have large sums at his disposal. (The British ambassador reported he owed 300,000 thalers and couldn't even pay his washerwoman.)

So great was Wilhelmina's influence on the then Prince of Prussia that his uncle, Frederick the Great, had to issue orders that his agencies were "no more to heed the recommendations of a certain high personage with regard to appointments"; he even arranged for Wilhelmina to be married to Rietz, in the hope this would estrange her from his nephew. The uncle couldn't have picked a worse character. No sooner was Frederick II dead and his nephew on the throne than Rietz moved into power. He was made privy steward and was even placed in charge of the palace household treasures, a case of putting the fox in charge of the hen house if ever there was one. He endured the new king's cuffs, kicks, and blows patiently, for Frederick William II was as "choleric" as so many other Hohenzollerns; Rietz passed the kicks on down the ladder with interest. "The happiness of Rietz," wrote one who knew him, "consisted in eating and drinking, in the gratification of his insatiable vanity, and in the hoarding of capital for his old age."

As soon as Frederick William II was on the throne, splendid and palatial homes were established for Wilhelmina and for her sister. Wilhelmina's two brothers were made equerry to the king and chief ranger, respectively, and even Rietz's brother got an influential job as the king's *valet de chambre* and secretary. More was soon to come to all of them, in bountiful measure.

Wilhelmina, however, had to face an unpleasant fact at this time: She was thirty-four, had been Frederick William's mistress for almost twenty years, and his eyes were straying. She promptly made herself invaluable to him by procuring for him three new mistresses: a laundrymaid, an actress, and a ballerina. But others who were Wilhelmina's enemies were at work on the king's appetites as well and arranged two bigamous, morganatic marriages in succession, first with Julia von Voss (who became Countess Ingenheim) and then, on her death, with a Countess Sophia Dönhoff. The queen approved of these marriages, hoping they would finish Wilhelmina off; the court pastors approved them, having found a precedent in Martin

Luther's approval of the bigamous marriage which Philip of Hesse had contracted.

An early enemy of Wilhelmina was Bischoffswerder, the king's old crony, who maintained his power over Frederick William by catering to his superstitions and sexual appetites. (When Frederick William was still Prince of Prussia, Bischoffswerder had even staged a séance in which the shades of Leibnitz, Marcus Aurelius, and the Great Elector urged the prince to rid himself of Wilhelmina; the experience, which frightened the prince half to death, ended by sending him into Wilhelmina's arms for comfort.) Bischoffswerder—and Wöllner—introduced Frederick William into the Freemasons, the Rosicrucians, and into a secret order called the Illuminati; they also introduced him to an Italian sexual stimulant called Diavolini which flogged his jaded appetites. "You will die a beggar," Bischoffswerder's wife warned her husband, "unless you make use of the last days of the king to do something for your family." Bischoffswerder succeeded so well that Colonel Christian von Massenbach noted in his memoirs that he had "leaped on Frederick's throne . . . [and become] at last King of Prussia."

Everyone else did well, too, as Frederician austerity was abandoned. The highest decoration Prussia bestowed, the *Pour le mérite,* had gone to only seventy men during Frederick the Great's long reign; under Frederick William II, every favorite seemed to get it, along with lands, palaces, mansions, pensions, and new titles. To the horror of the old, hereditary, noble families, about sixty commoners were ennobled, twenty-three of them raised to counts. One observer said that Rietz sold such patents of nobility (along with decorations) and added, "Many a Prussian nobleman whose sons now boast of the glory of their ancestors, has been ennobled, not by the king, but by the valet." [98]

While Bischoffswerder ran Prussian foreign affairs, domestic matters were controlled by Wöllner, a former pastor who had distinguished himself early in his career by running off with the daughter of his patron, whose son he was tutoring. Frederick William ennobled him and put him in charge of Prussian finances and royal buildings. As a sideline, Wöllner collected those of Frederick the Great's confidential letters and verses which were attacks on individuals and religion and printed them to blacken the dead king's name. As minister of state and head of the Department of Clerical Affairs, Wöllner reversed every enlightened decree Frederick II had ever issued in this field. However much of an autocratic state Prussia was, it was also unique in Europe in the matter of religious freedom, which was guaranteed to all. This was abandoned. Wöllner decreed a strict orthodoxy and led the court—frivolous and dissolute as it was—into a fervent fundamentalism. Those who deviated were punished harshly; this example led Wöllner to increase the severity of all punishments, for whatever offenses had been committed. Entire communities, including children and the aged, were made to run the gauntlet—an old Prussian (and Iroquois) punishment in which victims ran repeatedly between two rows of soldiers who beat them with birch rods all along the way. Flogging of peasants had been forbidden by Frederick the Great (and even by his brutal father); under the genial and fun-loving Frederick William II, all Prussia became subject to it once again.

Mayr, Wöllner's bald, cadaverous, stooped secretary, was another baleful and bizarre influence at court. An active Rosicrucian, he took part in many occult ceremonies and walked about the palace in strange occultist costumes. Obsessed with religion, he once tried to achieve a vision by swallowing most of a Bible; he ended up with a high fever rather than higher consciousness as a result of this experiment. Soon he developed even more acute symptoms of religious mania. Preaching from a pulpit on one occasion, he fired two pistols into the congregation, shouting, "I shall for once awaken you!" Instead, he ended up wounding one of the worshipers. Shortly afterward he was chained up in an insane asylum, after which he recovered enough to be made a pastor in Königsberg, East Prussia.

Bischoffswerder married Frederick William II's Prussia to the Austrians, which meant against Revolutionary France. (Sentiment in Prussia was largely favorable to France, but this as usual meant little.) When the French declared war against Austria in April, 1792, 45,000 Prussian troops joined 56,000 Austrians to smash "those lawyers in Paris," as the court called the revolutionaries. The aged Duke of Brunswick was placed in charge of the combined force, and the King of Prussia set out for the Rhine to join the expedition. Countess Dönhoff, then the king's morganatic wife, wrote her husband: "I shall entirely give you up if you thus heedlessly enter upon so difficult and arduous an undertaking. Unless you march at the head of 200,000 Prussians and 250,000 Austrians, you may renounce every hope of victory. With a handful of people, you will only risk your life and compromise your honor. You will be driven back from the frontiers. Your chivalrous whim makes you a Don Quixote. . . ."

She proved to be a better military analyst than his foreign minister, Bischoffswerder, who advised Colonel von Massenbach not to buy too many horses, since "the comedy cannot last long and we shall be home again in autumn."

At the instigation of aristocratic French refugees, who crowded the Austro-Prussian field headquarters, the Duke of Brunswick on July 25 issued an unfortunate memorandum which was published in Paris and which he regretted ever afterward. It threatened punitive action against the rebels and warned that Paris would be leveled to the ground in the event of resistance. Far from terrifying the revolutionaries, it mobilized them in an effort to ward off the coalition armies. These entered France on August 19, 1792, the Prussians led by the King of Prussia, by his cousin, the nineteen-year-old Prince Louis Ferdinand, and by Bischoffswerder. The entire force entering France under the Duke of Brunswick consisted of 42,000 Prussians, 29,000 Austrians, and between 4,000 and 5,000 French *émigré* soldiers. They were in a dreamworld, basking in the glories of Frederick the Great, when they no longer had him around. After capturing Verdun on August 20, they encountered resistance a month later at Valmy, a small village on the road to the Paris they meant to conquer. There they were defeated —that is to say, they retreated from the field of battle, in perfect Prussian marching order of course. A murderous cannonade continued until nightfall, 40,000 rounds being fired by both sides, but only about 200 casualties were inflicted on either set of combatants.

That evening the Prussian officers debated how they could

have lost this engagement against a rabble which was only their equal in strength.* Some blamed the artillery, some the mud; others said they had lost because they had not attacked. In fact, the Prussian army lost because they didn't press the attack with resolution, not having much resolution left. They had an army, but no generals with boldness; they had a science of warfare, but it was half a century old. Facing them was something completely new. The threats against Paris had led thousands of Frenchmen to volunteer. A wave of patriotic and revolutionary fervor had erupted; volunteer battalions formed everywhere. When these faced the disciplined but lackluster Prussians, their spirit caused the Prussians to falter and retreat. Despair and confusion, a sense of having been humiliated, swept through the Prussian camp. Unable to understand what had happened, Prussian officers sat about glumly, asking the opinion of their friends. One whom they questioned that evening was the aide to the Duke of Weimar, the poet Goethe.

"The greatest dismay spread throughout the army," Goethe reported later. "As late as that morning, one had thought nothing of spitting all those Frenchmen and devouring them; indeed, I myself had been lured into this dangerous expedition only out of complete trust in such an army and in the Duke of Brunswick; now, however, everyone walked about dejectedly, one avoiding the eyes of others, or if one met, it was but to curse or hurl imprecations. As night fell . . . I was called upon and asked what I thought of this, for I had so often been able to cheer and refresh the troops with a few brief remarks; this time, I told them: 'This place and day marks the beginning of a new era in world history—and you will be able to say that you were there!' "[99]

Goethe had been right. On the next day the National Convention in Paris abolished the monarchy and proclaimed a republic; four months later Louis XVI was executed.

The Prussian army began its retreat a few days after Valmy, recrossing the French border on October 23. Utterly dispirited, without supplies, half-starved, drinking muddy water, and with half their number shoeless, they by then sought only to save themselves.

* Thirty-four thousand Prussians were pitted against 52,000 Frenchmen, but only 36,000 of the latter actually took the field against the Prussian attackers.

Frederick William II did better; he spent a dissolute and gay year in Frankfurt-am-Main. The Frankfurters, who came to call him "our dear fat William," profited from his generosity. He had his court with him, including Wilhelmina and her quasi-husband, the valet and privy steward. At that time Goethe even encountered this Rietz in a tavern. Rietz, who was very fat, noted that Goethe was very tall and robust, whereupon he told the poet, "People always imagine that men of genius must be of small and sickly frame; now here are *two* living examples proving the contrary."

In 1793, a second campaign brought a minor success to the Prussians. They recaptured Mainz, which the French had taken the year before. Again, they failed to press on; instead, they spent two months doing nothing, while their diplomats succeeded at least in partitioning Poland. When Massenbach urged Frederick William to press on against Revolutionary France, the king demonstrated again where the interests of Prussia and the Hohenzollerns lay. "We have got what we wanted," he said. "We have got part of Poland." Thereupon he returned to Berlin, and although a third French campaign followed in 1794, Prussia hardly participated at all, having no money left. The Peace of Basel, which concluded these wars, moved the French border to the banks of the Rhine, with fateful consequences, for Prussia was now wedged between two potential enemies: France and Russia.

Shortly after Frederick William II returned to his Potsdam palace, he ended his relationship with Countess Dönhoff. (Their son, the Count of Brandenburg, later became prime minister of Prussia.) Now that both morganatic marriages had ended, Wilhelmina Rietz, *née* Encke, assumed full charge of the king again. Indeed, her power had been great throughout the campaign against France, and she had played as large a part in involving Prussia in this venture as Bischoffswerder, perhaps even more; now that the king had come home, her influence reached new peaks. So sure did she feel about her situation that she left Prussia for a year's tour of Italy. Her health required it, she told the king; indeed, she spent the trip in beds, from one end of the Italian boot to the other. Young and old, noblemen swooned over her; even the Italian courts fawned upon her as though she were a queen. Only the Queen of Naples refused to do so. It was Wilhelmina's position, not her profession, which bothered Queen Caroline· she would have been happy to receive the courtesan, if she were only not a commoner. Hurt, Wilhelmina wrote her king about the awkward situation: doubly awkward, since the king had titled Wilhelmina's daughter a countess, while she herself was still just Madame Rietz. The king's heart was touched. He had her divorced from Rietz (despite the fact that the marriage had never legally taken place) and then sent his equerry, Wilhelmina's brother, to Venice with the patent of nobility. There the trumpeter's daughter became the Countess Lichtenau and was given a coat of arms bearing the Prussian eagle and the Prussian crown.

Hearing that her lover had taken ill, Countess Lichtenau raced back to Potsdam to nurse him—and to bask in her new glory. She had a theater built into her house and forced the entire court, even the queen, to attend. She received three estates from the king, various annual maintenances, and, finally, a gift of 500,000 thalers in Dutch bank shares which the king transferred to her name. He once even offered to buy her the entire county of Pyrmont, a sovereign state; she refused this gift, fearing "vertigo" at "the summit," as she said. Another offer which she turned down, out of loyalty to him in his last illness, was a gift of 2,000,000 thalers in British bank notes, so that she could ultimately settle in Britain; to her credit, she refused to leave his side until he had breathed his last.

Death approached in late 1797. Berlin came to be jammed with quacks, magnetizers, occultist doctors, as well as physicians, each attempting to save the king. It was urged that the king (who suffered from heart disease) inhale the exhalations of newborn calves; others urged him to breathe the "pure exhalations" of two children, between eight and ten years of age, between whom he was supposed to sleep each night; it was also suggested that wind instruments be constantly played at him, but that under no circumstances was he to hear the sound of violins.

None of these prescriptions helped. On November 12, at dinner, the sound of a champagne bottle cork popping startled him into a faint; three days later, he said his farewells to his queen and to the crown prince. While addressing them, he was held upright in the arms of Countess Lichtenau; suddenly, overcome with sentiment, the queen embraced her husband's mistress, kissed her, and thanked her for the way she nursed him selflessly during his last illness, but the crown prince watched with hatred and contempt.

Countess Lichtenau was not by the king's side when he died at nine in the morning of November 16; the strain had begun to show on her, and she was ordered to bed by the king's physician. Only Rietz and two servants were there. One of them, watching his monarch suffer, remarked out loud, "Isn't he through yet? Doesn't he ever want to croak?" The king, who heard it, despaired; he turned to another servant and begged him not to abandon him at this time. That plea was his final statement.

The first thing the new king did was order the arrest of Countess Lichtenau. Then he was asked what name he would choose. He picked the name of his father, whom he hated, saying that "Frederick is unattainable for me."

Frederick William III never forgot two conversations he had had with his great-uncle, Frederick the Great, although the lessons did not sink in too well. The first encounter he remembered occurred when he was still a toddler, playing with a ball. This had landed on his great-uncle's desk, and Frederick II had confiscated it from him. The old man was amused to note with how much resolution the child demanded it back. He returned it, and as he did, he quietly and firmly said to the boy, "You will *not* allow Silesia to be taken from you."

The second encounter had taken place when the boy was in his teens, shortly before Frederick the Great's death. He told him that he must always be "sincere and honest and never try to appear what you are not, but always be more than you appear." Dismissing him later, the old man added: "Well, Fritz, try to be a sterling character, *par excellence*. Great things await you. I am at the end of my career, and my day's work will soon be accomplished. I am afraid that things will, after my death, go on pêle-méle [*sic*]. There are elements of ferment everywhere. . . . The masses are already beginning to make a move, and, if this comes to a head, it will be the devil let loose. I am afraid you will some time be in a very perilous and difficult position. Well, then, prepare yourself; think of me; watch over our honor and our glory; commit no injustice, nor submit to any. . . . The supporting foundation is the people in its unity. Stand by it faithfully, that it may love you and confide in you; thus only can you be strong and happy." [100]

Frederick William III later claimed that the advice "made an imperishable impression upon me, and dissimulation and lies have ever been hateful to me";[101] this is true enough, for Frederick William III was a good and gentle ruler who could not bear to inflict pain, a virtuous husband who never once dallied even while Berlin society became more licentious than ever, and a good father. But that is all that can be said of him. Great things did indeed await him; but he waited as they passed him by. He was indeed cast into a perilous position: He could not save himself or his nation but had to be pulled out of it against his will. He did watch over Prussia's honor and glory, but watch is all he did; since he failed to act, the honor and the glory died for a time, to be redeemed by others. As for the people in their unity, he failed utterly to stand by them faithfully, as his great-uncle had urged; they came to be united under him, but that merely frightened and bewildered this king. Ultimately, he betrayed the aspirations of the very subjects who had rescued him in his extremity.

It had been the same old Hohenzollern story of the neglected prince shunted aside to brood and grow melancholy in the shade. His dissolute father vastly preferred his mistresses' children to his queen's; he was kind enough to the prince when near him, but this proved rare indeed. Even his mother ignored him for long periods. Constantly closeted with loan sharks, to help meet the palace bills (the king having squandered the treasure), she had little time for "Fritz" and left him with his governor, an ulcerous misanthrope named Benisch who suffered interminably from stomach pains and could not bear the sight or sound of children.

The prince grew up shy and without self-confidence. He was more than modest: He was resigned. There was no arrogance in him, but there was also no strength; there was no envy, but also no ambition; there was no frivolity, but also no joy. There was just passivity. "It was indescribably hard for him to form a resolution," says the Prussian historian Heinrich von Treitschke.

"He delayed, reflected, allowed things to slip, was long-suffering of what he disliked because he had not sufficient confidence in his judgment." Just before his father died, he assured an official, "I shall fulfill my duty," but he never developed a clear idea of what that might be. Of only one thing he was certain: He wanted to reverse the dissolute tendencies in society; he wanted to be virtuous. So much did things change after his accession that: "From being a cesspool of vice, Berlin became like a dull copy of Miss Twinkleton's academy."[102] This, however, held true only for King Frederick William III and his queen; they were lilies of purity floating on scum.

When Frederick the Great died, his grandnephew became crown prince at the age of seventeen. He created enough of a good impression to cause Mirabeau to exclaim, "This man may have a great future before him," and he created an even better impression on becoming betrothed to Louisa of Mecklenburg-Strelitz, a princess destitute of money but rich in everything else: intelligence, spirit, compassion, virtue, and beauty.

Louisa's father was so poor that he earned his living as a British general; since he could not afford to bring her up in elegant court society, the princess cultivated a knowledge of German, not only of French. This later led her to become a champion of German national identity, more than her husband ever was. She came to be loved in Prussia as no princess before her was ever loved. An incident which occurred the year after she had become Queen of Prussia made her famous. Louisa had been introduced to countless titled ladies at a ball in Magdeburg and asked each their name and family particulars; then she happened to be introduced to an officer's wife whose father had been a merchant and no aristocrat at all. "Let me hear about your family—your birth," Louisa asked. The merchant's daughter flushed and stammered out in confusion, "Oh, Your Majesty, I am a nobody—of no birth at all!" (In German, it sounded worse yet, as though she had said, "not born at all.") This reply evoked malicious smiles and snickers among the nobles standing about, but Queen Louisa said very gently—in a voice everyone could hear—that insofar as *she* was concerned, "all of us, without exception, are equal." Then she thanked the woman for having given her an opportunity to express herself on this matter, that "outward show and worldly advantage" might be inherited, but that only a person's character was of any importance whatever. This little speech made her more than famous; it was felt she had proclaimed a new gospel of liberty—as indeed she had, for Prussia.

The marriage made her all the more popular; it seemed that this love match, graced as it was with an uncommon amount of domestic tranquillity, was an example for every one of her subjects. Although the king was not at first fond of the theater, the arts, or festivities, Louisa more than made up for his somewhat priggish nature, always with complete propriety and without a breath of scandal. So much were the new king and queen admired in these first years that everyone copied their taste in literature (novels of an ostentatiously noble and romantic sort) and their dress. (The king had abandoned knee breeches for "American pantaloons" and boots.)

Not quite everyone was in love with Queen Louisa; the military party at court disliked her popularity, the fact that she seemed to eclipse the king completely, and the influence she was suspected of exerting on him. Frederick William III was as frugal and plain-living as his father had been profligate and dissolute. He announced he would live "on the revenues of the crown prince" and, indeed, remained with his queen in Berlin's crown prince's palace, to cut costs. He was devout, preferred prayer meetings with his servants to his queen's balls and fetes, and although she apparently tried to enliven him, her efforts merely increased his melancholia. He found his adjutant, a man named Köckeritz, better company than most; this man was described by the Duke of Brunswick as having a head like a "scooped-out pumpkin, without a light inside." Köckeritz was loyal to the king in his fashion: he betrayed him only over dinner or wine, and then unintentionally. He was consulted in military matters because he was an officer, although he was generally believed to be "entirely destitute of any military talent." Since the king was irresolute, he left the ministers to shift for themselves; they, however, were in many cases his father's men, meaning they were mediocre or worse. Bischoffswerder, it is true, was retired, but three bunglers and schemers were retained: Count Christian von Haugwitz, the architect of Prussia's vacillating foreign policy; Cabinet Councilor Johann Lombard, a notoriously dissolute, though intelligent, man who was the gray eminence behind Haugwitz and who delayed Prussian mobilization against Napoleon until it was far too late; and, finally, the Marchese Girolamo Lucchesini who served as Prussian ambassador in Vienna and in Paris (where he alienated Napoleon, who came to despise him and therefore the court he represented).

Frederick William III had also inherited a dispirited and increasingly undisciplined army, a ruined treasury, and a demoralized society. In just twelve years his father had brought Prussian society to such a low state of personal morals that the public welfare was completely neglected in favor of private pleasure. Young officers who were invited to Frederick William III's court no longer behaved as restrained gentlemen: it was said that they ransacked the buffets and tables as though they were pillaging a town. The very probity of Frederick William III's personal life increased the immorality all around him; people complained that his court was the dullest in Europe and tried to make up for the deficiency. Privy Councilor von Cölln noted that "the debauched rakes in Berlin rail at the sober steadiness of the king; they are prying everywhere, in the hope of finding out some irregularity or some secret love intrigue of the king or of the queen; and they are dying with malice at not being able to find a flaw in this mirror of virtue. Frederick William's great popularity is an eyesore to them: in their opinion, he ought to surround himself with pomp and state, and keep a brilliant court, with plenty of jobs, intrigue, and scandal."

The rakes in question were predominantly Prussian officers, debauching themselves when they ought to have been preparing to defend the nation against the Napoleonic holocaust. "Their wives," says Cölln, "they treat as common property, which they sell and barter. . . ." Aristocratic ladies played at being procuresses, corrupting girls from the land and staging orgies; things had come to such a pass, says Cölln, that the honest burghers, still "exceedingly respectable," could not, try as they might, find girls to marry "whose honor and innocence have not been corrupted, or at least attempted, by those rank profligates." Officers who had been cashiered for incompetence, even for cowardice, were reinstated, thanks either to family influence or the kindness of the king; a decree exempted bureaucrats who earned less than a stipulated sum from paying their debts. Unlike the burghers, the peasantry had become as corrupted as the nobility, heeding neither clergy nor the law. "All the bonds which fettered the people are loosened," Von Cölln noted with horror; he was dismayed that such a "gentle, good-natured, kind" king ruled over "such abandoned wretches." They needed a tyrant, he said. This opinion was even shared by Baron Heinrich Friedrich Karl vom und zum Stein, a civil servant soon to emerge as a major reformer. "Despotic governments," he said, "destroy their peoples' character by denying them participation in public affairs and by entrusting such affairs entirely to an army of professional, intriguing bureaucrats." He said he loved Frederick William for his benevolence but said the king was not the man for such "an iron age." Writing after Napoleon had swept Prussia to destruction, Stein bemoaned the lack of a brilliant Prussian leader who "crushes and tramples underfoot everything, to raise a throne on corpses." [103]

Frederick William III, however, was not the man for this. He had a horror of physical pain and of inflicting it; indeed, he could not even hurt someone's feelings, though his own were brutally used. Prussia, which now had 10,000,000 inhabitants and an army of 250,000 soldiers, could have led the resistance to Napoleon; those soldiers might have been more than a match for the Grande Armée, had Frederick the Great been leading them—or even just a few competent generals. Instead, the king pursued a policy of strict neutrality. Ever since 1793 France had added to her territory, mainly by annexing German lands; as it did so, Napoleon let Prussia share a little in the feast, thus corrupting its policies. An uneasy peace and a false sense of security resulted. The Prussian generals, many of them almost senile veterans of Frederick the Great's wars, summed up their delusions when they later told Queen Louisa, "What if Napoleon has whipped the Austrians, the Russians, the Italians, and the Dutch? What are those compared to the battalions of Frederick?" [104] It was enough to make Frederick II turn over in his grave at Potsdam.

Prussia, the strongest German state, was rudderless and vacillating. It sought neutrality by riding the tiger; this led it to be incapable of influencing events. It had "a king of threads and patches, unable to resolve on a definite course of action and to hold it; unable even to know his mind for two weeks together. . . ."[105] The great Prussian sculptor Johann Gottfried Schadow, whose works had been commissioned by Frederick William II and his son and who knew both of them well, told the writer Karl August Varnhagen von Ense his view of Frederick William III. "Basically," said Schadow, "he was not a pleasant ruler. The queen had to endure a great deal—and in this showed best her loving nature. He was always dry, shy and unbearably dull, and particularly indecisive—*ach,* how that man was indecisive! There was not the smallest thing which did not cause him doubts, which he would not have liked to shove aside and postpone as long as possible; he had to be crowded and pushed to take any action at all, and still he searched for a way out, until the very last moment. . . ."[106]

Two years before he defeated Prussia, Napoleon Bonaparte destroyed North German neutrality by seizing Hanover, but even this move, next door to Prussia, could not rouse the king to action. Prussia was hypnotized by the hissing viper; it seemed in a trance, bewitched or perhaps accursed. In fact, it was stagnating, a prisoner of the state machine built by Frederick the Great, the apparatus of autocracy. But no one supervised the machine to control it, so it served itself and its own interests alone. Its bureaucrats were now either corrupt or powerless, being left to their own devices; since no one governed, the state was merely administered. Superficially, the machine seemed in good order, good enough to deceive the king; in fact, it was corroded and ready to disintegrate.

Summoned to Berlin in 1805, Baron vom Stein found the city in a chaotic condition. Only a few seemed to sense what was brewing; these patriotic voices were dubbed the war party, however, and were drowned out by the chorus of appeasers and neutralists in court. When Russia joined Austria to fight the French, that was the signal for the king to act by mobilizing his army; mobilize he did, but he faced the army to the East, against the czar. A short while later, when Napoleon seized the Hohenzollern duchies of Ansbach and Bayreuth, the king swung about again; now he prepared to be resolute. Haugwitz was dispatched to hand Bonaparte an ultimatum; Bonaparte asked Haugwitz to wait because he was busy. Then Bonaparte turned to face the

Austrians and Russians at Austerlitz, defeating them in his greatest victory yet, after which he said he had time for Haugwitz. Predictably, that Prussian minister and his ultimatum had vanished, as though in the smoke of Austerlitz—and with him, all pretensions about Prussian power. Instead of an ultimatum, the Prussians had disaster on their hands. Napoleon ordered them to demobilize, and demobilize they did. Then they signed a pact with Bonaparte which, they hoped, would guarantee their safety; it guaranteed them just a few more months of dances and delusions.

The war party in Berlin was horrified. This included not only Stein and a few resolute generals like Gerhard von Scharnhorst, but the scholar Alexander von Humboldt and even a Hohenzollern, the thirty-three-year-old cousin of the king, Prince Louis Ferdinand. Meeting either in Louis Ferdinand's home or in the home of his brother-in-law, Prince Anton Radziwill, they planned (plotted, really) what might be done.* Stein had a list of reforms ready, which might have rallied the people by giving them a voice, however small, in the affairs of state, while Scharnhorst had a list of military reforms which might have modernized that ancient and lumbering instrument in which nothing had changed for fifty years. These proposals were offered twice, in different forms; they were heeded not even once. The signers were reprimanded for proposing to counsel the king; they were told they were impertinent.

Finally, in September, 1806, Frederick William prepared to make a stand, but the prospect just amused Napoleon. "The idea that Prussia will venture to attack me single-handed," he wrote Charles Maurice de Talleyrand on the twelfth, "is so ridiculous that it deserves no notice. My alliance with Prussia is based upon her fear of me. That cabinet is so contemptible, the King so devoid of character. . . ." [107]

Prince Louis Ferdinand left for the front as the Prussian

* Louis Ferdinand had also been a cousin to King Frederick William II, since he was the son of Augustus Ferdinand, the youngest brother of Frederick the Great. Radziwill, scion of an aristocratic Polish family in Berlin, was married to Louis Ferdinand's sister, Prince Louisa. (Radziwill's title in Prussia was Fürst, not Prinz, since only the sons and daughters of monarchs were "princes"; outside Germany, however, the titles were interchangeable, and any Fürst called himself Prince once he crossed the borders, just as everyone in later years who had a "von" to his name and thus was aristocratic, used the title of baron when he left Germany, whether in fact he was a German baron or not.)

armies began to move; as he suspected, he was riding to his death in battle. The king, still annoyed at that impertinent memorandum, made a point of not saying farewell to him. Shortly after the prince arrived at field headquarters, he wrote his friend, Massenbach, "We have no ruling system left, nor any government at all!" [108]

On the nineteenth, Queen Louisa accompanied her cuirassier regiment as far the Brandenburg Gate. The fact that she did so, wearing the regimental uniform, struck the citizenry as ominous. Even more ominous was the sight of both the king and the queen leaving the city late the next day—fleeing Berlin, it was supposed, though in fact they were heading for the front. "The Queen of Prussia is with the army," said a Napoleonic bulletin issued on October 8, "dressed as an Amazon, and wearing the uniform of her dragoon regiment. She writes twenty letters a day to fan the flames in all directions. . . ." [109] The French identified her as a leader of the war party (although in fact she had discouraged Stein, Scharnhorst, and the other reformers, saying the king would never heed their demands, this despite the fact that she sympathized with them). French cartoons showed her as an "unsexed Amazon" and as a camp follower wearing a hussar's jacket open to expose her breasts.[110]

Once more, the king placed his entire trust in the Duke of Brunswick, who was appointed Prussian commander. This veteran of many a glorious battle in the dim and forgotten past was just as confident about his army. On the eve of the Battle of Jena, the Duke of Brunswick told Prussian officers that theirs was, "in spite of all that has happened of late and even without improvements, unquestionably the first army of the world." [111]

The facts, however, did not correspond with that statement. While Napoleon and most of his marshals were between thirty-five and thirty-seven years of age, the Prussian officer corps creaked with old age and fossilized ideas. Two-thirds "were either nearing the biblical age [seventy] or had long since passed it," a military historian notes. Field Marshal Wichard von Möllendorf, one of the field commanders facing Napoleon, was past eighty; the Duke of Brunswick, who was past seventy, was unable to sit his horse. Of regimental and battalion commanders, one-fourth were past sixty and unable to meet the physical exertions of battle as it was fought then; company and squadron commanders were not much younger. Out of 66 colonels of line infantry, 28 were over sixty; of 281 majors, 86 were over fifty-five and 190 others more than fifty.[112] The Napoleonic soldiers were well fed and well clothed, while the Prussians were hungry and cold. For twelve months preceding the Battle of Jena, Prussian soldiers had neither overcoats nor waistcoats; sham waistcoat pockets were stitched onto their jackets instead. Their tight breeches burst when any violent movement was made and their shoes constantly stuck in the mud. Their hats and their pigtails were Frederician, the latter making no sense and the former affording no protection against the weather.

Napoleon left Paris six days after Frederick William III and Queen Louisa had left Berlin. He reached the Rhine in two days and then gave his troops nine days to cover the twelve-day march from Bonn to Würzburg; they accomplished it in eight. On October 13, Napoleon reached Jena, expecting to find the area bristling with Prussian cannon. To his amazement, it was undefended. The Prussian king was only twelve miles away, at Auerstädt, but he was completely unaware that Napoleon's armies were in the area, for he had not bothered to send out scouts. For one thing, the Prussian generals didn't know the region, not having any maps (though these were on sale at Schropp's map shop in Berlin); the only map of the area his generals owned dated to 1763 and failed to cover much essential terrain. It goes without saying that Napoleon was well equipped with accurate topographical maps of the region. (Later his officers were Schropp's best customers.)

While Napoleon seized, manned, and fortified every strategic position around the Prussians, virtually cutting off their retreat to Berlin, King Frederick William III and his generals spent the evening talking. The pass at Kösen was undefended; one Prussian general, Schmettau, knew it but went to bed, deciding it could wait until the morning, by which time it had been seized by the French. The Duke of Brunswick also went to bed; he had already slept through most of the meeting with his king and fellow officers, late hours being tiring to old gentlemen. Prince Friedrich Ludwig von Hohenlohe, the field commander at Jena, also went to bed; so did the king. Gebhard Leberecht von Blücher, one of Prussia's few wide-awake generals, arrived during the night with an urgent message for him, but was told it would have to wait until morning, as the king had left orders not to be disturbed.

Napoleon, Marshal Louis Nicholas Davout, their officers, and their men stayed awake, however; they spent the night capturing one undefended position after another, until they had the Prussians almost completely surrounded. The Prussian soldiers slept until Napoleon awakened them with cannon.

Four days earlier and some miles west of Jena, Prince Louis Ferdinand of Hohenzollern was killed. On October 9 he had spent the evening at Rudolstadt Castle; there, like so many other Hohenzollerns on the eves of their deaths, he had seen the "White Lady." The next day he and his men confronted elements of Marshal Jean Lannes' corps; the prince was killed by a French sergeant named Guindey and left among the dead. In the confusion of the thousands of milling soldiers, the French lost sight of him. The next day his body was found. The stark naked corpse, half-buried in the ground, had been plundered. Napoleon paid tribute to the prince for dying "as all good soldiers would like to die." Louis Ferdinand's father, on the other hand, shrugged off his son's death with the remark that he had helped bring the war about and had therefore decided his own fate. His mother only fussed protectively over her younger son, the one she preferred. The only member of the House of Hohenzollern who mourned this prince was his sister Louisa.[113]

Hermann von Boyen, Prussian general and war minister, remarked, "At Auerstädt it required considerable cleverness on the Prussian side to succeed in losing this battle—for we had the advantage in all things." Marshal Davout's 27,300 men faced 50,000 Prussians under the king and the Duke of Brunswick. There were 1,300 French horsemen against 8,800 Prussians; the French had 44 cannon, while the Prussians had 230. Twelve miles away, at Jena itself, the French field commander (Napoleon) had a 1,000-man superiority, but this was canceled out by Prussian superiority in cavalry and cannon (8,450 French vs. 10,500 Prussian horsemen; 108 French cannon vs. 175).

The French tactics consisted merely in seeking the Prussians out and attacking them; Napoleon had no "Napoleonic tactics" at all. The Prussians, on the other hand, took their cue from their indecisive king and failed to respond. Their infantry fought well—or as well as could be expected under such leadership. By noon the king was hard pressed at Auerstädt; by two o'clock, his armies were fleeing so fast that they reached Weimar, seven miles away, two hours later. Then the refugees from Auerstädt were joined by those from Jena. A panic developed: Equipment was left abandoned; cannon remained behind; knapsacks and rifles were thrown away. Prince Hohenlohe, having no knapsack to abandon, abandoned his troops instead, taking eight squadrons of cavalry as a personal bodyguard; he galloped away so fast that when he reached Sondershausen, he had with him only sixty troopers, having outdistanced the rest of his guard.

As for King Frederick William III, he never even knew what was going on. His 100,000 men were at times less than five miles apart, divided into two forces, but the king, who was at Auerstädt, never received a communication to tell him what was going on at Jena. The Duke of Brunswick was wounded; anyone who could even think of an order to give now gave it, but because no plan had been made, complete confusion reigned. Finally, the king ordered a retreat to Weimar, and this turned into a wholesale rout. The Prussian army consisted of "mobs of frightened men, who, some hours ago, were masquerading in the livery of Frederick the Great." [114]

The king, who should have led them into battle, led the escape instead, surrounded by picked cavalrymen. Suddenly, in flight, he actually became involved in action, for some French hussars surprised him, and he and his men had to fight their way clear with their swords, in hand-to-hand combat. Meanwhile, Queen Louisa was in a coach, flying over the road to Weimar and also narrowly averting capture by the French. The king rode through the whole night, completely separated from his armies; he rode on until he finally reached Sömmerda, 20 miles away from Auerstädt, after blundering about for hours, not possessing a map of the region. Now, when he might have bemoaned the disaster, he turned to Blücher and said, "Let us congratulate ourselves upon having got out of the scrape so well."

* * *

Three days after Jena, Baron von Dorville came galloping through the Brandenburg Gate, down Unter den Linden, and up the Behrenstrasse to the military governor's palace. What he blurted out to Count Friedrich Wilhelm von der Schulenburg frightened the governor half to death. Schulenburg knew that all was lost, but he kept the news from the king's subjects. The next day he issued a statement, posted all over Berlin, which said, "The king has lost a battle. Calm is the first duty of all citizens!" * Then Schulenburg fled the city.

Five days after Schulenburg's escape, the first Frenchmen entered the capital. This was a small advance guard of the Grande Armée, led by the adjutant to General Pierre Augustin Hulin. They seized all palaces and public buildings. Later that day, advance elements of Marshal Davout's army marched in through the Brandenburg Gate; Davout himself arrived on October 26.

Napoleon, who had arrived in Potsdam, asked the sacristan, Gleim, of the Potsdam Garrison Church to show him the tomb of Frederick the Great, who lay there beside his father, Frederick William I. The sacristan showed it to Bonaparte and to his brother Jérôme. *"Sic transit gloria mundi!"* Bonaparte announced. He is also supposed to have said, on looking at the tomb of Frederick the Great, "If he were alive, we would not be standing here today." He then signaled his brother, the sacristan, and the others to leave him alone, and he stood gazing at Frederick II's tomb for a full ten minutes. Afterward he told Marshal Géraud Christophe Michel Duroc to leave the church unmolested. On October 27 he made his triumphal entry into Berlin, greeted by shouts of *"Vive l'Empereur!"* ("For heaven's sake," people said, "cry *Vive l'Empereur* at the top of your voice or we are lost!" [115])

King Frederick William III, who had fled to Küstrin, left that city the day before Napoleon entered Berlin. Before departing with his queen, the king told the Küstrin commandant, Colonel von Ingersleben, a nobleman of ancient family, to hold out with his 3,000 to 4,000 men to the last. Then the king departed for Memel, the most northeasterly border town of his kingdom (in what later became Lithuania). Ingersleben promptly showed how wrong Frederick the Great had been in

* *Ruhe ist die erste Bürgerpflicht!* means more than "Calm is the first duty of all citizens," for *Ruhe* implies silence, as well as calm.

putting so much faith in the honor of his aristocratic officers—if he was not around to spur that sense of honor on. When 300 French hussars approached, Ingersleben surrendered more than ten times that many Prussians without a shot. Prince Hohenlohe, the one who had fled Jena and Auerstädt in such unseemly haste, surrendered 16,000 men at Prenzlau without resistance, even sending the king's own guards regiment into captivity. On October 29 a young French hussar lieutenant rode into the fortress at Stettin, entirely unaccompanied, and demanded the surrender of its 5,000 troops; the governor, an eighty-one-year-old general, at first refused, then thought it over, and also surrendered without a shot being exchanged. Baron von Benkendorf surrendered Spandau Fortress outside Berlin the same way; Baron von Pruschenk surrendered Erfurt; General von Reinhardt, who wore the *Pour le mérite,* surrendered Glogau, the second most important fortress in Prussia; Baron von Thiele opened the Breslau gates to the French, and Baron von Haake, the gates at Schweidnitz. Zorndorf fell to the French because Frederick William III had appointed as its governor a man who had already been convicted as unfit for any post whatsoever. (Küstrin's governor also had once been dismissed—and for cowardice—being reinstated because of family influence.) The most abject surrender took place in Magdeburg, the most important city in Prussia outside Berlin; this was Prussia's strongest fortress, one which had only once been captured and that during the Thirty Years' War. Franz Kasimir von Kleist, general of infantry, knight of the Black Eagle, and son of a distinguished general, was in command there; he had vast stores of reserves, 800 cannon, 800 officers, and 22,000 soldiers and had promised to defend the city "until gunfire set his pocket handkerchief on fire." When Marshal Michel Ney arrived, with just 10,000 men and a few pieces of light field artillery, he changed his mind. He called a military council of his nineteen senior officers, whose combined ages totaled 1,400 years. When one seventy-two-year-old general urged resistance, Count von Kleist, seventy-three years old, shut him up with, "You are the youngest here. You will give your opinion when it is asked!"

What was very clear from all this was that the kingdom of Prussia had reverted to the anarchic condition of the Mark Brandenburg before the first Hohenzollerns moved in; the landowning nobles cared for nothing but their own hides and their own welfare and, in the absence of a strong king, were reverting to type. All that enormous devotion, selflessness, and self-sacrifice which Frederick II had discovered in his Junker officers had in actual fact been inspired into them by his own greatness; it could not outlast him, since these officers were in themselves less than great. As an American, Poultney Bigelow, wrote in the late nineteenth century, "The American war of independence developed one Benedict Arnold in seven years, but this short campaign developed a dozen in as many weeks."[116]

Being generous, one can say that these officers were being merely prudent in the face of Napoleon's reputation in war or that they were following the example of their king, for Frederick William III certainly never rallied his soldiers as had Frederick II in many a lost cause, leading them personally into the enemy guns. But it is interesting to note that those honorable exceptions to this saga of surrender which existed—for example, Kolberg, Graudenz, Pillau, Cosel, and Glatz—involved commanders who were *not* of ancient noble families, but were either commoners or newly created nobles. The defense of Kolberg by the seventy-six-year-old commoner Joachim Nettelbeck became legendary. He created a burghers' guard and protected the town against the French—and the violent opposition of the Prussian army commander, who wanted to surrender and loathed Nettelbeck's civilian militia. (Nettelbeck was afterward supported by a Prussian major named August Neithardt von Gneisenau, then in his forties, who will be encountered again.) Of the cowardly commanders, a number of them were court-martialed in later years and even sentenced to death, but their sentences were in almost every case commuted by the king, since they were, after all, aristocrats. Prince Hohenlohe, who retired to his estates after deserting Prenzlau, was never even called to account at all.

Memel on the Baltic had been chosen as the king's refuge, since even Königsberg, the traditional Hohenzollern headquarters in calamity, was unsafe. Queen Louisa arrived in January, 1807, sick with typhoid fever, starved, and half-frozen. Her children were with her, including the crown prince (later Frederick William IV) and his little brother William (the later

German emperor); William was dressed in a guards uniform, complete with Frederician pigtail and accompanied by all that remained of the king's guards: twenty-nine men. Alexander I of Russia came to nearby Tilsit to embrace Frederick William and to tell him, "We shall not fall singly—either we fall together or not at all." He betrayed this soon enough, but it so encouraged Louisa that she moved back to Königsberg, where she tended the wounded, while the king joined the czar's headquarters. Blücher arrived, pleading for 30,000 men, but the czar withheld them.

Six months later Königsberg fell; Louisa raced back to Memel. All Prussia was occupied; the king ruled only at Memel, over a strip of land 15 miles wide next to the Russian border. Then, on June 21, Russia signed an armistice with Napoleon, and Prussia was sold out. On the twenty-fifth the two emperors met on a raft in the middle of the Niemen River and conferred for three hours, as they divided the world up between them. Frederick William III, who had not even been invited to attend, sat his horse on the riverbank throughout that talk, impatiently awaiting word of the outcome. At the end of the talk the czar asked Napoleon if he wouldn't at least say hello to the King of Prussia. Napoleon agreed to do so the next day. He treated Frederick William with contempt, spoke only an hour with him, and addressed most of his remarks to Alexander I. He had no respect for the Hohenzollerns or their Prussia, having first watched Frederick William's indecisiveness and, later, the cowardice and treachery in the aristocratic Prussian officer corps. He ordered him to dismiss his new prime minister, Karl August von Hardenberg, of whom he knew only that he was anti-French. Hardenberg, a reformer like Stein, found refuge with the Russians. Then Napoleon prepared to conclude a peace with both Russia and Prussia, at the town of Tilsit.

Unable to shake himself from his melancholia, indecisiveness, and inactivity, Frederick William III now did a remarkable thing: He sent his queen to plead with Napoleon for Prussia, despite the fact that Napoleon had ordered the most scurrilous attacks to be published against Louisa, even claiming that the virtuous queen was a mistress of Alexander I. Napoleon met her in a small village house and began by treating her so casually as to show contempt. Finally, he demanded, "How could you conceive the idea of making war against me?" Louisa replied, "It was excusable enough, that remembering the glory of Frederick the Great, we deceived ourselves." Then, in tears, she begged him for an honorable peace and spoke of mercy, God, conscience, justice, her voice choking. Napoleon replied, "You are asking a great deal, but we shall see." As it turned out, he took away almost everything the House of Hohenzollern had garnered for itself over all the centuries since Burgrave Frederick first ventured into the Mark Brandenburg from distant Nuremberg. Frederick William III issued a statement to his former subjects in the lands he ceded, saying that because of "dire necessity," he released them from their duties to his house; that he separated from them "as a father from his children"; and that their memory would be forever dear to him. He was saying farewell to 5,000,000 people, living on 2,500 square miles of land, half his territories. Further, Napoleon demanded 146,000,000 French francs before he would evacuate the Prussian estates which still belonged to the Hohenzollerns. The state was near bankruptcy; only obstinacy and pride dissuaded the king from declaring it. Louisa wrote Baron vom Stein, "Great heavens, where are we now? What have things come to? Our sentence of death is pronounced!" That, it should be remembered, was written just twenty-three years after Prussia had reached its greatest glory under Frederick the Great.

In April, 1809, Major Ferdinand Baptista von Schill led the Second Brandenburg Hussars down Unter den Linden in Berlin and out through the Brandenburg Gate. No one, not even Bärsch or Lützow, the officers flanking Schill, knew where they were going; only Schill knew. He was taking his regiment out of French service, to be the advance guard of an army of liberation, for Schill was aflame with patriotic sentiments. The philosopher Johann Gottlieb Fichte had delivered his rousing *Speeches to the German Nation* in Berlin in 1807 and 1808; they were inspiring, especially since Fichte had not yet become the apologist for despotism into which he developed. His words reflected a growing patriotism which was rooted less in Prussia than in a vague concept called Germany: the idea that all who spoke the common German tongue belonged together. This was, to be sure, a larger and therefore more inspiring cause in which to serve, a nobler vision than any which Prussia had ever provided, for self-sacrifice in a grand, almost-mystical cause seemed far finer than mere service to the House of Hohenzollern, lately so discredited.

That such talk was going on at all was due to a number of factors. For one, the Hohenzollern court was still far away, in Königsberg, to which it returned after the peace of Tilsit; a gag had been removed from the mouths of the people. For another, not only were liberal reforms in the air, but some had taken place. They had not come thanks to the House of Hohenzollern, but in spite of it.

When Frederick William III dismissed Haugwitz, he offered Baron vom Stein the post of prime minister. Stein, however, hoped that Karl von Hardenberg would get the post, so that the two of them might work together in tandem to reform the state. Always incisive, blunt, frank and ruthlessly honest, Stein pushed his suggestions in very outspoken letters to the king. Outraged, Frederick William III responded by firing Stein from the government altogether, calling him "a refractory, insolent, obstinate, and disobedient official." Having no other choice, he appointed Hardenberg. When Hardenberg, however, was dismissed on Napoleon's orders six months later, Frederick William appointed Stein to be the new prime minister, again having no other choice, especially since Napoleon suggested Stein's name.

Stein went to work furiously. Five days after taking office, he initiated wide-ranging reforms throughout Prussia, making them retroactive to the day before, so much was he in a hurry to rip out the rot. He abolished serfdom throughout all Prussia, canceled all legal distinctions regarding landownership (as between lands held by peasants and those held by aristocrats), and he did away with class distinctions of all kinds respecting employment, trades, or occupations of all sorts. Then he further strengthened Cabinet reforms initiated under Hardenberg and, a year later, granted local self-government along progressive lines to every Prussian city and town.

He understood why Prussia had been defeated: because it had not been willing to enlist the service or enthusiasm of the people. The peasantry and commoners in general had been by far its most loyal and steadfast subjects; it had been the nobility in the officer corps and the court who had become weak, dissolute, treacherous, and corrupt.

The spirit of reform now infected the army as well. A special commission was created to reorganize the army along modern and efficient lines. Stein was a member, as were Gneisenau, Karl Wilhelm von Grolman, Boyen, and others. It was headed by Major General Gerhard von Scharnhorst, the man who in earlier years, as a lieutenant colonel at the War Academy, had taught the art of war to the officer who would write about it definitively Karl von Clausewitz. Though trained in Frederician traditions, Scharnhorst knew they were obsolete. The army which had been so terribly defeated at Jena and Auerstedt could not effectively confront French Revolutionary soldiers, the result of the French *levée en masse*. Prussian soldiers were still flogged and beaten and deserted in vast numbers; worse yet, their officers had become so dissolute and soft that the Duke of Brunswick had come to Auerstädt with his mistress and another officer had brought a piano along. It was clear that a professional army which was deliberately cut off from the population, which was hostile to civilians and hated by them in turn, could not enlist popular enthusiasm in these times. An army with roots in the citizenry was needed: a national army.

These Prussian officers, plotting among themselves, began to worry Napoleon Bonaparte. Suspicious, he ordered Frederick William III to dismiss the commission, which he did each time it convened; under more pressure, the king ordered its recommendations torn up.

Napoleon now realized that Stein was interested in reforming Prussia so that it could free itself from the Napoleonic yoke. Some letters of Stein's, expressing hope of a national uprising, had been captured, and Napoleon responded by seizing all of the baron's properties in Westphalia and by pressuring Frederick William III to dismiss Stein from the government. When Napoleon entered Madrid shortly thereafter, he declared "that man Stein" to be "an enemy of France" and an enemy of the Confederation of the Rhine, Napoleon's union of vassal German states. Then Bonaparte seized all of Stein's property within the territory of the confederation, and Stein was persuaded that his life was in grave danger. He fled to Prague and, from there, to the Russians.

Berlin was now filled with reports of the Spanish revolt, of unrest in the Tirol, as well as with rumors that the Westphalians were preparing to revolt against their new king, Napoleon's brother Jérôme. Patriotic hotheads, members of a Society of Friends of the Fatherland, were active and vocal. It was they who persuaded Major Ferdinand von Schill that he could spark the Westphalian revolt if he marched his regiment there, that he might even start the entire European liberation movement.

The news of Schill's desertion was immediately brought to King Frederick William's attention at Königsberg. Far from cheering this patriot on, he issued a Cabinet order which was later posted on the Brandenburg Gate. "It is with indescribable displeasure that I have noted reports concerning matters in Berlin," the king announced, going on to order Schill to report immediately to Königsberg. A few days later, a Napoleonic decree hung on the gate. "A certain Schill," it read, "a sort of highwayman who rose in rank by virtue of one crime after another during the last Prussian campaign, has deserted Berlin with his entire regiment, has moved toward Wittenberg on the Saxon border, and has surrounded this town. . . . This ridiculous enterprise was plotted by those who want to set fire to everything in Germany. . . ." Schill's capture was ordered, and a reward of 10,000 francs was offered. Finally, another Hohenzollern decree went up. "On orders of His Royal Majesty the King of Prussia, Our Gracious Lord," it said, "everyone is herewith most seriously warned not to make themselves guilty of similar actions. . . ."

Schill, meanwhile, had had a brief skirmish with the garrison at Magdeburg, after which he headed north to try to obtain British support. His small force was soon overwhelmed by Danish and Dutch troops at Stralsund, on May 31, 1809. It was during this action that Schill was killed at the age of twenty-three. His body is said to have been returned to the Berlin Rathaus, where a physician severed Schill's head. This trophy, placed inside a large glass jar, was then delivered to Jérôme, who paid 10,000 francs reward for it. So much for patriots. Queen Louisa, writing about Schill's death, could report only that the king was terribly upset about both it and the general unrest. "How is Napoleon to trust in the king's innocence?"

she asked. "It would be Napoleon's greatest but most ghastly triumph if he could destroy this friendship, which is made to last forever, for its basis is virtue. . . ."

Frederick William III melted down his golden dinner service, and Queen Louisa sold her jewels in order to support themselves at Königsberg, where they lived in a simple farmhouse. From here, Louisa encouraged Stein, Scharnhorst, and Gneisenau in their reforms, pleading with them to be patient with her vacillating husband, who would yet come around to their thinking, or so she hoped. Yet Scharnhorst's plans for a citizen army in which commoners might become officers and in which promotions were actually to be earned frightened the king. Commoners had never been made officers, except temporarily; after saving their king, they had always been cashiered. A citizen army, the king was convinced, was potentially a revolutionary mob. The Prussian army, after all, had always been the king's defense against his people as much as it had ever been the nation's defense against foreign attack. Its noble officers had always regarded the people as canaille. Scharnhorst's reliance on the rabble angered the king; Scharnhorst's plan to stop all flogging of soldiers frightened the officer corps.* How could the king trust his army to guard him against the mob, when the mob was to be uniformed and armed in the king's service?

On the queen's birthday in 1809, Königsberg gave a ball for her; she attended it, brokenhearted. "To whom will Prussia belong a year from now?" she wrote. "When shall we all be scattered? Father Almighty, take pity on us!" That spring Napoleon was threatening to take away Prussia's richest remaining province, Silesia; it was a spring when Frederick William III must certainly have recalled the words spoken to him as a small child, "You will *not* allow Silesia to be taken from you."

Louisa kept busy by interesting herself in the ideas of a Swiss educational reformer, Johann Heinrich Pestalozzi, who entertained the eccentric idea that the state should interest itself in producing educated citizens. She pestered and badgered her hus-

* Gneisenau, one of Scharnhorst's reformers, had learned the merits of a citizen army during the Revolutionary War in America, where he served the British, as well as at Kolberg.

band until he finally agreed to establish a school in Königsberg, embodying Pestalozzi's principles; it was the most "republican" gesture of his life.

In December, 1809, the King and Queen of Prussia were able to return to Berlin, the French having vacated that city. They arrived on the twenty-third, being greeted with wild enthusiasm —but the cheers were *not* for their Hohenzollern king, but for his queen, who had become the very embodiment of all patriotic sentiments and the repository of all national and libertarian hopes. She had secured the reappointment of Hardenberg as prime minister; Napoleon countenanced it because he had such a low regard for Prussia that he did not believe Hardenberg mattered any longer. Her influence on Prussian affairs had been great, far greater than was then suspected. But now she was dying of a heart ailment—or, as was supposed, of a broken heart. She died at the age of thirty-five, on July 19, 1810. Dr. Ernst Heim, a celebrated Berlin physician, conducted a post-mortem examination. She had said, after the loss of Magdeburg, "that if she could lay open her heart, the name of that city would be written on it in letters of blood." This did not prove to be the case. But a growth was found at her heart, and it was noted that its shape resembled the initial letter of Napoleon. Her body was taken to a park at Charlottenburg; her grave became a shrine almost immediately, thousands of people visiting it on pilgrimages as though it were the shrine of a saint.

Hardenberg, wielding extensive powers, abolished the exemption of the nobility from taxes, confiscated church properties to pay the public debt, and did away with the medieval system of guilds and corporations so as to allow anyone who wished to do so to enter trade. He also established universities at Berlin and Breslau along liberal lines; these came to be centers of patriotic feeling, agitation, and, finally, enlistment.

Yet the final humiliation of the ineffectual King of Prussia was yet to come, in 1812, when Napoleon forced him to surrender the whole of Prussia, with minor exceptions, to the service of the campaign against the czar; in May, at a meeting in Erfurt, Frederick William III appeared among the French marshals and generals almost like a servant, kept in an anteroom, cooling his heels. He was forced to conclude an alliance with

France against Russia and to give Napoleon all the troops he had left—20,000—for the Russian campaign. The pact dismayed the reformers. A fourth of the officer corps, including Scharnhorst, Gneisenau, Boyen, Clausewitz, and other competent officers, resigned; 300 officers in all left the service. Those who remained marched with General Hans Yorck von Wartenburg as far as Riga; Frederick William had written Yorck of "the close union which existed between the interests of himself and the Emperor of France." Yorck, who had never disobeyed before in his life, chose to do so on December 30, 1812. Napoleon was retreating, the wind was different, a chorus of patriotic voices was raised, and Yorck made his decision: He took his Prussian army out of French service, "neutralizing" it, and he allowed the czar's soldiers into West and East Prussia. Czar Alexander's army had become the army of liberation for Europe; in its advance guard rode the czar's new administrator for West and East Prussia, that "insolent and disobedient" Baron vom Stein. Stein immediately summoned the representatives of the local estates and formed Prussia's first parliament; then, in February, 1813, Stein ordered the establishment of a citizen army: a national militia and a reserve.

Yorck's defection was "enough to strike one with apoplexy," the king noted in Berlin, which by then was again under French occupation. However, he did what he knew best how to do: nothing at all. Then, on January 22, he allowed himself to be swept along by the fever igniting Prussia; it swept him to Breslau. Scharnhorst and Blücher were there, as was Hardenberg; Gneisenau was on his way; enormous excitement and expectancy were all about. Everyone waited for the king to call his people to arms. Thousands of officers and soldiers, retired from service on French orders, awaited the call; vast stores of British arms and large amounts of British money were at hand. With Stein pushing and Hardenberg tugging, the king finally and reluctantly issued a proclamation on February 3, asking the citizenry to arm themselves for the protection of the nation (although even then he could not bring himself to mention Napoleon as the enemy). Everyone understood, and everyone armed. Nine thousand Berliners volunteered in three days; thousands everywhere rose to save their lands—and even to save the House of Hohenzollern. Frederick William ought to have been grateful; when Napoleon declared war on Prussia in 1813, Napoleon stated, "The House of Hohenzollern is not fit to have a throne; it is hereby dethroned, and the provinces are distributed as follows: all Prussia and Lithuania falls to Poland; Silesia to Austria; Brandenburg to Westphalia." But in fact, the king was not grateful or happy; the idea of arming "the people" was so loathsome to him that he agreed to do it only after Yorck argued that volunteers were cheaper than regular troops.

The French evacuated Berlin at the beginning of March; on the twenty-third, Frederick William returned again to his capital. On the seventeenth, the king's proclamation promising his people liberty from both foreign *and domestic* oppression had been published, a remarkable document indeed, coming from a Hohenzollern hand. The Wars of Liberation now began. By October 19, 300,000 Prussians (of whom 10,000 were volunteers, the first Prussia had ever enlisted) helped defeat Napoleon at Leipzig's Battle of the Nations, after which the marketplace in Leipzig positively swarmed with potentates. The czar, the Austrian emperor, the Swedish crown prince, the King of Saxony were there—and Frederick William III. They all embraced and gave thanks to God; the nightmare almost seemed over. Blücher, the hero of Leipzig, arrived at the town gate, and the czar, who was overcome with emotion or perhaps delusions, introduced Blücher to his king by saying Frederick William III was "the Liberator of Europe." This was nonsense, but Frederick William was touched. In fact, his people had helped liberate Germany from Napoleon and would be rewarded badly for this service. When Prussia lost at Jena, only 1 Prussian in 50 was in arms; now every twelfth man in Berlin went out to fight the French. The Berlin police chief had to plead with the king to stop recruiting, there being so many volunteers that the army would swell to 400,000 men. Eleanora Renz of Potsdam joined a volunteer regiment disguised as a man and was killed in battle, a Prussian "Joan"; 160,000 gold and silver wedding rings were donated in exchange for "rings of iron"; people gave horses, silver spoons, even their hair to be sold in order to buy freedom. The French did not understand this enthusiasm, nor did the Prussian king. A regiment of volunteers under a Major Lützow, in which the poet Karl Theodor Körner served, unfurled a banner the king thought ominous: not the Prussian flag of the Hohenzollerns, but the black, red, and gold banner of a "united Germany," of a unified German Reich. In December, 1813, Lützow received orders to disband his force; he protested to the king, who replied the next month without a word of praise, dissolving the unit by incorporating its men into regular regiments, which flew the black-and-white flags of Prussia. Frederick William III was no "Liberator" nor any repository of patriotic hopes; the dead Queen Louisa inflamed all hearts. Körner made her out to be a Madonna. *"Du heilige, hör' deine Kinder flehen!"* he wrote: "Holy One, hear your children pleading!" The poet Heinrich von Kleist had already summed it up after Jena: "She gathers about her all the great men whom the king neglects. She it is who holds together what has not yet fallen to pieces." Körner rallied the people, predicting great things after victory: "A golden future lies before us—a heaven full of the sweets of liberty!" It was fortunate for him that he did not survive the war to test the accuracy of his prediction.

Blücher pursued the French to Paris and in 1815 helped Wellington seal Napoleon's doom at Waterloo. In May of that year, France received a constitution and was even granted more territory than it owned at the beginning of 1792; the German soldiers also wanted a constitution, giving them at least as many liberties as the Prussian king and his allies were now allowing the French. Frederick William on June 3 issued a Cabinet order vaguely referring to a constitution and to "representation," saying he would consider them when he got home. The day after, the king issued a proclamation to his people. "Great have been your exertions and great your sacrifices," it said. "I know them, and I acknowledge them, and God, who rules above us, has also recognized them. We have achieved what we desired."

The people disagreed. As Blücher put it, they had fought for *Freiheit und Vaterland*—for "freedom and fatherland"—it seemed the king was satisfied with "fatherland" alone.

Now restless students left their classrooms and formed patriotic student societies (which later developed into dueling fraternities), shouted slogans, demonstrated in the streets. Hardenberg had already proposed a representative assembly such as existed in France. Hopes ran high that the House of Hohenzollern would abandon autocracy, would rid itself of rule by an aristocratic military dictatorship, would set Prussia on the path toward a constitutional monarchy. It only remained for the king to act. He did; he substituted tyranny and despotism for mere autocracy. Prussia, which had risen for freedom, was made a police state instead.

Fateful changes had occurred in the European order—and were continuing to take place. In 1804 the last Holy Roman Emperor of the German Nation, the Habsburgs' Francis II, assumed the title "Hereditary Emperor of Austria" and on August 6, 1806, resigned the title of Holy Roman Emperor for the reason that he was powerless to defend it against Napoleon. (Holy Roman Emperor Francis II thereupon retitled himself Emperor Francis I of Austria.)

The Napoleonic empire had collapsed, and those who had destroyed it—Austria, Prussia, Russia, and Great Britain—assembled in September, 1814, in Vienna, to remake the face of Europe. Metternich represented Austria at this Congress of Vienna, and Hardenberg acted on behalf of Frederick William III of Prussia. Czar Alexander I of Russia was his own diplomat, and Britain was represented first by Lord Castlereagh, then by Wellington, and finally by Lord Clancarty. Louis XVIII of France, restored to the throne, sent Talleyrand. The Congress was historic in many ways and not only in terms of the boundaries it set; it was in fact the first major European summit and foreign ministers' conference.

Prussia did well, but in ways it had not expected. It had wanted all Saxony (the Saxon king having been among Napoleon's most loyal vassals); it got only two-fifths of that state. But it received extensive portions of Westphalia, as well as lands along the Rhine, after having to give up much of its eastern, Polish territories. The acquisitions along the Rhine forced Prussia to guard that river against any future French threat (Britain had supported and urged it for that very reason); it also significantly changed the character of Prussia. Three million Polish serfs had been replaced by 3,000,000 Rhinelanders, all of them "contaminated" by French liberal ideals, as well as by Roman Catholicism. The Prussian Junkers, who were thus deprived of a labor force, "lamented the empty acres of the Vistula," as Taylor put it;[117] they did not know that those

Rhinelanders sat atop the Ruhr Basin, one of the world's richest deposits of coal and iron. This reservoir would ensure Hohenzollern greatness in years to come.

Most significant, however, was the ethnographic change which had taken place. Prussia's population had increased from 6,000,000 to 10,000,000, and Prussia itself now straddled all northern Germany, from Memel (later Lithuania) to west of the Rhine, including not only Cologne but also Aix-la-Chapelle (Aachen). By means of the agreements reached at the Congress of Vienna, Prussia ceased to be what it had always been: an "Eastern" kingdom.

That major fact was not recognized by those who ruled Prussia—or, in any event, was not allowed to influence policy. Prussia continued as before to be ruled by a nobility whose ties remained overwhelmingly Eastern, whose lands lay in West and East Prussia, in Pomerania, and in the Mark Brandenburg, itself largely "Eastern" in character. Königsberg, in East Prussia, and not Cologne on the Rhine, continued to be the shrine of Prussianism, the ancient home of the Teutonic Order, and its mystical bulwark against liberal infection. It was there and in Potsdam that the Prussian kings felt secure, and it was from the Eastern part of the expanded kingdom that Prussia would continue to be governed to the satisfaction of the king and his Junker landowners.

This Eastern orientation was further strengthened when the monarchs of Russia, Austria, and Prussia joined in a Holy Alliance in 1818. (France was admitted but virtually seceded from it shortly afterward.) This was supposed to be a community of Christian nations; it turned into an alliance of archreactionaries who were determined to maintain the status quo, to deter the liberalization of their lands. An event which took place a year later committed these reactionaries along the road toward outright tyranny.

On March 23, 1819, a theology student named Karl Sand assassinated a German dramatist named August von Kotzebue, who had ridiculed national (*i.e.,* liberal) feeling in Germany and was suspected of being in the pay of Russia. This murder seemed to the aristocrats like the fall of the Bastille; the students would next be upsetting governments and killing kings, or so they claimed to believe. In any event, Sand made a convenient scapegoat, an excuse to launch an era of repression. Austria's Metternich called a conference at Carlsbad to discuss what countermeasures could be taken. In fact, Frederick William III had already assented in advance to the suppression of all liberal and "national" ideas. The Carlsbad Decrees bound the signatories not to grant any popular representation, to suppress all liberal newspapers, and to dismiss all liberal professors and teachers. Frederick William III made the decrees public on October 18, choosing the anniversary of the Battle of Leipzig, when, six years earlier, his people had fought and died for "freedom and fatherland." A ruthless suppression of all liberal and similarly subversive elements followed; it was a foretaste of twentieth-century totalitarianism. Bigelow, the nineteenth-century American, called it "a period of political darkness which can be compared with the days when women were burned at the stake because they knew a little about herb-tea." In Germany, he said, "the whole machinery of government . . . was but a tool in the hands of a secret police whose duty it was to sniff about the premises of scholars in order to be able to denounce them as demagogues guilty of high-treason." [118]

What happened to Ernst Moritz Arndt was typical. Arndt was a German poet and patriot who had to flee to Sweden to escape Napoleonic revenge for his anti-French sentiments; throughout his exile, he continued to fire German patriots by means of songs, poems, and pamphlets he sent back home. A close associate of Baron vom Stein and of Generals Blücher and Gneisenau, Arndt was summoned to Russia in 1812 to help Stein organize the struggle against Bonaparte. When the University of Bonn was founded in 1818, Arndt became its professor of modern history, and in that same year he published the fourth part of his *Spirit of the Times* (*Geist der Zeit*), which denounced the reactionary policies in Germany. Like many another liberal patriot, he had also called for a constitution; these were crimes enough for him to be hounded, despite his eminence and service against Napoleon. He was arrested by the police, and his study was torn apart by officials hunting for subversive writings; Arndt had occasion to be grateful that most of his letters and papers had earlier been lost at sea. He was soon released but kept under surveillance for a full twenty years. Another prominent man who was hounded was Friedrich Ludwig Jahn, who had established gymnastic societies which developed into patriotic clubs during the Wars of Liberation. "*Turnvater*" Jahn was imprisoned for six years for speaking out in favor of a constitutional monarchy—despite the fact that he had uttered sentiments like these in 1817: "God save the king and preserve the House of Hohenzollern; protect our country; increase the German people; purify our nation from the aping of things foreign; make Prussia a shining pattern for the united Germany. . . ." But this call also included suspect words: ". . . bind this union to a new Reich, and grant graciously and speedily the one thing of pressing need—a wise Constitution!"

His remarks about what he called *Zollern's Haus* were patriotic enough, but the words about a German "nation" were suspect, and the call for a constitution was almost treasonous. Everyone who had received a letter from Jahn made certain to burn it.

Other prominent patriots were treated similarly. The poet Fritz Reuter was imprisoned simply for being a member of a student fraternity which advocated a united Germany; he was kept without trial for years and was finally sentenced to thirty years' imprisonment. Even Fichte's speeches were banned from circulation; the sermons of the theologian Friedrich Schleiermacher in Berlin were screened for subversive content. Reform in agriculture was stopped; reform in the army ended even faster. Generals von Boyen and Grolman resigned, being unwilling to disband the Landwehr reserve and militia; they were treated as though they were revolutionaries, when in fact they were Prussian officers. Angered and disgusted, Baron vom Stein retired altogether from public life and established a society for historical research. Retreat into scholarship became a refuge for many another statesman made impotent by the despotic regime. Hardenberg, for his part, swung over to archconservatism and supported his king against the people's aspirations until his death in 1822. The illustrious scientist Alexander von Humboldt agonized in his post as court chamberlain to Frederick William; he tried to help artists and scientists, for he carried about the reactionary court a heart filled with the ideals of the French Revolution. His older brother Wilhelm, a philologist, writer, diplomat, and privy councilor, had also retired in protest against the reactionary regime; he sought comfort in the study of the Basque tongue.

Frederick William III took a great personal interest in the implementation of the Carlsbad Decrees. He rose early, worked hard all day long, labored constantly: at repression. He also began to long for female company again. Gneisenau put this into an odd context, saying, "The king is suffering from abdominal complaints and from the development of a deplorable hypochondria. He believed that he could no longer do without affectionate feminine company. . . ." For a time, the king, then fifty-four, considered an Irish countess named Dillon, but later chose Countess Augusta von Harrach, whom he married morganatically, which meant she had no claim to his inheritance. He treated her badly, worse than he'd treated Queen Louisa. Countess Bernsdorff wrote in her memoirs that his "manner toward her in public savored of scandalous coldness" and that he mortified her constantly. He sought "every opportunity of forcing her back into the position of a private person" and seated her at meals—and even in church—in an inferior position. She was only twenty-four when she married the king and thus evoked a good deal of sympathy in court circles. Countess Bernsdorff noted that the king shut her off from society and seemed to delight in humiliating his wife. The times had changed him, for he had once been noted for his inability to hurt anyone; the suffering he had undergone at the hands of Napoleon had not matured him, but had made him petty. He spent his remaining sixteen years slipping slowly into senility. He went out daily, driving through his capital in a modest carriage, and he maintained a modest establishment; since people found few virtues to ascribe to him, they extolled at least his modesty, thrift, and punctuality. He came to be obsessed with rooting out all threats to Hohenzollern absolutism, with persecuting "demagogues," as liberal thinkers were called; sniffing out subversion was the only activity which fully engaged the king's energies and intellect. So little did Prussia sparkle during this time that the period from 1819, when the repressive Carlsbad Decrees were issued, to 1840, when this king died, came to be called the Quiet Years—or, alternatively, the Biedermeier years, this being the term for a Prussian-style Victorian propriety. The people settled for trivial amusements: Fashion, music, dance and love affairs flourished, as did the first tenements, seedbeds of future revolts. This was, wrote Gustav Freytag, a time of "false refinement . . . overloaded with ornament," and romance was a way in which "men wished to raise themselves and those they loved out of the common realities of life into a purer atmosphere." Freytag discerned another yearning as well. "These aspirations," he wrote in his *Pictures of German Life,* "were not altogether estimable, by turns they became vague, childish, fanatical, stupid, sentimental, and at last dissolute; but beneath might always be discovered the feeling that there was something wanting in German life. Was it a higher morality? Was it gaiety? Perhaps it was the grace of God? The beautiful or the frivolous? Or perhaps that was wanting to the people, which the princes had long possessed, political life. . . ."

It was denied them still. They made the best of things, even of their king. As Frederick William III grew older, they found a new virtue could be ascribed to him: his age. The king came to be called the Old Gentleman and was respected for his years, if for little else. He has been called "the first real citizen-king of Prussia" (*Bürgerkönig Preussens*)[119] because his character was essentially bourgeois, but he lacked all sympathetic connection with the very people he epitomized. He mistrusted them and cheated them of the "freedom and fatherland" they had sought; all that the Prussians got out of their War of Liberation was universal military service. Some of Stein's reforms lasted; the abolition of serfdom is one. But the quarter century which ended in 1840 was a time of "restoration," a time when liberty was strangled, not given a new birth. Prussia emerged from Frederick William III's reign vastly larger and more influential than it had ever been, even under Frederick the Great, but the fact that it now stretched from Russia to Holland and France was not due to this king or to his Prussian Junkers, who never welcomed this extension of Prussia toward the West; Prussia could thank Britain for these acquisitions, for the British had wanted a counterweight to French power west of the Rhine.

The Hohenzollerns seldom understood and almost never responded to the sentiments of their people or even to the *Zeitgeist* animating the times in which they reigned. Frederick William III was no exception. Even some Prussian generals were far more responsively liberal; one example is Neithardt von Gneisenau. On May 15, 1815, Gneisenau drafted a plan whereby Prussia could "conquer" all Germany in an enlightened manner, rather than by force of arms. Most Germans, he wrote, looked to Prussia with admiration and looked to her for leadership as well; this situation gave Prussia an unprecedented opportunity. Because most German governments, he said, were "despotic and hated by the people," Prussia should very quickly draft a constitution, which the Prussian king should then grant his people, thereby setting an example for other German states which would prove irresistible to them. These other states would then seek union with Prussia; Prussia could grow "less through force of arms than through the liberalism of its fundamental principles." Further, Gneisenau suggested that a large sum of money be made available in order to further the arts and education. All men of learning and talent should be drawn to Prussia by high salaries and specially created posts; the court should do everything in its power to provide a welcome for excellence and to create a climate in which new talents could flourish. "Prussia," he concluded, "would soon be recognized as the model state, thrice-glorified by those things which alone aid a people in achieving progress: fame in war, constitution and law, and care for the arts and sciences." [120]

Such were the hopes even of Prussian generals. What actually took place, of course, was diametrically opposed to Gneisenau's genial vision. The arts and sciences were fettered, not fostered; instead of becoming a model state, Prussia developed into a model police state. This happened in the nineteenth century, not the eighteenth, which was so often called the age of absolutism. The pattern of the future was being set—ironically, by a Hohenzollern who could not bear to be decisive.

New York Public Library

THE HOHENZOLLERNS

FREDERICK WILLIAM II
FREDERICK WILLIAM IV
FREDERICK II

THE GREAT ELECTOR
FREDERICK I
WILLIAM II
WILLIAM I

FREDERICK WILLIAM III
FREDERICK III
FREDERICK WILLIAM I

A contemporary print shows the start of Hohenzollern rule over Brandenburg. Burgrave Frederick of Nuremberg is shown receiving the lands his descendants would rule for more than 500 years.

New York Public Library

The Great Elector, Frederick William, a Hohenzollern "Sun King." "One of the shiftiest of men," said Carlyle, adding, "not unjust by any means."

New York Public Library

e Elector George William, o did little but suffer. When ındenburg needed a great ctor, it got George William, o was merely the Great Elec-'s father.

New York Public Library

The first Hohenzollern King "in" Prussia, Frederick I, a vain, mis-shapen fop, crowns his queen at Königsberg. "He was," said his grandson, Frederick the Great, "little in great things, great in little things."

New York Public Library

Frederick William I, the fa of Prussianism and the Prus army, a sadistic boor who the laughingstock of Europ courts and a holy terror to people, his soldiers, and family, but who paradoxic was great in accomplishm and good for his lands.

New York Public Library

Frederick William I at his favorite occupation: inspecting and drilling his Giants' Guard. Thousand of tall men were dragooned into these monstrous regiments; the height of some of them, to the top of their tall hats, came to ten feet.

The Bettmann Archive

Frederick II—Frederick the Great—standing before Sans Souci Palace in Potsdam, his favorite residence. The intense eyes came to be legendary as "the Fritzian look." The simple tricorn hat he wore recalls his comment: "A crown is only a hat that lets the rain in."

The Bettmann Archive

Frederick the Great playing the flute, characteristically surrounded by dogs and disarray.

New York Public Library

New York Public Library

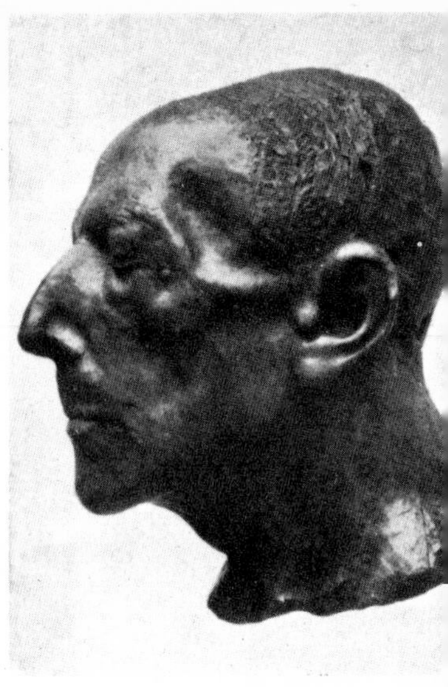

New York Public Librar

Above: A bust based on the deat mask of Frederick the Great.

Above left: Elizabeth Christin whom Frederick the Great wa forced to make his queen an whom he ignored throughout hi reign. It was "the mating of th eagle and the dove." Frederick in sisted she was pretty, though other thought differently, but he adde "True, she has no breeding an dresses very badly. . . ."

New York Public Library

Left: Frederick William II, slav of mistresses, sex drugs, and charla tans, who had a mania for govern ing by himself without doing any thing and who never conducte business or opened a letter "as n human power could induce him read forty lines at a time. . . ."

Frederick William III, whom Napoleon humiliated and who later was persuaded against his will to humiliate Napoleon. Under him, the Prussian army became a mob "of frightened men . . . masquerading in the livery of Frederick the Great." After Waterloo, he betrayed his people's fight for liberation and turned Prussia, for the first time, into a "modern" police state.

New York Public Library

ueen Louisa, the beautiful and
normously popular wife of Fred-
rick William III. The memory of
is queen inflamed the hearts of
e Prussians during the Wars of
iberation against Napoleon; they
ade her into a Madonna, and the
oet Karl Körner wrote, "Holy
ne, hear your children pleading!"
hey begged for *Freiheit und
aterland* ("freedom and father-
nd"); her widowed king gave
em fatherland alone.

New York Public Library

New York Public Library

Prince Louis Ferdinand of Hohenzollern at the Battle of Saalfeld, 1806, cut down by a French sergeant named Guindey. Like many another Hohenzollern on the eve of his death, Louis Ferdinand was visited the night before by the family ghost, the "White Lady."

New York Public Library

Frederick William IV, "the first master of what became a specialty of German politics—the meaningless but inspiring phrase." In 1848, with Berlin in revolt, the king captured the revolution by seeming to join it, after which he slowly sank into madness.

New York Public Library

New York Public Library

The future German Emperor William I as crown prince, with his wife, the liberally inclined Augusta of Saxe-Weimar, a friend of Goethe's. His staying power was remarkable: He was born the month George Washington retired to Mount Vernon and died six years after the birth of Franklin D. Roosevelt.

New York Public Library

New York Public Library

Left: Emperor William I on maneuvers. At eighty years of age, he mounted his horse at six each morning and needed only five hours of sleep a night; his officers attributed his stamina to lobster salad.

Right: Emperor William I. By the time he died, at ninety-one, he was such a Berlin landmark that Baedeker guidebooks listed the hour he could be seen at his palace corner window, watching the changing of the guard.

New York Public Library

King William I of Prussia being proclaimed German emperor at Versailles, January 18, 1871. Otto von Bismarck, who ruled while William reigned, stands in white uniform at foot of steps. "His Majesty," Bismarck said after the reluctant emperor accepted his new title, "bore me such a grudge for this course of events . . . he ignored me . . . and persisted in this attitude for several days."

New York Public Library

The future Emperor Frederick III as crown prince, with his wife, Britain's princess royal, Victoria, at the time of their marriage. A strong-willed girl, she wrote him forty-page letters before their wedding and overwhelmed him intellectually after it.

Emperor Frederick III. Empress Eugénie of France described him as "a tall, handsome man . . . slim and fair . . . in fact, a Teuton such as Tacitus describes them; he is chivalrously polite and with a touch of Hamlet about him."

New York Public Library

Empress Frederick, the widow of Emperor Frederick III, daughter of Britain's Queen Victoria (note resemblance), and uncompromisingly stern mother to the future Emperor William II. Watching her while her husband was dying of cancer, Count von Waldersee said, "My impression was that she revelled in being the center of attention. . . ."

New York Public Library

Emperor William II painted by Max Koner, showing him shortly after his accession to the throne—and showing him as he liked to see himself. His withered left hand is not hidden here as it is in photographs—and has been transformed to show a powerful martial grip on the sword he rattled for so much of his reign.

The Bettmann Archive

"Dropping the Pilot," a famous contemporary *Punch* cartoon, shows the young Emperor William II firing the aged Iron Chancellor, Otto von Bismarck. The real circumstances were not revealed to the emperor's subjects until many years later.

The Bettmann Archive

New York Public Library

Emperor William II and Empress Augusta (Dohna, as she was nicknamed). When he acceded to the throne, Queen Victoria commented, ". . . with such a hot-headed conceited and wrong-headed young man [good Anglo-German relations] may at ANY moment become *impossible*."

The Bettmann Archive

Emperor William II during 1908 maneuvers in Stettin. The pose is that of the supreme warlord of the nation, a role which William II enjoyed playing in peacetime but which he could never fulfill during World War I.

Three of the emperor's six sons salute Emperor William II. All Hohenzollern princes were commissioned at the age of ten. The emperor had so many uniforms that it was said he had a special admiral's uniform tailored for use only when attending performances of *The Flying Dutchman*.

New York Public Library

The ex-Kaiser in exile at Doorn, The Netherlands. After being compelled to abdicate in 1918, the last reigning Hohenzollern became what he had always secretly wanted to be: a benign English country gentleman.

The Bettmann Archive

Illustrated London News

Former Crown Prince William in Nazi storm trooper uniform in 1934, flanked by two of his sons, Herbertus (left) and Frederick (right). "Where a Hitler leads, a Hohenzollern can follow," said Prince Augustus William in 1931, but the family's enchantment with Nazism died quickly.

New York Public Library

The former Crown Prince William shortly before his death. Note the startling facial resemblance to Frederick the Great.

Illustrated London News

Prince Louis Ferdinand of Prussia, head of the House of Hohenzollern today, shown wearing Luftwaffe uniform at the time of his 1938 marriage to Grand Duchess Kira, a Romanov. World traveler and onetime Ford assembly-line worker, Louis Ferdinand became for a time the hope of German anti-Nazi conspirators, who planned to make him head of state after a coup deposed Hitler.

11

A Medieval Monarch Meets a Modern Mob

A PARISIAN fortune-teller, Madame Lenormand, confirmed Frederick William III's premonitions in 1815, when she gave him twenty-five more years in which to live. He had already noted the pattern in the House of Hohenzollern: The Great Elector's father died in 1640, Frederick the Great's father died in 1740; he was sure that he himself would die in 1840. On March 28 of that year, he left a dinner dance complaining of a cold; soon he had a fever and became a helpless invalid. Within weeks, he seemed to everyone decrepit, imbecilic, senile. In the beginning of June his daughter Charlotte and her husband, Czar Nicholas of Russia, visited him; they arrived just in time to witness his death on the seventh. Charlotte and the czar left the morbid surroundings and hurried back to Potsdam, where the czarina stripped off her mourning clothes the moment she was behind closed doors. The citizens did much the same; now that the Old Gentleman was dead, they looked with hope and expectancy to the new king. Frederick William IV, then forty-five years old, threw himself, sobbing, into the arms of a family friend, acting almost as though he had lost someone especially dear to him, when in point of fact the old king and the crown prince had barely been on speaking terms for some time past. The gesture, however, was typical of the new king: highly emotional, very dramatic, surprising all those present, and inconsistent with his previous actions. Death had replaced a bluff, straightforward, if indecisive king with a flamboyant ham actor who wanted desperately to play the romantic lead to his nation but who consistently blurted out all the wrong lines.

His mother, Queen Louisa, worried about him as soon as he was more than just a toddler. Although intelligent and even "good-hearted," he had an uncontrollable temper; wild rages fluctuated in him with wild joys. He regularly beat up his brother William (two years his junior) and later tried to do the same with Charles, who was six years younger, although Charles gave back as much as he got. All the princes and princesses avoided their older brother's company, staging a nursery boycott of the crown prince. Louisa feared he was being spoiled, as indeed he was. Like many another parent, she laid most of the blame on his teachers, most of them disasters in one way or another. A "benevolent philanthropist," Friedrich Delbrück, was the first; Major Gaudy, a confirmed invalid, was tried next and General Dierecke, the crown prince's military governor, became the third in line, but he turned out to be an old woman and had to be replaced by a general named Luck, who proved equally unfortunate. Young "Fritz" was simply too much for all of them: bright, temperamental, imaginative, absentminded, alert, vain, eager to learn, yet indulging every trivial whim and interest.

In 1810, when the crown prince was fifteen, a new tutor was found: J. P. F. Ancillon, then the official historian at Berlin's military academy and a former Huguenot pastor. He put his stamp on the crown prince: he confirmed him in his romantic attachment to the German Middle Ages and taught him to loathe all revolutionary—and even liberal—ideas; he shaped this prince into an anachronism in a time of turbulent change. Owing in part at least to Ancillon's influence, Frederick William IV never was the man for the time in which he lived. He might have been a perfectly acceptable seventeenth- or even eighteenth-century monarch, but in the nineteenth he proved unable to lead and unwilling to follow. He lived in the past, when he might have broken into the future. None of those around him helped plant his feet on the ground. Ancillon encouraged his medievalism, as did Karl von Roeder, his aide-de-camp, a loyal and devout officer with a dreamy attachment to things mystical and mysterious; his later military governor, General Schack, was of the same mold: romantic and sentimental, as well as slightly hysterical by nature.

When the crown prince was about twenty years of age, he fell in love, but with a piece of statuary. It was the head of an idealized princess and, as one observer, Caroline von Rochow, put it, "he was continually haunted by fear of the passionate love he must necessarily feel if he ever met her, which he never did." These flights of fancy extended in all directions. He was forever disappointed, for reality never measured up to what he imagined.

As prince, he was popular, even among Berlin's intellectuals, for he enjoyed their company and had a great interest in the arts, particularly in architecture. He was somewhat of a social butterfly, alighting at one party and then abruptly moving on to another; the fact that he showed himself at so many made him well liked, as did his fondness for speaking in the Berlinese argot. Frederick William was dearly in love with the sound of his voice and the mellifluous flow of his articulated fancies; it enchanted many, although it usually bewildered most. Berlin, after all, had for two reigns been accustomed to kings who could hardly bear to finish a sentence, being both of the snorting, harrumphing, "stuff-'n'-nonsense" school of oratory: strangulated, inarticulate, apoplectic officers. This crown prince, on the other hand, produced a delightful, diverting torrent of words, many demonstrating what Frau von Rochow calls his "lofty aims," all glitteringly formulated. But what he said in the salons often proved startlingly irrelevant or frivolous; it became clear he was a dilettante and—as people were beginning to whisper—"inconsequential."

Elizabeth of Bavaria was found for him, and the idea of being betrothed so enchanted the romantic crown prince that he deluged her with passionate love letters, although he had only met her briefly. These declarations puzzled her, but she was even more bewildered on her honeymoon, when her bridegroom, lately so ardent, suddenly proved indifferent. Those accompanying them heard him declare—with a yawn—that he was "transported with bliss." In fact, he was more in love with love, with the ideal, than with the flesh-and-blood Elizabeth. The couple stayed together harmoniously enough, though they never did produce any children—despite even the prompting of their brother-in-law, Czar Nicholas, who in the hope that it might promote procreation, sent them a beautiful bronze statuette of a baby boy. The sculpture remained in their Potsdam bedroom, but it was the only infant ever to inhabit that room; it was an idealized conception, preferred over one ideally conceived.

His interests broadened to include the classics, thanks to an 1828 trip he took to Italy with Prince John of Saxony, his brother-in-law; he called John Gianettino and Giovanni and called himself "the fat mad friend from Cölln on the Spree." Indeed, he was becoming fat and flabby in these years (though he slimmed down later); as for the reference to "mad," that may have been a premonition.

His obsession with the medieval past proved fateful for Prussia, for while this Hohenzollern sincerely wished to be a kindly, generous king, he also was unable to respect his people's longing for liberty. He lived in a stained-glass world of elaborate pageantry and he regarded his future subjects as "the gaudy peasantry of light opera . . . ever wreathed in smiles" and grateful for the briefest glimpse of their great king.[121] He came to believe in Metternich's conspiracy theory: that an international plot existed to overthrow and murder kings. Liberals and democrats were the Communists of a pre-Communist era; indeed, as scapegoats and victims, they were the Jews of a pre-Nazi time. "World liberalism" was said to have already captured control of Britain; if liberalism weakened the Continental monarchies, so went the argument, Britain might gain the advantage. The Holy Alliance, which ensured Christian rule by suppressing ungodly liberalism, greatly appealed to the crown prince; Frederick William came to believe that God had assigned to the House of Hohenzollern the work of governing Prussia, that he, as king, would be God's vicar in north Germany. "I know I hold my Crown from God alone and that I have the right to say, 'Woe to him who attacks it!' " he procaimed on his accession. The remark seemed preposterously anachronistic; the divine right of kings was being proclaimed in Prussia at a time when hardly anyone believed in it any longer. Even Frederick William III had never gone that far, had never called himself king "by the grace of God."

The festivities hailing his accession to the throne began at

Königsberg, East Prussia, on August 29, 1840. There was much pomp and circumstance, all the local guilds being assembled, butchers out front, but there was also impertinence as well. Privy Councilor Heinrich von Schön, president of the local Prussian Diet, or Parliament, chose this occasion to tell the king his people desired "a general representative parliament that shall be in a position to give its opinion when called upon." It was a modest enough request and made by men who had more to lose in a revolution, as Schön pointed out, "than the monarch had to fear": gray-haired, conservative property owners, hardly young hotheaded liberals. But the request was dismissed as completely unacceptable. "I consider it most disloyal," said the king's brother, William, who had now become Prince of Prussia, "to demand guarantees from a new sovereign on his accession. . . ." He pointed out that the late king had never convened the provincial Diets into a United Diet because he had wisely discerned that "such institutions in other countries . . . led to nothing but harm, unrest, and discontent on all sides." King Frederick William IV said much the same thing in an address to the delegates in Königsberg. "I declare myself opposed to every written constitution," he told them. "This sort of thing destroys the natural relation between prince and people."

At the public *Huldigung* ceremony in Königsberg, when the oath of allegiance to the new monarch was given, a woman screamed out in the crowd, "Don't swear! Don't swear!" but she was found to be crazy. The rest of the Prussian people—sober, hardworking, God-fearing, and loyal—all swore. So did Berlin, where two ceremonies were held, a fact which aroused much anger: The nobles were invited inside the palace, while the representatives of the people, the delegates from the provincial Diets, had to remain standing in front of the building, on the Schlossplatz.

The new king addressed the crowd in the square, giving them an example of his verbal pyrotechnics. He had a high-pitched voice, liked to throw an arm heavenward while speaking in public, as though pointing to the source of his inspiration, and he generally conveyed an impression of ecstasy—or suppressed hysteria. He was, as A. J. P. Taylor put it, "the first master of what became a specialty of German politics—the meaningless but inspiring phrase. . . ."[122]

"Will you stand by me," he asked the vast throng on the square, "and help me to develop and strengthen the splendid qualities which have been the means of associating Prussia, whose population is only fourteen millions, with the great powers of the earth: namely, honesty, loyalty, yearning for light and truth, the ever-increasing wisdom of age, combined with the ardor of youth? Will you persevere with me in this effort through good and evil days? If so, then answer me in the clear beautiful tones of the mother tongue, answer me with an honest, resolute 'Yes!'."

How could one not shout *Ja* to honesty, light, truth, the wisdom of old age—even to loyalty in such a noble context? A thunderous "Yes!" rolled across the Schlossplatz toward the king's gold and scarlet throne. Overcome with emotion, with the result of his own inspiring but essentially meaningless oratory, Frederick William exclaimed: "That 'Yes!' was for me. I shall remember it to my dying day. I will keep the vow I have made today, so help me God. In token thereof I raise my right hand to heaven, and may the blessing of God rest on this hour!"

Equally moved, the king's subjects broke out in a hymn, "Now Thank We All Our God!" nor did anyone ask: for what?

Toward the end of the year, the king rebuffed Privy Councilor von Schön's overtures again, offering a coherent statement of the absolutist position, a subject which always brought out the best in the king in terms of clarity.

"I feel myself absolutely king by the grace of God," he wrote Schön, "and with His help I shall feel that to the end. Take my royal word for it: no prince, no peasant, no farm laborer, no diet, no clamor will succeed in dispossessing me of any prerogative rightly or wrongly appertaining to the crown unless I first renounce it. I leave brilliance and astuteness, without envying them, to the so-called constitutional princes, who have become an abstract idea to the people through the instrumentality of a scrap of paper. The way of German princes is to rule as a father, and as I have inherited the sovereignty of my forefathers, I have confidence in my people. Therefore I can and will guide children of tender age, punish those who have been corrupted and, on the other hand, give those who are worthy of it a share in the administration of my domains, see that they receive their due, and protect them against insolence from subordinates."

A brochure urging constitutional rule, called *Four Questions,* came to the king's attention and infuriated him. He demanded that the minister of justice discover the identity of the author and charge him with treason; the author stepped forward voluntarily, writing the king a letter. He presented himself as Dr. Johann Jacoby, a Jewish physician from Königsberg. The king responded by writing to Schön, who was also in Königsberg, "See that the disgrace brought upon East Prussia by circumcised Jews is repaired by uncircumcised men of long-standing loyalty who have confidence in me!" But Schön was the wrong man to ask to do such work; the king had to dismiss him a few years later and for much the same reason, for Schön had by then also published a tract deemed treasonous. Jacoby was charged with *lèse-majesté,* or *Majestätsbeleidigung,* as well as with high treason; when the highest appeals court in Prussia, the Kammergericht, found Jacoby innocent, the outraged king attempted to interfere with the independence of the judiciary. This prompted a newly appointed Silesian judge, Heinrich Simon of Breslau, to resign in protest. Simon, who was also Jewish, penned a pamphlet suggesting that governments ought to exist for the well-being of the governed; he even sent it to the king, whose secretary returned it unread, "by order of the Most High." The fact that democratic sentiments were voiced by Jews like Simon and Jacoby particularly aroused the suspicions of the king; he completely missed the point that they were only giving voice to the sentiments of most others.

Shortly after acceding to the throne, Frederick William IV made one gesture toward constitutional rule—and this he regarded as being almost revolutionary. The provincial Diets, he said, would be allowed to establish committees which might or could be summoned by him if "matters of national importance" arose and if he thought the advice of such United Committees might be useful.

"In short," he said, "I have laid the foundations of an institution which may achieve real freedom without the iniquitous farces, the utter unreality, and the hideous claptrap of other constitutions and badly organized legislatures. Now, I say it boldly, none but Jacobins, periwigs, or donkeys can doubt my belief in freedom!"

The next year, after forming a new and even more reactionary government, the king actually issued an order summoning the United Committees to Berlin; the order, however, was withdrawn before it was ever circulated, since the king was persuaded that the sovereignty of a monarch should not be "subordinated to the sovereignties of majorities." Another new period of repression began; subversives were hunted everywhere, newspapers were suppressed, and a central censorship bureau was established. Professors such as Hoffmann von Fallersleben, public servants like Heinrich von Schön were dismissed from their posts. "Revolutionaries must not shelter in Prussia under the wing of the government," the king announced late in 1843. They took his advice and left. The early 1840's saw 50,000 German immigrants come to the United States each year. One of those who sailed was Karl Heinzen, later a newspaper publisher in Louisville and Boston. "Farewell, happy Prussia, with your secret trials, with your hellish administration of laws and your direct and indirect *lèse majestés,* with your press censorship and police!" Heinzen wrote. "Farewell, Prussia, with your unromantic bureaucracy and your 'romantic despotism' [a reference to the king]. Fare you well, with your secrecies, your tricks of despotism, your hypocrisy, your thinly-veneered scoundrelism without end! Farewell, my German Fatherland!" [123]

In Prussia's Silesian provinces at this time, children were forced to go to work at the age of four; scores of families starved to death; a whole people were in rags, brutally exploited by local employers. When these employers cynically lowered wages even more, the starving linen weavers revolted in 1844, but nothing was done to ameliorate their lot. The Prussian infantry shot them down; those who escaped were allowed to starve. A month later a man stepped forward on the Schlossplatz in Berlin just as the king was entering a carriage and fired a pistol twice; the king, protected by a heavy cloak, was only superficially wounded. The assassin was the former burgomaster of Storkow, a man named Tschech and the son of a pastor; he had a personal grievance against his king and was not acting out of political motives. Accordingly, Frederick William offered to commute his death sentence and only signed it "with streaming eyes" when Tschech proved defiant. The tears reflected a growing mawkishness; presently the king came to the conclusion that he was personally inspired by God. He told one official in December, 1844, that he appreciated his services but that "there are things one only knows as king that I did not even know myself as crown prince and have only now learned as king." Hearing this, General Leopold von Gerlach commented dryly, "The ways of the Lord are marvellous." [124]

They came to be even more marvelous: The reactionary Junkers were suddenly and miraculously transformed into champions of parliamentarianism, if only briefly and for particular reasons. It was stated earlier that the only time the Junkers clashed with the House of Hohenzollern was when the interests of their estates conflicted with the interests of their king or kingdom; this time had now come. They were promoting the idea of an *Ostbahn,* a railroad linking Berlin with their distant fiefs in West and East Prussia; the House of Rothschild, however, refused Prussia further credits to finance this unless these credits were approved and guaranteed by a Prussian Parliament. (This embarrassing situation developed because the previous king in 1820 had promised not to increase the national debt without the consent of the people's representatives in Parliament.) As a result, a United Diet was actually convened. It was hoped the delegates would approve the loan and then disband, never to be heard of again. Liberals were outraged. "We asked for bread," Heinrich Simon wrote in *Accept or Reject,* counseling the latter course, "and you have given us a stone.

"So be it," Simon continued, "we are at a crisis in Prussia—nay, in German history! Let the king show confidence in his people. Let him break once for all with the idea that any one person has rights of an exclusive nature as against the rights of fifteen million. . . . I abjure you [the king] to listen. . . . Cast from you the idea of 'absolute monarchy'—the idea that you are responsible to God alone for your actions. . . ."

The United Diet, which the Prussian people promptly called Absolutism's House of Borrowing, met in April, 1847, to hear the king address the delegates in person. He took this opportunity to seal its doom.

"One portion of the press," he said, "is demanding of me revolution in church and state, but of you they are demanding acts of ingratitude, of unlawfulness—even of disobedience.

Many and respectable men seek . . . an alteration of the relations between prince and people; they demand a relationship based on a contract, stamped and sealed under oath. My noble lords and faithful estates, I am constrained to make this solemn declaration: No power on earth shall ever persuade me to alter the natural relation between prince and people into one of contract and constitution; I shall never permit a sheet of written paper to intrude itself—as though it were a second Providence—between God in heaven and this people, to govern us by means of its provisions, substituting them for the old-time, sacred loyalty."

The delegates rallied, but not in support of their king. To everyone's amazement, they demanded the right to meet at regular intervals and further demanded that no taxes be levied in Prussia without their consent. The king responded by dissolving the United Diet; the delegates revenged themselves by not authorizing the debt increase. This parliamentary rebellion profoundly upset the king. By November his anxieties had increased, for there had been hunger riots in Berlin and trouble from Swiss radicals. "If they gain the upper hand there," the king wrote to Queen Victoria in Britain, "torrents of blood will flow in Germany too. . . . The murder of kings, priests and aristocrats is no idle threat with them. . . . This godless gang will gain ground in Germany because, although they are only a small body, their unity and pertinacity give them strength."

While the king's words and actions horrified democrats, they displeased the reactionaries in Prussia just as much. His inconsistency worried them. He persecuted some liberals but freed others. Arndt had been reinstated; Hermann von Boyen had been appointed minister of war, and the liberal scholar Alexander von Humboldt was a member of the Council of State. The fact that the king had convened a United Diet at all also deeply disturbed the archconservatives; such a move represented the kind of creeping liberalism which they feared. What they wanted was a king who would be utterly ruthless in suppressing all liberal thought and action, a warlord who would cause blood to flow in defense of the absolutist monarchy. Frederick William IV was not willing to go that far. He was by nature courteous, well meaning, and kind (despite his rages) and also had no stomach for such resolute action; further, he could not trample underfoot a people who, he was convinced, dearly loved him. That "old-time, sacred loyalty" of which he spoke was not one-sided; because it existed in his people (or so he was convinced), it had to be reciprocated.

There was, however, still one other reason why he could not act with dogged resolution: It would have required consistency and steadfastness. The king was poorly endowed with either quality. He constantly lost track of the train of his thought while speaking and shot off into dizzying flights of fancy. No one knew what he might think next, for the simple reason that he himself did not know it. He had a profound distrust of men of intellect, the exception being Humboldt, who was somewhat of a crony; while easily swayed, the king rarely listened attentively. This was not apparent at first; he would sit quietly enough, as though listening to an adviser's address—he sat so quietly that the adviser often thought he'd won the king over. In fact, the king had not been at all attentive behind those glassy eyes which everyone noted in him; he was merely formulating his own rebuttal. There was no hope of converting the king because his mind was utterly closed; the answer for his people lay in revolution.

News of the February, 1848, Revolution in Paris only moved Frederick William IV to reaffirm the divine right of kings; even with Louis Philippe in flight, this Hohenzollern did not sense the temper of the times. He immediately shot off a letter to Queen Victoria; it was a strange mixture of whimperings and bluster. "If the revolutionary party carry out their program," he wrote, "my relatively unimportant crown will be shattered, but so will Your Majesty's more powerful crown, and a terrible scourge will be inflicted on the nations: A century of turmoil, lawlessness and godlessness will follow. The late king did not venture to write 'by the grace of God'; we, however, call ourselves king 'by the grace of God' because it is true. Well, then, most gracious Queen, let us now show the people . . . that we know our sacred duty and how to do it."

Berlin quickly caught the contagion emanating from Paris. Street demonstrations erupted; thousands of people massed in the Tiergarten park to be harangued by revolutionary orators. On one occasion, a government minister named Bodelschwingh, attired in the uniform of a reserve major, rode up to the demonstrators and told them they ought to be ashamed of themselves and go home; they answered, impertinently, "We're free to do as we like now. Don't you know that?" Bodelschwingh, who most certainly did not, shook his head and rode off in confusion. By March 13, the police chief urged the Berlin military governor to bring troops into the Hohenzollern palace, to protect the king, because the people had grown increasingly defiant; the king's brother William that day uttered his forebodings. The way things went, he said, Germany would very soon be a republic. Crowds whom the troops had driven along Unter den Linden were massing in front of the palace, chanting, "Away with the soldiers!" Two days later the first flimsy barricades were built and the first stones were hurled at sentries.

On the sixteenth a courier arrived from Vienna with the news that Metternich had resigned and was fleeing from the revolution in Austria; Prince William, who received these dispatches in Berlin (the king being in Potsdam), told the war minister to give each soldier who turned out a modest bonus. "There is nothing left to be done," he murmured, "but to put oneself at the head of the movement." [125] He scribbled a note which a major, Oelrichs, took to the king in Potsdam. Oelrichs was flabbergasted to find his king in a small room, busy drying his socks and a pocket handkerchief. Frederick William cast a disinterested look at William's urgent note. "Come and have some soup with us, my dear Oelrichs," the king said. During the meal, the king asked for news from Vienna; when Oelrichs protested that the dispatches which had been sent separately from Berlin must have reached the king already, the king replied, "Good heavens, I've had nothing at all. This is really a dog's life; no one in the world is as badly served as I am. We must find out at once where the dispatches are. I thought that what the prince [William] said merely referred to what might possibly happen." When the dispatches arrived the next moment, the king was confronted with reality. "This is really *too* bad!" he said. "I can't eat any more."

He decided to leave for Berlin: for the palace, if the way were clear; as far as the railway station, if there were danger. At six in the evening, when he arrived in the palace, shots rang out in the city. Soldiers had fired on rioters for the first time. Two civilians were killed; several were wounded; the rest ran away, shrieking with rage. The next day the king thanked the troops involved for their discipline and loyalty.

March 18 was a warm Saturday; before it was over, it turned into what is now called a long, hot summer. Defiant crowds milled about the Schlossplatz all morning; shortly after one o'clock in the afternoon, the king and Burgomaster Naunyn appeared on the palace balcony to conciliate the mob. The king, said Naunyn, had agreed to reconvene the United Diet. Furthermore, the king now favored complete press freedom, agreed to a constitution along liberal lines, favored abolition of German customs barriers, sanctioned a German national flag, and wanted Prussia to lead the movement. As the king showed his assent by waving a handkerchief at the crowd, there were wild cheers, though not from the workers, only from the bourgeois. As Naunyn and his king reentered the palace, the crowd flared up in anger over another issue: Soldiers from the Potsdam garrison were spotted inside the palace gates. "Away with the soldiers!" they chanted. By 2 P.M. the king was convinced by his generals the mob might storm the palace. "Take some cavalry," said Frederick William IV, "and put an end quickly to that scandalous business out there!" [126]

"Dear me," Prince William said some minutes later. "Two rifles have gone off in the air. It is to be hoped that no one has been wounded in the houses over there: the windows are full of people." [127]

It was much worse than that. The two shots sparked an uprising. By the time it ended 18 soldiers and 183 civilians had been killed on that day alone.

"A moment ago," said an eyewitness, "there had been cheers and cries of 'hurrah!' A few minutes later, furious howls of protest and calls for revenge." [128] Furniture was hauled out of houses, paving stones were torn up, and wagons were overturned; barricades formed on every street corner and public square in the center of the city. Tens of thousands of citizens of all classes were up in arms; men everywhere forged bullets for themselves or fashioned lances.

"Never have I lived through a day of such fear and turmoil," said a distinguished professor and member of the Academy of

Sciences, the sixty-two-year-old Wilhelm Grimm, of *Fairy Tales* fame. "At two o'clock, still cheers hailing goals attained; by three, the tragic battle had begun. For fourteen solid hours, 2,000 or 2,500 men battled the people in the streets. The crackle of gun-fire, the explosions of cannon balls and the sound of grapeshot was dreadful. . . . In addition, fires raged, and whenever the sound of gunfire died down for a few moments, then one heard the frightening sound of the alarm-bells tolling. . . ."[129]

The Prince of Prussia stood beside General von Gerlach and personally led an artillery battery on the Schlossplatz. Gerlach told Prince William he was happy it had come to this. "We have the enemy facing us this time, not beneath us as in the morning," he said. His was a perfect expression of the relationship between the Hohenzollerns and their people, for the "enemy" referred to were the subjects of the Prussian king. William replied that his brother ought to withdraw every concession in the light of this rebellion. Inside the palace, however, the king was in no mood for such resolute action. He sat with his face buried in his hands and winced every time he heard a shot go off outside. "No, it cannot be!" he groaned. "My people love me!" Watching him, his queen worried about his courage. "If only the King does not give in!" she was heard to say anxiously.[130] That, however, was precisely what he did. On the nineteenth he promised to withdraw most troops from Berlin if the barricades were dismantled; by the twentieth he had agreed to withdraw all troops from the city, unconditionally. "All is lost now!" Prince William groaned.

The soldiers were supposed to march out with bands playing; they were lucky to get out alive. His men, said General von Prittwitz, had been "insulted in the most shameful manner, had been spat upon and splattered with mud." Other soldiers were stoned. Frederick William was shattered. Reality had turned out not in accordance with his dreams; the king had been catapulted in one day from the German Middle Ages into modern Germany.

He surrendered to demands that he free all political prisoners; some of those taken during the uprising had been savagely mistreated by soldiers at Spandau Fortress. In releasing them, he could not resist hurling a sarcastic gibe at the crowd from the palace balcony just before ducking back inside. "When you have got the prisoners back," he said, "see if you want to keep them!" Fists were shaken up at him; then the freed prisoners were led in triumph through the streets. Finally, the citizens brought wagons filled with their dead to the palace, to confront the king with what his regime had wrought. They demanded his appearance; shaken, huddled in a gray cloak, he appeared, accompanied by his queen. "Nothing is lacking now but the guillotine," Elizabeth murmured. The king had the presence of mind and the courtesy to remove his cap before the dead; the citizens thought he was saluting them, so they cheered. Then they all burst out into song, but they did not sing a revolutionary anthem such as the "Marseillaise" or a German workers' song; they sang, instead, a hymn, *"Jesus, meine Zuversicht,"* one in which the king and queen could join as well.

Officers inside the palace were wrapping themselves in their cloaks preparatory to spiriting the king away to Potsdam, by force if need be. The king, having returned from saluting the dead, walked aimlessly from room to room, not knowing what to do, unable to act, unable even to decide on escape. Prittwitz said he could hold Berlin for twenty-four, possibly thirty-six, hours; meanwhile, carriages assembled for the flight out of the city. Utterly confused, the king encountered one of his ministers on a palace staircase. He succeeded in rallying the king for a moment by stretching the truth a bit. "No Hohenzollern," said Count Arnim-Boitzenburg, "has ever yet run away from danger!" The queen afterward announced, "Arnim will not let us go," a phrase which also expressed the extent of the king's authority at that moment. Then, because a decision was urgently needed, it was decided to have a light meal.

The dinner was spoiled, however, by news that popular rage had turned against Prince William, rumored to be responsible for the killing of civilians. There were demands he be surrendered to the people; the court camarilla urged that he be spirited to safety. William took note of reports that the people were demanding he renounce the succession to the throne, and he offered to do so if it would help his brother; alternatively, he would leave if that might help. Prince William was now a real liability, but the king was not ready to have him renounce the succession; he told his brother to flee. William and his wife,

Princess Augusta, had to sneak down back stairs dressed, respectively, as a footman and a ladies' maid. William was taken to Spandau, she to Potsdam; when the citizens learned his whereabouts, he was spirited off again, to an island on the Havel River. There he received word to go on to London. "What have I done that I should have to leave my country in this way?" he said, with tears in his eyes. "How is it possible for such loyal people to be so misguided?" Then he shaved off his beard, put on a disguise, and hurried off. At one point, he lost his companion, Major von Oelrichs, and had to flee pursuing horsemen by running cross-country through wet meadows, leaping ditches, finally finding refuge with a country pastor. Reunited with Oelrichs by chance, William reached Hamburg aboard a train; he was greeted by thousands of local citizens, all cursing and threatening him. His railway carriage had to be uncoupled outside the city, and he and Oelrichs had to hide in the attic of an inn during the night, until they could reach the steamer *John Bull* the next morning. This docked at London on March 27, five days past Prince William's fifty-first birthday.

Berlin was now a city which seemed to belong to the revolutionaries completely, the soldiers having all left. Angry citizens threatened to set Prince William's palace on fire, but it was saved at the last moment by university students who posted a hand-lettered sign above its portals, proclaiming it the "property of the nation" (*Nationaleigentum*).* A revolutionary people's militia, the Bürgerwehr (Civic Guard), had been formed after the troops had left. It would not have taken much of a bold stroke for its members to do any of a number of revolutionary things: arrest the king, chase him into exile, conceivably send him to his death, force him to institute a genuine constitutional monarchy along democratic lines, or proclaim a republic. Instead, fearing disorder (the bugaboo of the bourgeois mind), the Civic Guard told the king they would protect him and all public buildings. An eyewitness noted that these revolutionaries

* Reminding one irresistibly of two gibes: that revolutions cannot succeed in Germany because the police would issue a prohibition against them, and that revolutionary mobs storming through a German city are inconceivable because of the signs which read KEEP OFF THE GRASS!

showed no real disposition toward revolution. "In all the history of revolts," he commented, "this was unique!" [131]

By March 21 Frederick William IV had regained much of his composure. There were to be no tumbrils after all. His people loved liberty, especially the idea of it, but clearly many of them loved order more. Thanks to the state's disproportionately large army, there was scarcely a man in Prussia who had not learned loyalty to the king and obedience to authority within its ranks; thanks to the established church, the schools, and the bureaucracy, obedience was by this time a habit 400 years old. The subjects of this king had blundered onto the stage in a great act; still blundering, they forgot their lines. As for the king, his performance was to prove masterful for once; as his brother suggested, there was nothing to be done but to put oneself at the head of the movement. Frederick William IV captured the revolution by seeming to surrender himself to it.

The people waved black-red-gold *Reichsbanner* flags, instead of Hohenzollern Prussia's black-and-white banner, so the king and his ministers wrapped black-red-gold ribbons around their sleeves and rode out among the people on the twenty-first. Flanked democratically by two commoners, one of them a wagon driver, the king proceeded behind civic guards bearing more revolutionary banners and was cheered by tens of thousands. "I see you are on guard here," he told the armed civilians standing watch outside the New Guardhouse, a Roman-style building on Unter den Linden, between the Zeughaus and the university, which Friedrich Schinkel built thirty years earlier to replace the *Königswache,* or Royal Guardhouse. "Believe me, I can't find words enough to express how much I want to thank you!" The king had recognized them for what they were: less revolutionaries than burghers protecting the king's property against disorder.

A student honor guard led the king to the university, where the entire student body and the professors had breathlessly assembled in neat rows, waiting for authority personified to appear. They seemed to have forgotten their revolutionary ideals; what they remembered was to be deferential before their uniformed king. That day the House of Hohenzollern might have been toppled like the Bastille; instead, the warden was allowed to modernize and extend his prison.

Frederick William IV enthralled his people that day, speaking in his splendidly obfuscating style of oratory. "My heart beats high," he proclaimed to the assembled multitudes, "to see that it is in my capital that one can witness such strong convictions. Today is a great, unforgettable, decisive day. The future, gentlemen, lies in your hands, and if in the middle or at the end of your lives you look back on its events, you must never forget this day! I wear your colors—but I do not wish for a crown or any dominion. I wish only for Germany's freedom, Germany's unity, and order!"

Then he raised his hand heavenward and pronounced that he had "grasped the banner" and placed himself at the head of the "entire people." Finally, he announced that "Prussia is merged into Germany."

This was the statement all had hoped to hear, for it seemed to proclaim German unification—and, just possibly, freedom—in a new, constitutional German Reich; Frederick William briefly seemed to them like Frederick Barbarossa come to life to save his long-suffering people.

Riding back to his palace, the king was accompanied on foot by a veterinary surgeon named Urban who held aloft a sheet of cardboard on which an imperial crown had been scrawled; this was the closest the king would ever get to one, for he afterward rejected the real thing. Urban entered the palace with the king and later emerged with instructions to lead the Czar Alexander Guards Regiment back into the city from Potsdam. It almost seemed as though the revolution had ended, but this was not the case, and in any event, it might be said never to have started at all. There had been an angry uprising, provoked by shots accidentally fired; there had been a riot, but never a revolt specifically against the House of Hohenzollern or aimed at removing from power the oppressive aristocratic-military cabal. The king was not in hiding or in exile, but safe among the "revolutionaries," and what freedoms Prussians won (such as the right to smoke in the streets) either were trivial or were to last for only seven months.

Just how safe the king felt himself to be in this "revolutionary capital" may be gauged from his own words, as related by Prince Frederick Charles of Hohenzollern, one of the king's army officers in Potsdam, who heard the king utter them. The king had gone to Potsdam to squelch plans which loyal officers were making for his "rescue" and to calm the large numbers of other royalists who wanted to resign their commissions, feeling that honor had been lost when they were forced to "retreat" from Berlin. The king appeared and provoked "protests, indignation, sympathy, and tears" when he announced to his officers that "he was free in Berlin and felt just as safe under the protection of the citizens as in [their] midst."[132]

It is at this point that the greatest Prussian since Frederick the Great stepped onto the stage. He was a thirty-three-year-old Junker who in 1847 had been spokesman for the absolutist and most reactionary faction in the United Diet, a man of tremendous energies and appetites: Otto Bismarck-Schönhausen. Out in the countryside when the revolt began, he briefly entertained the idea of rallying the king's "faithful peasantry" to rescue Frederick William IV from the clutches of the less faithful citizens in the capital; when this proved unrealistic and quixotic, he hurried to Berlin to try to rally the king's generals. So unpopular were his views that he shaved off his mustache and hid himself under a large, floppy hat (which he even decorated with a tricolor revolutionary cockade) before he entered Berlin; as fate would have it, at the Berlin railway station a civic guard who had known him recognized him immediately, looked him over and asked Bismarck what kind of *Schweinerei*—swinish business—he meant by his disguise.

Bismarck quickly discovered that unquestioning military obedience, the Prussian ideal, had its drawbacks: He could not rouse the king's generals to take action (although he played them a cavalry charge on a piano, hoping to do so), simply because they were incapable of acting without orders. Failing there, Bismarck went to see the king briefly and then the queen; she complained to him that Frederick William IV had not slept in three nights. "A king *must* be able to sleep!" Bismarck protested—or possibly he said, "A king must *not* sleep!"; he later gave out both versions. (A. J. P. Taylor, one of his biographers, remarked, "Perhaps the whole dialogue only occurred to him some forty years later."[133]) Augusta, wife of the exiled Prince William of Prussia, was visited next and offered a radical plan: The king should abdicate, her husband should renounce the succession, and her son, Prince Frederick, should be put on the throne in order to restore royal absolutism in a more acceptable guise. Augusta thought this proposal too radical and indignantly rejected it as disloyal.* Bismarck had no recourse after this but to drift about all summer, vainly trying to rally all the reactionaries he could find. Finally, unable to do anything more, he added his father's aristocratic prefix to his own name, calling himself Otto *von* Bismarck, just to show where he stood.

The first Parliament to unite the German people in their 2,000-year history met in May, at St. Paul's Church in Frankfurt-am-Main, proposing a liberal, constitutional German Empire. Thanks to the March "revolution," Prussia also had a National Assembly by this time, meeting in Berlin; its delegates were even more radical, antimonarchical, and republican than those in Frankfurt. On June 8, a new delegate entered the Prussian chamber, introduced as "the member from Wirsitz"; he was the Prince of Prussia, Prince William, who had just returned from Britain. His appearance provoked catcalls and hissing, especially since he had defiantly entered wearing the hated Prussian officers' uniform; when asked if he had anything to say, he replied that he would adhere to the constitutional government since the king supported it, but he hoped that the delegates would not forget the fine old Prussian army slogan "With God, for King and Fatherland!" This brought on more hooting and hissing, although a few cheers were heard as well; the member from Wirsitz left immediately afterward and went to Potsdam to join his family in seclusion, never to return. Wirsitz, which had elected him, remained unrepresented, a fact which did not matter for long, for soon all Prussia was in the same straits.

In October, 1848, the commander of the Civic Guard raced to the Assembly to blurt out the news that General Friedrich von Wrangel was at that very moment marching 15,000 troops on the city's five gates. The citizen militia was ready to fight, but its commander wanted the National Assembly to give him the command to do so. The Assembly established a five-man

* Had this been proposed a few months later, it might have had more appeal, for then there would have been a lofty precedent: just such a maneuver brought Emperor Francis Joseph to the throne of Austria in December, 1848.

committee to consider the matter; a majority of three opposed offering resistance, and Hohenzollern absolutism thus regained power by means of a democratic majority vote. Wrangel's men were greeted with flowers after having been sent out of the city with spit; they had, after all, come to "reestablish order" in a city unaccustomed to the "chaos" of freedom. Order required the imposition of martial law; it was accepted, as everyone was accustomed to more or less that kind of military rule for 400 years. Count Frederick William of Brandenburg (that semi-legitimate son of Frederick William II and Countess Dönhoff) was put at the head of a new, reactionary cabinet; the members of the Prussian National Assembly were dispersed by force of arms, and the Assembly itself was presently dissolved by order of the king on December 5. A new and severely restricted Parliament convened, and one of the members who squeaked in by a narrow vote was Bismarck. He remained as unpopular as ever; even the king had his doubts about him. "Red reactionary, smells of blood," the king remarked. "Only to be used when the bayonet rules." The time for that was fast approaching.

"The world rests not more surely on Atlas' shoulders than the state of Prussia on the shoulders of its army," wrote Prince Frederick Charles, summing up the aftermath of the 1848 uprising.[134] Because this state was not just the instrument of the Prussian army, but the army's own creation, it remained under army rule for the next seventy years, despite the Parliaments which served as window dressing. Now that Prussia had been subjugated, the King of Prussia lent his army out to serve absolutism elsewhere. Two Prussian army corps under Prince William moved against Karlsruhe; other Prussian soldiers replaced the dethroned King of Saxony on his seat of power. Only the impotent Frankfurt Assembly remained; it even had the cheek to send a delegation to Potsdam to ask the king to replace the Count of Brandenburg with a liberal prime minister. "Does Your Majesty care to listen to the delegation?" asked its leader, who happened to be that Jewish democrat from Königsberg, Dr. Jacoby. The king roared, "No!"—beside himself with rage at this impertinence.

"That is the tragedy of kings," Jacoby replied quietly. "They do not wish to listen to the truth."

No one in German history, writes Emil Ludwig in *The Germans,* had ever spoken like that to a German prince in the presence of others. Frederick William IV exploded and stormed out of the room (but Jacoby's portrait, together with his statement, hung in the homes of thousands of German democrats throughout later years).

Having abandoned democracy as its goal, the Frankfurt Assembly aimed at least at unification under a constitution of some type. It found the Habsburgs unwilling to accept the imperial crown, so it offered it to Frederick William IV of Prussia on April 3, 1849. The idea tempted the king and many of his Junkers, who recognized that it meant an opportunity for a massive Prussian land grab, but the king was dissuaded by his ministers, who warned him he would be smothered in a liberal, constitutional embrace. The king told the delegates, headed by Eduard Simson, the president of the Assembly, that he might have accepted the crown had it been offered to him by other German princes, but that he would not deign to "pick up a crown from the gutter"—meaning from the people. This *Kaiserkrone,* or emperor's crown, was just "an imaginary circlet made of scum and mud," he told his intimates.[135] On April 21 the king declared that Prussia could not accept the constitution proposed by the Frankfurt Assembly.

That refusal finished the Frankfurt Assembly, which petered out—but too slowly, and so the Prussian army moved in to chase the delegates home by force of arms. The years which followed were so dismal to liberty-loving Germans that they marked the peak of German emigration to the New World. From the end of 1848 through the 1850's more than 250,000 annually sailed to America. Those liberals who remained behind went into retirement or became practical moderates. Only the old cabal of aristocratic officers and ministers had power, guarding the lands of the House of Hohenzollern against the plague bacillus of liberal thought. In 1850 the king made as though to provide his people with a constitution; it was a bogus document, yet they would be governed by most of its significant provisions until the end of World War I, seven decades later. The most notorious provision was the three-class franchise on which representation was based. Those citizens who paid the two top categories of taxes received two-thirds of the votes and, therefore, two-thirds of the seats in Parliament; the overwhelming majority of the people, who received only one-third of the votes, could never assert its voice. Yet even this was granted grudgingly. The king's last testament pleaded with his successors to ignore the constitution as soon as they felt able to do so.

The remaining decade of Frederick William IV's reign failed to crown him with success. He had submitted to foreign pressure and withdrawn his troops from their 1848 involvement in a dispute over Schleswig-Holstein; during 1849 and 1850 he endured the collapse of his Erfurt Union and suffered what came to be called the "humiliation of Olmütz." Both matters resulted from advice given the king by General Joseph Maria von Radowitz, a conservative who believed concessions had to be made to liberals if Germany were to be saved from revolution. Since the King of Prussia had already refused the Frankfurt Assembly's offer to crown him emperor over a "little Germany" which excluded the Austrian Empire, Radowitz proposed that Prussia head a union of North and Central German states. On May 29, 1849, Prussia, Hanover, and Saxony concluded an alliance to further this project, and a conference was to be held at Erfurt the following March to discuss a constitution. By the year's end, however, Austria had convinced Hanover and Saxony to withdraw, even before the Erfurt Congress took place. Embarrassed by this failure, Radowitz nevertheless continued to promote the idea of some sort of German union under Prussian leadership. What followed, however, proved to be an even greater embarrassment to the Prussian king.

An internal conflict in Hesse-Kassel had prompted Elector Frederick I to invite Austrian and Bavarian troops into his state at the end of October, 1850; Prussian troops marched in as well, to protect Prussia's existing lines of communication. This brought the Prussians face to face with the Austrians. The Count of Brandenburg raced to Warsaw to enlist the czar's support for Prussia, while Radowitz urged Frederick William IV to prepare for war against Austria.

The czar turned Brandenburg down; in Berlin, conservatives such as Bismarck counseled the king not to break with the other traditionally conservative German state, Austria. Frederick William readily agreed, leaning as always toward the conservative position and loath in any event to begin a war between German states. Radowitz was compelled to resign on November 3, and Count von Brandenburg unexpectedly died three days later. The king formed a new government under Otto, Freiherr (Baron) von Manteuffel, who signed a humiliating agreement with the Austrians at Olmütz on November 29, by which Prussian troops were withdrawn from Hesse. Finally, in 1856–1857, he suffered another humiliation in Switzerland, being compelled to give up the canton of Neuchâtel, which had been nominally under Prussian rule since the days of Frederick I, the first King "in" Prussia. In 1854 he had decorated his quasi-Parliament with what he liked to think of as a British-style upper house, but since the Prussian "Commons" was a farce, his "House of Lords" was merely a chamber filled with aristocratic landowners in a nation already governed by such people.

His decline was at hand. He remained in Sans Souci Palace, avoiding Berlin ever since the uprising. It was said he drank a good deal more than was good for him; on the other hand, he was so excitable that he was also known to become animated and gay after drinking a cup of beef tea. He worked much of the day and spent the rest of the time speaking volubly and charmingly with his friends. The intellectual Humboldt was one of these; another was the almost-illiterate General von Wrangel who liked to insult Humboldt by calling him the "court sage." Others of his court included a famous artillery general, Prince Kraft zu Hohenlohe-Ingelfingen, who was the king's loyal aide-de-camp, and Count Keller, an odd choice for court marshal, for he had nothing but contempt for the etiquette which was his daily concern.

The king enjoyed taking solitary walks at night in the Sans Souci Palace gardens, but since he was getting on and was more nearsighted than ever, he was forever bumping into trees and falling down. Worse yet, he collided with his own sentries and never could remember the sign and countersign for that day, causing much confusion. On one occasion, in midwinter, a sentry challenged him and refused to believe him when he identified himself as "the king." "Anyone can say that," the soldier replied and prodded the cloaked stranger into his guard hut, where he kept him, shivering in the cold, for an hour, until the sergeant arrived with the relief.

In late spring, 1857, medical advisers said he was suffering from "nervous exhaustion" and needed the baths at Marienbad. He stayed there from mid-June to July 5, then went to Vienna in oppressive heat, and, on his return, suffered a stroke. Symptoms of what physicians called "softening of the brain" became apparent; within months, he was diagnosed as "incurably insane." Prince William, his brother, was named vice-regent. The last official act of King Frederick William IV, who already had his mental faculties impaired, was to study thirteen death sentences put before him for his approval. The sentences were ratified by an imbecile.

12

"Outward Obedience, Secret Kicks"

It's hard to beat William I of Hohenzollern for sheer staying power: He was born in the candlelit eighteenth century and died just short of the twentieth, after gasoline-powered cars had been invented. In fact, he was born the same month George Washington retired to Mount Vernon, and he died six years after the birth of Franklin D. Roosevelt. Not even Emperor Francis Joseph in Vienna matched that record, for he died when he was eighty-six, while William remained alive and vigorous until just before his ninety-second birthday.*

William never expected anything like that to happen. "Moses's eighty years are not to my taste," he said when he reached sixty, adding that he thought "the best of life is already behind one at that age. . . ."[136] As it turned out, the best was yet ahead. William never expected to outlive his brother and become King of Prussia, but he ended up more than that, for he became German emperor. He was a modest man, yet he was to raise the House of Hohenzollern to its greatest glory. He thought of himself as a simple soldier, yet he came to be regarded as a conqueror, as the Prussian who defeated the Habsburgs at Königgrätz and the French at Sedan. He was so frugal that he marked the level of wine in a bottle with a pencil after

* Francis Joseph's reign was considerably longer, however, stretching sixty-eight years from 1848 to his death in 1916. William was sixty-six years old when he became king in 1861 (the year Lincoln was inaugurated), and he reigned for twenty-seven years.

every meal and so unostentatious that, when traveling by train, he ate his meals in the ordinary railway station restaurants, yet his imperial court attained a wealth and magnificence unparalleled in Hohenzollern history before his reign. Yet, in a sense, few of these accomplishments were his. William earned the name of soldier king, but he never created an army, as had Frederick William I; he was a bold and fearless officer, but not a brilliant one, like Frederick the Great. William's great age, like his crown, came "by the grace of God"; most of the rest, including his imperial crown, came to him by the grace of Bismarck.

The vice-regency he assumed in October, 1857, was for three months only. Briefly, the court camarilla plotted to divest him of his position, by getting the king to proclaim himself able to rule; this would allow them to rule, by working through Queen Elizabeth. The move, however, was thwarted. After William's ninety-day term was renewed twice, the ministry agreed in September, 1858, to make him full regent. The king signed the abdication instrument in silence, then collapsed, sobbing; afterward he and his queen went to Italy, abandoning all hope. William took the oath as prince-regent on October 26, swearing that he would "firmly and unswervingly maintain the constitution" and that he would reign "in accordance with it and the laws," an oath he soon enough felt compelled to break. Now that he had assumed all the powers of the king, he proposed a policy of "moral conquests" and began by replacing the old conservative ministers with new, more liberal men. Rumors had it that his wife, Augusta, had "dictated" the list of new appointees.

One victim of the reshuffle was Bismarck, who was packed off to St. Petersburg as the Prussian ambassador. Hearing the news, Bismarck came to see the regent on January 26, 1859, angry at being "ostracized." He proceeded to tell William what he thought of his new ministers. There wasn't "a single capable statesmen" among them; all were "mediocrities, narrow minds." William became irritated and protested that War Minister Eduard von Bonin was no narrow-minded man. "Not that," Bismarck conceded. "But he can't even keep a drawer in order, much less a ministry—and Schleinitz [the new foreign minister] is a courtier, not a statesman."

"Perhaps you regard me as a dummy?" Prince William snapped back. "I mean to be my own foreign minister and minister of war—that's understood!"

Three days later Bismarck's post in Russia was confirmed, and a "new era" of liberalism was thought to have arrived. The prince-regent, who had been hated after March, 1848, as "the Cartridge Prince," a name he earned by leading troops against the rioters, was suddenly, if briefly, popular.

William, like Theodore Roosevelt, had to overcome a delicate, weak, and sickly constitution in order to lead the vigorous life he loved. By the time the prince was seven years old, he drilled daily under the command of a sergeant in the guards; three years later, he was a guards cadet officer, all Hohenzollern princes being commissioned at the age of ten. His mother thought of him as "simple, straightforward, and sensible" and as a marked contrast with his volatile, romantic, more intellectual brother, then crown prince. It became apparent early that William was cut out for army life. As an eleven-year-old lieutenant, he kept a diary which lovingly recorded the military drill and ceremonials he observed, and by the time he was sixteen, he had become fascinated with—and expert at—the colorful details of military dress. He accompanied the Prussians in the War of Liberation and quickly distinguished himself for personal bravery in battle. In 1814 he joined a furious Russian cavalry charge at the Battle of Bar-sur-Aube and, shortly afterward, rode unaccompanied through murderous gunfire to obtain intelligence requested by his father, which action earned him a Russian decoration and the Iron Cross. The acclaim he received surprised him; characteristically, he thought he'd done nothing noteworthy. He was only sixteen but had none of the arrogance of youth.

After the Peace of Paris came a triumphal visit to London, to celebrate the apparent end of "Nöppel," as the Prussians called Napoleon. Frederick William III had taken both his elder sons, as well as Blücher and Gneisenau, to Britain; the czar was also there. William watched a Portsmouth naval salute, Highland pipers, celebrations in London, and met Wellington.

"I prefer London to Paris," he wrote afterward. "England is almost a garden. None of the pictures one sees are exaggerated.

There are horses, cattle, deer, rabbits, etc., all running together in the parks. And the English turf! One is continually sinking into it, it is so soft. But I must not say more, or I shall long to be back in England."

Shortly after his eighteenth birthday, he was confirmed by the court chaplain at the Charlottenburg palace. This ceremony required of every Hohenzollern prince that he write down his own profession of faith, in his own words. William penned thirty-six articles which were simple, straightforward, and sensible, and which reflected that sense of duty and commitment to service which guided him throughout his life.[137] Much of it is as idealistic as one might expect in a young man of his age and time; some of it shows a youthful naïveté, but adorned with noble, even knightly, sentiments. He would cultivate "a kindly disposition to all men," he said, "for are not all men my brethren?" He would never "overbearingly or unduly assert" his rank; if he had to "demand or exact submission and obedience," he would do so "kindly and affably." He said he wished to be "beloved" rather than feared or honored simply for his rank; he would "unceasingly labor" to improve his heart "and mend" his life; he would "resolutely" turn away "corrupt men and flatterers" and would seek out his friends "among the good, the true-minded, the upright, the sincere." Article 36 declared, "I accept the laws and constitution of the state in every respect." It also stated he would "scrupulously obey" his father, a statement which soon enough was to be tested brutally. At the age of twenty-two, Prince William fell in love with a seventeen-year-old girl who, it was claimed, was beneath his station. He was a Hohenzollern, a son of a ruling house, while she was a Radziwill, a princess of a lesser house.

The Radziwills were descended from the Polish ruling house before the partitioning of Poland; although rich, theirs was no longer a reigning family. There had been past Hohenzollern-Radziwill marriages, so there was some precedent and reason to hope that another would be permitted. Louis, the younger son of the Great Elector, had married a Radziwill; Elisa Radziwill's mother, Princess Louisa, was also a Hohenzollern, being a cousin of King Frederick William III and the sister of that Prince Louis Ferdinand of Prussia who was killed at Saalfeld in 1806. The marriage of Louis, however, had taken place a long time before; the marriage of Louisa, a Hohenzollern daughter, was not as important as the marriage of William, a Hohenzollern son. There was a feeling that a marriage between Elisa Radziwill and Prince William would be a *mésalliance;* the Hohenzollerns were forever speaking of their ancient royal house, though in fact they had achieved royal status only in the eighteenth century and Frederick William III was only the fifth Hohenzollern king.

In the spring of 1822 a commission appointed to approve or disapprove the match turned thumbs down, and William was ordered to renounce the girl. He obediently submitted; later that year, the king allowed William to appeal the decision. The affair ran on interminably, for years, keeping the young lovers in an agony; there was even talk of Elisa's being adopted by the czar and then, when the czar refused, by a Hohenzollern, so as to give her regal rank. All these schemes failed. After five years of uncertainty, William finally gave up trying and pledged himself to obey his father. The Radziwills and others respected his decision but not his "lack of courage." They could understand his obedience but half hoped he might have proved a bit more rebellious. Others of royal birth, in Austria, had successfully battled the court; why was William unable or unwilling to do so? The thing was simply not in his nature. To act more nobly toward Elisa would have meant having to act "ignobly" toward his father; further, William was committed to subordinating his own desires to his sense of duty. Devoted as he was to her, he was not passionate by nature; she, in turn, was far more romantic than he, although, ironically, much less in love. After William's marriage to Princess Augusta in 1829, Elisa entertained plans for another marriage for herself, this time to Prince Friedrich Schwarzenberg, a Byronesque romantic who was the son of the famed Austrian field marshal, but this also came to nothing. A few years after that, Elisa died in Berlin, spitting up blood, and William, who attended the funeral, looked shattered. Her portrait remained on his desk for the rest of his life. The whole affair, a Prussian soap opera par excellence, had been heart-rending; as usual in Prussia, obedience emerged victorious even over love.

Augusta of Saxe-Weimar turned out to be an unusual choice, in any event: intellectual, pro-Catholic, and liberal. Goethe bade her farewell at Weimar; he regarded her highly and remained a friend until his death. William was thirty-two and she barely eighteen when they married in Berlin on June 11, 1829; William's sister Charlotte was present, in new grandeur, for the death of Alexander had raised her husband, Nicholas, to the Russian throne, and she was now the czarina. The couple moved into a new palace, once it was completed in 1836. Built by Karl Ferdinand Langhans on the south side of Unter den Linden, this was to be William's home until his death, for William declined to move into the Berlin Palace, the traditional Hohenzollern residence, even after acceding to the throne.

Augusta began to collect a literary and artistic circle; her youth had been spent in the proximity of Goethe, and she was determined to continue the intellectual tradition of her parents' Weimar court. Her ambitions outpaced her abilities, however, and courtiers soon snickered that she was forever quoting the opinions of others as though they were her own. Furthermore, her liberal politics failed to sit well in Prussia. She was referred to as "a little Jacobin," and it is a fact that during the 1848 uprising and the constitutional crises which followed, Augusta sided with the parliamentarian faction. It was no wonder that Bismarck hated her and that she reciprocated the feeling. Nor did she become more conservative as she grew older: by the time she was seventy, she was even vaguely "Socialistic," hoping idealistically that the rich might voluntarily part with some of their money. The same sentiments impelled her to take a great interest in the plight of the sick, of wounded soldiers, and of victims of disasters; she visited Florence Nightingale every time she visited England. Inevitably, the differences between her and her conservative husband caused an estrangement. They were married almost sixty years (she died nine months after his death) but quarreled constantly—some say daily. Bickering grew to be such a habit that when she became ill in 1887, William was extremely worried about her—because, said one Prussian general, the prospect of the quarrel ending was intolerable. Some of their arguments became common knowledge. On one occasion, Augusta, already empress, was at Baden-Baden and wanted to go to Geneva incognito. She sent a telegram to her husband, the emperor, asking, "May I go to Geneva?" The reply came back immediately: "Go!" From Geneva, she wanted to go to Turin and again asked permission. Once more the reply came back: "Go!" A few more telegrams of the same kind followed, each time eliciting the same one-word response, until the final reply came: "Go, and be hanged!" On another occasion, when Bismarck was fighting the Roman Catholic Church, Augusta was concerned about the nuns at a Coblenz convent, who were to be turned out of their home and of whom the empress was fond. "William," she said threateningly to the emperor, "if the nuns have to leave Coblenz, I shall stay with you." The nuns did not have to leave. Half the time William did not even speak to Augusta; if she addressed him, he would turn to some court official standing nearby and ask him to repeat her words. "What did she say?" he would ask, directly in front of her. William called her "hotheaded," and Bismarck referred to her as strong-minded: she annoyed them both, but both respected her. Their only children were Frederick and Louisa, born 1831 and 1838; Frederick became the tragic and liberally inclined Emperor Frederick III and the father of the last reigning Hohenzollern, William II. Louisa married the Grand Duke of Baden.

When William's father died, the childless new king, Frederick William IV, named his brother Prince of Prussia and heir presumptive; William was appointed governor of Pomerania and, during the king's brief visit to England in 1842, acted as regent. During the years preceding the March, 1848, uprising, the Prussian conservatives regarded Prince William as their champion in court, the king being mistrusted by both reactionaries and democrats. William and Augusta also visited Britain in these years, where they were overwhelmed by the hospitality of Queen Victoria and the Prince Consort, Albert, and where William received a doctor's degree at Oxford, from the chancellor of the university, Wellington, whom he had met after the Napoleonic Wars. He returned to Prussia bearing warnings from Wellington, Peel, and others against the democratic elements with which the British monarchy had to contend; they advised him to tell the King of Prussia not to take English conditions as a guide. William was opposed to forming the 1847 United Diet and in 1846 had declared it was his "sacred duty" to see that the crown "is handed down to the heirs to the throne with undiminished rights. . . ." But the growing pressure of democratic elements brought him around a bit, and in 1847 he predicted the birth of "a new Prussia"; he said he hoped that whether it be constitutional or not, it would be "as great and illustrious" as the old absolutist state had been. The following year he was back in Britain as a refugee from popular wrath. At a dinner given in Carlton House Terrace, William met another *émigré,* a Herr von Meyer and his wife. "Meyer" turned out to be Prince Metternich, who had been chased out of Vienna.

William now resigned himself to constitutionalism and approved most of the draft constitution which Friedrich Christoph Dahlmann proposed at the Frankfurt Assembly, though he objected to the idea that monarchs become members of an upper house, since they might conceivably be outvoted and could be drawn into undignified debates.

En route home on May 30, William wrote the king that he would fully abide by the constitution and later told officers who greeted him that he accepted the new conditions "wholeheartedly," but when Wrangel disbanded the Prussian National Assembly, he quickly forgot these earlier pronouncements. "Our coup with the National Assembly has succeeded," he wrote to his younger brother. "It had been set up on the illegal basis of disobedience. This could not be tolerated." A year later William led the Prussian forces into Baden and the Palatinate, reestablishing autocracy, and again played the role of Cartridge Prince. "Germany must be conquered before she can be governed," he wrote, innocently summing up the attitude of his entire dynasty toward the people over whom this House of Hohenzollern ruled. For his services, William received the *Pour le mérite* medal and was appointed governor of Prussia's Rhineland and Westphalia. The next seven years went quietly enough, the restoration of reaction always bringing "quiet years" in Prussia. William visited Russia once and Britain twice, in 1851 and 1853. He celebrated his silver wedding anniversary in 1854 and was made a field marshal. In 1857 he celebrated his fiftieth year in the Prussian army; Queen Victoria decorated him in honor of that jubilee. The next year, William's twenty-seven-year-old son, Frederick, married Victoria's daughter, Britain's princess royal (also named Victoria), who was then eighteen.

Then, at the age of sixty-one, William was installed as prince-regent of Prussia, replacing his brother, the king. Three years later the king who had been "a living corpse" died. William, now sixty-four years old, ascended the Hohenzollern throne on January 2, 1861. He brought to a Prussia whose character was changing in those industrial times a character molded in the unchanging traditions of the army. Fifty years of active army service had shaped this monarch. He was a soldier king in actual fact; he was an army officer enthroned. He was flexible enough to accept the limited constitutionalism his brother had granted, but the interests of the army were foremost in his mind. A conflict was brewing between the parliamentarians and Minister of War (later Field Marshal and Count) Albrecht von Roon, who had been planning a reorganization of the army. The effect of this was to be far-reaching.

At the coronation ceremonies in Königsberg in mid-October, William addressed a delegation of officers headed by old Wrangel. He spoke to them in his capacity as Prussia's "war-lord," this being the traditional role each Hohenzollern king felt compelled to play with varying degrees of success. His talk reflected his deep belief in absolutism; here, among those who had sworn to defend the House of Hohenzollern, he did not need to mince words. "The crown," he stated, "has come to me from the hands of God, and when I shall have taken it from His consecrated table and placed it on my head, it will be His blessing that will preserve it for me." He then reminded the officers that they were to help this godly work along. "It is for the army to defend it," he said, referring to the crown, "and Prussia's kings have never known the army to waver in its loyalty. It was the army that saved the king and fatherland in the disastrous outbreaks [of 1848], and if I should have to call it up against enemies, I count upon its loyalty and devotion, no matter from what quarter they may come." It was a reminder, not very thinly veiled, that the Prussian army might again be called on to shoot down Prussians, to "conquer Germany," as William had earlier said.

The actual coronation ceremony was so moving that William was seen to wipe his eyes with a pocket handkerchief afterward, while Augusta dissolved into tears. As he held aloft his scepter and sword of state, sunlight fortuitously streamed in on him through the Schlosskirche's stained-glass windows, a gorgeously mystical scene afterward immortalized by the painter Adolph Friedrich Erdmann von Menzel. William waved his scepter three times at the crowd outside, then moved in procession to the palace, amid the pealing of bells, the crash of cannon, and the singing of the national anthem, *"Heil Dir im Siegerkranz."** When he received professions of loyalty from the Diet parliamentarians, William reminded them of the divine authority of the Hohenzollern crown. "I am the first king to ascend the throne since it has been invested with institutions in conformity with the spirit of the times," he said. "But mindful of the fact that the crown comes from God alone, I have shown that I receive it humbly from Him by being crowned in sacred precincts. . . . The might and rights of the throne are secure whilst the harmony between king and people, which has made Prussia great, continues to exist. . . ." A few weeks later new parliamentary elections were held. The Conservatives won 24 seats, while the Progressive Party won 100. Within three months there developed a parliamentary crisis.

Parliament had been cynically invested with no effective powers at all. Its sole meaningful function was to *approve* the expenditure of government funds, which always meant the army budget, for this was the only fund seriously engaging the attention of the king or his ministers. To make certain that Parliament could not exercise any effective power over the government's purse strings, the constitution set up a complex system of raising tax revenues permanently and independently of Parliament. This, however, did not stop the delegates from moving boldly in 1862. They demanded that revenues and expenditures be accurately accounted for in the future, a demand which put the Hohenzollern ministry into a panic. It seemed an innocent-enough request, but in fact it posed a threat, for

* "Hail to Thee in the Victor's Laurels," sung to the melody of "God Save the Queen" (or "My Country 'Tis of Thee"), became the anthem of all Germany after William became emperor in 1871. It was not until 1922 that Weimar Germany's Socialist president, Friedrich Ebert, chose *"Deutschland, Deutschland über Alles"* as the official national anthem. This song had been composed by Hoffmann von Fallersleben in 1841; the reference to "Germany above all" was a then-subversive call for German unity. It cost Hoffmann his professorial post at Breslau, from which he was discharged for "demagogic activity." The fact that he had set it to the music which Joseph Haydn had composed for the Austrian anthem, "God Preserve Emperor Francis," made it doubly suspect.

the government had secretly been diverting funds toward army use. William reacted to the crisis by dissolving Parliament on March 11 and by blaming his ministers for not having exerted enough influence on that election which had resulted in so large a Progressive vote. His liberal ministers resigned and were replaced with Conservatives. The "new era" of liberalism had officially ended. His brother-in-law, Grand Duke Charles Alexander, at Weimar, protested; he wrote William, warning him not to disregard the spirit of liberalism in Germany, for to "go back to the methods of bygone days must necessarily be disastrous. . . ." William replied that he was sorry that the grand duke agreed "with the democratic newspapers, which conjure up visions of reaction and heaven knows what." The former ministers, he said, had been replaced only because they could no longer deal with Parliament and could not govern. "We are doing it now," William added, "by actively and resolutely opposing the democracy—nothing more."

New elections had been called for May 6, but the outcome was disappointing to the king, for the conservatives were completely beaten, and the army budget remained in jeopardy. This budget was loathsome to most of the delegates in Parliament not only because it would have doubled the army's size, but because it would have done so at the expense of the reserve Landwehr, that principal benefit which the Prussians had received for their sacrifices in the war against Napoleon. The Landwehr's middle-class officers had always been despised and distrusted by the aristocratic officers of Prussia's professional standing army, first of all because these had been schooled in Frederick II's dictum that only nobles were noble enough to command, secondly for a more modern reason. Bourgeois reserve officers might vote in parliamentary elections in their private lives, a notion which horrified the General Staff. Officers were sworn to serve and obey their king, if need be against his own people; they had no business voting "like democrats," possibly even for liberal delegates who were thorns in the king's side. "The armed forces," said Roon, "do not deliberate; they obey!" The conflict caused William to sink into such despair that he planned to abdicate if his ministers left him in the lurch; in any event, he could not permit Parliament to "ruin" the army. At the last moment, Roon produced a secret weapon:

Bismarck, whom Roon championed as prime minister. Bismarck, who had been in France, hurried to Berlin and met the king; he was shocked and horrified to find an act of abdication written out and lying on the table in front of King William. "If I cannot come to an understanding with you," William said, "I shall have this document published in the *Staatsanzeiger,* and then my son can see how he can get on. I should be acting against my conscience if I were to sacrifice the reorganization of the army, and that would seem to me wrong." Bismarck begged the king to abandon all plans of abdication, but William picked up the sheet of paper, still toying with it and the idea. "Will you govern without a majority?" the king asked Bismarck. Without hesitating for a moment, Bismarck replied, "Yes." William then asked him if he would govern without a budget, meaning without Parliament's authorization to spend the tax revenues. Again Bismarck replied, "Yes."

"Well, then," William said, breathing a sigh of relief, "everything's all right!" He and Bismarck left for a walk in the gardens. William showed Bismarck several sheets of paper covered with his own handwriting: the king's program. Bismarck studied it briefly, noted it contained concessions to the liberals, and urged the king to tear it up. "It is really no longer a question of whether the townspeople or the landed gentry predominate in the provincial Diets," Bismarck said, "but of whether the crown or the majority in the Chamber of Deputies is to govern Prussia. . . . I would rather perish with the king than leave Your Majesty in the lurch in a struggle with Parliament." It might be necessary to institute a period of outright dictatorship, he said; what was essential in any event was that parliamentary rule must be avoided.

William agreed completely and tore up the list of concessions, letting the little scraps of paper drift over the edge of the bridge on which they were standing, into a small gully in the park. Bismarck picked them up, warning the king that his handwriting would be recognized. "Would not Your Majesty prefer to trust them to the fireplace?" he asked. William assented and afterward revived his spirits at the spa in Baden-Baden, where Augusta was celebrating her birthday.

In Berlin, Bismarck prepared to address Parliament; he was

now both Prussian minister-president (or prime minister) and minister for foreign affairs. The first speech he gave before the parliamentary budget commission, however, backfired sensationally. Bismarck's enemies saw to it that his words were published and attacked them as scandalous. Even Roon was alarmed at Bismarck's tone, and when William heard of the matter at Baden-Baden, he prepared to board a train for the capital, to dismiss his new head of government. All seemed to agree that Bismarck had blundered badly. What he had told the parliamentarians was this: "Germany does not look to Prussia's liberalism, but to her strength. The great questions of the day will not be decided by speeches and the resolutions of majorities—that was the great mistake of 1848 to 1849—but by iron and blood!"

On the face of it, it was a perfectly reasonable statement, reflecting the actual truth: No one in his right mind looked to Prussia for liberalism, and, just as certainly, the fate of the king's subjects would not be determined by a majority of them. But this was no defense, for the remark was intemperate and inflammatory; the king liked his absolutist sentiments decked out prettily with constitutional talk, not revealed to the world in so bald a fashion. Bismarck, who knew that there were many people in Berlin who would counsel the king to dismiss him, decided to head his monarch off, by meeting William at a remote railway junction. Bismarck arrived first and waited for the king in a corner of the platform, seated atop an overturned wheelbarrow, watching workmen and third-class passengers milling about. The king's train arrived; more properly, it was not the king's at all, but an ordinary train, in which the frugal monarch simply occupied a private first-class compartment. Bismarck had some difficulty finding him, then had even more difficulty winning him over. His remarks had not been intemperate at all, he said, but had merely reasserted the supremacy of the House of Hohenzollern. William was extremely depressed (as a result of his having been with Augusta, Bismarck thought) and cut off Bismarck's remarks by saying, "I know exactly how this will end! They will cut off your head and later on mine, on the Opernplatz, beneath my windows. You'll end up like Stafford and I like Charles I!"

Bismarck didn't argue. "And afterward, Sire?" he said to William in French, which must have made William think of the fate of Louis XVI.

"Yes," William replied impatiently. "*Après* we shall be dead!"

"Yes, we shall be dead," Bismarck agreed. "But we must die sooner or later and can we perish more creditably? I myself in fighting for the cause of my king; Your Majesty in sealing your divine right with your blood? Whether shed on the scaffold or on the battlefield . . . you would be gloriously staking your life for the rights conferred on you by the grace of God."

Those were words to checkmate this king. William could not find a rebuttal which didn't seem cowardly; furthermore, Bismarck had cleverly appealed to an old soldier's readiness to die gloriously in battle, to a high-principled gentleman's readiness to sacrifice his life for a cause which he regarded as noble. William reacted like the soldier he was. As Bismarck related it, the king pulled himself together and responded by standing stiff, almost at attention, "like an officer answering a superior's command." [138]

King William I did not realize it yet, but he had been taught a lesson which was to last him for a quarter of a century. Bismarck would rule while William reigned.

Bismarck next taught Parliament a lesson, by governing as though it didn't exist. The fact that he was acting illegally and unconstitutionally bothered neither him nor the king. William was able to reorganize the Prussian army, and Bismarck would soon enough give him the opportunity to use that weapon. The king's chief minister was so much in the ascendant that for the rest of William's reign, he tended to eclipse the king. William, in any case, was no longer in the prime of vigorous life. Now in his late sixties, he was far from senile, but equally far from reality. Small incidents showed just how simple, almost simple-minded, this king was. He once attended a lecture on the "poetry of sorrow" and afterward told the speaker, a Jewish writer named Berthold Auerbach, that his remarks had astonished him; this was the first time he had ever heard the expression, had never known there was such a thing, and had never had any personal experience of sorrow. For the son of the grief-stricken Queen Louisa and the frustrated suitor of Elisa Radziwill, that was a strange comment indeed or, in any event, one which showed just how deep his capacity for deep feelings was. The same inability to comprehend real emotion was demonstrated in 1863, when he attended a play, *The Secret Agent*. The audience burst into applause when an actor demanded "that the ministry must be changed," but William completely misunderstood. He told Bismarck the audience applauded another line altogether: "You know that I have the good of the people at heart." He even wanted to rise in his box and bow, but fortunately he didn't.

The unpopular ministry of Bismarck abolished the constitutional freedom of the press two months later, and when the liberal-minded crown prince protested vigorously, the king sharply rebuked his son for stating his views. Crown Prince Frederick, however, stood his ground, saying he could not in all conscience have done otherwise, and suggested that his father divest him of his political and military positions. Bismarck, who was aware of the fact that liberal clergymen were already referring to this Frederick as a David, urged the king not to make his son a martyr; he reminded the king of how much sympathy had gone out to Crown Prince "Fritz" when his father, Frederick William I, imprisoned him at Küstrin. The squabble was allowed to die down, Frederick removing himself to Scotland for a holiday in the Highlands.

Bismarck's contempt for Parliament was demonstrated even more dramatically when he waged a war in 1864 without Parliament having voted any war credits. The revenues, as stated, were at his disposal in any case; he simply didn't bother getting parliamentary approval for their disbursement. This war was a joint Austro-Prussian venture against Denmark, over the long-disputed duchies of Schleswig and Holstein; it resulted in the joint Austro-Prussian occupation of those territories. This was the last cooperative venture of these two German powers, for Bismarck was now determined to contest Austria's preeminence among the German states.

War between Austria and Prussia had to come sooner or later. Austria was still regarded as the strongest German power and generally accepted as spokesman for all other German states. Prussia was ready to contest that position. In fact, the two states had been rivals for more than 100 years, ever since Frederick II attacked Silesia. Only their mutual hatred of Revolutionary

France had made them allies; they remained allied after Napoleon's defeat to prevent German liberalization and unification. The old system they helped crystallize had existed for half a century and was ready for the trash can. Bismarck was ready to sweep it away in 1866. General Helmuth Karl Bernhard von Moltke, the brilliant chief of the Prussian General Staff, late in life summed up the situation and the underlying causes in just two sentences: "The war of 1866 was entered on not because the existence of Prussia was threatened, nor was it caused by public opinion and the voice of the people; it was a struggle long foreseen and calmly prepared for, recognized as a necessity by the cabinet, not for territorial aggrandizement, but for an ideal end—the establishment of power. Not a foot of land was exacted from conquered Austria, but she had to renounce all part in the hegemony of Germany." [139]

The war flared up in June, after both parties had mobilized and gathered supporters among the German states. The decisive battle was fought at Sadova, or Königgrätz, as it was called in German. It was the first big modern battle, involving 440,000 to 460,000 troops, more than had fought at Leipzig against Napoleon in the Battle of the Nations and many more than Frederick the Great had ever put into the field. It was also the first modern battle in the sense that the products of the Industrial Revolution were involved: the telegraph and railroads, modern cannon, breech-loading rifles, and so forth. Few people expected the Prussians to win; the Austrians were generally—and mistakenly—regarded as having the stronger and better army. When it was all over, the world was staggered by the result. London's *Spectator* said, "Thirty dynasties have been swept away, the fate of twenty millions of civilized men has been changed for ever, the political face of the world has changed as it used to change after a generation of war. . . . Prussia has leaped in a moment into the position of the first Power in Europe." [140] The *Illustrated London News* was equally surprised. "Events of so startling a character have taken place in the theater of war," it wrote, "and present such an aspect of importance toward the future that the mind is dizzied. . . ." [141] *Revue des deux mondes,* in Paris, was not quite willing to accept the idea that Prussia was now the "first Power in Europe," there still being France to contend with, but it admitted that this one battle "has revealed the armed might of Prussia and has struck a perhaps irrevocable blow at the political power of Austria." [142]

It should not have surprised people that much. Europe ought to have learned a lesson from the success of Frederick the Great, when that Hohenzollern defeated the Habsburgs' Maria Theresa against all expectations; the Prussians were not Viennese, and they studied the science of warfare as thoroughly as the Austrians did the fine art of living. In Prussia there was universal military service, and the best families sent their best sons to pursue what they thought was the best profession, the army; in Austria all university graduates were exempt from military service, and anyone with money could buy his way out. The educational level of the Austrian soldiers was lower; furthermore, the Austrian officers preferred dash and personal bravery to careful study and methodical planning. The difference between the two armies was dramatically shown by the difference between Moltke and his Austrian counterpart, Ludwig von Benedek. Moltke was sixty-six and a professor of war, rather than a battlefield commander; he had spent six years planning every detail of this war with Austria and was quiet, self-confident, and unshakable in a crisis. Benedek was a brave and loyal combat officer who had fought with distinction but who had almost no military education at all; he was neither a strategist nor a good tactician. When Benedek was appointed at the age of sixty-two to face the Prussians, he grumbled, "So now I am supposed to study the geography of Prussia! What do I know about a Schwarze Elster and a Spree? How can I take in things like that at my age?" To a visitor, he said, "How could we prevail against the Prussians? We have learned little, and they are such studious people!" [143] An example of this was provided in 1864, when the Geographical Bureau of the Austrian General Staff was planning to prepare military maps of Germany, basing them on reports sent in by an Austrian officer who had been sent to Germany to study the terrain. That officer, however, preferred to attend the gambling casinos and irritably replied to Vienna's requests for information that they could find all they wanted in Baedeker's guidebooks. Quartermaster Friedrich von Beck admitted that the staff of the Vienna army command contained only one or two officers who even had a rudimentary understanding of military science and tactics. On the other hand, the Prussians not only had Moltke, a strategist whom military historians consider a military genius, but had three Hohenzollerns in the field, all of them capable and brave, and, in one case, even outstanding. The head of the entire Prussian force was, of course, the seventy-year-old King William I; the head of the first Prussian army was the king's nephew, Prince Frederick Charles of Prussia, and the head of the second Prussian army was the crown prince, Frederick William. Frederick Charles, like his uncle, had spent his whole life in Prussian military service and was an officer of skill and determination. The crown prince, also a capable officer, was brave, quiet, self-confident, and unflappable in crises. King William, despite his age and his early reluctance to accede to Bismarck's plans for war, could hardly contain himself when he heard the cannon thunder. Bismarck had come along, hastily promoted for the occasion from lieutenant in the reserve to major general. One of his main jobs was to control that old war-horse, the king, a formidable task under the circumstances. At one point, William refused to withdraw although under fire, not even being persuaded to do so with the argument that he was endangering his civilian prime minister by remaining exposed. Bismarck finally kicked William's horse with his boot, sending it off; the king, realizing what had happened, accepted the implied rebuke. "It was a perfect parable of relations between king and minister," says A. J. P. Taylor, "outward obedience, secret kicks." [144]

After the battle had been won, Bismarck found himself again at odds with the king. William simply never understood any of Bismarck's long-range political plans for Germany; he was a highly moral, almost simpleminded officer who was persuaded to fight only after Bismarck convinced him that the Austrians and their allies were threatening to attack Prussia, which was untrue. He had entered into the war with righteous anger, whereas Bismarck had entered it calmly; now that it was over, William felt that Austrian "wickedness" must be severely punished. Several other Prussian generals, equally simpleminded in their moral judgments, wholeheartedly agreed, but Bismarck was horrified, since he knew Austrian wickedness had never been involved. He did not want an inch of Austrian territory; he only wanted Austrian influence completely withdrawn north of the Main River and was willing to admit, as he did to William, that "Austria was no more in the wrong in opposing our claims than we were in making them." William didn't agree because he didn't understand; he wanted at the very least to humiliate the Austrians by leading his army in triumph through Vienna. Bismarck argued for two full days to prevent such an act of revenge; when arguments didn't win, he tried hysterics, tears, threats of suicide. These dramatics and the arguments of the crown prince, who supported Bismarck, finally won out. Austria was asked to pay an indemnity, nothing more; a few of its allies also paid indemnities; Prussia annexed only Schleswig-Holstein, Hanover, Hesse-Kassel, and Frankfurt-am-Main. A North German Confederation was established under Prussian domination, and the way was readied for the next move. This was to come within less than a handful of years. One Frenchman who watched the news from Königgrätz anticipated it by saying that it was the French, not the Austrians, who were beaten in that battle. For a long time, France had maintained its position in Europe by keeping rivalry between the two German powers alive. Now there was no rivalry left, Austria having given way to Prussia as the first German power. Only France was left as a rival, and the struggle against Napoleon III, which would soon come, would resolve that.

13

A Flourish of Trumpets

BACK in the fifteenth century, when Burgrave Frederick of Nuremberg traveled north to become the first Elector of Brandenburg, some of the Hohenzollern family remained behind. These South German and Roman Catholic Hohenzollerns continued the Swabian line of the family, and because the seat of some of them was Sigmaringen on the Danube, they were known as the princes of Hohenzollern-Sigmaringen. In the mid-nineteenth century, the head of this branch of the family was Prince Charles Anthony (Karl Anton), the father of six children, four of them sons. It was now their turn to emerge from obscurity.

Far from Germany, the leaders of two newly united principalities, Moldavia and Walachia, were in search of a foreign prince who could come to the Balkans and rule as Prince of Rumania, it being a common practice to import princes to fill vacant thrones. The position was ultimately offered to the second son of Charles Anthony, this being Charles Eitel, who later ruled Rumania as Carol I.

Rumania was fiercely Francophile, and the choice of a Hohenzollern seemed odd, but Napoleon III had given his tacit assent to the move and Charles Eitel (or Carol) had indirect ties to the French. His mother was the daughter of Grand Duke Charles of Baden and of Stéphanie de Beauharnais, the descendant of a prominent French family and the adopted daughter of Napoleon Bonaparte.

The new Prince of Rumania had served as a Prussian army officer and had participated in the Prussian war against Denmark in 1864, when he was twenty-five years old. He went to Rumania two years later—he had to be smuggled into the country because of the hostility of Austria, Russia, and Turkey. In April, 1866, he was unanimously elected prince, and in July he was given wide powers, which he used with great tact and wisdom, instituting wide-ranging reforms and improving the country's economy. He later briefly encountered anti-German sentiment during the Franco-Prussian War of 1870–71, for his pro-Prussian sympathies were severely at odds with the sentiment of his people, but he regained great popularity a few years later, when he fought successfully against the Turks. Ultimately, this led to Rumania's being proclaimed a kingdom completely independent of Turkey, and Carol I became king of his adopted country. His queen, who wrote poetry under the pen name of Carmen Sylva, bore him only one child, a daughter who died in 1874; as a result, King Carol chose his nephew, Ferdinand, to be his crown prince. When Carol I died in 1914, Ferdinand of Hohenzollern-Sigmaringen became King Ferdinand I of Rumania.

Thus the prestige of the House of Hohenzollern was soaring in 1866 for two reasons: First, in chronological order, was the election of a Hohenzollern-Sigmaringen as Prince of Rumania in April; next was the victory of the Prussians at Königgrätz. Bismarck, who was anxious to unite Germany under Hohenzollern rule, sought other opportunities for increasing the prestige of the house. His chance came in Spain, when the Cortes offered the vacant Spanish throne to the eldest son of Prince Charles Anthony of Hohenzollern-Sigmaringen, Prince Leopold.

Spain was an infinitely more prestigious prize than Rumania; Spain, after all, had once virtually ruled the world. Queen Isabella of Spain had been expelled in 1868, her son Alfonso was too young to reign, and it was felt, in any event, that the Bourbons who had ruled Spain since 1700 had been failures. General Juan Prim, the most influential Spaniard, approached Charles Anthony about his son. One might have thought that this relatively obscure branch of the Hohenzollerns would have leaped at the opportunity to seize yet a second throne, but this was not the case. Both Prince Leopold and his father disliked the idea. Spain was too unfamiliar to Leopold, he didn't like the idea of leaving home, and Spain, furthermore, had such a turbulent political history that he feared he might never last. Prince Charles Anthony decided to do what King William I of Prussia wanted him to do, since William was the head of the entire House of Hohenzollern, the Sigmaringen branch included. William also didn't like the Spanish venture but felt this was a matter Charles Anthony should decide on his own.

This of course did not sit well with the energetic Otto von Bismarck, who had his own ideas and who wrote them down in a long memorandum addressed to his king. Trade between Prussia and Rumania had already begun to flourish, thanks to there being a Hohenzollern on the Rumanian throne; trade between Prussia and Spain would flourish equally if Prince Leopold became King of Spain. Germany was then in the heyday of industrial expansion and needed new markets; Spain would provide vast commercial opportunities. Furthermore, if Leopold became King of Spain, then the House of Hohenzollern would have three reigning monarchs—kings in Prussia and Spain and a ruling prince in Rumania—and its prestige would have increased enormously. The dynasty would seem to match that of the Habsburgs. Bismarck pointed out that it was imprudent to turn down the offer. It would wound Spanish pride; Spain would almost certainly then seek a Bavarian prince, and these were too friendly to the Austrians, the French, and the Vatican. Worse yet, if the Spaniards failed to find a foreign prince who would accept their throne, they might establish a republic, which would strengthen the antimonarchist cause in neighboring France.

France, however, was not indifferent to what was going on. It already felt deeply threatened by the emerging power of Prussia. After the defeat of the Austrians, King William I had become leader of a vast North German Confederation, composed of states either annexed by Prussia or rendered into vassal states by it. Of 68,000,000 Germans, 40,000,000 had been forcibly Prussianized, and France was no longer able to play Austria and Prussia off against each other, the Austrians having been completely canceled out of German affairs. The idea of being surrounded by Hohenzollerns—one to the south, in Spain; the other to the west, in North Germany—reminded the French of when they had been wedged in between the Habsburgs in the Netherlands and in South Germany. The French, therefore, were furious when Bismarck's arguments finally prevailed and when Prince Leopold agreed to accept the Spanish throne. Napoleon III could not afford to let this pass, for he had already suffered one humiliation at the hands of the House of Hohenzollern. This had come about after the Battle of Königgrätz, when the French had barged in, offering to negotiate the peace between the combatants; when Prussia formed the North German Confederation, Napoleon had tried to grab first the west bank of the Rhine, then Luxembourg, failing in both endeavors. Sick physically and politically declining, Napoleon needed a diplomatic victory to shore himself up at home. The Hohenzollern candidacy for the Spanish throne (as this affair came to be called) provided a legitimate opportunity. He threatened war.

War was just what Bismarck and the Prussian generals wanted, for they were confident they could beat the French army and establish Prussia as the greatest single power in all Europe; furthermore, this war might lead to German unification under a Hohenzollern king. "If I could only have the handling of our army in this war," said Moltke, "the devil is welcome to these old bones as soon as it is over." But war was *not* what either King William or Prince Charles Anthony wanted; they were peaceable men. When the French threatened war, the head of the House of Hohenzollern-Sigmaringen promptly withdrew Prince Leopold's acceptance.* Emboldened by this diplomatic triumph, Napoleon III hoped for even greater victories and demanded that William I of Prussia give his royal word that any future offer of the Spanish throne would *never* be accepted. That was a bit too much for a Hohenzollern, and this bit of presumption ultimately cost the French Alsace and part of Lorraine.

While events in Spain and the French reaction to them were preparing to elevate the House of Hohenzollern to its greatest majesty yet, other events in Prussia itself were no less fateful.

* The Spanish throne was afterward accepted by a member of the House of Savoy, the Duke of Aosta. Leopold never attained royal status, nor did he live to see his son Ferdinand become King of Rumania in 1914.

Bismarck had ruled for four years without the participation of Parliament; at no time before had the court showed such contempt for the constitution it ostensibly espoused. In 1862 the liberal delegates to Parliament had attempted to assert themselves against the crown; for four years, they had watched impotently as the crown effectively governed the nation both illegally and unconstitutionally. This infuriated the delegates, and a crisis might conceivably have been reached which would have led Prussia—and ultimately Germany—toward a constitutional monarchy along British lines: a government by ministers responsible to Parliament, with a figurehead monarch who stood above the factional disputes of political parties and could unite the nation in spirit. This, however, did not happen, largely because of Königgrätz.

The Habsburgs, who seemed to symbolize reaction even more than did the House of Hohenzollern (being wedded not only to absolutism, but also to clericalism and the Vatican), had been replaced in German affairs by a vigorous, forward-looking (if not politically progressive) North German Confederation. Now that 40,000,000 Germans were subjects of or allied to the Prussian king, the dream of German unification almost seemed realized. It was now felt that the Habsburgs had been the chief obstacle to German unity and that the Hohenzollerns were more attuned to the spirit of the times. In any event, unification was two-thirds accomplished; the South German states which remained independent of Prussia after 1866 allied themselves swiftly to the North German Confederation, seeking the protection and security of the strongest German power. It was a time of great national pride in Prussia; a wave of passionate patriotism rolled across the land and swept away all those who, in this time of glory, wished to restrict the glorious, victorious king.

William I appeared before Parliament, speaking from the throne, not as a constitutional ruler, but as the traditional Prussian warlord, whose crown derived from the god of battles and who had just proven the justice of his cause by slaying the Habsburg dragon in three weeks.* He asked Parliament for in-

* The Austro-Prussian War of 1866 is called the Seven Weeks' War, but it took only three weeks to finish the Austrians off, the remaining four simply being the period prior to the formal end.

demnification—in effect, for parliamentary approval of the illegal way the government had been run for four years. The king told the delegates in the palace's White Hall that he felt confident the conflict between Parliament and the crown would now end because of past successes and future prospects. A few days later, Bismarck himself addressed Parliament, asking for an act of indemnity. "Absolutism on the part of the crown is just as little defensible," he said, "as absolutism on the part of parliamentary majorities!" What did these words mean? They were, on the one hand, a rejection of parliamentary democracy and, on the other, a slap at the crown, which Bismarck now blamed for the way in which he had ruled unconstitutionally. He meant to profit from the delegates' conflicts with the king: those conflicts kept him in power throughout William I's reign. "Kind words cost nothing," he added at the time. In fact, they paid off handsomely. Parliament granted him the Act of Indemnity by a vote of 230 to 75 on September 3, 1866. That vote was as fateful for Prussia as Runnymede had been for Britain, but in this case, the crown had won.

The vote was a complete surrender by delegates who had been swept away by patriotic emotion. Bismarck, who had for four years been almost universally disliked, even hated, in Prussia, was a popular hero after Königgrätz; he did not have to conquer Parliament, but merely needed to urge it on to suicide or to political castration. With this vote, Parliament announced it had settled for less than effective power and would not even try for sovereignty. It had declared that it was ready to swallow even illegal actions by the crown; in return, it happily received vague assurances from Bismarck that he would govern "in a liberal spirit."

This marked the end of liberalism's hopes. There were still many liberals left, and some retained their principles, but most joined the conservatives in cheering Bismarck. It soon became evident that a political career could not lead to power, since Parliament was in itself powerless; as a result, the vigorous, able, and ambitious in Germany began to enter industry instead. Parliament developed into a conglomeration of powerless interest groups, of lobbies hoping to gain minor concessions from the crown and its ministers; inevitably, this led to a popular contempt for politicians and a respect for the repository of actual power, the ministers of the absolutist king. It could be said that this September 3, 1866, vote also carried with it the first cracks in the House of Hohenzollern, for while it perpetuated the crown's absolutism, it was this very absolutism which would lead to the ultimate collapse of the dynasty. The House of Hohenzollern might have survived into the present day had it been transformed in the nineteenth century into a British-style constitutional monarchy; instead, it became a lumbering dinosaur which tumbled to its death in 1918. Absolutism continued to work during the reign of William I because Bismarck guided it with great care; it began to collapse under William II because it permitted a vain, blundering monarch to rule without checks, balances, or even a sense of direction.

King William I of Prussia was taking the waters at the spa at Ems in July, 1870, when the French overplayed their hand. On the morning of the thirteenth, the French ambassador, Vincent Benedetti, took a stroll in the Ems park, hoping to encounter the King of Prussia during William's customary morning walk. Seeing the king, Benedetti stood still and saluted courteously; William shook his hand and invited him along. The conversation immediately turned to the Spanish throne and to the fact that Prince Leopold had renounced it; William ventured that all the ambassador's worries were now over. Not so, for this was the moment when Benedetti asked the king to give his word that should such an offer ever be made in the future, it would not be accepted. William responded with the statement that a promise for all time ("*à tout jamais*") was impossible. Irritated, he beckoned to an adjutant, turned his back on the ambassador, and left. Later he advised the ambassador that he had no further communication to make to him at this time, and then he sent a telegram to Bismarck in Berlin, advising him of what had happened and asking if this exchange ought to be made public in the newspapers.

Bismarck was dining with Roon and Moltke that evening. Both the war minister and the chief of the General Staff were "very downcast" (as Bismarck described them) at the way the Hohenzollerns had surroundered to French pressure in the matter of the Spanish throne. It was during these discussions that the king's telegram, dictated by William and dispatched by

Privy Councilor Heinrich Abeken, arrived. This was the famous Ems dispatch. Bismarck had been ready to resign because of the way his king had received the French ambassador on several previous occasions at Ems, "exposing his monarchical person to disgraceful treatment from these foreign agents, without official support," which meant without Bismarck's being around. Roon and Moltke had urged him to stay; Bismarck thought it over while he restudied the Ems dispatch. Then, in the presence of his companions, he began to cut it down. It had earlier sounded somewhat conciliatory, as though the king might be ready to discuss the French proposals in the future, but Bismarck's edited (not rewritten) text now concluded with the sentence: "Upon this His Majesty refused to receive the French ambassador again, and sent him word through the aide-de-camp in attendance that His Majesty had no further communication to make to the minister." That version was released to the newspapers. "That sounds better!" Roon said, enormously relieved. "It sounded like a signal of surrender before," Moltke added. "Now it is like a flourish of trumpets." [145]

It had just that effect on the French. Napoleon III did not want war any more than William I did, but the French emperor's objections were swept away by his ministers, who nearly slavered for a conflict with Prussia, wishing to humiliate it. The day after, Napoleon signed a declaration of war, his hands trembling. In Prussia, Queen Augusta pleaded with King William to avert the conflict, tearfully reminding him of Prussia's defeat at the hands of the French in 1806. William departed from Ems for Berlin, was met at Brandenburg by Bismarck, Roon, Moltke, and the crown prince. At the railway station in Berlin, beneath the chandelier of the waiting room, the tall, blond crown prince struck Roon as "a flaming god of war . . . a perfect type of Teutonic fury." Total mobilization was decided upon in that railway station. The crown prince was embraced by the king "with the greatest emotion," as he afterward noted in his diaries; then he hurried out and told the news to the people milling about on the platform. That evening large crowds gathered in front of the palace, shouting "Hurrah!" and singing "I Am a Prussian!" until late at night. King William, however, was not swept away. "The enthusiasm fills me with anxiety," he wrote his wife, "for what chances are there not in war which might and must silence all this jubilation?" As for the simultaneous mobilization ordered by the independent South German states, William worried about how such "national feeling" could possibly be fulfilled.

With "a heavy heart," the king accompanied the troops, being nominally their field commander. The crown prince was given supreme command of all South German troops, as well as of several Prussian corps. Then news arrived that Italy, England, Russia, and Austria would remain neutral. On July 31, the king and Bismarck left for the front, at Mainz; Queen Augusta, seated in a carriage at that corner of Unter den Linden where the Café Kranzler was located (the Kranzler Corner), wept as she saw them off. Then she went home and began bombarding William with letters on how to conduct the war.

Losses on both sides were very heavy right from the start. "All the troops accomplished miracles of valor against an equally brave enemy," William wrote Augusta after the battles around Metz. Throughout the war, William was generous with his praise for the French; he was an old gentleman of Christian sentiments, modest and kindly, surrounded by officers who were snorting for blood and revenge. He disliked the war; he even blamed it on the French Revolution. At Varennes, he was shown the place where the house stood in which Louis XVI spent the night after his arrest; he afterward wrote Augusta, "Everyone is impressed by the thought that this arrest, which brought the royal couple to the scaffold, whereby all religion and the foundations of the kingdom were uprooted, is, for that reason, one of the causes of our now being at war here! ! For since that terrible time France has never had permanent peace!"

The French emperor, suffering from stones in the bladder, anemia, hemorrhoids, gout, and other painful ailments, surrendered himself (and 80,000 French troops) into William's hands after the Battle of Sedan. William treated him with great courtesy, while Bismarck, Roon, and Moltke handled him with a brusqueness tantamount to showing contempt. Bismarck did not trust his king to deal with Napoleon; he suspected William would be too easy. He arranged for William to meet Napoleon III only after the terms of surrender had been agreed on by the military, who could act harsher, as Bismarck put it. Finally, their majesties met. William greeted Napoleon by holding out his hand and saying, *"Sire, le sort des armes a décidé entre nous, mais il m'est bien pénible de revoir Votre Majésté dans cette situation."* William proposed a new home for the defeated emperor: Wilhelmshöhe, to which, upon Napoleon's request, he could take his entourage and servants. Both monarchs were very much affected by the meeting, Napoleon leaving in tears. William said to him that he knew him well enough to be sure he had not wanted the war, but that he had been forced into it. Napoleon claimed public opinion had forced him to declare war. William said that this public opinion had been created by Napoleon's ministers. The emperor admitted it, shrugging his shoulders. "The whole conversation seemed to do him good," William told Augusta afterward, clucking over his captive in good-natured fashion. Others in the king's entourage were not as generous. When Napoleon left William and passed through Donchery, he noticed Bismarck and Moltke watching him from a window. The defeated emperor saluted them. "He is now saluting his gravediggers," Moltke said.

Within days, Empress Eugénie, who had urged this war on her husband, was forced to flee to Britain from its consequences, crowds in Paris shouting, *"Vive la République!"* at the news that Napoleon had been taken captive. Her American dentist, a Dr. Evans, sent her in his carriage to his wife, who was vacationing at the Casino Hotel in Deauville; from there, Sir John Burgoyne hid her aboard his yacht, the *Gazelle,* and got her across the Channel and into two attic rooms in the York Hotel, Ryde. In March, 1871, Napoleon III followed her to England, where he died two years later.

His capture, however, had not marked the end of the war, although Paris had been surrounded by October, 1870, and the Bavarian armies were already tiring of the struggle and ready to go home. King William I's headquarters were moved to Versailles. "His Majesty," wrote the crown prince in his diary, "looks as blooming as though he were at home, in spite of his taking no exercise here either, never riding and always sitting in overheated rooms. He enjoys the daily dinners at four o'clock and tea at nine o'clock in the evening, when the whole Headquarters Staff and the Princes attached to the Royal suite always appear." [146]

Metz capitulated on October 27, and both Crown Prince Frederick William and Prince Frederick Charles were raised to the rank of field marshals, while Otto von Bismarck was created count. Now plans were being forged to raise King William to imperial rank. There followed sixty days of discussions and negotiations, not only to have William elected emperor by the various German kings, grand dukes, and princes, as well as by their Parliaments, but just to get William to accept the title, even grudgingly. The head of the North German Reichstag decided on December 6 to insert the words "German Emperor" and "German Empire" into the constitution; the crown prince commented, "It seemed as though he had pulled the poor German imperial crown out of his trousers pocket, wrapped in old newspaper." This objectionably democratic initiative was followed by yet another: The Reichstag sent a delegation to the king. William refused to meet the delegates, being afraid it might look as though the imperial crown had come from the people and not from the princes, the same grounds on which his brother, Frederick William IV, had rejected the imperial crown in 1849. William insisted he would see the parliamentary delegation only after King Ludwig II of Bavaria had notified him that all the German princes agreed to his elevation. Negotiations concerning this were complex and lengthy. Concessions had to be made to the South German states, such as permitting Bavaria to retain lower duties on beer, the national industry (and obsession) of that kingdom. Bavaria also kept its own postage and railways; in time of peace, it was also to be allowed to keep its own army. Bismarck flattered the King of Bavaria to win him over; behind his back he remarked, "Such idiocies have their effect on the king." Finally, he tried bribery, promising him a secret pension equivalent to 20,000 pounds sterling a year, out of funds sequestered from the Hanoverians. That argument proved decisive, and the Bavarian wrote a letter to William—which Bismarck dictated—offering him the imperial crown. This happened on December 18; on the same day, from Windsor Castle, Queen Victoria wrote her "dear brother" William that public sympathy had been entirely with Germany throughout the war "and still is, in the case of all well-informed people," but she warned him that this might change if the war dragged on still further. The king, tired of fretting for weeks on whether to bombard Paris or not, ordered the cannon to fire, it being a matter of either taking this course or starving the Parisians into surrender. What was known as the English faction in Prussia was at first passionately opposed to bombardment; this faction included the crown prince and his British-born crown princess, as well as Queen Augusta herself. As the weeks dragged on, however, even the crown prince was converted to bombardment, which began on January 5, 1871, and had the effect of swinging European public opinion against the Prussians, although it had precious little effect on Paris itself. It was dramatic but, compared to today's bombardments of cities, trifling. Paris was at the end of its rope in any event: torn with internal strife, demonstrations, minor uprisings, and running out of food. On January 19 the Parisians attempted an attack against the surrounding Germans, using 90,000 men, but it failed; on the twenty-eighth, an armistice was signed and the final Treaty of Frankfurt which ended the war was completed on May 10.*

Once William had made his decision to shell Paris ("Blaze away there," he had ordered, "and make a terrific noise!"), he was again immersed in the matter of the imperial crown. He objected to it passionately, though he could see that it was a dread inevitability. This crown, insofar as he was concerned, meant little or nothing and was a thing empty of honor, while the Prussian crown had earned its reputation by means of blood and glory. He wrote his son: "I, with my inherently Prussian heart, am to live to see the name which has achieved and created such greatness give place to another, which was hostile to the Prussian name, almost deathly hostile, for a whole century. . . . Once more the fates conspire against me, and force me into something to which I can only agree with a heavy heart, and yet must no longer refuse." [147]

But what was his exact title to be? He himself had no doubt that the old title must come first. He would sign himself "We, William by the grace of God King of Prussia, elected Emperor of Germany." Bismarck promptly voiced his objections. The word "elected" might evoke mistaken ideas that this imperial crown was not to be a hereditary title for the House of Hohenzollern; the words "Emperor of Germany" had in them too

* The Commune revolt in Paris occurred on March 18, and the German armies surrounding Paris watched as Parisians fought Parisians for two months.

much of a suggestion that William's domains covered all Germany. A compromise was found: William was to be "German Emperor"; all the other German princes and kings would be board members, with the Kaiser acting more or less as chairman.

This satisfied most of those concerned, although William continued to be unhappy. When all the Prussian princes asked to be retitled imperial princes, as the crown prince was to be retitled, William exploded. He wrote his brother Charles that he didn't even like the idea of the crown prince being addressed as "Imperial and Royal Highness."

"I consider that the Prussian family holds such a high position in history," he wrote, "and has gained such renown through its deeds . . . that it grieves me to the heart to see the Prussian royal title taking the second place! ! Therefore I wish the family to remain the Prussian royal family, in order to show clearly that there is absolutely nothing in the way in which the imperial dignity falls to me which could be a slight to the Prussian name. I can only consider that I receive the title of Emperor (just as one is entitled Lieutenant Colonel, etc.), for it is expressly stated: The King of Prussia bears the title of Emperor as the supreme presidential power. From this it is clear that it only applies to the King in person [and not to the princes]. . . ."[148]

As the time approached for his acceptance of the new title, William sank ever further into gloom. He spoke endlessly of Frederick I, the very first King "in" Prussia, and of his other Hohenzollern ancestors, as though this imperial title would besmirch their honor. Bismarck and the crown prince attempted to soothe him by assuring him that in principle, emperors are *not* given precedence over kings, but William saw annoyances everywhere. The ancient Prussian colors, black and white, were to be replaced by imperial colors of black-white-red: better than the "republican" black-red-gold banner, but objectionable enough to a king almost seventy-four years of age and sixty-four years in the uniformed service of the black-and-white Prussian banner. The day before he was named emperor, he wept, he sobbed, and he even threatened to abdicate in favor of his son, for the crown prince "was heart and soul with the new state of affairs," he said, "while I care not a jot about it and cling only to Prussia." This union with Germany seeemed to the aged monarch as though he were marrying beneath his station, wedding some low-class wench who'd ruin the name of Hohenzollern.

At noon the next day, however, the ordeal was undertaken, in Versailles' Hall of Mirrors. January 18 had been chosen, this being the one hundred and seventieth anniversary of that day in Königsberg when Elector Frederick III crowned himself King Frederick I. A short divine service was followed by an irritatingly long sermon; then the king read out the instrument constituting the German Empire and ordered Count Bismarck (elevated to full general that day) to read out the proclamation to the German people. Bismarck looked "black as thunder" and read his paper "quivering with emotion," but it evoked no great response from the assembled sovereigns, princes, and officers. Then the new Kaiser's brother-in-law, the Grand Duke of Baden, seized the initiative, raised his hand high, and called out a cheer for "His Majesty Emperor William the Victorious!" The tension in the room broke. The grand duke had avoided the words "Emperor of Germany," thus subtly reassuring all those present who feared the territorial implications that particular title would have carried. Everyone was now willing to cheer "Emperor William." The crown prince dropped to one knee and kissed his father's hand; then the others paid homage as well. William stepped off the dais to the tune of the "Hohenfriedberg March," to speak with the officers who stood behind Count Bismarck. He pointedly ignored his imperial chancellor, as Bismarck was now titled, for he was angry at not having had his way in the matter of the title. "His Majesty bore me such a grudge for this course of events," Bismarck wrote later, "that . . . he ignored me . . . and persisted in this attitude for several days."

On March 3 the German emperor drove through defeated Paris. Though he was now being referred to in Germany as William the Conqueror, he did not ride in at the head of his troops. He passed through the streets almost unnoticed, seated beside Anton Radziwill in a modest open carriage drawn by only a pair of horses, with only one coachman up front. The Hohenzollern Empire had begun modestly enough, though it would soon develop into something else.

* * *

Four days after the French had crushed the Prussian army at the Battle of Jena in 1806, a tearful, distraught Queen Louisa confronted her sons at the castle of Schwedt, in the presence of their tutor, who noted down her words. The future Frederick William IV was eleven years old at the time; the future Emperor William I was only nine. "Prussia is no more," she told them. What the Hohenzollerns had built over the centuries had been "overthrown and demolished" in one day. "Our national glory is departed," she said, urging them to tears—and then to something more. "Strive to rescue your people from the disgrace of this hour, from the burden of humiliation under which this nation is now groaning," she said. "Aspire to reconquer from the French the glory of your forefathers, now clouded and obscured, in the same way as your ancestor, the Great Elector, avenged his father's shame and humiliation upon the Swedes at Fehrbellin. . . ."

The defeat of Napoleon I a few years later was only a partial satisfaction; this victory over the French in 1871 seemed to redress the balance, for France had been toppled from her preeminence in Europe, just as Austria had been toppled in Germany in 1864. Simson, the president of the North German Reichstag, proclaimed that this victory would assure the German people "the unification of our fatherland in constitutional liberty." The "universal uprising" of all German states swept away divisive boundaries, and "the old curse is removed. . . ."[149] William I, who had certainly never yearned for German unity, was, however, conscious of having discharged a debt to the mother he revered; the Kaiser's triumphal return to Berlin was climaxed by the unveiling of a monument to his father, Frederick William III, whereupon the captured French battle standards were deposited at the feet of the man whom Napoleon had humiliated.

The city of Berlin was now the capital of the *Kaiserreich,* and the imperial capital was appropriately decked out for William's glorious return.* The Kaiser entered at the head of 42,000

* William had been decked out gloriously, too. Excluding military and honorary academic titles, as well as his countless honorary citizenships, his list of titles now read as follows:

"German Emperor, King of Prussia, Margrave of Brandenburg, first sovereign Duke of Silesia as well as the County of Glatz, Grand Duke of Posen and of the troops, preceded by that ancient field marshal von Wrangel and then by that trio of instigators, Bismarck, Roon, and Moltke. Bismarck had been elevated to the rank of prince of the German Empire, was given the title of Fürst and then the Grand Cross of the Hohenzollern Order in diamonds. Of the first honor he remarked, "I was a rich Junker and have become a poor prince"; of the second, he said with equal candor, "I'd sooner have had a horse or a barrel of good Rhenish wine." [150]

The city was *en fête;* not a meter of public road had escaped the bunting drapers. Huge statues, as hastily sculpted as ugly, were everywhere, holding aloft laurel wreaths and towering over hundreds of French cannon. On the Askanischer Platz, 10,000 schoolchildren stood on a platform and sang "The Watch on the Rhine"; pretty young ladies in white were assembled at strategic places to recite poems to the emperor as he passed. That evening the city was brilliantly illuminated; there was dancing in the streets and on the squares and, as the keeper of the royal archives, Dr. Julius von Pflugk-Harttung, put it, "abundant libations of beer." The celebrations and the heat of that June 16 caused three princes to faint dead away, but old Kaiser William I, now seventy-four, sat his horse patiently in full uniform for three hours, never flagging once.

Three years later, Bismarck told some politicians, "I am bored. The great things are done. The German Reich is made." Every single day, as long as William I lived, he visited his emperor at the palace when both of them were in Berlin; together, they imposed the Bismarckian system on Germany, but there were no further grand events. The war that had been won in 1871 was the last between the great powers in Europe until 1914, nor were there even internal constitutional fights, for the German people had to live under the old constitution until

---

Lower Rhine, Duke of Saxony, Engern and Westphalia, Duke in Geldern and at [*zu*] Magdeburg, Cleves, Jülich, Berg, Stettin, Pomerania, of the Kashubians and Wends, at Mecklenburg and Crossen, Burgrave of Nuremberg, Landgrave at Thuringia, Margrave of Oberlausitz, Prince of Orange, Neuenburg and Valangin, Fürst at Rügen, Paderborn, Halberstadt, Münster, Minden, Cammin, Wenden, Schwerin, Ratzeburg, Mörs, Eichsfeld and Erfurt, Count at [*zu*] Hohenzollern, of the Mark, at Ravensburg, Hohenstein, Tecklenburg, Schwerin, Lingen, Sigmaringen and Wehringen, Pyrmont, Lord of the Lands [*Herr der Lande*] of Rostock, Stargard, Lauenburg, Bütow, at Haigerloch and Werstein."

1918. The years which followed were filled with events significant to the history of Germany, such as the policy of "Socialism from above" which Bismarck rained down upon the Germans in order to take the wind out of the sails of the Socialists, but they were events which only marginally affected the Hohenzollerns. Kaiser William and the Austro-Hungarian emperor, Francis Joseph, met at Gastein and agreed to leave each other alone, which was the best assurance of future friendship and alliance; then the czar and Francis Joseph traveled to Berlin, followed shortly afterward by the Persian shah and by Victor Emmanuel of Italy. These travels were evidence of the importance of Germany now; Berlin was a new Rome.

In 1877, when the emperor became eighty years of age, the day was celebrated as a national festival; characteristically, the old Kaiser opened every one of the 1,000 telegrams he received with his own hands. Prince Henry, fifteen, and Prince Waldemar, nine, the two younger sons of the imperial crown prince and the younger brothers of the future Emperor William II, presented gifts to their grandfather: an engraving and a hand-bound book executed by themselves, it being a curious Hohenzollern custom that princes learned handicrafts in their youth. That same year the emperor celebrated the seventieth anniversary of his military career. He chose the occasion to restate the origin of Prussia: "Prussia has become what she was chiefly through the army." That summer he visited the provinces of Alsace and Lorraine, now so sullenly German that the municipal councilors at Metz refused even to allocate funds for a civic reception for him. From there, William journeyed to Essen, where Krupp showed him a huge new siege gun; then he joined extensive maneuvers. Despite his great age, he was mounted on his horse at six every morning and needed only five hours of sleep a night. His officers were amazed at his stamina; some of them attributed it to the midnight supper of lobster salad which he invariably ate.

Nothing seemed to faze the octogenarian, not even assassination attempts. There had been one in the year of his accession; a student named Oscar Becker, from Odessa, had tried to kill him for not doing enough toward German unity. That bullet had ripped William's coat collar and necktie and grazed his neck. Now, in 1878, after having fulfilled Becker's demands for

German unity, William suffered two assassination attempts within a few weeks. On May 11, at 3:30 P.M., William was driving along Unter den Linden with his daughter Louisa, the Grand Duchess of Baden. A demented mechanic named Hödel, hiding behind a cab, fired a six-shooter at the emperor but hit only his carriage. He fired again, but this shot also missed. William, astonished, asked his coachman to stop. "Were those shots fired at me?" he asked. A total of four shots were fired before Hödel was seized by a civilian named Dittmann and by a soldier assigned to William's carriage. Hödel afterward announced he wished to draw attention to the plight of the working classes: Industrialization had brought misery and slums. Hödel had once been a Socialist but had been expelled because of his eccentric behavior; he now said he hated the Socialists because they hadn't kept any of their promises. He was chained to a wall and afterward executed. Bismarck thundered about "Socialist outrages," but William characteristically was more kindly disposed. It was the act, he said, "of a man who had strayed into the wrong path. . . ."

On June 2, as the emperor again drove along Unter den Linden, raising his arm and saluting the passersby, Dr. Karl Nobiling, a man of education and "good family," fired a load of swan shot at him, then attempted suicide. This time, William was hit; anywhere from eighteen to thirty pellets entered his head, face, arms, and back. The emperor, streaming blood, was raced back to the palace, where physicians began to remove the swan shot wherever they could find it; it was later said that he carried some of it in his body to the grave. The crown prince acted for his father while William recovered, which took some months. In the autumn, he still felt like "a semi-invalid." When he returned to Berlin in December, he made a curiously humble address to the city authorities who had come to greet him. "When I was saved," he said, "I took it as a warning to ask myself whether I had so ordered my life and done my duty as to be worth saving."

Bismarck was in a less contemplative mood after the assassination attempts. He seized the opportunity to ram anti-Socialist laws through Parliament, beginning a witch-hunt for all dissidents. This police terror was unleashed under William's name. Germany came to be divided about the venerable old soldier:

He was regarded in his later years as truly the "father of his country" and venerated both for this and for his character; at the same time, however, he was held responsible for the form of government Germany inherited under him, that "Chancellor Absolutism" which the press denounced.

Bismarck and William quarreled often, but not for long. If William resisted Bismarck's proposals, the chancellor merely needed to threaten to resign to bring the emperor around, for it seemed to William that nothing stood between Germany and the "utter chaos" of liberalism and Socialism but this "Iron Chancellor." "It is not easy to be emperor under such a chancellor," William once said, admitting frankly who was on top. Bismarck made a great show of being the instrument of his monarch, but he was also given to admitting the true relationship. "I cannot be the servant of princes," he once snarled after leaving a meeting with William. "There are white men," he also said, "there are black men, and there are monarchs." The crown prince summed up the relation between his father and Bismarck in these words, uttered in 1866: "If Bismarck proposed an alliance with Garibaldi—well, he's at least a general. But if he proposed an alliance with Mazzini, the king would at first walk up and down the room in distress and would exclaim, 'Bismarck, Bismarck, what are you turning me into?' Then he would stop in the middle of the room and say, 'But if you believe that it is absolutely necessary in the interests of the state, there's nothing more to be said.' " In 1872, Bismarck once complained to Roon that he didn't understand why he did not please the king. "I only want to obey him," the chancellor said. Roon replied, "Certainly you want to, but you don't do it." Quarrels between William and his chancellor usually ended with William surrendering and Bismarck acting outraged at the opposition he received. He loathed the influence the empress was suspected of having on her husband. "Either marriage or monarchy," he said, "but both together are impossible!" The fund of royalist sentiment with which he entered office, he once stated, was rapidly running out, but this did not mean that Bismarck was becoming a "republican," only that he found managing his monarch tiring. "The emperor," he once said, "does not smoke, reads no newspapers, only documents and dispatches; it would be more useful if he played patience."

When Dr. Nobiling severely injured the emperor, Bismarck's first thoughts were not for the old man. He exclaimed with delight, "Now we'll dissolve the Reichstag!" He didn't even bother to visit his monarch for a week; he was only interested in the anti-Socialist laws by which he also meant to crush the National Liberals in Parliament, despite the fact that most National Liberals voted for these very laws. Four years later he put out a different picture of these events. "I thought in 1877 that I was entitled to resign," he said. "But after I had seen my lord and king lying in his blood, I felt that I could never desert this lord, who had sacrificed body and life for his duty to God and men, against his will." This was nonsense, of course; by the time he saw the wounded emperor, William had stopped bleeding. Bismarck, who had suffered from fainting spells and other ailments before the assassination attempt, said afterward, "Nobiling was the best physician I ever had!"

William's later life was a succession of jubilees and anniversaries; in 1887, he celebrated the most remarkable of all, his ninetieth year. He rose at eight o'clock that day, considerably later than he had been accustomed to do while still in his seventies and eighties, and then received the congratulations of his personal servants. At nine thirty the empress appeared and led him to a room filled with birthday presents. The emperor's daughter and her husband, the Grand Duke of Baden, gave him a large clock of Black Forest workmanship; its gilded face was decorated with portraits of his seven great-grandchildren. There followed festivities resplendent with royalty. Two kings and two queens, five crown princes, four grand dukes, two Russian grand dukes, eleven royal princes, five reigning dukes, four hereditary grand dukes, and about fifty assorted German princes showed up. Britain sent the Prince of Wales; even Japan was represented by a prince and princess. "Ninety years!" William exclaimed in a letter to Bismarck written for publication. "A lifetime, and what a long span! . . ." He hoped he might be granted another year of life. At seventy-five, he'd voiced surprise at being called an old gentleman. "Do I give the impression of being aged?" he asked then. "It is to be hoped that I don't look it when I am on duty. . . ."

As he grew older and older, the passage of time caused him

to be greatly revered, an odd development for one who had been hated as "the Cartridge Prince" in 1848 and as "the butcher" for his suppression of revolutionaries elsewhere a year later. The modesty and dignity surrounding his later life appealed enormously to the public. He was never disagreeable to his servants, was always courteous and considerate of others, and continued to be chivalrous, even gallant, to ladies. He could be bitterly vexed by Bismarck, but the strongest sign of disapproval others received from him was a gruff *Hmph!* and a flash of displeasure from his eyes. He remained simple in his habits, to the point of parsimoniousness: the envelopes he received in the morning mail were never thrown away; the emperor simply crossed out the inscription on them, readdressed them himself, and used them again. He liked going to the theater but would not use his good dress trousers for that; they were too valuable. Yet he was always meticulous about his appearance and his uniforms. He occasionally walked about the palace with his jacket undone, but the moment he heard the band coming for the changing of the guard, he buttoned himself up and went off to put on the *Pour le mérite* order, to be in regulation dress. He traveled modestly in old carriages which were not even equipped with rubber tires; he slept on a plain metal camp bed, in a narrow palace room which had only one window; he was to the very end an army officer who happened to be a Hohenzollern monarch. The last year of his life was tragic—but because of the tragic illness of his son, the crown prince, not because of his own sufferings. William I died peacefully at 8:20 A.M. on March 9, 1888, after a few days of illness. During the night of the eighth, he sat up and sobbed, "My son, my poor Fritz!" thinking of the incurably ill crown prince, slated to reign so briefly as Emperor Frederick III. His daughter, the grand duchess, urged him to rest. "I have no time for that now," William said a few hours before dying. He became confused periodically and thought he was a boy again at the Battle of Bar-sur-Aube, charging through shells; at other moments he murmured the names of old officers, old comrades in battle, with whom he had served during those Wars of Liberation against Bonaparte. Hearing the guards march past his palace windows, he roused himself to say, "I hope the companies are following each other in the proper numerical order." Assured that they were, secure in the belief that the Prussian army would never falter or ever change, he died at peace, contentedly. Bismarck left the palace for the Reichstag, to announce the Kaiser's death to Parliament. His voice broke as he told them the news; he even wept. He had lost an old companion, but what was even worse, he knew in his heart he would lose power.

14

"He Is a True Knight!"

"My pulse," said Bismarck after Frederick III acceded to the throne, "goes an average fifteen beats in the minute faster than in the previous reign." [151] No wonder: A German emperor reigned who was an anomaly in the House of Hohenzollern—a liberal who denounced war as a ghastly "butchery" and who was suspected of wanting a parliamentary democracy along British monarchical lines.

The new Kaiser and his consort, Victoria (the daughter of Queen Victoria of Britain), were considered so pro-British that the old Prussian reactionaries maligned Friedrich *der Dritte* ("the Third") as Friedrich *der Britte* ("the Briton"); the Junkers distrusted their emperor and loathed their empress with a virulent passion. Field Marshal Count Alfred von Waldersee remarked that the new Kaiser had "made many plans for the future, which were much inspired by liberal ideas," yet despite the evidence of Bismarck's pulse, the conservatives had nothing to worry about. Frederick III would articulate none of his plans. Dying of cancer of the larynx, he could not speak at all by the time he acceded to the throne.

He reigned for only ninety-nine days, but the principal reason why his reign was so short was his father's exceptionally long life, not his own illness. "Don't you think one can live too long?" the old emperor had asked a friend when he reached ninety, and whatever the friend may have replied, the son certainly agreed. "If the emperor lives much longer," Count

Waldersee noted on the same anniversary, "the crown prince will go to pieces altogether." When Crown Prince Frederick William was forty-one years old, in 1873, he already "thought it unfair of Providence to let his father live so long," Waldersee remarked;[152] as it turned out, he had to wait another fifteen years, a total of twenty-seven after he became crown prince, before he took his father's place.

Bismarck, who despised Victoria and loathed her influence on her husband, liked to denigrate Frederick William as a "mediocrity" who wanted merely "to amuse himself, not to govern," who preferred "a pleasant life without much thought or care, plenty of money, and praise from the newspapers" to work of any substance. Yet he admitted that Emperor William I "seldom or never" spoke to his son on matters of state and would not allow Bismarck to communicate with the crown prince "on subjects of the kind." There had been, he said, an "uninterrupted struggle" between father and son ever since 1863, when the crown prince had denounced restrictions on freedom of the press; at times, said Bismarck, the crown prince was "in despair" at the course of government. Although he disliked the crown prince, Bismarck called him "unaffected and straightforward," as well as "more human . . . more upright and modest" than his father; still, he denigrated him by comparing him with King Frederick William III. "The old king," said Bismarck, "used to drive seven times a week from the Pfaueninsel or the palace at Potsdam to the theater in Berlin in order to see worthless commonplace pieces, and afterwards to go behind the scenes and chuck the actresses under the chin, and then drive back the long dusty road he came. That is also the crown prince's style. . . ."[153]

He had no choice. There was not much else Crown Prince Frederick William could do. He languished for almost thirty years in what Emil Ludwig called "semi-thraldom,"[154] attending maneuvers or weddings, opening exhibitions, traveling abroad—a vice-president at odds with the administration he represented, yet powerless either to speak or to act.

He was an enigma; everyone speculated on what he might do on becoming emperor. Even today, there is speculation on what course German history would have taken had he reigned for, say, fifteen years. There were many apparent contradictions.

He believed in the divine right of kings, yet entertained liberal politicians. Handsome, tall, blond, he was hailed as the personification of Germanic virtues, yet he and his consort were suspected of "selling" Germany to Britain. He was generous and modest, yet fond of imperial display. He was unaffectedly kind and considerate to people below his rank, yet he often treated his eldest son poorly—"incredibly badly," as Waldersee put it. He was, says Ludwig, "a not wholly Prussian Hohenzollern," and the "not wholly" perhaps sums it up. He was less provincial than the Junkers about him and might have transformed the House of Hohenzollern into a modern dynasty, one which could even have escaped oblivion in 1918. In the end, however, he lost his resolve even before he lost his life. He asked Bismarck to stay on—on Bismarck's terms (no parliamentary democracy, no interference in foreign affairs). The long agony of waiting for the throne had defeated him as much as the final agony of cancer.

The birth of Frederick William took place on October 18, 1831, and thus seemed propitious; it was the anniversary of Napoleon Bonaparte's defeat at the Battle of the Nations in Leipzig. (Frederick William was buried on an equally historic anniversary, June 18, 1888, commemorating Napoleon's defeat at Waterloo.)

King Frederick William III still reigned at the time; nine years later, the prince's uncle ascended the throne as Frederick William IV, an event which elevated the young prince as well, placing him in the direct line of succession to the throne. This was communicated to the young prince by a tutor; he had the tutor chastised for even bringing up a subject remotely connected with his father's death. "To have such a son is a blessing from God!" William was told by the prince's military governor, and he merely expressed what was on everyone's lips at the time. He struck all who met him as lovable, courteous, considerate, and utterly selfless. So many Hohenzollerns seem almost to have been born apoplectic, given to early tantrums and late rages, but Frederick William was filled with enough sweetness and light to make up for an army of the enraged.

At ten, he was commissioned in the guards, like all other Hohenzollern princes; in accordance with another tradition in the family, he was assigned to learn a craft or two. Diligently, he applied himself to three: printing on a small, hand-operated printing press, bookbinding, and carpentry, even making his father a chair for Babelsberg Castle, where William, Augusta, and their children spent much time. (In later life, he met a master carpenter—a *Kunstschreiner,* or cabinetmaker—and told him with an ironic smile that he had also once been a carpenter but had never succeeded in becoming a master at the craft.)

A noted Hellenic scholar, Ernst Curtius, supervised his studies from the time the prince was thirteen, teaching him literature, art, history, and classical languages; at sixteen, Frederick William impressed the poet Emanuel Geibel with his "clear intellect" and "innate regard for spiritual matters." A year later Frederick William startled (indeed, horrified) his military governor at a guards officers' dinner by saying he thought " a representation of the people would become a necessity. . . ."[155]

Frederick William was a close friend of Prince Frederick Charles of Hohenzollern; this was his cousin, the son of Prince Charles, a younger brother to Kings Frederick William IV and William I. Frederick Charles, three years older, had been enrolled at the University of Bonn, thanks to the persistent efforts of Augusta, Frederick William's mother; she wanted to see her nephew there so that he would provide a precedent and ease the way for the later matriculation of her son. Other princes had studied at Bonn in the past, but a university education was unheard of for the House of Hohenzollern, a military education being thought sufficient. Augusta's unremitting efforts bore fruit, and Frederick William entered the university three weeks after his eighteenth birthday.* He studied literature, history, and law, while an English tutor was found to teach him English, as well as English literature and history, three times a week. Although his pro-British sentiments were later attributed to his British wife, it seems clear they developed earlier. "His love for England," wrote Copland Perry, his English tutor, "and his profound admiration for our Queen, were most remarkable. . . . Whatever information I was able to afford him about

* Enrolling him was more radical than it may perhaps appear. It took the British royal family another century before it sent an heir to the university, this taking place when Prince Charles, the Prince of Wales, was enrolled at Cambridge.

English political and social life was received by him with the greatest eagerness, and, when more solid study was concluded, we amused ourselves by writing imaginary letters to ministers and leaders of society." [156]

In his third term, the prince wrote of the value of a university education and why tutoring could not take its place.

"No one can deny that no true picture of the life and doings of man can be gained at court," he wrote, "and that it can only be acquired from the frequent intercourse with persons of all classes. At court one is surrounded by people who invariably meet royalty with politeness, with the observance of ancient traditional forms, and only too frequently with deceitful flatteries, so that habit gradually leads one to think of life in no other way, and to estimate all men with whom one comes into contact by the same standard.

"Men are not accustomed to these forms by nature; on the contrary, in public life they speak freely and candidly, and one must early become accustomed to realize that a very thoughtful man of learning and purpose is often concealed by a rough and awkward exterior. The world happens to be so, and it is the first duty of princes, especially in these days, to get to know it thoroughly. . . ."

Summer holidays were spent traveling, and in 1851 he went to Britain, where Queen Victoria noted in her diary that the nineteen-year-old prince seemed "so good and amiable" and where she introduced him to her daughter Vicky, then ten years old.

A torchlight procession and a serenade by the student body ended the prince's university education in 1852. He returned to the First Guards Infantry Regiment, in which he was now a captain and company commander. The following year he was promoted to major and introduced by his father into a Masonic lodge. Late in 1853, he toured Italy for several months, establishing a cordial relationship with Pope Pius IX, after an awkward initial scene. The Pope met the prince by holding out his ring finger for the prince to kiss, but the Protestant Hohenzollern decided this would not be good form and instead grasped the papal palm, shaking it heartily. (Whenever they met subsequently, the Pope greeted Frederick William with his hands clasped firmly behind his back.) This Italian journey also involved artistic and archeological explorations, in which the prince came to be very interested, later developing into an influential patron of the arts and archeology.

In the summer of 1855, Frederick William was invited to Balmoral in Scotland, to stay with Queen Victoria and Prince Albert. On September 20 he asked them for the hand of their daughter Vicky, who had just turned fifteen. Frederick William had already obtained the approval of his own parents and of his uncle, then reigning as King Frederick William IV; Victoria and Albert agreed immediately but said there was to be no marriage until Vicky turned seventeen and asked him also not to propose to her until she was confirmed the following spring. "I have been much pleased with him," Albert wrote to a friend about the young prince. "His prominent qualities are straightforwardness, frankness and honesty. He appears to be free from prejudices and preeminently well-intentioned. He speaks of himself as personally greatly attracted by Vicky. I regard it probable that she will have no objection to make." [157]

He was right, as was shown on September 29, when hope of his restraining the prince's ardor until the following spring went amiss. Frederick William and Princess Victoria were riding up Craig-na-ban together when the prince plucked some white heather, symbolic of good luck. Luck in what, she wondered as he handed it to her; on the ride back down Glen Girnoch, he explained, and she accepted. "It is not politics, it is not ambition," he later told Copland Perry. "It was my heart."

That may have held true for the couple now secretly engaged, but others took a political view of it. Duke Ernest of Saxe-Coburg-Gotha, the brother of Prince Consort Albert, said Albert was filled "with fatherly ambition" for his daughter, hoping to set her "upon a mighty throne." Frederick William, standing in the line of succession to the throne of Prussia, the duke wrote, "inspired the greatest hopes for the future." At the same time, the duke noted opposition in Germany, as rumors of the engagement flew about. "The more the Liberal papers of Germany applauded," he wrote, "the more disagreeably was the other side affected." [158] This had the odd effect of reinforcing King Frederick William IV's support for the match; he liked to do anything his ministers opposed. General von Gerlach came to the king waving a copy of the *Kölnische Zeitung* and indignantly complaining of "absurd reports" that the prince had become engaged to a British princess. "Well, yes," the king finally replied, laughing out loud. "That is really the case!"

A year later the prince was back in Britain for Vicky's sixteenth birthday; on his return, he stopped at Paris, to pay a visit to the French court. Emperor Napoleon III treated him with great courtesy, although he was apprehensive about the Prusso-British match. Empress Eugénie expressed her own views in a letter to a friend, in which she described her German visitors, the prince and Moltke, those two men who fourteen years later would help drive both her and Louis Napoleon into exile.

"The Prince," she wrote, "is a tall, handsome man, almost a head taller than the Emperor; he is slim and fair, with a light yellow moustache—in fact, a Teuton such as Tacitus describes them; he is chivalrously polite and with a touch of Hamlet about him.

"His companion, Herr von Moltke (or some such name), is a man of few words, but nothing less than a dreamer, always on the alert, and surprises one by the most striking observations. An imposing race, the Germans. Louis says it is the race of the future. Bah! We have not come to that yet!" [159]

In May, 1857, after more than eighteen months had passed since the secret engagement, the Prussian king published an official announcement of it in the *Preussische Staatsanzeiger*; a month later the prince and Moltke again visited Britain. The entire country was by now aglow with Victorian tintype sentiment concerning the engagement; even the *Times,* earlier hostile to the match, was coming around. Once back in Prussia, the prince began receiving letters from his fiancée. She was a very opinionated and energetic girl, who soon came to overwhelm her husband intellectually. That summer the prince told Moltke he'd received a letter from Vicky which was forty pages long.

The wedding took place in early 1858, in St. James's Palace. "You ask me in your letter what I have to say to the English marriage," Bismarck wrote a friend at that time. "In order to give my opinion, I shall have to separate the two words. I do not care for the English part of it, but the marriage itself may be quite a good one. . . ." That more or less summed up the position of the Prussian conservatives, as well as that of the

French. Everyone was in favor of love, and most agreed that a prince was a better man for having a happy home life, but a wedding between Great Britain and emerging Prussia was something else.

A hundred Eton boys cheered the bride and bridegroom under a banner reading CONGRATULATUR ETONA, and a further bevy of Etonian boys met them at Windsor, unharnessing the royal carriage and pushing it from the railway station to the castle. That day the *Times* commented that both nations may have benefited by the marriage, but in any event it could say with "confidence" that "an English Princess [was] a gain to the Prussian Court."

There followed the usual British honors: Frederick William was made a Knight of the Garter and a member of the Guild of Fishmongers.* On February 2, en route to the *Victoria and Albert* on which they sailed from Gravesend, the couple passed under arches bearing signs reading: FAREWELL, FAIR ROSE OF ENGLAND! and WE GIVE HER TO YOUR CARE! Sixty young girls scattered flowers as they boarded the vessel; dockworkers yelled instructions to Frederick William: "Keep her well!" and even "Be true to her!" The *Times* reported there was hardly a dry eye to be found.[160] In fact, the British not only feared that they might miss the princess royal, but also half feared she was entering a barbarian land.

The welcome she received in her new home was so warm and enthusiastic that "Papa Wrangel," the doddering old field marshal, sat down to greet the bride in his gala uniform, only to discover he had sat down on a layer cake covered with whipped cream. The couple briefly settled in the Berlin Palace until they moved into the crown prince's palace, which became their winter residence. The future Emperor William II, the first of their eight children, was born twelve months later; instruments needed to be used and more than just physical damage was done to the infant boy.

The New Palace, near Potsdam, became the couple's summer home. The British-born princess cultivated English gardens

* The only foreigners eligible for the Garter were crowned heads, but Frederick William was found to be eligible because he was a descendant of George I of Britain.

and, at their nearby farm, managed dairy and chicken farming in the manner of a British country estate. The villagers living nearby were surprised to find Victoria interested in the sanitary facilities of their homes, in their schools and children's holidays; even Frederick William began to adopt the manners of a British country squire, to the extent of entering the village school and taking the lesson at times. Standing before the children on one occasion, he touched a medal on his chest and asked the pupils, "To what kingdom does this belong?" A little girl replied, "To the mineral kingdom." "And this?" the prince asked, pointing to a flower. "To the vegetable kingdom."

"And I, myself?" he asked, according to a story which quickly became famous throughout Prussia. "To what kingdom do I belong?"

"To the kingdom of heaven," the child replied prettily.

On January 18, 1861, Prince William was crowned king, and his son, Frederick William, became Crown Prince of Prussia. Already a lieutenant general, he now became Statthalter of Pomerania as well.

As the new reign became more and more reactionary, the crown prince withdrew into inactivity rather than clash with his father. He attended ministerial meetings, but said nothing and in October, 1862, withdrew completely. By May, 1863, as the king's conflicts with Parliament increased, the crown prince nevertheless became more and more embroiled; letters and memorandums flooded in on him from the progressives, who saw him as their champion, and from the conservatives, who pleaded with him to save his house from the lower house of Parliament. He himself had been persuaded by Victoria that the monarchy must move with the times, if only to save itself, and that absolutism endangered the stability of the throne. He wrote to Max Duncker, an historian and his counselor on state matters: "I am silent, and live in a state of passive neutrality." A few days later he broke his silence and pleaded with his father not to infringe the law in the matter of the press ordinances. William I shot back a reply: "You say you do not intend to offer any opposition. Then you cannot have used sufficient care, for opposition speeches of yours have got abroad and found their way to me. You now have an occasion for making amends by expressing yourself in a different way, by keeping aloof from the progressives and by turning toward the conservatives. . . ."

On June 3 the crown prince protested the press ordinances in a letter to Bismarck and, on June 4, in another letter to his father, saying that the restrictions were illegal, unconstitutional, and dangerous.

The storm that was brewing was caused not only by his letters but even more so by a speech he had made on May 5, in Danzig. The mayor of that city had pleaded with the crown prince, asking him to defend the constitution; Frederick William's reply to the mayor and the councilors, afterward reported in the press, included words very embarrassing to the court and the government. He had told them that the decrees had been issued without his knowledge, a statement which clearly implied his personal disapproval of them; he had also said he regretted the "conflict between the government and the people," a comment which lent support to those who argued that the government of the King of Prussia was not just unpopular, but fundamentally unrepresentative of the interests of the Prussian people.

The king wrote his son that he would be deprived of all military commands and be recalled to Berlin if there were any further remarks of that kind. The crown prince responded by saying he could not retract anything he had said, because the ministry had taken "a step imperiling my future and that of my children"; that comment demonstrated he correctly understood that the House of Hohenzollern could survive in modern times only if it acted in the best interests of the people and became more constitutionally disposed. The prince offered to resign his commission and go into foreign exile.

Such a move would have created a major scandal; no less of a scandal would have been caused had the king made good on his own threats and stripped his son of all military commands. King William I prudently had a talk with Bismarck on June 10, before acting. They talked while riding in a carriage, speaking in French "on account of the footmen on the box," as Bismarck reported later. "In the interest of the dynasty," Bismarck said, "I set myself the task of appeasing the king." He urged him not to make his son a popular martyr. William, impressed with that argument, forgave his son but warned him to keep silent in the future.

Chafing under this implied reproof, the crown prince fired off a bitter letter to Bismarck on June 30. "I will tell you what results I anticipate from your policy," he said. "You will go on quibbling with the constitution until it loses all value in the eyes of the people. In that way, you will on the one hand arouse anarchical movements that go beyond the bounds of the constitution, while on the other hand, whether you intend it or not, you will pass from one venturesome interpretation to another, until you are finally driven into an open breach with the constitution. I regard those who lead . . . my most gracious father into such courses as the most dangerous advisers for crown and country."

During the Danish War of 1864, the crown prince was attached to the staff of the commander in chief of the Austro-Prussian forces, Field Marshal von Wrangel. On September 11 of that year, after this brief war ended, the crown princess gave birth to her fourth child, Sigismund (Charlotte and Henry having been born in 1860 and 1862 respectively). Sigismund would die within two years. "The history of the family of Hohenzollern is full of strange coincidences," wrote Britain's Rennell Rodd in 1888, noting that this Prince Sigismund had the Emperor of Austria for his godfather and died "almost on the very day his native land had drawn the sword against Austria." [161]

The war against Denmark provided a martial respite from the war the crown prince waged with his father's prime minister. Bismarck's foreign intrigues troubled him particularly, and he warned Bismarck they would "probably lead to our downfall in Europe."

He added: "It would not be the first time that Prussia had attempted to outwit the world with the result of finding herself in the end between two stools."

When Bismarck was provoking war with Austria in 1866, Frederick William said, "We are surrendering ourselves bound hand and foot to a blind fate. I for my part shall leave no means untried to meet, to avert, to warn, to obviate this mischief. . . ." He told Duncker that he thought Bismarck was "a criminal trifling with sacred things" and he insisted that the only proper way for Prussia to achieve her supremacy over Germany was by "a definitely liberal system of government, conforming to the requirements of the time"; force needed to be used, if necessary, against any princes who resisted the establishment of a liberal German confederation.

Yet the immediacy of war preparations swept the crown prince along, for these appealed to his military and patriotic instincts. He was appointed commander in chief of the Second Army, and since he was only a talented, but not brilliant, commander, he was given Major General Leonhard von Blumenthal as his chief of staff. Prince Frederick Charles of Hohenzollern, the crown prince's cousin, was to head the First Army.* The Second Army established headquarters at Neisse on June 14, readying itself for action. Four days later, Queen Augusta arrived to tell him that two-year-old Prince Sigismund had died of meningitis.

Activity roused him from depression, for battles had begun. After the Prussian victory at Königgrätz on July 2, the crown prince again began to bicker with Bismarck and his father and became involved in their arguments as well. As noted, the king wanted to pursue and punish the Austrians, against Bismarck's advice. Thinking he had lost his argument with King William, Bismarck even threatened to leap out of a fourth-floor window; the crown prince entered Bismarck's room in the nick of time, as it were, and laid a hand on his shoulder. He told him, "I am ready to support you and your opinions with my father." He thus became peacemaker and won his father's assent to Bismarck's plan not to humiliate the Austrians.

"Inasmuch as my Minister-President has left me in the lurch in the face of the enemy," William grumbled, "I have discussed the question with my son, and . . . find myself reluctantly compelled, after such brilliant victories on the part of the army, to bite into this sour apple and accept a disgraceful peace." [162]

At the peace negotiations, the crown prince met Moltke.

* The careers of both princes were closely bound. Both were army commanders in the Austrian War; both were named field marshals on the same day during the Franco-Prussian War of 1870–71. Their deaths took place on the same day of the month, and at the same hour of the day, at the same three-year interval which separated their births, Frederick Charles dying in 1885 and Frederick William in 1888.

"You will find a fine state of things up there," Moltke told him. "The king and Bismarck are not on speaking terms." On his arrival at the castle, the crown prince found that the king and Bismarck had shut themselves in their rooms "and neither would go to the other," he reported. Again, the crown prince acted as mediator.

All this resulted in a temporary rapprochement between the crown prince and Bismarck. He had seen how successful Bismarckian policy could be; he was thrilled by the greater glory of Prussia; he had no intention of losing any of the fruits of victory. As for the crown prince's role in this campaign, Napoleon III is said to have struck his fist on a table, exclaiming, "The future King a good general too! That is the last straw!" [163] But when war later threatened with France over Luxembourg, the prince exploded. "You have not seen war!" he told a Prussian who spoke of it to him with enthusiasm. "If you had seen it, you would not utter the word so calmly. . . ."

That war was averted; the clash with France was postponed until 1870. The prince undertook a trip to Italy in 1868, to strengthen the Italian nationalist ties with Prussia and to counter the Francophile faction in Italy. He met with ovations everywhere; the Italians even shouted, *"Evviva Prussia, l'angelo protettore d'Italia!"* Back in Berlin, Bismarck was pleased; he told Professor Johann Kaspar Blüntschli that an Italian ministry hostile to Prussia was no longer possible. Frederick William had proved to be the kind of prince the Italians appreciated. One newspaper said he smiled "almost constantly" and called him "a fine-looking man, tall and well-built, with a martial air." They were charmed not only by his appearance, but by his almost Italian courtliness. This became famous throughout Italy after a certain court ball. Princess Margherita, the bride of the Italian heir apparent, Prince Humbert, was dancing with a banker's son named Cassano when a catastrophe occurred which caused the room to gasp with horror: Cassano stepped on Margherita's gown and tore off the trim. Frederick William whipped a small case out of his pocket, slipped off the rubber band around it, produced a pair of scissors, and knelt down on one knee to cut off the torn trim. When Margherita extended her hand for the fragment of cloth, Frederick William refused; he gallantly pressed it to his heart instead and then folded it carefully, putting it into his pocket. Everyone was agog at such chivalry, although the South German *Stuttgarter Beobachter* reported it with the crack: "Those Prussians are sharp fellows: always armed and ready for anything!"

Forcible Prussianization after the Austrian War had made many a Swabian and Hessian more anti-Prussian than ever. The aged grandmother of Baron Hugo von Reischach, a man who later served the Hohenzollern court, said, for example, that she'd crawl ten miles on her knees to see Bismarck hanged.[164] But the Franco-Prussian War of 1870–71 changed all that. The choice of the genial crown prince to lead the South German armies was a fortunate one. So much were the non-Prussian soldiers converted that, during the Battle of Wörth, while bullets whistled over their heads, they cheered the prince's presence and sang *"Heil Dir im Siegerkranz,"* firing all the while.

Gustav Freytag, a friend of the crown prince, accompanied him to his headquarters. "I detest this butchery," Frederick William told him. "I have never longed for war laurels. . . . Yet it is just my fate to be led from one war to another, and from battlefield to battlefield, before I ascend the throne of my ancestors." On reaching France, he issued a proclamation that "Germany is at war with the emperor of the French, not with the French people," and assured them they would need to fear "no hostile measures." He carried out his promise in any event. He took over the Villa des Ombrages on the outskirts of Versailles as his headquarters; his "hostess" there later wrote of him as "that stately and friendly gentleman . . . who warded off mischief from our household."

She then wrote: "Although, according to the laws of war, he was our master and the owner for the time of all that we had, he behaved himself always as if he were our guest. I can never forget the gentleness with which he used to ask for anything, whether for himself or for his Adjutant, apologizing for giving us trouble, fearful of causing any inconvenience, and inquiring whether this or that would interfere with our own arrangements. . . . On the terrible 19th of January, 1871, when there was fighting at Mount Valérien, Bougival, and St. Cloud, and our troops were driven back upon Paris, many thousands of my fellow-countrymen were taken prisoners. At six o'clock in the evening the Crown Prince had learned that among them there were several men who were not professional soldiers—lawyers, artists, teachers, merchants, and others. He asked the French officers who were taken prisoners to notify these civilians that . . . he would place escorts at their service, so that they might return to their homes and work. This generous *noblesse* . . . has never been forgotten. . . ." [165]

Those who had seen Frederick William kneel to repair Princess Margherita's torn gown had exclaimed the sentiments of that age: "He is a true knight!" In fact, Frederick William was a chivalrous Victorian gentleman and the kind of nineteenth-century aristocrat for whom *noblesse oblige* meant an obligation to treat everyone below his station with elaborate courtesy. He was, in this respect, his father's son, for William I invariably was kind to those beneath his rank; unfortunately, Frederick William's courteous treatment did not always extend to his own eldest son.

Elevated to the rank of imperial crown prince in 1871, Frederick William waited for the Kaiser's crown to pass to him. He was forty years old, vigorous and handsome; he had added a full beard to the mustache and sideburns he had worn earlier, and since the beard was as blond as his hair had been in youth, he looked more majestic than ever. But his military career was over, now that he was a field marshal, and he had nothing to do except perform ceremonial functions for his aged father. Victoria, the imperial crown princess, was far more vigorous than he by nature and encouraged him to plunge himself into the kinds of activities with which her father, Prince Albert, had occupied himself: the encouragement of the arts, industry, and social welfare. Frederick William became seriously interested in the acquisition of new collections for the Berlin museums, and every report dealing with them first passed through his hands.

The Hohenzollerns had never been art collectors or great patrons of art; this made Frederick William somewhat of an exception. The Hohenzollern palace contained a few Cranachs, deposited in one room, the *Schöne Kammer* ("Beautiful Chamber"), which the Great Elector had established. Frederick the Great had built a library but had never been a serious collector of art. The Royal Museum had been put up by Frederick William III, but largely because the marshy site on which it stood needed to be drained in any case and the cost of that operation was so enormous that putting up a museum didn't seem to matter financially. His successor was the first to provide a meaningful impetus to art collection; it was he who designated the island in the Spree River as a "sanctuary for art and learning" and who put up the New Museum, completed in 1859. He is said even to have sketched preliminary plans for the National Gallery, which was completed in 1876. Crown Prince Frederick William ordered the construction of a Handicrafts and of a Folklore Museum, and he became the patron of the German Anthropological Association. He also established the Hohenzollern Museum in 1877, although he maintained a relatively sober view of his ancestors. The patriotic fervor convulsing Germany after unification prompted Prussian historians to paint all Hohenzollerns in golden colors: Frederick William I was portrayed as almost kindly, and Frederick William III, so well known for his irresolution, was presented as having cleverly saved Prussia by means of sly tactics. The crown prince announced that he "decisively" rejected such evaluations and "desired no floweriness and no concealment, but the simple historical truth. . . ." Countless other Victorian-age activities were fostered by the crown prince and his Victoria: the Society for the Promotion of Health in the Home, the Victoria School for the Training of Nurses, the Victoria Foundation for the Training of Young Girls in Domestic and Industrial Work, "workmen's colonies" designed to rehabilitate and retrain tramps, as well as the unemployed, and night schools for workers. This was a time, after all, when the upper classes were dedicated to giving the industrial masses uplift and improvement—anything but a meaningful say in their own affairs.

Victorian paternalism was most at home in William I's Berlin Palace, where it was coupled with starchy North German formality. Bismarck said he disliked foreign courts because the guests all too often sat down at table wherever they liked; in the Berlin Palace, he said, it was always easy to find one's accustomed seat at table, everything being regulated and orderly. The crown prince's palace, a short distance away, was less "Prussian"; even Jews were invited in. As a matter of fact, a welcome was offered to any person of cultural or industrial achievement, particularly those who worked to better social conditions or for "the refinement of the masses," as one courtier recalled.[166] This palace was also gayer, the balls given by Frederick William and Victoria being brilliant and elaborate fetes. At one costume ball given in 1875 for 1,000 guests, one old gentleman who wore a mask and a simple hood received a sharp, if playful, poke in the ribs from a masked courtier and was asked, "Well, old fellow, how are you?" The octogenarian, who was actually Emperor William I, drew himself up to his full height and rumbled, "Say what you like—but hands off!" [167]

Festivities like these were interrupted in 1879, when the death of eleven-year-old Prince Waldemar shattered his parents. Victoria took her English maid and one lady-in-waiting and left for Wiesbaden and, afterward, Italy, not even returning for the old emperor's golden wedding anniversary. The engagement in 1880 of Prince William (the future emperor) did not alleviate the pain; Waldemar had been the couple's favorite.

In 1878, when his father was wounded by an assassin and Frederick William had to act for the king, he had "an almost impossible task before him," as Prince Charles Anthony of Hohenzollern-Sigmaringen remarked at the time, being "obliged to carry on the government in accordance with his father's ideas and . . . against his most cherished convictions." Frederick William did, however, accede to Bismarck's anti-Socialist laws, for while he was no reactionary, he was no radical either. He regarded the Social Democrats as an "evil," an "abortion," and hoped the laws would prove to be "a radical cure." Liberalism went only so far in any Hohenzollern who was raised in the military, absolutist, monarchical tradition; the tutor to Prince Waldemar, who lived with the crown prince's family for some years, says that Frederick William was imbued with nothing more than middle-class liberalism; he opposed the Prussian reactionaries not because he was any less nationalistic than they, but because they were "particularists" who believed the king should heed only the advice of the Junkers. Certainly Crown Prince Frederick William and his wife were remarkably fond of the glitter, pomp, and display of their imperial position, far more so than King William I ever was. Where the old king remained simple in his tastes and modest in his ways, his son and the crown princess were intoxicated by the "glory" implicit in ostentatious display. They enjoyed the trappings of power, he more than the exercise of it. Bismarck, who had noted this early, was sanguine; such rulers, he thought, would prove easy to rule. Indeed, even before Frederick William acceded to the throne, he had reconciled himself to keeping the Iron Chancellor around on Bismarck's own terms; who else was there? He and Victoria planned to influence German society by establishing a glitteringly cultural court, with "democratic" trappings: a Camelot where poets would have equal place with Prussian generals. Professor Michael Freund calls both Frederick William and Victoria "noble, magnanimous, and generous"; says they wanted to free Germany from its enslavement to Junkers, soldiers and bureaucrats; adds that they hoped to create a "free and democratic Germany" ruled by a meritocracy—but that neither knew how to achieve any of these ends. They did not even appreciate, he says, what enormous fundamental changes in Germany's economic, political, and sociological structure were required for such change. Frederick William's personal diaries, which he kept up virtually to the moment he died and which encompass thirty-seven volumes, contain *not a single* suggestion on what policies he might pursue once he became emperor. The general belief during his lifetime was that he would follow Victoria's advice in all matters.

Thanks in large part to the press campaign of defamation which Bismarck fomented against "that Englishwoman," the imperial crown princess became one of the most hated women in Germany, even after she had become empress of the nation. She regarded Bismarck as "that evil man" and hated him passionately; he icily returned the hatred. People knew she kept an "English home" and believed, with some justification, that she preferred anything English over most things German; it outraged just about everyone in her adopted country, for Germany was then developing a strong sense of national identity. Yet in fact, while it was true that she and her husband followed English customs in the heart of Prussia, part of the reason seems to be pure perverseness. "She was English in Germany and German in England," said Baron von Reischach, her lord chamberlain. Victoria's brother, King Edward VII, agreed. "When in England," he later told Reischach, "my sister always fought Germany's battles and praised everything German to the skies." [168]

It did not make her popular in Germany, however, for none

of that was known. As the years went by and Emperor William I seemed determined to deny them the throne by living forever, she and her husband became increasingly depressed. Father William was by now so much an institution in Berlin that Baedeker's guidebooks listed the exact hour (noon) when the emperor could always be seen at what came to be called "the historic corner window" of his study, watching the changing of the guard outside. He had developed into a major tourist attraction, people coming to watch him as much as the soldiers; indeed, he had become a monument, immune to change, apparently immune to death.

The same did not hold true for the crown prince. He became hoarse enough in January, 1887, to summon his physician. He was already depressed enough to tell companions, "I am an old man; I stand with one foot in the grave." To General von Schweinitz, he said: "The future? No—that belongs to my son. My time has passed away."

A growth was found on the larynx and was treated daily. A glowing platinum wire was used to burn it away—all this without any effective local anesthetic. This went on throughout March and April, 1887; the crown prince stoically endured the daily torment. An examination in mid-May showed, however, that the growth had returned. Cancer was assumed for the first time. A group of German doctors, desiring to consult with a specialist, proposed Britain's Harley Street physician Morell Mackenzie to Crown Princess Victoria, knowing she would trust an Englishman. Mackenzie came, removed a portion of the growth, and sent it to Professor Rudolf Virchow in Berlin for examination. Virchow and Mackenzie then reported that there was no evidence of malignancy and no immediate need for an operation to remove the larynx or part of it. It was an illusion, however, and one which eventually cost Mackenzie (not Vinchow) his reputation.

Frederick William seemed well enough to attend the jubilee of Queen Victoria in June, 1887, after which he spent some time on the Isle of Wight. He returned to the Continent in September and, in order to avoid the German winter, proceeded to Venice, from there to Lago Maggiore, and eventually to the Villa Zirio in San Remo, where he arrived on November 4. It was there that he received the news from Professor von

Schroetter of Vienna that he definitely did have cancer and did not have much longer to live. It was too late for an operation to save him, he was told; in fact, it was too early in medical history for that kind of operation to have had much success.

By January the crown prince was encountering such difficulty in breathing that a tracheotomy had to be performed. Frederick William began reading Thomas à Kempis' *Imitation of Christ* and wrote Pastor Persius of Potsdam: "You are right in speaking of patience and resignation, for without [this] . . . it would not be easy to lead the life that is imposed on me. . . ." Then, on March 9, 1888, Frederick William was walking in the garden of the villa when a servant brought a telegram to him on a silver salver. He had no idea what it might be, but on glancing at the address, he knew instantly and collapsed in tears. The telegram was addressed to him as "His Majesty the German Emperor." His father had died, only to be succeeded by a dying man.

Two days later Frederick William set out for Berlin as Frederick III. His son William, now the crown prince, met him there in a closed carriage; no public welcome was permitted. On the twelfth, the *Reichsanzeiger* published an imperial proclamation and Frederick III's charge to Chancellor Bismarck. It confirmed Bismarck in his post and asked him to promote economic welfare, education, the military strength of the country, religious toleration, peace, and prosperity—as well as the "mutual rights" of the emperor and the nation's constitutional system. The German liberals were crushed; they had hoped for parliamentary government and had been given pretty generalities. Frederick III was simply too weak to force through any substantial change. He had time only to elevate or decorate a host of his liberal friends, to bequeath several million marks on his wife and on his daughters, and to force Robert von Puttkamer, the reactionary minister of the interior, into resigning.* Meanwhile, the new German empress, Victoria, not only reigned but seemed to rule, determined to take her husband's place. He admired her conscientiousness, but others were disgusted. Count von Waldersee, "reading" her face at the time,

* Frederick's diary shows a distribution of 9,000,000 marks, while Bismarck claims sardonically that 12,000,000 were handed out. As for Puttkamer, he returned to power after the emperor's death.

said "my impression was that she reveled in being the center of attention." She used wine and stimulants to force her collapsing husband into public appearances; three weeks before his death, he was compelled by her to attend a wedding at Charlottenburg, gasping piteously during the ceremony and collapsing afterward. Victoria, who could not bear the thought that she was empress to a dying emperor, continued to deny that he suffered from cancer. She insisted he was "merely ill" until two weeks before he died. The night before his death, she visited him with Bismarck. Frederick William summoned up just enough strength to press Victoria's hands into the hands of her archenemy. To what other person could he entrust her future? In the wings waited their son William, contemptuous of his father and filled with a consuming hatred for his mother. Victoria and Bismarck left Frederick III, and even as they listened to his groans and gasps for air through the door separating them from the dying man, they bargained for the morrow. Victoria knew her Camelot had eluded her and now demanded that Bismarck give her funds for a castle on the Rhine—a house, she said, where she could do as she wished without having always to consult the government. This became Friedrichshof, a magnificent palace near Kronberg. There she retired in elegant seclusion. There, thirteen years later, in 1901, after two months of great suffering, she died. Another strange Hohenzollern coincidence had taken place: Like her husband, she died of cancer of the larynx.

15

"My Son Will Never Mature"

The death of Frederick III had been another body blow to liberal hopes in Germany; those who had banked on this most democratically inclined of all the Hohenzollerns even felt it as a death blow. The question which intrigued historians afterward might be summed up in the phrase, "What if." No one, in fact, could answer it, for no one knew what policies Frederick III might have pursued had he reigned for any length of time. But the general thrust of his thinking had been essentially, if moderately, democratic, as may be seen from his early strife with Bismarck over constitutionalism and freedom of the press. He could have put Germany on the road toward meaningful parliamentary rule, have given it a constitution of substance, and thus have changed German, European and even world history. As it was, however, the fate of Germany, of Prussia, and of the House of Hohenzollern was not his to determine. Events which had taken place inside his palace in Berlin during the early afternoon of January 27, 1859, were to prove more significant in the long run.

For two days, batteries of artillery had been waiting for the birth of a royal child: the first child of Princess Victoria and her husband. Snow was falling, and crowds stood in the drifts, anxious for a signal, hopeful that a male heir would be given to the royal family. Shortly after three o'clock, the cannon began to roar. Without waiting to hear whether 101 salutes would be fired, signaling the birth of a prince, or thirty-six, for a princess, the child's grandfather, the prince regent, William, raced from a conference in the Wilhelmstrasse, flagged down a passing cab, and charged off to his son's palace. He learned it was a boy; the crowds outside the palace learned it from old Papa Wrangel, who could not contain himself long enough to open a window. He shoved his fist through a pane of glass and yelled, "It's all right, children! It's a fine, young, new recruit!"

He was a little premature, however. The eighteen-year-old mother seemed near death, and the doctors paid attention only to her; when they finally turned to the young prince, they were horrified to find him lying lifeless, or so they thought. The prince really would have died, had it not been for Fräulein Stahl, the midwife, who frightened the attending courtiers even more by grasping the royal infant firmly and slapping it soundly until it cried. The prince was alive; he stirred; then he was promptly abandoned in the doctors' efforts at reviving his mother. No one noticed for almost a month that the child could not move his left arm. The shoulder socket had been injured and the elbow joint dislocated, either by the energetic midwife or by the doctor who had aided the birth with instruments. Both the left arm and the hand were perfectly formed, but almost paralyzed. Little was known of orthopedics then, and no one dared attempt an adjustment of that arm. In later years it failed to match the other arm in size; the hand just reached the jacket pocket, where it usually remained. Nor was this the only damage done. William's left leg never reacted quite as well as did his right one, and he also suffered periodically from pains in his left ear and on the left side of his head.

All these disabilities were ignored as though they did not exist, at least in terms of what was expected of the boy. No allowance was made for the fact that he was half-crippled: he was to be drilled and bullied until the withered arm conformed or, as it happened, was overcome. On the other hand, he was continually reminded of its existence, of the fact that it was a trial sent to test the young prince. The arm was massaged and manipulated, subjected to agonizing electric treatment, wrapped in flannel, worked over endlessly, while the young boy was all the time subjected to admonitions, pleas, urgings, and preachings. He had to try to lift a spoon with it, had to try to hold a horse's reins with it, had to march, drill, and shoot as though the deformity were not there. His father watched ineffectually and urged the boy to become "vigorous and upright"; his mother, after ignoring William for the first years of his life, turned the full force of her domineering personality on him after the death of Sigismund in 1866.

Two years later, on the advice of Sir Robert Morier, a British diplomat who was a close friend of the family, William received a new tutor: Georg Hinzpeter, thirty-nine, a Westphalian Calvinist. Hinzpeter, who remained with William until the prince was twenty, treated the withered arm as though it were perfectly normal, though he admitted that this "incurable disability . . . was a very particular hindrance to his physical and psychical development." The boy was forced to ride, for was he not after all destined to become an army officer at the age of ten and, eventually, the warlord of the nation? The fact that he could not keep his balance or hold his reins did not trouble Hinzpeter or Victoria. William fell off the horse and was put back on again by Hinzpeter, though he shook with terror. Hinzpeter ordered him to trot and canter without stirrups for long, agonizing weeks and months; Hinzpeter never praised the boy's achievements, never acknowledged the tremendous efforts the young prince made, but always demanded more. Victoria watched, even as her son crashed to the ground again and again; she was determined that this loathsome defect would somehow or other be corrected until none could notice it. At the table, even in his later years, William's food would be cut up as discreetly as possible by his neighbor, or he somehow managed eating with a special tool devised for him: a knife and fork combined together. Eventually, he became amazingly proficient. His cousin King George V once said that William "shot remarkably well considering he has only one arm"; in fact, his gunbearer would hold up the barrel while William sighted and squeezed the trigger. Yet there is no doubt he conquered his deformity to a surprising extent: he rowed, swam, and played both tennis and the piano. Hinzpeter, whom William once described as that "gaunt, dry figure with the parchment face," drove the prince mercilessly, even invoking the brutal eighteenth-century curriculum devised by that archbully Frederick William I for his own son. Throughout all this, says British historian Sir

John W. Wheeler-Bennett, the prince cooperated "with an unusual energy and resolution" and "displayed a fortitude which must evoke our admiration and sympathy."

Hinzpeter and Victoria represented a harsh punishment to the boy, for some sin he knew he had never committed; his father was a neuter to the prince, for he left his son's education in the hands of Victoria and seemed completely overshadowed by Bismarck and the prince's grandfather. This grandfather, William I, whom the prince always called the Great Kaiser even after he himself had ascended the throne, became the object of his hero worship: a distant, noble, Germanic soldier king, the repository of all royal attributes and virtues. In 1871, when William I returned to Berlin as German emperor, the twelve-year-old prince watched him worshipfully from atop his pony. He was the kind of Kaiser the prince hoped to become.

Everyone acknowledged that Prince William was very bright indeed, but his mother did not. She told Queen Victoria of Britain that William had neither "brilliant abilities nor any other strength of character or talent."

She wrote: "I watch over him myself and every smallest detail of his education. He possesses a strong constitution and would be a handsome lad if it were not for this unfortunate left arm which becomes more and more noticeable, affects his facial expression, his stance, his walk and his deportment, makes all his movements clumsy and gives him a feeling of shyness. . . ." [169] Her mother, Queen Victoria, replied with a warning. "I am sure you watch over your dear boy with the greatest care," she wrote, "but I often think too great care, too much constant watching, leads to the very dangers hereafter which one wishes to avoid." Then she added that she hoped the prince might be allowed to mix with all classes. "Mere contact with soldiers *never* can [benefit] . . . for they are bound to obey and *no independence of character* can be expected in the ranks." Another admonition, delivered in 1865, was that Prince William be brought up "simply, plainly" and "not with that terrible Prussian pride and ambition which grieved dear Papa so much and which he always said would stand in the way of Prussia taking that lead in Germany which he ever wished her to do. . . ." [170]

The pressure on the prince inevitably evoked resistance.

When he was only four years old, he threw a tantrum during the marriage of his "Uncle Bertie" (later King Edward VII); a painter, commissioned to immortalize the droll scene, wrote, "Of all the little Turks, he is the worst." Filled with an overwhelming sense of inadequacy, William began early to assert himself. Hinzpeter wrote that "one was struck by the resistance called forth in him by any sort of pressure, any attempt to form his deeper nature. . . . It was extraordinarily difficult to reach the inner being. . . . This stubborn nature was extremely resistant even to the discipline of thought." Yet Hinzpeter kept applying the pressure relentlessly. "Only the utmost severity," the tutor wrote, ". . . availed to overcome the resistance. . . ."[171]

"We tortured ourselves," William wrote in his later years, "over thousands of pages of grammar, we applied its magnifying glass and scalpel to everything from Phidias to Demosthenes, from Pericles to Alexander, and even to dear old Homer. . . ."[172] The lessons started at six in the morning in summer and at seven in winter; they went on for twelve hours. "Life," Hinzpeter told the prince, "means labor," and he worked the prince mercilessly. No Prussian prince was ever pampered (although some had been spoiled); William's normal Prussian "Spartan upbringing," says Wheeler-Bennett, demanded in his special case "an additional measure of loving kindness on the part of his parents," to help him overcome his disability. "But Victorian parents were not accustomed to make life easy for their offspring," he continues, "and the Crown Princess, herself brought up in a strict school, was not inclined to relax the rigid code in regard to her own children."[173] Hinzpeter was not what the doctor ordered for such a boy as William, but he certainly was what his mother prescribed. Twice a week Hinzpeter took William to inspect museums, factories, or mines; Hinzpeter insisted that wherever they visited, William must make an appropriate speech of thanks to the manager or director. Hinzpeter made nothing but demands and he incorporated in his person the stern Calvinist teacher, the harsh Prussian drillmaster, and Victoria's ideal, the British public school headmaster who canes his charges. Like many a product of all these systems, William rebelled against the discipline, but never against the disciplinarian. He liked his torturer.

Hinzpeter and Victoria did not know it, but they were actually producing the effect Queen Victoria had warned against: the very dangers one wished to avoid. Rebellious and resentful, William grew to be a mass of complexes; fearfully insecure and frightfully self-assertive by way of compensation, he was consumed with a sense of inadequacy which he was unable to face. In consequence, he exalted himself, developed an exaggerated sense of his importance, glorified himself, swaggered, and strutted. He became a poseur, striking martial attitudes; even more than he revered his grandfather, he worshiped Frederick the Great and hoped to emulate that embodiment of Hohenzollern military genius.

Victoria became alarmed and belatedly followed her mother's advice. She sent William to school at Kassel, into a Gymnasium, or public secondary school, so that he might mix with lesser mortals, but it was too late. Count Leo von Caprivi wrote later that William played "quite the future emperor" there, showing an "overbearingness" which led even Hinzpeter to exclaim, "You have no idea of what an abyss I have looked into!" [174]

He graduated at eighteen, taking tenth place in a class of seventeen, and was awarded a certificate marked only "Satisfactory." Hinzpeter later tacitly acknowledged his own failure, by stating William had "never learned the first duty of a ruler: hard work." At that time a Prussian nobleman spoke to William's father about the boy's progress. "Don't congratulate me, dear Count," Frederick William replied. "My son will never mature, will never come of age." So it proved to be. A rigid Victorian upbringing had molded a highly intelligent boy who only had a physical handicap into an emotional cripple. Unfortunately for Germany, Europe, and even the House of Hohenzollern, this neurotic inherited an absolutist state.

After six months as a lieutenant in the First Guards Regiment, an experience he enormously enjoyed, William was sent off for four terms at the University of Bonn, where his father also had been educated. Instead of receiving a concentrated dose of one, two, or three subjects, which might have given him a taste for concentration, William was assigned to study eight, which made him the master of none but allowed him to speak glibly on each for the rest of his life. One of his teachers, Rudolf von Gneist, said William was typical of members of royal families: He knew everything without having learned anything. One thing, however, he did learn at Bonn, and that was to admire the achievements of the man his parents detested: Bismarck.

On the Rhine, shimmering with ancient Germanic legends and a sense of imperial traditions, William's romantic patriotism came to be as much stimulated as his love of military display had earlier been stimulated among the guards in Potsdam. The sycophantic press adulated him, as did everyone with whom he came into contact. "Rejoice ye hills!" miners exclaimed to him on one of his inspection visits. "Rejoice, ye vaulted caverns! Noble Prince, Star of Germany, protect our mines at home and afar!"[175]

He literally fell in love with himself—or with his image. The real William, that sensitive, shy, intelligent, and handicapped boy, hid behind the imperial William, Knight of the Order of the Black Eagle, descendant of Frederick the Great and of his grandfather, the "Great Kaiser." Wherever he traveled or stayed, at Wilhelmshöhe or, in 1878 for the first and last time, to Paris and Versailles, he was attracted by the portraits and memorabilia of great monarchs and warlords, all of them posturing, posing, strutting, and sneering in countless adoring pictures. The more he became inflamed with monarchical, even absolutist, zeal, the more he became hardened toward his parents, whose liberal friends he believed wished to undermine the House of Hohenzollern. He, after all, had sworn the sacred knight's oath at eighteen, "to maintain the honor of the royal house and guard the royal privileges." His parents seemed to him to have betrayed their trust, to have betrayed even imperial Germany.

But there were early signs of that inconsistency or duality which consistently manifested itself in him in countless contradictions. Although he was later to become passionately anti-British, for most of his reign he fervently admired the British aristocracy and played the British lord; he told Theodore Roosevelt in 1911, "I *adore* England!" Although he treated his mother abominably after acceding to the throne, he boasted to the British ambassador that he had inherited his mother's "good stubborn English blood." Yet Herbert von Bismarck, the Iron Chancellor's son and heir presumptive, said, "Prince William can never hear enough against England. . . ." In fact, William vacillated, being as rudderless in youth as he would always prove to be in what passed for his mature years.

His mother called him "selfish, domineering, and proud," but he could also be the exact opposite. He often struck people as devastatingly charming and considerate. He never knew what to be and often had to repair the damage done by his proud nature with an elaborate show of kindness. Sarah Bernhardt, spotting the fact that William was always onstage, said she got along with him splendidly because they were "both troupers." He was even playfully charming, although he could overdo this just as he could his saber rattling; he once caused an international uproar by tweaking the King of Bulgaria in the behind.

That monarch was not the only man to get such treatment; William often patted the behinds of young officers and tweaked their cheeks. This and his extremely close friendship with Count Philipp zu Eulenburg, a happily married man who had occasional homosexual relationships, ultimately led the enemies of William II to spread rumors that the Kaiser himself was a homosexual. Certainly he had a strong streak of the feminine about him, but he appears to have had a vigorous heterosexual appetite as well—and one which his wife entirely satisfied, for even those of his enemies who would have been delighted to find a scandal never found the slightest indication that William had been unfaithful to his wife.

This was Augusta Victoria of Schleswig-Holstein-Sonderburg-Augustenburg—Dona, as she was called—whom he married in February, 1881. In later years, as William became distrustful of his ministers and advisers, he leaned on Dona for advice. But Dona was not like his mother; Dona was not only illiberal, but stupid. Princess Daisy of Pless said Dona was "just like a good, quiet, soft cow that has calves and eats grass slowly and ruminates"; her eyes "might have been glass," so expressionless were they.[176] Yet they were turned on William with adoration, that which he needed most. A court official who observed her both before and after her elevation to German empress called her "always very small-minded" and jealous of her mother-in-law's position. No sooner had William acceded to the throne than Dona, with his consent, ousted Victoria from most of her posts of honor, even from patronage of the Red Cross Society and the like. The way she acted, he said, was not only "often very petty" but "the case of a beggar on horseback." [177]

Bismarck recognized early that the beggar to be set on horseback was really Crown Prince William, the champion of authoritarianism at odds with his liberal parents. Although Bismarck was now in his seventies, he planned for his son, Count Herbert, to succeed him in a sort of hereditary chancellorship. Bismarck was keenly aware that he came from a family as old as the Hohenzollerns, whom he once referred to as "a Swabian family no better than mine"; in fact, Bismarck's name of Schönhausen had ironically come from an estate given the family as compensation, after a Hohenzollern elector had robbed the Bismarcks of their original lands.[178] The chancellor began in the 1880's to curry favor with young William. He sent William to Russia to visit the future Czar Nicholas II in 1884; two years later he sent him to meet Emperor Francis Joseph at Bad Gastein in Austria and then to Russia again. William, not even crown prince yet, but just the son of the crown prince, became the focus of Bismarck's anti-British, pro-Russian, jingoist, and absolutist policies. Crown Princess Victoria complained bitterly that neither she nor her husband were consulted and that these trips were arranged between the Kaiser and young William. During that autumn of 1886, Bismarck even got the ancient emperor to order the employment of his grandson in the Foreign Office, but this the twenty-eight-year-old prince's father prevented. "In view of the immaturity as well as the inexperience of my eldest son," Frederick William wrote to Bismarck, "together with his tendency towards over-bearingness and self-conceit, I cannot but frankly regard it as dangerous to allow him at present to take any part in foreign affairs." [179]

That remarkable analysis of the future Kaiser deepened the rift between William and his parents and tied him ever closer to the Bismarcks, father and son. It was not difficult for William to become convinced that his "pro-British" mother was virtually a traitor and that his father had been led into weakening the throne and the nation by adopting liberal ideas. William heard this talk all the time, from the Bismarcks and from his fellow officers at Potsdam. Then, shortly before the death of the old emperor, Bismarck did an apparent *volte-face:* He wanted better ties with Britain, and since he could make use of Victoria in this connection, he improved his relations with her and the crown prince. Prince William was shattered. The man whom he admired most in Germany, aside from his grandfather, had joined the enemy. "No one is irreplaceable," William told a government minister at that time. Bismarck, he said, would of course "be needed for some years," but after that, "the monarch must himself take a larger part. . . ." These were prophetic words, as were the ones Bismarck had once spoken to William, "Someday you must be your own chancellor."

Meanwhile, William waited, satisfied with his life in the army and among his friends, Eulenburg and Count von Waldersee, happy at the Guards Club, and pleased that Dona was producing sons at the rate of one a year: William in 1882, Eitel Frederick in 1883, Adalbert in 1884, after which she rested until 1887, when Augustus William was born. Oscar followed in 1888, Joachim in 1890, and an only daughter, the couple's seventh and last child, Victoria Louisa, in 1892.

Crown Prince Frederick William being ill at San Remo in March, 1888, it was Prince William who watched with tears in his eyes as old Emperor William I slipped loose from life with great dignity, after taking a little champagne. During the ninety-nine days which followed, William watched icily as his father died. He had at first resented the fact that his father was allowed to assume the throne in such a pitiful physical condition; then, after a friend suggested an interregnum would probably be of benefit to him, William happily agreed that Frederick III and Victoria would most likely blunder so badly that their brief reign would make his all the more welcome. He spent the ninety-nine days distributing busts and autographed pictures of himself. There were plenty of officials and officers happy to receive them. Isolated by disease, Frederick III was powerless; his empress was hated; neither seemed to matter at all. All eyes were turned on the "Rising Sun," the thirty-year-old crown prince. On June 15 this prince became William II, the third of his house to become German emperor, the ninth to become King of Prussia, and the last of his house to reign in the lands which the Hohenzollerns had subdued some four centuries before.

The new reign had not even begun before ominous omens were read. For twenty-four hours before Frederick III died in the New Palace in Potsdam (Friedrichskron, as he had retitled it), officers who had never before been seen within the palace appeared in groups of two or three, demanding food and lodging. A few hours before Frederick III's death, a man appeared who announced he was, by order of Crown Prince William, the new master of the household. As soon as the emperor's death had been confirmed, hussars clattered up to the palace at the trot, battalions of soldiers surrounded it and the palace gardens, sentries were posted everywhere, and the mysterious officers were barking out commands. On order of the master of the household, no one was permitted contact with the outside world, and no one was permitted to leave the palace or its gardens. This applied to the new emperor's mother; it applied even to the physicians who had attended Frederick III. When the surgeon general was sent to summon Professor Virchow for a postmortem examination, he was halted by a sentry with a loaded gun and could not embark on his errand. The palace was hermetically sealed, as though a coup were taking place; the new emperor had begun his reign by making everyone his personal prisoner.

His motives, however, were less sinister and even understandable, especially if one takes into account his almost pathological suspicion of his mother. William was convinced that for weeks state papers had been smuggled to Britain; he was going to hold everyone prisoner while he personally hunted for evidence in his father's desk. It has also been suggested that he feared the existence of a will which would have cut him out of the inheritance altogether or perhaps would have given his mother too much of that money which frugal old William I had saved.

Something had in fact been smuggled to Britain the day before Frederick III died. It was a package containing his war diary for the years 1870–71 and his diaries for many of the succeeding years; the Berlin correspondent for the New York *Herald* had carried the packet from Potsdam to the British Embassy, which in turn forwarded it to Windsor. This was a precaution aimed at avoiding censorship; when the diaries ultimately did appear in Germany, they proved harmless enough and not dangerous to the new Kaiser. Empress Victoria (who now assumed the title Empress Frederick) had also put her husband's will beyond the reach of her son, for it made her independent of her son's largess.

William found nothing in his father's desk which would have proved a treasonable connection between his mother and Britain, nor anything else of interest except family memorabilia. A major named Normann, who watched the young Kaiser ransack the desk, says William came upon a telegram sent to his parents on the day of his birth. As he read the text—"Is it a fine boy?"—William, he said, clutched his withered left hand convulsively about his sword hilt.

He was then handed an envelope which, by tradition, was given to each Hohenzollern ruler on his accession. This contained that plea from King Frederick William IV urging his successors to tear up the constitution which had been wrung out of him by force. Instead of saving the document for his successor, William destroyed it. He then also destroyed the deathbed hope of his father, who had charged William "as a filial duty" to assent to the engagement of William's sister with the man she passionately loved, Prince Alexander of Battenberg. This betrothal had been opposed on political grounds by Bismarck and on social grounds by most German society, the Battenbergs (future Mountbattens) not being considered of sufficient rank to marry the sister of a reigning emperor.

Disrespect, not dignity, was the keynote of his father's funeral. No foreign princes were invited to attend; not even the German public was allowed to come near. While the chapel was being decorated by hammering workmen, the coffin containing Frederick III's body lay about among them "like a toolchest." [180] When the ceremony took place, the only ones acting with dignity, says Eulenburg, were the troops. The others seemed to take their cue from the young Kaiser. Eulenburg noted with distress that "the clergy were laughing and chattering" and Field Marshal von Blumenthal was "reeling about, talking. . . ." Afterward the new Kaiser tried to forget his father altogether.

The first statement issued by the new Kaiser was to the army; the second was to the navy; only the third did he address to his people.

"We belong to each other—I and the army—we were born for each other and will cleave indissolubly to each other, whether it be the will of God to send us calm or storm," he told his troops.

In his pronouncement to his people, William II vowed "before God" to do everything "in piety and godly fear," to be just, merciful, a guardian of the right, a succorer of the poor and oppressed, a champion of peace—all this "with eyes raised to the King of Kings."

Hearing this, the German people hoped he would be a religious prince, filled with Christian humility, but they were to be disappointed. Old William I had interpreted the title *Dei gratia imperator* as meaning that he owed his imperial rank to the grace of a God to whom he was accountable, but William II reversed its meaning. For him the title meant that God Himself had invested him with the rank of emperor and that he was, thus, heaven's vicar in Germany. It was a subtle point, but one which influenced the vain emperor's actions. An early example of this came during the visit to Berlin of the Prince of Wales, William II's "Uncle Bertie." Despite the fact that no foreign princes had been invited to Frederick III's funeral, the future Edward VII had appeared for his sister's sake; this immediately led him to be regarded as his sister's champion and William's enemy. The nephew demanded that the uncle, who was a mere heir apparent, treat him in private, as well as in public, with the respect due an emperor. This, said Queen Victoria of Britain, "is *perfect madness*!" She added that if her grandson William had such notions, he had better never come to England. The political relations between Britain and Germany, she hoped, would not be affected "by these miserable personal quarrels," but she feared "that, with such a hot-headed conceited and wrong-headed young man, this may at ANY moment become *impossible*." [181]

The British, noting the Kaiser's behavior to his uncle, huffed, "No English gentleman would behave like [that]. . . . But we must not forget that none of them [William II and the two Bismarcks] happen to be *English Gentlemen*, and we must take them as we find them—pure Prussians." [182]

None of this, of course, was apparent to the German people, who saw only the Kaiser's bravura performances. A week after his father's funeral he dressed the palace guard in the ceremonial uniforms of Frederick the Great's age, dressed himself in a stunning uniform with a scarlet cape, dressed his pages in black knee breeches, and opened the Reichstag with a speech delivered in a majestic, military manner, after which he grasped Bismarck's hand warmly and the old chancellor kissed his Kaiser's hand. This scene was what the German people wanted: the old chancellor, whom they by now mistook for honest old virtue itself, united with the vigorous young symbol of the future.

In fact, the Kaiser's arrogant self-assertiveness perfectly mirrored the mood of Germany. Ever since unification had been achieved, German commerce and industry had enjoyed an unprecedented boom, and the future not only looked glorious, but limitless. It seemed to many Germans that this had not come about by accident, but that God must have blessed the land and its wise rulers. Frederick III, with his liberal airs, had seemed like an aberration and had been in any event only a brief interruption in a glorious monarchical drama. The venerable William I was now succeeded by someone who seemed his rightful son and heir; the grandson seemed to express national pride and unbounded confidence by his every gesture. Those enormous mustaches, with which William emblazoned his initial on his face and which recalled those worn by the men of the Giants' Guard, seemed to express perfectly the brash and bumptious assertiveness of the times.

The frugality of William I's court was immediately abandoned. The Berlin Palace, with its 650 rooms, became the new emperor's main residence and hardly seemed big enough for all the courtiers flooding in. One day's food consumption in the palace, when there were *no* visitors, came to 100 pounds of butter, 100 pounds of beef, 200 pounds of pork and mutton each, and 350 pounds of veal, not to speak of fish, game, poultry, and vegetables in the same proportions. More than sixty palaces, scattered around Germany, were maintained for Kaiser William's periodic visits. A twelve-carriage royal train, with blue silk upholstery, chandeliers, and special carriages for the emperor's entourage, was kept in constant readiness for his incessant travels. On his first trip, to Vienna and Rome, William carried with him 80 diamond rings, 150 silver orders, 50 breastpins, 30 gold watches and chains, 100 small chests, 20 diamond-encrusted Orders of the Black Eagle, 3 gold photograph frames—all these to be given as gifts. He traveled about in a solid-gold helmet, dressed in a wardrobe of specially designed uniforms. An imperial yacht, the *Hohenzollern,* was built at a cost of 4,500,000 marks during William's second year "as a prototype for the navy" it was explained at first, although later admitted to be a "pleasure boat" for himself and his family. Just five months after acceding to the throne, William horrified Bismarck by demanding an increase in salary of 6,000,000 marks a year.

He rose at six in the morning each day, early rising being a Hohenzollern tradition sanctified by the example of Frederick the Great, and like his ancestor, William began work immediately after morning coffee. But he was constitutionally unable to take a serious interest in anything; he never even read the newspapers, but only those inoffensive press clippings which had been cut out for him. Any letter of any length—which usually meant any letter of importance—went into the wastebasket. Dispatches and memorandums prepared for his study were glanced at and scribbled on. The emperor's marginal comments, most of them silly expletives and intemperate reactions, could fill volumes on their own, as could the emperor's speeches, his bombastic *Kaiserreden,* delivered everywhere in Germany, during trips which often consumed thirty weeks out of the year.

Yet the real master of Germany was still Bismarck. He was imperial chancellor, Prussian prime minister, president of the Ministry of State, minister of trade and commerce, the man who was in complete charge of all foreign affairs, and the unsurpassed manipulator of the Reichstag delegates. Bismarck was happy to encourage the emperor's vanity and to urge him to travel, to attend countless ceremonials, to spend weeks on maneuvers, to review troops, to visit the growing fleet—anything to keep him out of Berlin, out of the center of power. William, who shared the public's admiration of the man who had single-handedly created the German Empire and who even seemed personally responsible for German prosperity, was happy to keep Bismarck on. Others, however, plotted. Bismarck alone determined who held any position of importance in the government; his removal would eliminate an obstruction to wealth and power. Count von Waldersee, who longed to replace the

Iron Chancellor, whispered in William II's ear: "Frederick would never have become great, if on his accession he had found and retained in power a minister of Bismarck's authority and prestige."

On the anniversary of Frederick the Great's birthday in January, 1890, William called the Crown Council to announce what was to be, in his words, "historically a very significant new departure." He had decided to become *roi des gueux,* he said, "king of beggars"; he would champion the working class and lure them away from Social Democracy. "The employers," he told the council, "have squeezed the men like lemons and then let them rot on the dung heaps." He demanded an end to child labor, an end to Sunday working, a greater share for the workers in the profits of their employers, and cancellation of the deportation clause in the anti-Socialist laws. Bismarck warned against any such surrender to the Reichstag, and when William at first remained adamant, Bismarck threw out the trump card which had always brought Emperor William I around. "If Your Majesty attaches no weight to my advice," he said, "I do not know whether I can remain at my post."

The threat worked for the time being, and Bismarck began to subvert the emperor's plans. Both men retreated from the Crown Council feeling they had lost. Bismarck lay on his sofa and complained that not one man in the Cabinet had supported him. The Kaiser, furious that he had been forced into a corner by Bismarck, shook his fist in the face of the minister of war and complained that *he* had been left in the lurch. Finally, the emperor's proclamation was prepared, although Bismarck pleaded that William consign it to the flames. That evening William said proudly that the workers would now "know that I think for them," and indeed, the democratic papers the next day praised the emperor. Like all praise, it swept all restraint away. "The old man is crawling," William gloated, referring to Bismarck. "I'll leave him a few weeks to recover his breath; then I'll govern!"

On election day, the young Kaiser showed he had his doubts about the workers after all. He placed the army on the alert and spent the day among his officers, reviewing the guards on parade at Tempelhof. His suspicions proved to be justified. The Social Democratic Party had in 1884 polled 550,000 votes and in 1887, 763,000; on this February 20, 1890, the SPD doubled its mandate, to 1,427,000 votes. William muttered that the workers had betrayed him, but when Bismarck urged that all Socialists be treated as enemies of the state, William, who longed to be loved, said, "I won't be called the Cartridge King, like my grandfather!"

"Better sooner than later," Bismarck shot back. "Social Democracy cannot be reformed out of existence—someday it will have to be shot out of existence!"

"I will *not* wade in blood!" William exclaimed, almost completely out of control.

Again Bismarck hinted at resigning, and again William capitulated, although he afterward told friends, "He is almost impossible! He can't bear for me even to express a wish or an intention!" Bismarck said later, "On sleepless nights, I used to debate with myself whether I could endure it any longer under him. My love for my country said, 'You must not go. You are the only man who can keep that willful nature in equilibrium.' But I also knew the monarch's mental condition, which seemed to me potentially capable of bringing about the most deplorable developments. The spectacle which had been presented in Bavaria by [the insane] Ludwig II passed off smoothly enough, but in a military state like Prussia a similar entertainment would have fatal effects."

The suggestion that William was mad was a slander; he was always unstable, but never insane. It showed, however, how intemperate the reactions of both the emperor and his chancellor were toward each other by this time. Soon there were fresh clashes. Bismarck had entertained a Catholic Centrist leader; when he told the Kaiser about this, he was surprised to hear that he ought to have received William's permission first. "If you make this a reproach to me," Bismarck said, "Your Majesty might as well forbid your chief of staff in wartime to make reconnaissances of the enemy. I can by no means submit to such control in matters of detail and my personal meetings at my own house."

"Not even if your sovereign commands you?" William asked.

"Not even then, Your Majesty!"

Again William capitulated. "It is not a question of a command," he murmured, flinching before the steely gaze of the

Iron Chancellor, "but of a desire. It surely cannot be your intention to stir up the people. . . ."

"That is precisely my intention!" Bismarck replied triumphantly. "Such confusion shall prevail in the country, such a hullabaloo, that not a human being shall know what the emperor is at with his policy!"

William protested that he wanted the exact opposite. "My policy shall lie open and plain. . . . I desire no conflict with the Reichstag. . . ." He told the chancellor he had asked General Falkenstein to negotiate with the Parliament about the army bills. Bismarck, affronted, again offered to resign—and again the emperor flinched and hesitated. He seized on another issue which annoyed him. He said he never received reports from ministers and asked Bismarck to cancel a regulation dating to 1852 which compelled ministers to funnel all reports to the emperor through the prime minister's office. Bismarck refused to do so, saying he could not remain in charge of the government if the monarch made decisions "on the advice of all and sundry." Then he switched the subject to the impending visit of the czar, against which he warned, and began rummaging among some papers for a specific sheet containing some remarks the czar had made about the Kaiser, comments which had been reported to the British court. Watching the paper dangle tantalizingly from the chancellor's fingers, William exclaimed, "Well? Can't you read it out?" Bismarck looked horrified and said he could never do that, since the words would wound the Kaiser. William grabbed the paper from the chancellor's hand and read it himself. The czar, it revealed, had said of William, *"Il est fou. C'est un garçon mal élevé et de mauvaise foi."* William blanched, quivered, yet controlled himself. He knew he had been humiliated, not so much even by the czar as by his chancellor. How could he shake Bismarck's hand after this? The emperor left, clutching his helmet so as to avoid giving the chancellor his hand; he extended two fingers to him instead. Then he hurried off to his friend Waldersee, who was delighted to provide him with more fuel for his fires. These consisted of some reports from the German consul at Kiev, referring to Russian troop movements—reports which Bismarck had deliberately and deceitfully withheld from the emperor, Waldersee was happy to suggest.

William was elated; it seemed to him that he had found the weapon with which to gun Bismarck down. He shot off a letter to all government offices saying there was no doubt whatever that the Russians were "in full strategic disposition for war," called for countermeasures, and publicly stated that he very much deplored having been kept in the dark. Once more he demanded that Bismarck declare the 1852 regulation null and void, and once more Bismarck refused. The chancellor was quite right in doing so, of course, for if every department of the government began dealing with the emperor directly, rather than through the prime minister, complete chaos would result. Not only would it have stripped Bismarck's office of any meaningful authority, but it would also have put all affairs of government into thoroughly inexperienced and immature hands. Furthermore, nothing would ever get done, for, as has been noted, lengthy dispatches ended up in the Kaiser's wastebasket or, at best, were scanned so flightily that any decisions the emperor arrived at after casting his eyes over them were hasty and dangerous.

William, of course, saw the matter differently. His grandfather's stories, of victory over Napoleon I and over Napoleon III, as well as of his Hohenzollern heritage, had gone to his head. "A pageant of all that Prussia had been, a vision of all that she was to become, opened before the eyes of the young Prince as he listened to these stories and realized that one day the mantle of all this greatness would fall upon his own shoulders," writes Wheeler-Bennett.[183] Simultaneously, the sufferings he had endured as a child, his own determination to excel in everything despite his physical handicap led him to shield "his natural timidity with a protective and compensating covering of aggressive self-assertion." [184] Thus, when Bismarck balked in this instance, William declared, "My old Hohenzollern family pride was up in arms. Now it was a question of compelling the old hothead's obedience, or parting once and for all. Now it was simply, 'Emperor or Chancellor on top?' " [185]

William II sent a general to see Bismarck on March 17, again to demand the withdrawal of the 1852 regulation or, alternatively, the immediate resignation of the imperial chancellor. When Bismarck refused to accede, the general told him, "Your

Serene Highness will be good enough to be at the palace at two o'clock, to hand over your office."

"I am not well enough," Bismarck muttered. "I'll write."

This was an impertinence; to use Frederick the Great's phrase, the monarch was being treated as though he were "some little Prince of Zerbst and Köthen." But William was no Frederick II, so he just cooled his heels in the palace, while nervously waiting for his chancellor to write. When no word arrived, an official was dispatched to ask Bismarck why he had not tendered the farewell visit which the emperor had demanded.

"The emperor, as you know, can dismiss me at any moment," Bismarck replied wearily. "I stand ready to countersign any straightforward dismissal without delay. But I do not, on the other hand, propose to absolve the emperor from the responsibility for my retirement, but rather to give full publicity to its true source. After twenty-eight years in office, which have not been without their influence in Prussia and the empire, I require time to justify myself in the eyes of posterity—as well as at a farewell visit."

That evening Bismarck had still not made his appearance at the palace. William fretted, worried that the chancellor might force him to dismiss Bismarck in public, which would cause an uproar. Finally, on the next day, the longed-for letter arrived. William noted that it was in fact a resignation and wrote "Accepted!" on it in great haste, as though fearful it might still be withdrawn. Because its six pages attributed all the blame for the enforced resignation on the emperor, those pages were consigned to the vaults, and the emperor's subjects had to wait years before they got to read the text of Bismarck's letter. What was published immediately was completely different. It was the emperor's statement about the matter, brilliantly executed in its way, for William II was a master at hyperbole, as skilled an orator as Frederick William IV had been, and a propagandist par excellence. He told his people that he regretted that "poor health" had forced Bismarck to resign, that he hoped Bismarck would remain available to the nation, and that he was even offering to make him a duke and a major general. "I feel as sad at heart," he wrote, "as if I had lost my grandfather all over again. But we must submit to God's will, even though it destroy us. The duty of the officer on the watch upon the ship of state has now fallen to me. Our course is the old course. Full steam ahead!"

When William accepted Bismarck's resignation, it was said at the time that he had "dropped the pilot." But it was more serious than that. The ship's new master had no charts, and far from merely dropping the pilot, the Kaiser had left both rudder and keel behind.

16

Pomp Without Circumstance

THE year in which William II acceded to the Hohenzollern throne also happened to be the year Unter den Linden received its first electric lights, which seems appropriate, for this new Kaiser stepped—or swaggered—out of his grandfather's gaslit era onto a brilliantly illuminated stage. He was now its center, for Bismarck had sullenly retired to his estate, Friedrichsruh. His departure was cheered by most officials and army officers; they flocked sycophantically about the vain young emperor, satisfied to note that he was amenable to even the grossest flattery.

All the restraints Bismarck's iron grip had imposed were being slipped. The old chancellor, after all, had always known Germany's limits, though he recognized none for himself; those who followed him were men of limited ability who, under William II, were to know no limits at all. Ironically, the Kaiser's ordinary subjects wept as the grizzled old chancellor rode in an open carriage through Berlin to the railway station where he would embark for his estate. The man they had once hated now seemed venerable behind his enormous, drooping mustaches; they seemed to forget he had made them sacrifice parliamentary government for the gift he had bestowed: Prussian glory. William Gladstone summed Bismarck up by saying he had made Germany great but had made the Germans small.

Compared to the blustering young emperor, however, Bismarck appeared to be virtue personified. What his departure meant to Germany became clear as an attempt was made to replace the Iron Chancellor. Bismarck had held power for almost three decades; in the three decades which followed his departure, eight men tried—and failed—to fill his shoes. The first whom the Kaiser appointed was an utterly inexperienced officer named Leo von Caprivi, and his first foreign minister was equally ill equipped for the job he held. William II thought that appointing inexperienced men would allow him to rule alone, but in fact, it threw everything into the hands of a baleful, bearded baron named Friedrich von Holstein, an eccentric misanthrope who ruled from a minor desk. There followed a succession of other imperial chancellors: Prince Chlodwig Karl Viktor von Hohenlohe-Schillingfürst, Bernhard von Bülow, Theobald von Bethmann-Hollweg and others—but always the government pursued a zigzag, erratic course, for the imperial "helmsman" periodically lurched to grab the wheel, swerving the state into a new direction. Yet a sort of consistency became apparent: The brig they sailed was called absolutism, its direction was toward destruction, and the ultimate harbor was chaos.

William II was unable to develop any consistent policies, having no consistency in himself, nor any belief, conviction, or personal philosophy which might have given him direction. He never had a star to guide him other than the divine right of kings, and he finally had to make do with that monarchical principle, which did not get him far when he was at sea. He settled on bluster to fill the sails of his ship of state. He was happy to pose endlessly for photographs or friends: on parade in an endless succession of new uniforms "at work" at his desk (*i.e.,* adding marginal comments to dispatches about to be filed away); playing the warlord behind those huge waxed mustaches which Berlin's hairdresser, Friseur Haby, created for him anew each morning; or surrounded by his six gaudily uniformed sons. Accompanied by his ever-smiling, vacuous Augusta and protected by his glittering guards officers, he spent most of his time moving around his provinces in that special train of his, acting the top banana in an imperial road show designed to impress yokels only recently Prussianized.

His travels became a joke or, at any rate, the subject of jokes. Because his grandfather had been called *der weise Kaiser* ("the wise emperor") and his father *der leise Kaiser* ("the silent emperor"), the rhyme was continued by calling William II *der Reisekaiser* ("the traveling emperor"). People said that Germany's anthem, *"Heil Dir im Siegerkranz"* ("Hail to Thee in the Victor's Laurels"), ought now to be entitled *"Heil Dir im Sonderzug"* ("Hail to Thee in Thy Special Train"). William II was so much en route that Chancellor Caprivi often did not know where the emperor was to be found, and he was often happy to hear that William, when he was needed, was at least somewhere in Germany and not abroad.

The ostentatiousness of the new imperial court contrasted so much with the modest establishment kept by the emperor's grandfather, William I, that it surprised many. Yet it had all been predicted years earlier by Gustav Freytag, in a letter the novelist had written to William II's father. He warned that gaining imperial rank would tempt the House of Hohenzollern to abandon all Frederician simplicity, would heighten the arrogance of the aristocracy and military, would breed sycophancy among officers and officials, and would lead the German people to become more servile than ever. Finally, Freytag warned the then Crown Prince Frederick William that a "strong democratic undercurrent" existed threatening the monarchy. Germany's rulers he said, were like actors on a stage who postured before the applause and tributes they received, but who did not note the "demons of destruction" lurking behind the wings. Frederick William was shocked. "Imperial pomp and heightened arrogance," he said, would not get out of hand, for his father, William I, was "too kindly" and he himself was "too well intentioned." He did not foresee the reign of his own son.

Ironically, the new monarch, for all his blustering and saber rattling, also came to be called *der Friedenskaiser* ("the emperor of peace"), although it could be argued that the peace William kept for twenty-five years had been built by Bismarck and that William merely occupied the structure. The fact that he kept the peace made William less than popular with the military party in Berlin; as for the younger officers, most of them fanatical Kaiser supporters, these soon began to grumble that they had "to bear the expense of continual changes in their uniforms and outfits, ordered by the Kaiser." [186] Their pay was as low as ever, yet in the first seventeen years of William II's reign, the Kaiser redesigned their uniforms thirty-seven times.

Ever since the day Frederick William I had doffed his peruke and put on the uniform of an army officer, Hohenzollern males, be they eighteen or eighty, wore uniform almost every day of their lives, from the moment they rose to the moment they retired. They climbed out of their sheets straight into their boots; as a matter of fact, William II's enormous wardrobe did not even include a dressing gown. (This was because his grandfather had once refused the gift of a costly silk robe by harrumphing, "Hohenzollerns wear no dressing gowns!" [187]) William II, like his father and grandfather, owned a few civilian suits (tailored in London), but these were for country wear or foreign travel. Military uniform was palace dress. No matter how stifling the heat, the stiff, thick military collar, as a court official noted, had to be worn as a sign "of *noblesse oblige,*" as a hair shirt designed to make the wearer feel nobler, not humbler. No Hohenzollern, however, had ever owned a wardrobe such as William II collected once he became Kaiser. He didn't just wear the regulation army uniform, as his grandfather had done; he abandoned Frederician simplicity to such an extent that several tailors had to be permanently quartered in the palace just to keep pace with his requirements. There were countless gala uniforms, a different one for each occasion; there were naval uniforms and uniforms of every one of his regiments; there were foreign gala uniforms in which to greet visiting royalty; there were interim uniforms for informal use within the palace. It was even joked that the emperor owned a special admiral's uniform, for use only when he attended *The Flying Dutchman* at the opera.

The palace also contained an extensive dressmaking establishment. A dozen seamstresses labored constantly in an effort at making Empress Augusta look as elegant as the Kaiser wished her to look, but it was a thankless task. Although the emperor himself chose the luxurious materials for her dresses, Augusta always looked badly dressed, "without either taste or distinction," a court official noted. "She looked like any simple, middle-class girl from the provinces" and, even after being decked out in silks, furs, and jewels, never looked much better. She simply did not understand how to wear clothes; furthermore, she resented lavishing money on the wardrobe when it might be put to better uses. By this she meant building ugly churches, which was her principal interest and activity in Berlin.

The Kaiser's own principal activity was excitation; he was a perpetual-motion machine, a whirlwind of inactivity. The only time he ever remained in any one place for long was when he was aboard the yacht *Hohenzollern,* on which he paid twenty-five consecutive annual visits to Norway. Aboard ship, he himself conducted the Sunday divine service, writing his sermon and prayers, the latter being "more a command to the Almighty than a petition." [188] Worship was handled briskly and efficiently, as were the calisthenics which the emperor led and which he insisted everyone perform (even if he creaked with age).

All this activity and the many sports which he successfully pursued were calculated to convince everyone in Germany that he was as physically robust as anyone else. Many were indeed convinced that this was so, but the Kaiser himself was perhaps not so sure. Compensating for that withered arm would remain a lifelong activity for him. One means of proving his prowess was by establishing himself as a mighty hunter. In one year (not his best), he personally slaughtered 44 deer, 56 roebuck, 400 hares, 12 sows, 120 pheasant, 200 partridges, 8 blackcocks, and 1 fox. Hunting wild boar was one of his favorite pastimes, though the boar was a sow whose tusks had been broken and filed in advance. After the dogs had worried it, the Kaiser arrived in great style and a long, sharp sword called a *Saufeder* was ceremonially handed to him. With this, he stabbed the wounded animal over and over, until it was dead. Afterward he received applause for the performance, and the *Saufeder* was given to an honored guest to keep as a memento of what a court official called "this disgusting and degrading spectacle." [189]

He had other talents: He sang ballads in a pleasing baritone and even composed a fantastic opera called *Der Sang an Aegadia,* which the Royal Opera was compelled to perform lavishly, which the audience politely applauded, and which the music critics skillfully damned by praising only the production and by only mentioning the author's "enthusiasm." William also tried his hand at painting and designing; the effect was often ludicrous, not because William lacked talent, for in fact, he had a great deal of that, but because he utterly lacked taste.

He was in general a difficult man with whom to deal: always unpredictable, sometimes charming, often nasty and rude. He humiliated guests at the table, and if he forced people to play cards with him, he could never bear to lose, although the stakes were always low. His statesmen were frightened of his impetuosity, his generals were contemptuous of his military talents, and the only ones who seemed to have genuinely liked Kaiser William II were his young officers, who saw him as their champion, and those of his subjects who simply and uncritically worshiped every Hohenzollern. "Fear was the leading characteristic of those who served him in any capacity," said a court official, "fear of his sharp tongue, of his curt, arbitrary manner, and his sudden dislikes." [190] His early aggressive self-assertion, says Wheeler-Bennett, "later developed into a certain boorish brutality." An example which became particularly notorious is given by Wheeler-Bennett as characteristic of the Kaiser. "There was that habit, for example," he says, "of which his Chancellor, Prince Hohenlohe, writes so feelingly, of turning inwards the stones and seals of the many rings which he wore on his right hand, and thereby crushing in a grip of agony the fingers of the person whom he might be greeting." [191]

But there were some who feared the emperor though they never had to fear his handshake: the Social Democrats, whom William II came to hate passionately. Even the eminent Professor Rudolf Virchow fell in disgrace for holding "Socialistic views"; William once had a statue of Heinrich Heine removed, because the poet caused double offense: because of his "Socialist" ideas and his Jewish birth. (Ultimately, *wealthy* Jews were accepted by the Kaiser and exempted from the general anti-Semitic atmosphere of the Berlin court). The Social Democrats kept gaining votes, even adherents in the army, and William II attributed every evil in the nation to them. He even blamed their growing influence for an unprecedented event: a court proceeding, instituted against the Kaiser by tenant farmers, which the emperor lost. William II was even forced to pay court costs in this case—an example of the best kind of Prussian justice in the Frederician tradition, which delighted the public and predictably outraged him.

He was not accustomed to losing or to being criticized. The law against *lèse-majesté—Majestätsbeleidigung*—was brutally enforced during his reign. Those who informed on their neighbors to report remarks critical of the emperor received financial rewards, and the informer's word was frequently accepted without supporting evidence. One officer's wife was reported to have said at a tea party that she thought the Kaiser wasn't very intelligent and that "some even call him a softy." She was sent to prison, her husband was transferred to a remote frontier post where there was no chance of promotion, and their two sons were expelled from cadet school. Another case concerned two small boys who were overheard by a policeman to say that their father called the Kaiser a *Windbeutel*—a cream puff or bag of wind. The father was imprisoned for two years and the family rendered destitute. As a result of this, people spoke of the Kaiser without using his name; he became "Herr Lehmann."

The police-state atmosphere fostered by Prussian militarism was nothing new, but under William II, it received more royal support than ever. The emperor publicly asserted that the German aristocracy was not only the nobility of the nation, but consisted of the noblest individuals in Germany; as the officer class was almost exclusively dominated by nobles, it made the military more arrogant toward commoners than ever. There were more officers than ever before, for William II increased the peacetime strength of the army officer corps from 23,317 in his first year to 36,693 in 1913 (when total army strength was almost 800,000 men). The emperor, writes Wheeler-Bennett, "delighted in military display, gave full reign to the martial ambitions of his generals, and regarded with favour the tendency of his Officer Corps to look upon themselves as knightly paladins. . . ."[192] Although a gradual *embourgeoisement* of the officer corps was taking place, guards and cavalry regiments remained exclusive preserves of the nobility and allowed only a tiny sprinkling of bourgeois officer cadets to enter their ranks. (Regimental commanders and their officers as a body continued, as they had for two centuries, to have the right of accepting or rejecting an officer seeking to join the regiment.)

Military officers had been arrogant enough toward the population in previous reigns, but their enhanced status under William II made them even more arrogant. The emperor set them an example of the kind of behavior now sanctioned. A typical instance took place at a dinner to which an elderly government official was invited; being accustomed to homely mannerisms, he tucked his napkin into his collar instead of laying it on his lap. The emperor, seated far down the table, saw the "bib" and shouted, "I suppose you're going to be shaved!" This remark evoked gales of laughter from the courtiers at the table. The mortified official afterward said that the Kaiser was no gentleman, but a boor.

That sort of thing was bad enough inside the palace, but on the national and the international stage it proved more than an embarrassment to Germany: it was a positive liability. "There is only one master in the Reich and that is myself. I will tolerate no other!" he declaimed. "I look on my position as decreed for me by heaven," he said. "I act on behalf of a higher power!" The list of such statements was endless, for the Kaiser felt the constant need to reassert his position in the face of those "disobedient" masses who voted for the Social Democrats; he even told a contingent of Potsdam guards recruits that he might call on them to shoot down their own relatives, brothers, "or even—God forbid—your parents," but that they would have to do so, having surrendered themselves to him "body and soul."

Meanwhile, he was bungling in foreign affairs. Bismarck's ingenious Reinsurance Treaty with Russia was not renewed when it was due for renegotiation in 1890. William had been warned by his grandfather to maintain ties with Russia; indeed, even Frederick the Great had warned that such ties were essential; it was now more important than ever, for Germany and Russia were the two strongest military powers in Europe. Bismarck had been determined to keep Russia out of the embrace of France; William ended up officiating at their marriage. Within two years of his failure to renew the treaty with the czar, a French fleet had visited Kronstadt, and Czar Alexander, to William's horror, had saluted that anthem of the regicides, the "Marseillaise." Then a Russian squadron paid a return visit to Toulon, and the two countries signed a pact promising military aid to each other if attacked. William frantically shored up his ties with Britain, sat at the feet of his grandmother, Queen Victoria, even buttered up his Uncle Bertie—Edward, the Prince of Wales—whom he detested, paraded in his British admiral's uniform, and had himself made a colonel in the First Royal Dragoons. "I hope Britannia will continue to rule the waves," he said during an 1894 visit to Britain, only to be appalled shortly afterward when the Prince of Wales, attending the coronation of Nicholas after Czar Alexander's death, made the new czar colonel in chief of the Scots Greys.

Relations between William and his British grandmother became more testy each year, largely because they were seeing too much of each other. The Kaiser had developed a passion for yacht racing at Cowes; he came each year, to the consternation of Victoria. Annual visits, she said, "are not quite desirable"; in fact, the more one saw of the Kaiser, the more one found him tiring and unpleasant. He had to be treated with extreme care all the time, for he would fly into a fury or dissolve into a pout at the slightest provocation. Of course, he himself was unaware that his personality was difficult; the problem, he said, was dynastic. "The Hohenzollerns have never been popular in England," he told Caprivi when that minister tried to urge him to stay away. "I am going to Cowes for the races, and that is all there is to it!" When Lord Salisbury suggested to Queen Victoria that she might cure William of some of his wild notions if she had a good long talk with him, she replied, "No, no, I really cannot go about keeping everybody in order." [193] By 1894 William was tired of Caprivi's lack of "imagination" and the fact that Caprivi did not understand his "wider thoughts"; in fact, he was frightened of unrest within Germany and of the fact that Caprivi seemed unwilling to crush it ruthlessly. The emperor who had told Bismarck he would "*not* wade in blood" was now so jittery that he was ready to do just that.

"Into battle for religion, morality and order against the parties of revolution!" he exclaimed in East Prussia at this time. "As the ivy clings to the gnarled oak and protects it while storms howl through its topmost branches, so the Prussian nobility gathers round my House. Let us enter the battle together! Forward with God! And dishonorable he who leaves his King in the lurch!" [194]

As it turned out, the only blood William waded in was that of Caprivi, who was dismissed—and who was happy to go. The thundering call to battle delivered to the Prussian nobles was just talk, just William being swept away by the majesty of his own rhetoric. In content, it was a ringing cry worthy of a fifteenth-century king, which is precisely the role William often liked to play, just as Frederick William IV enjoyed it. (William

II even saw himself as a Crusader; several heroic paintings and statues of him in medieval armor appeared in consequence.)

He approached every question, not with an open mind, but as Michael Balfour puts it, "with an open mouth." He had enormously wide interests and could declaim about music, naval strategy, architecture, archeology, the Hittite language, the origin of the world. Having an extremely retentive memory and a very quick and nimble mind, William often dazzled slower or even more thoughtful thinkers with a display of verbal pyrotechnics which could not help impressing and even charming a good many visitors. If he liked someone, he could give that person his undivided attention, at least for a moment, for he was forever charging off to talk to someone else. One British envoy found this particularly disconcerting. He said that if one were asked a question by the Kaiser, one never had time to formulate even the beginning of an answer before William II began talking to someone else. Holstein, who hated William, said he had "the unfortunate habit of talking all the more rapidly and incautiously the more a matter interests him." Since most subjects on earth seemed to interest the Kaiser, he spoke in this manner most of the time.

Unfortunately, however charming he could be, he could be just as sadistic. His habit of crushing a guest's hand in the grip of his abnormally strong right hand and his habit of doing so with rings turned inward have been mentioned, but his words often hurt just as much. They often even hurt German foreign relations, for no one was spared when the words tumbled forth uncontrolled. He called the King of Italy "the dwarf" and his queen "a peasant girl," the "daughter of a cattle thief"; he mocked Prince Ferdinand of Bulgaria as being decorated "like a Christmas tree" with medals (a description applicable to William as well) and called him "unscrupulous." He insulted the German Catholics as "the purest pagans" for "praying to their saints," and he once even threatened war against South Germany. He had, in short, no tact whatever. As might be expected, he delighted in nasty practical jokes, some of which later embarrassed him. On one occasion, when he met Archduke Francis Ferdinand at the railway station, William told him, "Don't imagine that I've come to meet *your* train.

I'm expecting the Crown Prince of Italy!" The archduke was not amused. Nor were elderly men whom he pushed over while they were doing calisthenics aboard the *Hohenzollern* or teammates whom he slapped on the back during a game of tennis, using a racket. He treated Lord Salisbury so arrogantly that he had to be reminded that Salisbury was the British queen's prime minister, not his own; he then insulted his uncle the Prince of Wales by reminding him that he had never been a soldier and by letting him know that he thought him to be "a peacock." Edward, in turn, said Nephew William was "the most brilliant failure in history," a phrase which recalls Winston Churchill's own estimate of William II. "The defense which can be made [of the Kaiser] will not be flattering to his self-esteem. . . . 'Look at him; he is only a blunderer.' "[195]

A court official who lived in the Berlin Palace until his death shortly before the outbreak of World War I was hard put to enumerate the Kaiser's concrete accomplishments. All he could say was that William II took an interest in improving the congested traffic in Berlin, that he introduced railway safety measures, encouraged Count Ferdinand von Zeppelin's experiments, and brought some paintings to Berlin. He also mentions the Kaiser's acquisition of Helgoland, an island which came to be a white elephant, costing millions to stop erosion; the building of the Kiel naval canal which almost immediately proved too narrow (after the steamer *Deutschland* stuck fast in it) and had to be dug out again; and the changes wrought in the Tiergarten, into which the Kaiser planted countless statues of his Hohenzollern ancestors and of Prussian generals, utterly ruining the charming woods. Although this official neglected to mention it, another of the Kaiser's achievements was the expansion of the German navy. Just as he liked to make his courtiers squirm by calling them "you old swine," he desperately wanted to make Britain squirm by matching it in battleships. To start with, he had a tiny force designed for coastal defense and an officer named Alfred von Tirpitz. Within sixteen years Tirpitz took Germany from sixth place among naval powers to second; it was a fantastic accomplishment, one which has been compared to Peter the Great's overnight creation of a Russian fleet. Inevitably, this program of naval expansion provoked a response from Britain, which built a competitive navy to counter the emerging threat.

"The British navy," said Winston Churchill in 1912, "is to us a necessity, and from some points of view the German navy is to them more in the nature of a luxury." The idea that theirs was a *Luxusflotte* outraged the Germans, but there was some truth in it. The reason given for an expanding German fleet was German colonialism and German commerce, but in fact, the reason may also be found in William's desire to match or outdo Britain and in his compulsive need for an outlet for his own inner aggressions. Dreadnoughts, blistering with guns, were power and aggressiveness personified. In the absence of a coherent foreign policy, these monsters gave William a sense of security, just as in the absence of a popular domestic policy he sought security in the constant company of his guards.

The *Luxusflotte* was dignified by the appellation *Risikoflotte,* meaning a deterrent fleet so strong that none would attack Germany. This idea, which was bolstered by the fallacious assumption that France and Russia would remain hostile to Britain, fascinated the German people; it seemed to them a guarantee of the peace they desired, and the naval program therefore became enormously popular. Ironically, Tirpitz himself attributed its construction to a blunder committed by William in 1896 which almost plunged Germany into war with Britain: the episode of the Kruger telegram. William had congratulated the Boer president on having repulsed British invaders and had asserted the "independence" of the Transvaal; privately, William told Hohenlohe he was ready to send troops down there to make it a German protectorate, not independent at all. The British exploded at the Kaiser's remarks and sent a squadron to the North Sea. The German ambassador in London called the Kruger telegram "incomprehensible insanity" and pointed out that it increased Britain's "evident desire to draw nearer to France." As usual, William II frantically tried to obliterate his blunder. He wrote a letter of apology to his grandmother, Queen Victoria, telling her that the British invaders—a few hundred horsemen, under Dr. Leander Starr Jameson, who were repudiated by the British government—

had, after all, violated Victoria's own "peaceful intentions and instructions." William said he had only expressed his "indignation with the rabble" and then ended lamely by saying, "I challenge any gentleman to point out to me wherein this was in any sense offensive to England." [196] The Kaiser's grandmother did not reply. Instead, Tirpitz responded. The Kruger telegram had "shown the nation the necessity of the battlefleet." What this incredible statement in fact meant was that the German people were to finance a huge navy so as to save themselves from the effects of their Kaiser's big mouth. William's friend Eulenburg commented, "The poor Kaiser makes the whole world nervous."

The government in Berlin was more than nervous; it was at its wits' end. "There is a lack of unity of direction because His Majesty lacks unity in himself," Eulenburg had noted in his diary in 1894. "The picture as a whole lacks any sort of harmony and this harmony cannot be created. It was only possible under the ideal figure of the old Kaiser, for every horse was *glad* to be pulling his carriage, which was the coach of State. But now? Everyone is biting each other, beating each other, hating each other, lying and cheating each other." [197]

Bülow, who was chancellor from 1900, noted three years earlier, on becoming foreign minister, that there was a terrible danger if William was not surrounded by the most prudent of advisers, for the advice the impressionable Kaiser received would determine whether his reign would be "glorious or melancholy."

Bülow, who knew how to manipulate the Kaiser with flattery and who adroitly restrained him, was an enormous change for the better after Caprivi and Hohenlohe. William thought him a "glorious chap"; no wonder, for Bülow as early as 1897 called the Kaiser "charming, touching, irresistible, adorable. . . ." A year later Bülow wrote a friend (in a letter he made sure was later seen at the palace): "He is so remarkable! Together with the Great King and the Great Elector he is far and away the most remarkable Hohenzollern that has ever existed. He combines . . . the most sound and original intelligence with the shrewdest good sense. He possesses an imagination which can soar on eagle-wings above all trivialities, and with it the soberest perception of the possible and the attainable; and—what energy into the bargain! What a memory! What swiftness and sureness of comprehension!"[198]

Court circles were amazed. They knew that "Bülow is perpetually humbugging him" and thought the romance between the new chancellor and the Kaiser could not last long. As for that, Waldersee said he was of "a different opinion: the Emperor can never have too much of that kind of thing."[199]

Count Bülow (later promoted to Fürst) was married to a beautiful Italian, a woman of great wit and reputedly greater intelligence than he possessed; they made "a very happy couple, and the Kaiser was the third in the family," as a court official wrote. Almost each day, William II stopped by at the chancellor's residence near the Tiergarten, en route to his morning ride in the park; "I want to see my Bernhard," William announced, whether it was convenient or not, and stayed for breakfast.[200] Eulenburg, watching, noted with relief that foreign relations were under control. "No more explosive dispatches," he said. Yet the damage had been done. Rival blocs had been formed which would prove disastrous for Germany in World War I. The Kaiser counted on his Triple Alliance with Italy and Austria-Hungary, but facing him was a Franco-British entente and a Franco-Russian alliance. By giving Tirpitz a completely free hand in building up the German navy, Bülow increased British fears of Germany to the boiling point. The very deterrent which was to keep the peace exacerbated tensions.

Bülow defended his outrageous flattery by pointing out he had "to consolidate" his position with the Kaiser if he were to have any influence at all; this was true enough, but unfortunately, the technique made it impossible for him ever to stand up against the Kaiser effectively.

Matters were little better when it came to domestic policies, for the Kaiser, though he was now in the twentieth century, continued to act like a sixteenth-century monarch. Eulenburg warned him not to repress libertarian strivings too harshly; he even spoke darkly of the possibility that the people might try to force his abdication or restrict his power. William was amazed. "Oh? Who could harbor such thoughts? And how would they go about it?" he asked. Later, he told Eulenburg that parliamentary government was discredited, public opinion was deranged, and the nation needed a dictatorial monarch. "Really, when I look at the behavior of the people at home I lose all desire to rule," he said. "The only course is to pay no attention to them at all."

The Kaiser was a typical bully, not only in bluster, but in retreat; challenged, he almost invariably became conciliatory. In fact, though he had a passion for the army and for war games, he had an absolute horror of starting a war. Thus, during the Boer War, while the German press went into an absolute hysteria of anti-British propaganda and sentiment could easily have been ignited in favor of war. William became uneasy and conciliated Britain, although he privately gloated over British reverses. In June, 1900, William finally had his chance at easy military glory and seized it with glee. In China the Nationalist Boxers had destroyed all foreign embassies in Peking and murdered the German minister. William wired Bülow to send out battleships and an expeditionary force. Peking, he thundered, was to be "razed to the ground . . . blotted out." Waldersee was made a field marshal and sent out to China—too late, since British, American, and Japanese troops had already freed the diplomatic quarter. Waldersee arrived in time only to stage a parade in subdued Peking and to demand Chinese indemnities.

The experience of seeing the Kaiser in a real war fever for the first time frightened his associates. Eulenburg told Bülow that he had "gazed into a bottomless pit of hatred and bitterness." Indeed, there had been a scene at Wilhelmshaven, when the German troops left for China, which frightened wider circles. The Kaiser had climbed a scaffold at the quay and told the troops: "No mercy will be shown. No prisoners will be taken. As a thousand years ago the Huns under King Attila made a name for themselves still powerfully preserved in tradition and legend, so through you may the name 'German' be stamped on China for a thousand years, so that never again may a Chinese dare to look askance at a German." [201] Bülow and Eulenburg were aghast and even tried to suppress these words, but an enterprising reporter had got them all down on paper. Soon they were flashed around the world and fourteen years later the word "Hun," first used by the Kaiser in such a connection, would be hurled back in the Kaiser's face.

A year later, in Bremen, a man subsequently found deranged and not responsible for his action hurled something at the Kaiser: a small metal fragment which scratched the imperial cheek but left a scar of apprehension in the imperial soul. Two weeks later William addressed his troops.

"My Alexander Regiment is called upon to act to some extent as a bodyguard both by day and by night—to be ready, if occasion arises, to fight to the death for the king and his household," William stated. "And if the city of Berlin should ever again revolt against its sovereign, as in the year 1848, then, grenadiers, you will be called upon to drive those insolent and unruly subjects in pairs before you with your bayonets." Later there were disturbances in Berlin, and thirty men were wounded, whereupon the Kaiser said he was "well satisfied" with the police, but ordered them next time to strike with the sharp edges, not the flat sides, of their sabers.

"He doesn't really mean it," a courtier protested when William threatened to lead his guards personally against the disorderly Berliners. "The emperor talks like that, but nothing ever comes of it!" That applied generally, but still had disastrous results for his nation. Russia, as Waldersee noted in 1892, was increasing its armaments, thinking Germany was aggressively inclined, thanks to William's saying "how he would like to give the Russians a beating" and so on. "My conviction," said Waldersee, "is that all these sayings are the outcome of uneasiness, just as a child will scream to keep up its courage. . . . But as our monarch would not on any account have this suspected, he gets more and more obstinate and violent about trifles, and talks himself into the idea that he is a very mettlesome person." Waldersee also noted his "popularity hunting," the fact that nothing delighted William more than "a frantically cheering mob." He squandered money "recklessly," Waldersee noted, and mainly on his vanities. These and his conceits were legion. Told he had "a little cold," the Kaiser sternly advised his physician, "I have a great cold! I am great in everything!" It was partly a joke, but mostly a statement of his beliefs. When he became a field marshal in 1900, in deference to the "pleas" of senior generals, he announced that he could manage very well with a few aides-de-camp and no longer needed a General Staff. He told his war minister and chief of the Military Cabinet they were "old donkeys" who thought themselves wiser than the Kaiser because they were older; he greeted a much-respected fifty-three-year-old count at a hunt by calling out, "What, you old swine, have you been asked here, too?" He hit the Russian Grand Duke Vladimir in the back with a baton, merely in fun; deadly serious for once, he humiliated one of the German princes to such an extent that he almost sparked a Fronde type of rebellion. He meddled in army affairs so much that the attitude of the military, said Waldersee, was one of "resignation," which described quite well the attitude of most others whose fate it was to work with the emperor in governing Germany. If he did not have some project immediately in sight, he grew despondent and then chased after yet other new excitements or novelties, which Waldersee said were absolute necessities for him. He could not bear to remain long at home; Augusta's eternal reading and embroideries drove him to distraction, drove him on yet another *Sonderzug* to yet another German city for yet another gala appearance and intemperate, unpredictable speech.

"God preserve us from war while this Emperor is on the throne!" said an old Junker, Köller, to Hohenlohe. "He would lose his nerve. He is a coward at heart." [202] He put his finger on it: A weak, vain, half-crippled prince had been placed on the throne of a nation which was the most militaristic on earth at the time, of an absolutist military state, and was compelled in the face of his deformity to prove himself more manly than any officer in the nation. Yet despite the frenzied activity, he did nothing. Count Robert von Zedlitz-Trutzschler, who described typical days spent with the Kaiser, concluded "his life is in fact one continuous idleness." He added, "And compare this with what the gazettes say of him!" [203] Waldersee said much the same. William was so busy with amusements "that in fact he [had] hardly any time left for work. . . . It is really scandalous how the court gazettes deceive the public about the emperor's industry—according to them, he is hard at work from morning till night."

There were some who saw the portents of the future. Waldersee warned that William's "extreme vanity" had actually accelerated the danger of Socialism; he mentioned that not a single one of the Kaiser's counselors faced the future with confidence and that the German princes were "equally uneasy"; he did not even entertain hope that the emperor might change. "Only some great reverse will bring that about," he said. "When so markedly egotistical a nature dominates a realm," wrote Eulenburg to Bülow, "the consequences can be nothing but catastrophic. . . ." William's mother, the Empress Frederick, shared in the gloom. She warned of historical "retribution and judgment" and that "every day that dawns may be disastrous." The monarchy, she wrote a friend, "is about to be put to a test and I tremble lest the issue be a woeful one." [204]

The fault was not entirely his, however. "The real tragedy of Wilhelm II," writes Wheeler-Bennett, "is that he should ever have been Emperor at all. Nature had designed him for a life of intellectual and artistic activity; Fate destined him for a soldier and a Sovereign. As a private individual his quick intelligence and brilliant, if unstable, intellect, might well have out-weighed his capriciousness and lack of judgment. As a public figure his every defect became magnified, his every waywardness a common topic. Upon this Prussian youth, with his withered arm, the floodlight of publicity beat relentlessly almost from his birth, until he found his only comforting warmth within its blaze. . . . Few were more unsuited to the throne than Wilhelm II; few were more pitiable among the playthings of destiny . . ." [205]

The emperor was sometimes aware of his shortcomings. He once told a friend that he was what he was and that he could not change. The sad fact of the matter is that he might have been helped to change by advisers who stood their ground. The younger Moltke, on being appointed chief of staff, spoke very directly to the emperor, insisting he stay out of military maneuvers, and William, duly impressed by Moltke's arguments, behaved for a full three years. But there were not many Moltkes or many occasions for taking such strong stands. The Kaiser was mainly surrounded by courtiers, advantage seekers, and sycophants, who flattered and glorified him always; it got to the point that August von Mackensen, as a general in 1904, set a new custom for the army by kissing the emperor's hand. The entire nation—with one exception—exalted him to the position of demigod; it is no surprise that he was severely affected. The exception was the working class. They, by and large, voted Social Democratic, causing the Kaiser to consider them traitors.

William II's lack of any coherent personal, foreign, or domestic policies, together with his inability to study a problem in depth, put him at the mercy of his advisers. Those closest to him and most able to win his ear with flattery were able to do with him more or less what they pleased—but only for a time, for soon other voices, equally flattering, would be heard and adhered to. It was not William's policies which governed Germany and her foreign affairs, but the policies of others combined with his disruptive whims, which often undid all that he or his advisers meant to achieve. The best example of this is to be found in William II's continuing efforts at achieving a *rapprochement* with Britain on the one hand and with Russia on the other. Historical ties with Russia meant a great deal to him, as did the fact that the Russian czar represented the monarchical principle as he, William, saw it: that of an absolutist monarch ruling through an aristocratic civil service and military caste, resisting the encroachments of constitutionalism and parliamentarianism, not to speak of republicanism. As for Britain, William had a love-hate relationship with it, for his admiration for England was very real and as strong as his envy and hate. What he could not bear was what he considered to be Britain's arrogance and sense of superiority; he felt they humiliated him and Germany. Yet Queen Victoria died in his arms, and when he attended her funeral, he was so devoted a grandson that he was cheered throughout London. Afterward he surprised his German officer companions by pointing to the tower of Windsor Castle and announcing with admiration that it was from there that the world was governed. No sooner was he back in Berlin and the garrison town of Potsdam, however, than his resentment took over again. Ultimately, every effort he made at achieving a *rapprochement* with Britain and Russia not only failed, but backfired.

A series of blunders—some of them his own, some of them caused by his advisers—had the effect of isolating Germany.*

* William let himself be persuaded by Holstein and Bülow to reject Joseph Chamberlain's offer of a German-British alliance in 1898. In 1905 he let himself be dragged against his own right inclinations into interfering in Morocco; this established ties between France and Britain which lasted into World War I.

Ties were established by France with both Russia and Britain, with disastrous results for his nation.

The British, however, did not desire a complete rupture of their relations with Germany. They hoped to prevent it by means of an international agreement which would limit the armaments of both nations; the British *sine qua non* was a reduction in the Kaiser's naval armaments program. Bülow would have been happy to agree, but the Kaiser in this case listened to Admiral von Tirpitz, who argued that any such British demand was incompatible with German honor. In 1908 the first crisis developed between the Triple Alliance of Germany, Italy, and Austria-Hungary on the one hand and Russia on the other. Austria had seized Bosnia, and when Serbia protested, Russia supported the latter. William, whom the Austrians had not informed in advance, was shocked at the annexation and felt betrayed, but Bülow argued him into supporting the Austrian move nevertheless. He was afraid that if Germany failed to do so, she would be left without *any* allies at all in Europe. It had come to that, two decades after William acceded to the throne, eighteen years after Bismarck had left power.

In retrospect, it almost seems incredible that matters had come to such a pass. The grandson of Queen Victoria might naturally have been expected to establish the closest possible ties with Great Britain, while at the same time maintaining Germany's close traditional ties with Russia; the "traditional enemy," France, would then have been isolated. Instead, all traditional and natural ties were severed by blunder and bluster. Ties between Britain and Germany could have been re-established as late as 1912, when the British war minister, Lord Haldane, held conversations in Berlin with William II, Admiral Tirpitz, and Chancellor Bethmann-Hollweg. Indeed, these conversations were so friendly that William naïvely thought the talks were a complete success, failing to understand the British insistence that German naval power be limited. Even as the talks were going on, William and Tirpitz were drafting legislation to expand the German navy to forty-one battleships and sixty cruisers by 1920, a fact which not only subverted Haldane's visit, but prompted a friendly British overture to turn into a hostile British reaction.

William II's closest friend, "Phili" Eulenburg, was dropped like a hot potato in 1907, after the Kaiser was shown evidence of homosexual acts the prince had conducted ten, twenty, thirty years earlier. True, he could not have continued his association with Eulenburg, for the news was out and widely known, but the way in which he abandoned this dearest (and often frankest) of his advisers shocked his circle. William, after all, had handled another homosexual scandal in a completely different manner. When the heir to the Krupp empire was driven to commit suicide after his gaudy homosexual activities became known, William attended his funeral and angrily charged the Socialists with slandering Krupp. Privately, William now gave vent to his outrage about "Phili," but publicly he did nothing; he did not even summon Eulenburg for a last visit, in order to ask him to reply to the charges. He simply called the interior minister and told him that a number of prominent people, Eulenburg included, "are perverts [and] I have no further use for them." He told Zedlitz to make "a moral example" of them "before all the world . . . without any consideration of persons." Lawsuits followed in the wake of the scandal, and for once, the Kaiser read the papers line by line. "If the newspapers don't stop this kind of thing," he told Zedlitz, "I'll send an aide-de-camp to blow the editor's brains out!" That same month, December, 1907, he wrote to Houston Stewart Chamberlain (husband of Wagner's daughter and the "Aryan" philosopher whose rabid anti-Semitism became part of the Nazi cult): "It has been a very difficult year which has caused me an infinite amount of acute worry. A trusted group of friends was suddenly broken up through Jewish insolence, slander and lying.* To have to see the names of one's friends dragged through all the gutters of Europe without being able or entitled to help them is terrible. It upset me so much that I had to have a holiday and rest. The first after nineteen years of hard uphill work." [206]

Much of the emperor's character and psychology is revealed

* The original revelations had appeared in *Die Zukunft* ("The Future"), a weekly founded by Maximilian Harden, this being the nom de plume of a Jewish Berlin journalist named Witkowski. First in the service of Bismarck, Harden was soon a champion of Holstein, who had been fired (by the homosexual Eulenburg, he suspected); some of the fines Harden was compelled to pay after the subsequent lawsuits were reimbursed by Bülow out of public funds.

in those preposterous lines. He refused to face the facts about his friends; instead, he blamed "Jewish slander," although he knew better. He hypocritically posed as one who wished that he were "able or entitled to help" these friends, for he knew that would have been the gentlemanly, kindly, chivalrous, princely thing to do; rendering such help was what one might have expected from "a Christian king," as William considered himself to be. But in fact, although he might have helped Eulenburg with nothing more than a private, unpublicized gesture showing consideration, understanding, and loyalty, he never even tried to do anything for his friend. As for the reference to "nineteen years of hard uphill work," that is perhaps the most preposterous of the lot. There is in its phrasing the characteristic whine of the man who has so successfully and completely deceived himself that he cannot even be accused of deliberately lying. Illusions and self-pity filled the imperial breast. No wonder that dispassionate observers, like those British whom he visited in November, 1907, during that "holiday and rest" of which he wrote Chamberlain, saw him more clearly than did many of his own people. Foreign Secretary Sir Edward Grey thought William was "not quite sane and very superficial"; Lord Esher, who also met him at Windsor during this holiday, said he lacked any "real grasp of the facts." Empress Augusta, on the other hand, impressed Esher a great deal, even as being well dressed, which was either a sign that her wardrobe had improved or an indication of British tastes.[207] In any event, Augusta was now drawing closer to her husband than ever before. William had lost confidence in Bülow and lost Eulenburg altogether. He was now alone, with no one to tell him the truth ever, for Augusta, of course, had no more comprehension of reality than he himself had.

Reality, in truth, was becoming more dismal. The British had responded to Tirpitz's naval construction program by launching the first dreadnought in February, 1906. This warship made all existing battleships—German *and* British—obsolete overnight; the dreadnoughts which followed escalated the armaments race. By 1908 tensions had also escalated to the point where the Kaiser for the first time spoke about Germany's being "encircled." He meant it to justify his policies; it understandably frightened his subjects half to death.

Britain's continuing attempts to slow down German naval construction had the effect of outraging the emperor, who saw these British demands as a personal affront. The idea that peace had to be secured by German naval limitation was an "impertinence," the Kaiser said, and he advised his ambassador in London to tell the British "to go to hell." Edward VII and the Kaiser met briefly afterward; William took the opportunity to bluster that Germany was ready to fight to retain its navy, for this was a matter of German honor and dignity. He even produced the lame excuse that in any event, he was powerless to curtail German naval construction, for the terms of the construction program had been written into law by the Reichstag. Coming from a Hohenzollern who had such a deep contempt for Parliament, this was a surprising statement indeed, and Edward VII remarked dryly that Parliament ought to be able to amend or alter the laws it made. The two monarchs parted at loggerheads. William II followed the meeting up with another of his incendiary, preposterous, and inaccurate pronouncements. He told his people that the British had handed him an ultimatum (untrue) and that he had rejected it. The way "I had shown my teeth did not fail to have its effect," he boasted, adding, "That is always the way to deal with Englishmen." [208]

Shortly afterward William II made an attempt to damp down the fires, but the extinguisher he used turned out to be filled, as might have been expected, with gasoline. This was the *Daily Telegraph* incident of 1908, which had its roots in a visit William paid the previous year to the home of Colonel Stuart-Wortley, at Highcliffe Castle, Hampshire. The atmosphere there had been delightful; William had grown enthusiastic about "the delights and comforts of English home and country life." He referred to his hosts as "the great British people" and said he enjoyed mixing with "excellent people in all walks of life, with all classes giving clear evidence of culture. . . ."

After he had returned home, and in the midst of the Bosnian crisis of 1908, William received a typewritten manuscript based on comments he had made at Highcliffe Castle, with a request that these be approved for publication in the *Daily Telegraph*. William thought this was a fine idea since it would allow him to reassure the British that German naval armament was in no way meant as a threat to Britain. These remarks of his, he told Colonel Stuart-Wortley, would demonstrate the "Anglophile views" held by himself and his house. Bülow was first asked to approve it, but while the Kaiser was having a holiday shooting, Bülow was having a holiday bathing at Nordeney on the North Sea, and he passed the manuscript on to the Foreign Office. But the secretary of state to whom he had sent it was also having a holiday, at Berchtesgaden, and the head of the press section was similarly on vacation, whereupon the typescript went to an undersecretary of state named Stemrich. Stemrich, however, was busy with the Bosnian crisis, and he passed it on to a privy councilor named Klehmet with the remark that it seemed "rather rocky." Klehmet, a conscientious official, read it and had grave doubts about publication but felt it was not his prerogative to oppose "the emperor's express wish"; furthermore, he was under the impression that Bülow had already approved the typescript and wanted only errors of fact to be corrected. Klehmet made a few corrections and then sent the typescript back to Stemrich, who neatly avoided responsibility by not reading it. Stemrich sent it to Nordeney, to the emperor's aide, an ambassador named Müller, who also didn't read it and who passed it on to Bülow. The chancellor glanced at it, noted that some corrections had been made, and sent it back to the Foreign Office after having signed his approval on the document. Once more, the state secretary was too busy to read the typescript and sent it back again to Bülow. The chancellor remarked that he'd already seen the document and gave it to the emperor. From him it went to Colonel Stuart-Wortley and the *Daily Telegraph,* which published it on October 28, 1908; a German translation appeared in the *Norddeutsche Allgemeine Zeitung* a day later.

It was a long article and consisted of a hodgepodge of ill-considered statements. There was a strange reference to the German fleet's protecting British interests against Japanese and Chinese threats, a suggestion which naturally outraged Japan and which prompted the *Times* to point out that the German fleet was in fact situated in the North Sea and that many of its ships didn't have the coal capacity to steam to the Pacific. There was a remark that William alone had refused to support the Boers during the Boer War, despite public opinion in

Germany, and that he had turned down a Russian and French offer "to humble England to the dust"; this, of course, didn't sit well with the Russians or the French, or with the British, for that matter. William also had written that he'd gone so far as to have sent a "sympathetic" letter to his grandmother, Queen Victoria, when Britain suffered reverses in the Boer War; furthermore, he said he'd proposed a strategic plan which could win that war for Britain, this being a plan which, by "an extraordinary coincidence," the British had actually used to attain victory. Thus he was claiming credit for British successes, which hardly made him popular with the British public. "And now I ask you," he concluded, "is this not the behavior of a man who wishes England well? Let England give a fair answer!"

But there was even more to it than that. "You English are like mad bulls," he had written, "you see red everywhere! What on earth has come over you, that you should heap on us such suspicions as is unworthy of a great nation? What *can* I do more? I have always stood forth as a friend of England. . . . Have I ever once broken my word? . . . I regard this misapprehension as a personal insult! . . . You make it uncommonly difficult to remain friendly to England! . . ." [209]

The Kaiser's ambassador in London almost had a stroke when he read the *Telegraph* article. "Now we can close up shop!" he exclaimed. A howl of protest arose in newspapers everywhere: in Paris, Rome, St. Petersburg, London, Tokyo—and, most remarkably, Germany as well. Bülow was horrified when he saw the text in print (although he had approved it). Klehmet, who was being groomed for a scapegoat, pleaded innocent by saying that he thought his emperor had insisted on its being published. "Haven't you realized yet," Bülow snapped back, "that His Majesty's personal wishes are often the purest nonsense?" [210] The state secretary in the Foreign Office, Schön, who had been on holiday at Berchtesgaden, reported later that the public indignation in Germany was so great that there was even talk among the ministers of asking William to abdicate. Those who were indignant even included the conservatives, for everyone was suddenly disgusted with William's volubility, with his intemperate comments, with his irrepressible blustering. For the first time, the emperor was lampooned in the

German press; one cartoon showed him receiving a muzzle as a present. It seems in retrospect that someone might have made him a present of some conscientious and efficient advisers, the kind who would have had the sagacity—and the courage—to prevent their emperor from embarrassing himself and the nation.

Nothing came of all the indignation. Schön was even assured of the emperor's complete support. "The affair will turn out more harmless than at first appeared," William II said to Schön, clapping him on the shoulder. Bülow made the gesture of tendering his resignation, but the Kaiser refused to accept it and even issued a statement assuring Bülow of his full confidence. This was published on October 31, after which the Kaiser left Berlin for a hunting holiday. Bülow was left alone to face the wrath of the Reichstag. The German press, the German people, and the delegates to the German Reichstag were still fed up.

Bülow faced the delegates on November 11. The hostility of the Social Democrats had been expected, but now the conservatives were also enraged with the Kaiser, for they felt he was undermining the prestige of the monarchy. But there was absolutely nothing these delegates could do. Only a revolution (whether violent or not) could have changed Germany this late in the game, for Germany remained an authoritarian state resting on monarchy, army, and bureaucracy. This was the fruit of centuries of Hohenzollern rule. The Reichstag could not censure the Kaiser or the chancellor, and only the emperor could appoint the chancellor and his ministers. The chancellor was not in the least responsible to Parliament, as Bülow well knew. Still, the delegates had to be satisfied somehow, and Bülow promised them that henceforth the Kaiser would exercise greater restraint.

William, meanwhile, was plunged into deep depression and despair. This was his first experience in being criticized, and it disturbed him greatly. He had fled the turmoil by going to the home of an old friend, Prince Maximilian Egon zu Fürstenberg at Donaueschingen, for the autumn shoot, but the experience of bringing down sixty-five stags in two days didn't relieve his anxiety. Fürstenberg wrote, "If you met Kaiser William, you would not know him," and one of the other guests said, "I had the feeling that . . . I had before me a man who was looking with astonishment for the first time in his life at the world as it really is. Brutal reality has swum into his ken and struck him as a horrible caricature." [211]

William remained in the company of Fürstenberg and his friends throughout this entire crisis. The emperor, a man of "brilliant if unstable intellect," had for his companions these men whose intellectual level was low, according to Count Zedlitz, and whose coarse stories "degrade the narrators." Zedlitz added, "Still worse are the idiotic pranks to which they lend themselves." [212] Shades of the original "soldier king," one thinks, and of his *tabagie* at Königswusterhausen, with poor Gundling causing the generals to roar with laughter! But an even stranger prank occurred during the farewell evening which Emperor William II spent at Fürstenberg Castle; during this gala, Count Hülsen-Haeseler, a general and chief of the Military Cabinet, appeared dressed in a tutu as a ballerina, dancing a *pas seul* before the delighted guests. This had not been the first time the general had publicly performed as a female impersonator. The performance on that evening, however, was marred by the fact that the general collapsed immediately after his dance, dead of a heart attack. Doctors, then a priest, were summoned to attend the dead general, after his body had been hastily put back in uniform; the whole affair was just as hastily hushed up. William returned to Berlin more shaken than before, pouting and irritable. His depression mounted over the next days, for he simply could not understand how he could have outraged the German people. "What is going on?" he asked the head of his Civil Secretariat after the first Reichstag debate on November 11. "What is the meaning of all this?" He called his crown prince to him and spoke of abdicating. He knew now that his people thought of him as a blunderer and a failure, knew it for the first time in his life, could not understand why they should think this way and finally, in a letter, said his advisers were "people whose cowardice and lack of responsibility has deprived me of the protection which anyone else would have accorded to the head of state as a matter of course."

There! He had found the answer! The fault lay with Bülow. William believed his chancellor had betrayed him. He, the emperor, had acted in full accord with the constitution, for had he not shown Bülow the text before authorizing publication? It was outrageous that Bülow should not have taken full public blame for the *Telegraph* incident, and William II even came to believe Bülow might have rigged the whole affair in order to embarrass him. The following July, William II dismissed his chancellor. With that, he cut the last tie holding him back from war. Bülow, the best of William's chancellors, had "kept the coach from overturning," had "skirted the abyss," as Zedlitz put it; those who followed him hardly even tried. A great opportunity had been missed by everyone but the Kaiser in 1908. The despairing emperor could have been brought to heel by a stronger, more self-confident chancellor, and again Germany might have found a form of government wherein the chancellor was responsible to Parliament alone, but neither Bülow nor the Reichstag felt confident enough to press for such a radical change. Since no change came and since William II justified his actions to himself and regained what courage he had, it was inevitable that he would emerge victorious. After this crisis, it has been said, Germany was administered, not governed. The House of Hohenzollern had triumphed—just ten years before it would collapse.

17

"I Am Hated Everywhere in the World"

In 1906, Winston Churchill, then British undersecretary of state for the colonies, attended the German army maneuvers in Silesia, as a personal guest of the Kaiser. In *Thoughts and Adventures,* he provides a vivid portrait of the German emperor and of German armed might:

> Magnificent was the spectacle of German military and Imperial splendour so brilliantly displayed to foreign eyes. Several scenes linger in my memory which illustrate the pomp and power of the German Empire. When the Emperor, resplendent in the uniform of the White Silesian Cuirassiers, rode through the streets of Breslau at the head of a sparkling cavalcade, he was rapturously welcomed by his dutiful subjects. A large portion of the road was lined, not by troops, but by many thousands of elderly men obviously belonging to the poorer classes, all dressed punctiliously in ancient black frock-coats and tall hats. These were the old soldiers, to whom special positions of honour were accorded, and indeed they formed a striking background of sombre civic strength to the white uniforms of the Emperor and his Cuirassiers.
>
> In the Review which preceded the manoeuvres 50,000 horse, foot and artillery marched past the Emperor and his galaxy of kings and princes. The Infantry, regiment by regiment, in line of battalion quarter columns, reminded one more of great Atlantic rollers than human formations. Clouds of cavalry, avalanches of field-guns and—at that time a novelty—squadrons of motor cars (private and military) completed the array. For five hours

the immense defilade continued. Yet this was only a twentieth of the armed strength of the regular German Army before mobilization; and the same martial display could have been produced simultaneously in every province of the Empire. I thought of our tiny British Army, in which the parade of a single division and a brigade of Cavalry at Aldershot was a notable event. I watched from time to time the thoughtful, sombre visage of the French Military Attache, who sat on his horse beside me absorbed in reflections it would not have been difficult to plumb. The very atmosphere was pervaded by a sense of inexhaustible and exuberant manhood and deadly panoply. The glories of this world and force abounding could not present a more formidable, and even stupefying, manifestation.

On the evening of this Review the Emperor gave his dinner to the Province. . . . The Emperor spoke with his usual facility and with the majesty that none could deny. The German staff officer at my side translated in a whisper sentence by sentence into excellent English. It was the year 1906, the Centenary of the Battle of Jena. "A hundred years ago," said William II, "Germany was reduced to the abyss of ruin. Our armies were everywhere captured or dispersed, our fortresses taken, our Capital captured by hostile troops, the very structure of our State broken into fragments, long years of foreign domination ahead." Only a hundred years ago! It seemed incredible that a single century, four fleeting generations, should have sufficed to raise the mighty fabric of power and wealth, energy and organization, of which we were the awe-struck witnesses. What an amazing contrast: 1806–1906! What a contrast also between the bounding fortunes of martial Germany and the slow-growing continuity of British national life, which after 900 years of immunity from foreign invasion still wore a modest and self-questioning garb. But more amazing still would have been the contrast if the curtains of the future could for a moment have been swept aside, and if that glittering throng could have perceived that scarcely ten years separated triumphant Germany from a collapse, subjugation and prostration, far more complete and lasting than any that had darkened the morrow of Jena.

The maneuvers were impressive in their size but showed the anachronistic tactics then still in use by the Germans. Churchill noted that several German officers were impatient; three years later, attending similar maneuvers near Würzburg, Churchill noted that all the shortcomings had been corrected.

The 1906 maneuvers ended with a display rather characteristic of Kaiser William II. Churchill writes:

> At the Grand Finale the Emperor led in person a charge of 30 or 40 squadrons of cavalry upon a long line of field guns in the centre of the enemy's position. We all galloped along in the greatest glee, and the surging waves of horsemen soon overwhelmed and swept through the rows of venomous-looking little cannons which presumed to confront them. "Do you think it is all right?" we asked an Artillery officer whose battery the Umpire had loyally adjudged to be captured. "Certainly it is all right," he replied. "They are His Majesty's own guns. Why shouldn't he capture them? It is an honour for us to serve His Majesty in this manner." But there was a twinkle in his eye.
>
> After the bugles had sounded the "Cease Fire" . . . [the] Emperor welcomed his personal guests with that unaffected and easy grace which was habitual to him, and added so much to his charm and popularity. He talked to foreign visitors with the freedom and manner of an agreeable host at an English country-house party, while all around the stiff uniformed figures of his Generals and Aides-de-Camp stood immobile and passive, each rooted to his particular spot. . . .

After the 1909 maneuvers, which Churchill attended as cabinet minister and president of the Board of Trade, he reflected on how the European scene would look ten years later, after the end of World War I:

> Indeed these Wurzburg manoeuvres make in my mind the picture of a Belshazzar feast. Upon how many of those who marched and cantered in that autumn sunlight had the dark angel set his seal! . . . All the Kings and Princes of Germany, all the Generals of her Empire, clustered around the banqueting tables. Ten years were to see them scattered, exiled, deposed, in penury, in obloquy—the victims of a fatal system in which they were inextricably involved. And for the Kaiser, that bright figure, the spoilt child of fortune, the envy of Europe—for him in the long series of heart-breaking disappointments and disillusions, of failure and undying self-reproach, which across the devastation of Europe was to lead him to the wood-cutter's block at Doorn—there was surely reserved the sternest punishment of all.

A German physician named Renvers had a less charitable view of the Kaiser. "If the Kaiser were an ordinary patient," he told Bülow, "I should diagnose *Pseudologia phantastica*—a tendency to live in phantasy or, putting it bluntly, to lie. Such tendencies are common enough in all neurasthenic patients. . . . Remedy? Bodily and mental quiet: composure: self-discipline. If you could persuade the Kaiser to read a serious book alone for two hours every day—the sort of book on which one had to concentrate—you would have done a great deal." [213]

Bülow, after losing first favor and then his job, could, of course, do nothing. Instead, as the emperor's neurasthenic symptoms of fright, anxiety, inadequacy, and compensating bluster increased after the *Daily Telegraph* affair, other standing orders were issued in the Berlin Palace: From the moment the Kaiser rose in the morning, he was to be engaged in conversation so that he might be given *a sense* of being active. It was not inactivity, however, that troubled William II most. It was boredom, by which he meant his reaction to that bodily and mental quiet Dr. Renvers had suggested. A moment spent alone was for him a moment of uncertainty and fear; since serious work such as the careful study of dispatches required him to have more than a moment alone, he abandoned all serious work, even all pretense at it. And since he could not, of course, face his fears, he hid them behind a show of self-confidence. "Leave foreign affairs to me!" William II had said with a laugh when he sacked Bülow aboard the *Hohenzollern* at Kiel in July, 1909. "I have learned something at your school. It will be all right." Then, when Bülow seriously urged him to come to terms with the British about naval armament and to be careful in the Balkans, William stamped about impatiently, explained he had a luncheon date with the Prince of Monaco, couldn't "keep Monaco waiting," and walked off, telling Bülow, "All right, all right. I won't forget what you say. You can be quite happy." William the Second soon came to be dubbed William the Sudden.

For him to say "Leave foreign affairs to me!" after the *Telegraph* affair showed the measure of William II's self-deception. He was utterly incapable of suspecting that he might have committed an error. The outrage unleashed against him had indeed shown him that his press and even his people thought him a blunderer, but this made him only feel a martyr to his people's ingratitude. Now that Bülow and Eulenburg were gone and there was only the simpleminded Augusta to advise him in private, he became romantic and religious, seeing above him a pantheon filled with all the old, great Hohenzollern kings and Kaisers, who watched benignly and protectively as this, their progeny, strengthened German might and power and heightened German glory in the world.

A conscientious, scholarly civil servant named Theobald von Bethmann-Hollweg was appointed chancellor in July, 1909. He knew absolutely nothing about foreign affairs. William II was happy ("Leave foreign affairs to me!"); soon there developed *two* governments in Berlin, the Kaiser's and Tirpitz's on the one hand, the indecisive and powerless chancellor's on the other. Bethmann-Hollweg knew that the Kaiser did not want war, so his policy was to try to undo all his warlike actions; Tirpitz knew the Kaiser wanted an ever-stronger navy, and he gave it to him, undoing all of Bethmann-Hollweg's work. Bethmann-Hollweg did not even understand why Germany needed *any* fleet at all; he supposed it was "for the general purposes of Germany's greatness." When the British, having failed again to limit German naval armament through agreement, remarked politely that they were at least convinced that Bethmann-Hollweg wanted peace, the Kaiser exploded, saying that they obviously had no idea "who is the master here" and that he knew better than anyone else "how to handle the British." Foreign Minister Alfred von Kiderlen-Wächter was not even consulted in negotiations with Britain.

After twenty years of reigning and having reached the age of fifty, William was becoming somewhat bored with affairs of state. That talk of handling the British was just talk. William would periodically inject himself into foreign affairs, muddying the waters and rocking the boat, but he was hurt by his lack of success in anything he did. The Social Democrats continued ominously amassing more votes in Germany, despite the cheers which greeted the gold-helmeted Kaiser everywhere on his travels; he could not understand the phenomenon and feared it. In fact, aside from the military aristocrats, it was largely the middle classes who supported the Hohenzollern monarchy with any real enthusiasm. They found the last decades of the *Kaiserreich* reassuring. Just as each man knew his place, so all men had their settled places. Probity led them to have a horror of disorderly reform, just as piety led them to remember that the godly obeyed constituted authority. They had enormously increased in wealth since William I had become emperor in 1871; it seemed to them that benefits rightly flowed downward from above, like manna bestowed by Nordic gods. It was like the German storybook *Schlaraffenland,* in which no one worked and in which roast geese with cutlery attached floated gently down from the skies into one's mouth, just as all desirable social changes also ought to drift down, neatly packaged, from *die Obrigkeit,* those in positions of authority. Who, then, were those shoving up from the bottom of the social heap, agitating for workers' rights, even parliamentary democracy? A few Marxists only, or so one hoped; dangerous types all of them, one knew for certain! The workers' "red ballots," cast for the SPD, alarmed the solid citizens, for this proletariat of course outnumbered them and, as was correctly pointed out, had no experience of political responsibility. No wonder many burghers were grateful that there was a three-class franchise to keep this mob in its place and property values on the climb. Despite the fact that they were annoyed with the Kaiser's loose tongue, the upper and middle classes regarded the authoritarian state and its monarchy—even the unstable monarch—as both symbol and guarantee of national stability. They knew, or believed at any rate, that the alternative would be chaos.

Furthermore, they were feeling their oats. Germany's growing prosperity and military power had unleashed aggressive ambitions. Pan-Germanists, industrialists, and colonialists screamed, "Forward!" in their newspapers and howled that Tirpitz's men-of-war seemed to be rusting from disuse. Proud of their mighty naval force, proud of their victory-laden armies, conscious of their wealth, they chafed over the fact that Germany still seemed to them to be regarded as a second-rank world power. To them, this was a humiliation which needed to be redressed by means of action.

As for the reigning Hohenzollern emperor, he chafed just as much as did many of his supernationalist subjects, but he "wanted the gladiator's rewards without the battle," as Barbara Tuchman remarks.

"More cosmopolitan and more timid than the archetype Prussian, he had never actually wanted a general war," Miss Tuchman writes. "He wanted greater power, greater prestige, above all more authority in the world's affairs for Germany, but he preferred to obtain them by frightening rather than fighting other nations. . . ."[214] His navy he sincerely regarded as a defensive force and as a peaceful symbol of German might (even of the power of the House of Hohenzollern); he never thought of it as an instrument to be used to attain "world domination" or "world conquest." As usual, however, he was not the master of his policies because he was not the master of his mind.

What was called the First Moroccan Crisis occurred in 1905, when William II landed at Tangier, ostentatiously recognized the Sultan of Morocco as an independent monarch, and protested French economic domination of that territory. The motives had been expansionist, imperialist, and colonialist; Germany was simply late in the colonialist game and wanted a share of the spoils. It needed to assert its new power and flex its muscles; it also badly needed, or thought it needed, room for its expanding population, markets for its burgeoning industries, and outlets for German energy. The Kaiser had not been enthusiastic about the Moroccan adventure but had let himself be persuaded into embarking on it. It failed in its purpose; France continued to dominate Morocco, and the affair proved embarrassing to Germany. Six years later, however, voices were again suggesting to the Kaiser that Germany stake a place in the sun for itself; once more, he let himself be persuaded against his own better judgment. Tirpitz's huge navy was finally unleashed—or, rather, one gunboat was set in motion. This was the *Panther*. Internal unrest in Morocco had provided the pretext; the *Panther* landed at Agadir on July 1, 1911, ostensibly "to protect German lives and property," but actually to extort substantial concessions in Africa from the French. The German press, slavering for international adventures, went hysterical and screamed that "the leap of the *Panther*" would capture West Morocco for the nation.

It did nothing of the kind (although Germany did manage to extort from France a small portion of the French Congo). Because Britain stood firmly by the side of France during this Second Moroccan Crisis, Germany once again was compelled to trim her sails and her ambitions. The *Panther* did succeed, however, in causing a serious war scare. This, of course, was not what the emperor had wanted at all. Happily, war was averted by means of lengthy negotiations. These dragged on forever, it seemed, and were so laconic that the Kaiser began to lose his nerve.

"What the devil is to be done now?" he wrote at the time. "It's a pure farce. Negotiations go on and on, and nothing comes of it. . . ." Unhappy about ever having been persuaded into the greedy adventure (by Kiderlen), the emperor accurately predicted that the British and Russians would "stiffen the backs" of the French. David Lloyd George warned that British interests could not be ignored; British interests at the time consisted in keeping Germany in an inferior place. The jittery Berlin government assured the French that Germany had no actual territorial claims to make on Morocco, which seemed to satisfy Paris. Four months after the *Panther* "leaped," Germany and France signed an agreement so unfavorable to Germany that the Kaiser's colonial secretary—who had never been consulted about the adventure—resigned in protest.

Embarrassment, humiliation, and frustration only heightened the impatience of the Pan-German imperialist and colonialist faction. The German press noted that a fortune was being spent on German armaments: Was the "leap" of the *Panther* the best William II could do with Tirpitz's huge navy? The French press mocked the Kaiser and called him William "the timid"; worse yet, the German press did much the same by implication. One German paper asked: "Have we become a generation of women? . . . What is the matter with the Hohenzollerns?" [215]

What indeed? Nothing, in fact; William II of Hohenzollern was simply the "plaything of destiny," as Wheeler-Bennett calls him, a blunderer incapable of conciliation or conciliatory remarks, being hurtled along by ambitious, imperialistically minded men. Lord Haldane rightly remarked that the entire Agadir episode had driven the Kaiser away from Bethmann-

Hollweg and into the arms of Tirpitz and the generals; in being more "warlike," he sought again to hide his inadequacies.

A last attempt at halting the Anglo-German naval armaments race, which, said Churchill at the time, "must lead to war within the next two years," was made in 1912. Lord Haldane, the British war minister, came to Berlin only to find that the German naval party—the Kaiser, Tirpitz, and others—was dead set against sacrificing a single gunboat unless it could extract from Britain major political concessions.

What the Kaiser wanted from the British was nothing less, he admitted, than "a reorientation of her whole policy"—a guarantee of British neutrality in a European war. But the British were afraid of antagonizing their French and Russian allies; such an agreement would have broken up their Triple Entente—although it can be argued that it might have prevented World War I. Haldane had become convinced the Kaiser really *did* want to reach an agreement, for which he was castigated as being pro-German when he got home. When Sir Edward Grey, the foreign secretary, afterward remained inflexible, William again anguished over the way he and his nation were being treated by what he regarded as the insufferably arrogant English. "This is not the way in which the German Kaiser and his German people can and must expect to be approached. . . . They dictate and we are to accept! There can be no question of this. *We must be approached and taken at our own worth** . . . there is nothing to be done—except to arm." (Even Augusta was urging him on. "Your Majesty," she pleaded with her husband, "the throne of your children is at stake!")

The inherent weaknesses of the system which the House of Hohenzollern had lived with and had perfected were now manifesting themselves. All decisions in the state were being made by the emperor and his camarilla of advisers, without being in any way influenced by moderate public opinion. The Kaiser in his palaces, surrounded always by the same old clique of Junker reactionaries and professional, aggressively minded military men, was completely sealed off from his people, who had neither the emperor's ear nor his respect. The situation was movingly described by Emil Ludwig:

* Emphasis is the emperor's.

> No majority in the Reichstag, no overwhelming expression of public opinion, demanded an accelerated [naval] programme from the Government; nobody was putting pressure on the Emperor beyond a dozen naval men, supported by a few hundred thousand whooping civilians. Tirpitz once dismissed, the Emperor could have appointed any of his moderate men from one day to another—and a sigh of relief would have gone up from his people, more audible far than the trumpeting of the Pan-Germans. The English would not have decided against Germany in 1914, and the War would have been avoided.[216]

The conciliatory course was closed to William, however. He was as consumed with jealousy of England as England was by now consumed with apprehension about Germany. Yet William's feelings toward Britain continued ambivalent in the extreme, as was shown when he attended the funeral of his uncle, Edward VII, in 1910. He had earlier written a comment on a document which expressed his loathing of "Uncle Bertie": "Lies! The dog is lying! England! Uncle! A most charming fellow, this King E. VII! Ineffable cheek! Pharisee! Rot! Twaddle! Bunkum! Hurrah, we've caught the British scoundrels out this time!" Then, when he heard of Edward's death, he wrote, "Edward VII's chief mourners, besides his own people, will be the Gauls and the Jews." Yet after the funeral, Lord Esher remarked, "My firm belief is, that of all the royal visitors the only *mourner* was this extraordinary Kaiser." Indeed, William wrote Bethmann from Windsor Castle that he was immensely moved by being again in his parent's old apartments, "where I often played as a little boy. . . ." He again had "the old sense of being at home here," and he even said, "I am proud to call this place my second home, and to be a member of this royal family. . . ." [217] He longed to love what he hated, and he was impelled to loathe what he secretly loved.

William II began the year 1912 by blustering that he was quite prepared "to let it come to war" (*"Es komme ruhig zum Krieg!"*). That year, war did begin in the Balkans, and William characteristically shrank back in horror lest Germany be dragged in.

Serbia, Greece, and Bulgaria effectively routed the Turks from Europe in the First Balkan War of 1912; they then quarreled over the spoils, which launched the Second Balkan War in 1913. The result of these wars was a great increase in the size of Serbia, and since Serbia was hostile to Austria-Hungary, Germany's ally, William feared the consequences. The changes in the Balkans might be uncomfortable for Austria-Hungary, he said, but he could not justify to his people or his conscience exposing Germany to the risk of war because of these. Russia, he knew, was Serbia's champion, and William warned that "Germany might possibly go down to ruin" if it fought a two-front war with Russia to the East and with Britain (possibly a Russian ally) to the West.

A general war was avoided because the Russians were uncertain about British support; peace even survived the Second Balkan War of June–August, 1913. (Serbia emerged enlarged, as did Greece, whose queen was William II's sister Sophia, married to Constantine of the Hellenes.) But peace was less assured than was the general slide toward war. Lloyd George afterward remarked that "no one at the head of affairs quite meant war" but that "it was something into which they glided, or rather staggered and stumbled." William nervously watched Russia furiously arming and, with French money, building railroad lines west toward Europe. Increasingly apprehensive, he allowed Bethmann-Hollweg to lead him to unqualified support for Austria-Hungary, which was Germany's only ally, except for Italy and a greatly weakened Turkey. He began to think that a general European war was, perhaps, an inevitability. The prospect made him gloomy, as well it might; a British bishop who met him at the time said he felt the Kaiser was under the influence of "a great fear." In November, 1913, the French ambassador in Berlin wrote: "The Kaiser . . . has come to think that war with France is inevitable. As he advances in years, the reactionary tendencies of the court, and especially the impatience of the soldiers, obtain a greater hold over his mind. . . ." Three months later, William did indeed predict the inevitability of war with France. Moltke, chief of the General Staff, urged a "preventive" war immediately, because delays would only strengthen Germany's enemies, all of them busily arming. Colonel Edward M. House, President Wilson's adviser and emissary to Germany in 1914, reported back that Germany was "charged with electricity," that "everybody's nerves are tense," and that "it only needs a spark to set the thing off."

The times called for icy nerves, but no one had them, least

of all the jumpy Kaiser. Germany was an armed camp, a garrison state, and he was the "All-Highest," the "Supreme Warlord" to whom everyone turned, whom everyone sought to influence and prod. How can a supreme warlord act in a crisis, when all spotlights in the nation are turned on him? For William II, who was always onstage, always striking an attitude, there was no doubt. The spark came soon enough, when a Serbian named Gavrilo Princip assassinated the Austro-Hungarian Archduke Francis Ferdinand and his wife, in Sarajevo, on June 28, 1914. William knew where his loyalties lay: with the bereaved old emperor, Francis Joseph, who had already lost his eldest son and whose wife, the empress, had been assassinated in 1898. Sarajevo seemed the last of a series of ominous regicides. The Kings of Italy, Portugal, and Greece all had been killed, in 1900, 1908, and 1913. Two days after Sarajevo, William fired off a letter to Emperor Francis Joseph, urging him to act against the Serbs, despite the danger that Russia might respond on Serbia's side. Germany would stand by its ally, he said. It was "now or never" in the fight against the godless, the terrorists, the revolutionaries, the anarchists—all of whom he lumped together in his mind with the Socialists back home. The Serbs, he said, were "dogs," "a pack of criminals" to be punished, who needed now "to knuckle under." Having got that off his chest, having belatedly asked Bethmann-Hollweg whether he agreed with the letter to Francis Joseph (he did), having received assurances from the generals that the German army was fit to fight, he then sauntered aboard the *Hohenzollern* for his leisurely annual cruise to Norway.

On July 23, Vienna shot off an ultimatum to Serbia, making impossibly humiliating demands. It did not bother to consult its German ally beforehand; as a matter of fact, Bethmann-Hollweg was assuring European capitals that the Austrian demands were moderate, although in fact he did not even know what they were. To everyone's amazement, Serbia accepted the terms, a move which infuriated Vienna, for the Austrians had mobilized for war and wanted to march on the Serbs to teach them a lesson. William breathed a sigh of relief. Every reason for war had disappeared, he said, since the Serbs had announced to the world "a capitulation of the most humiliating kind." He said he was now ready "to mediate for peace."

But war, not peace, was coming, for Bethmann-Hollweg, urged on by the German General Staff, was in turn urging the Austrians to invade Serbia in order to eliminate the dangers Pan-Slavism posed for the dual monarchy; the Germans were afraid their Austrian ally would turn out to be an albatross unless the Southern Slav agitators were checked. Meanwhile, William II was being kept completely in the dark, at least until Vienna had indeed declared war on Serbia. Dispatches were being kept from him, and even as the Kaiser was wiring the czar that he was trying to induce Austria to come to a settlement with Russia, his chancellor was sending threatening messages to the same address.

On the morning of July 30, William received news that the Russians had ordered a partial mobilization; he wrote on the dispatch that he too must now mobilize. He was under enormous pressure from his generals to do so, for they were anxious to win a victory in the West before the czar's armies—that "Russian steamroller" all Germany feared—got under way. That same day William received more ominous news. Sir Edward Grey had told the German ambassador in London that Britain might not be able to be passive in a conflict between Germany and France. William II exploded when he heard that, for just two days earlier he had been led to believe King George said Britain would remain neutral. "I have the word of a king," William had said with satisfaction, only to have to call this king "a liar" forty-eight hours later. All the hatred this ambivalent emperor felt for Britain boiled over. He wrote that it was clear to him that England, France, and Russia had agreed among themselves "to use the Austro-Serb conflict as a pretext for waging a war of annihilation against us.

". . . So the celebrated *encirclement* of Germany has finally become an accomplished fact. . . . The net has suddenly been closed over our head, and the purely *anti-German policy* which England has been scornfully pursuing all over the world has won the most spectacular victory. . . . Even after his death Edward VII is stronger than I, though I am still alive! . . . And we fell into the net. . . . Now our job is to show up the whole business ruthlessly and tear away the mask of Christian peaceseeking and put the pharisaical hypocrisy about peace in the pillory! ! ! And our consuls in Turkey and India, agents, etc., must get a conflagration going throughout the whole Mohammedan world against this hated, unscrupulous, dishonest nation of shopkeepers—since if we are going to bleed to death, England must at least lose India." [218]

This was the anguished cry of a despairing "neurasthenic" whose nerves had snapped and who was no longer able to assess the situation accurately. Russia, which had mobilized and which was preparing to move West, was the threat—and the only immediate threat at that moment—but Russia could not capture his attention. Nor could William admit to himself that he and his governments had destroyed the carefully built Bismarckian balance of power, which had kept the peace, that he had lost those allies Bismarck had carefully cultivated over the years, Russia and Britain. He could not face the fact that the policy of encirclement was largely his own monstrous creation, that he had made Europe so jittery over the decades that France, Britain, and Russia all forgot age-long enmities and realigned themselves as allies, to protect themselves against this particular German. Even the British foreign secretary, Grey, was only briefly mentioned in William's lengthy tirade, and George V, the reigning British monarch, was merely dismissed as the king who was completing a policy set long ago. All William's wrath, all his self-righteous and self-pitying anger, all his neurotic fury, poured forth onto a corpse, onto the dead Edward VII, his hated "Uncle Bertie" and all that he symbolized to the Kaiser: the "insufferable" British superiority of Edward's sister Victoria, the Kaiser's own mother, and the colossal figure of that frightening *grande dame,* the Kaiser's grandmother, Queen Victoria. For William II of the House of Hohenzollern, German Emperor and King of Prussia, the war which would destroy the lives of 1,773,700 of his subjects and wound or maim 4,216,058 more, was something in the nature of a family feud.*

"You will be home before the leaves have fallen from the

* Casualties as estimated by the United States War Department, including deaths from all causes. Barbara Tuchman says that the known dead per capita of population were 1 to 28 for France, 1:32 for Germany, 1:57 for Britain, and 1:107 for Russia. Of 11,000,000 German combatants, more than 7,000,000 were casualties (killed, died, wounded, missing, and prisoners of war). Total casualties for Russia and France were even higher; in percentages, the Austro-Hungarian casualties were highest of all.

trees," the Kaiser told his departing soldiers during the first week in August, 1914. Germans, including the members of the Reichstag, were exhilarated by the war fever. German arms had proved themselves invincible against the Habsburgs in 1866 and the French in 1870–71; the spirit of Frederick the Great was yet alive, one and a half centuries after his death, or so they were convinced. No one could deter the martial juggernaut now. U.S. Ambassador James Watson Gerard, who tried to do so (acting on his own responsibility), never even received an answer to the letter he sent to Chancellor Bethmann-Hollweg on August 1, asking, "Is there nothing that my country can do? Nothing that I can do towards stopping this dreadful war?" It was too late; that day, war was declared on Russia. Three days later Gerard and the rest of the diplomatic corps filed into the White Hall of the Berlin Palace, to hear the emperor speak from the throne to the assembled Reichstag delegates. Chancellor Bethmann was dressed in the uniform of the Dragoon Guards during this ceremony; although he was the "civilian" head of government, he never put on civilian clothes again for the remainder of his term in office. The Kaiser for once eschewed the gala uniform and appeared in field gray, wearing his spiked helmet, and read his speech standing, his withered left hand clutching a sword no longer rattled but unsheathed. When he concluded his speech, he added extempore remarks. Henceforth, he called out, he no longer recognized any political parties, "but only Germans!" Then he offered to shake the hands of any political leaders who joined him in these sentiments. All of them rushed forth to have their hands crushed by the imperial palm, although the Social Democrats were spared, for none of the Socialist delegation had been invited to the palace. That afternoon, however, the SPD's Reichstag delegation proved as patriotic as the others by betraying its pacifist principles and voting the Kaiser the war credits he wanted. The Kaiser had been proved right: There were no political parties left, for all the politicians had joined the war party. (The Social Democrats justified their action by the fact that German arms might overthrow the despotic regime of the czar, but since they continued to support the war even after the czar had been toppled, their moral position came to be badly eroded.)

The Kaiser's optimism was dampened very soon, for the

British declared war on Germany on the evening of August 4, after German troops had crossed the borders of Belgium, the inviolability of which had been guaranteed by Britain. Six days later, when Ambassador Gerard visited the Berlin Palace, he found the emperor dispirited. The Kaiser sat at a green iron table in a little garden beside the bank of the Spree River, which flows past the palace. He was reading telegrams under a garden umbrella, his two dachshunds at his feet, as Gerard approached him.

"The Kaiser spoke rather despondently about the war," Gerard reported. "I tried to cheer him up by saying the German troops would soon enter Paris, but he answered, 'The British change the whole situation—an obstinate nation. They will keep up the war. It cannot end soon.' "[219] Later in the war, William once remarked that no one had told him Britain would enter a continental conflict, but he dropped the subject when someone remarked that Count Paul Wolff-Metternich, the German ambassador in London, had been warning all along of the danger of war with Britain. As a matter of fact, the ambassador had got the sack in 1912 for making just such gloomy predictions.[220]

William left for the front, as a supreme warlord would have to do. His was the unquestioned power of command over the army and the navy, wrote Erich Ludendorff in his war memoirs. All decisions needed to obtain royal approval; all officers, even the chief of staff, were his actual, not nominal, subordinates. For the first time in his life, William II was the *complete* autocrat, unfettered by politicians, untroubled by constitutional restrictions, bound only to prove himself master in the field.

He failed the test right from the start. He shrank from the exercise of personal responsibility now that it was his, just as he had always shrunk from the consequences of the actions he had taken. The younger Moltke, field marshal and chief of the General Staff, was an irresolute intellectual given, when crossed, to tears and to pouting in his room, where he sometimes stayed alone for hours, doing nothing, deep in dejection; still, the Kaiser could not even assume mastery of the situation in the face of such a man, although he tried feebly at first. Then came Erich von Falkenhayn and, afterward, Paul von Hindenburg and Ludendorff; soon the supreme warlord came to be merely a supreme embarrassment around headquarters.

As early as August 29, 1914, Moltke wrote to his wife, "It is heart-rending to see how entirely he [the Kaiser] fails to comprehend the gravity of the situation. Already there is a certain 'Hooray!' mood that I hate like hell!" [221] Yet that hooray mood lasted only as long as good news was fed to him; privately, he often had grave doubts about the outcome of the war. During the war's first winter, Admiral von Tirpitz, who felt the war was moving too slowly, wrote:

"I came home after seeing the Emperor, much depressed. . . . Imagine his grandfather in the same situation! . . . The chief mark of his character is that he will make no decision, take no responsibility. . . . The Emperor sees colossal victories in every direction, but I think it is only to allay his uneasiness. . . . The Staff-Surgeon says that the Emperor definitely begged to be relieved of his responsibility; but then he was brought up short by the wall he has built around himself, and ran his head against his sense of personal dignity."

In March, 1915, Tirpitz went so far as to try to help the emperor relieve himself of his responsibilities. "I see only *one* way out," the admiral wrote. "The Emperor must give out that he is ill for eight weeks or more. He must go to Berlin to begin with. Kessel . . . too was in a fright about the Emperor, and suggested that the King of Bavaria should be persuaded to ask him to let it be supposed for some time that he was ill. If we could contrive it, it ought to come from himself. . . . It seems as if only a still greater disaster would bring about any change in him, but then it would be too late." [222]

The staff surgeon refused to join in any such plot, although two years later he thought it probable that "this highly nervous man" might have a nervous breakdown.

There was enough evidence to support such conjectures. William privately admitted in 1916 that "this war will not end in a great victory," yet publicly he was compelled by his position to keep up morale and bolster national confidence. As his nerves were unable to stand four years of these psychological *volte-faces,* his staff fed him continuous reports of victories, real and imagined, "whereupon everyone sings Hosannah," as Tirpitz caustically remarked. "To keep up this mood," wrote a liaison officer who was often the Kaiser's guest, "he was told innumerable stories of trenches, in which the German soldier always appeared in the best possible light. . . ." General Hugo von Freytag-Loringhoven said that the Kaiser "refused to face facts and entrenched himself in optimism. . . ." William, he wrote, was no warlord like his grandfather and daily showed a growing "absence of any real force of character."

He had never grown up at all, as a remark attributed to him on the outbreak of war shows. "To think that George and Nicky [the czar] should have played me false!" he is said to have complained. "If my grandmother had been alive, she would never have allowed it." [223] But it was more than immaturity, more than neurotic behavior, that were showing themselves now. Ludwig referred to the Kaiser as "a civilian to the marrow" oppressed by the military traditions of his Hohenzollern ancestors, hiding his fateful weakness under the uniform coat of the soldier king he was compelled to play. [224] At one moment, he would delight in tales of corpses piled up as high as a man and tell his soldiers to take no prisoners; at the next moment, he would consent to the bombing of London, after resisting it for some time, only if targets of important military value were chosen. He agonized over dragging Germany into a war with the United States but then said that, as the first order of business, President Wilson's throat ought to be cut.

"The emperor traces the progress of the war upon the maps," Tirpitz wrote in 1915. "The whole company around him gradually falls asleep."

"If people in Germany think I am the supreme commander," William told Prince Max von Baden in 1914, "they are grossly mistaken. The General Staff tells me nothing and never asks my advice. I drink tea, go for walks, and saw wood. . . ." He was surrounded by a suite of elderly officers and officials, who warned visitors to tell him only good news. "It was the business of the entourage to discover a pretext for . . . excursions—something that would interest him and keep him in good spirits," wrote Count Karl von Stürgkh. The monotony of the days was broken by "simple" wartime lunches of only three courses, plus wines, cigars, and beer. The Kaiser, who actually had no idea of how the British blockade was affecting rations back home, liked to tell his dinner guests he ate no better than any of his subjects.

Since he was usually far from Berlin and even from Germany, he did not know what was going on at home; since headquarters for him had to be safely far removed from the front lines, he did not know what was going on there either. His generals briefed him from twelve noon to one o'clock, but sometimes he could spare them only a few minutes because others wanted to see him too or because "the luncheon table could be seen through the open folding doors," as Tirpitz reported.

Seeing their warlord at the front (poring over maps and making decisions—in photographs) and seeing furthermore that he exuded confidence, the naturally German people exuded confidence as well. None of them had been told of German failures; they were instead fed propaganda in doses even heavier than those given to William himself. Every wall in Germany, it seemed, was emblazoned with that slogan which perfectly mirrored William II's hatreds: *Gott strafe England!* ("May God punish England!"); the words were even printed on the nation's money. As early as 1914, Ernst Lissauer had composed a song entitled "Hymn of Hate Against England" (*Hassgesang gegen England*), and while it may not be surprising that the song was circulated to the troops, what was unusual was the fact that Lissauer received from William II the coveted Order of the Red Eagle, Second Class, for his paranoid lyrics.*

Albert Ballin, chairman of the Hamburg-American Steamship Company, one of the Kaiser's few Jewish friends, was of the opinion that William felt "he had been betrayed by his

* Excerpt:

French and Russian, they matter not,
A blow for a blow and a shot for a shot;
We love them not, we hate them not,
We hold the Weichsel and Vosges gate,
We have but one and only hate,
We love as one, we hate as one,
We have one foe and one alone. . . .

We will never forgo our hate,
Hate by water and hate by land,
Hate of the heart and hate of the hand,
Hate of the hammer and hate of the crown,
Hate of seventy millions, choking down.
We love as one, we hate as one,
We have one foe and one alone—ENGLAND!

English relatives and therefore had to fight with England to the bitter end." Ballin says that even Empress Augusta had caught the fever. He saw her "cry with both hands clenched and lifted: 'Make peace with England? Never!' " Yet to Tirpitz's despair, the indecisive Kaiser did make one decision: The German fleet was to remain in harbor, rather than risk being destroyed by Britain. War would be won on land and the fleet reserved either to extort a favorable peace or to wage a future war against Britain. He had never meant the fleet for war and now, perversely, was being consistent. The fleet was his special love, his pet or toy, and he was as unwilling to risk it in action as his ancestor, Frederick William I, had been to risk his Giants' Guard in war. Only the submarines were let loose, introducing a form of warfare which a British admiral, Sir Arthur Wilson, called "damned un-English." [225] Yet even the submarines were from time to time restricted to their bases, and Tirpitz was never able to influence the course of the conflict his policies had helped unleash. He saw the land war grind to a virtual stalemate; he wanted to win the war at sea; when he finally found it impossible to do so, he resigned from his office, in March, 1916. In his way, he had been the dominant figure in Germany since Bismarck's departure, although a baleful influence. (Bismarck, who spoke with him just before the turn of the century, said afterward that Tirpitz's view of the European situation was thirty to forty years behind the times.)

William II would have dearly loved to use his navy to humiliate the British fleet, but as much as he adored his navy, he lacked confidence in it as well. The British navy was more powerful; what was even more powerful was William's hidden, deep-seated, and lifelong admiration for Britain. It was this that sapped him of resolution; thus, even after his navy had performed creditably at Jutland in 1916, he ordered it pulled back to harbor afterward. He never allowed it to make a concerted effort at breaking the British blockade, though this was starving Germany and depriving her of war matériel.

Throughout the long months and years of this war, William II proved an utter failure at the one job he ought to have performed well: playing monarch, even if he could not play warlord. The function of a monarchy is to unite a nation, to provide a focus for interests loftier than partisan, factional, or regional, and perhaps to inspire and uplift a people. Yet William hardly ever showed himself to his people and took no real interest whatever in the fact that they were overworked, undernourished, and exhausted. As the war went on, even his troops began to see him less and less, for William rightly gathered the impression that front-line officers resented his visits, not because they feared for his safety, but because they thought him in the way. Periodically, he would address a contingent of soldiers, but since he had no conception of or interest in what they were thinking, he made them feel ill at ease, even aghast, with his bloodthirsty admonitions. He never even tried to inspire them with the hope of an honorable peace, of an end to the slaughter, for which they longed, nor did he even confine himself to patriotic platitudes or lofty bromides. They saw before them not a majestic leader, but still another petty officer screaming at them to sacrifice and die. When he was once told that there were people in Germany who were dismayed by his performance during the war, he shot back, "What do I care what the people think?" There were times when he did realize what the British blockade meant in terms of curtailed rations in Germany, but even then he thought of it largely in terms of the Hohenzollerns, which led him again to rant against his British cousins. Gerard reports one such occasion, after a visit to the Kaiser in the Ardennes, at Charleville-Mézières, where he occupied a large villa. The Kaiser, Gerard wrote, "referred to the efforts to starve out Germany and keep out milk, and said that before he would allow his family and grandchildren to starve he would blow up Windsor Castle and the whole Royal family of England." [226] There was, of course, little chance of the Hohenzollerns' doing without, as the rest of the Germans were doing, for even those of the Hohenzollern princes who were in the field occupied palaces and châteaus wherever they went, one to each prince; those back home managed quite nicely in the sixty-odd Hohenzollern palaces scattered throughout the realm. As for William II personally, this Kaiser who dearly loved to cite Frederick the Great to his troops never even once tried to emulate the example of that battlefield commander, who slept on straw in barns, ate the sour bread of his officers and men, and inspired rather than demanded sacrifice.

The Kaiser abdicated his authority some time before he abdicated his throne. His last intervention in the war was taken around the turn of the year 1916–17. He made a lame offer to end the war, telling Chancellor Bethmann this must surely show him to be "a ruler who possesses a conscience, feels responsible to God, has compassion for his own and the enemy peoples, and . . . the will to free the world from its sufferings. . . ." Yet he refused to spell out details, and when President Woodrow Wilson asked him for specific proposals, William replied with an intemperate letter stating that the Entente powers—"a band of robbers" who had been "beaten off and crippled"—must state their intentions first. Germany, "the party attacked, being on our defensive purely," would then offer its own proposals—"as victors."

An offer of peace negotiations couched in such bellicose language was turned down, as might be expected. Chancellor Bethmann, who had been behind the peace feeler, lost even more of his eroding influence.

The Reichstag had no more idea of the realities of this war than the German people in general had; both groups were the victims of propaganda. Accordingly, in October, 1916, the Reichstag had already passed a motion stating that it had confidence in Chancellor Bethmann so long as Bethmann enjoyed the confidence of the High Command. Generals, not civilians, were the heroes of the hour in Germany, especially since Falkenhayn had been replaced in August, 1916, by Hindenburg, with Erich von Ludendorff as his quartermaster general. Hindenburg was one of the nation's most idolized heroes; he and Ludendorff could do no wrong. Even the emperor was swept along by the enthusiasm and, on January 10, 1917, turned over all political control in Germany to these two men. When the *Frankfurter Zeitung* protested that even Bismarck had always insisted on political control over a war, the emperor called this a "fallacy" which needed immediately to be "stamped out." The warlord added, "Politicians hold their tongues in wartime, until strategists permit them to speak!" Bethmann remained but was virtually powerless; a naked military dictatorship had been established over a nation which, in these latter years of the war, was seething with Socialist and Communist revolutionary sentiment.

It was the logical culmination of centuries of absolutist power. The men who held this power, the Hohenzollerns, were, after all, always soldier kings, uniformed from the age of ten, and brought up to loathe constitutionalism. When William II said, on the outbreak of war, that he no longer recognized any political parties, but only Germans, this was merely another formulation of his earlier remark that he had never even read the German constitution. His faith lay only in his officers, not in the "particularists" in the Reichstag. It had been much the same with his grandfather, but the system had worked under a giant like Bismarck, whereas it no longer did with Bethmann. Once again, the parallel with earlier times may be seen: The absolutist system of Frederick II worked under a man who could be called Frederick the Great, but it collapsed under lesser men after his death. One might have thought William II would have learned something from his family's history, but the tragedy of the Hohenzollerns is that they never benefited from experience at all.

William II surrendered to Hindenburg and Ludendorff's demand that unrestricted submarine warfare be resumed. It had earlier been called off because of America's objections, but although many in Germany, Bethmann included, felt certain that resuming this type of warfare would bring the United States into the war, an event which might spell defeat for the Central Powers, Hindenburg and Ludendorff argued that a U-boat counterblockade of Britain was essential. Gerard was summoned to the Foreign Office in the Wilhelmstrasse at 6 P.M. on January 31, 1917, and given the news that the U-boats would be unleashed at midnight.

"Give us only two months of this kind of warfare, and we shall end the war and make peace within three months," he was told by State Secretary Arthur Zimmermann. On Saturday, February 3, Zimmermann told Gerard, "As you will see, everything will be all right. America will do nothing, for President Wilson is for peace and nothing else. Everything will go on as before. I have arranged for you to . . . see the Kaiser next week, and everything will be all right." The next day, February 4, Gustav Stresemann addressed a National Liberal Party rally, assuring the members that, after careful study of the Americans, he could assure them America would never break off relations with Germany. After stormy applause died down, a man in the back of the hall rose and read aloud from that day's issue of *B.Z. am Mittag*; it reported that Wilson had broken off diplomatic relations with Germany the day before.

This break, says Gerard, "came as an intense surprise" to the ruling circles.[227] * On the other hand, when William II was warned that the next step was war with America, he replied with resignation, "It's all the same to me." The declaration of war duly followed, on April 6. Ludendorff forecast that no American troops would land in Europe before 1918; by that time, he said, Britain would have been forced to its knees. The first American troops, however, landed early in July, 1917, and General John Pershing arrived in France on June 13.

Meanwhile, other problems beset the Kaiser at the beginning of 1917. In Russia after the March Revolution, the czar had abdicated. Anxious to help ignite still more bombs, the German Foreign Office arranged to get Lenin from Switzerland to Russia, without letting the Kaiser know, of course, for they knew how he felt about revolutionaries and regicides. As Winston Churchill put it in *The World Crisis*: "It was with a sense of awe that they turned upon Russia the most grisly of all weapons. They transported Lenin in a sealed truck like a plague bacillus from Switzerland into Russia." That same March the radical wing of the Social Democrats had broken off and formed itself into the Independent Socialist Party. If the loyalty of the German masses was to be retained, the government had to make some dramatic move, some major concession. Bethmann, still chancellor, proposed the immediate introduction of universal suffrage on April 5; three days later the Kaiser in his Easter message referred to his people's "massive contributions . . . in this terrible war" and said, rather vaguely, that, after these, "I am sure there is no room left for Prussia's class suffrage"—for that three-class franchise. Privately, he spoke of this, in patronizing terms, as his "Easter egg" to the people.

But it was not enough. Times had changed. The Socialists spoke out for peace "without annexations or reparations." The Reichstag set up a committee to study a revision of the con-

* Stresemann recovered from his *gaffe*, became party chief and, during the Weimar era, German chancellor and foreign minister. In 1926 he was awarded the Nobel Peace Prize.

stitution. In May it decided that the chancellor must be responsible to Parliament and that army and navy appointments be made by the minister concerned and no longer by the Kaiser personally. Strikes flared up throughout Germany's munitions factories, and rebellion was in the air.

The Conservatives in the Reichstag had become alarmed, however, and protested against the Easter message and all liberalization attempts. Emboldened, the Kaiser angrily rejected the Reichstag committee's proposals. In July, Hindenburg and Ludendorff demanded that the Kaiser get rid of Chancellor Bethmann altogether; this he did, although he refused the generals' suggestion that Bülow be given the job again. A number of other candidates were proposed, but these were objectionable to Hindenburg or Ludendorff or someone else. Officials were finally reduced to checking the *Almanach de Gotha* and the *Official Directory* to come up with new names. A certain Georg Michaelis was finally proposed. William II had never heard of the man and so had no objections; Hindenburg and Ludendorff also agreed to him. They notified Michaelis, who was Prussian food controller, and brought the dumbfounded official to supper with the Kaiser. Unfortunately, he was such a nonentity that he lasted only three months, after which Count Georg von Hertling, seventy-four years of age and so near to blindness that papers had to be read to him, was appointed for a year. It did not matter: Ludendorff was the dictator and had stamped out all attempts at liberalizing Prussia's suffrage or anything else. "With this franchise, we cannot live," he said, meaning the officer corps and the Establishment. He was even ready to conclude "any kind of peace" so long as it would help prevent changes in the voting laws. The Kaiser, of course, shared these sentiments, as may be seen from an incident which occurred after Bethmann had gone. The emperor deigned to meet a parliamentary delegation which even included a Socialist, a type of human being William had never before received. He could not, of course, have suspected it, but this man, Friedrich Ebert, would become imperial chancellor (for a day) and eventually President of Germany. William proceeded to make fun of a peace resolution the Reichstag had drafted, and he then predicted not only victory in the war but also a subsequent agreement with France, whereupon "all Europe under my leadership will begin the real war with England—the Second Punic War." Then he concluded his talk with these delegates by saying, "Where my guards are, democracy is not!"

"The consternation among us members," wrote Matthias Erzberger of the Center (Catholic) Party, "got greater and greater. . . ."

At the beginning of the war the Reichstag had proclaimed a *Burgfrieden*—meaning a peace within "Fortress Germany"; this peace was gradually disintegrating. Mutinies, strikes, protest demonstrations had to be ruthlessly suppressed. In the Reichstag only a left-wing coalition could muster a majority, for the Social Democrats were now the single most powerful delegation, with 110 seats. Yet they were ignored by the government as though they did not exist, causing the delegates to despair and the voters to raise voices in anger. A book which ostensibly dealt with Caligula sold 150,000 copies within a month; the nation knew which emperor the author had in mind.

The Bolshevik Revolution took place in November, 1917, and Trotzky negotiated peace terms at Brest-Litovsk. The Reichstag's call for a peace without annexations was ignored. Hindenburg said he needed to annex much of the Baltic states "for the maneuvering of my left wing in the next war." The Allies watched the negotiations for a sign of how Germany would act at a peace conference. What they saw made them fight all the harder. The Kaiser was not kept informed about the details of the negotiations, and when he on one occasion produced a map which, he said, showed his ideas about the frontier, Ludendorff actually shouted him down, saying he had no right to ask the views of others before the High Command had reflected on the matter. Shaken, the emperor retreated. Ludendorff then drafted a letter for Hindenburg, in which the field marshal told the Kaiser he could accept either their advice or their resignations. William turned to Richard von Kühlmann, state secrectary for foreign affairs, whom the generals hoped to have sacked, and Kühlmann drafted a letter for his emperor which put the generals gently back in their place. But the generals recognized how much of a figurehead monarch this Kaiser had become and reacted to this nastily, by demanding that the emperor dismiss Rudolf von Valentini, the head of his Civil Secretariat, whom they blamed for "liberal tendencies" in the government. William exploded at this impertinence, calling Ludendorff "a malefactor" whose hand he would never again shake; though for the most part he did as Ludendorff "suggested," William loathed this coarse general and referred to him as "the man with the sergeant's mouth" (*Feldwebelfresse*). On this occasion, William even slammed a door in the face of the venerable Hindenburg, shouting, "I don't want your paternal advice!" Valentini, however, knew what was at stake; to defuse the crisis before the generals quit, he resigned, to be replaced by a reactionary anti-Semite named Friedrich von Berg-Markienen.

William II sulked; the generals were now even dictating to him what people he might have in his personal entourage. He knew how powerless he had become; what he was unwilling to admit was the reason—his failure to assert his power. On an article which stated that the equilibrium between civil and military forces had been disturbed in Germany, he added the notation "because on both sides the emperor is ignored." That remark was characteristic not only of his self-pity, but of his self-deception, for the equilibrium had been disturbed when the Kaiser weighted the scales by throwing all power to the generals. At one point, the emperor had irritated the officers so much that there was even brief talk in the operations section of arresting the Kaiser, but it came to nothing, and indeed there was no need to go that far. William II was already the prisoner of the High Command, locked away where he could not interfere, and fed a ration of stale victories.

At last, on March 21, 1918, the Kaiser had something to celebrate: a huge German offensive, code-named Michael, had begun on the western front. Eight hundred thousand German soldiers charged out of their trenches in what was to be the last German push of the war, aimed at crushing the British and French armies before the full weight of American reinforcements could make itself felt. William raced to Avesnes to be with his troops on the twenty-first; after inspiring them by letting them see his person, he raced back to the headquarters at Spa, where he jubilantly toasted complete victory with champagne. The British, he said, were "totally defeated" and it had all been a great victory of "monarchy over democracy," as though this were the cause uppermost in the minds of those of his soldiers who were sacrificing themselves for their homeland. If a British parliamentary delegation now came to beg for peace, William added jubilantly, its members would first have to kneel on the ground before the imperial battle standards.

His elation is understandable, for Ludendorff's Michael Offensive at first was brilliantly successful and cost the British a staggering 300,000 casualties. German newspapers reported that the victories had been achieved "under the personal command of His Majesty," but the emperor was not so willing to accept responsibility for the fact that the German advance was soon stopped. Ludendorff sought to regain the initiative by attacking first here, then there, and finally by launching another major drive, the Blücher attack, on May 27, throwing fifteen German divisions against seven. This drive reached the Marne three days later, but there it ground to a halt, stopped both by the river and by determined resistance, not least by American divisions at Château-Thierry. As German reserves dwindled in the weeks which followed, Allied reserves increased. British casualties had been partly replaced, and fresh American troops were arriving. "Americans are springing up like mushrooms everywhere," wrote a German army captain in July.[228]

British fliers began bombarding German soldiers with leaflets, carefully phrased to produce disaffection and revolutionary sentiment in German ranks. A typical one promised the soldiers they, too, would soon be free men, "for the revolution is coming." It revealed corruption among officers and asked, *"Soldat, o deutscher Soldat, was hätte wohl Friedrich dazu gesagt?"* ("Soldier, Oh German soldier, what would Frederick [the Great] have said to that?")[229]

The Allied armies were strong enough to launch their own great offensive at 4:20 A.M. on August 8, 1918. Almost 500,000 troops were hurled against the German lines, augmented by tanks, these being a weapon the Germans had neglected. "Six to seven divisions allowed themselves to be overrun by tanks in the fog," wrote Ludendorff; August 8, he said, was "the blackest day in the history of Germany." That comment alone, from an officer who knew the history of Jena and Auerstädt, when Napoleon smashed the Prussian armies, is an index of the calamitous defeat German arms suffered. The day was not over before Ludendorff admitted that "the war has to be ended." He was a broken man, for all his grand stratagems, as well as the great advances of the spring, had dissolved to nothing; he knew that more than the German lines had broken, knew that the fighting spirit of the German soldier had begun to crack. The German lines held after reeling backward and surrendering large territories, but the stand was desperate, reserves were nonexistent, and a counterattack was as impossible to launch as victory was to achieve. Soldiers were brave enough, but they were simply fed up, both with war and with fighting for a regime they had begun to loathe. Too much had been demanded of them for four years, and it seemed to them that their officers were prepared to let endless thousands more be slaughtered, although the prospects were hopeless. Some soldiers threw away their guns and shouted revolutionary slogans at their officers; German units which chose to fight or which merely moved up to front-line positions were denounced as "strikebreakers" and *Kriegsverlängerer* ("war lengtheners") by their own comrades.

The Kaiser's personal illusions were also beginning to crack. Hindenburg confessed to him that Germany's last gamble at achieving victory had now definitely failed, and the Kaiser admitted that it seemed as though the country had "reached the limit of its endurance capacity." But a clear conception of the magnitude of the disaster continued to elude him. Major August Niemann, the emperor's devoted adjutant, said, "It was infinitely difficult to give the emperor a clear idea of the situation without disturbing his mental equilibrium."[230] William's friend the Jewish shipowner Ballin was summoned to the emperor's side but was warned against making him "too pessimistic." Ballin was surprised to hear William still talking of that "Second Punic War" in which he would defeat Britain; he afterward commented that the Kaiser "seemed very much misled . . . so humbugged that he has no idea how catastrophic things have become." Humbugged perhaps, but for good reason. His aides feared he might suffer a complete "mental and physical collapse" if he heard bad news.[231] * In actual fact, when

* Ballin was himself a measure of the emperor's capacity to deceive himself, for when William II was once asked how he reconciled his anti-Semitism with

the worst news possible arrived on September 2, he did not collapse. That day, Captain Sigurd von Ilsemann, one of his adjutants and Niemann's assistant, informed him that British tanks had broken into the Siegfried Line. The Kaiser banged his fist on the table and snapped, "Now we have lost the war! Poor Fatherland!" Then he hurried through the room, tore open a door to the dining room and told the assembled dinner guests that he had "serious, shattering news" to give them. "It means nothing more or less than that we have lost the war!" he concluded. Ilsemann reports that this was greeted with consternation and a deathly silence; the Kaiser, he says, ate hardly anything throughout the meal and, what was more unusual, said hardly a word.

Seven days after the British tanks attacked, William had recovered his voice enough to address 1,500 Krupp steelworkers in the vestibule of their works in Essen, standing among them dressed in his field-gray uniform, the symbol of all that these workers had disliked and which they by now had come to loathe. Adjutant Ilsemann handed him the speech his Civil Secretariat had prepared; but it remained in its folder, and the Kaiser spoke extemporaneously—and so excitedly that his brow became wet with perspiration. "It would have been better had he not said some of the things he did," Ilsemann afterward noted in his diary.

The men he was addressing were foremen; the Kaiser called them "my dear friends," a fact which must have amazed them, for if there was one thing William was not, it was a friend of the industrial proletariat, most of them "traitors" who voted Social Democratic. He then amazed them even more, by swinging casually from one end of the political spectrum to the other. At one point in his thirty-minute address, he even sounded pro-Communist, for he denounced the Allied intervention in Russia as an attempt "to overthrow the ultrademocratic government" of the Bolsheviks. Hardly had he finished posturing as a champion of the working class than he warned the workers to beware of discouraging rumors with which "the Anglo-Saxons . . . are trying to foment disturbances," adding that anyone even listening to such rumors "is a traitor and

---

his friendship, William expostulated, "Ballin a Jew? No such thing! Ballin is a Christian!" 232

worthy of appropriate punishment." Finally, he spoke to them paternalistically, even patronizingly. "To every single one of us, his task is given," the emperor said. "To you with your hammer, to you at your lathe, to me upon my throne." This was imperial egalitarianism, the claptrap nobility then enjoyed mouthing. The workers saw through it; some of them even snickered. The speech was followed not by applause or cheers, but by an awkward silence. Niemann, who was there, reported, "The men's faces were expressionless, and the more eloquent the Emperor became, the more apparent was the coolness." [233]

He left, but not for headquarters, which had become intolerable. That restless spirit which had for thirty years charged through Germany on countless ego-building ceremonial trips now set forth again, and for the same reasons: to bask in the warmth of publicity, to strut so that he might not falter, to keep on the move so that he might avoid work. Medals were bestowed and troops inspected far from the front, at the Kiel naval base, even in the Baltic provinces. Germany—not just the German armies—was collapsing all around him, but Emperor William II was unaware of the fact, for everywhere he went all seemed so normal, as during the halcyon quarter century of peace: bowing, scraping, deferential officers and officials, cannonades, flags, banners, trumpets, drums, smart military reviews, toasts given in fine champagnes, bunting, rostrums, civic receptions, endless words of fealty and of praise. Furthermore, much of the Hindenburg Line still held fast, and the Allies had paused in their attacks, preparing for an all-out offensive.

It began on September 26, and the German lines wavered and threatened to snap. Meanwhile, on September 15, Allied forces on the Bulgarian front had mounted an offensive which split the Bulgarian army into two parts and caused the war-weary Bulgarians to give up the fight and surrender. When this news reached Ludendorff, he said it sealed Germany's fate. With its Bulgarian ally out of the war and the Turks ready to capitulate to the British, it seemed to him clear that Austria-Hungary, already exhausted, would also sue for peace. The Kaiser returned to headquarters at Spa on September 29, the day after Bulgaria surrendered and the day on which it signed an armistice. Hindenburg and Ludendorff wasted no time in telling the emperor the unpleasant truth. "The High Command and the

German armies are finished," they said that morning. "Not only is victory out of the question, but Germany faces immediate, final, and inevitable defeat." German troops were "poisoned" with Socialist ideas and were no longer reliable, they confessed; if the war were permitted to continue, the Allies would undoubtedly succeed in breaking through the German lines, sending hundreds of thousands of German soldiers fleeing across the Rhine, "carrying revolution into Germany." This, they said, "must be prevented at all cost." Since Wilson would never negotiate an armistice with the present military dictatorship, Ludendorff said it was essential that a democratic government be formed.

It seemed incredible to the emperor to hear of revolutionary sentiment among burghers and workers whom he had always thought of as loyal, having recognized only smiling faces. News of strikes and mutinies, of revolts which had needed to be suppressed, and of protest meetings all had been kept from him lest he become too upset, lest he panic and have that breakdown everyone feared might come. Now, all of a sudden, the full measure of the German collapse had at least been referred to, if not spelled out for him. After the generals left, Foreign Minister Paul von Hintze said William had two choices: either democratize the government or establish a dictatorship to suppress all revolutionary agitation. William II had toyed with the idea of a dictatorship before, it being after all merely an absolute form of the absolutist monarchy already existing and fully in harmony with his contempt for Parliament or the popular will, but he brushed the suggestion aside as "Nonsense!" To become dictator where he had been emperor would have meant standing up to Hindenburg and Ludendorff, meant turning aside their demands, meant taking personal command of both the home front and the western front, meant taking the ultimate gamble so as to establish his authority like *un rocher de bronze,* as Frederick William I had said. William II of Hohenzollern was a dilettante who was not man enough to be a *Wilhelm Eisenzahn,* an "Iron Tooth." And so it was that he did the decent thing. He listened to Hintze's proposal for a democratic government "with suppressed emotion, with kingly dignity, and declared himself in favour of the program suggested."[234]

That afternoon, the chancellor laid before the emperor a document dated the next day, September 30: "It is my wish that the German people should take a more active part than heretofore in deciding the fate of the fatherland. It is therefore my pleasure that men who are supported by the confidence of the people should have a larger share in the rights and duties of the government."

William read it over, thought it over, and could not bear to sign it. Ninety minutes later he summoned Hintze and told him he'd like to ponder it for two weeks. "This revolution business hasn't gone so far, after all," he said. Hintze was aghast and again reminded the emperor that Hindenburg and Ludendorff had both warned that there would be total collapse if an immediate armistice were not arranged. William listened in silence, but when the foreign minister finished, he walked away from the table on which the document lay and headed for the door, hoping still to escape signing it. To his amazement—and very likely for the first time in his adult life—an official interposed himself: Hintze politely barred the door and would not let him leave. Again Hintze predicted disaster if the Kaiser did not sign; wearily, the emperor turned, walked to the table, and affixed his name. Then he hurried off to dress for dinner, for it was already seven. In actuality, however, as his new chancellor put it two weeks later, it was "five minutes past midnight," too late to save the House of Hohenzollern, even if Germany might still be saved.[235]

In Constantinople a German officer named Hans von Seeckt, the man who would come to head the Weimar-era Reichswehr, wrote a letter on October 1, the day on which a kindly, liberal aristocrat named Prince Max von Baden was chosen as the emperor's new chancellor.

"Just now received the telegraphic news," Seeckt wrote. "So, we have a parliamentary regime. I shall have to keep silent, as it is the will of the All-Highest." [236]

The "All-Highest" was that day traveling from Spa back home to the New Palace in Potsdam. Prince Max arrived in Berlin and met with representatives of the Reichstag to form the first government which would be responsible, not to the emperor, but to Parliament, the first which included two Social

Democrats (Friedrich Ebert and Philipp Scheidemann), and which finally abolished Prussia's three-class franchise, that travesty of parliamentarianism which was so monstrous that even Bismarck, who found it useful, admitted that "a crazier, more contemptible electoral law had never been thought of in any country." [237]

"I only became aware of how completely the old Prussian system had collapsed after I arrived here," Prince Max wrote to his cousin, from Berlin. "Frightened, I wanted to shrink back, because I realized that no military might stood behind my policies and that we are bankrupt on the field of battle. . . . We're in the middle of a revolution. If I succeed in making it a peaceful revolution, the state will continue after the conclusion of peace. If I fail, it means bloody revolution and total ruin." [238]

The revolution of which Prince Max wrote was a revolution in attitudes. The leaders of the Reichstag party delegations had all along been confident of German victory; they had been victims of propaganda as much as the Kaiser ever was. On October 1, the day Prince Max was appointed chancellor, a representative of the High Command met the party leaders and told them the truth. To say that it came as a shock is to understate the matter: These men simply could not believe their ears. Yet they had the word of Hindenburg and Ludendorff for it: German defeat was absolutely certain, and only an immediate armistice could save the nation from a bloody revolution.

Once these words had been absorbed and once the home front became convinced that a continuation of the war was hopeless, there was no halting their quest for peace. Prince Max had already cabled President Wilson, asking for an armistice, during the night of October 3–4; while Germany waited for an answer, an unexpected development occurred.

Ludendorff changed his mind. Once again, the Allied advance had slowed; the Hindenburg Line, though pierced, had not collapsed. Ludendorff became convinced by October 17 that his troops could be withdrawn to a shortened line of defense; from there, they might offer determined resistance, and this, in turn, could extort better peace conditions from the Allies. Ludendorff no longer wanted an armistice, at least not one which was requested in words which admitted defeat, such as Max von Baden's telegram had done.

The fact of the matter is that Ludendorff's nerves had snapped when Bulgaria surrendered on September 29. He was a "neurasthenic" like his emperor—a brilliant but neurotic man of enormous energy, boorish habits, profound depressions, and occasional hysterias. He wallowed in self-pity at the slightest reverses and tended to go to pieces very easily. (Already in July, after his Michael Offensive had bogged down, Ludendorff had begun to crack; Colonel Mertz von Quirnheim noted down in his diary that month, "His Excellency completely broken up.") He was unstable, a fact which emerged with even greater clarity after the war, when he associated himself with Hitler and developed such a distorted "conspiracy theory" of history that he saw international plots against Germany from every quarter: from Jews, Rosicrucians, and even the Dalai Lama, who he came to believe was the man behind Stalin. After the Allied offensive of August 8, Ludendorff's intimate and aide, Colonel Max Bauer, wrote, "Ludendorff has got to go. His nerves are completely finished. . . ." By mid-September he was under treatment; it was this distraught man, who showed all the symptoms of a manic-depressive, who assessed the situation of the German armies on September 29, when he went to the Kaiser with his amenable nominal superior, Hindenburg. It was in this state that Ludendorff swung about again in mid-October, sailing upward on his manic-depressive cycle, and suggesting that the war ought to be continued.

Washington responded on October 23 to Prince Max's appeal for an armistice. It demanded guarantees that the changes in Germany were real and permanent and warned that it would demand German surrender, not peace negotiations, if it had to "deal with the military masters and the monarchical autocrats of Germany." William II exploded when he read this note. "The hypocritical Wilson has at last thrown off his mask," he said. "The object of this is to bring down my house, to set the monarchy aside." The empress, just as angered, ranted that Wilson was a "parvenu" who had the effrontery "to humiliate a princely house which can look back on centuries of service to people and country."

Faced with these peace terms, the High Command suddenly

denied brazenly that it had ever urged an immediate armistice, and Ludendorff prepared to send telegrams to all army commanders ordering all possible resistance since U.S. conditions were "impossible for us soldiers to accept." An army telegraph operator who was to send off this message noted that Ludendorff was still acting as though he were running Germany and that he was in effect subverting Chancellor Prince Max's government; the man happened to be a member of the radical Independent Socialists, so he first sent the text of Ludendorff's message to his party leaders in Berlin. When they got the news to Prince Max, the chancellor went to the Kaiser and demanded that Ludendorff be dismissed immediately, or the Cabinet would resign. "Now the whole structure threatens to collapse," the Kaiser groaned. "Still, it *is* an impossible state of affairs that such a manifesto can come out without my consent and the chancellor's. I see nothing for it but to comply with the chancellor's request." On October 26, William II summoned Hindenburg and Ludendorff before him. When it was over, the Kaiser seemed relieved to see the *Feldwebelfresse* go. "I have separated the Siamese twins," he announced. Hindenburg would stay as chief of the general staff; General Wilhelm von Groener took Ludendorff's place as quartermaster general.

On the next day the Austrian emperor told William II that Austria was ending all hostilities. Prince Max knew this meant Germany would have to accept Wilson's conditions, for the Allies would now be able to press an attack on Germany from Austrian territory, using Austrian rail lines. Even the Kaiser saw the inevitability and agreed to Wilson's terms.

The question of William's abdication remained acute. Prince Max had urged the emperor to abdicate, German ambassadors cabled Berlin urging the same, the public demanded abdication, and even monarchists were pressing William to resign the throne in order to secure a better peace for Germany and even to save the monarchy itself. It was agreed generally that *both* the emperor and his thirty-six-year-old crown prince would have to quit, the one to abdicate, the other to renounce the succession. (Crown Prince William was so much disliked in the Allied camp that he was a distinct liability; once, when both the Kaiser and his son had been out shooting game with British hosts, one senior Englishman said to another, "For God's sake, don't shoot the Kaiser; his son is worse yet!") If both quit, then the monarchy might yet be saved under a regency, until the Kaiser's grandson, another William, then twelve, came of age.

Depressed by all this agitation and pressure, the emperor slipped out of Berlin on October 29, returning unannounced and unexpected to military headquarters at Spa. "Prince Max's government," he told his generals, "is trying to throw me out. At Berlin I should be less able to oppose them than in the midst of my troops."

Back in Berlin, Prince Max was in a coma for thirty-six hours, having swallowed too strong a sleeping medicine for an attack of influenza; when he awoke and returned to his office on November 3, he found out that both Austria-Hungary and Turkey had surrendered. The next day, there was even worse news. The bloody revolution he had expected broke out throughout the nation. The Kiel naval base was in the hands of sailors, and revolutionary mobs in several cities had seized complete control. Had the Kaiser been in Potsdam or Berlin, he never would have been able to resist the public clamor calling for him to abdicate the throne; it was on everybody's lips, and the roar would have reached even his reluctant ears. But he was at Spa, in far-off Belgium, and he was surrounded by officers who had sworn eternal loyalty to their supreme warlord, their "All-Highest." There he felt safe again; there he was sealed off from reality; there he could continue for a few days at least to pose as absolute monarch; there he was receiving the deference due a German Emperor, a King of Prussia, and the head of the House of Hohenzollern.

But his obstinate refusal to abdicate in time spelled doom for the House of Hohenzollern. Not Wilson, but the Kaiser, brought down this house and set the monarchy aside, for the Allies had never asked that a republic be established, had only indicated that this blusterer who had become the focus of all their anti-German hatred, must go. The Social Democrats in Berlin were no republicans; as Wheeler-Bennett says, "Ebert and his colleagues moved heaven and earth to secure the establishment of a constitutional monarchy in Germany with a regency acting in the name of one of the sons of the Crown Prince."[239] The *sine qua non* was that the emperor sacrifice himself for the good of his house if he was unwilling to do so for the good of the nation; William II could not bring himself to do so until it was too late.

On November 9, at 10 A.M., several elite units, such as the Czar Alexander Guards Regiment, joined the revolution, and the emperor's world began to collapse. For days he and his generals had been plotting how to march on Berlin, overthrow the democratic government the Kaiser himself had established under Prince Max, shoot down all the striking and demonstrating workers, but the defection of crack units on November 9 put an end to all such dreams. Field Marshal Hindenburg said he was still in favor of marching on Berlin but admitted he didn't think such a venture would have much success; then he asked the Kaiser to excuse him. The emperor was rattled. He said he wanted to spare his country a civil war; all he wanted to do, he said, was return to Berlin at the head of his returning armies. It was at this point that General Groener rose to speak. Groener was an officer William had liked ever since 1914, for Groener had been one of the few who bothered at the start of the war to keep the emperor informed of developments; William referred to Groener as "the jolly Swabian." This time, however, Groener shocked the Kaiser by telling him the truth. "Sire," he said, "you no longer have an army. The army will march home in peace and order under the command of its officers and commanding generals, but not under the command of Your Majesty, for it no longer stands behind Your Majesty."

Eyes blazing with fury, William II walked up to Groener and snapped, "I require that statement in writing. I want all the commanding generals to state in black and white that the army no longer stands behind its supreme warlord. Has it not sworn loyalty to me in its military oath?"

"Sire," said Groener, "today oaths are but words."

This reply, delivered in Groener's soft, quiet Swabian accents, was the unkindest cut of all. Who stood behind him now? His people were in arms, vast armies of ordinary citizens tore through the streets of his cities, army officers who had the effrontery to appear in uniform were shot down in the streets, Socialist governments were being proclaimed everywhere, and now he was informed that his army had rejected him. A few officers were loyal still, but that was all; it was not enough.

Prince Max telephoned from Berlin to describe the revolution which had broken out in the capital; he told the emperor that only his immediate abdication could satisfy the people and prevent civil war. Any further obstinate clinging to the throne, he told William II, would only bring the emperor the hatred of his people, while abdication would earn him their gratitude.

But William temporized, even as more people were arriving at Spa to add to the pressures being put on him. The crown prince arrived, clearly unwilling to renounce the succession to the throne. Some officers suggested that the emperor must, under these circumstances, seek an honorable death befitting a Prussian king and supreme warlord, that he should place himself at the head of his troops on the western front and allow himself to be killed leading them in a foray on the field of battle. The idea was briefly entertained, then quickly rejected. William II was neither the man to make himself a martyr nor the man to lead his troops back home to crush the rebels, although he entertained both ideas. That day, he even contemplated suicide. En route to the royal train, in which he would deliberate whether he should flee or not, he told two of his adjutants, Major Georg von Hirschfeld and Captain von Ilsemann, that he was ready to fight to the last even if he only had a few loyal men left to support him. ". . . And even if we are all slain," he said, "I am not afraid of death! No, I shall remain here!" Then he paused for a moment, uttered what Ilsemann calls "a terrible sigh," and said, "The best thing would be if I shot myself dead."

He certainly had absolutely no wish to earn the gratitude of his subjects by stepping off the stage. His enemies were all "Bolsheviks"; of that he was convinced. At one point he even uttered the fantastic idea that the British might yet lend him troops with which to put down the Bolsheviks in Germany. (That same delusion was to imbue Adolf Hitler with hope in 1945.) In one casual remark, made to Adjutant von Ilsemann, however, the Kaiser betrayed the fact that he knew it was the German people, not just the German Bolsheviks, who now wanted him to abdicate; in that remark, William II also betrayed his loathing for his subjects. "Who would have thought," he said, "that it would come to this? The German people are . . ." He left the sentence unfinished, recovered his composure, and warned his adjutants to be well armed.

Abdication he regarded as pandering to the mob. He saw himself as lord and master of his people and not, as Frederick the Great had, as the "first servant" of the state. He regarded himself as king and emperor not by the will of the people, but by "the grace of God"; how, then, could these people take away from him a crown they had never given, a crown which neither he nor any of his house had ever "picked up from the gutter"? William II wanted to assert his "rights"; it was for this reason that he had fled to Spa. In this time of national upheaval, William II thought only of his own position, not of the survival of the House of Hohenzollern, to say nothing of the survival of Germany.

An officer arrived with anxiously awaited news. He had been sent to poll front-line officers concerning the emperor's chances with his troops. He had asked them whether their troops would follow their Kaiser back into Germany to smash the revolution; of thirty-nine officers, *only one* thought the troops would obey such a command. William was told his troops wanted an immediate armistice, wanted to stop dying and bleeding to death in a forlorn cause, and would in any event fight no more.

Again Berlin telephoned, saying that it was now a matter of minutes before the government buildings were seized by revolutionary mobs. All eyes turned to William II to gauge his reaction; his eyes sought those of the aged Hindenburg, hoping to find comfort there, but finding none. William nodded to Hintze; he would resign, he said, but only as German emperor, never as King of Prussia. It still had not dawned on him that he personally, he alone, had to go, that he was offensive and objectionable, that none wanted him around, although the throne of Prussia might yet be saved for his grandson.* Prince Max, in Berlin, however, knew it. Disaster was certain unless he acted at once, so he gave the German press agency a statement announcing that William II had abdicated and that the crown prince had renounced the succession. A moment later Prince Max surrendered the government he could no longer lead to Friedrich Ebert, the Social Democrat. Ebert issued a

* Bavaria having already declared itself a republic, the German Empire was dissolving.

proclamation, urging officials throughout the nation to stay at their posts to save Germany from "anarchy" and "the most terrible misery"; he told them that he knew it would not be easy for them to work for his new government, but he appealed "to their love of our people."

Karl Liebknecht, the radical left-wing Socialist who headed the nucleus of the German Communist Party, ignored Friedrich Ebert's government and proclaimed "a Socialist Republic" from the balcony of the Berlin Palace; Scheidemann, Ebert's colleague, sought to nullify this action by proclaiming a republic on his own, from a window in the Reichstag Building. When Ebert heard of this, he exploded in anger and faced Scheidemann seething with rage. "You have no right," he told his colleague, "to proclaim a republic. Whatever will become of Germany, whether a republic or what have you, is a matter for a constituent assembly to decide!"

But the decision had in fact been taken, for the revolutionary armies in the street had embraced it. William, still at Spa, did not know of these events, for they were happening too fast. All he knew was that Prince Max had announced his abdication as emperor and king, as well as the crown prince's renunciation of the throne. "Barefaced, outrageous treason!" William called it. "I am King of Prussia, and I will remain king. As such I will stay with my troops."

But this was an illusion, for the troops were not staying with him. Finally, it was Hindenburg who delivered the *coup de grâce;* the field marshal told William he had better abdicate both positions, as Berlin had already announced. "I cannot," said Hindenburg, "accept the responsibility of seeing Your Majesty haled to Berlin by mutinous troops and handed over as a prisoner to the revolutionary government." It was a reminder of Ekaterinburg, of what had happened to William's cousin Czar Nicholas II and his family on July 16. The chief of the naval staff hastened to agree with Hindenburg, telling the Kaiser he also didn't have the navy behind him any longer —that navy he had created and on which he had lavished so much love. This hurt more than the loss of the army's loyalty —and that had hurt far more than the loss of his people's affection, about which he cared amazingly little.

The Kaiser was warned that the only road of escape left

open, the one to Holland, might be cut at any moment and that mutinous troops might be on their way to Spa, to seize him. Wearily, he agreed to leave after hearing this doleful news, but only the next morning.

En route to the frontier in automobiles at 5 A.M. on November 10, the Kaiser and his party were extremely apprehensive. A solitary German soldier at a bridge, who stopped the cavalcade with a red flag, made everyone jumpy, until it proved to be a normal inspection, not a Bolshevik ambush. At the frontier, officers told Bavarian Landwehr border guards that the party consisted of officers traveling to Holland on urgent business; the soldiers, who thought this might be connected with peace negotiations and who never recognized the Kaiser, waved the cars through. Baron Werner von Grünau of the Foreign Office entered a Dutch border guard building to talk to the frontier officials, while the Kaiser and his adjutants paced about, smoking cigarettes. At eight that morning, a Dutch diplomat, Verbrugge van 'sGravendeel, arrived, together with some Dutch officers; the diplomat had left Brussels at eleven the previous night to alert the border post of the impending arrival of the emperor, but the Kaiser had reached the border first. The Dutch politely suggested the Kaiser and his party go to Eijsden railway station, to await the arrival of the imperial train, which had traveled from Spa empty (because of the danger that it might be stopped by revolutionary soldiers).

Casual onlookers at the Eijsden platform recognized the Kaiser. *"Ah, Kamerad kaputt!"* they shouted, shaking their fists at him; some called out, *"Vive la France!"* Once inside the train, the Kaiser still seemed in danger, his adjutants fearing that factory workers (Belgians, they claimed) might throw stones at the windows; it took hours for police to arrive and clear the platform.

It took even longer—most of the day—for news to arrive from The Hague, concerning the Kaiser's request for asylum. His adjutant, Captain von Ilsemann, says waiting was "torture." The Kaiser spent the agonizing hours doing what he did best: talking fast and furiously and justifying himself. He blamed fate for the fact that his father had died too soon; this, he said, had catapulted him to the throne at too young an age, forcing him to spend most of his reign being unduly influenced by older men. Bitterly, he said that he was now the elder and his ministers were the younger; just now, when he might have been able to enforce his wishes over younger men, he was being chased out of the country. His own conscience was clear, as he was to announce solemnly the next day: "The Lord God knows I never wanted this war!" A few days later, he blamed Ludendorff—whom he called "a tyrant"—for everything, including his dynasty's fall. He compared himself to a gardener who raises a pet bear (Ludendorff); the bear, wishing to protect its master, kills the master instead, by trying to swat a fly which has landed on its master's face. Then he compared the British and the Germans, saying that the British had become so mighty because Englishmen think of their country ahead of themselves. The fault of the Germans, William said, was that they always think of their own welfare first, before they think of their fatherland's.

It was of course his own personal welfare and safety which interested Kaiser William II during these days; he spoke of nothing else to his intimate circle, referring to his subjects only in the angriest, most derisive ways. Finally, the personal comfort of Kaiser William was assured. Queen Wilhelmina sent word that a ministerial council had voted unanimously to grant him asylum and that, until a permanent home was found, he should go to Amerongen Castle, the home of Count Godard von Aldenburg-Bentinck.

The train trip there was another nightmare. Although curtains were drawn whenever the train passed through Dutch villages and towns, the Kaiser was well aware of the fact that crowds had gathered on platforms en route to shake their fists at him, even to draw their fingers across their throats. "Leave the curtains alone," the Kaiser said after a time. "What does it matter anymore?" (This remark reminded Ilsemann of something the Kaiser had said at Spa: "It doesn't matter where I go. I am hated everywhere in the world." *)

* Whether the Kaiser's asylum had been prearranged remains a mystery, for Dutch archives on the matter are still sealed. Philipp Scheidemann claimed (but never substantiated) that Britain's George V had asked Holland's Queen Wilhelmina to grant asylum to his cousin William. A former governor general of the Dutch East Indies visited Spa during the night of November 8, and as early as November 7, rumors circulated in Holland to the effect that the Kaiser would settle there; furthermore, the arrival of the Dutch diplomat from Bel-

At three in the afternoon of November 11, the train pulled into Maarn, where Count Bentinck waited on a platform crowded with onlookers. Wearily, the Kaiser laid a hand on the count's shoulder and said, "Now show me where I have to go." Because the count was a widower, his daughter, Countess Elisabeth (who later married Ilsemann), greeted the Kaiser at the castle doors. "Excuse me that I have to trouble you," William said, "but it is not my fault." Then he entered what would be his home until May, 1920. Although he was still uncertain about his ultimate fate and although he was fearful of assassination attempts, he now began to relax, surprising everyone with his calmness and composure. As Ilsemann had noted much earlier, the Kaiser easily resigned himself, for he was no fighter or even a decisive individual. Those who met him for the first time at Amerongen Castle found him unaffected, charming, supremely courteous, and kindly; again he was as Winston Churchill had seen him: exhibiting "the freedom and manner of an agreeable host at an English country-house party," that easy charm he always displayed when in informal circumstances and not compelled to act the warlord. Softly, the Kaiser now uttered his first request after leaving the lands of his Hohenzollern forefathers: "What I should like, my dear count, is a cup of tea—good, hot English tea."

---

gium who met William at the border indicates previous knowledge of the Kaiser's intentions. However, as Ilsemann makes abundantly clear in *Der Kaiser in Holland,* the Kaiser and his officers, both at Spa and on the royal train, were not at all sure that asylum would be granted; in fact, they had their gravest doubts, fearing the Dutch would succumb to Allied pressure. The fact that the Dutch queen had to tell William she'd have to call a ministerial council and the fact that she kept the Kaiser waiting anxiously for hours until the council had decided indicate that the final decision to grant asylum was made after the Kaiser had entered Holland, not in advance of the trip.

18

"I Take My Stand Before the Throne of My Fathers. . ."

"IN peace," said the emperor's erstwhile Chancellor von Bülow, "the Kaiser was a war-lord; in war, he evaded taking decisions, and in defeat, he fled." [240] It was an unkind cut: The Kaiser had no choice but to flee, for the Germans were sick of him. To the surprise of everyone, all of William's best characteristics emerged once he had been forcibly retired. Since there was no need for him to bluster and posture, he became an English country gentleman, the role he secretly liked most. The belligerent mustaches, which had defiantly etched his imperial initial on his uncertain face, now began to sag; soon a gray, pointed beard was added, giving him the appearance of a kindly grandfather happy to play with small children. His energies were still prodigious, but channeled differently. In his first eighteen months at Amerongen, he felled more than 1,000 trees. More followed at Haus Doorn, the villa into which he moved in mid-1920; there were so many that he occasionally autographed logs for visitors to take home as souvenirs, while others went to heat the homes of villagers.

The Dutch government courageously refused to extradite him when the Allies wanted to put the ex-Kaiser on trial as a war criminal. They extracted from William and his former crown prince a promise that they would not engage in political activities while in Holland. Both men kept their word, and the former Kaiser soon proved to be a model exile. To keep himself in trim, he continued to cut down trees, even in his seventies; to keep his mind active, he wrote apologias and formed a local literary society, reading papers on historical, scientific, and other subjects to the local intelligentsia and visitors. He was shattered by the death in 1921 of his wife, Augusta, to whom he had been married for forty years, but he was soon consoled by a thirty-five-year-old widow with five children, Princess Hermine von Schönaich-Carolath, who was born a Princess of Reuss, an ancient Thuringian house. He married her in 1923, outraging some monarchists at home and distressing his eldest son, the former crown prince, but assuring him a happy and tranquil old age surrounded not only by his own grandchildren but by those children his new wife brought to Haus Doorn.

Former Crown Prince William returned to Germany in 1923, on the promise of good behavior; he quickly became known as the "crown prince of sport," as a playboy and skirt chaser. This being a time of turmoil, he rose to its challenges by becoming trivial. Finally, he associated himself with the right-wing Stahlhelm ("Steel Helmet") organization, and two of his brothers—Oscar and Augustus William ("Auwi")—joined the Nazi Party in 1931. Two years later the former crown prince also put on the brown uniform of the Nazis, although he characteristically restricted himself to joining one of their most trivial formations, the NSKK, or National Socialist Motorists' Corps. Two of his sons also joined the party.

It is a commonplace to say that Nazism was built on the ruins of Weimar; it is more accurate to say it was built on the ruins of the House of Hohenzollern. The constitutional monarchy which had been set up in October, 1918, under Prince Max of Baden was not destroyed by the fact that Scheidemann proclaimed Germany a republic from the Reichstag window a month later. It was destroyed because a revolutionary situation had been allowed to develop, making Scheidemann's pronouncement imperative. This revolutionary situation developed because Kaiser William II obstinately refused to abdicate in time. When he did abdicate, it was too late. Because he was interested only in preserving the rights and privileges of his house, he failed to preserve the constitutional monarchy; because he was interested in saving his own prerogatives, he failed to save Germany. The trend of the Weimar Republic was immediately apparent. It may even be discerned in Ebert's proclamation of November 9, 1918. In it, he had to *plead* with German officials to serve a system which he knew they abhorred; their abhorrence of the republic continued until Hitler killed it off on January 30, 1933. The entire *Führungsschicht*—leadership caste—of Germany had been in the service of the autocratic, absolutist, authoritarian monarchy; from the day the month-old constitutional monarchy died, they either tried actively to subvert the democratic republic or helped Hitler kill it by withholding from the republic their active support. As economic crises radicalized the German proletariat and the German lower middle classes, these leaders of German life and public opinion—officials, officers, judges, press czars, financiers, educators, etc.—gave moral support to the "nationalist" extremists. When the ex-crown prince joined the Stahlhelm organization and his brothers Oscar and Auwi joined the National Socialist German Workers Party (NSDAP), they were at one and the same time merely following the example of other German "nationalist patriots" and, by dignifying these groups with their presence, also setting the mass of the Germans an example.

It became clear how greatly the fall of the House of Hohenzollern was convulsing the nation. If the Kaiser had granted his people a constitutional monarchy in 1916, most of the future would have looked completely different. The Nazi future would almost certainly have been avoided even if the Kaiser had stepped down in favor of one of his grandsons in October, 1918, a month before he was compelled to abdicate. The constitutional monarchy would have been given a very good chance at survival, and the constitutional monarchy would have survived the political crises of the 1920's. The left-wing radicals would still have been active, of course, but the greatest danger in Germany in the past, in the present, and in the future comes from the *right,* not from the left, and the thrust of the right wing would have been blunted with a Hohenzollern on the throne. The entire German *Führungsschicht,* conservative, nationalist, and even reactionary almost to a man during the 1920's, would have remained loyal. It would have supported a Hohenzollern constitutional monarchy, and grown accustomed to a parliamentary democracy sanctioned by a Hohenzollern regent acting on behalf of a Hohenzollern heir. The nationalists and conservatives would not have helped extreme right-wingers overthrow such a constitutional monarchy; they would have defended it against the "plebeian" Nazis, whom they would have recognized as dangerous revolutionaries. If the Nazis had tried to storm the House of Hohenzollern, they would have been smashed quickly; the Reichswehr, which never could reconcile its monarchist loyalties with service to the republic, would have rallied to save the government of their Hohenzollern sovereign.

Because the conservative nationalists hated the democratic republic, they let the Nazis destroy it; indeed, many among them financed the process and cheered it on. So, too, with the Hohenzollerns; instead of defending the German republic against the Nazi onslaught, they helped the Nazis along. They did so, apparently, out of the misguided idea that Hitler might reestablish the monarchy; when that proved a vain hope, they continued to do so out of the shabby hope that they, their families and their properties might profit. In June, 1931, Prince Augustus William, son of the former Kaiser, proclaimed, "Where a Hitler leads, a Hohenzollern can follow." A year later, former Crown Prince William did precisely that, supporting Hitler as presidential candidate, against Field Marshal Hindenburg (the man whom his father, the former Kaiser, now hated, blaming Hindenburg for chasing him out of the country against his will). In 1933 the Hohenzollern princes lent themselves to Nazi propaganda displays, further dignifying the Nazi thugs by their presence and tacit approval. They ultimately broke with the Nazis—that is to say, they "kept themselves aloof" (*distanzierten sich*). The opportunity now arose for the Hohenzollerns to assume again their historic role as German leaders. No evaluation of their dynasty could be complete without a glance at how the Hohenzollerns met the greatest threat Germany ever encountered, the threat of Nazi tyranny, and how they responded to the greatest challenge Germans met at the time: the challenge of resistance.

Resistance groups of various shadings were forming throughout Germany during the 1930's; a number of these groups began to consider the possibility of either restoring the Hohenzollern monarchy after staging a successful *coup d'état* against Hitler or making one of the Hohenzollerns leader of the nation temporarily, until the final form of a post-Nazi government might be decided by means of free elections. Professor Johannes Popitz, Prussian finance minister since 1933, was one of those most anxious to restore the House of Hohenzollern. The former Kaiser and former Crown Prince William having, respectively, abdicated and renounced the succession, Popitz's thoughts were not directed toward either of these; in any event, he and most of the others in the resistance movement discounted using the former crown prince, for reasons associated with his character and style of life. Count Fritz von der Schulenburg, another conspirator, had already been warned against making use of the former crown prince by his own father, who had been the former crown prince's chief of staff in World War I. Those who knew the former crown prince best were precisely the ones most skeptical about his usefulness. Despite this, the leaders of the conspiracy—specifically Carl Goerdeler and Colonel General Ludwig Beck—wanted to satisfy themselves about the attitudes toward Nazism displayed by the former crown prince; they apparently came to the conclusion that he was "sufficiently skeptical" not to be written off entirely as a possibility, despite his 1932 support of Hitler. Beck was willing to consider him, although he regarded him as "a most questionable figure" because of his notorious private life. Beck discussed the former crown prince with several officers, and Goerdeler even discussed using him with Colonel Count Claus Schenk von Stauffenberg, the man who ultimately planted the July 20, 1944, bomb; Count von Stauffenberg was not very enthusiastic about former Crown Prince William. As we shall see, however, that particular Hohenzollern was nevertheless given a chance to serve the anti-Nazi cause.

Very briefly, Popitz's thoughts turned to making use of Prince Oscar of Prussia, one of the former crown prince's brothers and one of the two who had joined the Nazis in 1931, only to be disillusioned and disgusted by them afterward. Oscar, however, was soon replaced in the thoughts of the conspirators by the former crown prince's sons. The eldest of these was Prince William, born 1906, as heir apparent to the succession; however, he contracted a morganatic marriage and, in accordance with Hohenzollern custom, renounced his rights as head of the house in 1933, in favor of his next-eldest brother, Prince Louis Ferdinand, born in 1907.

Louis Ferdinand was by far the most interesting Hohenzollern possibility. He had completed his studies in Berlin in 1929 and had then gone on an extended trip through North and South America. He worked for a time on the assembly line of the Ford Motor Company, had met people of all walks of life, was reputedly liberal and intelligent and cultured; he had even come to know President Franklin D. Roosevelt personally, a fact which weighed heavily in the minds of the anti-Nazi Germans, especially in later war years, when they thought this might ameliorate peace conditions for Germany once Hitler was removed from power. When Louis Ferdinand's eldest brother, William, renounced his rights to the succession as head of the house, his grandfather, ex-Kaiser William, ordered Louis Ferdinand back home to Germany. The Nazis had just come to power and tried to win his allegiance, but Louis Ferdinand's eyes had been opened and his mind enlarged during years of travel, and he refused any association with the Nazi leaders. This, of course, quickly became known, causing the conspirators to approach this prince in the hope he might associate himself with them.

None of the active conspirators was a nationally well-known figure in Germany, and the idea of restoring the monarchy was motivated principally by this fact. It was not just a matter of staging a successful *putsch* against Hitler, of throwing the Nazis out of office, but in this heyday of Nazi successes it was necessary to replace Hitler with a figure which could unite the nation. Furthermore, there was the crucial question of how to justify overthrowing Hitler, a question which became even more acute from 1938 to 1942, the period of Hitler's greatest diplomatic and military successes. The conspirators were prepared to lay before the German people the monstrous catalogue of Nazi crimes, of murders kept secret from them by the Goebbels-ruled press, but wondered if the German people would even believe them. Beck, chief of the General Staff until his reassignment in 1938, was a respected figure, but if he staged a *putsch,* many Germans might simply regard it as a usurpation of legitimate authority by a junta of power-hungry generals. The conspirators believed the catalogue of Nazi crimes would be best released over the signature of a Hohenzollern heir, whose word would tend to be believed.

Louis Ferdinand was initiated into the plans of the conspirators by Dr. Otto John, a Lufthansa executive, in 1937. A year later these plans took definite form. It seemed to the conspirators that Hitler was bent on dragging Germany into a war which they could not justify to their consciences and which they felt sure would be ruinous for Germany. Beck resigned from the General Staff in protest against these plans, and General Franz Halder took his place. Halder was already convinced of the need for "practical opposition" against Hitler and prepared for a *coup d'état* in the event Hitler actually went to war. Plans were ready in 1938; troops stood by, prepared to move on Berlin and capture the capital; all that was required was for the British and French to stand fast and threaten war against Germany if Hitler insisted on annexing the Sudetenland. Emissaries were sent to London to urge Neville Chamberlain and Lord Halifax to do just that; they even went to see Churchill, then out of power. The trigger for the coup was to be an Anglo-French threat of war; the conspirators in Berlin felt certain they could "justify" overthrowing Hitler if they told the German people they did it to save the peace. The British and French, however, collapsed at the Munich Conference, and Hitler staged his greatest bloodless victory since the Anschluss of Austria; as far as the German people were concerned, he had triumphed and at the same time had saved the peace. The conspirators were dismayed; the rug had been pulled out from under them.

The reaction of the two leading Hohenzollerns—the ex-Kaiser in Holland and the ex-crown prince in Potsdam—to this disaster was revealing. Former Crown Prince William sent a secret letter to Chamberlain, thanking him "for saving the peace"; the ex-Kaiser sent a letter (in indelible pencil) to Queen Mary, saying he had not the slightest doubt that Chamberlain "was inspired by heaven and guided by God" for averting "a most fearful catastrophe." Both men clearly wanted to have the peace maintained, both men rejected the idea that it had been Hitler who had saved the peace, but both men completely failed to understand the implications of the Anglo-French surrender at Munich.

In November, 1938, when anti-Semitic measures escalated furiously in Nazi Germany, the former Kaiser is said to have remarked that he felt ashamed of being a German.[241] How much his attitude toward the world had changed and how much the Nazis now came to dislike the Hohenzollerns were made clear by events surrounding the ex-Kaiser's eightieth birthday in January, 1939. Queen Mary having already broken the ice by responding to the ex-Kaiser's penciled letter, the British royal family sent him congratulatory telegrams. By way of contrast, all German officers, active and reserve, were specifically forbidden by Hitler to send greetings to their exiled former commander in chief. Only two aged field marshals were allowed to visit the ex-Kaiser at Haus Doorn, these being Rupprecht, former Crown Prince of Bavaria, and the eighty-nine-year-old Mackensen, the man who had initiated the custom of German officers kissing William II's hand.

Two Englishmen, Robert Bruce Lockhart and John W. Wheeler-Bennett, stayed as guests at Haus Doorn for a weekend during August, 1939. Wheeler-Bennett found the Kaiser greatly changed. In Edwardian English, peppered with such adjectives as "ripping" and "topping," the former emperor spoke frankly about the world situation. Wheeler-Bennett found him to be "a charming, humorous and courteous old gentleman—though full of guile." Providence, the ex-Kaiser said, allotted all peoples only a certain amount of *Lebensraum;* nations and peoples must defend and develop this living space but not take more than their allotted share. He told his British visitors that all great empires had failed because their rulers had not been content with their allotted space and added that others would fail for the same reason. Wheeler-Bennett asked him if he meant by these future failures the British Empire or the Third Reich, and the ex-Kaiser responded archly, "You may take it whichever way you choose." On bidding his visitors farewell, William said, "Come back and see me again next Summer, if you can. But you won't be able to, because the machine is running away with *him* as it ran away with *me.*" [242]

A week later, war broke out. The Netherlands' Queen Wilhelmina offered the ex-Kaiser a refuge on one of the Dutch colonial islands, and the British suggested sending him to Sweden or Denmark, but all these offers were politely declined. In Germany, fifteen Hohenzollern princes went into active service in the armed forces, and the first Hohenzollern prince to be killed, during the Polish campaign of 1939, was one of Prince Oscar's sons. Louis Ferdinand, who had once worked for Lufthansa, entered the Luftwaffe. By November, 1939, Lufthansa's Dr. John had brought him into close contact with some of the leaders of the anti-Nazi underground: with Colonel General Kurt Freiherr von Hammerstein-Equord, with jurist Hans von Dohnanyi, with theologian Dr. Dietrich Bonhoeffer and his brother, Dr. Klaus Bonhoeffer, with attorney Joseph Wirmer and merchant Justus Delbrück. It was during this time that Louis Ferdinand also came to know Jakob Kaiser, postwar West German minister for all-German affairs, a trade-union leader who was among the most active anti-Nazi conspirators during the Hitler era.

Not much developed from these early contacts. Hitler's blitzkrieg had been too successful; the conspirators wanted to wait until the first front-line reverses dampened the enthusiasm of the German people. Meanwhile, they tried to gain adherents to their cause.

This cause was damaged by Hohenzollern blunders in 1940. The year began with the ex-Kaiser acquitting himself well. In the early hours of May 10, German armies invaded the Netherlands, and on that same day, Winston Churchill asked Lord Halifax whether the ex-Kaiser ought not to be told that he could seek refuge in Britain and that he would be treated "with consideration and dignity" by his English cousins. King George VI agreed to this, and the invitation was duly extended. But William replied courteously that he would not desert the Dutch people "in their misfortune"; he also said at the time that he did not want "to run away" again, having been charged with doing that in November, 1918. A German army guard was placed before Haus Doorn—to keep German soldiers away—but the place soon became a shrine for German officers and men stationed in or traveling through Holland.

Two weeks later, on May 25, the French campaign cost another Hohenzollern his life. This was a lieutenant and company commander, Prince William, the eldest son of the former crown prince, who was severely wounded on that day and died of his wounds three days later. His body was taken to Potsdam, and the funeral turned into a gathering of monarchists, "old Prussian" officer families, and anti-Nazi conspirators. The fact that

50,000 Berliners flocked to pay their last respects was taken by Hitler as a monarchist—or at any rate "disloyal"—demonstration; to forestall any future occurrences of this kind, Hitler issued orders that no Hohenzollerns were to be allowed near the front after that.

On June 14, 1940, the Nazi armies marched into Paris, to the accompaniment of a monumental Hohenzollern blunder. The ex-Kaiser sent Hitler a personal telegram, congratulating him on his victory. This was accompanied by two separate telegrams sent by the former crown prince (in May and in June), in which he addressed the Nazi dictator as "my Führer," which he closed with the Nazi phrase *"Sieg Heil!"* and in which he expressed admiration for Hitler's "genial leadership," even saying he wished he could shake Hitler's hand. These telegrams, published in Germany, shattered the monarchists in the anti-Nazi resistance movement. Why had the former Kaiser and his son sent these telegrams to a man they both despised? It is possible that the ex-Kaiser was simply swept away by enthusiasm over French "humiliation," although Wheeler-Bennett suggests that the initiative for his telegram might have come from the "gentlemen of his *Umgebung,*" of his entourage, who were more enthusiastic about the Nazis than was the former emperor himself. As for the two telegrams sent by the former crown prince, they seemed to have been motivated by rather shabby reasons: by his wish to ingratiate himself with Hitler so as to improve the position of the Hohenzollern family and its properties in Nazi Germany.

The ex-Kaiser died on June 4, 1941, and redeemed himself once more. Hitler had wanted to bury him in Germany, in ceremonies which would clearly establish Hitler's claim as successor to the late emperor, but this was stopped on the ex-Kaiser's personal instructions. He had asked to be buried near where he had lived for twenty years, in the grounds of Haus Doorn, among his Dutch neighbors; this last wish of his was granted.

In July, 1942, resistance leader Carl Goerdeler visited Prince Louis Ferdinand on his estate, coming away very much impressed with the young man's cosmopolitan air, his cultural and intellectual level, and his democratic attitudes. Certain doubts existed whether he might not have lost some of his "majesty" and "dignity" during his adventurous years, but Goerdeler felt these were more than compensated for by the positive sides of his character, as well as by the fact that he knew President Roosevelt. Most important was the fact that Louis Ferdinand stated flatly that he was ready to place himself at the disposal of the conspirators in the event of a successful *coup d'état,* even if only as "a private person." In the months that followed, Jakob Kaiser met Louis Ferdinand several times. In December, 1942, Kaiser met with a Herr von Knebel-Döberitz, a representative of the old Prussian landowning families in the resistance movement, and Knebel-Döberitz told him that Prince Louis Ferdinand could probably be won over to issuing a proclamation to the German army, reiterating his renunciation of the throne but saying that he was taking over the command of the army temporarily in order to save Germany and make possible a speedy end to the war. Knebel-Döberitz suggested to Kaiser that Louis Ferdinand be named *Reichsttathalter* ("Reich governor") for ten years, after which the people would vote on the future form of the German state. This latter aspect of the plan didn't appeal to the other conspirators, but they were still agreed that some use should be made of the Hohenzollerns. Jakob Kaiser was asked if the German Catholics would accept a Hohenzollern; Kaiser, the Catholic trade unionist, replied in the affirmative. When asked if the German working classes would accept a Hohenzollern, Wilhelm Leuschner, the SPD trade unionist in the conspiracy, said they would, if this were the only way one could get rid of the Nazi tyranny.

Prince Louis Ferdinand, however, was reluctant to usurp the rights of his father, the former crown prince who had become head of the House of Hohenzollern upon the death of the ex-Kaiser. Further, the officers in the conspiracy were not as enthusiastic about Louis Ferdinand as they might be about his father; whatever faults the former crown prince possessed, he at least had been an army commander in World War I and was known to them, whereas Louis Ferdinand was an unknown quantity to the military. It was therefore decided that former Crown Prince William should make the first move, and a proclamation was drafted (presumably by Knebel-Döberitz) in the winter of 1942–43. This document, which was found among Goerdeler's papers after the Gestapo murdered him, has a wonderfully monarchical ring about it. Excerpts:

> When I renounced the crown of Prussia and the German imperial dignity, I did not do so in order to clear the way for a development which now has destroyed the blameless reputation of the German people and besmirched its spotless shield of honor. A condition of injustice, of tyranny and of moral savagery has developed, such as has never before existed in the history of our people. . . .

The statement then catalogued many examples of bestial Nazi crimes and murders and stated that "the blood of German soldiers and the happiness of German families can no longer be spilled and destroyed, so as to enable inhuman criminals to conduct such cowardly crimes." German youngsters must no longer be forced, the statement continued, "to obey the bloodthirsty commands of conscienceless leaders."

> When my forefathers took over the Mark Brandenburg, they enforced law and order upon the selfish nobility. Justice and decency came to be the pride of the German people. I have not renounced the throne in order to deliver the Reich to madmen and criminals. . . . The Führer broke his oath to the German people by means of secret murders.
>
> I take my stand before the throne of my fathers, before which injustice had not been tolerated, before the labors of our ancestors, in order to save their achievements. . . .
>
> I have assumed the leadership of the Reich and the supreme command of the Wehrmacht. Soldiers and officials will give an oath which they can keep with an upright heart, even as I swear before God to lead the Reich in justice and decency, in faithfulness and honesty. I shall therefore command that the responsible criminals are to be seized and placed before courts. The German people shall be given the opportunity of judging the size and extent of the crimes and danger.
>
> We are still at war, but we shall work together for a peace which fulfills our national requirements, which guarantees the freedom of the nation and of every German in a state based on justice and decency, and which does not destroy the freedoms or happiness of other peoples. . . . As soon as this goal has been achieved, my son Prince Louis Ferdinand will take my place. . . .[243]

Not only might this ringing document have rallied the entire Wehrmacht behind the conspirators, for a large percentage of senior army officers were already either in the resistance or sympathetic to it, but it might have rallied the entire German people. Its unequivocal admission of monstrous Nazi crimes and its declaration that the criminals would be punished by the Germans themselves would have done much to alter the future. The Germans would have saved themselves and their nation, as well as countless hundreds of thousands of Jews and other victims of Nazism as yet not murdered by that year. Unfortunately, former Crown Prince William never signed that document or issued it. Dr. Otto John declared afterward that the former crown prince was later very angry at the "presumptuousness" of the monarchists in the resistance movement.*

It became abundantly clear to the German anti-Nazi resistance movement that it could expect nothing from the former crown prince, and so it once again turned directly to Prince Louis Ferdinand, his eldest surviving son. Two meetings were held with the prince, first in the home of Professor Karl Bonhoeffer, father of the two Bonhoeffers in the resistance movement, Klaus and Dietrich, and second in the home of Dr. Klaus Bonhoeffer himself. Those present included Goerdeler, Jakob Kaiser, Wilhelm Leuschner, Dr. Wirmer, and Ewald von Kleist-Schmenzin, the last-named being a Prussian conservative who was one of the most passionate anti-Nazis among the conspirators, a man who had published anti-Nazi tracts before Hitler came to power and who had been plotting against Hitler ever since 1933. Ulrich von Hassel, the German ambassador in

* It might be noted, however, that the Allies were not ready to welcome a German anti-Nazi initiative. In November, 1941, Jakob Kaiser called together a meeting of prominent German anti-Nazis in the home of attorney Wirmer, to which the American journalist Louis P. Lochner was invited. Lochner was asked to test out President Roosevelt's reaction to a restoration of the Hohenzollern monarchy under Louis Ferdinand, and Lochner agreed to visit the White House when next in the United States. Pearl Harbor delayed his return to America until July, 1942, and Lochner never succeeded in gaining Roosevelt's ear. Lochner's report on the German resistance movement was buried, and Lochner was told that such information had to be kept secret because it was "highly embarrassing" to the war effort. Official policy was that all Germans, especially all German conservatives and officers, were Nazis, when in actual fact, the officers and conservatives, the Junkers and landowners, the monarchists and the nobility were least taken in by the Nazis and resisted them far more strenuously than did the average "little German."

Rome, also attended the second meeting. All these men pleaded with Prince Louis Ferdinand to take radical action: to announce himself as pretender to the throne of his forefathers and to "give the signal for a revolt of the generals." Louis Ferdinand, however, could not bring himself to usurp his father's claims to the throne and refused to do so without his father's express permission. It was not that he believed his action would not achieve the stated goal, and it certainly was not that he was afraid to act, for he had been risking his life for years by attending secret meetings of the anti-Nazi underground movement; it was simply that he could not do otherwise than place his obligations toward the dynasty ahead of his obligations to the German people.

Former Crown Prince William told his son that he "rejected the dangerous adventure" and warned him earnestly and successfully "not to meddle in such conspiracies." [244]

Carl Goerdeler thereafter discounted the Hohenzollerns, though he himself would have preferred a restoration of the monarchy. In the extensive notes he left behind, which plot out the course of the Germany he and General Beck hoped to establish after their coup against Hitler, the only Hohenzollern name he mentioned as being conceivably "worthy" of leading the German people was that of the crown prince's youngest son, Prince Frederick. But that prince was never seriously considered.

The last chance at redeeming Hohenzollern honor in this time of the greatest national need had been passed by, as had the last chance at a restoration of the House of Hohenzollern. At a time when the historic leaders of Germany should have led, they failed to do so. They remained passive and inconsequential. The former crown prince thought of himself as head of an ancient Christian royal house, but he could not find the same Christian motivation to resist Nazism which moved Germany's lesser nobility to action; he could not even find patriotism enough to make him move or to let his son take action. Anyone wishing to build a case against the idea that monarchies produce men of majesty need only look at the action of the former crown prince during this time of terrible need; anyone wishing to argue that noble blood produces noble men need only look at the long list of German counts, barons, and others of noble birth who risked everything to fight Hitler and who sacrificed their lives for humanity, as well as Germany. The tables had turned on the Hohenzollerns. This was a time when the Prussian Junker nobles whom they once suppressed proved to be more noble than the heir to their former sovereign house.

While these conspirators acted and later paid for their actions, the former crown prince frittered away his time with his twenty-five-year-old mistress, Gerda Puhlmann, a former entertainer at Berlin's Skala. He was captured by the French on May 4, 1945. Some weeks later, at Lindau, he complained to General Jean de Lattre de Tassigny that he had lost all his "acceptable dwelling places." The general replied, "You have lost above all, monsieur, the sense of dignity. After the collapse of your country, at the age of sixty-five [actually sixty-three], the father of six children, you have no other interest than for your own comfort, the house of your idle hours, the woman of your pleasures. You are to be pitied, monsieur, that is really all I have to say to you."

The woman of his pleasures left him in 1947, and the former crown prince consoled himself with a hairdresser and chambermaid named Stefi Ritl, who stayed with him until he died on June 21, 1951. Five days later his body, clad in the uniform of the Death's Head Hussars, was put to rest in the family vault of Hohenzollernburg Castle near Hechingen. Four Hohenzollern princes mounted guard about his coffin; every German royal house was represented, and for the first time in the history of such occasions, all those present were in civilian clothes. Among the wreaths displayed, many of which bore the names of illustrious old regiments, was one which bore the Napoleonic initial N, surmounted by a crown, and was sent by the pretender to the throne of France.

A year later, the bones of two other Hohenzollerns were laid to rest in the same castle. Their two coffins had been removed from Potsdam during the war, had remained in Thuringia until 1945, and had then been transported, by courtesy of the United States Army, to the American Zone of Occupation. They contained the remains of Frederick William I, Prussia's Soldier King, and of his son, the greatest Hohenzollern of them all, Frederick the Great. They rested in Marburg until 1952, when they were placed in the family vault in the Hohenzollernburg, that majestic castle which had been built near the site of ancient Zolorin Castle. The Hohenzollerns had returned home to Swabia, whence they had originally come.

Dynasties such as the Hohenzollerns are governed by life cycles, even as are families and individual men: They thrive during a vigorous youth, grow great during a time of challenge and enormous effort, become settled in success, grow rigid in old age, and finally wither and die, to become part of the mulch in which new and often vigorous forms of life spring up. As in William Shakespeare's "seven ages of man," the succession of men who made up the House of Hohenzollern seemed to have moved, almost inexorably, toward "mere oblivion," in stages which can be clearly discerned and which reflect the dynamics of evolution and involution, as well as of struggle, progress, and decay. Throughout the 900 years of this dynasty's life, great periods of exertion and effort were followed by periods of torpor and passivity; dynamic growth gave way to stagnation and the capacity for forceful change relapsed into recidivism. The seed-time of this dynasty consisted of those several hundred years in which it gathered strength prior to moving to the Mark Brandenburg, the place of its manifest destiny, the arena in which it would build itself by pitting itself against great odds. The tasks demanded of the Hohenzollern margraves in the dynasty's second phase produced forceful and energetic men; this was the time when the family consolidated its power within its new lands, disciplined its refractory Junker nobility, and subdued its independent-minded towns. A third phase was ushered in after the Thirty Years' War: it also was a time of enormous exertions. The Great Elector and the first two Prussian kings set their stamp on this time by means of vast administrative reforms, cultural adornments, and the fostering of trade and commerce. However "monstrous" the person of King Frederick William I may seem, as a public person he looms as one of the great Hohenzollern monarchs, for he built not only the kingdom's instrument for greatness, its army, but a state machine which was efficient and incorruptible, loyal and hard-working, frugal, alert, wakeful, and enterprising. He had no aggressive ambitions or instincts and was content to see Prussia hum with industry and enterprise.

It seems clear that stagnation could have set in at precisely this point in the career of the Hohenzollerns, for Frederick William I was content to husband and defend his lands and lacked the vision to see what Prussia might become. Had his successor been anyone except Frederick the Great, Prussia might have remained only one of several important German states and never have attained its dominant position. The vigorous young king, however, was the instrumentality needed to prevent crystallization at this point: a shock which maintained the forward thrust.

Frederick II's audacious (if outrageous) attack on the Habsburgs, followed by his survival in the face of a mighty European coalition determined to destroy Prussia forever, put Prussia finally on the map as one of the great powers and gave it, in Silesia, both the additional manpower it needed and the agricultural and mineral wealth which helped ensure its growth. The cynical partitioning of Poland which took place in the latter part of his reign not only expanded the Hohenzollern lands, but gave them some cohesion.

It was Frederick II, even more than his Soldier King father, who also gave Prussia the character of a military garrison state, animated by a military ethos. This forceful, indefatigable king, whose reputation rests so heavily on feats of arms, was not, however, principally a warlike example to his people. His long reign, most of which passed in peace, determined and actuated the beliefs, standards, and ideals of his subjects, for Frederick, whose life was effort personified and the very embodiment of struggle, set the Prussian ethos the example of his own spirit. He taught his people industriousness and incorruptibility, modesty and frugality, just as his father had done, but he also set on the Prussian ethic the stamp of his own cultured and often-enlightened personality. Prussia, under the Great Elector, had already become a haven for religious refugees; Frederick the Great reinforced this tradition of tolerance and set Europe the example of liberality by abolishing torture and establishing freedom of the press. Prussianism, as it was now being shaped, included not only its most obvious external characteristic, militarism, but its most unusual feature: a devotion to the rule of law, to which even the king was subject. In Prussia, even the humblest citizen could demand satisfaction from his king through the courts; he was not restricted to petitioning the king, but could sue him. (As noted, Kaiser William II lost such a court action and was compelled to pay the court costs of the plaintiff, an action which outraged him, but to which he had to submit under the system his forefathers had wrought.)

A foretaste of the fate of Prussia once the dry rot had begun to settle in the House of Hohenzollern was provided, though briefly, by the short-lived collapse of Prussia under the onslaught of Napoleon Bonaparte. A smug satisfaction had replaced industriousness, slumber had replaced wakefulness, and Prussia was conquered. But so great was the velocity inherent in Frederick the Great's reign that enough of the spirit he had inculcated into the land survived, enabling Prussia to emerge a generation after his death and after the humiliation of Jena with greater lands and powers than it ever possessed. By a stroke of luck, it was given the Ruhr Basin, generator of Prussian strength in years to come.

Four phases of the life of the House of Hohenzollern had passed. All had been activist phases, consolidating the machinery of the state: an efficient, hardworking, and honest administration; a disciplined army rich in triumph and refreshed after Napoleon's defeat by means of a broadened base among the people; and a population devoted to work and struggle, trained in obedience on countless barracks squares and proud of a heritage of hard-fought greatness. It was on this foundation that Bismarck could construct Hohenzollern imperial majesty, first defeating the Habsburgs and ousting them from power in German affairs and then defeating the French in a war which rallied all German kingdoms behind the Hohenzollern shield. Centuries of dynamic forward thrust had made it possible to create a Second German Reich, the first German Empire in almost a millennium. No other German royal house had attained to such heights over so many centuries; no other German dynasty had achieved such great success.

In the long run, however, there is nothing that fails like success. Where there had once been nothing but tasks, work and challenges, calling forth great efforts and raising the Hohenzollerns to meet those tasks, there now came completion and fulfillment and, with completion, decline. Imperial rank had been attained in the fifth phase of the life of the Hohenzollerns

William I, their first Kaiser, slipped into a pouchy old age. All the Prussian—or Spartan—qualities on which Hohenzollern might had been constructed were now gradually becoming just old saws; an industrial boom and a prosperous, fat, gouty old age took the place of intense effort. The peak had been reached, and although there seemed to be no more worlds to conquer, the Hohenzollerns continued to retain a system no longer serviceable for the age in which they now lived. Like Shakespeare's justice, "his youthful hose well sav'd, a world too wide for his shrunk shank," the Hohenzollerns clothed themselves in the trappings of the Frederician tradition and maintained a fundamentally authoritarian eighteenth-century state even into the twentieth century. Rigidity had set in, and old forms had crystallized because the Hohenzollerns feared to jolt them. A second shock, as vivifying as that which Frederick the Great had given, was needed now and might have awakened the happily sleeping giant Germany, sliding to decay in a time of great material progress and spiritual illusion. The shock needed was a radical change in the old system: the creation of a genuine, parliamentary, constitutional monarchy, invested with the confidence of the people as a whole and responsive to the people's needs and aspirations. Such a shock would have jolted the state into a new direction, would have kept the Hohenzollerns flexibly attuned to their times, and would have thrust the state away from its progression toward decay. But the Hohenzollerns in the late nineteenth century were like hypnotized monarchs, performing their roles, as Gustav Freytag had warned, before applauding audiences and not perceiving the demons of destruction lurking in the wings. Military virtues now gave way to military pomp and panoply, hardworking officials merely became harsh, and Frederician simplicity gave way to overweening arrogance and childish show. Evolution had given way to involution—the regressive alteration of an organism characteristic of senility.

The final note in the seven ages of this dynasty was struck by the last Kaiser, a sensitive, almost effete, though blustering travesty of a Prussian soldier king—"*sans* teeth, *sans* eyes, *sans* taste, *sans* everything." His exaggerated personality set a terrible example to the German people, and his demagogic oratory inflamed bellicosity and unrestraint in them. Fabian von

Schlabrendorff, one of the officers who tried to kill Hitler, wrote of this spirit in explaining "the other side of the coin" of German civil obedience. "It becomes apparent to any serious student of German history," he writes, "that one of the basic flaws in the character of the German people is a lack of feeling for form, poise, and balance. They are comparable to a torrent of water without a river bed to contain it and give it form and direction . . . the average German's lack of natural poise led him to . . . excessive civil and military obedience, with the inherent danger of accepting and obeying *any* law and *any* authority, whether good or bad. . . ."[245]

In this last phase of the career of the Hohenzollerns, only the outer forms remained, and when forms take the place of the enlivening spirit they are meant to contain and represent, then only a travesty remains. Ever since challenges and the sheer necessity to survive in a land without natural frontiers had been removed, ever since fulfillment had taken the place of striving, ever since wakeful animation had given way to self-satisfied torpor, ever since action had been replaced by posturing, the House of Hohenzollern began to rot. "A crown," said Frederick the Great, who wore only a battered tricorn, "is just a hat that lets the rain in." By way of contrast, William II struck poses in a huge gold helmet; it failed to save him from the storms sweeping his land. Ultimately, the process of deteri oration brought down the House of Hohenzollern, a blighted if gilded, structure whose crash convulsed Germany. A nation had been deluded and put to sleep by a dynasty which in it later years was too creaking to transform itself, too enthralled with past glories to seize future opportunities. No wonde Hitler chose as his rallying cry *Deutschland Erwache!* ("Ger many, awaken!") This rootless Austrian, filled with frightfu dynamic urges, had sprung out of the manure of a ramshackl house, striking a new note which would send the lands of th Hohenzollerns along a new and more terrible course.

But it is a dreadful oversimplification to suggest, as has bee fashionable lately, that Nazism was a logical outgrowth of Pru sianism, the inevitable result of Hohenzollern rule, a "continu tion of German history," as Shirer suggests. Nazism was a gro tesque exaggeration, really a perversion, of only the autocrati aspect of Hohenzollern rule in Prussia; Nazism did away wit religious tolerance and equality of all men before the law, which were aspects of Hohenzollern rule as well. Ultimately, the best of the "Prussian spirit" showed itself on July 20, 1944, in those thousands of officers and civilians who were prepared, as a service to their nation, to risk torture and death, to risk even being branded traitors before an uncomprehending public.

Total defeat swept away almost everything the Hohenzollerns had built up, leaving it cleft in chunks for victors to devour. In 1947, Prussia was wiped off the face of the map by order of the Allied Control Council; the name Prussia no longer appears even to designate an administrative province. The lands of the Junkers have been lost to the Poles and to the Russians, perhaps for centuries, perhaps forever. What remained of the Reich over which the Hohenzollerns had reigned was split in two; Potsdam, home of the Hohenzollern kings outside Berlin, became home to the Soviet military administration in East Germany. "The accomplishments of the past," writes Prince Louis Ferdinand of Prussia, today's head of the House of Hohenzollern, ". . . cannot be obliterated: the name Hohenzollern remains indissolubly associated with the history of Germany."[247] Indeed, the Hohenzollerns were not just the makers of much of German history, but teachers to the German people, shapers of the German character, and molders of the German ethos. Much of their influence lives on even today, although much has also been lost. Those who today search for the spirit of the Hohenzollerns will find it no longer at Sans Souci Palace, but in the best and in the worst within the German people.

Genealogical Table

BRANDENBURG LINE

- Burchard I (d. 1061), Count of Zollern
  - Frederick I (d. 1115)
    - Frederick II (d. 1145)
      - Frederick III (d. *c.* 1200) Burgrave of Nuremberg as Frederick I
        - Conrad I of Nuremberg (d. *c.* 1260)
          - Frederick III (d. 1297) Burgrave of Nuremberg
            - Frederick IV (d. 1332)
              - John II (d. 1357)
                - Frederick V (1333–98) Burgrave of Nuremberg 1357–97 Prince of the Empire from 1363
                  - John III (*c.* 1369–1420) Burgrave 1397–1420
                  - Frederick VI (1371–1440) Burgrave 1397–1440 Elector of Brandenburg as Frederick I 1415–40
                    - John the Alchemist (d. 1464)
                    - Frederick II, "Iron Tooth" (1413–71), Elector of Brandenburg 1440–70
                    - Albert III, "Achilles" (1414–86), Elector of Brandenburg 1470–86
                      - John Cicero (1455–99) Elector of Brandenburg 1486–99
              - Conrad II (d. 1334)
        - Frederick IV of Zollern, II of Nuremberg (d. 1251 or 1255), founder of Swabian line
    - Burchard (d. 1150)
      - Burchard I (d. 1193) of Zollern-Hohenberg (males of senior Hohenberg line extinct 1393)

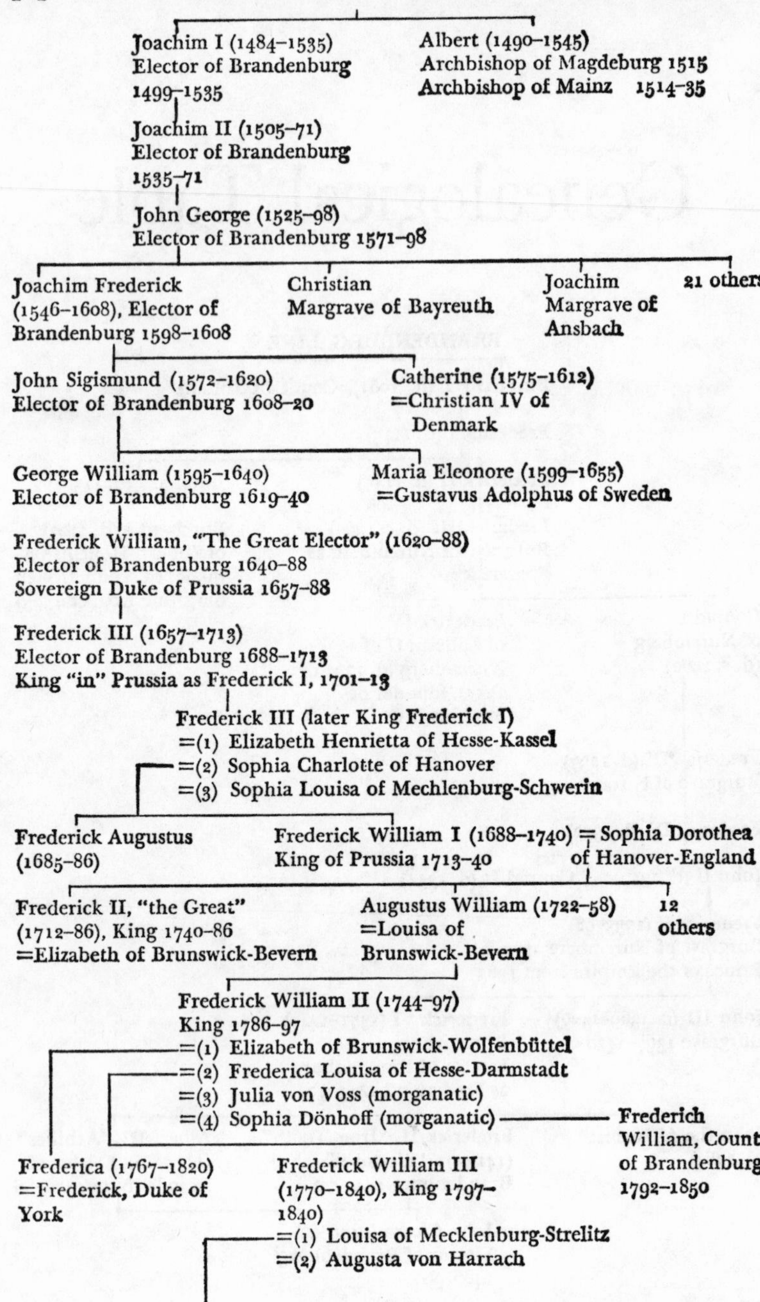
Joachim I (1484–1535)
Elector of Brandenburg
1499–1535
Albert (1490–1545)
Archbishop of Magdeburg 1515
Archbishop of Mainz 1514–35
Joachim II (1505–71)
Elector of Brandenburg
1535–71
John George (1525–98)
Elector of Brandenburg 1571–98
Joachim Frederick
(1546–1608), Elector of
Brandenburg 1598–1608
Christian
Margrave of Bayreuth
Joachim
Margrave of
Ansbach
21 others
John Sigismund (1572–1620)
Elector of Brandenburg 1608–20
Catherine (1575–1612)
=Christian IV of
Denmark
George William (1595–1640)
Elector of Brandenburg 1619–40
Maria Eleonore (1599–1655)
=Gustavus Adolphus of Sweden
Frederick William, "The Great Elector" (1620–88)
Elector of Brandenburg 1640–88
Sovereign Duke of Prussia 1657–88
Frederick III (1657–1713)
Elector of Brandenburg 1688–1713
King "in" Prussia as Frederick I, 1701–13
Frederick III (later King Frederick I)
=(1) Elizabeth Henrietta of Hesse-Kassel
=(2) Sophia Charlotte of Hanover
=(3) Sophia Louisa of Mechlenburg-Schwerin
Frederick Augustus
(1685–86)
Frederick William I (1688–1740) = Sophia Dorothea
King of Prussia 1713–40
of Hanover-England
Frederick II, "the Great"
(1712–86), King 1740–86
=Elizabeth of Brunswick-Bevern
Augustus William (1722–58)
=Louisa of
Brunswick-Bevern
12
others
Frederick William II (1744–97)
King 1786–97
=(1) Elizabeth of Brunswick-Wolfenbüttel
=(2) Frederica Louisa of Hesse-Darmstadt
=(3) Julia von Voss (morganatic)
=(4) Sophia Dönhoff (morganatic)
Frederich
William, Count
of Brandenburg
1792–1850
Frederica (1767–1820)
=Frederick, Duke of
York
Frederick William III
(1770–1840), King 1797–
1840)
=(1) Louisa of Mecklenburg-Strelitz
=(2) Augusta von Harrach

Frederick William IV (1795–1861)
King 1840–61
=Elizabeth of Bavaria

William I (1797–1888)
King 1861–88
German Emperor 1871–88
=Augusta of Saxe-Weimar

7 others

Frederick III (1831–88)
King and Emperor 1888
=Victoria of Great Britain

Frederick Charles
(1828–85), Prince
son of Charles (1801–83)
and Maria of Saxe-Weimar

William II (1859–1941)
King and Emperor 1888–1918
=(1) Augusta Victoria of Schleswig-Holstein=Sonderburg
=(2) Hermine von Schönarch=Caroloth

William (1882–1951)
Crown Prince 1888–1918
=Cecilie of Mecklenburg-Schwerin

6 others including Princes Eitel Frederick, Adalbert, Augustus William, Oscar, Joachim, and Princess Victoria Louisa

William (1906–1940)
renounces rights 1933
=Dorothea v Salviati

Louis Ferdinand (1907–)
=Grand Duchess Kyra Kirilovna
of Russia

4 others

2 Princesses of Hohenzollern

Frederick William (1939–)

Michael (1940–)

Maria Cecilia (1942–)

Kyra (1943–)

Ludwig Ferdinand (1944–)

Christian Sigmund (1946–)

Xenia (1949–)

FAMILY TIES OF WILLIAM II, GERMAN EMPEROR 1888–1918, WITH GREAT BRITAIN

Mary, Queen of Scots
1542–1567, d. 1587

James I
1603–1625

Elizabeth=Frederick V, Elector Palatine
d. 1662

Sophia =Ernest Augustus, Elector of Hanover
d. 1714

Elector Frederick III=Sophia Charlotte
of Brandenburg (King Frederick I from 1701)
1688–1713
d. 1705

George I of
England
1714–1727

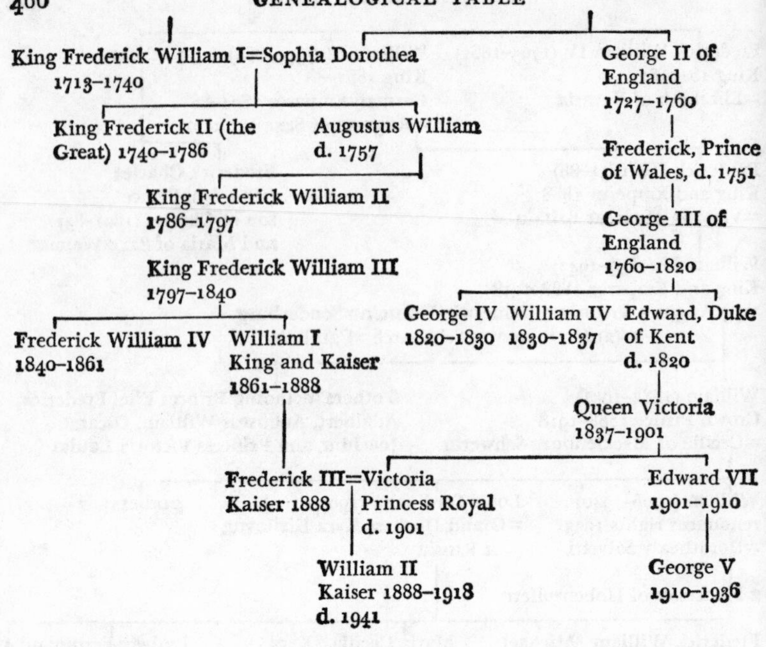
King Frederick William I=Sophia Dorothea
1713–1740
George II of England
1727–1760
King Frederick II (the Great) 1740–1786
Augustus William
d. 1757
Frederick, Prince of Wales, d. 1751
King Frederick William II
1786–1797
George III of England
1760–1820
King Frederick William III
1797–1840
George IV
1820–1830
William IV
1830–1837
Edward, Duke of Kent
d. 1820
Frederick William IV
1840–1861
William I
King and Kaiser
1861–1888
Queen Victoria
1837–1901
Frederick III=Victoria
Kaiser 1888
Princess Royal
d. 1901
Edward VII
1901–1910
William II
Kaiser 1888–1918
d. 1941
George V
1910–1936

FAMILY TIES OF WILLIAM II, GERMAN EMPEROR 1888–1918, WITH RUSSIA

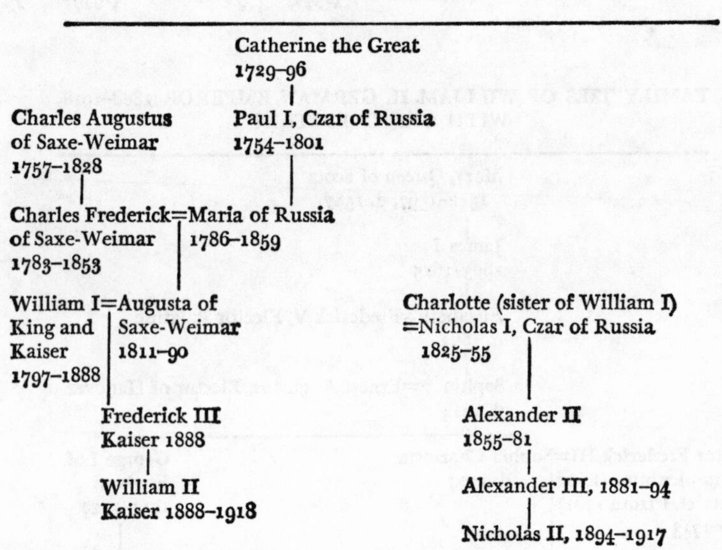
Catherine the Great
1729–96
Charles Augustus
of Saxe-Weimar
1757–1828
Paul I, Czar of Russia
1754–1801
Charles Frederick=Maria of Russia
of Saxe-Weimar
1783–1853
1786–1859
William I=Augusta of
King and
Kaiser
1797–1888
Saxe-Weimar
1811–90
Charlotte (sister of William I)
=Nicholas I, Czar of Russia
1825–55
Frederick III
Kaiser 1888
Alexander II
1855–81
William II
Kaiser 1888–1918
Alexander III, 1881–94
Nicholas II, 1894–1917

PRINCIPAL FIGURES IN THE SWABIAN LINE

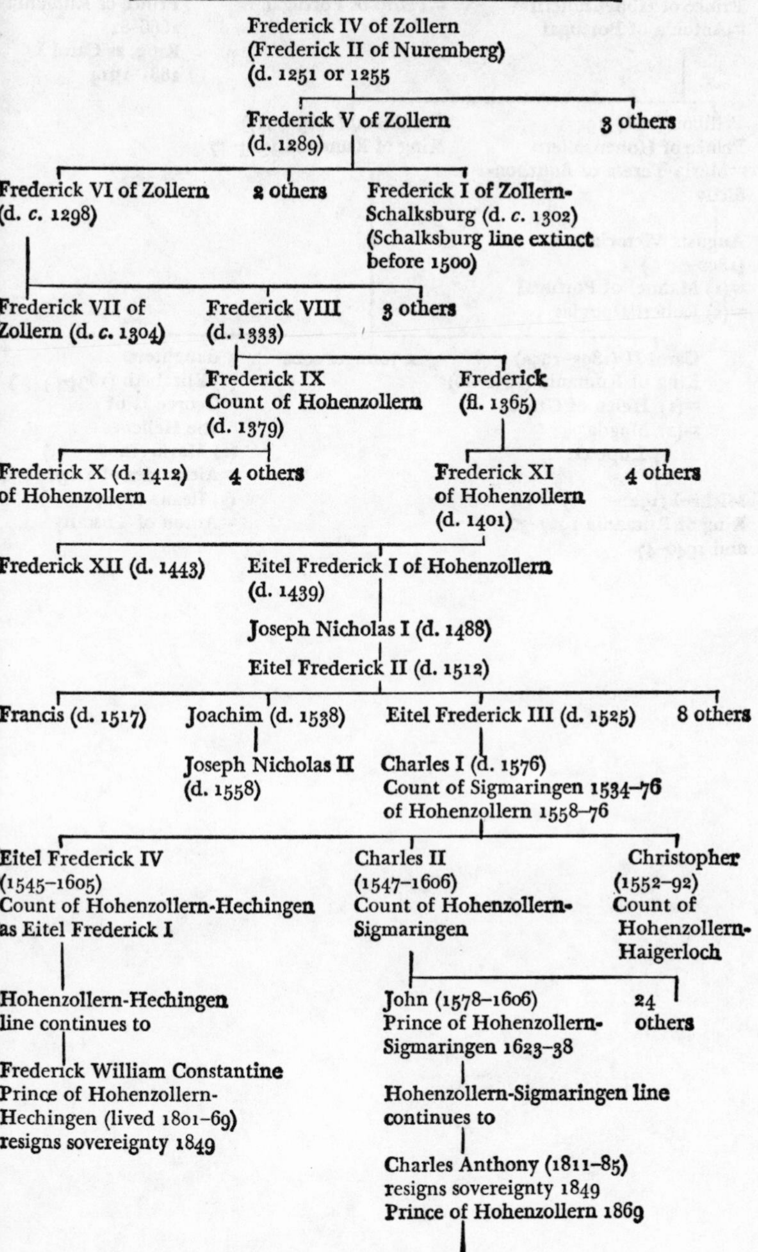
Frederick IV of Zollern
(Frederick II of Nuremberg)
(d. 1251 or 1255
Frederick V of Zollern
(d. 1289)
3 others
Frederick VI of Zollern
(d. c. 1298)
2 others
Frederick I of Zollern-Schalksburg (d. c. 1302)
(Schalksburg line extinct before 1500)
Frederick VII of Zollern (d. c. 1304)
Frederick VIII
(d. 1333)
3 others
Frederick IX
Count of Hohenzollern
(d. 1379)
Frederick
(fl. 1365)
Frederick X (d. 1412)
of Hohenzollern
4 others
Frederick XI
of Hohenzollern
(d. 1401)
4 others
Frederick XII (d. 1443)
Eitel Frederick I of Hohenzollern
(d. 1439)
Joseph Nicholas I (d. 1488)
Eitel Frederick II (d. 1512)
Francis (d. 1517)
Joachim (d. 1538)
Eitel Frederick III (d. 1525)
8 others
Joseph Nicholas II
(d. 1558)
Charles I (d. 1576)
Count of Sigmaringen 1534–76
of Hohenzollern 1558–76
Eitel Frederick IV
(1545–1605)
Count of Hohenzollern-Hechingen
as Eitel Frederick I
Charles II
(1547–1606)
Count of Hohenzollern-Sigmaringen
Christopher
(1552–92)
Count of
Hohenzollern-Haigerloch
Hohenzollern-Hechingen
line continues to
John (1578–1606)
Prince of Hohenzollern-Sigmaringen 1623–38
24
others
Frederick William Constantine
Prince of Hohenzollern-Hechingen (lived 1801–69)
resigns sovereignty 1849
Hohenzollern-Sigmaringen line
continues to
Charles Anthony (1811–85)
resigns sovereignty 1849
Prince of Hohenzollern 1869

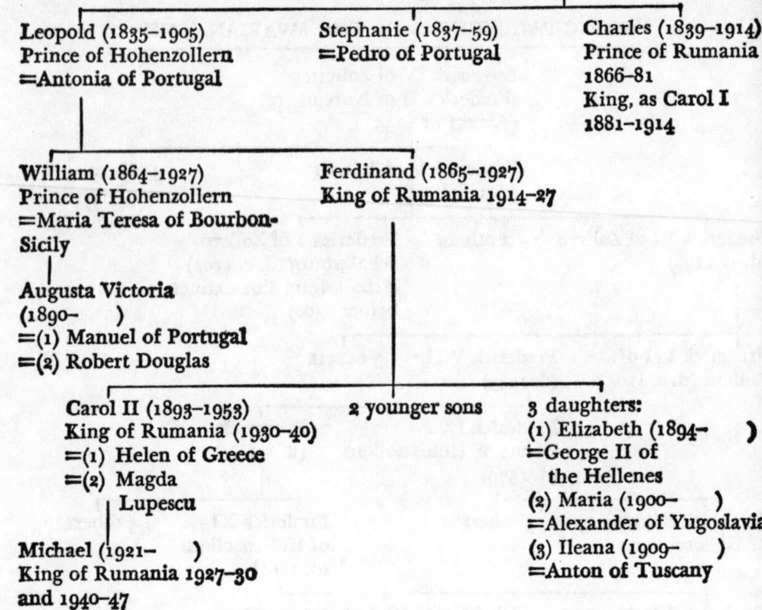
Leopold (1835–1905)
Prince of Hohenzollern
=Antonia of Portugal
Stephanie (1837–59)
=Pedro of Portugal
Charles (1839–1914)
Prince of Rumania
1866–81
King, as Carol I
1881–1914
William (1864–1927)
Prince of Hohenzollern
=Maria Teresa of Bourbon-Sicily
Ferdinand (1865–1927)
King of Rumania 1914–27
Augusta Victoria
(1890–)
=(1) Manuel of Portugal
=(2) Robert Douglas
Carol II (1893–1953)
King of Rumania (1930–40)
=(1) Helen of Greece
=(2) Magda Lupescu
2 younger sons
3 daughters:
(1) Elizabeth (1894–)
=George II of the Hellenes
(2) Maria (1900–)
=Alexander of Yugoslavia
(3) Ileana (1909–)
=Anton of Tuscany
Michael (1921–)
King of Rumania 1927–30
and 1940–47

Notes

1. G. P. Gooch, *Frederick the Great: the Ruler, the Writer, the Man* (London, Longmans, 1947), pp. 1 and v–vi.
2. Baroness Deichmann, *Impressions and Memories* (London, John Murray, 1926), p. 119.
3. A. J. P. Taylor, *The Course of German History* (London, 1966), p. 17.
4. As given in Sidney B. Fay, *The Rise of Brandenburg-Prussia to 1786,* revised by Klaus Epstein (New York, Holt, Rinehart & Winston, 1937; rev. ed. 1964), p. 8.
5. Attributed to Haftitz in Hans Ludwig, *Altberliner Bilderbogen,* (Berlin, Altberliner Verlag, 1965), p. 14; also, see Anton Ritthaler, *Die Hohenzollern: Eine Bilderbogen* (Frankfurt-am-Main and Bonn, Athenäum Verlag, 1961), p. 34.
6. Quoted in Fay, *op. cit.*, p. 32.
7. Ritthaler, *op. cit.*, p. 36.
8. Fay, *op. cit.*, p. 32.
9. Dr. Carl Friedrich Pauli, *Allgemeine Preussische Staatsgeschichte* (Halle, 1760–69), Vol. IV, p. 604, as given in Thomas Carlyle, *History of Friedrich II of Prussia, called Frederick the Great* (London, Chapman & Hall, 1858–65), Vol. I, Bk. III, Ch. XVII.
10. Carlyle, *op. cit.*, Vol. I, Bk. III, Ch. XVI.
11. J. D. E. Preuss, *Friedrich der Grosse, eine Lebensgeschichte* (Berlin, Nauck, 1832–34), Vol. I, p. 270.
12. C. Edmund Maurice, *Life of Frederick William: The Great Elector of Brandenburg* (London, 1926), p. 30: *"Ex moerore animi, et perturbatione sensuum."*
13. Förster, *Friedrich Wilhelm I, König in Preussen* (Potsdam, 1834), cited in Carlyle, *op. cit.*, Vol. I, Bk. III, Ch. XVIII.
14. Maurice, *op cit.*, p. 129.
15. Carlyle, *op. cit.*, Vol. I, Bk. III, Ch. XIX.
16. Edith Simon, *The Making of Frederick the Great* (London, Cassell, 1963), p. 8.
17. J. D. E. Preuss, *Friedrich der Grosse (Historische Skizze,* Berlin, Duncker & Humblot, 1838), p. 380, cited in Carlyle, *op. cit.*, Vol. I, Bk. III, Ch. XX. (Translated by W. H. N. from German text cited by Carlyle.)

18. Taylor, *op. cit.*, p. 18.
19. *Ibid.*, p. 19.
20. According to Frederick the Great's sister Wilhelmina, in her memoirs: Wilhelmine (Frédérique Sophie) de Prusse, Margrave de Bareith etc., *Mémoires, écrit de sa main* (Brunswick, Paris, and London, 1812).
21. According to a letter written by Field Marshal Schulenburg to his nephew, as quoted in Dr. Edward Vehse, *Memoirs of the Court of Prussia*, trans. by Franz C. F. Demmler (London, T. Nelson & Sons, 1854), p. 26.
22. Vehse, *op. cit.*, p. 28.
23. *Ibid.*, p. 29.
24. *Ibid.*
25. Harald von Koenigswald, *Preussisches Lesebuch* (München, Biederstein Verlag, 1966), p. 46.
26. Vehse, *op. cit.*, p. 42.
27. J. R. Hutchinson, *The Romance of a Regiment* (London, Sampson Low, 1898), p. 18.
28. Quoted in Koenigswald, *op. cit.*, pp. 60–63.
29. Hutchinson, *op. cit.*, p. 29.
30. *Ibid.*, p. 33.
31. *Ibid.*, pp. 97–98.
32. Vehse, *op. cit.*, p. 49.
33. *Ibid.*
34. *Ibid.*, p. 76.
35. F. L. Carsten, *The Origins of Prussia* (London, Oxford University Press, 1954), p. 276.
36. *Ibid.*, p. 277.
37. Letter of May 3, 1732, as given in Koenigswald, *op. cit.*, pp. 64–65.
38. As given in Fay, *op. cit.*, p. 92.
39. *Ibid.*
40. Ludwig Reiners, *Frederick the Great: An Informal Biography*, trans. by Lawrence P. R. Wilson (London, Oswald Wolff, 1960), p. 13.
41. *Ibid.*, p. 20.
42. *Ibid.*, p. 19.
43. *Ibid.*, p. 20.
44. Carlyle, *op. cit.*, Bk. I, Ch. IV, p. 429.
45. Vehse, *op. cit.*, p. 78.
46. Cited by Carlyle, *op. cit.*, Bk. IV, Ch. VII.
47. Simon, *op. cit.*, p. 40.
48. Carlyle, *op. cit.*, Bk. VI, Ch. II.
49. Simon, *op. cit.*, p. 54.
50. As given in Koenigswald, *op. cit.*, pp. 52–53. (Translated from the German by W. H. N.)
51. Reiners, *op. cit.*, p. 24.
52. *Ibid.*, p. 25.
53. Carlyle, *op. cit.*, Bk. VI, Ch. IV; also, Simon, *op. cit.*, pp. 60–61; Reiners, *op. cit.*, p. 28.
54. *Ibid.*

55. Report of Suhm, October, 1728, to Augustus the Strong, as given in Koenigswald, *op. cit.*, pp. 51–52; also, Simon, *op. cit.*, 61–62, and Reiners, *op. cit.*, p. 29.
56. Simon, *op. cit.*, p. 66.
57. *Ibid.;* also, Wilhelmina, *Memoires,* as quoted in Carlyle, *op. cit.*, Bk. VI, Ch. VIII.
58. *Ibid.*
59. Letter of Sir Charles Hotham in Berlin to Lord Harrington, as given in Carlyle, *op. cit.*, Bk. VII, Ch. IV; also, Simon, *op. cit.*, p. 72, and Reiners, *op. cit.*, p. 35.
60. See Carlyle, Bk. VII, Ch. VI and VII; also, Simon, *op. cit.*, pp. 80 *et seq.;* Reiners, *op. cit.*, pp. 39 *et seq.;* Vehse, *op. cit.*, pp. 117 *et seq.;* Gooch, *op. cit.*, pp. 108 *et seq.*
61. J. D. E. Preuss, *Friedrich der Grosse: Eine Lebensgeschichte* (Berlin, Nauck, 1834), I, p. 44; also, Reiners, *op. cit.*, pp. 42 and 47; Simon, *op. cit.*, pp. 92 and 98; Koenigswald, *op. cit.*, pp. 55–56.
62. Given in Koenigswald, *op. cit.*, p. 55.
63. Wilhelmine, *op. cit.*, i, p. 307, and Preuss, *op. cit.*, I, 45; cited also in Carlyle, *op. cit.*, Bk. VII, Ch. IX; also, Vehse, *op. cit.*, p. 126; Simon, *op. cit.*, p. 100, and Reiners, *op. cit.*, pp. 49–50.
64. Vehse, *op. cit.*, p. 130; also, Reiners, *op. cit.*, p. 57, and Simon, *op. cit.*, p. 109.
65. Given in Reiners, *op. cit.*, p. 58.
66. *Ibid.*
67. Vehse, *op. cit.*, p. 132.
68. Given in Simon, *op. cit.*, p. 115.
69. Letter of Frederick William I to crown prince, as given in Reiners, *op. cit.*, p. 64; also, Vehse, *op. cit.*, pp. 132–33 and Simon, *op. cit.*, pp. 116–17.
70. Letter of Seckendorff to Prince Eugene of Savoy, as given in Simon, *op. cit.*, pp. 117–18; see also, Wilhelmine, *Mémoires.*
71. Letters to Grumbkow and Wilhelmina, given in Simon, *op. cit.*, p. 118.
72. Gooch, *op. cit.*, p. 111.
73. *Ibid.*
74. Alfred Arnath, *Prinz Eugen von Savoyen* (1858), Vol. III, p. 432, as given in Nicholas Henderson, *Prince Eugen of Savoy* (London, Weidenfeld & Nicholson, 1964), p. 282.
75. *Ibid.*, pp. 282–83.
76. Vehse, *op. cit.*, p. 157.
77. Hutchinson, *op. cit.*, p. 247.
78. Attributed to Knobelsdorff in Reiners, *op. cit.*, p. 83, and in Simon, *op. cit.*, p. 160.
79. Frederick II, *History of the Seven Years War,* Vol. IV, p. 25, in *Complete Works of Frederick II,* J. D. E. Preuss, ed., 30 vols. (Berlin, 1846–57).
80. Vehse, *op. cit.*, p. 161.
81. *Ibid.*

82. Simon, *op. cit.*, p. 197; also, Reiners, *op. cit.*, p. 99.
83. Gooch, *op. cit.*, pp. 10–11.
84. *Trenck: Memoiren und Kommentar,* Eberhard Cyran, ed. (Berlin, 1966).
85. Taylor, *op. cit.*, p. 21.
86. Reiners, *op. cit.*, pp. 115–16, and Simon, *op. cit.*, p. 247.
87. Simon, *op. cit.*, p. 254.
88. Vehse, *op. cit.*, pp. 210–30; also, Simon, *op. cit.*, p. 240 *et seq.*, and Reiners, *op. cit.*, p. 115 *et seq.*
89. Gordon A. Craig, *The Politics of the Prussian Army 1640–1945* (New York, Oxford University Press, 1964), p. 16.
90. *Aus dem Nachlasse Friedrich August Ludwigs von der Marwitz* (Berlin, 1852), i, 407.
91. Gordon A. Craig, *The Politics of the Prussian Army 1640–1945* (New York, Oxford University Press, 1964), p. 16.
92. Franz Schnabel, *Deutsche Geschichte im 19. Jahrhundert* (Freiburg im Breisgau, 1925 ff.), I, p. 97.
93. Craig, *op. cit.*, p. 19.
94. Given in Reiners, *op. cit.*, p. 293.
95. From Malmesbury's *Diaries and Correspondence,* Vol. I, as given by H. Wickham Steed, "From Frederick the Great to Hitler: The Consistency of German Aims," *International Affairs* (London, The Royal Institute of International Affairs), Vol. XVII, No. 5 (September–October, 1938), p. 660.
96. Frederick II to Minister Hoym, in 1785, as given in Vehse, *op. cit.*, pp. 315–16.
97. Given in Vehse, *op. cit.*, p. 317.
98. Prussian Councilor of War von Cölln, *Confidential Letters,* as given in Vehse, *op. cit.*, p. 350.
99. Johann Wolfgang von Goethe, *Campaign in France in 1792 and 1793.*
100. Related by Frederick William III to Bishop Eylert in 1823 and given in Vehse, *op. cit.*, pp. 386–87.
101. *Ibid.*
102. C. Sheridan Jones, *The Story of the Hohenzollerns* (London, Jarrold & Sons, 1915), p. 197.
103. Von Cölln, *op. cit.;* also, Stein to Prince Louis Ferdinand, as given in Hans von Arnim, *Prinz Louis Ferdinand von Preussen* (Berlin, Haude & Spenersche Verlagsbuchhandlung, 1966), p. 60; also, Stein to Princess Marianne, 1810, as given in Vehse, *op. cit.*, p. 390.
104. Poultney Bigelow, *History of the German Struggle for Liberty* (New York and London, Harper & Bros., 1896), p. 29.
105. Jones, *op. cit.*, p. 211.
106. Given in Koenigswald, *op. cit.*, pp. 143–44.
107. Given in Bigelow, *op. cit.*, p. 35.
108. Arnim, *op. cit.*, p. 81.
109. Bigelow, *op. cit.*, p. 38.
110. *Ibid.*, p. 39 n.

111. *Ibid.*, pp. 33–34.
112. *Ibid.*, p. 34; also, Karl Demeter, *The German Officer Corps in Society and State 1650–1945* (Frankfurt-am-Main, 1962; English translation by Angus Malcolm, London, Weidenfeld & Nicholson, 1965), p. 8.
113. Arnim, *op. cit.*, pp. 92–100.
114. Bigelow, *op. cit.*, p. 49.
115. Vehse, *op. cit.*, p. 424; also, Walther Schimmel-Falkenau, *Kommen und Gehen Unter den Linden* (Berlin, Rembrandt Verlag, 1963), pp. 101–7.
116. Bigelow, *op. cit.*, p. 71.
117. Taylor, *op. cit.*, p. 44.
118. Bigelow, *op. cit.*, Vol. III, p. 77.
119. Walther Hubatsch, *Hohenzollern in der deutschen Geschichte* (Frankfurt-am-Main and Bonn, Athenäum Verlag, 1961), p. 77.
120. Letter of Gneisenau (probably to Hardenberg), written in Paris, as given in Koenigswald, *op. cit.*, pp. 173–74.
121. Bigelow, *op. cit.*, Vol. III, p. 308.
122. Taylor, *op. cit.*, p. 66.
123. Bigelow, *op. cit.*, p. 322.
124. Paul Wiegler, *William the First, His Life and Times*, trans. and ed. by Constance Vesey (London, George Allen & Unwin Ltd., 1929), pp. 100–1.
125. *Ibid.*, p. 112.
126. *Ibid.*, p. 113; also Schimmel-Falkenau, *op. cit.*, p. 217.
127. Wiegler, *op cit.*, pp. 113–14.
128. As quoted in Schimmel-Falkenau, *op. cit.*, pp. 217–18.
129. Letter to Ludwig Grimm in Kassel, dated Berlin, March 20, 1848, given in Wilhelm Schoof, *Die Gebrüder Grimm in Berlin* (Berlin, Haude & Spenersche Verlagsbuchhandlung, 1964), p. 55.
130. Wiegler, *op. cit.*, p. 114.
131. As given in Schimmel-Falkenau, *op. cit.*, p. 219.
132. Prince Frederick Charles, "The Origins and Development of the Spirit of the Prussian Officer, Its Manifestations and Its Effects," dated Stettin, January 3, 1860, given in Demeter, *op. cit.*, p. 257.
133. A. J. P. Taylor, *Bismarck: The Man and the Statesman* (London, Hamish Hamilton, 1955), p. 25 n.
134. As given in Demeter, *op. cit.*, p. 260.
135. Taylor, *Course*, p. 91; also, Emil Ludwig, *The Germans*, trans. by Heinz and Ruth Norden (London, Hamish Hamilton, 1942), p. 251.
136. Wiegler, *op. cit.*, p. 175.
137. *Ibid.*, p. 42; also, E. A. Brayley Hodgetts, *The House of Hohenzollern: Two Centuries of Berlin Court Life* (London, Methuen, 1911), p. 356; also, Archibald Forbes, *William of Germany* (London, Cassell, 1888), pp. 58–60; also, G. L. M. Strauss, *Emperor William* (London, Ward & Downey, 1888), pp. 105–8.
138. Taylor, *Bismarck*, p. 57; also, Wiegler, *op. cit.*, p. 211; also, Dr. Moritz Busch, *Bismarck: Some Secret Pages of His History* (New York and London, Macmillan, 1898 and 1899), pp. 306–7 and 460.

139. Helmuth von Moltke, *Gesammelte Schriften und Aufsätze,* III, pp. 426–27, as given in Gordon A. Craig, *The Battle of Königgrätz* (London, 1965), p. 15.
140. *The Spectator,* London, July 7, 1866.
141. *Illustrated London News,* July 14, 1866.
142. *Revue des deux mondes,* Paris, July 14, 1866.
143. *Benedeks nachgelassene Papiere,* Heinrich Friedjung, ed., p. 406, cited in Craig, *op. cit.,* pp. 28 and 196.
144. Taylor, *Bismarck,* p. 84.
145. *Ibid.,* pp. 120–21; also, Wiegler, *op. cit.,* p. 297; also, Dr. Julius von Pflugk-Harttung, "Origin of the War," in *The Franco-Prussian War,* trans. and ed. by Major General J. F. Maurice, CB, Wilfred J. Long, and A. Sonnenschein (London, Swan Sonnenschein, 1900), pp. 22–23 and 34 n.; also Forbes, *op. cit.,* p. 215.
146. Frederick III, *Das Kriegstagebuch von 1870/71,* H. O. Meissner, ed. (Berlin, K. F. Koehler, 1926); English translation, *The War Diary of the Emperor Frederick III, 1870–1871* (London, Stanley Paul, 1927).
147. Wiegler, *op. cit.,* pp. 319–20.
148. *Ibid.,* p. 322.
149. Dr. Theodor Flathe, "The Political History of the War," in J. F. Maurice, *op. cit.,* p. 613.
150. Taylor, *Bismarck,* p. 134.
151. Busch, *op. cit.,* p. 490.
152. Field Marshal Count Alfred von Waldersee, *Denkwürdigkeiten* (Stuttgart, Deutsche Verlags-Anstalt, 1922–25).
153. Busch, *op. cit.,* pp. 60, 356, 375, and 509.
154. Emil Ludwig, *Wilhelm Hohenzollern: The Last of the Kaisers,* trans. by Ethel Colburn Mayne (New York and London, G. P. Putnam's Sons, 1926–27), p. 6.
155. Margaretha von Poschinger, *Kaiser Friedrich: In neuer quellenmässiger Darstellung* (Berlin, Richard Schroeder, 1898–1900); English translation with an introduction by Sidney Whitman, ed., *Life of the Emperor Frederick* (New York and London, Harper & Brothers, 1901), p. 21.
156. Quoted in Rennell Rodd, *Frederick, Crown Prince and Emperor: A Biographical Sketch Dedicated to His Memory, with an Introduction by Her Majesty the Empress Frederick* (London, David Stott, 1888), pp. 37–38; also Poschinger, *op. cit.,* pp. 30–31.
157. Letter to Baron von Stockmar, dated September 20, 1855, given in Poschinger, *op. cit.,* pp. 54–55.
158. *Memoirs of Ernest II, Duke of Saxe-Coburg-Gotha* (London, Remington & Co., 1888).
159. Poschinger, *op. cit.,* p. 79; also, Rodd, *op. cit.,* p. 49.
160. London *Times,* February 23, 1858.
161. Rodd, *op. cit.,* p. 77.
162. Marginal comments penciled by William on a Bismarckian memorandum, cited by Poschiner, *op. cit.,* p. 279.

163. This remark was reported by members of the French court to Princess Biron of Courland, cited in Poschinger, *op. cit.*, p. 287.
164. Baron Hugo von Reischach, *Under Three Emperors*, trans. by Prince Blücher (London, Constable & Co., Ltd., 1927), pp. 10–11.
165. Given in Rodd, *op. cit.*, pp. 131–32.
166. Anonymous, *Recollections of Three Kaisers* (London, Herbert Jenkins Ltd., 1929), p. 71.
167. *Ibid.*, p. 73.
168. Reischach, *op. cit.*, pp. 91 and 139.
169. As given in Lawrence Wilson, *The Incredible Kaiser: A Portrait of William II* (London, Robert Hale Ltd., 1963), pp. 17–18.
170. *Letters of the Empress Frederick*, Sir H. Ponsonby, ed., cited in Michael Balfour, *The Kaiser and His Times* (London, Cresset Press, 1964), pp. 75–76; also, Egon Cesar, Count Corti, *The English Empress: A Study in the Relations Between Queen Victoria and Her Eldest Daughter* (letter of January 27, 1865), given in Balfour, *op. cit.*, p. 76.
171. Cited by Ludwig, *William Hohenzollern*, pp. 5–6; also, Wilson, *op. cit.*, p. 18.
172. Article by William II in *Biographisches Jahrbuch und Deutscher Nekrolog*, XII, 1907, cited by Balfour, *op. cit.*, p. 77.
173. J. W. Wheeler-Bennett, *Three Episodes in the Life of Kaiser Wilhelm II*, The Leslie Stephen Lecture, 1955 (Cambridge, Syndics of the University Press, 1956).
174. Hinzpeter, in letter to Morier, given in Ludwig, *William Hohenzollern*, p. 9.
175. *Ibid.*, p. 10.
176. *Princess Daisy of Pless*, by Herself, p. 260, cited in Balfour, *op. cit.*, p. 87.
177. Anonymous, *Recollections*, pp. 114–15.
178. Taylor, *Bismarck*, *op. cit.*, p. 10.
179. Wilson, *op. cit.*, p. 22; also, Ludwig, *William Hohenzollern*, p. 23 and Wheeler-Bennett, *op. cit.*, p. 12.
180. Ludwig, *William Hohenzollern*, p. 63.
181. Letter of Queen Victoria, given in Balfour, *op. cit.*, p. 123.
182. Ponsonby, *Letters*, given in Balfour, *op. cit.*, pp. 121–22.
183. Wheeler-Bennett, *op. cit.*, p. 10.
184. *Ibid.*, pp. 6–7.
185. Ludwig, *William Hohenzollern*, pp. 91–115.
186. Baroness Deichmann, *op. cit.*, pp. 187 and 281.
187. Anonymous, *Recollections*, p. 169.
188. *Ibid.*, pp. 177–78.
189. *Ibid.*, p. 181.
190. *Ibid.*, p. 262.
191. Wheeler-Bennett, *op. cit.*, p. 7.
192. J. W. Wheeler-Bennett, *The Nemesis of Power: The German Army in Politics 1918–1945* (New York, Viking Press, Inc., 1964), p. 8.
193. Balfour, *op. cit.*, pp. 180–81.

194. Wilson, *op. cit.*, p. 57.
195. Winston S. Churchill, *Great Contemporaries,* given in *Maxims and Reflections,* Colin Coote & Daniel Batchelor, eds. (London, Eyre & Spottiswoode, 1947), p. 46.
196. Ludwig, *William Hohenzollern,* pp. 194–201; also Wilson, *op. cit.*, pp. 66–68.
197. Wilson, *op. cit.*, pp. 69–71.
198. Ludwig, *William Hohenzollern,* pp. 235–36.
199. Waldersee, *Denkwürdigkeiten,* Vol. III, p. 176.
200. Anonymous, *Recollections,* p. 189.
201. Wilson, *op. cit.*, p. 90.
202. Prinz Alexander von Hohenlohe, *Aus Meinem Leben,* Gottlob Anhäuser, ed. (Frankfurt am Main, Frankfurter Societäts-Druckerei, 1925), p. 338.
203. Count Robert von Zedlitz-Trützschler, *Zwölf Jahre am deutschen Kaiserhof* (Stuttgart, Deutsche Verlags-Anstalt, 1925), pp. 212 and 230.
204. Letter to Baroness von Schrader, dated 1893, given in Ludwig, *William Hohenzollern,* p. 330.
205. Wheeler-Bennett, *Three Episodes,* pp. 11–12.
206. H. S. Chamberlain, *Briefe,* Vol. II, pp. 226–27, cited by Balfour, *op. cit.*, p. 277.
207. *Ibid.*
208. *Ibid.*, p. 286.
209. Ludwig, *William Hohenzollern,* pp. 385–86; also, Wilson, *op. cit.*, pp. 111–12, and Balfour, *op. cit.*, pp. 289–90.
210. Wilson, *op. cit.*, p. 113.
211. Balfour, *op. cit.*, p. 291, and Wilson, *op. cit.*, p. 117.
212. Zedlitz, *op. cit.*, p. 231.
213. Memoirs of Prince von Bülow, 1903–9 vol., p. 410, given in Balfour, *op. cit.*, p. 297.
214. Barbara W. Tuchman, *The Guns of August* (London, Four Square Books, 1964), p. 95
215. Balfour, *op. cit.*, p. 317.
216. Ludwig, *William Hohenzollern,* p. 426.
217. *Ibid.*, pp. 322–27; also, Balfour, *op. cit.*, pp. 307–8; also, Wilson, *op. cit.*, p. 133; also, Tuchman, *op. cit.*, p. 15 *et seq.*
218. *Die Deutsche Dokumente zum Kriegsausbruch 1914,* II, p. 132, given in Balfour, *op. cit.*, pp. 350–52; also, Wilson, *op. cit.*, p. 141, and Ludwig, *William Hohenzollern,* pp. 447–48.
219. James W. Gerard, *My Four Years in Germany* (London, New York and Toronto, Hodder & Stoughton, 1917), pp. 88, 90, 138–44; also, Tuchman, *op. cit.*, p. 151.
220. Tuchman, *op. cit.*, p. 143.
221. Ludwig, *William Hohenzollern,* p. 457.
222. *Ibid.*, pp. 457–58.
223. Princess Blücher, cited in Balfour, *op. cit.*, p. 355.
224. Ludwig, *William Hohenzollern,* pp. 358–59.

25. Quoted in Marder, *Dreadnought to Scape Flow,* I, 332, cited in Balfour, *op. cit.,* p. 366.
26. Gerard, *op. cit.,* p. 243.
27. *Ibid.,* pp. 271–82, 284.
28. Letter of a captain, dated July 13, 1918, as given in documentation published by *Frankfurter Allgemeine Zeitung* (*F.A.Z.*), November 5, 1968.
29. As given in *F.A.Z.,* November 5, 1968.
30. Ludwig, *William Hohenzollern,* p. 476.
31. *Ibid.,* p. 477.
32. *Ibid.*
33. Niemann, quoted *ibid.,* p. 479.
34. *Ibid.,* p. 461.
35. Prince Max of Baden, letter dated October 15, 1918, to Grand Duke of Baden, as given in *F.A.Z.,* November 5, 1968.
36. As given in *F.A.Z.,* November 5, 1968.
37. Taylor, *Bismarck,* p. 97.
38. Prince Max, letter, *op. cit.*
39. Wheeler-Bennett, *Three Episodes,* p. 14.
40. *Ibid.,* p. 22.
41. Quoted in Balfour, *op. cit.,* p. 419.
42. Wheeler-Bennett, *Three Episodes,* pp. 22–24.
43. As given in Gerhard Ritter, *Carl Goerdeler und die deutsche Widerstandsbewegung* (Stuttgart, Deutsche Verlags-Anstalt, 1954), Appendix IV, pp. 567–68, trans. by W.H.N.
44. *Ibid.,* p. 292.
45. Fabian von Schlabrendorff, *The Secret War Against Hitler,* trans. by Hilda Simon with a foreword by Terence Prittie (London, Hodder & Stoughton, 1966), pp. 24–25.
46. Henry Ormond, "Juden als Soldaten," *Allgemeine unabhängige jüdische Wochenzeitung,* Düsseldorf, July 5, 1968.
47. Preface by Louis Ferdinand, Prince of Prussia, to Ritthalter, *op. cit.,* p. 5.

Bibliography

Anderson, Matthew S., *18th Century Europe: 1713–1789.* New York and London, Oxford University Press, 1966.

Anker, Kurt, *Kronprinz Wilhelm.* Berlin, E. S. Mittler & Sohn, 1919.

Archenholz, Johann Wilhelm von, *Geschichte des Siebenjährigen Krieges in Deutschland.* Berlin, Haude & Spener, 1793–1830.

Arnim, Hans Von, *Prince Louis Ferdinand von Preussen.* Berlin, Haude & Spenersche Verlagsbuchhandlung, 1966.

Ausubel, Nathan, *Superman: The Life of Frederick the Great.* New York, Ives Washburn, 1931.

Baden, Prince Max von, *Erinnerungen.* Stuttgart, Deutsche Verlags-Anstalt, 1927.

Balfour, Michael, *The Kaiser and His Times.* London, Cresset Press, 1964; New York, Houghton Mifflin, 1964.

Barnes, Harry Elmer, *Genesis of the World War.* New York and London, Knopf, 1926.

Bartholdy, Gustav Mendelssohn, ed., *Der König: Friedrich der Grosse in seinen Briefen und Erlassen, sowie in zeitgenössischen Briefen, Berichten und Anekdoten.* Munich and Leipzig, Wilhelm Langewiesche, 1913.

Beheim-Schwarzbach, Max, *Friedrich Wilhelms I. Colonisationswerk in Lithauen, vornehmlich die Salzburger Colonie.* Königsberg, Hartung, 1878.

Benson, Edward Frederick, *The Kaiser and English Relations.* London, Longmans, 1936.

Bentinck, Lady Norah Ida Emily, *The Ex-Kaiser in Exile.* London, Hodder & Stoughton, 1921.

Berner, Ernst, *Geschichte des preussischen Staates.* Munich, Verlagsanstalt für Kunst & Wissenschaft, 1891.

Besterman, Theodore, *Voltaire Essays, and Another.* New York and London, Oxford University Press, 1962.

Bigelow, Poultney, *History of the German Struggle for Liberty.* New York and London, Harper & Bros., 1896–1903. 3 vols.

Bismarck-Schönhausen, Prince Otto Eduard Leopold von, *Bismarck: The Man and the Statesman—Being the Reflections and Reminiscences of Otto Prince von Bismarck, Written and Dictated by Himself After His Retirement from Office,* trans. under the supervision of A. J. Butler, etc. London, Smith, Elder, 1898. 2 vols.

———, *Briefe,* Hans Rothfels, ed. Göttingen, Vandenhoeck & Ruprecht 1955.

———, *Erinnerung und Gedanke* [Vol. 3 of *Gedanken und Erinnerungen*] Stuttgart and Berlin, J. G. Cotta, 1921.

———, *Gedanken und Erinnerungen.* Stuttgart and Berlin, J. G. Cotta 1916. 2 vols.

———, *Gedanken und Erinnerungen,* an abbreviated and critically an notated edition by A. M. Gibson. New York, Columbia University Press 1940.

———, *The Kaiser vs. Bismarck: Suppressed Letters of the Kaiser and New Chapters from the Autobiography of the Iron Chancellor, with an Historical Introduction by Charles Downer Hazin,* trans. by Bernard Miall New York and London, Harper & Bros., 1920

———, *Reflections and Reminiscences,* Theodore S. Hamerow, ed. New York, Torch-Harper & Row, 1968.

Bithell, Jethro, ed., *Germany: A Companion to German Studies.* London Methuen, 1932; rev. 1937, 1955.

Blücher, Princess Evelyn, *An English Wife in Berlin.* London, Constable 1920.

Bonnin, Charles, ed., *Bismarck and the Hohenzollern Candidature for th Spanish Throne: The Documents in the German Diplomatic Archives* trans. by Dr. Isabella M. Massey, with a foreword by Dr. G. P. Gooch London, Chatto & Windus, 1957.

Botzenhart, Erich, *Die Staats- und Reformideen des Freiherrn vom Stein* Tübingen, Osiander'sche Buchhandlung, 1927.

Boyen, Hermann von, *Denkwürdigkeiten,* F. Nippold, ed. Stuttgart, J. G Cotta, 1896.

Brandenburg, Erich, *From Bismarck to the World War: A History o German Foreign Policy, 1870–1914,* trans. by Annie Elizabeth Adams London, Oxford University Press, 1927; Mystic, Conn., Verry, Lawrence, 1927.

Braun, Freiherr Magnus von, *Von Ostpreussen bis Texas.* Stollhamm Oldenburg, Rauschenbusch Verlag, 1955.

Brimble, E. Lilian, *In the Eyrie of the Hohenzollern Eagle: Reminiscence of Life in the Household of the Crown Prince Frederick William o Germany.* London, Hodder & Stoughton, 1916.

Bülow, Prince Bernhard Heinrich Martin Carl von, *Denkwürdigkeiten* Franz von Stockhammern, ed. Berlin, Ullstein, 1930–1931. 4 vols.

———, *Memoirs,* trans. by F. A. Voight and G. Dunlop. New York an London, Putnam, 1931–1932.

Busch, Dr. Moritz, *Bismarck: Some Secret Pages of His History,* con densed ed. New York and London, Macmillan, 1898–1899.

Carlyle, Thomas, *History of Friedrich II. of Prussia, Called Frederic the Great.* London, Chapman & Hall, 1858–1865. 6 vols.

Carsten, F. L., *The Origins of Prussia.* London, Oxford University Pres 1954.

Catt, Henri Alexandre de, *Frederick the Great: The Memoirs of H*

Reader, Henri de Catt, 1758–1760, trans. by F. S. Flint, with an introduction by Lord Rosebery. London, Constable, 1916. 2 vols.

———, *Unterhaltungen mit Friedrich dem Grossen,* R. Koser, ed. Leipzig, S. Hirzel, 1884.

CECILIE, AUGUSTA MARY, CROWN PRINCESS OF PRUSSIA, *Erinnerungen.* Leipzig, K. F. Koehler, 1930.

———, *Erinnerungen an den deutschen Kronprinzen.* Biberach an der Riss, Koehler, 1952.

———, *The Memoirs of the Crown Princess Cecilie,* trans. by Emile Burns. London, Victor Gollancz, 1931.

CHURCHILL, WINSTON LEONARD SPENCER, *Thoughts and Adventures.* London, Thornton Butterworth, 1932; New York, Macmillan, 1942.

CLARK, R. T., *The Fall of the German Republic.* London, George Allen & Unwin, 1935.

CRAIG, GORDON A., *The Politics of the Prussian Army, 1640–1945.* New York and London, Oxford University Press, 1955; New York, Galaxy Book, Oxford University Press, 1964.

———, *The Battle of Königgrätz: Prussia's Victory over Austria, 1866.* London, Weidenfeld & Nicholson, 1964; Philadelphia, Lippincott, 1964.

CZERNIN, COUNT OTTOKAR, *Im Weltkriege.* Berlin, Ullstein, 1919.

DAWSON, WILLIAM HARBUTT, *The German Empire, 1867–1914, and the Unity Movement.* London, George Allen & Unwin, 1919; Hamden, Conn., Shoe String Press, 1919. 2 vols.

DEICHMANN, BARONESS, *Impressions and Memories.* London, John Murray, 1926.

DEMETER, KARL, *Das deutsche Heer und seine Offiziere: Das deutsche Offizierkorps in seinen historisch-soziologischen Grundlagen.* Berlin, Reimar Hobbing, 1930.

———, *The German Officer Corps in Society and State 1650–1945,* trans. by Angus Malcolm, with an introduction by Michael Howard. London, Weidenfeld & Nicholson, 1965.

DIESEL, EUGEN, *Germany and the Germans,* trans. by W. D. Robson-Scott. London, Macmillan, 1931.

DIETRICH, RICHARD, *Kleine Geschichte Preussens.* Berlin, Haude und Spenersche Verlagsbuchhandlung, 1966.

DROYSEN, JOHANN GUSTAV, *Das Leben des Feldmarschalls Grafen Yorck von Wartenburg.* Berlin and Leipzig, Veit, 1851–1852. 3 vols.

EASUM, CHESTER, *Prince Henry of Prussia, Brother of Frederick the Great.* Madison, University of Wisconsin Press, 1942.

ELLWEIN, THOMAS, *Das Erbe der Monarchie in der deutschen Staatskrise.* Munich, Isar Verlag, 1954.

ERGANG, ROBERT, *The Potsdam Führer: Frederick William I, Father of Prussian Militarism.* New York, Columbia University Press, 1941.

ERNEST II, DUKE OF SAXE-COBURG-GOTHA, *Memoirs.* London, Remington, 1888. 4 vols.

EULENBERG, HERBERT, *The Hohenzollerns,* trans. by M. M. Bozman, etc. London, George Allen & Unwin, 1929.

EYCK, ERICH, *Bismarck: Leben und Werk.* Zürich, Erlenbach, 1941–1944 3 vols.

———, *Bismarck and the German Empire.* New York, Macmillan, 1950 London, George Allen & Unwin, 1950.

EYLERT, RULEMANN FRIEDRICH, *Charakter-Züge und historische Fragmente aus dem Leben des Königs von Preussen Friedrich Wilhelm III—Gesammelt nach eigenen Beobachtungen und selbstgemachten Erfahrungen.* Magdeburg, Heinrichshofen, 1843–1846.

FAY, SIDNEY B., *The Rise of Brandenburg-Prussia to 1786,* rev. by Klaus Epstein. New York, Chicago, San Francisco, Toronto, London, Holt, Rinehart & Winston, 1937; rev. ed. 1964.

FONTANE, THEODOR, *Von Zwanzig bis Dreissig.* Berlin, S. Fischer Verlag, 1925.

———, *Wanderungen durch die Mark Brandenburg.* Stuttgart, J. G Cotta'sche Buchhandlung Nachf., 1925. 3 vols.

FORBES, ARCHIBALD, *William of Germany: A Succinct Biography of William I., German Emperor and King of Prussia.* London, Paris, New York and Melbourne, Cassell, 1888.

FREDERICK II (FREDERICK THE GREAT), KING OF PRUSSIA, *Die Briefe Friedrichs des Grossen an seinen vormaligen Kammerdiener Fredersdorf.* Johannes Richter, ed. Berlin, Verlagsanstalt H. Klemm, 1926.

———, *Der grosse König: Friedrich der Einzige in seinen Werken, Briefen, Erlassen und Berichten seiner Zeitgenossen,* Dr. Heinrich Schierbaum, ed. Bielefeld-Leipzig, Velhagen und Klasing, 1920.

———, *Memoirs of the House of Brandenburg from the Earliest Accounts to the Death of Frederick I., King of Prussia.* London, J. Nourse, 1757.

———, *ibid.,* but *to the Death of Frederick William I.* London, J. Nourse, 1758–1768.

———, *Posthumous Works of Frederic II, King of Prussia,* trans. from the French by T. Holcroft. London, 1789. 13 vols.

———, *Die Werke Friedrichs des Grossen in deutscher Übersetzung,* Gustav Berthold Volz, ed., trans. into German by Friedrich von Oppeln Bronikowski, Thassilo von Scheffer, and others; illustrated by Adolph von Menzel. Berlin, Reimar Hobbing, 1913–1914. 10 vols.

FREDERICK III, GERMAN EMPEROR AND KING OF PRUSSIA, *The Crown Prince Frederick William: A Diary.* London, Sampson Low, 1886.

———, *Diaries of the Emperor Frederick During the Campaigns of 1866 and 1870–71 as Well as His Journeys to the East and to Spain,* Margaretha von Poschinger, ed., trans. by Francis A. Welby. London, Chapman & Hall, 1902.

———, *The Emperor Frederick: A Diary—New Edition.* London, Sampson Low, 1888.

———, *Das Kriegstagebuch von 1870/71,* Heinrich Otto Meisner, ed Berlin, K. F. Koehler, 1926.

———, *Tagebücher von 1848–1866,* Heinrich Otto Meisner, ed. Leipzig K. F. Koehler, 1929.

———, *The War Diary of the Emperor Frederick III, 1870–1871,* trans and ed. by A. R. Allison, etc. London, Stanley Paul, 1927.

FREUND, MICHAEL, *Das Drama der 99 Tage: Krankheit und Tod Friedrichs III.* Cologne and Berlin, Kiepenheuer & Witsch, 1966.

FREYLINGHAUSEN, JOHANN ANASTASIUS, *Sieben Tage am Hofe Friedrich Wilhelms I., Tagebuch,* Bogdan Krieger, ed. Berlin, A. Duncker, 1900.

FREYTAG, GUSTAV, *The Crown Prince and the German Imperial Crown: Reminiscences,* trans. from the seventh ed. by G. Duncan. London, G. Bell & Sons, 1890.

———, *Die Erhebung Preussens gegen Napoleon im Jahre 1813,* Otto Siepmann, ed. London, Macmillan, 1914.

GABLENTZ, OTTO HEINRICH VON DER, *Die Tragik des Preussentums.* Munich, Verlag Franz Hanfstaengel, 1948.

GAXOTTE, PIERRE, *Frederick the Great.* New Haven, Conn., Yale University Press, 1942.

———, *German Diplomatic Documents 1871–1914,* selected and trans. by E. T. S. Dugdale, etc. London, Methuen, 1928–1931. 4 vols.

GERARD, JAMES W., *My Four Years in Germany.* London, Toronto, Hooder & Stoughton, 1917.

GOOCH, GEORGE PEABODY, *Franco-German Relations 1871–1914.* New York, Russell & Russell, 1923; London, Longmans, 1923.

———, *Frederick the Great: The Ruler, the Writer, the Man.* New York, Knopf, 1947; London, Longmans, 1947.

———, *Germany.* London, Ernest Benn, 1925.

———, *Germany and the French Revolution.* New York, Russell & Russell, 1920; London, Longmans, 1920.

———, *History of Modern Europe, 1878–1919.* New York, Holt, 1923; London, Cassell, 1923.

GRIEWANK, KARL, *Der Wiener Kongress und die europäische Restauration 1814/15,* 2d. rev. ed. Leipzig, Koehler & Amelang, 1954.

HAMEROW, THEODORE S., ed., *Otto von Bismarck: A Historical Assessment.* Boston, D. C. Heath, 1962, 1965. London, Harrap, 1962.

HANSEN, JOSEF, *Preussen und Rheinland von 1815–1915: 100 Jahre politisches Leben am Rhein.* Bonn, A. Marcus & E. Weber, 1918.

HARTUNG, FRITZ, *Deutsche Verfassungsgeschichte vom 15. Jahrhundert bis zur Gegenwart,* 5th rev. ed. Stuttgart, K. F. Koehler, 1950.

———, *König Friedrich Wilhelm I, der Begründer des preussischen Staates.* Berlin, De Gruyter, 1942.

HEIM, ERNST LUDWIG, *Aus den Tagebüchern des alten Heims,* G. Siegerist, ed. Berlin, Archiv der Brandenburgia; Gesellschaft für Heimatkunde der Provinz Brandenburg, 1901.

HEINIG, CURT, *Hohenzollern: Wilhelm II und sein Haus—Der Kampf um den Kronbesitz.* Berlin, 1921.

HENDERSON, NICHOLAS, *Prince Eugen of Savoy.* London, Weidenfeld and Nicholson, 1964; New York, Praeger, 1965.

HILLARD-STEINBÖMER, GUSTAV, *Herren und Narren der Welt.* Munich, List, 1954.

HINDENBURG, PAUL LUDWIG HANS ANTON VON BENECKENDORFF UND VON, *Aus meinem Leben.* Leipzig, S. Hirzel, 1920.

———, *Briefe, Reden, Berichte,* Fritz Enders, ed. Ebenhausen-Munich, W. Langewiesche-Brandt, 1934.

———, *Out of My Life,* trans. by F. A. Holt. London, Cassell, 1920.

Hinrichs, Karl, *Friedrich Wilhelm I.* Hamburg, Hanseatische Verlagsanstalt, 1941.

———, *Der Kronprinzenprozess: Friedrich und Katte.* Hamburg, Hanseatische Verlagsanstalt, 1936.

Hintze, Otto, *Die Hohenzollern und ihr Werk: 500 Jahre vaterländische Geschichte.* Berlin, P. Parey, 1915–1916.

Hinzpeter, G., *Kaiser Wilhelm II: Eine Skizze nach der Natur gezeichnet.* Bielefeld, 1888.

Hodgetts, E. A. Brayley, *The House of Hohenzollern: Two Centuries of Berlin Court Life.* London, Methuen, 1911.

Hohenlohe-Schillingfürst, Prince Alexander von, *Aus meinem Leben,* Gottlob Anhäuser, ed. Frankfurt am Main, Frankfurter Societäts-Druckerei, 1925.

Hohenlohe-Schillingfürst, Prince Chlodwig zu, *Denkwürdigkeiten,* Friedrich Curtius, ed. Stuttgart, Deutsche Verlags-Anstalt, 1906–1907. 2 vols.

———, *Denkwürdigkeiten der Reichskanzlerzeit,* Karl Alexander von Müller, ed. Stuttgart, Deutsche Verlags-Anstalt, 1931.

Horn, David Bayne, *Frederick the Great and the Rise of Prussia.* Mystic, Conn., Verry, Lawrence, 1964; London, English Universities Press, 1964.

Howard, Michael, *The Franco-Prussian War.* London, Rupert Hart-Davis, 1960.

Howard, Ethel, *Potsdam Princes.* London, Methuen, 1916.

Hubatsch, Walther, *Die Ära Tirpitz: Studien zur deutschen Marinepolitik 1890–1918.* Berlin and Frankfurt am Main, Musterschmidt, 1955.

———, *Hohenzollern in der deutschen Geschichte.* Frankfurt am Main and Bonn, Athenäum Verlag, 1961.

Humboldt, Alexander von, *Alexander von Humboldt und das preussische Königshaus: Briefe aus den Jahren 1835–1857,* Conrad Müller, ed. Leipzig, K. F. Koehler, 1928.

Hutchinson, J. R., *The Romance of a Regiment: Being the True and Diverting Story of the Giant Grenadiers of Potsdam, How They Were Caught and Held in Captivity 1713–1740.* London, Sampson Low, 1898.

Ilsemann, Sigurd von, *Der Kaiser in Holland: Aufzeichnungen des letzten Flügeladjutanten Kaiser Wilhelms II. aus Amerongen und Doorn 1918–1923,* ed. and with a foreword by Harald von Koenigswald. Munich, Biederstein Verlag, 1967.

Jany, Kurt, *Geschichte der Königlich Preussischen Armee bis zum Jahre 1807.* Berlin, K. Siegismund, 1928. 3 vols.

———, *Die Königliche Preussische Armee und das deutsche Reichsheer 1807–1914* [Vol. 4 of foregoing]. Berlin, K. Siegismund, 1933.

Jonas, Klaus, *The Life of Crown Prince William,* trans. by Charles W. Bangert. London, Routledge & Kegan Paul, 1961; New York, Hillary House, 1961.

JONES, C. SHERIDAN, *The Story of the Hohenzollern.* London, Jarrold & Sons, 1915.

KAUTSKY, CARL JOHANN, *The Guilt of William Hohenzollern.* London, Skeffington & Son, 1920.

KIAULEHN, WALTHER, *Berlin: Schicksal einer Weltstadt.* Munich and Berlin, Biederstein Verlag, 1958.

KLEIN, TIM, *Die Befreiung 1813, 1814, 1815: Dokumente.* Ebenhausen-Munich, W. Langewiesche-Brandt, 1913.

KLEPPER, JOCHEN, *Der Soldatenkönig und die Stillen im Lande.* Berlin, Eckart-Verlag, 1938.

KLOPP, ONNO, *Der König Friedrich II von Preussen und seine Politik,* 2d rev. ed. Schaffhausen, Hurter'sche Buchhandlung, 1867.

———, *Die preussische Politik des Friderizianismus nach Friedrich II.* Schaffhausen, Hurter'sche Buchhandlung, 1867.

KOENIGSWALD, HARALD VON, ed., *Preussisches Lesebuch: Zeugnisse aus drei Jahrhunderten.* Munich, Biederstein Verlag, 1966.

———, *Stirb und Werde: Aus Briefen und Kriegstagebuchblättern des Leutnants Bernhard von der Marwitz.* Breslau, W. G. Korn, 1931.

KOSER, REINHOLD, *Geschichte Friedrichs des Grossen.* Stuttgart, J. G. Cotta'sche Buchhandlung Nachf., 1921–1925. 4 vols.

KRAMMER, MARIO, *Alexander von Humboldt: Mensch, Zeit, Werk.* Berlin, Volksverband der Bücherfreunde, Wegweiser Verlag, 1951; Berlin and Munich, Weiss, 1954.

KUGLER, FRANZ THEODOR, *Life of Frederick the Great: Comprehending a Complete History of the Silesian Campaign and the Seven Years War,* trans. by E. A. Moriarty. London and New York, G. Routledge & Sons, 1877.

KÜNTZLER, GEORG, AND HASS, MARTIN, *Die Politischen Testamente der Hohenzollern.* Leipzig and Berlin, B. G. Teubner, 1919.

LAVISSE, ERNEST, *Youth of Frederick the Great.* London, Bentley & Son, 1891; New York, Reprint House International, 1892.

LEHNDORFF, E. A. HEINRICH VON, *Dreissig Jahre am Hofe Friedrich des Grossen,* K. E. Schmidt-Lötzen, ed. Gotha, F. A. Perthes, 1907.

LOCHNER, LOUIS P., *What About Germany?* New York, Dodd, 1942.

LONGMAN, F. W., *Frederick the Great and the Seven Years War,* 3d ed. London, Longmans, 1888.

LOUIS FERDINAND OF HOHENZOLLERN, PRINCE OF PRUSSIA, *The Rebel Prince: Memoirs,* with an introduction by Louis P. Lochner. Chicago, Regnery, 1952.

LUDENDORFF, FRIEDRICH WILHELM ERICH VON, *Meine Kriegserinnerungen, 1914–1918.* Berlin, E. G. Mittler & Sohn, 1919.

———, *My War Memories 1914–1918.* London, Hutchinson, 1919. 2 vols.

LOUISE SOPHIA, PRINCESS OF PRUSSIA, *Behind the Scenes at the Prussian Court.* London, John Murray, 1939.

LUDWIG, EMIL, *The Germans,* trans. by Heinz and Ruth Norden. Boston, Little, Brown, 1941; London, Hamish Hamilton, 1942.

———, *Wilhelm Hohenzollern, The Last of the Kaisers,* trans. by Ethel Colburn Mayne. New York and London, Putnam, 1926–1927.

LUDWIG, HANS, *Altberliner Bilderbogen,* illustrated by Klaus Ensikat. Berlin [East], Altberliner Verlag, Lucie Groszer, 1965.

LUTZ, RALPH HASWELL, ed., *The Fall of the German Empire, 1914–1918: Documents of the German Revolution.* Stanford, Calif., Stanford University Press, 1932.

MACKENZIE, SIR MORELL, *The Fatal Illness of Frederick the Noble.* London, Sampson Low, 1888.

MARWITZ, FRIEDRICH AUGUST LUDWIG VON DER, *Lebensbeschreibung,* F. Meusel, ed. Berlin, E. S. Mittler und Sohn, 1908.

MAURICE, J. F., LONG, WILFRED J.; SONNENSCHEIN, A., ed., *The Franco-Prussian War.* London, Swan Sonnenschein 1900.

MAYHEW, ATHOL, *The Emperor of Germany, William I: A Life Sketch.* London, T. Nelson & Sons, 1887.

MEINECKE, FRIEDRICH, *Preussisch-deutsche Gestalten und Probleme.* Leipzig, Koehler und Amelang, 1940.

———, *Das Zeitalter der deutschen Erhebung, 1785 bis 1815.* Bielefeld, Veldhagen und Klasing, 1924.

MENDELSSOHN, PETER DE, *Zeitungsstadt Berlin: Menschen und Mächte in der Geschichte der deutschen Presse.* Berlin, Ullstein, 1959.

MEYER, ARNOLD OSKAR, *Bismarck: Der Mensch und der Staatsmann,* with an introduction by Hans Rothfels. Stuttgart, K. F. Koehler, 1949.

MIRABEAU, HONORÉ GABRIEL RIQUETTI, COMTE DE, *De la monarchie prussienne sous Frédéric le Grand.* London and Paris, 1788.

MOLTKE, COUNT HELMUTH CARL BERNHARD VON, *Ausgewählte Werke,* Ferdinand von Schmerfeld, ed. Berlin, Reimar Hobbing, 1925. 4 vols.

———, *Erinnerungen, Briefe, Dokumente 1877–1916.* Stuttgart, Der Kommende Tag, 1922.

———, *Essays, Speeches, and Memoirs,* trans. by C. F. McClumpha, Major C. Barter, and Mary Herms. London, Osgood & McIlvaine, 1893. 2 vols.

———, *The Franco-German War of 1870–71,* trans. by C. Bell & H. W. Fischer. London, Osgood & McIlvaine, 1891. 2 vols.

———, *ibid.,* trans. rev. by Archibald Forbes. London, Osgood & McIlvaine, 1893.

———, *Gesammelte Schriften und Denkwürdigkeiten.* Berlin, E. S. Mittler & Sohn, 1891–1893. 8 vols.

———, *Geschichte des deutsch-französischen Krieges von 1870–71.* Berlin, E. S. Mittler & Sohn, 1895.

MÜLLER, GEORG ALEXANDER VON, *The Kaiser and His Court: The Diaries, Notebooks, and Letters of Admiral Georg Alexander von Müller, Chief of the Naval Cabinet 1914–1918,* Walter Görlitz, ed., trans. by Mervyn Savill. London, Macdonald, 1961.

———, *Regierte der Kaiser? Kriegstagebücher, Aufzeichnungen und Briefe des Chefs des Marine-Kabinetts, Admiral Georg Alexander von Müller, 1914–1918,* with a foreword by Sven von Müller, Walter Görlitz, ed. Frankfurt am Main, Musterschmidt, 1959.

MUSCHLER, REINHOLD, *Philipp zu Eulenburg, sein Leben und seine Zeit.* Leipzig, F. W. Grunow, 1930.

NAUMANN, FRIEDRICH, *Das blaue Buch von Vaterland und Freiheit*. Königstein-Taunus, K. R. Langewiesche, 1914.

———, *Freiheitskämpfe*. Berlin, Georg Reimer, 1911.

NAUMANN, VIKTOR, *Argumente und Dokumente*. Berlin, Rowohlt, 1928.

———, *Profile*. Munich, Duncker & Humblot, 1925.

NELSON, WALTER HENRY, *The Berliners: Their Saga and Their City*. New York, McKay, 1969; London, Longmans, 1969.

NETTLEBECK, JOACHIM, *Lebensgeschichte*. Halle, Rengersche Buchhandlung, 1820.

NETZER, HANS-JOACHIM, ed., *Preussen: Porträt einer politischen Kultur*. Munich, Paul List Verlag, 1968.

NICOLAI, CHRISTOPH FRIEDRICH, *Anekdoten von Friedrich dem Grossen*, Emil Schaeffer, ed. Leipzig, Insel-Bücherei, 1915.

NIEMANN, ALFRED, *Die Entthronung Kaiser Wilhelms II*. Leipzig, K. F. Koehler, 1924.

———, *Kaiser und Revolution: Die entscheidenden Ereignisse im Grossen Hauptquartier*. Berlin, A. Scherl, 1922.

———, *Wanderungen mit Kaiser Wilhelm II*. Leipzig and Berlin, K. F. Koehler, 1924.

NOSKE, GUSTAV, *Erlebtes aus Aufstieg und Niedergang einer Demokratie*. Offenbach, Bollwerk Verlag, 1947.

OLDENBURG-JANUSCHAU, ELARD VON, *Erinnerungen*. Leipzig, Hase & Koehler, 1938.

PASSANT, ERNEST J., *A Short History of Germany 1815–1945*. New York, Columbia University Press, 1962; London, Cambridge University Press, 1966.

PAULIG, F. R., *Friedrich der Grosse, König von Preussen. Neue Beiträge zur Geschichte seines Privatlebens, seines Hofes und seiner Zeit*, Vol. 3 of *Familiengeschichte des Hohenzollernschen Kaiserhauses*. Frankfurt an der Oder, 1892.

PHILIPPSON, MARTIN, *Der Grosse Kurfürst Friedrich Wilhelm von Brandenburg*. Berlin, S. Cronbach, 1897, 1902, 1903. 3 vols.

———, *Das Leben Kaiser Friedrichs III*. Wiesbaden, J. F. Bergmann, 1900.

POSCHINGER, MARGARETHA VON, *Life of the Emperor Frederick*, with an introduction by Sidney Whitman. New York and London, Harper & Bros., 1901.

———, *Kaiser Friedrich, in neuer quellenmässiger Darstellung*. Berlin, Richard Schroeder, 1898–1900. 3 vols.

PREUSS, JOHANN DAVID ERDMANN, *Friedrich der Grosse: Eine Lebensgeschichte*. Berlin, Nauck, 1832–1834. 5 vols.

———, *Friedrich der Grosse mit seinen Verwandten und Freunden: Eine historische Skizze*. Berlin, Duncker & Humblot, 1838.

———, *Oeuvres de Frédéric le Grand*, J. D. E. Preuss, ed. Berlin, 1846–1857. 30 vols.

RADZIWILL, PRINCESS MARIE DOROTHÉE ELISABETH, *Briefe vom deutschen Kaiserhof 1889–1915*. Paul Wiegler, ed. Berlin, Deutscher Verlag, 1936.

———, *This Was Germany: An Observer at the Court of Berlin. Letters of Princess Marie Radziwill to General di Robilant 1908–1915,* ed. and trans. from the French and with an introduction and notes by Cyril Spencer Fox. London, John Murray, 1937; Forest Hills, N.Y., Transatlantic Arts, 1938; Toronto, Musson Book Co., 1938.

RANKE, LEOPOLD VON, *Hardenberg und die Geschichte des preussischen Staates, 1793–1813.* Berlin, Duncker & Humblot, 1879.

———, *Zwölf Bücher preussischer Geschichte.* Leipzig, Duncker & Humblot, 1874.

RATHENAU, WALTHER, *Der Kaiser: Eine Betrachtung.* Berlin, S. Fischer, 1919.

Recollections of Three Kaisers ["by?"], *Being Reminiscences of a Court Employee under William I, Frederick III and William II.* London, Herbert Jenkins, 1929.

REDDAWAY, WILLIAM FIDDIAN, *Frederick the Great and the Rise of Prussia.* New York, Haskell House, 1904.

REINERS, LUDWIG, *Bismarck.* Munich, Beck, 1956–1958. 3 vols.

———, *Frederick the Great: An Informal Biography,* trans. and adapted by Lawrence P. R. Wilson. London, Oswald Wolff, 1960.

REISCHACH, BARON HUGO VON, *Under Three Emperors: Being Court Reminiscences Under William I, Frederick III and William II,* trans. by Prince Blücher. London, Constable, 1927.

RITTER, GERHARD, *Carl Goerdeler und die deutsche Wiederstandsbewegung.* Stuttgart, Deutsche Verlags-Anstalt, 1954.

RITTHALER, ANTON, *Die Hohenzollern: Ein Bildwerk,* with a foreword by Prince Louis Ferdinand of Prussia. Frankfurt am Main and Bonn, Athenäum Verlag, 1961.

———, *Kaiser Wilhelm II: Herrscher in einer Zeitwende.* Cologne, Verlag Tradition und Leben, 1958.

ROCHOW, CAROLINE LOUISE ALBERTINE VON, *née* VON DER MARWITZ, and MARIE DE LA MOTTE-FOUQUÉ, *Leben am preussischen Hofe 1815–1852.* Berlin, E. S. Mittler & Sohn, 1908.

RODD, SIR JAMES RENNELL, *Frederick, Crown Prince and Emperor: A Biographical Sketch Dedicated to His Memory, with an Introduction by Her Majesty the Empress Frederick.* London, David Stott, 1888.

ROON, COUNT ALBRECHT THEODOR EMIL VON, *Denkwürdigkeiten aus dem Leben des General-Feldmarschalls Kriegsminister Grafen von Roon,* Count Waldemar von Roon, ed. Breslau, E. Trewendt, 1892.

ROSENBERG, HANS, *Bureaucracy, Aristocracy and Autocracy: The Prussian Experience 1660–1815.* Cambridge, Mass., Beacon Press, 1966.

ROTHFELS, HANS, *Bismarck, der Osten und das Reich.* Stuttgart, Kohlhammer, 1960; 2d ed., 1962.

———, *The German Opposition to Hitler: An Assessment,* trans. by Lawrence P. R. Wilson. London, Oswald Wolff, 1961.

SCHADOW, GOTTFRIED, *Biographie in Aufsätzen und Briefen,* J. Friedländer, ed. Stuttgart, Ebner & Seubert, 1890.

SCHEIDEMANN, PHILIPP, *Memoiren eines Sozialdemokraten.* Dresden, C. Reissner, 1928. 2 vols.

———, *Memoirs of a Social Democrat,* trans. by J. E. Michell. London, Hodder & Stoughton, 1929. 2 vols.

SCHEVILL, FERDINAND, *The Great Elector.* Hamden, Conn., Shoe String Press, 1947.

SCHIEDER, THEODOR, *Das deutsche Kaiserreich von 1871 als Nationalstaat.* Cologne-Opladen, Westdeutscher Verlag, 1961.

SCHIMMEL-FALKENAU, WALTHER, *Kommen und Gehen Unter den Linden.* Berlin, Rembrandt Verlag, 1963.

SCHNEIDER, REINHOLD, *Die Hohenzollern.* Leipzig, Hegner, 1933; 2d rev. ed., Cologne & Olten, Hegner, 1953.

SCHOEPS, HANS JOACHIM, *Das war Preussen: Zeugnisse der Jahrhunderte, Eine Anthologie.* Honnef/Rhein, Dr. Hans Peters Verlag, 1955.

———, *Das andere Preussen.* Stuttgart, Friedrich Vorwerk Verlag, 1952.

———, *Die Ehre Preussens.* Stuttgart, Friedrich Vorwerk Verlag, 1951.

SCHOPPMEIER, KARL-HEINZ, *Der Einfluss Preussens auf die Gesetzgebung des Reiches.* Berlin, G. Stilke, 1929.

SCHÜSSLER, WILHELM, *Kaiser Wilhelm II, Schicksal und Schuld.* Göttingen, Musterschmidt, 1962.

SCHUSTER, GEORGE NAUMANN, *The Germans: An Enquiry and an Estimate.* New York, 1932.

SCHWERTFEGER, BERNHARD, *Kaiser und Kabinettschef: Nach eigenen Aufzeichnungen und dem Briefwechsel von Valentini['s] dargestellt.* Olden burg, Stalling, 1931.

SCHWIPPS, WERNER, *Die Garnisonkirchen von Berlin und Potsdam.* Berlin, Haude & Spenersche Verlagsbuchhandlung, 1964.

SIMON, EDITH, *The Making of Frederick the Great.* Boston, Little, Brown, 1963; London, Cassell, 1963.

SPENGLER, OSWALD, *Preussentum und Sozialismus.* Munich, C. H. Beck, 1920.

STEVENSON, R. S., *Morell Mackenzie: The Story of a Victorian Tragedy.* London, William Heinemann, 1946.

STRAUSS, G. L. M., *Emperor William: The Life of a Great King and Good Man.* London, Ward & Downey, 1888.

STÜRGKH, COUNT JOSEF, *Im deutschen grossen Hauptquartier.* Leipzig, P. List, 1921.

———, *Politische und militärische Erinnerungen.* Leipzig, P. List, 1922.

SYBEL, HEINRICH VON, *Die Begründung des Deutschen Reiches durch Wilhelm I.* Munich, Oldenbourg, 1890. 5 vols.

SYDOW, ANNA VON, *Gabrielle von Bülow, Tochter Wilhelm von Humboldts: Ein Lebensbild, aus den Familienpapieren Wilhelm von Humboldts und seiner Kinder, 1791–1887.* Berlin, E. S. Mittler & Sohn, 1893.

Taylor, A. J. P., *Bismarck: The Man and the Statesman.* London, Hamish Hamilton, 1955; New York, Knopf, 1955.

———, *The Course of German History.* London, Hamish Hamilton, 1945; New York, Coward-McCann, 1946.

———, *The Habsburg Monarchy, 1809–1918: A History of the Austrian Empire and Austria-Hungary.* London: Hamish Hamilton, 1948; New York, Macmillan, 1949.

TEMPERLEY, HAROLD, *Frederick the Great and Kaiser Joseph: An Episode of War and Diplomacy in the Eighteenth Century*. London, Duckworth, 1915; 2d ed., New York, Barnes & Noble, 1968.

TIRPITZ, ALFRED PETER FRIEDRICH VON, *Deutschlands Ohnmachtpolitik im Weltkriege*. Hamburg, Hanseatische Verlagsanstalt, 1926.

———, *My Memoirs*. London, Hurst & Blackett, 1919. 2 vols.

TREITSCHKE, HEINRICH VON, *History of Germany in the Nineteenth Century*, with an introduction by W. H. Dawson, trans. by Eden and Cedar Paul. London, Jarrold & Sons, 1915–1919. 7 vols.

———, *Treitschke's Origins of Prussianism: The Teutonic Knights*, trans. by Eden and Cedar Paul. London, George Allen & Unwin, 1942.

TUCHMAN, BARBARA W., *The Guns of August*. New York, Macmillan, 1962; London, Constable, 1962.

VALENTIN, VEIT, *The German People from the Holy Roman Empire to the Third Reich*, trans. by O. Marx. New York, Knopf, 1946.

———, *Geschichte der Deutschen*. Berlin and Stuttgart, Pontes Verlag, 1947; 2d ed., 1949.

VEHSE, DR. CARL EDUARD, *Memoirs of the Court of Prussia*, trans. by Franz C. F. Demmler. London, T. Nelson & Sons, 1854.

VIERECK, GEORGE SYLVESTER, *The Kaiser on Trial*. London, Duckworth, 1938.

VOGEL, WERNER, *Führer durch die Geschichte Berlins*. Berlin, Rembrandt Verlag, 1966.

VOLTAIRE, FRANÇOIS MARIE AROUET DE, *Mein Aufenthalt in Berlin*. Hans Jacob, ed. Munich, O. C. Recht, 1921.

WALDERSEE, COUNT ALFRED HEINRICH CARL LUDWIG VON, *Denkwürdigkeiten des General-Feldmarschalls Alfred Grafen von Waldersee. Auf Veranlassung des General-Leutnants Georg Grafen von Waldersee bearbeitet*, Heinrich Otto Meisner, ed. Stuttgart, Deutsche Verlags-Anstalt, 1922–1925. 3 vols.

———, *A Field-Marshal's Memoirs*, condensed and trans. by Frederic Whyte. London, Hutchinson, 1924.

WARD, SIR ADOLPHUS WILLIAM, *The Origins of the Kingdom of Prussia: The Great Elector and the First Prussian King*, Vol. IV of *The Cambridge Modern History*. London, Cambridge University Press, 1902–1911.

WEDGWOOD, CICELY V., *The Thirty Years War*. London, Jonathan Cape, 1938; New Haven, Conn., Yale University Press, 1939.

WESTARP, COUNT KUNO FRIEDRICH VICTOR VON, *Das Ende der Monarchie am 9. November 1918*, Werner Conze, ed. Berlin, Rauschenbusch, 1952.

WHEELER-BENNETT, SIR JOHN W., *Hindenburg: The Wooden Titan*. London, Macmillan, 1936.

———, *The Nemesis of Power: The German Army in Politics, 1918–1945*. London, Macmillan, 1953; New York, Compass Books, Viking Press, 1967.

———, *Three Episodes in the Life of Kaiser Wilhelm II*. The Leslie Stephen Lecture, 1955. London, The Syndics of Cambridge University Press, 1956.

WIEGLER, PAUL, *William the First: His Life and Times,* trans. and ed. by Constance Vesey. London, George Allen & Unwin, 1929.

WILHELMINE [actually Fréderica Sophia Wilhelmina], PRINCESS OF PRUSSIA, Consort of Frederick William, Margrave of Brandenburg-Bayreuth, *Mein Bruder Fritz: Denkwürdigkeiten aus dem Leben der Markgräfin Wilhelmine von Bayreuth,* Georg Heinrich, ed., Vol. 1 of *Friedrich der Grosse in seiner Zeit.* Leipzig, Georg Kummers Verlag, 1928.

———, *Memoirs of Frederica Sophia Wilhelmina, Princess Royal of Prussia,* with an introduction by William D. Howells. Boston, J. R. Osgood, 1877.

———, *Memoirs, Written by Herself,* trans. from original French. London, H. Colburn, 1812. 2 vols.

WILLIAM HOHENZOLLERN, former Crown Prince of Germany (1882–1951), *Erinnerungen,* Karl Rosner, ed. Stuttgart, J. G. Cotta'sche Buchhandlung Nachf., 1922.

———, *I Seek the Truth: A Book on Responsibility for the War,* trans. by Ralph Butler. London, Faber & Gwyer, 1926.

———, *Ich Suche die Wahrheit!—Ein Buch zur Kriegsschuldfrage.* Stuttgart, J. G. Cotta'sche Buchhandlung Nachf., 1925.

———, *Meine Erinnerungen aus Deutschlands Heldenkampf.* Berlin, E. S. Mittler & Sohn, 1923.

———, *The Memoirs of the Crown Prince of Germany.* London, Thornton Butterworth, 1922.

———, *My War Experiences.* London, Hurst & Blackett, 1932.

WILLIAM I, GERMAN EMPEROR AND KING OF PRUSSIA, *The Correspondence of William I and Bismarck, with other letters from and to Prince Bismarck,* trans. by J. A. Ford. London, William Heinemann, 1903, 2 vols.; one-volume ed., 1915.

———, *Wilhelm's des Grossen, Kaiser, Briefe, Reden und Schriften,* Ernst Berner, ed. Berlin, E. S. Mittler & Sohn, 1906. 2 vols.

———, *Wilhelms I. Briefe an seinen Vater König Friedrich Wilhelm III (1827–1839)*, Paul Alfred Merbach, ed. Berlin, K. Curtius, 1922.

———, *Wit and Wisdom of the late Emperor William* (Extracts from speeches and telegrams, etc.), trans. by J. Liebe. London, Ward & Downey, 1888.

WILLIAM II, GERMAN EMPEROR AND KING OF PRUSSIA, *The Emperor's Speeches: Being a Selection from the Speeches, Edicts, Letters and Telegrams of the Emperor William II,* trans. by L. Elkind. London, Longmans, 1904.

———, *Ereignisse und Gestalten aus den Jahren 1878–1918.* Leipzig, K. F. Koehler, 1922.

———, *The German Emperor as Shown in His Public Utterances,* Christian Gauss, ed. London and New York, William Heinemann, 1915.

———, *My Ancestors,* trans. by W. W. Zambra. London, William Heinemann, 1929.

———, *My Early Life.* London, Methuen, 1926.

———, *The War Lord: A Character Study of Kaiser William II by Means of his Speeches, Letters and Telegrams,* compiled by J. M. Kennedy. London, F. & C. Palmer, 1914.

WILSON, LAWRENCE, *The Incredible Kaiser: A Portrait of William II.* London, Robert Hale, 1963.

WOLFF, RICHARD, *Vom Berliner Hof zur Zeit Friedrich Wilhelms I., Berichte des Braunschweiger Gesandten in Berlin.* Berlin, E. S. Mittler und Sohn, 1914.

ZEDLITZ-TRÜTZSCHLER, COUNT ROBERT, *Zwölf Jahre am deutschen Kaiserhof: Aufzeichnungen.* Stuttgart, Deutsche Verlags-Anstalt, 1925.

Index